John Gower's English Works.

G. C. MACAULAY.

VOL. I.

Early English Text Society.
Extra Series, No. LXXXI.

1900 (reprinted 1957)
Price 40s.

[These volumes are issued by the Early English Text Society in arrangement with the Delegates of the Clarendon Press.]

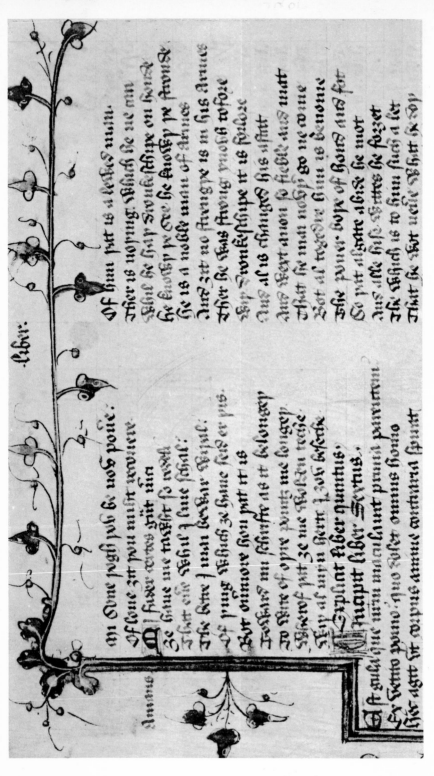

MS. Fairfax 3, f. 125 vᵒ. (UPPER PORTION)

The
English Works of John Gower.

EDITED FROM THE MANUSCRIPTS,

WITH INTRODUCTION, NOTES, AND GLOSSARY.

BY

G. C. MACAULAY, M.A.,

FORMERLY FELLOW OF TRINITY COLLEGE, CAMBRIDGE.

VOL. I.

(CONFESSIO AMANTIS, PROL.— LIB. V. 1970.)

'O gentile Engleterre, a toi j'escrits.'

Published for
THE EARLY ENGLISH TEXT SOCIETY
by the
OXFORD UNIVERSITY PRESS
LONDON   NEW YORK   TORONTO
1900 (reprinted 1957)

REPRINTED LITHOGRAPHICALLY
IN GREAT BRITAIN AT THE UNIVERSITY PRESS, OXFORD
BY CHARLES BATEY, PRINTER TO THE UNIVERSITY

PREFATORY NOTE.

No apology is needed for a new edition of the *Confessio Amantis*, which has long been among the desiderata of the Early English Text Society. The work of the present editor dates from the discovery, made some six years ago, that the best authorities for the text were to be found in the Bodleian Library, and consequently that the main part of the work ought to be done at Oxford. At the same time all due attention has been paid to the manuscripts which are to be found elsewhere, and thanks are due to many Librarians and private owners for the help which they have given.

It may be added here that the editor has become more and more convinced, as his work went on, of the value and authentic character of the text given by the Fairfax MS. of the *Confessio Amantis*, which as proceeding directly from the author, though not written by his hand, may claim the highest rank as an authority for his language.

It is hoped that the list of errata, the result chiefly of a revision made during the formation of the Glossary, may be taken to indicate not so much the carelessness of the editor, as his desire to be absolutely accurate in the reproduction of this interesting text.

The analysis of the *Confessio Amantis* which is printed in the Introduction, was undertaken chiefly at the suggestion of Dr. Furnivall. With reference to this it may be observed that in places where the author is following well-known sources, the summaries are intentionally briefer, and in the case of some of the Biblical stories a reference to the original has been thought sufficient.

G. C. M.

CONTENTS

INTRODUCTION

THE *Confessio Amantis* has been the subject both of exaggerated praise and of undue depreciation. It was the fashion of the fifteenth and sixteenth centuries to set Gower side by side with Chaucer, and to represent them as the twin stars of the new English poetry, a view which, however it may be justified by consideration of their language and literary tendencies, seems to imply a very uncritical estimate of their comparative importance. Some of these references are collected below, and they serve to indicate in a general way that the author had a great literary reputation and that his book was very popular, the latter being a conclusion which is sufficiently vouched for also by the large number of manuscripts which existed, and by the three printed editions. We shall confine ourselves here to drawing attention to a few facts of special significance.

In the first place the *Confessio Amantis* is the earliest English book which made its way beyond the limits of its own language. There exists a Spanish translation, dating apparently from the very beginning of the fifteenth century, in which reference is made also to a Portuguese version, not known to be now in existence, on which perhaps the Castilian was based. This double translation into contemporary languages of the Continent must denote that the writer's fame was not merely insular in his life-time.

Secondly, with regard to the position of this book in the sixteenth century, the expressions used by Berthelette seem to me to imply something more than a mere formal tribute. This printer, who is especially distinguished by his interest in language, in the preface to his edition of the *Confessio Amantis* most warmly sets forth his author as a model of pure English, contrasting his native simplicity with the extravagant affectations of style and

language which were then in fashion.   In fact, when we compare
the style of Gower in writing of love with that which we find in
some of the books which were at that time issuing from the press,
we cannot help feeling that the recommendation was justified.

Again, nearly a century later a somewhat striking testimony to
the position of Gower as a standard author is afforded by Ben
Jonson's *English Grammar.*   The syntax contains about a hundred
and thirty illustrative quotations, and of these about thirty are
from Gower.   Chaucer is cited twenty-five times, Lydgate and
Sir Thomas More each about fourteen, the other chief authorities
being Norton, Jewel, Fox, Sir John Cheke and the English
Bible.

Finally, our author's popularity and established position as
a story-teller is decisively vouched for by the partly Shakesperian
play of *Pericles.*   Plots of plays were usually borrowed without
acknowledgement; but here, a plot being taken from the *Confessio
Amantis*, the opportunity is seized of bringing Gower himself on
the stage to act as Prologue to four out of the five acts, speaking
in the measure of his own octosyllabic couplet,

> ' To sing a song that old was sung
> From ashes ancient Gower is come,' &c.

The book was so well known and the author so well established
in reputation, that a play evidently gained credit by connecting
itself with his name.

The following are the principal references to Gower in the fifteenth and sixteenth centuries.   The author of *The King's Quair* dedicates his poem to the
memory (or rather to the poems) of his masters Gower and Chaucer. Hoccleve
calls him ' my maister Gower,'

> ' Whos vertu I am insufficient
> For to descrive.'

John Walton of Osney, the metrical translator of Boethius, writes,

> ' To Chaucer, that is flour of rhethorique
> In english tonge and excellent poete,
> This wot I wel, no thing may I do like,
> Though so that I of makinge entermete ;
> And Gower, that so craftely doth trete
> As in his book⟨es⟩ of moralite,
> Though I to hem in makinge am unmete,
> Yit moste I schewe it forth that is in me.'

Bokenham in his *Lives of the Saints* repeatedly speaks of Gower, Chaucer
and Lydgate, the last of whom was then still living, as the three great lights

of English literature. Caxton printed the *Confessio Amantis* in 1483, and it seems to have been one of the most popular productions of his press.

In the sixteenth century Gower appears by the side of Chaucer in Dunbar's *Lament for the Makaris* and in Lindsay's poems. Hawes in the *Pastime of Pleasure* classes him with Chaucer and his beloved Lydgate, and Skelton introduces him as first in order of time among the English poets who are mentioned in the *Garland of Laurel*,

'I saw Gower that first garnysshed our Englysshe rude,
And maister Chaucer,' &c.,

a testimony which is not quite consistent with that in the *Lament for Philip Sparow*,

'Gower's Englysh is old
And of no value is told,
His mater is worth gold
And worthy to be enrold.'

Barclay in the Preface of his *Mirour of Good Manners* (printed 1516) states that he has been desired by his ' Master,' Sir Giles Alington, to abridge and amend the *Confessio Amantis*, but has declined the task, chiefly on moral grounds. The work he says would not be suitable to his age and order (he was a priest and monk of Ely),

'And though many passages therin be commendable,
Some processes appeare replete with wantonnes :

.   .   .   .

For age it is a folly and jeopardie doubtlesse,
And able for to rayse bad name contagious,
To write, reade or commen of thing venerious.'

Leland had some glimmering perception of the difference between Chaucer and Gower in literary merit ; but Bale suggests that our author was ' alter Dantes ac Petrarcha ' (no less), adding the remark, taken perhaps from Berthelette's preface, ' sui temporis lucerna habebatur ad docte scribendum in lingua vulgari [1].' In Bullein's *Dialogue against the Fever Pestilence* (1564) Gower is represented as sitting next to the Classical poets, Homer, Hesiod, Ennius and Lucan. Puttenham in the *Art of English Poesie* (1589), and Sidney in the *Defence of Poesie* (1595), equally class Gower and Chaucer together. The latter, illustrating his thesis that the first writers of each country were the poets, says, ' So among the Romans were Livius Andronicus and Ennius, so in the Italian language . . . the poets Dante, Boccace and Petrarch, so in our English, Gower and Chaucer, after whom, encouraged and delighted with their excellent foregoing, others have followed to beautify our mother tongue, as well in the same kind as in other arts.'

In Robert Greene's *Vision*, printed about 1592, Chaucer and Gower appear as the accepted representatives of the pleasant and the sententious styles in story-telling, and compete with one another in tales upon a given subject, the cure of jealousy. The introduction of Gower into the play of *Pericles, Prince of Tyre* has already been referred to.

The uncritical exaggeration of Gower's literary merits, which formerly prevailed, has been of some disadvantage to him in

[1] In some unpublished papers kindly communicated to me by Miss Bateson.

modern times.   The comparison with Chaucer, which was so
repeatedly suggested, could not but be unfavourable to him ; and
modern critics, instead of endeavouring to appreciate fairly such
merits as he has, have often felt called upon to offer him up as
a sacrifice to the honour of Chaucer, who assuredly needs no such
addition to his glory.   The true critical procedure is rather the
opposite of this.   Gower's early popularity and reputation are
facts to be reckoned with, in addition to the literary merit which
we in our generation may find in his work, and neither students
of Middle English, nor those who aim at tracing the influences
under which the English language and literature developed during
the fifteenth and sixteenth centuries, can afford to leave Gower's
English work out of their account.

THE ENGLISH WORKS.

   i. LITERARY CHARACTERISTICS.—The reason of the success of
the *Confessio Amantis* was naturally the fact that it supplied a popular
need.   After endeavouring to 'give an account of his stewardship'
in various ways as a moralist, the author at length found his true
vocation, and this time happily in his native tongue, as a teller of
stories.   The rest is all machinery, sometimes poetical and interesting, sometimes tiresome and clumsy, but the stories are the
main thing.   The perception of the popular taste may have come
to him partly through the success of Chaucer in the *Legend of Good
Women*, and the simple but excellent narrative style which he
thereupon developed must have been a new revelation of his
powers to himself as well as to others.   It is true that he does not
altogether drop the character of the moralist, but he has definitely
and publicly resigned the task of setting society generally to
rights,

> 'It stant noght in my sufficance
> So grete thinges to compasse,
>
> .   .   .   .   .   .
>
> Forthi the Stile of my writinges
> Fro this day forth I thenke change
> And speke of thing is noght so strange,' &c. (i. 4 ff.)

He covers his retreat indeed by dwelling upon the all-pervading
influence of Love in the world and the fact that all the evils of
society may be said to spring from the want of it ; but this is little
more than a pretext.   Love is the theme partly because it supplies

a convenient framework for the design, and partly perhaps out of deference to a royal command. There is no reason to doubt the statement in the first version of the Prologue about the meeting of the author with Richard II on the river, and that he then received suggestions for a book, which the king promised to accept and read. It may easily be supposed that Richard himself suggested love as the subject, being a matter in which, as we know from Froissart, he was apt to take delight. 'Adont me demanda le roy de quoy il traittoit. Je luy dis, "D'amours." De ceste response fut-il tous resjouys, et regarda dedens le livre en plusieurs lieux et y lisy [1].' It was certainly to the credit of the young king that he should have discerned literary merit in the work of the grave monitor who had so lectured him upon his duties in the *Vox Clamantis*, and should have had some part in encouraging him to set his hand to a more promising task; and if it be the fact that he suggested love as the subject, we cannot but admire both the sense of humour displayed by the prince and the address with which our author acquitted himself of the task proposed.

The idea of the Confession was no doubt taken from the *Roman de la Rose*, where the priest of Nature, whose name is Genius, hears her confession; but it must be allowed that Gower has made much better use of it. Nature occupies herself in expounding the system of the universe generally, and in confessing at great length not her own faults but those of Man, whom she repents of having made. Her tone is not at all that of a penitent, though she may be on her knees, and Genius does little or nothing for her in reply except to agree rather elaborately with her view that, if proper precautions had been taken, Mars and Venus might easily have outwitted Vulcan. Gower on the other hand has made the Confession into a framework which will conveniently hold any number of stories upon every possible subject, and at the same time he has preserved for the most part the due propriety of character and situation in the two actors. By giving the scheme an apparent limitation to the subject of love he has not in fact necessarily limited the range of narrative, for there is no impropriety in illustrating by a tale the general nature of a vice or virtue before making the special application to cases which concern lovers, and this special application, made with all due solemnity, has often a character of piquancy in which the moral tale

---

[1] Froissart, *Chron.*, ed. K. de Lettenhove, vol. xv. p. 167.

pure and simple would be wanting. Add to this that the form adopted tends itself to a kind of quasi-religious treatment of the subject, which was fully in accordance with the taste of the day, and produces much of that impression of quaintness and charm with which we most of us associate our first acquaintance with the *Confessio Amantis.*

The success of the work—for a success it is in spite of its faults —is due to several merits. The first of these is the author's un-questionable talent for story-telling. He has little of the dramatic power or the humour which distinguish Chaucer, but he tells his tales in a well-ordered and interesting manner, does not break the thread by digressions, never tires of the story before it is finished, as Chaucer does so obviously and so often, and carries his reader through with him successfully to the end in almost every case. His narrative is a clear, if shallow, stream, rippling pleasantly over the stones and unbroken either by dams or cataracts. The materials of course are not original, but Gower is by no means a slavish follower in detail of his authorities ; the proportions and arrangement of the stories are usually his own and often show good judgement. Moreover he not seldom gives a fresh turn to a well-known story, as in the instances of Jephthah and Saul, or makes a pretty addition to it, as is the case in some of the tales from Ovid. Almost the only story in which the interest really flags is the longest, the tale of Apollonius of Tyre, which fills up so much of the eighth book and was taken as the basis of the plot of *Pericles* ; and this was in its original form so loose and rambling a series of incidents, that hardly any skill could have completely redeemed it. There is no doubt that this gift of clear and inter-esting narrative was the merit which most appealed to the popular taste, the wholesome appetite for stories being at that time not too well catered for, and that the plainness of the style was an advantage rather than a drawback.

Tastes will differ of course as to the merits of the particular stories, but some may be selected as incontestably good. The tale of Mundus and Paulina in the first book is excellently told, and so is that of Alboin and Rosemund. The best of the second book are perhaps the False Bachelor and the legend of Constantine and Silvester, in the latter of which the author has greatly im-proved upon his materials. In the third book the tale of Canace is most pathetically rendered, far better than in Ovid, so that in spite of Chaucer's denunciation his devoted follower Lydgate could not resist the temptation of borrowing it. The fourth book, which altogether is of special excellence, gives us Rosiphelee, Phyllis, and the very poetically told tale of Ceix and Alceone. The fifth has Jason and Medea, a most admirable example of sustained narrative, simple and yet effective and poetical, perhaps on the whole Gower's best performance: also the oriental tale of Adrian and Bardus, and the well told story of Tereus and Philomela. In the seventh we shall find the Biblical story of Gideon excellently rendered, the Rape of Lucrece, and the tale of Virginia. These may be taken as specimens of Gower's narrative power at its best, and by the degree of effectiveness which he attains in them and the manner in which he has used his materials, he may fairly be judged as a story-teller.

As regards style and poetical qualities we find much that is good in the narratives. Force and picturesqueness certainly cannot be denied to the tale of Medea, with its description of the summer sea glistening in the sun, which blazes down upon the returning hero, and from the golden fleece by his side flashes a signal of success to Medea in her watch-tower, as she prays for her chosen knight. Still less can we refuse to recognize the poetical power of the later phases of the same story, first the midnight rovings of Medea in search of enchantments,

> 'The world was stille on every side;
> With open hed and fot al bare,
> Hir her tosprad sche gan to fare,
> Upon hir clothes gert sche was,
> Al specheles and on the gras
> Sche glod forth as an Addre doth:
> Non otherwise sche ne goth,
> Til sche cam to the freisshe flod,
> And there a while sche withstod.
> Thries sche torned hire aboute,
> And thries ek sche gan doun loute
> And in the flod sche wette hir her,
> And thries on the water ther
> Sche gaspeth with a drecchinge onde,
> And tho sche tok hir speche on honde.' (v. 3962 ff.),

and again later, when the charms are set in action, 4059 ff., a passage of extraordinary picturesqueness, but too long to be quoted here. We do not forget the debt to Ovid, but these descriptions are far more detailed and forcible than the original.

For a picture of a different kind, also based upon Ovid, we
may take the description of the tears of Lucrece for her husband,
and the reviving beauty in her face when he appears,

> 'With that the water in hire yhe
> Aros, that sche ne myhte it stoppe,
> And as men sen the dew bedroppe
> The leves and the floures eke,
> Riht so upon hire whyte cheke
> The wofull salte teres felle.
> Whan Collatin hath herd hire telle
> The menynge of hire trewe herte,
> Anon with that to hire he sterte,
> And seide, " Lo, mi goode diere,
> Nou is he come to you hiere,
> That ye most loven, as ye sein."
> And sche with goodly chiere ayein
> Beclipte him in hire armes smale,
> And the colour, which erst was pale,
> To Beaute thanne was restored,
> So that it myhte noght be mored ' (vii. 4830 ff.),

a passage in which Gower, with his natural taste for simplicity,
has again improved upon his classical authority, and may safely
challenge comparison with Chaucer, who has followed Ovid more
literally.

It is worth mention that Gower's descriptions of storms at sea
are especially vivid and true, so that we are led to suppose that
he had had more than a mere literary acquaintance with such
things. Such for instance is the account of the shipwreck of
the Greek fleet, iii. 981 ff., and of the tempests of which Apollonius is more than once the victim, as viii. 604 ff., and in general
nautical terms and metaphors, of some of which the meaning is
not quite clear, seem to come readily from his pen.

Next to the simple directness of narrative style which distinguishes the stories themselves, we must acknowledge a certain
attractiveness in the setting of them. The Lover decidedly
engages our interest : we can understand his sorrows and his
joys, his depression when his mistress will not listen to the verses
which he has written for her, and his delight when he hears men
speak her praises. We can excuse his frankly confessed envy,
malice and hatred in all matters which concern his rivals in her
love. His feelings are described in a very natural manner, the
hesitation and forgetfulness in her presence, and the self-reproach

afterwards, the eagerness to do her small services, to accompany her to mass, to lift her into her saddle, to ride by her carriage, the delight of being present in her chamber, of singing to her or reading her the tale of Troilus, or if no better may be, of watching her long and slender fingers at work on her weaving or embroidery. Sometimes she will not stay with him, and then he plays with the dog or with the birds in the cage, and converses with the page of her chamber—anything as an excuse to stay ; and when it grows late and he must perforce depart, he goes indeed, but returns with the pretence of having forgotten something, in order that he may bid her good-night once more. He rises in the night and looks out of his window over the houses towards the chamber where she sleeps, and loses himself in imagination of the love-thefts which he would commit if by any necromancy he had the power. Yet he is not extravagantly romantic : he will go wherever his lady bids him, but he will not range the world in arms merely in order to gain renown, losing his lady perhaps in the meantime at home. We take his side when he complains of the Confessor's want of feeling for a pain which he does not himself experience, and his readiness to prescribe for a wound of the heart as if it were a sore of the heel. Even while we smile, we compassionate the lover who is at last disqualified on account of age, and recommended to make a ' beau retret' while there is yet time.

But there is also another character in whom we are interested, and that is the lady herself. Gower certainly appreciated something of the delicacy and poetical refinement which ideal love requires, and this appreciation he shows also in his *Balades* ; but here we have something more than this. The figure of the lady, which we see constantly in the background of the dialogue, is both attractive and human. We recognize in her a creature of flesh and blood, no goddess indeed, as her lover himself observes, but a charming embodiment of womanly grace and refinement. She is surrounded by lovers, but she is wise and wary. She is courteous and gentle, but at the same time firm : she will not gladly swear, and therefore says nay without an oath, but it is a decisive nay to any who are disposed to presume. She does not neglect her household duties merely because a lover insists upon hanging about her, but leaves him to amuse himself how he may, while she busies herself elsewhere. If she has leisure and can sit down to her embroidery, he may read to her if he will, but it must be some sound romance, and not his own rondels, balades, and virelays in praise of her. Custom allows him to kiss her when he takes his leave, but if he comes back on any pretext and takes his leave again, there is not often a second kiss permitted. She lets him lead her up to the offering in church, and ride by her side when she drives out, but she will take no presents from him, though with some of her younger admirers, whose passion she knows is a less serious matter, she is not so strict, but takes and gives freely. Even the description of her person is not offensive, as such descriptions almost always are. Her lover suspects that her soul may be in a perilous state, seeing that she has the power of saving a man's life and yet suffers him to die, but he admits there is no more violence in her than in a child of three years old, and her words are as pleasant to him as the winds of the South. Usurious dealing is a vice of which he ventures to accuse her, seeing that he has given her his whole heart in return for a single glance of her eye, and she holds to the bargain and will not give heart for heart; but then, as the Confessor very justly replies, 'she may be such that her one glance is worth thy whole heart many times over,' and so he has sold his heart profitably, having in return much more than it is worth.

However, the literary characteristic which is perhaps most remarkable in the *Confessio Amantis* is connected rather with the form of expression than with the subject-matter. No justice is done to Gower unless it is acknowledged that the technical skill which he displays in his verse and the command which he has over the language for his own purposes is very remarkable. In the ease and naturalness of his movement within the fetters of the octosyllabic couplet he far surpasses his contemporaries, including Chaucer himself. Certain inversions of order and irregularities of construction he allows himself, and there are many stop-gaps of the conventional kind in the ordinary flow of his narrative; but in places where the matter requires it, his admirable management of the verse paragraph, the metrical smoothness of his lines, attained without unnatural accent or forced order of words, and the neatness with which he expresses exactly what he has to say within the precise limits which he lays down for himself, show a finished mastery of expression which

is surprising in that age of half-developed English style, and
in a man who had trained himself rather in French and Latin
than in English composition. Such a sentence as the following,
for example, seems to flow from him with perfect ease, there
is no halting in the metre, no hesitation or inversion for the sake
of the rhyme, it expresses just what it has to express, no more
and no less :

> 'Til that the hihe king of kinges,
> Which seth and knoweth alle thinges,
> Whos yhe mai nothing asterte,—
> The privetes of mannes herte
> Thei speke and sounen in his Ere
> As thogh thei lowde wyndes were,—
> He tok vengance upon this pride.'   (i. 2803 ff.)

Or again, as an example of a more colloquial kind,

> 'And if thei techen to restreigne
> Mi love, it were an ydel peine
> To lerne a thing which mai noght be.
> For lich unto the greene tree,
> If that men toke his rote aweie,
> Riht so myn herte scholde deie,
> If that mi love be withdrawe.'   (iv. 2677 ff.)

There is nothing remarkable about the sentiment or expression
in these passages, but they are perfectly simple and natural, and
run into rhyming verse without disturbance of sense or accent; but
such technical skill as we have here is extremely rare among the
writers of the time.   Chaucer had wider aims, and being an artist
of an altogether superior kind, he attains, when at his best, to
a higher level of achievement in versification as in other things ;
but he is continually attempting more than he can perform, he
often aims at the million and misses the unit.   His command over
his materials is evidently incomplete, and he has not troubled
himself to acquire perfection of craftsmanship, knowing that other
things are more important,

> 'And that I do no diligence
> To shewe craft but o sentence.'

The result is that the most experienced reader often hesitates in
his metre and is obliged to read lines over twice or even thrice,
before he can satisfy himself how the poet meant his words to be
accented and what exactly was the rhythm he intended.   In fact,
instead of smoothing the way for his reader, he often deliberately

chooses to spare himself labour by taking every advantage, fair or unfair, of those licences of accent and syllable suppression for which the unstable condition of the literary language afforded scope. The reader of Gower's verse is never interrupted in this manner except by the fault of a copyist or an editor ; and when we come to examine the means by which the smoothness is attained, we feel that we have to do with a literary craftsman who by laborious training has acquired an almost perfect mastery over his tools. The qualities of which we are speaking are especially visible in the more formal style of utterance which belongs to the speeches, letters and epitaphs in our author's tales. The reply of Constance to her questioner (ii. 1148 ff.) is a good example of the first :

> ' Quod sche, " I am
> A womman wofully bestad.
> I hadde a lord, and thus he bad,
> That I forth with my litel Sone
> Upon the wawes scholden wone,
> Bot what the cause was, I not :
> Bot he which alle thinges wot
> Yit hath, I thonke him, of his miht
> Mi child and me so kept upriht,
> That we be save bothe tuo." '

And as longer instances we may point to the reflexions of the Emperor Constantine near the end of the same book (ii. 3243 ff.), and the prayer of Cephalus (iv. 3197–3252). The letters of Canace and of Penelope are excellent, each in its own way, and the epitaphs of Iphis (iv. 3674 ff.) and of Thaise (viii. 1533 ff.) are both good examples of the simple yet finished style, e. g.

> ' Hier lith, which slowh himself, Iphis,
> For love of Araxarathen :
> And in ensample of tho wommen,
> That soffren men to deie so,
> Hire forme a man mai sen also,
> Hou it is torned fleissh and bon
> Into the figure of a Ston :
> He was to neysshe and sche to hard.
> Be war forthi hierafterward ;
> Ye men and wommen bothe tuo,
> Ensampleth you of that was tho.'   (iv. 3674 ff.)

In a word, the author's literary sphere may be a limited one, and his conception of excellence within that sphere may fall very far short of the highest standard, but such as his ideals are, he is able very completely to realize them. The French and English elements of the language, instead of still maintaining a wilful strife, as is so often the case in Chaucer's metre, are here combined in harmonious alliance. More especially we must recognize the fact that in Gower's English verse we have a consistent and for the moment a successful attempt to combine the French syllabic with the English accentual system of metre, and this without sacrificing the purity of the language as regards forms of words and grammatical inflexion. We shall see in our subsequent investigations how careful and ingenious he is in providing by means of elision and otherwise for the legitimate suppression of those weak terminations which could not find a place as syllables in the verse without disturbing its accentual flow, while at the same time the sense of their existence was not to be allowed to disappear. The system was too difficult and complicated to be possible except for a specially trained hand, and Gower found no successor in his enterprise; but the fact that the attempt was made is at least worthy of note.

With considerable merits both of plan and execution the *Confessio Amantis* has also no doubt most serious faults. The scheme itself, with its conception of a Confessor who as priest has to expound a system of morality, while as a devotee of Venus he is concerned only with the affairs of love (i. 237–280), can hardly be called altogether a consistent or happy one. The application of morality to matters of love and of love to questions of morality is often very forced, though it may sometimes be amusing in its gravity. The Confessor is continually forgetting one or the other of his two characters, and the moralist is found justifying unlawful love or the servant of Venus singing the praises of virginity. Moreover the author did not resist the temptation to express his views on society in a Prologue which is by no means sufficiently connected with the general scheme of the poem, though it is in part a protest against division and discord, that is to say, lack of love. Still worse is the deliberate departure from the general plan which we find in the seventh book, where on pretence of affording relief and recreation to the wearied penitent, the Confessor, who says that he has little or no understanding except of love, is allowed to make a digression which embraces the whole field of human knowledge, but more especially deals with the duties of a king, a second political pamphlet in fact, in which the stories of kings ruined by lust or insolence, of Sardanapalus, Rehoboam, Tarquin, and the rest, are certainly intended to some extent as an admonition of the author's royal patron. The petition addressed to Rehoboam by his people against excessive taxation reads exactly like one of the English parliamentary protests of the period against the extravagant demands of the crown. Again, the fifth book, which even without this would be disproportionately long, contains an absolutely unnecessary account of the various religions of the world, standing there apparently for no reason except to show the author's learning, and reaching the highest pitch of grotesque absurdity when the Confessor occupies himself in demolishing the claim of Venus to be accounted a goddess, and that too without even the excuse of having forgotten for the moment that he is supposed to be her priest. Minor excrescences of the same kind are to be found in the third book, where the lawfulness of war is discussed, and in the fourth, where there is a dissertation on the rise of the Arts, and especially of Alchemy. All that can be said is that these digressions were very common in the books of the age—the *Roman de la Rose*, at least in the part written by Jean de Meun, is one of the worst offenders.

Faults of detail it would be easy enough to point out. The style is at times prosaic and the matter uninteresting, the verse is often eked out with such commonplace expressions and helps to rhyme as were used by the writers of the time, both French or English. Sometimes the sentences are unduly spun out or the words and clauses are awkwardly transposed for the sake of the uninterrupted smoothness of the verse. The attainment of this object moreover is not always an advantage, and sometimes the regularity of the metre and the inevitable recurrence of the rhyme produces a tiresome result. On the whole however the effect is not unpleasing, 'the ease and regularity with which the verse flows breathes a peaceful contentment, which communicates itself to the reader, and produces the same effect upon the ear as the monotonous but not wearisome splashing of a fountain [1].' Moreover, as has already been pointed out, when the writer is at his best, the rhyme is kept duly in the background, and the paragraph is constructed quite independently of the couplet, so that this

[1] B. ten Brink, *Geschichte der Engl. Litt.* ii. 141.

form of metre proves often to be a far better vehicle for the narrative than might have been at first supposed.

ii. DATE AND CIRCUMSTANCES.—The *Confessio Amantis* in its earliest form bears upon the face of it the date 1390 (Prol. 331 *margin*)[1], and we have no reason to doubt that this was the year in which it was first completed. The author tells us that it was written at the command of King Richard II, whom he met while rowing on the Thames at London, and who invited him to come into his barge to speak with him. It is noticeable, however, that even this first edition has a dedication to Henry earl of Derby, contained in the Latin lines at the end of the poem[2], so that it is not quite accurate to say that the dedication was afterwards changed, but rather that this dedication was made more prominent and introduced into the text of the poem, while at the same time the personal reference to the king in the Prologue was suppressed. If the date referred to above had been observed by former editors, the speculations first of Pauli and then of Professor Hales, tending to throw back the completion of the first recension of the *Confessio Amantis* to the year 1386, or even 1383, would have been spared. Their conclusions rest, moreover, on the purest guess-work. The former argues that the preface and the epilogue[3] in their first form date from the year 1386, because from that year the king (who was then nineteen years old) 'developed those dangerous qualities which estranged from him, amongst others, the poet'; and Professor Hales (*Athenæum*, Dec. 1881) contends that the references to the young king's qualities as a ruler, 'Justice medled with pite,' &c. certainly point to the years immediately succeeding the Peasants' revolt (a time when Gower did not regard him as a responsible ruler at all, but excuses him for the evil proceedings of the government on account of his tender age)[4],

---

[1] This date has hitherto been omitted from the text of the printed editions.

[2] The last two lines, which contain the mention of the earl of Derby, are omitted in some MSS. of the first recension, and this may be an indication that the author circulated some copies without them. A full account of the various recensions of the poem is given later, under the head of 'Text.'

[3] The term 'epilogue' is used for convenience to designate the conclusion of the poem after viii. 2940, but no such designation is used by the author: similarly 'preface' means here the opening passage of the Prologue (ll. 1–92).

[4] 'Minoris etatis causa inde excusabilem pronuncians.'

that the reference to Richard's desire to establish peace (viii. 3014* ff.) *must* belong to the period of the negotiations with the French and the subsequent truce, 1383–84, though Professor Hales is himself quite aware that negotiations for peace were proceeding also in 1389, and finally that the mention of 'the newe guise of Beawme' must indicate the very year succeeding the king's marriage to Anne of Bohemia in 1382, whereas in fact the Bohemian fashions would no doubt continue to prevail at court, and still be accounted new, throughout the queen's lifetime. It is on such grounds as these that we are told that the *Confessio Amantis* in its first form *cannot* have been written later than the year 1385 and was probably as early as 1383.

All such conjectures are destroyed by the fact that the manuscripts of the first recension bear the date 1390 at the place cited, and though this does not absolutely exclude a later date for the completion of the book, it is decisive against an earlier one. Moreover, the fact that in the final recension this date is omitted (and deliberately omitted, as we know from the erasure in the Fairfax MS.) points to the conclusion that it is to be regarded definitely as a date of publication, and therefore was inappropriate for a later edition.

This conclusion agrees entirely with the other indications, and they are sufficiently precise, though the fact that one of these also has unluckily escaped the notice of the editors has caused it to be generally overlooked [1].

The form of epilogue which was substituted for that of the first recension, and in which the over-sanguine praise of Richard as a ruler is cancelled, bears in the margin the date of the fourteenth year of his reign (viii. 2973 *margin*), 'Hic in anno quarto decimo Regis Ricardi orat pro statu regni,' &c. Now the fourteenth year of King Richard II was from June 21, 1390, to the same day of 1391. We must therefore suppose that the change in this part of the book took place, in some copies at least, within a few months of its first completion.

Thirdly, we have an equally precise date for the alteration in the Prologue, by which all except a formal mention of Richard II is

---

[1] Dr. Karl Meyer, in his dissertation *John Gower's Beziehungen zu Chaucer und König Richard II* (1889), takes account of these various notes of time, having made himself to some extent acquainted with the MSS., but his conclusions are in my opinion untenable.

excluded, while the dedication to Henry of Lancaster is introduced into the text of the poem ; and here the time indicated is the sixteenth year of King Richard (Prol. 25), a date which appears also in the margin of some copies here and at l. 97, so that we may assume that this final change of form took place in the year 1392–93, that is, not later than June 1393.

Having thus every step dated for us by the author, we may, if we think it worth while, proceed to conjecture what were the political events which suggested his action ; but in such a case as this it is evidently preposterous to argue first from the political conditions, of which as they personally affected our author and his friends we can only be very imperfectly informed, and then to endeavour to force the given dates into accordance with our own conclusions[1].

It will be observed from the above dates that we are led to infer two stages of alteration, and the expectation is raised of finding the poem in some copies with the epilogue rewritten but the preface left in its original state.   This expectation is fulfilled. The Bodley MS. 294 gives a text of this kind, and it is certain that there were others of the same form, for Berthelette used for his edition a manuscript of this kind, which was not identical with that which we have.

In discussing the import of the various changes introduced by the author it is of some importance to bear in mind the fact already mentioned that even the ·first issue of the *Confessio Amantis* had a kind of dedication to Henry of Lancaster in the Latin lines with which it concluded,

> ' Derbeie comiti, recolunt quem laude periti,
> Vade liber purus sub eo requiesce futurus.'

This seems rather to dispose of the idea that a dedication to Henry would be inconsistent with loyalty to Richard, a suggestion which would hardly have been made in the year 1390, or even 1393.

---

[1] This has been equally the procedure of Prof. Hales on the one hand, who endeavours to throw back the composition of the first recension to an extravagantly early period, and of Dr. Karl Meyer on the other, who wishes to bring down the final form of the book to a time later than the deposition of Richard II.   The theory of the latter, that the sixteenth year of King Richard is given as the date of the original completion of the poem, and not of the revised preface, is sufficiently refuted by the date ' fourteenth year' attached to the rewritten epilogue.

No doubt those copies which contained in the preface the statement that the book was written at the command of the king and
for his sake, and in the epilogue the presentation of the completed
book to him (3050* ff.), if they had also appended to them the
Latin lines which commend the work to the earl of Derby, may
be said to have contained in a certain sense a double dedication,
the compliment being divided between the king and his brilliant
cousin, and very probably a copy which was intended for the
court would be without the concluding lines, as we find to be
the case with some manuscripts ; but the suggestion that the expressions of loyalty and the praises of Richard as a ruler which we
find in the first epilogue are properly to be called inconsistent with
a dedication of the poem to Henry of Lancaster, his cousin and
counsellor, is plausible only in the light of later events, which could
not be foreseen by the poet, in the course of which Henry
became definitely the opponent of Richard and finally took the
lead in deposing him. It is true that the earl of Derby had been
one of the lords appellant in 1387, but after the king's favourites
had been set aside, he was for the time reconciled to Richard,
and he could not in any sense be regarded as the leader of an
opposition party. That Gower, when he became disgusted with
Richard II, should have set Henry's name in the Prologue in
place of that of the king, as representing his ideal of knighthood
and statesmanship, may be regarded either as a coincidence
with the future events, or as indicating that Gower had some
discrimination in selecting a possible saviour of society; but it is
certain that at this time the poet can have had no definite idea
that his hero would become a candidate for the throne.

The political circumstances of the period during which the
Confessio Amantis was written and revised are not very easy to
disentangle. We may take it as probable that the plan of its
composition, under the combined influence of Chaucer's *Legend of
Good Women*[1] and of the royal command, may have been laid
about the year 1386. Before this time Richard would scarcely
have been regarded by Gower as responsible for the government,
and he would naturally look hopefully upon the young sovereign,
then just entering upon his duties, as one who with proper admonition and due choice of advisers might turn out to be a good

---

[1] For the connexion between this and the *Confessio Amantis* see L. Bech
in *Anglia*, v. 313 ff.

ruler. During the succeeding years the evil counsellors of the king were removed by the action of the lords appellant and the Parliament, and in the year 1389 a moderate and national policy seemed to have been finally adopted by the king, with William of Wykeham as Chancellor and the young earl of Derby, who had been one of the appellants but had quarrelled with his uncle Gloucester, among the king's trusted advisers. By the light of subsequent events Gower condemned the whole behaviour of the king during this period as malicious and treacherous, but this could hardly have been his judgement of it at the time, for Richard's dissimulation, if dissimulation it were, was deep enough to deceive all parties. Consequently, up to the year 1390 at least, he may have continued, though with some misgivings, to trust in the king's good intentions and to regard him as a ruler who might effectually heal the divisions of the land, as he had already taken steps to restore peace to it outwardly. It is quite possible also that something may have come to his knowledge in the course of the year 1390–91 which shook his faith. It was at this time, in July 1390, just at the beginning of the fourteenth year of King Richard, that his hero the earl of Derby left the court and the kingdom to exercise his chivalry in Prussia, and for this there may have been a good reason. We know too little in detail of the events of the year to be able to say exactly what causes of jealousy may have arisen between the king and his cousin, who was nearly exactly of an age with him and seems to have attracted much more attention than Richard himself at the jousts of St. Inglevert in May of this year. Whatever feeling there may have been on the side of the earl of Derby would doubtless reflect itself in the minds of his friends and supporters, and something of this kind may have deepened into certitude the suspicions which Gower no doubt already had in his heart of the ultimate intentions of Richard II. The result was that in some copies at least of the *Confessio Amantis* the concluding praises of the king as a ruler were removed and lines of a more general character on the state of the kingdom and the duties of a king were substituted, but still there was no mention of the earl of Derby except as before in the final Latin lines. Two years later, 1392–93, when the earl of Derby had fairly won his spurs and at the age of twenty-five might be regarded as a model of chivalry, the mention of Richard as the suggester of the work was removed, and the name of Henry set in the text as the sole object of the dedication.

The date sixteenth year must certainly be that of this last change, but the occasion doubtless was the sending of a presentation copy to Henry, and this would hardly amount to publication. The author probably did not feel called upon publicly to affront the king by removing his name and praises, either at the beginning or the end, from the copies generally issued during his reign. Whether or not this conduct justifies the charge of time-serving timidity, which has been made against Gower, I cannot undertake to decide. He was, however, in fact rather of an opposite character, even pedantically stiff in passing judgement severely on those in high places, and not bating a syllable of what he thought proper for himself to say or for a king to hear, though while the king was young and might yet shake himself free from evil influences he was willing to take as favourable a view of his character as possible. Probably he was for some time rather in two minds about the matter, but in any case 'timid and obsequious' are hardly the right epithets for the author of the *Vox Clamantis*.

Before leaving this subject something should perhaps be said upon a matter which has attracted no little attention, namely the supposed quarrel between the author of the *Confessio Amantis* and Chaucer. It is well known that the first recension of our poem has a passage referring to Chaucer in terms of eulogy (viii. 2941*–57*), and that this was omitted when the epilogue was rewritten. This fact has been brought into connexion with the apparent reference to Gower in the *Canterbury Tales*, where the Man of Law in the preamble to his tale disclaims on Chaucer's behalf such 'cursed stories' as those of Canace and Apollonius, because they treat of incest. It has been thought that this was meant for a serious attack on Gower, and that he took offence at it and erased the praise of Chaucer from the *Confessio Amantis*.

It is known of course that the two poets were on personally friendly terms, not only from the dedication of *Troilus*, but from the fact that when Chaucer was sent on a mission to the Continent in 1378, he appointed Gower one of his attorneys in his absence. It is possible that their friendship was interrupted by a misunderstanding, but it may be doubted whether there is sufficient proof of this in the facts which have been brought forward.

In the first place I question whether Chaucer's censure is to be taken very seriously. That it refers to Gower I have little doubt, but that the attack was a humorous one is almost equally clear. Chaucer was aware that some of his own tales were open to objection on the score of morality, and when he saw a chance of scoring a point on the very ground where his friend thought himself strongest, he seized it with readiness. Some degree of seriousness there probably is, for Chaucer's sound and healthy view of life instinctively rejected the rather morbid horrors to which he refers; but it may easily be suspected that he was chiefly amused by the opportunity of publicly lecturing the moralist, who perhaps had privately remonstrated with him [1]. As to the notion that Chaucer had been seriously offended by the occasional and very trifling resemblances of phrase in Gower's tale of Constance with his own version of the same original, it is hardly worth discussion.

There is of course the possibility that Gower may have taken it more seriously than it was meant, and though he was not quite so devoid of a sense of humour as it has been the fashion to suppose [2], yet he may well have failed to enjoy a public attack, however humorous, upon two of his tales. It must be observed, however, that if we suppose the passage in question to have been the cause of the excision of Gower's lines about Chaucer, we must assume that the publication of it took place precisely within this period of a few months which elapsed between the first and the second versions of Gower's epilogue.

Before further considering the question as to what was actually our author's motive in omitting the tribute to his brother poet, we should do well to observe that this tribute was apparently allowed to stand in some copies of the rewritten epilogue. There is one good manuscript, that in the possession of Lord Middleton,

---

[1] Lydgate apparently did not take Chaucer's censure very seriously, for he quite needlessly introduced the tale of Canace into his *Falls of Princes*, following Gower's rendering of it.

[2] See for example the picture of Nebuchadnezzar transformed into an ox, 'Tho thoghte him colde grases goode,' &c. (i. 2976 ff.), the account of the jealous husband, who after charging his wife quite unreasonably with wishing she had another there in his stead, turns away from her in bed and leaves her to weep all the night, while he sleeps (v. 545 ff.), and the description of the man who entertains his wife so cheerfully on his return home with tales of the good sport that he has had, but carefully avoids all reference to the occurrence which would have interested her most (v. 6119 ff.).

in which the verses about Chaucer not only stand in combination with the new form of epilogue, but in a text which has also the revised preface, dated two years later [1]. Hence it seems possible that the exclusion of the Chaucer verses was rather accidental than deliberate, and from this and other considerations an explanation may be derived which will probably seem too trivial, but nevertheless is perhaps the true one. We know from the Fairfax MS. of the *Confessio Amantis* and from several original copies of the *Vox Clamantis* that the author's method of rewriting his text was usually to erase a certain portion, sometimes a whole column or page, and substitute a similar number of lines of other matter. It will be observed here that for the thirty lines 2941*– 2970*, including the reference to Chaucer, are substituted thirty lines from which that reference is excluded. After this come four Latin lines replacing an equal number in the original recension, and then follow fifteen lines, 2971–2985, which are the same except a single line in the two editions. It may be that the author, wishing to mention the departure of the Confessor and the thoughts which he had upon his homeward way, sacrificed the Chaucer verses as an irrelevance, in order to find room for this matter between the Adieu of Venus and the lines beginning 'He which withinne daies sevene,' which he did not intend to alter, and that this proceeding, carried out upon a copy of the first recension which has not come down to us, determined the general form of the text for the copies with epilogue rewritten, though in a few instances care was taken to combine the allusion to Chaucer with the other alterations. Such an explanation as this would be in accord with the methods of the author in some other respects ; for, as we shall see later on, the most probable explanation of the omission in the third recension of the additional passages in the fifth and seventh books, is that a first recension copy was used in a material sense as a basis for the third recension text, and it was therefore not convenient to introduce alterations which increased the number of lines in the body of the work.

[1] The reading in the Latin note at the beginning of 'quarto ⟨decimo⟩' for 'sexto decimo' is probably due to a mistake, for we find 'sextenthe' in the text of l. 25. It may be noted that the MS. mentioned by Pauli as containing the rewritten preface and also the Chaucer verses (New Coll. 326) is a hybrid, copied from two different manuscripts.

iii. ANALYSIS.

PROLOGUS.

1–92. PREFACE. By the books of those that were before us we are instructed, and therefore it is good that we also should write something which may remain after our days. But to write of wisdom only is not good. I would rather go by the middle path and make a book of pleasure and profit both : and since few write in English, my meaning is to make a book * for England's sake now in the sixteenth year of King Richard. Things have changed and books are less beloved than in former days, but without them the fame and the example of the virtuous would be lost. Thus I, simple scholar as I am, purpose to write a book touching both upon the past and the present, and though I have long been sick, yet I will endeavour as I may to provide wisdom for the wise. For this prologue belongs all to wisdom, and by it the wise may recall to their memory the fortunes of the world ; but after the prologue the book shall be of Love, which does great wonders among men. Also I shall speak of the vices and virtues of rulers. But as my wit is too small to admonish every man, I submit my work for correction to my own lord Henry of Lancaster, with whom my heart is in accord, and whom God has proclaimed the model of knighthood. God grant I may well achieve the work which I have taken in hand.

93–192. TEMPORAL RULERS. In the time past things went well : there was plenty and riches, with honour for noble deeds, and each estate kept its due place. Justice was upheld and the people obeyed their rulers. Man's heart was then shown in his face and his thought expressed by his words, virtue was exalted and vice abased. Now all is changed, and above all discord and hatred have taken the place of love, there is no stable peace, no justice and righteousness. All

---

* for King Richard's sake, to whom my allegiance belongs and for whom I pray. It chanced that as I rowed in a boat on the flowing Thames under the town of New Troy, I met my liege lord, and he bad me come from my boat into his barge, and there he laid upon me a charge to write some new thing which he himself might read. Thus I am the more glad to write, and I have the less fear of envious blame. A gentle heart praises without malice, but the world is full of evil tongues and my king's command shall nevertheless be fulfilled. Though I have long been sick, yet I will endeavour to write a book which may be wisdom to the wise and play to those who desire to play. But the proverb says that a good beginning makes a good end : therefore I will here begin the prologue of my book, speaking partly of the former state of the world and partly of the present.

kingdoms are alike in this, and heaven alone knows what is to be done. The sole remedy is that those who are the world's guides should follow good counsel and should be obeyed by their people; and if king and council were at one, it might be hoped that the war would be brought to an end, which is so much against the peace of Christ's religion and from which no land gets any good. May God, who is above all things, give that peace of which the lands have need.

193-498. THE CHURCH. Formerly the life of the clergy was an example to all, there was no simony, no disputes in the Church, no ambition for worldly honour. Pride was held a vice and humility a virtue. Alms were given to the poor and the clergy gave themselves to preaching and to prayer. Thus Christ's faith was first taught, but now it is otherwise. Simony and worldly strife prevail; and if priests take part in wars, I know not who shall make the peace. But heaven is far and the world is near, and they regard nothing but vainglory and covetousness, so that the tithe goes at once to the war, as though Christ could not do them right by other ways. That which should bring salvation to the world is now the cause of evil : the prelates are such as Gregory wrote of, who desire a charge in order that they may grow rich and great, and the faith is hindered thereby. Ambition and avarice have destroyed charity ; Sloth is their librarian and delicacy has put away their abstinence. Moreover Envy everywhere burns in the clergy like the fire of Etna, as we may see now [in this year of grace 1390] at Avignon. To see the Church thus fall between two stools is a cause of sorrow to us all : God grant that it may go well at last with him who has the truth. But as a fire spreads while men are slothfully drinking, so this schism causes the new sect of Lollardy to spring up, and many another heresy among the clergy themselves. It were better to dike and delve and have the true faith, than to know all that the Bible says and err as some of these do. If men had before their eyes the virtues which Christ taught, they would not thus dispute about the Papacy. Each one attends to his own profit, but none to the general cause of the Church, and thus Christ's fold is broken and the flock is devoured. The shepherds, intent upon worldly good, wound instead of healing, and rob the sheep unjustly of their wool. Nay, they drive them among the brambles, so that they may have the wool which the thorns tear off. If the wolf comes in the way, their staff is not at hand to defend the sheep, but they are ready enough to smite the sheep with it, if they offend ever so little. There are some indeed in whom virtue dwells, whom God has called as Aaron was called, but most follow Simon at the heels, whose chariot rolls upon wheels of covetousness and pride. They teach how good it is to clothe and feed the poor, yet of their own goods they do not distribute. They say that chastity should be preserved by abstinence, but they eat daintily and lie softly, and whether they preserve their chastity thereby, I dare not say :

I hear tales, but I will not understand. Yet the vice of the evil-doers is no reproof to the good, for every man shall bear his own works.

499–584. THE COMMONS. As for the people, it is to be feared that that may happen which has already come to pass in sundry lands, that they may break the bounds and overflow in a ruinous flood. Everywhere there is lack of law and growth of error; all say that this world has gone wrong, and every one gives his judgement as to the cause ; but he who looks inwards upon himself will be ready to excuse his God, in whom there is no default. The cause of evil is in ourselves. Some say it is fortune and some the planets, but in truth all depends upon man. No estate is secure, the fortune of it goes now up, now down, and all this is in consequence of man's doings. In the Bible I find a tale which teaches that division is the chief cause why things may not endure, and that man himself is to blame for the changes which have overthrown kingdoms.

585–662. NABUGODONOSOR in a dream saw an image with the head and neck of gold, the breast and arms of silver, the belly and thighs of brass, the legs of steel, and the feet of mixed steel and clay. On the feet of this image fell a great stone which rolled down from a hill, and the image was destroyed. Daniel expounded this of the successive kingdoms of the world.

663–880. These were the FOUR MONARCHIES, of Babylon, of Persia, of the Greeks, and of the Romans. We are now in the last age, that of dissension and division, as shown by the state of the Empire and the Papacy. This is that which was designated by the feet of the image.

881–1088. We are near to the end of the world, as the apostle tells us. The world stands now divided like the feet of the image. Wars are general, and yet the clergy preach that charity is the foundation of all good deeds. Man is the cause of all the evil, and therefore the image bore the likeness of a man. The heavenly bodies, the air and the earth suffer change and corruption through the sin of man, who is in himself a little world. When he is disordered in himself, the elements are all at strife with him and with each other. Division is the cause of destruction. So it is with man, who has within him diverse principles which are at strife with one another, and in whom also there is a fatal division between the body and the soul, which led to the fall from a state of innocence. The confusion of tongues at the building of the tower of Babel was a further cause of division, and at last all peace and charity shall depart, and the stone shall fall. Thenceforward every man shall dwell either in heaven, where all is peace, or in hell, which is full of discord.

Would God that there were in these days any who could set peace on the earth, as Arion once by harping brought beasts and men into accord. But this is a matter which only God can direct.

LIB. I.

1-92. I cannot stretch my hand to heaven and set in order the world: so great a task is more than I am able to compass: I must let that alone and treat of other things. Therefore I think to change from this time forth the style of my writings, and to speak of a matter with which all the world has to do, and that is Love; wherein almost all are out of rule and measure, for no man is able to resist it or to find a remedy for it. If there be anything in this world which is governed blindly by fortune, it is love: this is a game in which no man knows whether he shall win or lose. I am myself one who belongs to this school, and I will tell what befel me not long since in regard to love, that others may take example thereby.

93-202. I fared forth to walk in the month of May, when every bird has chosen his mate and rejoices over the love which he has achieved; but I was further off from mine than earth is from heaven. So to the wood I went, not to sing with the birds, but to weep and lament; and after a time I fell to the ground and wished for death. Then I looked up to the heaven and prayed the god and the goddess of love to show me some grace. Anon I saw them; and he, the king of love, passed me by with angry look and cast at me a fiery lance, which pierced through my heart. But the queen remained, and asked me who I was, and bade me make known my malady. I told her that I had served her long and asked only my due wage, but she frowned and said that there were many pretenders, who in truth had done no service, and bade me tell the truth and show forth all my sickness. 'That can I well do,' I replied, 'if my life may last long enough.' Then she looked upon me and said, 'My will is first that thou confess thyself to my priest.' And with that she called Genius, her priest, and he came forth and sat down to hear my shrift.

203-288. This worthy priest bade me tell what I had felt for love's sake, both the joy and the sorrow; and I fell down devoutly on my knees and prayed him to question me from point to point, lest I should forget things which concerned my shrift, for my heart was disturbed so that I could not myself direct my wits. He replied that he was there to hear my confession and to question me: but he would not only speak of love; for by his office of priest he was bound to set forth the moral vices. Yet he would show also the properties of Love, for he was retained in the service of Venus and knew little of other things. His purpose was to expound the nature of every vice, as it became a priest to do, and so to apply his teaching to the matter of love that I should plainly understand his lore.

289-574. SINS OF SEEING AND HEARING. I prayed him to say his will, and I would obey, and he bade me confess as touching my five senses, which are the gates through which things come into the heart, and first of the principal and most perilous, the sense of sight. Many a man has done mischief to love through seeing, and often the fiery dart of love pierces the heart through the eye. (289-332.)

Ovid tells a tale of the evils of 'mislook,' how *Acteon* when hunting came upon Diana and her nymphs bathing, and because he did not turn away his eyes, he was changed into a hart and torn to pieces by his own hounds. (333-378.)

Again, the *Gorgons* were three sisters, who had but one eye between them, which they passed one to another, and if any man looked upon them he was straightway turned into a stone. These were all killed by Perseus, to whom Pallas lent a shield with which he covered his face, and Mercury a sword with which he slew the monsters. (389-435.)

My priest therefore bade me beware of misusing my sight, lest I also should be turned to stone; and further he warned me to take good heed of my hearing, for many a vanity comes to man's heart through the ears. (436-462.)

There is a serpent called *Aspidis*, which has a precious stone in his head, but when a man tries to overcome him by charms in order to win this stone, he refuses to hear the enchantment, laying one ear close to the earth and stopping the other with his tail. (463-480.)

Moreover, in the tale of Troy we read of *Sirens*, who are in the form of women above and of fishes below, and these sing so sweetly, that the sailors who pass are enchanted by it and cannot steer their ships: so they are wrecked and torn to pieces by the monsters. Uluxes, however, escaped this peril by stopping the ears of his company, and then they slew many of them. (481-529.)

From these examples (he said) I might learn how to keep the eye and the ear from folly, and if I could control these two, the rest of the senses were easy to rule. (530-549.)

I made my confession then, and said that as for my eyes I had indeed cast them upon the Gorgon Medusa, and my heart had been changed into stone, upon which my lady had graven an eternal mark of love. Moreover, I was guilty also as regards my ear ; for when I heard my lady speak, my reason lost all rule, and I did not do as Uluxes did, but fell at once in the place where she was, and was torn to pieces in my thought. (550-567.)

God amend thee, my son, he said. I will ask now no more of thy senses, but of other things. (568-574.)

THE SEVEN DEADLY VICES.—PRIDE.

575-1234. HYPOCRISY. Pride, the first of the seven deadly Vices, has five ministers, of whom the first is called Hypocrisy. Hast thou been of his company, my son?

I know not, father, what hypocrisy means. I beseech you to teach me and I will confess. (575-593.)

**

c

A hypocrite is one who feigns innocence without, but is not so within. Such are many of those who belong to the religious orders, with some of those who occupy the high places of the Church, and others also who pretend to piety, while all their design is to increase their worldly wealth. (594-672.)

There are lovers also of this kind, who deceive by flattery and soft speech, and who pretend to be suffering sickness for love, but are ready always to beguile the woman who trusts them. Art thou one of these, my son?

Nay, father, for I have no need to feign: my heart is always more sick than my visage, and I am more humble towards my lady within than any outward sign can show. I will not say but that I may have been guilty towards others in my youth; but there is one towards whom my word has ever been sincere.

It is well, my son, to tell the truth always towards love; for if thou deceive and win thereby, thou wilt surely repent it afterwards, as a tale which I will tell may show. (672-760.)

Mundus and Paulina. At Rome, in the time of Tiberius, a worthy lady Pauline was deceived by Mundus, who bribed the priests of Isis and induced them to bring her to the temple at night on pretence of meeting the god Anubus. Mundus concealed himself in the temple and personated the god. Meeting her on her way home he let her understand the case, and she, overcome with grief and shame, reported the matter to her husband. The priests were put to death, Mundus was sent into exile, and the image of Isis was thrown into the Tiber. (761-1059.)

The Trojan Horse. Again, to take a case of the evil wrought by Hypocrisy in other matters, we read how, when the Greeks could not capture Troy, they made a horse of brass and secretly agreeing with Antenor and Eneas they concluded a feigned peace with the Trojans and desired to bring this horse as an offering to Minerva into the city. The gates were too small to admit it, and so the wall was broken down, and the horse being brought in was offered as an evidence of everlasting peace with Troy. The Greeks then departed to their ships, as if to set sail, but landed again in the night on a signal from Sinon. They came up through the broken gate, and slew those within, and burnt the city. (1060-1189.)

Thus often in love, when a man seems most true, he is most false, and for a time such lovers speed, but afterwards they suffer punishment. Therefore eschew Hypocrisy in love. (1190-1234.)

1235-1875. INOBEDIENCE. The second point of Pride is Inobedience, which bows before no law, whether of God or man. Art thou, my son, disobedient to love?

Nay, father, except when my lady bids me forbear to speak of my love, or again when she bids me choose a new mistress. She might as well say, ' Go, take the Moon down from its place in heaven,' as bid me remove her love out of my breast. Thus far I disobey, but in no other thing. (1235-1342.)

There are two attendants, my son, on this vice, called *Murmur* and *Complaint*, which grudge at all the fortune that betides, be it good or bad. And so among lovers there are those who will not faithfully submit to love, but complain of their fortune, if they fail of anything that they desire.

My father, I confess that at times I am guilty of this, when my lady frowns upon me, but I dare not say a word to her which might displease her. I murmur and am disobedient in my heart, and so far I confess that I am ' unbuxom.'

I counsel thee, my son, to be obedient always to love's hest, for obedience often avails where strength may do nothing; and of this I remember an example written in a chronicle. (1343-1406.)

There was a knight, nephew to the emperor, by name *Florent*, chivalrous and amorous, who seeking adventures was taken prisoner by enemies. He had slain the son of the captain of the castle to which he was led; and they desired to take vengeance on him, but feared the emperor. An old and cunning dame, grandmother to the slain man, proposed a condition. He should be allowed to go, on promise of returning within a certain time, and then he should suffer death unless he could answer rightly the question, ' What do all women most desire?' He gave his pledge, and sought everywhere an answer to the question, but without success. When the day approached, he set out; and as he passed through a forest, he saw a loathly hag sitting under a tree. She offered to save him if he would take her as his wife. He refused at first, but then seeing no other way, he accepted, on the condition that he should try all other answers first, and if they might save him he should be free. She told him that what all women most desire is to be sovereign of man's love. He saved himself by this answer, and returned to find her, being above all things ashamed to break his troth. Foul as she was, he respected her womanhood, and set her upon his horse before him. He reached home, journeying by night and hiding himself by day, and they were wedded in the night, she in her fine clothes looking fouler than before. When they were in bed, he turned away from her, but she claimed his bond; and he turning towards her saw a young lady of matchless beauty by his side. She stayed him till he should make his choice, whether he would have her thus by night or by day; and he, despairing of an answer, left it to her to decide. By thus making her his sovereign, he had broken the charm which bound her. She was the king's daughter of Sicily, and had been transformed by her stepmother, till she should win the love and sovereignty of a peerless knight. Thus obedience may give a man good fortune in love. (1407-1861.)

Know then, my son, that thou must ever obey thy love and follow her will.

By this example, my father, I shall the better keep my observance to love. Tell me now if there be any other point of Pride. (1862-1882.)

1883-2383. SURQUIDRY or PRESUMPTION holds the third place in the court of Pride. He does everything by guess and often repents afterwards : he will follow no counsel but his own, depends only on his own wit, and will not even return thanks to God.

When he is a lover, he thinks himself worthy to love any queen, and he often imagines that he is loved when he is not. Tell me, what of this, my son?

I trow there is no man less guilty here than I, or who thinks himself less worthy. Love is free to all men and hides in the heart unseen, but I shall not for that imagine that I am worthy to love. I confess, however, that I have allowed myself to think that I was beloved when I was not, and thus I have been guilty. But if ye would tell me a tale against this vice, I should fare the better. (1883-1976.)

My son, the proud knight *Capaneus* trusted so in himself that he would not pray to the gods, and said that prayer was begotten only of cowardice. But on a day, when he assailed the city of Thebes, God took arms against his pride and smote him to dust with a thunderbolt. Thus when a man thinks himself most strong, he is nearest to destruction. (1977-2009.)

Again, when a man thinks that he can judge the faults of others and forgets his own, evil often comes to him, as in the tale which follows.

The Trump of Death. There was a king of Hungary, who went forth with his court in the month of May, and meeting two pilgrims of great age, alighted from his car and kissed their hands and feet, giving them alms also. The lords of the land were displeased that the king should thus abase his royalty, and among them chiefly the king's brother, who said that he would rebuke the king for his deed. When they were returned, the brother spoke to the king, and said he must excuse himself to his lords. He answered courteously and they went to supper.

Now there was ordained by the law a certain trumpet of brass, which was called the Trump of Death : and when any lord should be put to death, this was sounded before his gate. The king then on that night sent the man who had this office, to blow the trumpet at his brother's gate. Hearing the sound he knew that he must die, and called his friends together, who advised that he with his wife and his five children should go in all humility to entreat the king's pardon. So they went lamenting through the city and came to the court. Men told the king how it was, and he coming forth blamed his brother because he had been so moved by a mere human sentence of death, which might be revoked. 'Thou canst not now marvel,' he said, 'at that which I did : for I saw in the pilgrims the image of my own death, as appointed by God's ordinance, and to this law I did obeisance ; for compared to this all other laws are as nothing. Therefore, my brother, fear God with all thine heart, for all shall die and be equal in his sight.' Thus the king admonished his brother and forgave him. (2010–2253.)

I beseech you, father, to tell me some example of this in the cause of love.

My son, in love as well as in other things this vice should be eschewed, as a tale shows which Ovid told.

There was one *Narcissus*, who had such pride that he thought no woman worthy of him. On a day he went to hunt in the forest, and being hot and thirsty lay down to drink from a spring. There he saw the image of his face in the water and thought it was a nymph. Love for her came upon him and he in vain entreated her to come out to him : at length in despair he smote himself against a rock till he was dead. The nymphs of the springs and of the woods in pity buried his body, and from it there sprang flowers which bloom in the winter, against the course of nature, as his folly was. (2254–2366.)

My father, I shall ever avoid this vice. I would my lady were as humble towards me as I am towards her. Ask me therefore further, if there be ought else.

God forgive thee, my son, if thou have sinned in this : but there is moreover another vice of Pride which cannot rule his tongue, and this also is an evil. (2367–2398.)

2399–2680. AVANTANCE. This vice turns praise into blame by loud proclaiming of his own merit ; and so some lovers do. Tell me then if thou hast ever received a favour in love and boasted of it afterwards.

Nay, father, for I never received any favour of which I could boast. Ask further then, for here I am not guilty.

That is well, my son, but know that love hates this vice above all others, as thou mayest learn by an example. (2399–2458.)

Alboin and Rosemund. Albinus was king of the Lombards, and he in war with the Geptes killed their king Gurmond in battle, and made a cup of his skull. Also he took Gurmond's daughter Rosemund as his wife. When the wars were over, he made a great feast, that his queen might make acquaintance with the lords of his kingdom ; and at the banquet his pride arose, and he sent for this cup, which was richly set in gold and gems, and bade his wife drink of it, saying, ' Drink with thy father.' She, not knowing what cup it was, took it and drank ; and then the king told how he had won it by his victory, and had won also his wife's love, who had thus drunk of the skull. She said nothing, but thought of the unkindness of her lord in thus boasting, as he sat by her side, that he had killed her father and made a cup of his skull. Then after the feast she planned vengeance with Glodeside her maid.

A knight named Helmege, the king's butler, loved Glodeside. To him the queen gave herself in place of her maid, and then making herself known, she compelled him to help her. They slew Albinus, but were themselves compelled to flee, taking refuge with the Duke of Ravenna, who afterwards caused them to be put to death by poison. (2459-2646.)

It is good therefore that a man hide his own praise, both in other things and also in love, or else he may fail of his purpose.

2681-3066. VAIN GLORY thinks of this world only and delights in new things. He will change his guise like a chameleon. He will make carols, balades, roundels and virelays, and if he gets any advantage in love, he rejoices over it so that he forgets all thought of death. Tell me if thou hast done so.

My father, I may not wholly excuse myself, in that I have been for love the better arrayed, and have attempted rondels, balades, virelays and carols for her whom I love, and sung them moreover, and made myself merry in chamber and in hall. But I fared none the better: my glory was in vain. She would not hear my songs, and my fine array brought me no reason to be glad. And yet I have had gladness at times in hearing how men praised her, and also when I have tidings that she is well. Tell me if I am to blame for this.

I acquit thee, my son, and on this matter I think to tell a tale how God does vengeance on this vice. Listen now to a tale that is true, though it be not of love. (2681-2784.)

There was a king of whom I spoke before, *Nabugodonosor* by name. None was so mighty in his days, and in his Pride he ruled the earth as a god. This king in his sleep saw a tree which overshadowed the whole earth, and all birds and beasts had lodging in it or fed beneath it. Then he heard a voice bidding to hew down the tree and destroy it; but the root (it said) should remain, and bear no man's heart, but feed on grass like an ox, till the water of the heaven should have washed him seven times and he should be made humble to the will of God. The King could find none to interpret this dream, and sent therefore for Daniel. He said that the tree betokened the king, and that as the tree was hewn down, so his kingdom should be overthrown, and he should pasture like an ox and be rained upon and afflicted, until he acknowledged the greatness of God. The punishment was ordained, he said, for his vain glory, and if he would leave this and entreat for grace, he might perchance escape the evil.

But Pride will not suffer humility to stand with him. Neither for his dream nor yet for Daniel's word did this king leave his vain glory, and so that which had been foretold came upon him.

Then after seven years he remembered his former state and wept; and though he might not find words, he prayed within his heart to God and vowed to leave his vain glory, reaching up his feet towards the heaven, kneeling and braying for mercy. Suddenly he was changed again into a man and received his power as before, and the pride of vain glory passed for ever from his heart. (2785–3042.)

Be not thou, my son, like a beast, but take humility in hand, for a proud man cannot win love. I think now again to tell thee a tale which may teach thee to follow Humility and eschew Pride.

3067–3425. HUMILITY. *The Three Questions.* There was once a young and wise king, who delighted in propounding difficult questions, and one knight of his court was so ready in answering them that the king conceived jealousy and resolved to put him to confusion. He bade him therefore answer these three questions on pain of death: (1) What is it that has least need and yet men help it most? (2) What is worth most and yet costs least? (3) What costs most and is worth least? The knight went home to consider, but the more he beat his brains, the more he was perplexed. He had two daughters, the younger fourteen years of age, who, perceiving his grief, entreated him to tell her the cause. At length he did so, and she asked to be allowed to answer for him to the king. When the day came, they went together to the court, and the knight left the answers to the maiden, at which all wondered. She replied to the first question that it was the Earth, upon which men laboured all the year round, and yet it had no need of help, being itself the source of all life. As to the second, it was Humility, through which God sent down his Son, and chose Mary above all others; and yet this costs least to maintain, for it brings about no wars among men. The third question, she said, referred to Pride, which cost Lucifer and the rebel angels the loss of heaven, and Adam the loss of paradise, and was the cause also of so many evils in the world.

The king was satisfied, and looking on the maiden he said, 'I like thine answer well, and thee also, and if thou wert of lineage equal to these lords, I would take thee for my wife. Ask what thou wilt of me and thou shalt have it.' She asked an earldom for her father, and this granted, she thanked the king upon her knees, and claimed fulfilment of his former word. Whatever she may have been once, she was now an earl's daughter, and he had promised to take her as his wife. The king, moved by love, gave his assent, and thus it was. This king ruled Spain in old days and his name was Alphonse: the knight was called Don Petro, and the daughter wise Peronelle. (3067–3402.)

Thus, my son, thou mayest know the evil of Pride, which fell from his place in heaven and in paradise; but Humility is gentle and debonnaire. Therefore leave Pride and take Humility.

My father, I will not forget: but now seek further of my shrift.

My son, I have spoken enough of Pride, and I think now to tell of Envy, which is a hellish vice, in that it does evil without any cause. (3403–3446.)

LIB. II.

1–220. SORROW FOR ANOTHER'S JOY. The next after Pride is ENVY, who burns ever in his thought, if he sees another preferred to himself or more worthy. Hast thou, my son, in love been sick of another man's welfare?

Yea, father, a thousand times, when I have seen another blithe of love. I am then like Etna, which burns ever within, or like a ship driven about by the winds and waves. But this is only as regards my lady, when I see lovers approach her and whisper in her ear. Not that I mistrust her wisdom, for none can keep her honour better; yet when I see her make good cheer to any man, I am full of Envy to see him glad.

My son, the hound which cannot eat chaff, will yet drive away the oxen who come to the barn; and so it is often with love. If a man is out of grace himself, he desires that another should fail. (1–96.)

Acis and Galatea. Ovid tells a tale how Poliphemus loved Galathea, and she, who loved another, rejected him. He waited then for a chance to grieve her in her love, and he saw her one day in speech with young Acis under a cliff by the sea. His heart was all afire with Envy, and he fled away like an arrow from a bow, and ran roaring as a wild beast round Etna. Then returning he pushed down a part of the cliff upon Acis and slew him. She fled to the sea, where Neptune took her in his charge, and the gods transformed Acis into a spring with fresh streams, as he had been fresh in love, and were wroth with Polipheme for his Envy. (97–200.)

Thus, my son, thou mayest understand that thou must let others be.

My father, the example is good, and I will work no evil in love for Envy. (200–220.)

221–382. JOY FOR ANOTHER'S GRIEF. This vice rejoices when he sees other men sad, and thinks that he rises by another's fall, as in other things, so also in love. Hast thou done so, my son?

Yes, father, I confess that when I see the lovers of my lady get a fall, I rejoice at it; and the more they lose, the more I think that I shall win: and if I am none the better for it, yet it is a pleasure to me to see another suffer the same pains as I. Tell me if this be wrong.

This kind of Envy, my son, can never be right. It will sometimes be willing to suffer loss, in order that another may also suffer, as a tale will show. (221–290.)

The Travellers and the Angel. Jupiter sent down an angel to report of the condition of mankind. He joined himself to two travellers, and he found by their talk that one was covetous and the other envious. On parting he told them that he came from God, and in return for their kindness he would grant them a boon: one should choose a gift and the other should have the double of what his fellow asked. The covetous man desired the other to ask, and the other, unwilling that his fellow should have more good than he, desired to be deprived of the sight of one eye, in order that his fellow might lose both. This was done, and the envious man rejoiced. (291-364.)

This is a thing contrary to nature, to seek one's own harm in order to grieve another.

My father, I never did so but in the way that I have said: tell me if there be more.

383-1871. DETRACTION. There is one of the brood of Envy called Detraction. He has Malebouche in his service, who cannot praise any without finding fault. He is like the beetle which flies over the fields, and cares nothing for the spring flowers, but makes his feast of such filth as he may find. So this envious jangler makes no mention of a man's virtue, but if he find a fault he will proclaim it openly. So also in Love's court many envious tales are told. If thou hast made such janglery, my son, shrive thee thereof. (383-454.)

Yes, father, but not openly. When I meet my dear lady and think of those who come about her with false tales, all to deceive an innocent (though she is wary enough and can well keep herself), my heart is envious and I tell the worst I know against them; and so I would against the truest and best of men, if he loved my lady; for I cannot endure that any should win there but I. This I do only in my lady's ear, and above all I never tell any tale which touches her good name. Tell me then what penance I shall endure for this, for I have told you the whole truth.

My son, do so no more. Thy lady, as thou sayest, is wise and wary, and there is no need to tell her these tales. Moreover she will like thee the less for being envious, and often the evil which men plan towards others falls on themselves. Listen to a tale on this matter. (454-586.)

Tale of Constance. The Roman Emperor Tiberius Constantinus had a daughter Constance, beautiful, wise, and full of faith. She converted to Christianity certain merchants of Barbary, who came to Rome to sell their wares, and they, being questioned by the Soldan when they returned, so reported of Constance that he resolved to ask for her in marriage. He sent to Rome and agreed to be converted, and Constance was sent with two cardinals and many other lords, to be his bride. But the mother of the Soldan was moved by jealousy. She invited the whole company to a feast, and there slew her own son and all who had had to do with the marriage except Constance herself, whom she ordered to be placed alone in a rudderless ship with victuals for five years, and so to be committed to the winds and waves. (587-713.)

For three years she drifted under God's guidance, and at last came to land in Northumberland, near a castle on the bank of Humber, which was kept by one Elda for the king of that land Allee, a Saxon and a worthy knight. Elda found her in the ship and committed her to the care of Hermyngheld his wife, who loved her and was converted by her. Hermyngheld in the name of Christ restored sight to a blind man, at which all wondered, and Elda was converted to the faith. On the morrow he rode to the king, and thinking to please him, who was then unwedded, told him of Constance. The king said he would come and see her. Elda sent before him a knight whom he trusted, and this knight had loved Constance, but she had rejected him, so that his love was turned to hate. When he came to the castle he delivered the message, and they prepared to receive the king; but in the night he cut the throat of Hermyngheld and placed the bloody knife under the bed' where Constance lay. Elda came the same night and found his wife lying dead and Constance sleeping by her. The false knight accused Constance and discovered the knife where he had placed it. Elda was not convinced, and the knight swore to her guilt upon a book. Suddenly the hand of heaven smote him and his eyes fell out of his head, and a voice bade him confess the truth, which he did, and thereupon died. (714–885.)

After this the king came, and desiring to wed Constance, agreed to receive baptism. So a bishop came from Bangor in Wales and christened him and many more, and married Constance to the king. She would not tell who she was, but the king perceived that she was a noble creature. God visited her and she was with child, but the king was compelled to go out on a war, and left his wife with Elda and the bishop. A son was born and baptized by the name of Moris, and letters were written to the king, and the bearer of them, who had to pass by Knaresborough, stayed there to tell the news to the king's mother Domilde. She in the night changed the letters for others, which said, as from the keepers of the queen, that she had been delivered of a monster. The messenger carried the letters to the king, who wrote back that they should keep his wife carefully till he came again. On his return the messenger stayed again at Knaresborough, and Domilde substituted a letter bidding them on pain of death place Constance and her child in the same ship in which she had come, and commit them to the sea. They grieved bitterly, but obeyed. She prayed to heaven for help and devoted herself to the care of the child (886–1083). After the end of that year the ship came to land near a castle in Spain, where a heathen admiral was lord, who had a steward named Theloüs, a false renegade. He came to see the ship and found Constance, but he let none else see her; and at night he returned, thinking to have her at his will. He swore to kill her if she resisted him, and she bade him look out at the port to see if any man was near: then on the prayer of Constance he was thrown out of the ship and drowned. A wind arose which took her from the land, and after three years she came to a place where a great navy lay. The lord of these ships questioned her, but she told him little, giving her name as Couste. He said that he came from taking vengeance on the Saracens for their treachery, but could hear no news of Constance. He was the Senator of Rome and was married to a niece of the Emperor named Heleine. She came to Rome with her child and dwelt with his wife till twelve years were gone, and none knew what she was, but all loved her well. (1084-1225.)

In the meantime king Allee discovered the treachery and took vengeance on his mother, who was burnt to death after confession of her guilt ; and all said that she had well deserved her punishment and lamented for Constance. Having finished his wars, the king resolved to go to Rome for absolution, and leaving Edwyn his heir to rule the land, he set forth with Elda. Arcennus reported to his wife and to Couste the coming of king Allee, and Couste swooned for joy. The king, after seeing the Pope and relieving his conscience, made a feast, to which he invited the Senator and others. Moris went also, and his mother bade him stand at the feast in sight of the king. The king seeing him thought him like his wife Constance, and loved him without knowing why. He asked Arcennus if the child were his son, and from him he heard his story and the name of his mother. The king smiled at the name ' Couste,' knowing that it was Saxon for Constance, and was eager to ascertain the truth. After the feast he besought the Senator to bring him home to see this Couste, and never man was more joyful than he was when he saw his wife. (1226-1445.)

The king remained at Rome for a time with Constance, but still she did not tell him who she was. After a while she prayed him to make an honourable feast before he left the city and to invite the Emperor, who was at a place a few miles away from the city. Moris was sent to beseech him to come and eat with them, which request he granted ; and at the time appointed they all went forth to meet the Emperor. Constance, riding forward to welcome him, made herself known to him as his daughter. His heart was overcome, as if he had seen the dead come to life again, and all present shed tears. So a parliament was held and Moris was named heir to the Emperor. King Allee and Constance returned home to the great joy of their land ; but soon after this the king died, and Constance came again to Rome. After a short time the Emperor also died in her arms, and she herself in the next year following. Moris was crowned Emperor and known as ' the most Christian.' (1446-1598.)

Thus love at last prevailed and the false tongues were silenced. Beware then thou of envious backbiting and lying, and if thou wouldest know further what mischief is done by backbiting, hear now another tale. (1599-1612.)

Demetrius and Perseus. Philip king of Macedoine had two sons,

Demetrius and Perseus. Demetrius the elder was the better knight, and he was heir to the kingdom ; but Perseus had envy of him and slandered him to his father behind his back, saying that he had sold them to the Romans. Demetrius was condemned on suborned evidence and by a corrupt judge, and so put to death. Perseus then grew so proud that he disdained his father and usurped his power, so that the father perceived the wrong which had been done ; but the other party was so strong that he could not execute justice, and thus he died of grief.

Then Perseus took the government and made war on Rome, gathering a great host. The Romans had a Consul named Paul Emilius, who took this war in hand. His little daughter wept when she parted from him, because her little dog named Perse was dead, and this seemed to him a prognostic of success, for Perseus had spoken against his brother like a dog barking behind a man's back. Perseus rode with his host, not foreseeing the mischief, and he lost a large part of his army by the breaking of the ice of the Danube. Paulus attacked him and conquered both him and his land, so that Perseus himself died like a dog in prison, and his heir, who was exiled from his land, gained his bread by working at a craft in Rome. (1613–1861.)

Lo, my son, what evil is done by the Envy which endeavours to hinder another.

I will avoid it, my father ; but say on, if there be more.

My son, there is a fourth, as deceptive as the guiles of a juggler, and this is called False Semblant. (1862–1878.)

1879–2319. FALSE SEMBLANT. This is above all the spring from which deceit flows. It seems fair weather on that flood ; but it is not so in truth. False Semblant is allied with Hypocrisy, and Envy steers their boat. Therefore flee this vice and let thy semblant always be true. When Envy desires to deceive, it is False Semblant who is his messenger ; and as the mirror shows what was never within it, so he shows in his countenance that which is not in his heart. Dost thou follow this vice, my son ?

Nay, father, for ought I know ; but question me, I pray you.

Tell me then, my son, if ever thou hast gained the confidence of any man in order to tell out his secrets and hinder him in his love. Dost thou practise such devices ?

For the most part I say nay ; but in some measure I confess I may be reckoned with those that use false colours. I feign to my fellow at times, until I know his counsels in love, and if they concern my lady, I endeavour to overthrow them. If they have to do with others than she, I break no covenant with him nor try to hinder him in his love ; but with regard to her my ears and my heart are open to hear all that any man will say,—first that I may excuse her if they speak ill of her, and secondly that I may know who her lovers are. Then I tell tales of them to my lady, to hinder their suit and further mine. And though

I myself have no help from it, I can conceal nothing from her which it concerns her to know. To him who loves not my lady, let him love as many others as he will, I feign no semblant, and his tales sink no deeper than my ears. Now, father, what is your doom and what pain must I suffer? (1879-2076.)

My son, all virtue should be praised and all vice blamed: therefore put no visor on thy face. Yet many men do so nowadays, and especially I hear how False Semblant goes with those whom we call Lombards, men who are cunning to feign that which is not, and who take from us the profit of our own land, while we bear the burdens. They have a craft called *Fa crere*, and against this no usher can bar the door. This craft discovers everything and makes it known in foreign lands to our grievous loss. Those who read in books the examples of this vice of False Semblant, will be the more on their guard against it. (2077-2144.)

Hercules and Deianira. I will tell thee a tale of False Semblant, and how Deianira and Hercules suffered by it. Hercules had cast his heart only upon this fair Deianira, and once he desired to pass over a river with her, but he knew not the ford. There was there a giant called Nessus, who envying Hercules thought to do him harm by treachery, since he dared not fight against him openly. Therefore, pretending friendship, he offered to carry the lady across and set her safe on the other shore. Hercules was well pleased, and Nessus took her upon his shoulder; but when he was on the further side, he attempted to carry her away with him. Hercules came after them and shot him with a poisoned arrow, but before he died he gave Deianira his shirt stained with his heart's blood, telling her that if her lord were untrue, this shirt would make his love return to her. She kept it well in coffer and said no word. The years passed, and Hercules set his heart upon Eole, the king's daughter of Eurice, so that he dressed himself in her clothes and she was clothed in his, and no remedy could be found for his folly. Deianira knew no other help, but took this shirt and sent it to him. The shirt set his body on fire, and clove to it so that it could not be torn away. He ran to the high wood and tore down trees and made a huge fire, into which he leapt and was burnt both flesh and bones. And all this came of the False Semblant which Nessus made. Therefore, my son, beware, since so great a man was thus lost. (2145-2312.)

Father, I will no more have acquaintance with False Semblant, and I will do penance for my former feigning. Ask more now, if more there be.

My son, there is yet the fifth which is conceived of Envy, and that is Supplantation, by means of which many have lost their labour in love as in other things. (2313-2326.)

2327-3110. SUPPLANTATION. This vice has often overthrown men and deprived them of their dignities. Supplantation obtains for himself the profit of other men's loss, and raises himself upon their fall. In the same way there are lovers who supplant others and deprive them of what is theirs by right, reaping what others have sown. If thou hast done so, my son, confess.

For ought I know, father, I am guiltless in deed, but not so in thought. If I had had the power, I would long ago have made appropriation of other men's love. But this only as regards one, for whom I let all others go. If I could, I would turn away her heart from her other lovers and supplant them, no matter by what device: but force I dare not use for fear of scandal. If this be sin, my father, I am ready to redress my guilt. (2327-2428.)

My son, God beholds a man's thought, and if thou knewest what it were to be a supplanter in love, thou wouldest for thine own sake take heed. At Troy Agamenon supplanted Achilles, and Diomede Troilus. *Geta* and *Amphitrion* too were friends, and Geta was the lover of Almena: but when he was absent, Amphitrion made his way to her chamber and counterfeited his voice, whereby he obtained admittance to her bed. Geta came afterwards, but she refused to let him in, thinking that her lover already lay in her arms. (2429-2500.)

The False Bachelor. There was an Emperor of Rome who ruled in peace and had no wars. His son was chivalrous and desirous of fame, so he besought leave to go forth and seek adventures, but his father refused to grant it. At length he stole away with a knight whom he trusted, and they took service with the Soldan of Persia, who had war with the Caliph of Egypt. There this prince did valiantly and gained renown; moreover, he was overtaken by love of the Soldan's fair daughter, so that his prowess grew more and more, and none could stand against him. At length the Soldan and the Caliph drew to a battle, and the Soldan took a gold ring of his daughter and commanded her, if he should fall in the fight, to marry the man who should produce this ring. In the battle this Roman did great deeds, and Egypt fled in his presence. As they of Persia pursued, an arrow struck the Soldan and he was borne wounded to a tent. Dying he gave his daughter's ring to this knight of Rome. After his burial a parliament was appointed, and on the night before it met, this young lord told his secret to his bachelor and showed him the ring. The bachelor feigned gladness, but when his lord was asleep, he stole the ring from his purse and put another in its stead. When the court was set, the young lady was brought forth. The bachelor drew forth the ring and claimed her hand, which was allowed him in spite of protest, and so he was crowned ruler of the empire. His lord fell sick of sorrow, caring only for the loss of his love; and before his death he called the lords to him and sent a message to his lady, and wrote also a letter to his father the Emperor. Thus he died, and the treason was known. The false bachelor was sent to Rome on demand of the Emperor, to receive punishment there, and the dead body also was taken thither for burial. (2501-2781.)

Thus thou mayest be well advised, my son, not to do so ; and above all, when Pride and Envy are joined together, no man can find a remedy for the evil. Of this I find a true example in a chronicle of old time, showing how Supplant worked once in Holy Church. I know not if it be so now. (2782-2802.)

Pope Boniface. At Rome Pope Nicholas died, and the cardinals met in conclave to choose another Pope. They agreed upon a holy recluse full of ghostly virtues, and he was made Pope and called Celestin. There was a cardinal, however, who had long desired the papacy, and he was seized with such envy that he thought to supplant the Pope by artifice. He caused a young priest of his family to be appointed to the Pope's chamber, and he told this man to take a trumpet of brass and by means of it speak to the Pope at midnight through the wall, bidding him renounce his dignity. This he did thrice ; and the Pope, conceiving it to be a voice from heaven, asked the cardinals in consistory whether a Pope might resign his place. All sat silent except this cardinal of whom we have spoken, and he gave his opinion that the Pope could make a decree by which this might be done. He did so, and the cardinal was elected in his stead under the name of Boniface. But such treason cannot be hid ; it is like the spark of fire in the roof, which when blown by the wind blazes forth. Boniface openly boasted of his device; and such was his pride that he took quarrel with Louis, King of France, and laid his kingdom under interdict. The king was counselled by his barons, and he sent Sir William de Langharet, with a company of men-at-arms, who captured the Pope at Pontsorge near Avignon and took him into France, where he was put in bonds and died of hunger, eating off both his hands. Of him it was said that he came in like a fox, reigned like a lion, and died like a dog. By his example let all men beware of gaining office in the Church by wrongful means. God forbid that it should be of our days that the Abbot Joachim spake, when he prophesied of the shameful traffic which should dishonour the Church of God. (2803-3084.)

Envy it was that moved Joab to slay Abner treacherously; and for Envy Achitophel hanged himself when his counsel was not preferred. Seneca says that Envy is the common wench who keeps tavern for the Court, and sells liquour which makes men drunk with desire to surpass their fellows. (3085-3110.)

Envy is in all ways unpleasant in love; the fire within dries up the blood which should flow kindly through his veins. He alone is moved by pure malice in that which he does. Therefore, my son, if thou wouldest find a way to love, put away Envy.

Reason would that I do so, father; but in order that I may flee from this vice, I pray you to tell me a remedy.

My son, as there is physic for the sick, so there are virtues for the vices, which quench them as water does a fire. Against Envy is set Charity, the mother of Pity, which causes a man to be willing to bear evil himself rather than that another should suffer. Hear from me a tale about this, and mark it well. (3111–3186.)

Constantine and Silvester. In Latin books I find how Constantine, the Emperor of Rome, had a leprosy which could not be cured, and wise men ordered for his healing a bath of the blood of children under seven years old. Orders were sent forth, and mothers brought their children from all parts to the palace. The Emperor, hearing the noise of lamentation, looked forth in the morning and was struck with pity. He thought to himself that rich and poor were all alike in God's sight, and that a man should do to others as he would that others should do to him. He resolved rather to suffer his malady than that so much innocent blood should be shed, and he sent the mothers and children away happy to their homes. In the night he had a vision of Saint Peter and Saint Paul, saying to him, that as he had shown mercy, mercy should be shown to him, and bidding him send to fetch Silvester from Mount Celion, where he was hiding for fear of the Emperor, who had been a foe to Christ's faith. They told him their names and departed, and he did as they commanded. Silvester came and preached to the Emperor of the redemption of mankind and the last judgement, and said that God had accepted the charity and pity which he had shown. Constantine received baptism in the same vessel which had been prepared for the blood; and as he was being baptized, a light from heaven shone in the place and the leprosy fell from him as it were fishes' scales. Thus body and soul both were cleansed. The Emperor sent forth letters bidding all receive baptism on pain of death, and founded two churches in Rome for Peter and Paul, to which he gave great worldly possessions. His will was good, but the working of his deed was bad. As he made the gift, a voice was heard from heaven saying that the poison of temporal things was this day mingled with the spiritual. All may see the evil now, and may God amend it. (3187–3496.)

I have said, my son, how Charity may help a man in both worlds; therefore, if thou wouldest avoid Envy, acquaint thyself with Charity, which is the sovereign virtue.

My father, I shall ever eschew Envy the more for this tale which ye have told, and I pray you to give me my penance for that which I have done amiss, and to ask me further.

I will tell thee, my son, of the vice which stands next after this. (3497–3530.) .

Lib. III.

There is a vice which is the enemy to Patience and doth no pleasure to nature. This is one of the fatal Seven and is called IRE, which in English is WRATH.

25-416. He has five servants to help him, of whom the first is MELANCHOLY, which lours like an angry beast and none knows the reason why. Hast thou been so, my son?

Yea, father, I may not excuse myself therof, and love is the cause of it. My heart is ever hot and I burn with wrath, angered with myself because I cannot speed. Waking I dream that I meet with my lady and pray her for an answer to my suit, and she, who will not gladly swear, saith me nay without an oath, wherewith I am so distempered that I almost lose my wits ; and when I think how long I have served and how I am refused, I am angry for the smallest thing, and every servant in my house is afraid of me until the fit passes. If I approach my lady and she speaks a fair word to me, all my anger is gone ; but if she will not look upon me, I return again to my former state. Thus I hurt my hand against the prick and make a whip for my own self ; and all this springs from Melancholy. I pray you, my father, teach me some example whereby I may appease myself.

My son, I will fulfil thy prayer. (25-142.)

Canace and Machaire. There was a king called Eolus, and he had two children, a son Machaire and a daughter Canace. These two grew up together in one chamber, and love made them blind, so that they followed only the law of nature and saw not that of reason. As the bird which sees the food but not the net, so they saw not the peril. At length Canace was with child and her brother fled. The child was born and the truth could not be hid. The father came into her chamber in a frenzy of wrath, and she in vain entreated for mercy. He sent a knight to her with a sword, that she might slay herself ; but first she wrote a letter to her brother, while her child lay weeping in her breast. Then she set the pommel of the sword to ground and pierced her heart with the point. The king bade them take the child and cast it out for wild beasts to devour. Little did he know of love who wrought such a cruel deed. (143-336.)

Therefore, my son, have regard to love, and remember that no man's might can resist what Nature has ordained. Otherwise vengeance may fall, as in a tale that I will tell. (337-360.)

Tiresias saw two snakes coupled together and smote them with his staff. Thereupon, as he had disturbed nature, so he was transformed against nature into a woman. (361-380.)

Thus wrote Ovid, and thus we see that we ought not to be wroth against the law of nature in men. There may be vice in love, but there is no malice.

**   d

My father, all this is true. Let every man love whom he will; I shall
not be wroth, if it be not my lady. I am angry only with myself,
because I can find no remedy for my evils. (381–416.)

417–842. CHESTE. The second kind of Wrath is Cheste, which has
his mouth ever unlocked and utters evil sayings of every one. Men
are more afraid of him than of thunder and exclaim against his evil
tongue. Tell me, my son, if thou hast ever chid toward thy love.

Nay, father, never : I call my lady herself to witness. I never dared
speak to her any but good words. I may have said at times more than
I ought, the best plowman balks sometimes, and I have often spoken
contrary to her command; but she knows well that I do not chide.
Men may pray to God, and he will not be wroth; and my lady, being
but a woman, ought not to be angry if I tell her of my griefs. Often
indeed I chide with myself, because I have not said that which I ought,
but this avails me nothing. Now ye have heard all, therefore give me
absolution.

My son, if thou knewest all the evils of Cheste in love, thou wouldest
learn to avoid it. Fair speech is most accordant to love ; therefore
keep thy tongue carefully and practise Patience.

My father, tell me some example of this. (417–638.)

Patience of Socrates. A man should endure as Socrates did, who
to try his own patience married a scolding wife. She came in on
a winter day from the well and saw her husband reading by the fire.
Not being able to draw an answer to her reproaches, she emptied the
water-pot over his head : but he said only that rain in the course of
nature followed wind, and drew nearer to the fire to dry his clothes.
(639–698.)

I know not if this be reasonable, but such a man ought truly to be
called patient by judgement of Love's Court.

Here again is a tale by which thou mayest learn to restrain thy
tongue. (699–730.)

Jupiter, Juno and Tiresias. Jupiter and Juno fell out upon the
question whether man or wife is the more ardent in love, and they
made Tiresias judge. He speaking unadvisedly gave judgement
against Juno, who deprived him of his sight. Jupiter in compensation
gave him the gift of prophecy, but he would rather have had the
sight of his eyes. Therefore beware, and keep thy tongue close.
(731–782.)

Phebus and Cornide. Phebus loved Cornide, but a young knight
visited her in her chamber. This was told to Phebus by a bird
which she kept, and he in anger slew Cornide. Then he repented,
and as a punishment he changed the bird's feathers from white to
black. (783–817.)

Jupiter and Laar. The nymph Laar told tales of Jupiter to Juno,
and he cut off her tongue and sent her down to hell. There are many

such now in Love's Court, who let their tongues go loose. Be not thou one of these, my son, and above all avoid Cheste.

My father, I will do so : but now tell me more of Wrath. (818–842.)

843–1088. HATE is the next, own brother to Cheste. Art thou guilty of this?

I know not as yet what it is, except ye teach me.

Listen then : Hate is a secret Wrath, gathering slowly and dwelling in the heart, till he see time to break forth.

Father, I will not swear that I have been guiltless of this ; for though I never hated my lady, I have hated her words. Moreover I hate those envious janglers who hinder me with their lies, and I pray that they may find themselves in the same condition as I am. Then I would stand in their way, as they stand in mine, and they would know how grievous a thing it is to be hindered in love.

My son, I cannot be content that thou shouldest hate any man, even though he have hindered thee. But I counsel thee to beware of other men's hate, for it is often disguised under a fair appearance, as the Greeks found to their cost. (843–972.)

King Namplus and the Greeks. After the fall of Troy the Greeks, voyaging home, were overtaken by a storm and knew not how to save their ships. Now there was a king, Namplus, who hated the Greeks because of his son Palamades, whom they had done to death, and he lighted fires to lure their ships towards his rocky coast. They supposed that the fires were beacons to guide them into haven, and many of their ships ran on the rocks. The rest, warned by the cry of those that perished, put forth again to sea.

By this, my son, thou mayest know how Fraud joins with Hate to overthrow men. (973–1088.)

1089–2621. CONTEK and HOMICIDE. Two more remain, namely Contek, who has Foolhaste for his chamberlain, and Homicide. These always in their wrath desire to shed blood, and they will not hear of pity. Art thou guilty of this, my son?

Nay, my father, Christ forbid. Yet as regards love, about which is our shrift, I confess that I have Contek in my heart, Wit and Reason opposing Will and Hope. Reason says that I ought to cease from my love, but Will encourages me in it, and he it is who rules me.

Thou dost wrong, my son, for Will should ever be ruled by Reason, whereof I find a tale written. (1089–1200.)

Diogenes and Alexander. There was a philosopher named Diogenes, who in his old age devised a tun, in which he sat and observed the heavens. King Alexander rode by with his company and sent a knight to find out what this might be. The knight questioned Diogenes, but he could get no answer. 'It is thy king who asks,' said the knight in anger. 'No, not my king,' said the philosopher. 'What then, is he thy man?' 'Nay, but rather my man's man.' The knight told the king, who rode himself to see. 'Father,' he said, 'tell me how I am thy man's man.' Diogenes replied, 'Because I have always kept Will in subjection to me, but with thee Will is master and causes thee to sin.' The king offered to give him whatsoever he should ask. He replied, 'Stand thou out of my sunshine: I need no other gift from thee.'

From this thou mayest learn, my son; for thou hast said that thy will is thy master, and hence thou hast Contek in thine heart, and this, since love is blind, may even breed Homicide. (1201–1330.)

Pyramus and Thisbe. In the city of Semiramis there dwelt two lords in neighbouring houses, and the one had a son named Piramus, and the other a daughter, Tisbee. These loved each other, and when two are of one accord in love, no man can hinder their purpose. They made a hole in the wall between them and conversed through this, till at length they planned to meet near a spring without the town. The maiden was there first; but a lion came to drink at the spring with snout all bloody from a slain beast, and she fled away, leaving her wimple on the ground. This the lion tore and stained with blood, while she lay hid in a bush, not daring to move. Piramus came soon and supposed she had been slain. Reproaching himself as the cause of her death, he slew himself with his sword in his foolhaste. Tisbee came then and found him dead, and she called upon the god and goddess of love, who had so cruelly served those who were obedient to their law. At last her sorrow overcame her, so that she knew not what she did. She set the sword's point to her heart and fell upon it, and thus both were found lying. (1331–1494.)

Beware by this tale that thou bring not evil on thyself by foolhaste.

My father, I will not hide from you that I have often wished to die, though I have not been guilty of the deed. But I know by whose counsel it is that my lady rejects me, and him I would slay if I had him in my power.

Who is this mortal enemy, my son?

His name is *Danger*, and he may well be called 'sanz pite.' It is he who hinders me in all things and will not let my lady receive my suit. He is ever with her and gives an evil answer to all my prayers. Thus I hate him and desire that he should be slain. But as to my lady, I muse at times whether she will be acquitted of homicide, if I die for her love, when with one word she might have saved me.

My son, refrain thine heart from Wrath, for Wrath causes a man to fail of love. Men must go slowly on rough roads and consider before they climb: 'rape reweth,' as the proverb says, and it is better to cast water on the fire than burn up the house. Be patient, my son: the mouse cannot fight with the cat, and whoso makes war on love will have the worse. Love demands peace, and he who fights most will conquer least. Hasten not to thy sorrow: he has not lost who waits.

Thou mayest take example by Piramus, who slew himself so foolishly. Do nothing in such haste, for suffrance is the well of peace. Hasten not the Court of Love, in which thou hast thy suit. Foolhaste often sets a man behind, and of this I have an example. (1495-1684.)

Phebus and Daphne. Phebus laid his love on Daphne and followed his suit with foolish haste. She ever said him nay, and at length Cupid, seeing the haste of Phebus, said that he should hasten more and yet not speed. He pierced his heart therefore with a golden dart of fire, and that of Daphne with a dart of lead. Thus the more Phebus pursued, the more she fled away, and at length she was changed into a laurel tree, which is ever green, in token that she remained ever a maid. Thus thou mayest understand that it is vain to hasten love, when fortune is against it.

Thanks, father, for this : but so long as I see that my lady is no tree, I will serve her, however fortune may turn.

I say no more, my son, but think how it was with Phebus and beware. A man should take good counsel always, for counsel puts foolhaste away.

Tell me an example, I pray you. (1685-1756.)

Athemas and Demephon. When Troy was taken and the Greeks returned home, many kings found their people unwilling to receive them. Among these were Athemas and Demephon, who gathered a host to avenge themselves and said they would spare neither man, woman, nor child. Nestor however, who was old and wise, asked them to what purpose they would reign as kings, if their people should be destroyed, and bade them rather win by fair speech than by threats. Thus the war was turned to peace: for the nations, seeing the power which the kings had gathered, sent and entreated them to lay aside their wrath. (1757-1856.)

By this example refrain thine heart, my son, and do nothing by violence which may be done by love. As touching Homicide, it often happens unadvisedly through Will, when Reason is away, and great vengeance has sometimes followed. Whereof I shall tell a tale which it is pity to hear. (1857-1884.)

Orestes. Agamenon, having returned from Troy, was slain by his wife Climestre and her lover Egistus. Horestes, his infant son, was saved and delivered into the keeping of the king of Crete. When he grew up, he resolved to avenge his father, and coming to Athens gathered a power there with the help of the duke. When he offered sacrifice in a temple for his success, the god gave him command to slay his mother, tearing away her breasts with his own hands and giving her body to be devoured. He rode to Micene and took the city by siege : then he sent for his mother and did as the oracle had commanded. Egistus, coming to the rescue of Micene, was caught in an ambush and hanged as a traitor.

Fame spread these deeds abroad, and many blamed Horestes for slaying his mother. The lords met at Athens and sent for him to come and answer for his deed. He told how the gods had laid a charge upon him to execute judgement, as he had done, and Menesteus, a duke and worthy knight, spoke for him and championed his cause. They concluded upon this that since she had committed so foul an adultery and murder, she had deserved the punishment, and Horestes was crowned king of Micene. Egiona, daughter of Egistus and Climestre, who had consented to the murder of Agamenon, hanged herself for sorrow that her brother had been acquitted. Such is the vengeance for murder. (1885-2195.)

My father, I pray you tell me if it is possible without sin to slay a man.

Yea, my son, in sundry wise. The judge commits sin if he spares to slay those who deserve death by the law. Moreover a man may defend his house and his land in war, and slay if no better may be.

I beseech you, father, to tell me whether those that seek war in a worldly cause, and shed blood, do well. (2196-2250.)

War. God has forbidden homicide, and when God's Son was born, his angels proclaimed peace to the men of good will. Therefore by the law of charity there should be no war, and nature also commends peace. War consorts with pestilence and famine and brings every kind of evil upon the earth. I know not what reward he deserves who brings in such things ; and if he do it to gain heaven's grace, he shall surely fail. Since wars are so evil in God's sight, it is a marvel what ails men that they cannot establish peace. Sin, I trow, is the cause, and the wages of sin is death. Covetousness first brought in war, and among the Greeks Arcadia alone was free from war, because it was barren and poor. Yet it is a wonder that a worthy king or lord will claim that to which he has no right. Nature and law both are against it, but Wit is here oppressed by Will, and some cause is feigned to deceive the world. Thou mayest take an example of this, how men excuse their wrong-doing, and how the poor and the rich are alike in the lust for gain. (2251-2362.)

Alexander and the Pirate. A sea-rover was brought before Alexander and accused of his misdeeds. He replied, ' I have a heart like thine, and if I had the power, I would do as thou dost. But since I am the leader of a few men only, I am called a thief, while thou with thy great armies art called an Emperor. Rich and poor are not weighed evenly in the balance.' The king approved his boldness and retained him in his service. (2363-2417.)

Thus they who are set on destruction are all of one accord, captain and company alike. When reason is put aside, man follows rapine like a bird of prey, and all the world may not suffice for his desires. Alexander overran the whole earth and died miserably, when he thought himself most secure. Lo, what profit it is to slay men for covet-ousness, as if they were beasts. Beware, my son, of slaying. (2418-2484.)

Is it lawful, my father, to pass over the sea to war against the Saracen?

My son, Christ bade men preach and suffer for the faith. He made all men free by his own death, and his apostles after him preached and suffered death : but if they had wished to spread the faith by the sword, it would never have prevailed. We see that since the time when the Church took the sword in hand, a great part of that which was won has been lost to Christ's faith. Be well advised then always ere thou slay. Homicide stands now even in the Church itself; and when the well of pity is thus defouled with blood, others do not hesitate to make war and to slay. We see murder now upon the earth as in the days when men bought and sold sins.

In Greece before Christ's faith men were dispensed of the guilt of murder by paying gold : so it was with Peleus, Medea, Almeus, and so it is still. But after this life it shall be known how it fares with those who do such things. Beasts do not prey upon their own kind, and it is not reasonable that man should be worse than a beast.

Solinus tells a tale of a bird with man's face, which dies of sorrow when it has slain a man. By this example men should eschew homi-cide and follow mercy. (2485-2621.)

I have heard examples of this virtue of MERCY among those who followed the wars. Remember, my son, that this virtue brings grace, and that they who are most mighty to hurt should be the most ready to relieve. (2622-2638.)

Telaphus and Theucer. Achilles and his son Telaphus made war on Theucer, king of Mese. Achilles was about to slay the king in the battle, but Telaphus interceded for him, saying that Theucer once did him good service. Thus the king's life was spared but the Greeks won the victory. Theucer, grateful for this and for other service before rendered by Achilles, made Telaphus heir to all his land, and thus was mercy rewarded. (2639-2717.)

Take pity therefore, my son, of other men's suffering, and let nothing be a pleasure to thee which is grief to another. Stand against Ire by the counsel of Patience and take Mercy to be the governor of thy con-science : so shalt thou put away all homicide and hate, and so shalt thou the sooner have thy will of love.

Father, I will do your hests ; and now give me my penance for Wrath, and ask further of my life.

My son, I will do so. Art thou then guilty of Sloth?

My father, I would know first the points which belong to it.

Hearken then, and I will set them forth : and bear well in mind that shrift is of no value to him that will not endeavour to leave his vice. (2718-2774.)

LIB. IV.

1–312. LACHESCE is the first point of SLOTH, and his nature is to put off till to-morrow what he ought to do to-day. Hast thou done so in love?

Yes, my father, I confess I am guilty. When I have set a time to speak to that sweet maid, Lachesce has often told me that another time is better, or has bidden me write instead of speaking by mouth. Thus I have let the time slide for Sloth, until it was too late. But my love is always the same, and though my tongue be slow to ask, my heart is ever entreating favour. I pray you tell me some tale to teach me how to put away Lachesce. (1–76.)

Eneas and Dido. When Eneas came with his navy to Carthage, he won the love of the queen Dido, who laid all her heart on him. Thence he went away toward Ytaile; and she, unable to endure the pain of love, wrote him a letter saying that if he came not again, it would be with her as with the swan that lost her mate, she should die for his sake. But he, being slothful in love, tarried still away, and she bitterly complaining of his delay, thrust a sword through her heart and thus got rest for herself. (77–146.)

Ulysses and Penelope. Again, when Ulixes stayed away so long at Troy, his true wife Penolope wrote him a letter complaining of his Lachesce. So he set himself to return home with all speed as soon as Troy was taken. (147–233.)

Grossteste. The great clerk Grossteste laboured for seven years to make a speaking head of brass, and then by one half-minute of Lachesce he lost all his labour. (234–243.)

It fares so sometimes with the lover who does not keep his time. Let him think of the five maidens whose lamps were not lit when the bridegroom came forth, and how they were shut out.

My father, I never had any time or place appointed me to get any grace: otherwise I would have kept my hour. But she will not alight on any lure that I may cast, and the louder I cry, the less she hears.

Go on so, my son, and let no Lachesce be found in thee. (244–312.)

313–538. PUSILLANIMITY means in our language the lack of heart to undertake man's work. This vice is ever afraid when there is no cause of dread. So as regards love there are truants that dare not speak, who are like bells without clappers and do not ask anything.

I am one of those, my father, in the presence of my lady.

Do no more so, my son, for fortune comes to him who makes continuance in his prayers. (313–370.)

Pygmaleon. There was one named Pymaleon, a sculptor of great skill, who made an image of a woman in ivory, fairer than any living creature. On this he set his love and prayed her ever for a return, as though she understood what he said. At length Venus had pity on him and transformed the image into a woman of flesh and blood. Thus he won his wife ; but if he had not spoken, he would have failed. By this example thou mayest learn that word may work above nature, and that the god of love is favourable to those who are steadfast in love. About which also I read a strange tale. (371–450.)

Iphis. King Ligdus told his wife that if her child about to be born should be a daughter, it must be put to death. A daughter was born, whom Isis the goddess of childbirth bade bring up as a boy. So they named him Iphis, and when he was ten years old he was betrothed to Iante. Cupid took pity on them at last for the love that they had to one another, and changed Iphis into a man. (451–505.)

Thus love has goodwill towards those who pursue steadfastly that which to love is due.

My father, I have not failed for lack of prayer, except so far as I said above. I beseech Love day and night to work his miracle for me. (506–538.)

539–886. FORGETFULNESS. There is yet another who serves Accidie, and that is Foryetelness. He forgets always more than the half of that which he has to say to his love.

So it has often been with me, father : I am so sore afraid in her presence that I am as one who has seen a ghost, and I cannot get my wits for fear, but stand, as it were, dumb and deaf. Then afterwards I lament and ask myself why I was afraid, for there is no more violence in her than in a child of three years old. Thus I complain to myself of my forgetfulness ; but I never forget the thought of her, nor should do, though I had the Ring of Oblivion, which Moses made for Tharbis. She is near my heart always, and when I am with her, I am so ravished with the sight of her, that I forget all the words that I ought to speak. Thus it is with me as regards forgetfulness and lack of heart.

My son, love will not send his grace unless we ask it. God knows a man's thought and yet he wills that we should pray. Therefore pull up a busy heart and let no chance escape thee ; and as touching Foryetelness I find a tale written. (539–730.)

Demophon and Phyllis. King Demephon, as he sailed to Troy, came to Rhodopeïe, of which land Phillis was queen. He plighted his troth to her, and she granted him all that he would have. Then came the time that he should sail on to Troy, but he vowed to return to her within a month. The month passed and he forgot his time. She sent him a letter, setting him a day, and saying that if he came not, his sloth would cause her death. She watched and waited, putting up a lantern in a tower by night, but he did not return. Then when the day came and no sail appeared, she ran down from the tower to an arbour where she was alone, and hanged herself upon a bough with a girdle of silk. The gods shaped her into a tree, which men called after her Philliberd, and this name it has still to the shame of Deme-phon, who repented, but all too late. Thus none can guess the evil that comes through Foryetelness. (731–886.)

887–1082. NEGLIGENCE is he who will not be wise beforehand, and afterwards exclaims, 'Would God I had known!' He makes the stable-door fast after the steed is stolen. If thou art so in love, thou wilt not achieve success.

My father, I may with good conscience excuse myself of this. I labour to learn love's craft, but I cannot find any security therein. My will is not at fault, for I am busy night and day to find out how love may be won.

I am glad, my son, that thou canst acquit thyself of this, for there is no science and no virtue that may not be lost by Negligence. (887–978.)

Phaeton. Phebus had a son named Pheton, who, conspiring with his mother Clemenee, got leave to drive the chariot of the Sun. Phebus advised him how he should do, and that he should drive neither too low nor too high. But he through Negligence let the horses draw the car where they would, and at last the world was set on fire. Phebus then caused him to fall from the car, and he was drowned in a river. (979–1034.)

Icarus. As in high estate it is a vice to go too low, so in low estate it does harm to go too high. Dedalus had a son named Icharus, and they were in prison with Minotaurus and could not escape. This Dedalus then fashioned wings for himself and his son, and he warned his son not to fly too high, lest the wax with which his wings were set on should melt with the sun. Icharus neglected his father's warning and fell to his destruction : and so do some others. (1035–1082.)

1083–2700. IDLENESS is another of the brood of Sloth and is the nurse of every vice. In summer he will not work for the heat and in winter for the cold. He will take no travail for his lady's sake, but is as a cat that would eat fish and yet not wet his claws. Art thou of such a mould? Tell me plainly.

Nay, father, towards love I was never idle.

What hast thou done then, my son?

In every place where my lady is, I have been ready to serve her, whether in chamber or in hall. When she goes to mass, I lead her up to the offering ; when she works at her weaving or embroidery, I stand by, and sometimes I tell tales or sing. When she will not stay with me, but busies herself elsewhere, I play with the dog or the birds and talk to the page or the waiting-maid, to make an excuse for my lingering. If she will ride, I lift her into the saddle and go by her side, and at other times I ride by her carriage and speak with her, or sing. Tell me then if I have any guilt of Idleness.

Thou shalt have no penance here, my son ; but nevertheless there are many who will not trouble themselves to know what love is, until he overcome them by force. Thus a king's daughter once was idle, until the god of love chastised her, as thou shalt hear. (1083-1244.)

Rosiphelee, daughter of Herupus, king of Armenie, was wise and fair, but she had one great fault of sloth, desiring neither marriage nor the love of paramours. Therefore Venus and Cupid made a rod for her chastising, so that her mood at length was changed. She walked forth once in the month of May, and staying alone under the trees near a lawn, she heard the birds sing and saw the hart and the hind go together, and a debate arose within her as to love. Then casting her eyes about, she saw a company of ladies riding upon white horses. They had saddles richly adorned and were clothed in the fairest copes and kirtles, all alike of white and blue. Their beauty was beyond that of earthly things, and they wore crowns upon their heads such that all the gold of Cresus could not have purchased the least of them.

The king's daughter drew back abashed and hid herself to let them pass, not daring to ask who they were. Then after them she saw a woman on a black horse, lean, galled and limping, yet with a richly jewelled bridle. The woman, though fair and young, had her clothing torn and many score of halters hanging about her middle. The princess came forth and asked her what this company might be, and she said these were they who had been true servants to love, but she herself had been slow and unwilling ; and therefore each year in the month of May she must needs ride in this manner and bear halters for the rest. Her jewelled bridle was granted her because at last she had yielded to love, but death came upon her too suddenly. ' I commend you to God, lady,' she said, ' and bid you warn all others for my sake not to be idle in love, but to think upon my bridle.' Thus she passed out of sight like a cloud, and the lady was moved with fear and amended her ways, swearing within her heart that she would bear no halters. (1245-1446.)

Understand then, my son, that as this lady was chastised, so should those knights take heed who are idle towards love, lest they deserve even a greater punishment. Maidens too must follow the law of love and not waste that time during which they might be bearing the charge of children for the service of the world. And about this I think to tell them a tale. (1447-1504.)

Jephthah's daughter. Among the Jews there was a duke named Jepte, who going to war against Amon, made a vow that if victory were granted to him, he would sacrifice to God the first who should meet him on his return. He overcame his foes and returning met his daughter, who came forth to welcome him with songs and dances. When she saw his sorrow and heard the vow that he had made, she bade him keep his covenant, and asked only for a respite of forty days to bewail her maidenhead, in that she had brought forth no children for the increase of her people. So with other maidens she went weeping over the downs and the dales, and mourned for the lost time which she never could now redeem. (1505–1595.)

Father, ye have done well to rebuke maidens for this vice of Sloth : but as to the travail which ye say men ought to take for love, what mean ye by this ?

I was thinking, my son, of the deeds of arms that men did in former times for love's sake. He who seeks grace in love must not spare his travail. He must ride sometimes in Pruce and sometimes in Tartary, so that the heralds may cry after him, 'Valiant, Valiant !' and his fame may come to his lady's ear. This is the thing I mean. Confess, if thou hast been idle in this. (1596–1647.)

Yea, my father, and ever was. I know not what good may come of slaying the heathen, and I should have little gain from passing over the sea, if in the meantime I lost my lady at home. Let them pass the sea whom Christ commanded to preach his faith to all the world ; but now they sit at ease and bid us slay those whom they should convert. If I slay a Saracen, I slay body and soul both, and that was never Christ's lore.

As for me, I will serve love, and go or stay as love bids me. I have heard that Achilles left his arms at Troy for love of Polixenen, and so may I do : but if my lady bade me labour for her, I would pass through sky or sea at her command. Nevertheless I see that those who labour most for love, win often the least reward, and though I have never been idle in deed, yet the effect is always idleness, for my business avails me nothing. Therefore idle I will call myself.

My son, be patient. Thou knowest not what chance may fall. It is better to wait on the tide than to row against the stream. Perchance the revolution of the heavens is not yet in accord with thy condition. I can bear witness to Venus that thou hast not been idle in love ; but since thou art slow to travail in arms and makest an argument of Achilles, I will tell thee a tale to the contrary. (1648–1814.)

Nauplus and Ulysses. King Nauplus, father of Palamades, came to persuade Ulixes to go with the Greeks to Troy. He, however, desired to stay at home with his wife, and feigning madness he yoked foxes to his plough and sowed the land with salt. Nauplus saw the cause and laid the infant son of Ulixes before his plough. The father turned the plough aside, and Nauplus rebuked him for thus unworthily forsaking the honour of arms and for setting love before knighthood. He repented of his folly and went forth with them to Troy. (1815–1891.)

Thus a knight must prefer honour to worldly ease and put away all dread, as did *Prothesilai*, whose wife wrote to him that he should lose his life if he landed at Troy ; and he took no heed of her womanish fears, but was the first to land, choosing rather to die with honour than to live reproved. (1892–1934.)

Saul too, when the spirit of Samuel told him that he should be slain in battle, would not draw back from the danger, but with Jonathas his son he met his enemies on the mountains of Gelboe, and won eternal fame. (1935-1962.)

Education of Achilles. Prowess is founded upon hardihood, and we know how Achilles was brought up to this by Chiro, called Centaurus. He was taught not to make his chase after the beasts that fled from him, but to fight with such as would withstand him. Moreover a covenant was set that every day he should slay, or at least wound, some savage beast, as a lion or a tiger, and bring home with him a token of blood upon his weapon. Thus he came to surpass all other knights. (1963-2013.)

Other examples there are, as of Lancelot and many more, which show how Prowess in arms has led to success in love. Let this tale be witness of it. (2014-2044.)

Hercules and Achelons. King Oënes of Calidoyne had a daughter Deianire, who was promised in marriage to Achelons, a giant and a magician. Hercules, that worthy knight who set up the two pillars of brass in the desert of India, sought her love, and the king dared not refuse him. It was ordained then that combat should decide between them. Achelons, stirred up to prowess by love, fought boldly, but Hercules seized him with irresistible strength. Then Achelons tried his craft, changing himself into a snake first and then a bull. Hercules, however, held him by the horns and forced him down, till at length he was overcome. Thus Hercules won his wife by prowess. (2045-2134.)

So *Pantasilee,* queen of Feminee, for love of Hector did deeds of prowess at Troy; and *Philemenis,* because he brought home the body of Pantasilee and saved some of her maidens, had a tribute granted to him of three maidens yearly from the land of Amazoine. *Eneas* also won Lavine in battle against king Turnus. By these examples thou mayest see how love's grace may be gained, for worthy women love manhood and gentilesse. (2135-2199.)

What is *Gentilesse,* my father?

Some set that name upon riches coming down from old time, but there is no true merit in riches; and as for lineage, all are descended from Adam and Eve. Rich and poor are alike in their birth and in their death; the true gentilesse depends upon virtue, and for virtue love may profit much. Especially love is opposed to Sloth, and Sloth is most of all contrary to the nature of man, for by it all knowledge is lost. (2200-2362.)

By *Labour* it was that all useful arts were found out, and the names of many inventors have been handed down by fame, as Cham, Cadmus, Theges, Termegis, Josephus, Heredot, Jubal, Zenzis, Promotheus, Tubal, Jadahel, Verconius, and among women Minerve and Delbora. Saturnus found out agriculture and trade, and he first coined money. (2363-2450.)

Many philosophers have contrived the getting and refining of metals and the science of *Alconomie*, by which gold and silver are multiplied, with the working of the seven bodies and the four spirits for the finding of the perfect Elixir.

The philosophers of old made three Stones : the Vegetable, by which life and health are preserved, the Animal, by which the five senses are helped in their working, and the Mineral, by which metals are transformed. This science is a true one, but men know not how to follow it rightly, so that it brings in only poverty and debt. They who first founded it have great names, as Hermes, Geber, Ortolan and others. (2451–2632.)

With regard to *Language*, Carmente was the first who invented the Latin letters, and then came those who laid down the rules of rhetoric, as Aristarchus, Dindimus, Tullius and Cithero. Jerome translated the Bible from Hebrew, and others also translated books into Latin from Arabic and Greek. In poetry Ovid wrote for lovers, and taught how love should be cooled, if it were too hot.

My father, I would read his books, if they might avail me ; but as a tree would perish if its roots were cut away, so if my love were withdrawn, my heart would die.

That is well said, my son, if there be any way by which love may be achieved ; and assuredly he who will not labour and dares not venture will attain to nothing. (2633–2700.)

2701–3388. SOMNOLENCE. The chamberlain of Sloth is Somnolence, who sleeps when he should be awake. When knights and ladies revel in company, he skulks away like a hare and lays himself down to rest ; and there he dreams and snores, and when he wakes, he expounds his dreams. If thou wilt serve love, my son, do not thou so.

Surely not, father ; it were better for me to die than to have such sluggardy, or rather it were better I had never been born. I have never been sleepy in the place where my lady was, whether I should dance with her, or cast the dice, or read of Troilus. When it is late and I must needs go, I look piteously upon her and take leave upon my knee, or kiss her if I may ; and then before I depart from the house, I feign some cause to return and take leave of her again. Then afterwards I curse the night for driving me away from her company, and I sigh and wish for day, or think of the happiness of those who have their love by their side all the long night through. At last I go to bed, but my heart remains still with her: no lock may shut him out, and he passes through the strongest wall. He goes into her bed and takes her softly in his arms, and wishes that his body also were there. In my dreams again I suffer the torments of love, or if I dream sometimes that I meet her alone and that Danger has been left behind, I wake only to find all in vain.

My son, in past times many dreams have told of truth, as thou mayest know by a tale. (2701–2926.)

Ceix and Alceone. Ceix, king of Trocinie, went on a pilgrimage for the sake of his brother Dedalion, and left at home Alceone his wife. She besought him to fix the time of his return, and he said 'Within two months.' The time passed and she heard no tidings, and Juno, to whom she prayed, sent Yris to the house of Sleep, bidding him show this lady by dream how the matter was.

Yris bent the heaven like a bow and came down, and she went to the place where Sleep had his dwelling, in a cave where no sun ever shone and no sound could be heard but the murmur of the river Lethes, which ran hard by. He himself was sleeping in a chamber strewn up and down with dreams, and long it was ere her words could pierce his ears. When he at length understood the message, he chose out three, Morpheus, Ithecus and Panthasas, to do this deed. Morpheus appeared to Alceone in the form of her husband lying dead upon the shore, while the other two showed her in action the scene of the tempest and the wreck. She cried out in terror and awoke, and on the morrow, going down to the sea, she saw his body floating on the waves. Careless of death she leapt into the deep, and would have caught him in her arms; but the gods pitied them and changed them into birds of the sea, and so they dwelt together lovingly. (2927-3123.)

Thus dreams prove sometimes true.

Father, I have said that when I am in my lady's company, I do not desire to sleep. But at other times I care little to wake, for I cannot endure to be in company without her. I know not if this be Somnolence.

I acquit thee, my son, and I will tell a tale to show how little love and sleep are in accord. (3124-3186.)

Prayer of Cephalus. He who will wake by night for love may take example by Cephalus, who when he lay with Aurora prayed to the Sun and to the Moon that the night might be made longer and the day delayed, in order that he might follow only the law of love. Sloth cares nothing for the night except that he may sleep, but Cephalus did otherwise. (3187-3275.)

My father, that is no wonder, since he had his love by his side. But this is never my case, so I have never need to entreat the Sun to stay his chariot, or the Moon to lengthen her course. Sometimes I have a dream that makes me glad, but afterwards I find it untrue: so that I know not of what use sleep is to man.

True, my son, except that it helps nature, when it is taken in due measure. But he who sleeps unduly may come by misfortune, as I can show by a tale. (3276-3316.)

Argus and Mercury. Jupiter lay by Io, wherefore Juno changed her into a cow and gave her into the keeping of Argus, who had a hundred eyes. Mercury came to steal the cow, and he piped so cunningly that Argus fell asleep. So Mercury smote off his head and took away Io. Therefore, my son, beware thou sleep not overmuch. (3317-3364.)

Love will not let me do so, father: but ask further, if there be more.
Yea, my son, one there is to tell of still. (3365-3388.)

3389-3692. TRISTESCE. When Sloth has done all that he may, he conceives Tristesce, which drives him to utter wretchedness. With Tristesce is Obstinacy, and despair follows them. So it is with some lovers, who lose all hope.

I am one of these, father, except that I do not cease to pray.

My son, do not despair; for when the heart fails, all is lost. Listen to a tale about this. (3389-3514.)

Iphis and Araxarathen. Iphis, son of king Theucer, loved a maid of low estate. Though a prince, he was subject to love, but she would not listen to his suit. At length being brought to despair, he came before her house in the night, and having bewailed his case and lamented her hardness of heart, he hanged himself upon the post of the gate. On the morrow the maiden took the guilt upon herself, and prayed that no pity might be shown to her, as she had shown no pity to him. The gods took away her life and changed her into stone; and men carried the body of Iphis to the city and set up the stone image of the maiden above his tomb, with an epitaph telling of their fate. (3515-3684.)

Thus, my son, despair, as I say, is a grievous thing.

Father, I understand now the nature of Sloth, and I will take heed.

LIB. V.

AVARICE is the root of all strife among men. He ever gets more and more and lets nothing go, and yet he has never enough. He has no profit from his riches any more than an ox from his ploughing or a sheep from his wool: instead of being master of his wealth, he serves it as a slave. Dost thou fare so in love, my son?

No, my father, for I was never in possession; but I cannot here excuse my will, for if I had my lady, I would never let her go; and herein I am like the avaricious man. Moreover, though I have not the wealth, yet I have the care, and am like that ox of which ye told before. Judge if this be Avarice.

My son, it is no wonder if thou art a slave to love; but to be a slave to gold is against nature and reason. (1-140.)

Midas. Bacchus had a priest named Cillenus, and he being drunk and wandering in Frige was brought in bonds before Mide, the king of that land. This king dealt with him courteously, and Bacchus in reward of this bade him ask what worldly thing he would. He debated long within himself between three things, pleasure, power and wealth; and at length he asked that all things might be turned by his touch to gold. The boon granted, he tried his power on stone and leaf, but when he at length sat down to meat, then he saw the folly of Avarice, and prayed Bacchus to take back his gift. The god took pity and bade him bathe in Paceole, and so he recovered his first estate; but the stones in the bed of the river were changed to gold. He went home and put away his Avarice, and taught his people to till the land and breed cattle rather than seek increase of gold. (141-332.)

Before gold was coined, war and usury were unknown, but now through Avarice all the world is out of joint. When thou seest a man have need, give him of thy substance, for the pain of *Tantalus* awaits those who will not give : they stand in a river up to their chin and yet cannot drink, and fruit hangs over and touches their lips, of which they cannot eat. Thus Avarice hungers ever after more, though he has enough, and gets no good from that which he has. If thou desirest to be beloved, thou must use largess and give for thy love's sake : if thou wilt have grace, be gracious, and eschew the disease of Avarice. Some men have no rest for fear their gold should be stolen, and so some lovers cannot be at peace for Jealousy. (333-444.)

What is this *Jealousy*, my father ?

It is like a fever, my son, which returns every day. It makes a man look after his lady wherever she goes, and if she make the least sign of countenance to another man, he turns it to a cause of quarrel. Nothing can please him that she does. If he goes from home, he leaves some one to report her doings, and finds fault where there is none. The wife who is married to such a man may well curse the day when the gold was laid upon the book. As the sick man has no appetite for food, so the jealous man has no appetite for love, and yet like the avaricious he is tormented with the fear of losing his treasure. Love hates nothing more than this fever of which I speak, and to show how grievous it is, I will tell thee an example. (445-634.)

Vulcan and Venus. Vulcan the smith had the fair Venus for his wife, whom Mars loved and was beloved again. Jealousy caused Vulcan to spy upon them, and he devised so by his craft that they were caught as they lay together and bound with chains. He called the gods to see, but was only rebuked for his pains. Hence earthly husbands may learn that by Jealousy they bring shame upon themselves. (635-725.)

This example, my father, is hard to understand. How can such things happen among the gods, when there is but one God who is Lord of all ? How come such gods as these to have a place ?

My son, such gods are received by the unwise in sundry places : I will tell thee how. (726-747.)

747-1970. THE RELIGIONS OF THE WORLD. There were four forms of belief before Christ was born.

The *Chaldees* worshipped the Sun, Moon and Stars and the Elements, which cannot be gods because they suffer change. (747-786.)

The *Egyptians* worshipped beasts, and also three gods and a goddess,

**   e

of whom the goddess, Ysis, came from Greece and taught them tillage. (787–834.)

The *Greeks* deified the men who were their rulers or who became famous, as Saturnus king of Crete and Jupiter his son,—such was their folly. Of gods they had besides these Mars, Apollo, Mercury, Vulcan, Eolus, Neptune, Pan, Bacchus, Esculapius, Hercules, Pluto, and of goddesses Sibeles, Juno, Minerva, Pallas, Ceres, Diana, Proserpine; also Satyrs, Nymphs and Manes,—it would be too long to tell the whole. (835–1373.)

Yes, father, but why have ye said nothing of the god and the goddess of love?

I have left it for shame, my son, because I am their priest, but since thou desirest it, I will tell thee. Venus was the daughter of Saturn, and she first taught that love should be common. She had children both by gods and men : she lay with her brother Jupiter and her son Cupid, and she first told women to sell their bodies. Therefore they called her the goddess of love and her son the god. (1374–1443.)

The Greeks took a god to help in whatsoever they had to do. Dindimus, king of the Bragmans, wrote to Alexander, blaming the Greek faith, and saying that they had a god for every member of their body, Minerva for the head, Mercury for the tongue, and so on. (1444–1496.)

Idol-worship came first through Cirophanes, who set up an image of his son, and after that Ninus made a statue of his father Belus, which he caused to be worshipped, and third came the statue of Apis or Serapis, who spoke to Alexander in the cave, when he came riding with Candalus. (1497–1590.)

Thus went the misbeliefs of Grece, of Egypt and of Chaldee. Then, as the book says, God chose a people for himself. Habraham taught his lineage to worship only the one true God, and after they had multiplied in Egypt, God delivered them wondrously by Moises and brought them into the land of promise. But when Christ was born, they failed and fell away; so that they now live out of God's grace, dispersed in sundry lands. (1591–1736.)

God sent his Son down from heaven to restore the loss which we suffered in Adam : so that original sin was the cause of man's honour at the last. By this faith only we can attain to Paradise once more, but faith is not enough without good deeds. Therefore be not deceived by Lollardy, which sets the true faith of Christ in doubt. (1737–1824.)

Christ wrought first and then taught, so that his words explained his deeds, but we in these days have the words alone. Our prelates are like that priest who turned away his eyes and let Anthenor steal the Palladion of Troy. Christ died for the faith, but they say that life is sweet, and they follow only their own ease. Therefore the ship of Peter is almost lost in the waves, and tares are sown among the corn. Gregory complains of the sloth of the prelacy, and asks how we shall appear beside the Apostles in the day of Judgement. We shall be like the man who hid his lord's besant and got no increase upon it. We are slow towards our spiritual work, but swift to Avarice, which, as the apostle says, is idolatry.

My father, for this which ye have said I shall take the better heed: but now tell me the branches of Avarice as well in love as otherwise. (1825-1970.)

1971-2858. COVEITISE. Avarice has many servants, and one of these is Coveitise, who is her principal purveyor and makes his gain in every place. He is as the pike who devours the smaller fishes: for him might is always right. I will tell thee a tale of the punishment of this vice. (1971-2030.)

Virgil's Mirror. Virgil made a mirror at Rome, wherein the motions of all enemies for thirty miles round might be seen. They of Carthage had war with Rome, and took counsel with the king of Puile how they might destroy this mirror. Crassus, the Roman Emperor, was above all things covetous. They sent therefore three philosophers to Rome with a great treasure of gold, which they buried in two places secretly. These men professed to the Emperor that by dreams they could discover ancient hoards of gold, and first one and then the other of these buried treasures was found. Then the third master announced a yet greater treasure, to be found by mining under the magic mirror. As they mined, they underset the supports of the mirror with timber, and on a certain night these three set fire to the timber and fled out of the city. So the mirror fell and was destroyed, and Hanybal slew so many of the Romans in a day, that he filled three bushels with their gold rings. The Romans punished their Emperor by pouring molten gold down his throat, so that his thirst for gold might be quenched. (2031-2224.)

Coveitise in a king or in those of his court is an evil thing, my son; but he who most covets often gains least, and Fortune stands for much as well in courts as elsewhere. (2225-2272.)

The Two Coffers. A king heard that his courtiers complained of unequal rewards for their service. He resolved to show them that the fault lay not with him, and he caused two coffers to be made in all respects alike, the one of which he filled with gold and jewels, and the other with straw and stones. He called before him those who had complained, and bade them choose. They chose the worthless coffer, and he proved to them by this, that if they were not advanced, their fortune only was to blame. (2273-2390.)

Like this is the story of the *Two Beggars* whom the Emperor Frederick heard disputing about riches, and for whom he prepared two pasties, one containing a capon and the other full of florins. (2391-2441.)

Thus it is often with love : though thou covet, yet shalt thou not obtain more than fortune has allotted thee. Yet there are those that covet every woman whom they see, finding something to their liking in each. They can no more judge in matters of love than a blind man can judge of colours.

My father, I had rather be as poor as Job than covet in such a manner. There is one whom I would have, and no more. (2442–2513.)

There are some also who choose a woman not for her face nor yet for her virtue, but only for her riches.

Such am not I, father. I could love my lady no more than I do, if she were as rich as Candace or Pantasilee ; and I think no man is so covetous that he would not set his heart upon her more than upon gold. To one who knows what love is, my lady seems to have all the graces of nature, and she is also the mirror and example of goodness. It were better to love her than to love one who has a million of gold. I say not that she is poor, for she has enough of worldly goods ; yet my heart has never been drawn to her but for pure love's sake.

It is well, my son, for no other love will last. Hear now an example of how coveitise prevailed over love. (2514–2642.)

The King and his Steward's Wife. There was a king of Puile, whom his physicians counselled to take a fair young woman to his bed, and he bade his steward provide. The steward had a wife whom he had married for lucre and not for love, and he set his coveitise before his honour. Having received a hundred pounds from the king to procure him the woman, he brought at night his own wife, against her will. Before the morning he came and desired to take her away, but the king refused to let her go, and at length the steward was compelled to tell him who she was. The king threatened him with death if he remained one day longer in the land, and afterwards he took the woman for his wife. (2643–2825.)

Beware, my son, of this, for it is a great evil when marriage is made for lucre.

Father, so think I, and yet riches may sometimes be a help to love. Now ask me more, if more there be. (2826–2858.)

2859–4382. FALSE WITNESS and PERJURY. Coveitise has two counsellors, False Witness and Perjury, who make gain for their master by lying. So lovers often swear faithful service to a woman, and it is all treachery.

I am not one of these, father : my thought is not discordant to my word. I may safely swear that I love my lady, and if other men should bear witness of it for me, there would be no false swearing.

My son, I will tell thee a tale to show that False Witness is at last found out. (2859–2960.)

Achilles and Deidamia. Thetis, in order that her son Achilles might not go to Troy, disguised him as a girl and put him to dwell with the daughters of king Lichomede. There he was the bedfellow of Deidamie, and so her maidenhead was lost. The Greeks in the meantime assailed Troy in vain, and it was told them by divination that unless they had Achilles, their war would be endless. Ulixes therefore was sent with Diomede to bring him, and coming to the kingdom of Lichomede he could not distinguish Achilles from the rest. Then he set forth the gifts which he had brought for the women, and among them a knight's harness brightly burnished. Achilles left all the rest and chose this, and then he came forth armed in it before them. He was glad enough, but not so Lichomede, who had been so overseen. Thus came out the treachery of False Witness; and if Thetis, who was a goddess, thus deceived Deidamie, what sécurity have women against the untruth of lovers? (2961–3218.)

My father, tell me some tale about Perjury.

I will tell thee, my son, how Jason did to Medea, as it is written in the book of Troy. (3219–3246.)

Jason and Medea. Jason was the nephew of king Peleus ; and desiring to achieve adventures and see strange lands, he took a company of knights, and among them Hercules, and sailed to the isle of Colchos to win the fleece of gold. On the way they touched at Troy, where the king Lamedon treated them discourteously, and then they came to Colchos. Oëtes, who was king there, endeavoured to persuade Jason to leave his adventure, but without success ; and then the princess Medea entertained him with welcome. Moved by love of him she offered him her help to win the fleece, and he plighted his troth to her and swore that he would never part from her. She taught him what to do, and gave him a magic ring and an ointment, telling him also what charms and prayers to use, so that he might slay the serpent which guarded the fleece, yoke the fire-breathing oxen to the plough, sow the teeth of the serpent and slay the knights who should spring up.

He took his leave of her, and passing over the water in a boat did as Medea bade him. Returning with the fleece he was welcomed back by Medea and the rest, and that night he took Medea and her treasure on board his ship and they sailed away to Greece. It was vain to pursue : they were gone.

When they came to Greece, all received them with joy, and these lovers lived together, till they had two sons. Medea with her charms renewed the youth of Eson, Jason's father, and brought him back to the likeness of a young man of twenty years. No woman could have shown more love to a man than she did to Jason ; and yet, when he bare the crown after his uncle Peleus was dead, he broke the oath which he had sworn and took Creusa, daughter of king Creon, to wife. Medea sent her the gift of a mantle, from which fire sprang out and consumed her ; then in the presence of Jason she killed his two sons, and was gone to the court of Pallas above before he could draw his sword to slay her. Thus mayest thou see what sorrow it brings to swear an oath in love which is not sooth. (3247-4229.)

I have heard before this how Jason won the fleece, but tell me now who brought that fleece first to Colchos.

Phrixus and Helle. King Athemas by his first wife had two children, Frixus and Hellen; but his second wife Yno hated them and contrived a device against them. She sowed the land with sodden wheat; and when no harvest came, she caused the priests of Ceres to say that the land must be delivered of these children. The queen bade men throw the children into the sea; but Juno saved them, and provided a sheep with golden fleece, which swam with them over the waves. Hellen for dread fell off his back and so was lost, but her brother was borne over to the isle of Colchos, and there the fleece was set, which was the cause why Jason was so forsworn.

My father, he who breaks his troth thus is worthy neither to love nor to be beloved. (4230-4382.)

4383-4670. USURY. Another of the brood of Avarice is Usury, whose brokers run about like hounds, hunting after gain. He has unequal weights and measures, and he takes back a bean where he has lent a pea. So there are many lovers, who though the love they gave will hardly weigh a mite, yet ask a pound again; and often by the help of their brokers these buy love for little.

My father, I am not guilty of this. That which I give is far more than ever I take again. Usury will have double, but I would be content with half. If my lady reward me not the better, I can never recover my cost. Nor yet have I ever used brokers in love. But thought is free, my father, and to me it seems that my lady herself cannot be excused of this that ye call Usury. For one glance of her eye she has my whole heart, and she will render me nothing again. She has all my love and I go loveless: she says not so much as 'Thanks.' Myself I can acquit, and if she be to blame in this, I pray God to give her grace to amend.

My son, thou speakest ill in that thou accusest thy lady. She may be such that her one glance is worth thy heart many times reckoned. Moreover in love the balance is not even: though thy love weigh more, thou must not ask for return as a debt that is due; for Love is lord and does after his own will. Be patient, and perchance all may turn to good. I am well pleased that thou hast used in love no brokerage to deceive. (4383-4572.)

Echo. Brokers of love receive at last that which they have deserved. Juno had Echo among her maidens, and she was of accord with Jupiter to get him new loves and to blind her lady's eyes. When Juno understood this, she reproved her and took vengeance, sending her to dwell in the woods and hills and repeat always the sound of the voices that came to her ears. (4573-4652.)

If ever thou be wedded man, my son, use no such means as this.

4671–4884. PARSIMONY or SCARCENESS. Another there is whom Avarice has for the keeper of his house, and his name is Scarceness. It is easier to flay the flint than to get from him the value of a rush to help another. How is it with thee, my son? Hast thou been scarce or free towards thy love?

My father, if I had all the treasure of Cresus or the gold of Octovien, I would give it all to her, if I might. But indeed I never gave her any gift, for from me she will not take any, lest I should have some small cause of hope. Yet she takes from others and gives again, so that all speak well of her. As for me, she knows that my heart and all that I have is at her command and will be while I live. (4671–4780.)

Babio and Croceus. Scarceness accords not with love, and often a man has lost the coat for the hood. With gift a man may do much, and meed keeps love in house. Babio had a love named Viola, who was both fair and free; but he was a niggard, and so she was ill served. Croceus, liberal and amorous, came in her way, and she left Babio loveless. (4781–4862.)

My father, if there be anything amiss in me toward my love in this matter, I will amend it.

Thou sayest well, and I will pass on. (4863–4884.)

4885–5504. INGRATITUDE or UNKINDNESS. This is a vice which repays no service, and when he has received a barnful, grudges to give a grain in return. God and Nature both condemn this vice, and even a beast loves the creature who does him kindness, as this tale will show by example. (4885–4936.)

Adrian and Bardus. Adrian, a great lord of Rome, while hunting in a forest, fell into a pit. He cried for help all day, but none heard till evening, when one Bardus, a woodcutter, came by with his ass, and heard Adrian promise to give half his goods to him who should help him. He let down a rope, and first an ape and then a serpent was drawn up by it. Bardus was terrified, but still the voice implored help, and at length Adrian was drawn up. At once this lord departed without thanks, and threatened Bardus with vengeance if ever he should claim the promise. The poor man went home, not daring to speak more, and on the next day, going to get wood, he found that the ape had requited his kindness by gathering for him a great heap of sticks, and so continued to do day by day; and the serpent brought him a precious stone in her mouth. This last he sold to a jeweller and afterwards found it again in his purse, and as often as he sold it, the same thing followed. At length this came to be known, and the Emperor heard of it. Calling Bardus before him he listened to his tale, and gave judgement that Adrian should fulfil his promise. (4937–5162.)

Flee this vice, my son, for many lovers are thus unkind.

Alas, father, that such a man should be, who when he has had what he would of love, can find it in his heart to be false. As for me, I dare not say that my lady is guilty of this Unkindness, but I for my part am free.

Thou must not complain of thy lady, my son. Perchance thy desire is not such as she in honour can grant. It is well that thou art not guilty of Unkindness, and I will tell thee a tale to keep thee in that course. (5163-5230.)

Theseus and Ariadne. Minos, king of Crete, having war with those of Athens, compelled them as a tribute to send nine men yearly, whom he gave to be devoured by Minotaurus. The lot fell at last upon Theseus, son of the king of Athens, and he went with the rest to Crete. Adriagne, daughter of Minos, loved him, and she gave him help to slay the monster. Then he took her away with him by ship, and her sister Fedra went in their company. They rested in the isle of Chio, and there he left Adriagne sleeping, and sailed away with Fedra. Thus by his ingratitude and falsehood he broke the law of love, and evil came of it afterwards. (5231-5495.)

5505-6074. RAVINE. Ravine, in whose service is extortion, seizes other men's goods without right and without payment. So there are lovers who will take possession by force. (5505-5550.)

Tereus. Pandion, king of Athens, had two daughters, Progne and Philomene. Progne was married to Tereus, king of Thrace, and desiring to see her sister, she sent Tereus to Athens to bring her. Coming back in company with Philomene he ravished her, and then maddened by her reproaches cut out her tongue, so that she could speak no articulate words. Then he shut her up in prison, and coming home to his wife, he told her that her sister was dead. Philomene in her prison prayed for deliverance, and at length weaving her story with letters and imagery in a cloth of silk, she sent it by a privy messenger to Progne. Progne delivered her sister, and together they concerted vengeance, with prayers to Venus, Cupid and Apollo. Progne slew the son which she had by Tereus and served up his flesh to him for meat, and when he would have pursued the sisters to take vengeance, the gods transformed them all three, Philomene to a nightingale, which complains ever for her lost maidenhead, Progne to a swallow, which twitters round houses and warns wives of the falsehood of their husbands, and Tereus to a lapwing, the falsest of birds, with a crest upon his head in token that he was a knight. (5551-6047.)

Father, I would choose rather to be trodden to death by wild horses or torn in pieces, than do such a thing as this against love's law. (6048-6074.)

6075-6492. ROBBERY. The vice of Robbery gets his sustenance by that which he can take on the high-roads, in woods and in fields. So there are lovers, who, if they find a woman in a lonely place, will take a part of her wares, no matter who she may be ; and the wife who sits at home waiting for her husband's return from hunting will hear from him nothing of this, but only how his hounds have run or his hawks have flown. (6075-6144.)

Neptune and Cornix. Cornix was a maid attendant on Pallas, and as she went upon the shore, Neptune thought to rob her of the treasure which passes all others and is called the maidenhead. She prayed to Pallas, and by her help escaped from him in the form of a crow, rejoicing more to keep her maidenhead white under the blackness of the feathers than to lose it and be adorned with the fairest pearls. (6145-6217.)

Calistona. King Lichaon had a daughter Calistona, who desired ever to be a maiden and dwelt with the nymphs of Diane. Jupiter by craft stole her maidenhead, and Diane discovering it reproached her, so that she fled away. She was delivered of a son, Archas, but Juno in vengeance transformed her into a bear. In that likeness she met her son in the forest, and he bent his bow against her, but Jupiter ordained for them both so that they were saved from misfortune. (6225-6337.)

Such Robbery, my son, is ever to be avoided, and I will tell thee how in old days VIRGINITY was held in esteem.

Valerius tells how the Emperor did honour to the virgin, when he met her in the way, and we hear also of *Phirinus*, who thrust out his eyes in order that he might the better keep his virginity.

Valentinian moreover, the Emperor, in his old age rejoiced more that he had overcome his flesh, than that he had conquered his enemies in battle. (6338-6428.)

Evil follows when Virginity is taken away in lawless manner, as when Agamenon took Criseide from the city of Lesbon, and plague came upon the host, so that they sent her back with prayer and sacrifice.

Therefore do no Robbery in love's cause, my son. (6429-6492.)

6493-6960. STEALTH. Coveitise has also a servant called Stealth, who takes his prey in secret, coming into houses at night, or cutting purses by day. Like the dog that comes back from worrying sheep, he looks all innocent, so that no man knows what he has done. There are lovers also who take by stealth, either kisses or other things. Hast thou done so ? (6493-6561.)

I dare not, father, for my heart is hers and will not do anything against her. Moreover Danger is so watchful a warden that none can steal anything from her. Strong locks make thieves into honest men, and by no lying in wait can I slip through his guard. Yet at night I often wake when others sleep, and I look out from my window upon the houses round, and mark the chamber where she lies. I stand there long in the cold and wish for some device of sorcery, whereby I might enter that chamber and steal. It brings me ease for the time to think of these things, but it profits me nothing in the end. It is for you to judge if I deserve penance for this or no.

Stealth does little good, my son, in the end. I will tell thee a tale from Ovid of stealth which was done by day. (6562–6712.)

Leucothoe. Phebus loved Leuchotoe, whom her mother kept close in chamber and seldom allowed to go forth. On a day he came in suddenly through her chamber wall and stole her maidenhead. Her father, when he knew, dared not take quarrel with Phebus, but without pity he caused her to be buried alive; and Phebus wrought so that she sprang up as a golden flower, which ever follows the sun. (6713–6783.)

No wonder that this came to evil, my father, because it was done in broad day, but lovers sometimes have kept their thefts more secret. Tell me of something done by night. (6784–6806.)

Hercules and Faunus. Hercules and Eolen, going together on a pilgrimage towards Rome, rested in a cave. Faunus, with Saba and her nymphs, were in a wood hard by, and Faunus, having had a sight of Eolen, thought to come by night and steal. Hercules and Eolen went to rest on separate beds, having to offer sacrifice on the morrow, and as they had exchanged clothes with one another in sport, she had his mace by her and his clothes upon her bed, and he her wimple round his face and her mantle over him. The servants slept like drunken swine. Faunus came into the cave, and feeling the mace and lion's skin, he left her bed alone and went over to the other: Hercules seized him and threw him on the floor, where he still lay helpless on the morrow, a laughing-stock to Saba and the nymphs.

I have too faint a heart, father, for any such michery. (6807–6960.)

6961–7609. SACRILEGE. God has laid down a law that men shall not steal, but work for their sustenance, and yet there are those who will even take the goods of holy Church, and this is called Sacrilege. [There are three kinds of Sacrilege, namely, theft of holy thing from holy place, of common thing from holy place, or of holy thing from common place. (7015*–7029*.)] Three princes especially in old days were guilty of this, Antiochus, Nabuzardan and Nabugodonosor. This last wrought sacrilege in the temple at Jerusalem, and Baltazar his heir paid the penalty. (6961–7031.) [A tale is told of one *Lucius* at Rome, who robbed the statue of Apollo of a ring, a golden mantle and a golden beard, and excused himself, saying that he took the ring because it was held out towards him and offered, the mantle because it was too heavy for summer and too cold for winter, and the beard because it was not fit that Apollo should have a beard, when his father, who stood near him, was beardless. Thus can men feign and excuse themselves. (7105*–7209*.)]

There are lovers who at mass will whisper in their lady's ear or take from her hand a ring or glove. Some go to churches to seek out women and to show themselves there in fresh array, looking round upon them all and sighing, so that each thinks it is for her; and yet such

a man loves none of them, but goes there only to steal their hearts.
All this is Sacrilege.

My father, I do not so : but when my lady goes to matins or to mass,
thither I go also ; and then my looks are for her alone, and my prayers
are that God may change her heart.   I watch and wait to steal from
her a word or look, and when I lead her up to the offering with my
hand about her waist, I win a touch as well.   Except in such things
I have done no Sacrilege, but it is my power and not my will that fails.

Thy will is to blame, my son ; the rest that thou hast said is of little
account.   Yet all things have their time and place : the church is for
prayer and the chamber for other things.   That thou mayest know how
Sacrilege is punished, I will spend on thee a tale.   (7032–7194.)

Paris and Helen.   Lamedon was king of Troy, and against him the
Greeks made war, and they slew him and destroyed his city.   With other
prisoners they took the fair Esiona his daughter, and she was given to
Thelamon.   Priamus, son of Lamedon, built up Troy again, and with
advice of his parliament he sent Antenor to demand back Esiona.   The
Greeks and Thelamon stoutly refused his request, and Priamus called
his parliament again to debate of war or peace.   Hector spoke for peace,
alleging grounds of prudence, though he was ever the first in war ;
but his brother Paris gave his voice for avenging the wrong.   He told
how, as he slept beside a well, three goddesses came before him in
a vision, and Venus, to whom he assigned the golden apple which was
the prize of beauty, had promised to give him in Greece the fairest
woman of all the earth.   Paris then went forth to Greece, though
Cassandra and Helenus lamented for the evil that was to come.
Landed in an isle he met the queen Heleine, who came to do sacrifice
there to Venus, and he stole her heart.   Heleine was in the temple all
the night, offering prayer to Venus, and Paris came all suddenly and
bore her to his ship.   This Sacrilege was the cause why the Greeks
laid siege about Troy, and at last burnt and slew all that was within
it.   (7195–7590.)

Note also how Achilles saw Polixena in the temple of Apollo, and
how Troilus first laid his love on Criseide in a holy place.   Take heed
therefore to thyself.

Thus Avarice has more branches than any other vice, and the working of it is everywhere seen ; but if a man would live rightly, he must
do Largess.   (7591–7640.)

7641–7844.   PRODIGALITY and LARGESS.   Virtue lies between two
extremes : here we see Avarice and Prodigality, and between them
Liberality or Largess, which holds the middle path between too much
and too little.   Where Largess guides a man, he does what is right
both to God and the world, and God rewards him with the gift of
heaven.   The world gives ever to him who hath ; but it is better to
give than to receive, to have thine own good than to crave that of

others. 'If thy good suffice thee not, then refrain thy desires and suffice to thy good.' Charity begins with itself: if thou enrich others making thyself poor, thou wilt have little thanks. 'Jack is a good fellow,' they say while his money lasts, but when that is gone, then 'Jack *was* a good fellow,' and they leave him to starve. (7641-7760.)

There are lovers who spend and waste their love with Prodigality, setting their heart upon many. But he who makes himself thus common, loses the special love of one, if she be wise. Hast thou thus wasted thy love?

Nay, father: I have tasted here and there, but never truly loved any excepting one. On her indeed my love is wasted, for it brings no return: I know not whether this is what ye mean by Prodigality.

My son, perchance thy love is not lost nor wasted. None can say how such a thing will end; therefore I know not whether thou hast lost or won. As summer returns after winter, so perchance thou mayest yet recover thy grace of love. (7761-7834.)

LIB. VI.

1-14. GLUTTONY. The great original sin which brought death on all mankind was Gule, that is, Gluttony. The branches of it are many, but I shall speak of two only.

15-616. DRUNKENNESS makes a wise man foolish and a fool think himself wise. The drunken man thinks that there is nothing that he does not know and nothing that he cannot do, yet he is withal so helpless that he can neither stand nor go; he knows not what he is, nor whether it is day or night. In the morning he calls again for the cup which made him lose his wits at night. The wine binds him fast and makes him a subject and a slave. (5-75.)

There are lovers so besotted with love, that they know no more than drunken men what reason is. The greatest men have been thus overcome: Salomon, Sampson, David, Virgil and Aristotle. Confess if thou art thus drunken, for I think by thy countenance thou art schapen to this malady.

It is true, my father: I confess that I am drunk with love, and often I know not what I do, so that men marvel at me. When I am absent from my lady I am drunk with the thoughts of her, and when I am present, with looking upon her. At times I am in Paradise, and then I wake and my joy is turned to woe. I suffer then the fever of hot and cold, and the evil is that the more I drink, the more I am athirst. Yet I think if I had truly a draught of the drink that I desire, I should be sobered and do well; but tasting of this is forbidden me. (76-305.)

Love-drunkenness, my son, is a grievous thing, and yet none can withstand it. It is not all of one kind, for Jupiter has two tuns full of love-drink in his cellar, the one sweet and the other bitter. Cupid is butler of both, and being blind he gives men to drink of them by chance, now of this and now of that, so that some laugh and others lower. I know by thy tale that thou hast drunk of the potion that is bitter. (306-390.)

Bacchus in the Desert. But thou must ever pray to attain to the other, whereby thy thirst may be allayed, as Bacchus prayed in the desert, when he and all his host were in danger of perishing by thirst. Jupiter sent a ram, which spurned the ground, and there sprang up a fountain of water. (391-439.)

Pray thou thus in thy need: a dumb man seldom gets land. Remember moreover that the butler is blind, and he may by chance give thee a drink of the sweet, which shall cause thee to grow sober.

Of love-drunkenness an example is Tristram, who drank with Bele Ysolde of the drink which Brangwein gave them : and that thou may. the more eschew the company of drunken men, hear this tale. (440-484.)

Marriage of Pirithous. The fair Ipotacie was wedded to Pirotoüs, and he invited his friends to the feast. They became drunk both with wine and with desire, and so they carried away the bride by violence from her husband. (485-529.)

Galba and Vitellus were rulers of Spain, and so drunken were they both that the land cried out against them. They ravished both wife and maid, but at length they were brought under the law and condemned to die. Then they filled full a great vessel of wine and drank until their senses left them, and so they were slain, being already half dead. (537-595.)

617-1260. DELICACY. The vice of Delicacy will not lack any pleasure which meat or drink can give, and desires always something new.

So he who is delicate in love cannot content himself with what he has; but though he have a fair wife, yet he will set his heart on others, and though his lady make him cheer, he must have more than she can with honour give.

I am not guilty of this, father : I would be satisfied if I could be fed at all, except with woe. Yet some dainties I pick which please me for the time. (617-752.)

My sight is fed with dainties when I look upon her face and form, yet it may never be fed to the full, but always longs for more. (753-826.)

My hearing has a dainty feast when men commend her worthiness and grace, and above all when I hear her speak, for her words are to me like the winds of the South. Or again, I feed my ears with tales of those who loved before I was born, of Ydoine and Amadas and of many more, and I think how sorrow endures but for a time. (827-898.)

Finally, I have a cook whose name is Thought, who keeps his pots ever boiling with fancy and desire, and sets before me on the table all the pleasant 'sights that I have seen and words that I have heard. Yet it is no full meal, but one of woulds and wishes, so that the food I have does me little good, and serves only to keep off starvation, till I have the feast which shall satisfy my hunger. (899-938.)

Such are my three delights, and I take my food thus of thinking, hearing and seeing, as a plover does of air. By Delicacy such as this I hope that I do no Gluttony.

It is in small things only that thou hast thy delight, my son; but remember always that the delights of the body do grievance to the soul. (939-974.)

Dives and Lazarus. Christ tells a tale against this vice, which is read in Latin, but for the better knowledge of the truth I will declare it in English. Christ saith, &c. (975-1109.)

Thus, my son, he who follows Delicacy and gives no alms shall fall into distress. He who has power over the good things of this world may wear the richest ornaments and eat the choicest food, yet he must put away Delicacy, if he would not starve his soul while feeding his body. (1110-1150.)

Nero followed his lusts against nature, and in regard to Delicacy he wrought a subtle thing to know how his stomach fared. He chose three men to eat and drink at his table. On a certain day after meat he caused one to ride, another to walk, and the third to sleep, and after this he killed them, in order that he might see which had best digested his food.

He refrained from nothing that was pleasant to him, and above all he set his heart on women, so that he spared neither wife nor maid. So drunk was he with his lusts. (1151-1226.)

Delicacy and Drunkenness go together and pass all bounds of reason. Thus too Love is at times so unrestrained that he takes no heed of God's law, but calls in the powers of heaven and earth and hell to achieve his purpose. (1227-1260.)

1261-2407. SORCERY. There is nothing that love will not dare. He follows no law but his own, and goes forth like Bayard the blind horse, till he fall into the ditch. Thus at times he follows Sorcery, whether Geomance, Ydromance, Piromance or Nigromance, with all the craft both of invocation of spirits and of natural magic.

I know nothing of this, father; but to win my lady I would once have done all that might be done, whether in hell or heaven.

That goes very near, my son: but I warn thee that he who does so is beguiled at last, and that Sorcery has no good end. (1261-1390.)

Ulysses and Telegonus. Of those that were at Troy Uluxes had a name above all for craft and magic arts. This king was vexed by storms as he returned, and in spite of needle and stone his ship was driven upon the strand of Cilly, where he found two queens, Calipsa and Circes. These were sorceresses and they changed many of his men to the form of beasts, but he overcame them with his sorceries, and at length he took his course for home, leaving Circes with child. His wife and all his people rejoiced at his home-coming, but when a man is most in his prosperity, then fortune makes him soonest fall. He had a dream, as he lay upon his bed, and he seemed to see a form of heavenly beauty. He embraced that image and it embraced him again, and it said to him : ' Our acquaintance shall be hereafter to our sorrow : one of us two shall take his death from this love in which we now rejoice.' It showed him then a sign, three fishes wrought upon a pennon, and so all suddenly went forth from him.

Uluxes started from sleep, and making his calculations upon this, he judged that the danger was to be feared from his son Thelamachus. Him therefore he shut up within castle wall, and he made for himself a stronghold and set his servants to keep guard. But none can make resistance against his fate : Thelogonus, his son by Circes, came to find his father, bearing as his ensign a pennon with three fishes upon his spear, and he came to this stronghold of Uluxes. The guards denied him entrance and an affray arose at the gate. The king came forth, and Thelogonus cast his spear at him, not knowing who he was. Uluxes was wounded to death, but he recognized the figure of his dream and the sign upon the pennon, and embraced his son, commending him to the care of Thelamachus before he died.

Lo, what evil came to him of Sorcery : by Sorcery he begat his son, and that which was done against nature was against nature avenged. (1391–1788.)

Nectanabus. The king of Egypt, Nectanabus, a great magician, fled from his enemies to Macedoine. In the chief city there the queen Olimpias kept the feast of her nativity and rode forth to be seen by the people. Nectanabus stood with the others, and gazed upon her so steadfastly, that the queen sent for him and asked him who he was. He replied that he was one who had a message for her, which must be said in private. She appointed a time, and he told her how the god Amos of Lybia desired to be her bedfellow and would beget a child of her who should subdue the whole earth. To prove his words he caused her by his magic to have a vision, which she took for prophecy ; and so at length, coming in the person of the god and transforming himself into various shapes, he had his will of her and begat a son. Nectanabus caused Philip the king, being from home, to have a vision whereby he supposed that a god had lain with his wife, and returning he found her with child. Still he doubted, but by further signs and wonders Nectanabus caused him to forget his jealousy. Amid portents of earthquake and of tempest the child was born, and his name was called Alexander. He grew up, and Aristotle taught him philosophy, while Nectanabus instructed him in astronomy. On a certain night, when they were upon a tower observing the stars, Nectanabus prophesied by them that his own death should be by the hands of his son. Alexander, to prove that he lied, threw him from the tower to the ground, asking what was the use of his art if he could not prophesy his own fate rightly. Nectanabus made known the truth, and Alexander was sorry, and told his mother how it was. Thus he died and was buried, and this was the reward of Sorcery. (1789–2366.)

Zoroaster too and *Saul* came to evil by Sorcery. I counsel thee never to use this, my son. (2367–2400.)

I will not, father. But I beseech you tell me something of that Philosophy which, as ye said, Aristotle taught to Alexander: for to hear of something new might ease my pain.

Thou sayest well; but I, who am of the school of Venus, know not much of this high lore. Yet, as it is comprehended in a book, I can in part show forth to thee how it is. (2401–2440.)

LIB. VII.

1–60. Thou hast prayed me to declare to thee the school of Aristotle, and how Alexander was taught. This is not the matter on which we were set to speak; yet since wisdom is to be desired above all things, I will tell thee of that which Calistre and Aristotle wrote to Alexander.

There are three principal points of Philosophy: Theoric, Rhetoric, Practic.

61–1506. THEORIC. The parts of Theoric are three: Theology, Physics and Mathematics. The first treats of God and things spiritual; the second of bodily things, such as man, beast, herb and stone; and the third has four divisions, Arithmetic, Music, Geometry and Astronomy. (61–202.)

Aristotle taught this young king of the four elements and the four complexions of man, of the principal divisions of the earth, and of the fifth element, Orbis, which contains the whole. (203–632.)

To speak next of *Astronomy*, this Orbis is that which we call the firmament, and in it are first the seven Planets, and then the twelve Signs of the Zodiac, about each of which Alexander was taught in turn. (633–1280.)

Nectanabus, teaching him natural magic, informed him of the Fifteen Stars and of the stone and herb appropriate to each, by means of which wonders may be worked. (1281–1438.)

The authors who taught this science of Astronomy were first Noë, then Nembrot, and after them many others, but principally Tholomee, who wrote the book of Almagest, and Hermes. (1439–1492.)

Thus these Philosophers taught Alexander in regard to that which is called Theoric. (1493–1506.)

1507–1640. RHETORIC. Speech is given to man alone and he must take heed that he turn it to no evil use. There is virtue in stones and in herbs, but word has virtue more than any earthly thing. But the word must not be discordant with the thought, as when Uluxes by his eloquence persuaded Anthenor to betray to him the city of Troy. Words are both evil and good, they make friend of foe and foe of friend. For a true example of Rhetoric read how Julius and the consul Cithero pleaded against one another when the treason of Catiline was discovered.

1641-5397. PRACTIC. This has three divisions, Ethics, Economics and Politics. A king must learn the first in order that he may rule himself in the way of good living, the second teaches him how to order his household, and the third how to govern his kingdom. (1641-1710.)

1711-1984. The first point of Policy is TRUTH, which above all things ought to be found in a king ; and this is in part signified by the jewels of his crown.

To show thee that Truth is the sovereign virtue of all, I will tell thee a tale. (1711-1782.)

King, Wine, Woman and Truth. Daires, Soldan of Perce, had three wise men about his chamber, Arpaghes, Manachaz and Zorobabel. To them he put the question, which is strongest, wine, woman, or a king. Of this they disputed in turn, and Arpaghes said, ' A king is the strongest, for he has power over men and can raise them up and cast them down : also he alone stands free from the law.' Manachaz said, 'Wine is the strongest, for this takes reason away from the wise and makes the fool seem learned, this turns cowardice to courage and avarice to largess.' Zorobabel said, ' Women are the strongest, for the king and all other men come of women and bow to the love of women,' and he told how he had seen Cirus upon his throne overcome by the love of Apemen, daughter of Besazis, so that she did with him what she would. Women too make men desire honour, and woman is next to God the greatest help of man, as *Alceste*, wife of Ametus, gave her life to save her husband. Thus Zorobabel told his opinion, but nevertheless he said that above all these the mightiest of all earthly things is Truth: and so the question was concluded, and Zorobabel was most commended for his judgement. (1783-1984.)

1985-2694. LARGESS is the second point of Policy. A king must be free from the vices both of Avarice and of Prodigality. As Aristotle taught by the ill example of the king of Chaldee, he must spend his own substance and not that of his people, he must do justice before he makes gifts, and his gifts must be to those who have deserved them. (1985-2060.)

Julius and the poor Knight. A knight came to plead his cause at Rome, where the Emperor Julius was in presence ; but he could get no advocate, because he was poor. He prayed for justice to the Emperor, and Julius assigned him an advocate. The knight was angry, and said, ' When I was with thee in Afric, I fought myself and put no man in my stead ; and so thou here shouldest speak for me

** f

thyself.' Julius took his cause in hand; and thus every worthy king should help his servants when in need. (2061-2114.)

Antigonus and Cinichus. A king should know how much to give. A poor knight asked King Antigonus for a great sum, and he replied, 'That is too much for thee to ask': then when the knight asked a very small gift, he said, 'That is too little for me to give.'

Kings must not exceed the due measure in giving, and especially they ought not to give to flatterers, who offend against God, against the prince and against the people. Yet flattery is always found in the courts of kings. (2115-2216.)

Diogenes and Aristippus. Two Philosophers went from Carthage to Athens to learn, and thence returned again. The one, Diogenes, was content to dwell apart and study, the other, Arisippus, went to court and got honour and wealth by flattery. Diogenes was gathering herbs in his garden and washing them in the river, when Arisippus passed by with a company, and said, 'If thou hadst known how to make thyself pleasing to thy prince, there would have been no need for thee to pick herbs.' The other replied, 'If thou hadst known how to pick herbs, there would have been no need for thee to make thyself pleasing by thy flatteries.' (2217-2317.)

But the example of Arisippus is chiefly followed, and flattery is that which makes men beloved. [Dante the poet said once to a flatterer, 'Thou hast many more servants than I, for a poet cannot find how to feed and clothe himself, but a flatterer may rule and lead a king and all his land.'] There was a custom among the Romans, which was established against flattery, as follows. (2318-2354.)

Roman Triumph. When an Emperor had a triumph after victory, he went in pomp with four white horses and the nobles of the land before and behind him: but one sat with him in his car, who said continually, 'Know thyself, and remember that good fortune is only for a time.' Moreover he and every other man might speak whatever truth he knew to the Emperor, whether good or bad. (2355-2411.)

The Emperor and his Masons. Again, when an Emperor was enthroned, his masons came to ask him how he would have the stone made for his tomb. There was no flattery then, to deceive princes. (2412-2448.)

Caesar's Answer. One came and did reverence to Cesar, as if he were a god: then he came and sat down by his side as an equal. 'If thou art a god,' he said, 'I have done well in worshipping thee, but if a man, in sitting by thy side.' Cesar answered that he was a fool, and had done ill in one of two things, either in sitting by the side of his god or in worshipping a mere man. They that heard this took it as a lesson against flattery. (2449-2490.)

The king who bestows his goods upon flatterers does harm to himself and his land. There is an example in the Bible. (2491-2526.)

Ahab and Micaiah. I Kings xxii. (2527-2694.)

2695-3102. JUSTICE is the third point of Policy. A land is nothing without men, and men cannot be without law. It is for the king above all others to guide the law, and though he is above the law, yet he must not do things which are against it. He must make his own life right towards God, and then endeavour to rule his people rightly, and he must see that his judges are both wise and true. (2695-2764.)

Maximin, when he appointed a judge, inquired carefully whether he were virtuous or no. Thus the course of law was not hindered by coveitise. (2765-2782.)

Gaius Fabricius, consul of Rome, when the Samnites brought him gold, tried it with taste and smell, and said he knew not for what it would serve. It was better, he said, to rule the men who had the gold, than to possess gold and lose the liberty to be just. (2783-2817.)

In those times none was preferred to the office of judge unless he were a friend to the common right. (2818-2832.)

Conrad ordered matters so that in his time no man durst set aside the law for gold. (2833-2844.)

Carmidotoire the consul slew himself rather than allow his own law to be broken, when by inadvertence he had come armed to the Senate-house. (2845-2888.)

Cambyses flayed a corrupt judge, and nailed his skin upon the chair where his son was set to judge in his place. (2889-2904.)

Ligurgius, prince of Athens, having established good laws in his city, took an oath from the citizens that they would change nothing during his absence ; and so he departed, never to return, desiring that Athens might still enjoy good laws. (2917-3028.)

The first Lawgivers. The names of those who first made laws ought to be handed down to fame. They are Moses, Mercurius, Neuma Pompilius, Ligurgius, Foroneus, Romulus. Kings ought to be led by law, and it is a scandal to a king if the law be not executed. (3029-3102.)

3103-4214. The fourth point of Policy is PITY. This is the virtue by which the King of kings was moved when he sent his Son down to this earth. Every subject should fear his king, and every king should have mercy on his people. [The apostle James says that he who shows no pity shall find none. Cassodre says that the kingdom is safe where pity dwells. Tullius that the king who is overcome by pity bears a shield of victory. We read how a knight appealed from the wrath of Alexander to his pity and so obtained grace. (3149*-3179*.)] Constantine said, 'He who is a servant to pity, is worthy to rule all else.' Troian said that he desired his people to obey him rather from love than fear. (3103-3162.)

[*The Pagan and the Jew.* Two travellers went through the desert together, and each asked the other of his belief. The one said, 'I am a Pagan, and by my faith I ought to love all men alike and do to others as I would they should do to me.' The other, 'I am a Jew, and by my faith I ought to be true to no man, except he be a Jew, as I am.' The day was hot and the Pagan rode on an ass with his baggage, while the Jew went on foot. The Jew asked the Pagan to let him ease his weariness by riding, and the other assented. So they went on, but when the Pagan desired his ass back, the Jew rode on, saying that thus he did his duty by his law. The Pagan prayed to God to judge his quarrel, and going on further he found the Jew slain by a lion and the ass with the baggage standing by him. Thus a man may know how the pitiful man deserves pity, and that lack of pity is the cause of evil. (3207*-3360*.)]

Codrus, king of Athens, having a war, was informed by Apollo that either he must perish in the battle or his people be discomfited. He had pity upon his people and gave his life for them. Where have we such kings now? (3163-3214.)

Pompey had war against the king of Ermenie, and having taken him captive, he gave him his crown again and restored him to his kingdom. (3215-3248.)

Cruelty is the opposite of Pity. (3249-3266.)

Leoncius the tyrant cruelly cut off the nose and lips of the merciful Justinian: he was so served himself by Tiberius, and Justinian was restored to the empire. (3267-3294.)

Siculus the cruel king caused Berillus to make a bull of brass, within which men should be burnt to death. Berillus was himself the first who suffered this torture. (3295-3332.)

Dionys fed his horses on man's flesh and was slain by Hercules. (3341-3354.)

Lichaon devoured the bodies of his guests and was changed into a wolf. (3355-3369.)

Tyranny may not last. The Lion will not slay the man who falls down before him to entreat mercy, and how then ought a Prince to destroy the man who asks his mercy? Yet some tyrants have been so cruel that Pity cannot move them. (3370-3416.)

Spertachus, a warrior and a cruel man, made war on the queen Thameris, and having taken her son prisoner, he slew him without mercy. The queen gathered a power and took the tyrant in an ambush. Then she filled a vessel with the blood of his princes and cast him therein, bidding him drink his fill of blood. (3417-3513.)

A king, however, must not fail to slay in the cause of Justice, and he must be a champion of his people without any weak pity. If he fears without cause, he is like those in the fable who were in dread when the Mountain was in labour, and at length it brought forth a mouse.

As there is a time for peace, so there is also a time for war, and here too virtue stands between two extremes, between foolish pity and rash cruelty. Of men who have undertaken war for a righteous cause there are examples in the Bible, and of those I will tell thee one. (3514-3626.)

Story of Gideon. Judges vii. (3627-3806.)

Saul and Agag. Saul failed to obey God's command to slay Agag, showing pity wrongfully : therefore he lost his life and his kingdom. (3807-3845.)

On the other hand *Salomon* obeyed his father David's command in slaying Joab, and yet he showed mercy in his reign and wrought no tyranny. Also he was wise and had worthy men about him, and there is nothing better for a ruler than Wisdom. Salomon asked for this gift from God, and this it is which a king chiefly needs in order to hold the balance even between Justice and Pity. (3846-3944.)

Courtiers and Fool. Lucius, king of Rome, asked his steward and his chamberlain what men said about him. The steward merely flattered in his reply, but the chamberlain answered that people thought he would be a worthy king if he had good counsellors. The fool, who played with his bauble by the fire, laughed at both, and said, ' If the king were wise, the council would not be bad.' Thus the king was instructed and put away his bad counsellors. (3945-4010.)

Folly of Rehoboam. 1 Kings xii. 1-20. (4027-4129.)

Counsel of young men thus leads to ruin. There is a question whether it is better that the king be wise or his council. The answer is that it is better to have wise counsellors. (4130-4180.)

The Emperor *Anthonius* said he would rather have one of his subjects saved than a thousand of his enemies slain. Mercy mingled with justice is the foundation of every king's rule. Thus I have spoken of four points, Truth, Largess, Pity and Justice. There is yet a fifth. (4181-4214.)

4215-5397. CHASTITY, the fifth point of Policy. The male is made for the female, but one must not desire many. A man must keep the troth he has plighted in marriage, and this all the more in the high and holy estate of a king.

Aristotle advised Alexander to frequent the company of fair women, but not to beguile himself with them. For it is not they who beguile the men, but the men beguile themselves. The water is not to blame if a man drown himself in it, nor the gold if men covet it. It is by nature that a man loves, but not by nature that he loses his wits : that is like frost in July or hose worn over the shoe. Yet great princes have been thus misled. (4215-4312.)

Sardanapalus lost his kingdom and his honour, because he became effeminate in his lusts. (4313-4343.)

David, however, though he loved many women, preserved the honour of knighthood. (4344-4360.)

Cyrus had a war with the *Lydians,* and he could not conquer them.

Then, feigning, he made a perpetual peace with them, and they fell into idleness and fleshly lust, so that he subdued them easily. (4361–4405.)

Balaam advised king Amalech to send fair women among the Hebrews, and these led them into lust, so that they were discomfited in battle, till Phinees caused them to amend their ways. (4406–4445.)

This virtue of Chastity belongs especially to a king.

Salomon took wives of sundry nations and did idolatry in his folly. Therefore after his death his kingdom was divided.

Antonie, son of Severus, gave an evil example of lust; and the tale which here follows will show what is the end of tyranny and lechery. (4446–4592.)

Tarquin the tyrant had many sons, and among them Arrons. He had a war with the Gabiens, and to their city Arrons went, showing wounds which he said he had received from his father and brethren. They took him as their leader, and he by his father's advice cut off the heads of their chief men, and so the Romans conquered the city. They made a solemn sacrifice in the temple of Phebus, and a serpent came and devoured the offerings and quenched the fires. Phebus said that this was for the sin and pride of Tarquin and his son, and that he who should first kiss his mother, should avenge the wrong. Brutus fell to the ground and kissed his mother Earth. (4593–4753.)

Tarquin had a war afterwards with Ardea, and they were long at the siege. A dispute arose between Arrons and Collatin as to the virtue of their wives, and they rode to Rome to see how they were employed. At the palace they found the wife of Arrons full of mirth and thinking nothing of her husband; at the house of Collatin, Lucrece was working with her women and praying for her husband's return. Arrons was smitten with love of her, and returning again the next day he ravished her. She on the morrow called her husband and her father, with whom came Brutus, and told them her tale. Refusing their forgiveness she slew herself, and they took the body into the market-place, where Brutus told the tale to the people. They remembered also the former evil doings of Tarquin and his son, and sent both into exile. (4754–5130.)

Virginia. When Appius Claudius was governor of Rome, he set his desire upon a gentle maid, daughter of Livius Virginius, and he caused his brother Marcus to claim her unrightfully as his slave. Her father was with the host, but he rode hastily to Rome; and when Appius adjudged her to his brother against the law, finding that he could save her from dishonour in no other way, he thrust her through with his sword and made his way back to the host. Thus the tyranny came to men's ears and the unrighteous king was deposed by the common consent. (5131–5306.)

As an example of chastity in marriage we read the story of *Sarra* the daughter of Raguel. Seven men who married her were strangled by the fiend Asmod, because they took her only for lust; but Thobie, taught by Raphael, had his will and yet kept the law of marriage. God has bound beasts by the law of nature only, but men must follow also the law of reason and do no lechery. Thus the philosopher taught to Alexander. (5307-5397.)

I thank you, father. The tales sound in my ears, but my heart is elsewhere; for nothing can make me forget my love. Leave all else therefore, and let us return to our shrift.

Yes, my son, there is one point more, and this is the last. (5398-5438.)

LIB. VIII.

1-198. LAWS OF MARRIAGE. God created Adam and Eve to repair the loss of Lucifer and his angels, and bade them increase and multiply. In the first generation by God's law brother and sister were joined in marriage, then afterwards cousin wedded cousin, as in the time of Habraham and Jacob. At last under Christian law Marriage was forbidden also in the third degree. Yet some men take no heed to kinship or religion, but go as a cock among the hens and as a stallion among the mares. Such love may be sweet at first, but afterwards it is bitter.

199-2008. EXAMPLES OF INCEST. *Caligula* the Roman Emperor bereft his three sisters of their virginity : therefore God bereft him of his life and of his empire.

Amon lay with his sister Thamar, and Absolon his brother took vengeance upon him.

Lot lay with his daughters, and the stocks which came from them were not good.

Thus if a man so set his love, he will afterwards sorely repent it; and of this I think to tell a tale which is long to hear. (199-270.)

Apollonius of Tyre. In a Chronicle called Pantheon I read how king Antiochus ravished his daughter and lived with her in sin. To hinder her marriage, he proposed a problem to those who sought her love, and if a man failed to resolve it, he must lose his head. At length came the Prince Apollinus of Tyre, and the king proposed to him the question. He saw too clearly what the riddle meant, and Antiochus fearing shame put off the time of his reply for thirty days. (271-439.)

The Prince feared his vengeance and fled home to Tyre, and thence he departed secretly in a ship laden with wheat. Antiochus sent one Taliart in all haste to Tyre, with command to make away with the Prince by poison. Finding that Apollinus had fled, he returned.

In the meantime the Prince came to Tharsis, and took lodging there with one Strangulio and his wife Dionise. The city was suffering famine, and Apollinus gave them his wheat as a free gift, in return for which they set up a statue of him in the common place. (440–570.)

A man came to him from Tyre and reported that king Antiochus desired to slay him. He was afraid and fled thence again by ship. A storm came upon him and the ship was wrecked : Apollinus alone came alive to land. A fisherman helped him and directed him to the town of Pentapolim, where he found the people gathered to see games, and the king and queen of the country there present. (571–695.)

He surpassed all others in the games, and the king called him to supper in his hall. At supper he was sad and ate nothing, and the king sent to him his daughter to console him. To her he told his name and country, and with that he let the tears run down his cheeks. She fetched a harp and sang to it, and he took it from her hand and played and sang divinely. They all saw that he was of gentle blood. (696–799.)

The king's daughter desired her father that he might be her teacher, and in the course of time she turned with all her heart to love of him. She so lost her appetite for meat and drink and sleep that she was in danger of her life.

Three sons of princes demanded her in marriage, and she by letter informed her father how the matter stood : if she might not have Apollinus, she would have none other. (800–911.)

The king sent for Apollinus and showed him his daughter's letter. He assented gladly, and the marriage took place with great festivity. Soon after this men came from Tyre reporting that Antiochus and his daughter were dead, having been both struck by lightning, and entreating him to return to his own people. All were rejoiced to hear that the king's daughter had married so worthy a prince. (912–1019.)

Apollinus sailed away with his wife, she being with child. A storm arose and she began to be in travail. In anguish she was delivered of a maid child, but she herself lay dead. (1020–1058.)

Apollinus sorrowed as never man sorrowed before, but the master of the ship required that the dead body be cast out of the ship, because the sea will not hold within itself any dead creature, and the ship would be driven on the shore if the body remained within her. They made therefore a coffer closely bound with iron and covered with pitch, in which they placed the corpse, with gold and jewels, and with a letter praying that she might receive burial ; and so they cast it overboard. Apollinus in the meantime sailed first to Tharsis. (1059–1150.)

The coffer was cast up at Ephesim and was found by Cerymon, a great physician. He by his art restored the seeming corpse to life, and she took upon herself the rule of religion and dwelt with other women in the temple of Diane. (1151–1271.)

Apollinus coming to Tharsis entrusted his infant daughter Thaise to the care of Strangulio and Dionise, and so he sailed on to Tyre. This daughter, until she was fourteen years old, grew up with the daughter of Strangulio, but Thaise was preferred to the other in all places where they went, and Dionise was therefore wroth. She bade her bondman Theophilus take Thaise down to the shore of the sea and there slay her. He brought her to the sea, but her cry called forth pirates from their hiding-place, who carried her with them away to Mitelene and sold her to Leonin, master of a brothel. (1272-1423.)

The young men who came to her were moved by compassion and did her no wrong, so that Leonin sent his own servant in to her. She entreated to be permitted to make gain for him in some other way, and being taken from the brothel and placed in security, she taught such things as gentlewomen desire to learn, and her name went forth over all the land. (1424-1497.)

Theophilus reported that he had slain Thaise, and Dionise, pretending that she had died suddenly, made a great funeral and set up a tomb with an epitaph. After this, Apollinus came to seek for his daughter at Tharsis, and hearing that she was dead, he put forth to sea again in grievous sorrow. He lay weeping alone in the darkness of the ship's hold, until under stress of storm they came to Mitelene. (1498-1617.)

Hearing of his grief, the lord of the city, Athenagoras, sent Thaise to comfort him. He at first rejected all her consolation, but then to his joy discovered that she was the daughter for whom he mourned. Athenagoras asked for her in marriage and was wedded to her. (1618-1776.)

They went forth all together with intent to avenge the treason at Tharsis, but Apollinus was warned in a dream to go to Ephesim, and there in the temple of Diane he found the wife whom he supposed to have been dead. Thence they voyaged to Tyre and were received with joy. Athenagoras and Thaise were there crowned king and queen, and Apollinus sailed away and took due vengeance upon Strangulio and Dionise. (1777-1962.)

When this was done, a letter came to him from Pentapolim, praying him to come and receive that kingdom, since the king was dead. They had a good voyage thither, and he and his wife were crowned there and led their life happily. (1963-2008.)

Thus, my son, thou mayest see how it is with those that love in a good manner, but it is not love when men take their lust like beasts.

2029-3172. CONCLUSION. Father, I may acquit myself in this, but I entreat your counsel as to what way I shall follow in my love.

I counsel thee, my son, to labour no more in things which bring thee no profit. The end of every pleasure is pain. Love is blind, and makes all his servants blind: thou mayest yet withdraw and set thyself under the law of reason.

It is easy to say so, father. My woe is but a game to you, feeling nothing of that which I feel. The hart that goes free knows not the sorrows of the ox under the yoke. But I entreat you to present for me a Supplication to Venus and Cupid, and bring me a good answer back. (2009-2188.)

Then arose a great debate between my Priest and me : my reason understood him well, but my will was against him. At length he agreed to deliver my Supplication, and with tears instead of ink I wrote the letter thus : 'The wofull peine of loves maladie,' &c. (2189-2300.)

The Priest went forth to present my petition, and I abode. Suddenly Venus stood by me, and I fell upon my knee and prayed her to do me grace. 'What is thy name ?' she said, as if in game. 'John Gower,' I replied. 'I have read thy bill,' she said, 'in which thou hast complained to Nature and to me. Nature is mistress where she will, and I excuse thee for following her law : but as for what thou sayest, that I am bound to relieve thee, because thou hast served in my Court, I will give thee medicine that will heal thy heart, but perchance it will not be such as thou desirest.' (2301-2376.)

Half in scorn she spoke to me of my age and hoary locks, and counselled me to make a 'beau retret,' while there was yet time ; for even though I should attain to my desire, I could not hold covenant duly with love.

I grew cold suddenly for sorrow of my heart, and lay swooning on the ground. Then methought I saw Cupid with his bow bent, and with him a great company, those gentle folk who once were lovers, arrayed in sundry bands. (2377-2459.)

Youth was the leader of one company, and these had garlands, some of the leaf and some of the flower. They went with piping and with song which resounded all about : they laughed and danced and played, and talked of knighthood and of ladies' love. There was Tristram with Ysolde, Lancelot with Gunnore, Jason with Creusa, Hercules with Eole, Troilus with Criseide, but in his mirth he was yet heavy of cheer because of Diomede. Those also I saw who died for love, as Narcissus, Piramus, Achilles ; and the women who were forsaken, Dido, Phillis, Adriagne, Deianire and Medea. Many others too I saw, but four women especially who were most commended as examples in marriage, Penolope, Lucrece, Alceste and Alcione. Youth, which led this company, took no heed of me. (2460-2665.)

Then came Eld, leading a company not so great. Their music was low and their dancing soft : they smiled, but they did not laugh aloud. There was David with Bersabee, and Salomon with his wives and concubines, Sampson with Dalida, and Aristotle with the queen of Greece ; Virgil also and Plato and Ovid the poet. (2665-2725.)

When this company was come to the place where I lay, they entreated Venus for me, and even some of the younger band said that it was great pity. Cupid came with Venus to me as I lay, and the lovers all pressed round to see. Some said that love was folly in the old, and others that no age could be free, and that while there was yet oil in the lamp, it might always be set alight. Cupid groped after me till he found me, and then he drew forth that fiery lance which before he had cast through my heart, and Venus anointed my wound with a cooling ointment and gave me a mirror in which I might behold myself. I saw my face wrinkled and my eyes dim, and I likened myself to that time of year when winter has despoiled the earth. Then Reason returned to me and I was made sober and sound. (2726–2869.)

Venus beheld me, and laughing asked me what Love was. I answered with confusion that I knew him not, and prayed that I might be excused from my attendance on her Court. As touching my Confession too, I asked an absolution, and the Priest gave it readily. Then the queen delivered to me a pair of beads to hang about my neck, and on them was written *Por reposer* in gold. 'Thus,' said she, 'have I provided for thine ease, and my will is that thou pray for peace. Stay no more in my Court, but go where moral virtue dwells, where are those books which men say that thou hast written : thou and I must commune together never again. *Adieu, for I must go from thee.' And so enveloped in a starry cloud, Venus was taken to her place above, and her Priest departed also at the same time. I stood for a while amazed ; and then I smiled, thinking of the beads that she had given me and of the prayers that I should say. And thus I took my way softly homeward. (2870–2970.)

To God, the Creator of all things, I pray for the welfare of this land, and that it may have peace and unity, which every estate should desire. I pray that the clergy may work after the rule of charity, that the order of knighthood may cause extortion to cease and defend the right of the Church, that merchants may follow honesty, and above all that the king may keep himself and all the other estates of the kingdom in the right way. The king who humbly follows the law of

---

* Adieu, for I must go from thee. And greet Chaucer well, as my disciple and my poet, who has filled the land with the songs which he made for my sake. And bid him in his later age make his testament of love, as thou hast made thy shrift.'

And so enveloped in a starry cloud, Venus was taken to her place above, and I turned homeward with my beads in hand. (2940*–2970*.)

To God, the Creator of all things, I pray for my worthy king Richard the Second, in whom has always been found Justice mingled with Pity. In his person it may be shown what a king should be, especially in that he sought no vengeance through cruelty. Though evil came upon the land, yet his estate was kept safe by the high God, as the sun is ever bright in himself, though the air be troubled. He sought love and peace and accord, not only here at home, but abroad also, following

God shall be blessed, and his name shall be remembered for ever. (2971-3105.)

I promised to make in English a book between play and earnest, and now I ask that I may be excused for lack of curious skill. I have written in rude plain words, as sickness and age would suffer me ; and I pray my lords that I may stand in their grace, for I desire to do pleasure to those under whose rule I am. (3106-3137.)

And now my Muse bids me rest and write no more of love, which turns the heart away from reason. Of this love then I take my final leave. But that love which stands confirmed by charity, which may save the body and amend the soul, such love may God send us, that in heaven our joy may be without end. (3138-3172.)

Christ's way, and therefore are we bound to serve him, and his name shall be ever remembered. (2971*-3035*.)

I, his subject, helpless with old age and sickness, desire to do him some pleasure, and therefore I present to him this poor book, made both for profit and for sport, and I ask that I may be excused for lack of curious skill. I have written, as I best might, in rude plain words.

And now that I am feeble and old, my Muse bids me rest and write no more of love. He who has achieved what he desired may fitly do his service to love in songs and sayings ; but if a man fail, it is otherwise : therefore I take now my final leave of love. But that love which stands confirmed by charity, which brings no repentance and charges not the conscience, this may God send us, that in heaven our joy may be without end. (3036*-3114*.)

iv. ORTHOGRAPHY AND PHONOLOGY.—In the remarks upon Gower's language which here follow there is no systematic completeness. Attention is called to such points as seem to be important or interesting, reference being made especially to the language of Chaucer, as dealt with in B. ten Brink's *Chaucers Sprache und Verskunst* (second edition, 1899). It is necessary perhaps to remark here upon a difference of procedure which distinguishes this investigation from those which have for their object the text of Chaucer or of other writers whose work is handed down to us in manuscripts which do not proceed from the author himself. In such cases we have first to ascertain what the author actually wrote, before we can draw any valid conclusions about the laws of his language. It may even be necessary to restrict the discussion to such forms as are authenticated by rhyme ; but when we are compelled to do this, we must remember that we are accepting a rather dangerous limitation. The conclusions drawn from the rhyme-words of a Middle English author will probably not be precisely applicable to his language in general. The sphere of our investigations will be that in which the licentious and exceptional is most likely to be found. If he has any tendency to borrow from other dialects than his own or to use irregular forms, this tendency will be most seen in his·rhymes, for it will probably be the exigencies of rhyme which suggest the variation. Chaucer repeatedly uses 'here,' in the sense of the modern 'her,' to rhyme with such words as 'bere,' 'spere,' but we should certainly not be justified in concluding that this and not 'hire' was the normal form of his language. Similarly in the case of Gower by examination of his rhymes alone we might be led to many very doubtful results. For example, we should gather that he almost always used the form *sinne* rather than *senne*, *wile* (verb) and not *wole* or *wol*, *axe* and not *aske, sek* (adj.) and never *sik, hond* and never *hand, couthe* and never *coude, sente* (pret.) rather than *sende*, the adverb ending *-ly* in preference to *-liche* or *-lich*. In these cases and in many others we might easily be misled, the forms of these words as used in rhyme being determined chiefly by the comparative frequency of the various rhyme-syllables. Most of the conclusions above mentioned, and others like them, have in fact been arrived at in a paper by K. Fahrenberg, published in the *Archiv für die neueren Sprachen*, vol. 89. The author of this paper, having only Pauli's text before him, very properly confines himself to an examination of the rhymes, and within these limits most of his results are sound enough ; but it would be very unsafe to treat them as generally applicable to the language of Gower. In our case it must be understood that the Fairfax manuscript is regarded (for reasons which will afterwards be stated) as a practically accurate reproduction of the author's original text, and consequently the occurrence of a particular form in rhyme is not held necessarily to be of any special significance.

ORTHOGRAPHY.—This being premised, we shall proceed to note first some points which call for attention in the orthography of the text.

In describing the British Museum MS. Harl. 3869, Pauli takes occasion to observe: 'This copy is very remarkable on account of its orthography, which has been carried through almost rigorously according to simple and reasonable principles.' This system he appears to attribute to the copyist of the manuscript in question, but it is in fact that of the author, the text being copied very faithfully from the Fairfax manuscript itself. Pauli appears to have been repelled by the outward appearance of this 'small stout folio' with its rather untidy writing. He did not take the trouble to examine the Oxford copies ; but he seems to have perceived that its orthography was the same as that of the Stafford manuscript, and this should have enlightened him. In fact, if instead of taking Berthelette as his basis, he had simply printed the text of the Harleian volume, there would hardly have been need of another edition.

The orthography of the Fairfax text, first hand, confirmed as it is in almost every particular by that of the Stafford manuscript, and supported also by the testimony of others, more especially of MS. Bodley 902, may be assumed to be that of the author ; and it is well worthy of our attention, for he evidently regarded exactness and consistency in spelling as a matter of some importance.

We may observe in the first place that it was not Gower's practice to mark vowel-length by doubling the vowel. Naturally there are some MSS. in which this is occasionally found, and in particular the third hand of A gives *caas, paas, glaade, maade, saake, waas, bee, breep, soo, aroos, moore, schoon, ooper, toold,* &c. with considerable frequency, while very many MSS. have *book, look, took, oon, heere, mateere,* and some other forms of the same kind ; but this is not in accordance with the author's rule. In the Fairfax MS. the cases of doubled vowel are only occasional, except in the instance of *good,* which is thus regularly distinguished from *god.*

Of *oo* there are very few cases except *good.* We have *oon* about three times for *on,* and *blood, brood, cooste, do* (= doe), *foode, hool, schoo, too* (= toe), *woot,* in isolated instances. The doubling of *e* is more frequent, as *beere, cheeke, cleene, dee* (pl. *dees*), *degree, eem, eer, fee, feede, feer, feere, feet, greene, meene, meete, pees, queene, scheete, see* (subst.), *seene, slee, spreede, thee, tree, weer, weere, wreeche, ȝee, ȝeer,* and a few more. Most of the above words, however, and in general all others, are written usually with a single vowel, and we have quite regularly (for example) *ded, dede, drem, ek, fend, fre, gret, hed, her* (= hair), *lef, red, slep, bok, bon, brod, fot, gon, hot, lok, non, schon, sone* (soon), *tok, wok,* and so on. Where there is variation of spelling in this respect, it is not felt to be a matter which concerns the rhyme ; for we have *weer : pouer, pees : reles, sene : meene, there : feere, good : stod, fode : goode, do : schoo,* &c., though sometimes the spelling of the rhyme-words is evidently brought into harmony, as *meene* : *Almeene*, ii. 2465 f., *beere* : *weere*, iv. 1323 f., *brood* : *good*, v. 4375 f., *goode* : *foode*, vii. 519 f. In a few cases however a phonetic distinction seems to be intended, as when we find *eet* as preterite of *ete*, and *beere* (also *bere*) pret. plur. of *beren*.

Maii (the month) is regularly written with *ii*, but rhymes with *mai*, *gay*, &c.

The doubling of final consonants, apparently to indicate vowel shortness, is more common, as in *all*, *bladd*, *charr*, *hadd*, *happ*, *madd*, *bedd*, *fedd*, *fett*, *spedd*, *bitt*, *bridd*, *chidd*, *godd*, *rodd*, beside *al*, *char*, *had*, *hap*, *mad*, *bed*, *fet*, &c.

The doubling of *s* in a final tone syllable seems to have no such significance, as in *Achilles* : *press*, iv. 2161 f., but *Ulixes* : *pres*, iv. 147 f., so *natheles* : *encress*, *pes* : *encress*, in all of which the vowel must be long.

One of the most noteworthy points of the orthography is the frequent use of *ie* in tonic syllables for close *ē*. This appears in French words such as *achieve*, *appiere*, *chief*, *chiere*, *clier*, *grieve*, *matiere*, *messagier*, *pier*, &c. (also in many of these cases *e*, as *chere*, *cler*, *matere*), but it is very commonly used also in words of English origin and seems invariably to be associated with the close sound of the vowel. Thus we have *hiede*, *spriede*, *lief* (but *levere*), *sieke*, *diel*, *stiel*, *whiel*, *dieme*, *sieme*, *diere*, *fiere* (= company), *hiere* (adv.), *hiere* (verb), *liere*, *stiere*, and others, which have in most cases the alternative spelling with *e*, as *hede*, *sprede*, *seke*, *del*, *stel*, *whel*, *deme*, *seme*, &c., but in all of which the vowel has the close sound.

It is impossible here to discuss the question how far this habit of spelling may have been introduced by analogy from French words with a similar sound of the vowel, and how far it may have grown out the Kentish use of *ie*, *ye* for O. E. *ēo*, *ē*, *ie*. Reference may be made to the remarks in the Introduction to the volume of Gower's French Works, p. xxi, where it is suggested that *ie*, having lost its value as a diphthong in later Anglo-Norman, came to be regarded as a traditional symbol in many cases for close *ē*, and hence such forms as *clier*, *clief*, *pier*, *prophiete*, &c., and as regards *ie* in the Kentish dialect there is a useful statement in the paper by W. Heuser, *Zum Kentischen Dialekt im Mittelenglischen*, published in *Anglia*, xvii, 78 ff.

In any case the fact is pretty clear that this variation was confined by Gower to words in which he gave to the vowel a close sound, and it is therefore useful as a distinguishing note, though there are few words in which this is the only form of spelling.

Both in stems of words and in their terminations *i* is on the whole preferred to *y*, so that we have *crie, hide, lif, like, mile, ride,* &c. more usually than *crye, hyde,* &c. (but perhaps *y* more often after *m, n,* as *knyht, myhte, nyht*), and also *arrai, mai, dai, hardi, ladi, worþi, mi, thi,* more often on the whole than *array, may,* &c., but *-ly* in adverbs more often than *-li*.

In some few cases it seems that a distinction is pretty consistently made, as between *wryte* (inf.) and *write* (past participle), and perhaps between *wite* (know) and *wyte* (blame).

Before *gh* followed by *t* we find *a, o* almost regularly in place of *au, ou*. Thus we have *aghte, straghte, taghte, boghte, broghte, doghter, noght, oghte, oght, soghte, wroghte,* &c., but occasionally *broughte, doughter, ought,* &c. Beside some of these there are forms in which *au* (*aw*), *ou* (*ow*) are written, but followed by simple *h*, as *strawhte, tawhte, douhter* (*dowhter*).

There is no difference between *-oun* and *-on* as terminations of such French words as *divisioun, complexioun,* &c., but *-oun* is much the more usual form [1]. Where they occur in rhyme, the rhyme-words are usually assimilated to one another in form of spelling, but sometimes *-oun, -on* rhyme together, as *division : doun,* ii. 1743 f., *toun : condicion,* v. 2551, *constellacioun : relaçion,* vi. 2253 f.

In the case of *an* followed by a consonant in a tone-syllable the variation to *aun* seems to be merely a question of spelling, and we have such rhymes as *chaunce : remembrance,* ii. 893 f., *demande : comaunde,* iv. 2794, *supplanted : enchaunted,* ii. 2491, *covenant : supplaunt,* ii. 2367. In the French terminations *-ance, -ant,* the simple form is decidedly preferred (but *gouvernaunce : porveaunce,* Prol. 187 f., *graunt : amblaunt,* ii. 1505 f.), and so also in many other words, as *change, strange, comande, demande, supplante* (also *comaunde, supplaunte*). In other cases *au* is either the usual or the only form, as *daunce, daunte, enchaunte, haunte, sclaundre.*

With regard to the consonants, it should be observed that Gower consistently wrote *sch* for *sh* initially, so that we have regularly *schal, schape, sche, schewe, schip, schrifte,* and also *lord-schipe, worschipe,* &c.[2], in other places usually *ssh,* as *bisshop* (also *bisschop*), *buissh, fissh, fleissh* (also *fleisch*), *freissh, reisshe, wisshe.*

The almost regular use of *h* for *gh* in such words as *hih, nyh, sih, kniht, liht, miht, niht, heihte, sleihte,* &c. will be spoken of later.

Gower did not use *ȝ* for *h* or *gh*. Such forms as *miȝte, riȝt,*

---

[1] The difference in the MS. usually consists only in the line drawn over the final *on*. So also often in the case of the words discussed below, *chaunce, daunce, enchaunte,* &c.

[2] Very seldom *sh* in F, as Prol. 938, i. 2171, i. 1458.

ouȝte, wrouȝt, are practically unknown in the best MSS. (F has *nouȝt* once.) On the other hand initially in such words as *ȝe, ȝer, ȝive (forȝive), ȝong*, &c., *ȝ* is regularly used. Only late and inferior MSS. have *y*. In regard to this letter Gower's usage is exactly the reverse of that which we find in the *Ayenbite of Inwyt*. We have þ for *th* regularly except in the case of a capital letter being required, as at the beginning of a line, or in connexion with some foreign words and names as *thalemans, thevangile, rethorique, Athemas, Anthenor, Thebith*. Cases of *th* for þ in ordinary English words are very rare in F (but i. 2890, v. 2319, vii. 4203).

In some words there is an interchange of *c* and *s*, as *decerte, pourchace pourchase, service servise, rancoun, suffice suffise, sufficant*, &c., and the French termination *-esse* is also spelt *-esce*, as *largesse largesce, simplesce simplesse* ; so also *encresce, redresce*, &c. In such points the orthography of Romance words is usually in accordance with that which we find in the author's French writings, in which also are found such etymological forms as *deceipte, doubte*.

Before quitting the general subject, we ought to note certain words of common occurrence which are spelt not quite in the usual way. The author regularly writes *bot* for *but*, *be* for *by*, when used as a preposition and unemphatic, *ous* for *us* (pers. pron.), *noght* for *not* (*not* being used for *ne wot*). Some forms of proper names, as *Habraham, Irahel*, are characteristic. In these points, as in many others, the writer evidently followed a definite system, and in spite of the variations recorded, the orthography of the Fairfax and Stafford MSS. certainly conveys to the reader the general impression of regularity and consistency.

PHONOLOGY. (1) O. E. SHORT VOWELS AND DIPHTHONGS.

O.E. **a, æ, ea**. In the case of *a* (*o*) before a lengthening nasal combination, *ld, nd, mb, ng*, &c., we may note that though *hond, honde, hondes* are preferred, as by Chaucer, yet *hand, handes* pretty frequently occur, as i. 2, 1807, 2994, ii. 574, iii. 116, v. 1505, &c. (also *handle*, iii. 1956, v. 1949), and that without any necessity of rhyme. In fact *hand* seems to be rather preferred except in rhyme. Contrary to what is apparently Chaucer's usage we find *thonk, thonke* as the regular forms in Gower, and only occasionally *thank*, as ii. 60, 2012. This may be due to the Kentish tendency to lengthen before *nk*, which perhaps was pronounced nearly as *ng* (see Morsbach, *Mittelengl. Gramm.*,

p. 128), and in this connexion we may note the fact that the Fairfax MS. twice has *þong* for *þonk*. On the other hand there is no definite trace of the principle which has been discovered in some of the Kentish texts of lengthening before these combinations when a vowel follows, while preserving *a* when the consonant group ends the word, *honde, stonde, þonke*, &c., but *hand, stand, þank*[1]. Gower uses *handes* as well as *hand*, and interchanges *hange* and *honge, sang* and *song*, according to convenience.

Note that *upon* rhymes freely with *on* (=one), *anon, gon*, &c., but the supposed rhyme *on* (*ăn*) : *mone*, i. 2179, noted by Fahrenberg, is really *one* (*ān*) : *mone*. In some cases of original *ǣ* shortened to *æ* Gower prefers *e* to *a*, as *eny*, only occasionally *any, eddre* beside *addre*, but *lesse, ledde* only for the sake of rhyme.

ea before *h* becomes *ī* in *sih* (from *seah, sæh*, pret. of *sēon*), which in Gower is the usual form of the word. *æg* forms *ai* (*ay*), as in *dai, lay, mai, fain, slain*, and other *ai* forms, which are not interchangeable with *ei* (but *said* with variant *seid* by influence of *seie*).

O. E. e. When we are dealing with so careful a rhymer as Gower, we need hardly remark upon the absolute distinction made between *ę̄* derived from O. E. *ĕ* and *ẹ̄* of whatever origin. The case of *skiereþ* : *hiereþ*, cited by Fahrenberg as an instance of the opposite, cannot be regarded as a real exception, in view of the uncertain derivation of *skiere*. His other cases of supposed *ę* : *ẹ* are instances of the pret. pl. *spieke* (*speke*), from *sprǣcon*, as *spieke* : *beseke*, ii. 959, *sieke* : *spieke*, ii. 1455. One is doubtful, viz. *seke* : *mispeke*, ii. 2007, where *mispeke* may be pret. subjunctive ; and besides these, *undergete* : *flete*, ii. 1133 f., is irregular.

There is, however, also a well-marked distinction between new-lengthened *ę̄* in words like *trede, stede, bere, spere*, &c., *forȝete, gete, begete* (inf. and partic.), *mete* (subst.), &c., and *ẹ̄* from *ǣ* or *ēa*, the distinction being due presumably to imperfect lengthening With the first class rank also words in which *e* is derived from O. E. *y* in open syllables, as *lere* (loss) from O. E. *lyre, stere* (stir) from *styrian, dede* (pret.) from *dyde*, and also *e* in *answere*.

Thus we find the following quite distinct sets of rhymes : *bede, forbede* (past participles), *bede* (subst.), *dede* (pret. = did), *stede* (stead), *trede,*

---

[1] M. Konrath in *Archiv für die neueren Sprachen*, 89, p. 153 ff.

forming one class and rhyming together, while they are kept entirely apart from *threde, drede, dede* (= dead), *rede*, pl. adj. (= red), which have *ẹ̄* from *ea* or *ǣ*. On the other hand, *bede* the pret. plur. of *bidde* (from *bǣdon*) rhymes with *dede* (dead), e.g. i. 2047.

So also *answere, bere* (subst.), *bere* (verb inf.), *forbere, dere* (destroy), *lere* (loss), *stere* (stir), *bestere, swere* (verb), *tere* (verb), *were* (wear), *were* (defend), form one class of rhyme-words as against *ere, fere* (fear), *there, were* (from *wǣron*), &c. But *eere* (verb) from *erian* rhymes with *there*, v. 819 f., and *scheres* with *teres*, v. 5691. The case of *bere* rhyming with *were* (from *wǣron*), i. 2795 f., vii. 1795 f., is not an exception to the rule, being the preterite plural, from *bǣron*.

Another group is *chele, fele* (many), *hele* (cover), *stele, wele*, as against *hele* (heal), *dele*, &c. : but we find *hele* (*hǣlo*) : *hele* (*helan*), iii. 2755 f.

Again we have *ete, gete* (inf. and partic.), *begete, forȝete, mete* (meat), *sete* (past partic.), kept apart from *grete* (great), *bete* (beaten), *strete, tete, lete* (*lǣtan*), *swete* (verb, = sweat), *threte, whete*, &c. It may be noted that *beȝete* (subst.) belongs to the class *grete, bete*, &c.

There is every reason to suppose that the same distinction would hold with other endings, in the case of which no sufficient rhyme-test is forthcoming, as *breke, speke* (inf.), *wreke* (inf. and past partic.), which have no other words with *ẹ̄* with which they could be rhymed, *eke, seke, meke*, &c., all having *ę̄*.

On the whole we may say that this distinction is very carefully kept in Gower's rhymes, and must certainly indicate a difference of pronunciation.

The adverb *wel*, also written *wiel*, has a double sound, as in Chaucer, either *ę̄* or *ẹ̄*, rhyming with *del* (*diel*), *stiel, whiel*, &c., and also with *naturel, Daniel*, and the substantive *wel* for *wele*.

eg forms *ei*, which is often interchangeable with *ai*, as *seie, leie, weie, aȝein*.

O. E. i. There is nothing in Gower's rhymes to lend support to the theory that *i* from O. E. *ĭ* in open syllables (i.e. before a single consonant followed by a vowel), as in the past participles *write, drive, schrive*, and the infinitives *ȝive, wite*, is of doubtful quantity. The past participle and plural preterite *write* have *ĭ* and rhyme with *wite* (know), while the infinitive *wryte* rhymes with *wyte* (blame), verb and substantive : the infinitives *live, ȝive, forȝive* and the participles *drive, ȝive, schrive*, &c. rhyme among themselves and not with *schryve* (inf.), *alyve, fyve* : the short vowel words *wile* (verb), *skile, bile* are separate from *wyle* (subst.), *whyle, ile*, &c. This would not be worth mentioning but for ten Brink's argument (*Chaucers Sprache*, §§ 35, 325), based on the very smallest positive evidence.

hire (*hir*) is used regularly for the personal and possessive pronoun of the third person sing. fem. (= her), and never *here*, as is Chaucer's usage in rhyme.

cherche is Gower's regular form from *cirice*, but *chirche* is common in the orthography of the *Praise of Peace*, e.g. 197, 210, 225, &c., beside *cherche*, 232, 254.

O. E. o. *wolde, scholde, golde, molde* rhyme with *tolde, holde, colde,* &c., but in open syllables a distinction is observed (as in the case of *e*) between new-lengthened *ọ̄* and *ǭ* from O. E. *ā*, so that *tofore, before, therfore, score* and the participles *bore, forbore, lore, schore, swore* are kept separate in rhyme from such words as *hore, more, lore* (subst.), *ore, rore, sore*, to which later group should be added *More* (Moor), and the Romance verb *restore*[1]. This distinction seems to be recognized by Chaucer, cp. *Troilus,* v. 22–26, but with a good many exceptions, as *Legend of Good Women,* 452 f., 550 f., 1516 f., *Cant. Tales,* A 1541 f., 3237 f., &c., chiefly, but not exclusively, in the case of *more*. Gower is very much stricter and allows very few exceptions (*overmore : tofore,* i. 3361 f., *nomore : therfore,* vii. 3279* f., *more : therfore,* vii. 3869 f., *more : fore,* viii. 991 f.), which must be regarded as imperfect rhymes. Considering the frequency with which words of these two classes occur in rhyme, it is remarkable that the distinction should be so well kept.

We may note that *bowe* (subst.) from *boga* rhymes with words like *knowe*, in which *ow* is from *āw*.

O. E. u. In some words *o* and *u* interchange, as *begonne begunne, conne cunne, coppe cuppe, dronkeschipe drunkeschipe, further forther, ronne* (*over*)*runne, sonne sunne, thurgh thorgh*(*soght*), *tonge tunge, tonne tunne,* &c., but we have without variation, *bole, hunger, note* (nut), *some, under, wonder,* &c. The regular rhyme *under : wonder* is enough to show that the sound was the same.

love, above rhyme together and not with any other word. (For the rhyme at v. 7047 f., see under ō.)

sone (from *sunu*), *wone* (custom), *astone*, rhyme only with one another: in the rhyme *wones : ones*, which occurs iv. 2217 f., viii. 611 f., we have to do of course with a different word.

---

[1] In other cases, as with the group *broke, loke, spoke, wroke* (past participles), and *ʒoke* (subst.), there are no rhyme-words with *ǭ* from *ā* by which a distinction can be established.

dore (*door*) rhymes with *spore* and *dore* (subjunctive of *dar*), *bole* with *wole* (verb).

O. E. **y**.   This is usually represented by *e* (except before *h, gh*), e. g. *abegge, berie, berthe, besy, bregge, dede* (did), *evel, felle* (also *fille*), *felthe, ferst, fest, hell* (also *hill, hull*), *ken* (also *kin*), *kende* (usually *kinde*), *kesse* (also *kisse*), *knette, krepel, lere, lest* (listen), *lest* (= pleases, also *list*), *mende* (also *minde*), *merie, merthe, pet* (also *pitt, put*), *scherte, schetten, senne* (also *sinne*), *stere* (stir), *thenke* (from *þyncan*), *werche* (also *worche*), *werse* (also *worse*): to these must be added *hedde, hed*, pret. and past partic. of *hyde*, in which original *ȳ* was shortened (also *hidde, hid*).   On the other hand, we have *gilt* (also *gult*), *gultif, lifte* (sky), *stinten* (not *stenten*), *thinne* (not *thenne*), *thurste, wierdes*.   Gower does not use the forms *birthe, bisy, dide* (did), *mirie, mirthe, stire*.

The results obtained for certain words from rhymes by Fahrenberg[1] are rather misleading.   For example, he suggests the conclusion that *fille* (subst.) and *fulfille* are used with *i* only, but of the nineteen instances which he quotes, all but two are in rhyme with *wille*, a natural combination (at least for *fulfille*), and one which has determined the form in most cases.   Apart from this, both *felle* (subst.) and *fulfelle* are found (*felle* in rhyme, iii. 2609).

Again, *senne* is much more common than would appear from the rhymes.   Fahrenberg can quote only one instance in rhyme, as against twenty-nine of *sinne*, but this is certainly due to the greater frequency of the words (such as *beginne, winne*, &c.), which give rhymes to *sinne*.   The word occurs seven times in the Prologue, once it is in rhyme, *Sinne* : *inne*, and of the other six instances five are of *senne* and one only of *sinne*.   On the other hand, *hell* (from *hyll*) alone appears in rhyme, but *hill* or *hull* are commoner forms in use.

The mistakes tell both ways, but on the whole the conclusion that *i* is much commoner than *e* in these words is seriously incorrect.

For the use in rhyme of the words of this class with open tone syllable, as *stere, lere* (from *lyre*), see under **e**.

(2) O. E. LONG VOWELS AND DIPHTHONGS.

O. E. **ā**.   The *ǭ* of *hom* rhymes, as in Chaucer, with the *ō* of the

---

[1] *Archiv für n. Sprachen*, 89, p. 392.   As I sometimes have occasion to criticize statements in this paper, I take the opportunity here of acknowledging its merit, as the only careful study lately attempted of Gower s language.

preterites *com*, *nom*, and also *fom* with *nom*, v. 4007. These must be regarded as imperfect rhymes, due to the want of strictly correct rhyme-words. Gower has regularly *most* (O. E. *māst*) and but once in rhyme *mest* (O. E. *mǣst*), *lest : althermest*, i. 3101 f. : also regularly *oght, noght*, and *oghte* (verb), but *tawht : awht*, i. 2770, and *aghte : betaghte*, viii. 747.

O. E. **ǣ**. This, when representing West-Germanic *ā*, Gothic *ē*, appeared as *ē* in the Old Anglian and Kentish dialects, and might naturally be expected to be sometimes close *e* in the language of Chaucer and Gower. It is well known that Chaucer uses many of the words which have this vowel in a variable manner.

The same is true to some extent also in words where the original *ǣ* corresponds to Germanic *ai*, and in which we find Old Kentish *ē*. Of these *leden, clene, menen, leeren* appear in Chaucer sometimes with *ẹ* (and *evere, nevere* always). For these and some other cases see ten Brink, *Chaucers Sprache*, § 25.

When we compare Chaucer's usage with that which we find in our author, we find what our former experience has prepared us to expect, viz. a greater strictness and regularity of usage in Gower. The examples of fluctuation between the two sounds are comparatively few.

Taking first the words in which *ē* is from *ǣ* corresponding to West-Germanic *ā*, we find the following with *ẹ*:

bede (pret. pl.), from *bǣdon*, (*dede : bede*, i. 2047 f.).

breth (: *deth*, i. 119, 2127, &c.).

fere, ' fear,' (: *ere*, i. 462, ii. 46).

her, ' hair,' (*heres : teres*, i. 2999).

lete, from *lǣtan*, (: *grete*, i. 3365, &c.).

lewed (: *thewed*, i. 274, *beschrewed*, iii. 479).

sete, pret. pl., (*sete : grete*, iv. 1309), but *siete* (not in rhyme), v. 3339.

strete (: *grete*, i. 938, *bete*, i. 1156).

there (: *ere*, i. 499, 558, &c.), but also *there : swere* (neck), iv. 859, and *hiere* (adv.) : *there, Praise of Peace*, 178.

were, from *wǣron*, (: *ere*, Prol. 235, i. 2808, &c.), but also *ẹ* in a few instances, as *hiere* (verb) : *were*, i. 2741 f., *hiere* (adv.) : *were*, v. 747 f.

where (e. g. *elleswhere : eere*, Prol. 9), but *here* (adv.) : *elleswhere*, v. 361 f.

The substantive and verb *red*, *rede* rhyme about equally with *ẹ* and *ẹ̄*, the latter cases being almost all with *ded, dede* (dead, sing. and pl.), as i. 1446, iv. 1940, 1960, &c. On the other hand, *rede : hiede*, i. 447 f., *rede : spede*, i. 1293 f., ii. 103 f., &c., *red : sped*, iii. 1991 f.

The following words of this class have as a rule *ẹ̄*:

cheke (*chieke*) (: *mieke*, v. 2471, *eke*, v. 3019).

dede, ' deed,' (: *fede*, Prol. 465, *mede*, i. 1553, &c., *spede*, i. 2653, &c., *ȝede*, ii. 855, *forbiede*, iii. 1122), but *dede* (dead) : *dede*, i. 1037 f.

drede (: *nede*, i. 1987, 2240 [1], : *spede*, iv. 629, : *hiede*, iv. 1448, &c.), but *dede* (dead) : *drede*, ii. 3405 f., *drede* : *rede* (from *rēad*), iv. 185 f.

leche (: *seche*, ii. 3220, *beseche*, iii. 413).

meete, 'dream,' (: *meete*, from *mētan*, iii. 51).

mete (*unmete*), adj. (: *mete*, from *mētan*, ii. 458, iii. 1100).

slep, *slepe*, subst. and verb, (*kepe* : *slepe*, Prol. 309 f., 475 f., *slep* : *kep*, i. 155, &c.), but *slep* : *hep* (*hēap*), iv. 3007 f.

speche (*spieche*) (: *seche*, Prol. 174, *beseche*, i. 1986).

spieke (*speke*), from *sprēcon*, pret. pl. (: *beseke*, ii. 959, *sieke*, ii. 1456).

thred (: *sped*, i. 1419).

ʒer, *ʒere*, (*ʒere* : *stiere*, ii. 2379, *ʒer* : *hier*, iii. 129, *ʒeeres* : *pleiefieres*, iv. 481), with no instances apparently of *ę̄*.

If we take now the words in which *ē* is from *ǣ* corresponding to Germanic *ai*, we obtain the following results.

With *ẹ̄* :

er (: *ner*, ii. 2285).

geth (: *deth*, ii. 1804, 2616, &c.).

lene, 'lend,' (: *bene*, v. 4407).

leve, ' remain,' (: *bereve*, Prol. 412).

se (*see*), ' sea,' (: *stree*, iii. 86, iv. 1715, *sle*, iv. 1664), but *be* : *se*, iv. 1625 f., *me* : *see*, viii. 1723 f.

ʒe (*ʒee*), 'yea,' (: *slee*, iii. 262, 2068, *stree*, iii. 668).

(*stre*, *slee*, have no *ẹ̄* rhymes, so we have no reason to suppose, as in the case of Chaucer, that final *e* has a close sound.)

With *ę̄* :

areche, from *ārǣcan*, (: *beseche*, ii. 666).

clene (: *sene*, ii. 3461).

del (*diel*), *somdiel*, &c. (: *whiel*, Prol. 137, *stiel*, Prol. 612, 828).

evere, *nevere*, (: *levere*, Prol. 38, ii. 5, ii. 2417, &c.).

-hede (*-hiede*) as a suffix : *hiede* : *godhiede*, Prol. 497 f., cp. i. 1211 f., 1719 f., v. 595 f., viii. 95 f., *mede* : *wommanhiede*, iii. 1607 f., *wommanhiede* : *fiede*, vi. 695 f., *maidenhede* : *spede*, vii. 5145 f., viii. 1419 f., and so on, but once *ẹ̄*, *Maidenhede* : *rede* (from *rēad*), v. 5987.

hete, subst. and verb, 'heat,' (: *swete*, 'sweet,' ii. 2740, vi. 249), but *hete* : *tobete*, iii. 121 f., *hete* : *bete*, viii. 1195 f.

lede (: *hiede*, v. 156, : *fede*, vii. 2336 *), but *dede* (dead) : *lede*, ii. 2779 f.

lere (*liere*), from *lǣran*, (: *hiere*, verb, i. 454, iii. 2204, v. 2029, *diere*, viii. 1462, *hiere* (adv.), viii. 1497, *unliered* : *stiered*, Prol. 233 f.).

mene (*meene*), verb, (: *sene*, ii. 2830, iv. 1645, *wene*, i. 1937, &c., *grene*, i. 777, &c., *tene*, iii. 771, *queene*, iv. 786).

sprede (*spriede*) (: *fede*, i. 2824, *spede*, ii. 504, *spredeth* : *nedeth*, v. 7679 f., *feedeth*, vi. 895 f.), but *sprede* : *hede* (head), vii. 845 f.

teche (: *beseche*, i. 590, 2260, iii. 132).

The above are the results arrived at by examination of the rhymes with vowels of undoubted quality ; i. e. *ę̄* from O. E. *ēa*,

---

[1] According to ten Brink, *nede* ought to be regarded as an uncertain rhyme because of the O. E. *nēades* beside *nīedes*, but Gower never rhymes it with open *ē*.

and *ę* from O. E. *ē̆*, *ēo*, *ie*. In addition to this, an investigation has been made of the rhyming of these words among themselves and with words of Romance origin, in the process of which some additional words with *ē* from *ǣ*, as *dele, hele, swete,* 'sweat,' *wete,* are brought in. This cannot here be given in full, but it may be said that in almost all points it confirms the results arrived at above. A few words, however, to which an open vowel is assigned above, rhyme with other words from *ǣ* which almost certainly have *ę̄*, and therefore must be set as having unstable pronunciation. Thus, in spite of the rhyme *lene* (lend) : *bene* mentioned above, we have *lene* : *mene* (both verb and subst.) and *lene* : *clene*, and though *fere* rhymes more than once with *ere*, we have *lered* : *afered* and *unlered* : *afered*, which suggest that the close sound was possible.

On the whole we may set down the following as the result of our examination.

With open vowel: of the *ǣ* (*ę̄*) class, *bede*, pret. pl., *breth, her* (pl. *heres*), *lete, lewed, strete* : of the *ā = ai* class, *er, geth, leve* (remain), *ȝee* (yea).

With close vowel: of the former class, *leche, meete* (dream), *mete* (fit), *slepe, speche, speke*, pret. pl., *thred, wete, wreche, ȝer*, and with one exception only in each case *dede, slep* : of the latter class, *areche, clene, del, evere, lere, mene, nevere, teche*, and with one exception in each case, *-hede* (*-hiede*), *lede, sprede*.

With unstable vowel: from *ǣ* (*ę̄*), *drede, eve, fere* (fear), *red* (sūbst.), *rede, there, were, where* : from *ǣ = ai*, *hete, lene, see* (sea).

The conclusions to which we are led are, first that in Gower's usage there is less instability of vowel-sound in these words than in Chaucer, the number of words with unstable vowel being smaller and the variations even in their case more exceptional; secondly that Gower's language has a strongly pronounced leaning towards *ę̄*; and finally that this tendency is quite as much visible in the words of the *ǣ = ai* class as in the others.

O. E. **ēa.** The substantive *believe* has *ę̄* by influence of the verb.

There is no use apparently of *nę̄de* from *nēad* or of *ȝę̄r* from *gēar*, and *ek, eke*, seems invariably to have *ę̄*.

From *ēage, flēah, hēah, nēah* we have *yhe, flyh, hih, nyh*.

There seems no reason to suppose that *stre, sle* had *ę̄*, as has been concluded for Chaucer's language because of such rhymes

as *sle* : *he, stre* : *she, stree* : *we,* see ten Brink, *Chaucers Sprache,*
§ 23.

It has already been shown that *see* (sea), which we have
supposed to have unstable vowel quality, very seldom rhymes
with words having *ē̜*, notwithstanding the frequent opportunity for
such rhymes, and *ȝee,* 'yea,' never.   It may be questioned whether
the rule laid down by ten Brink for Chaucer is a sound one, and
whether Chaucer's practice does not really depend simply upon
the larger supply of rhymes in *ē̜*, such as *he, she, me, thee, be, se*
(verb), *tre, three,* &c.   It is at least possible that the difference
here between Gower and Chaucer arises from the fact that the
latter was less strict in his rhymes, and certainly the later
developments of *sle, see, stre, ȝee* supply no confirmation of the
idea that they had *ē̜* regularly in Chaucer's language.

O. E. **ēo.**   By the side of *sek* (*siek*) there is occasionally *sik.*

The form *fil, fille* for *fell, felle,* pret. sing. and pl. from *falle,* are
not used by Gower.   He rhymes *fell* (*fēoll*) : *hell* (*hyll*) and *felle,*
pret. pl. : *felle* (*fyllan*).

The personal pronoun *ȝow* (*ȝou*) from *ēow* rhymes with *thou,
now,* &c.

O. E. **ī.**   Fahrenberg's instances of *ī* : *ē,* i. 177 f. and iii. 413 f.,
are both founded on mistakes.

O. E. **ū.**   The personal pronoun from O. E. *ūs* is always written
ous, but rhymes in some instances with -*us* in Latin names, e. g.
Tricolonius : *ous, Tereüs* : *ous.*

būtan is shortened to *bot,* not *but.*   It occurs also as a dissyllable in the form *bote.*

O. E. **ȳ.**   The only example of *ȳ* as *ē* is *fer* from *fȳr,* which
occurs in rhyme with *ȝer,* iii. 694, (elsewhere *fyr*).   Chaucer has
fere, dat., rhyming with *here,* adv., *Troilus,* iii. 978, and also *afere*
in rhyme with *stere,* 'stir,' *Troilus,* i. 229.

The cases of *hedde, hed,* pret. and past participle (from *hȳdan*),
are examples of shortened *ȳ* passing naturally to *e,* and so also
fest from *fȳst, felthe* from *fȳlþe, threste* from *þrȳsta.*

From *ȳg* in *drȳge* we have *dreie,* but also *drye.*

O. E. **ō.**   Gower, like Chaucer, rhymes the word *do* (*misdo,
undo,* &c.), and occasionally *to* in *therto,* with words that have *ọ̄*
derived from *ā,* not only *so, also, two, wo,* but also *tho,* adv. (i. 2609,
iii. 683, v. 5331, &c.), *go, ago* (ii. 2483, 3513, iv. 1161, 3465,

v. 5173, &c.), *overmo* (i. 2385), *no* (v. 4776), *fo* (iv. 3407).
These words also rhyme with proper names, such as *Juno, Lichao, Babio*. The other forms of *do*, as *doth, don*, rhyme nearly always
with *ọ̄*, but once we have *doth : goth*, v. 3967 f., and once *don : anon*, v. 3627 f. The rhyme *soth : goth* also occurs, v. 1579 f.
This latter class of rhyme, as *don : anon, don : gon, sothe : bothe,
soth : wroth*, occurs frequently in Chaucer's earlier work, as the
Book of the Duchess, but much less so in the later.

These rhymes, like those of *hom* with *com*, &c., noticed above
under *ā̆*, are to be explained as due to scarcity of exactly corresponding rhyme words. The only exact rhyme for *do* and *to* is in
fact *schoo*, which is found in Prol. 356, but obviously could not be
of frequent occurrence. The explanation given by ten Brink,
Chaucers Sprache, § 31, and repeated mechanically by others, is
that certain words which have *ọ̄* from *ā̆*, as *wo, two, so (swā̆)*, may
equally have *ọ̄* upon occasion owing to the influence of *w*. This
is shown to be wrong both by the fact that the rhymes in question
are, as we have seen, by no means confined to these words, and
by the absence of other evidence in the case of *wo* and *so* that
they ever had a tendency to *ọ̄*. The fact that the rhyme *do : so*
is by far the commonest instance is due simply to the more
frequent occasion for using the words.

In the rhyme *glove : love*, v. 7047 f., we have to deal with *ọ̄*,
and there can be no question here of *love* from *lufian*. Both
sense and rhyme point to a verb *love* corresponding to the
substantive *lof* or *love*, mod. *luff*, and signifying the action of
bringing a ship's head up nearer to the wind. The other rhymes
used with *glove* are *behove*, Prol. 357, *prove*, iii. 2153.

We may note that *wowe* from *wōgian* rhymes with *bowe* (būgan),
which does not fit in with ten Brink's very questionable theory
about the development of *ou (ow)*, *Chaucers Sprache*, § 46, Anm.

(3) ROMANCE VOWELS. A few notes only will be added here
to what has already been said in the Introduction to Gower's
French Works.

Words with *-oun (-on)* ending, as *condicioun (-on), opinioun (-on)*,
&c., rhyme only among themselves or with *toun, doun*, &c. There
are no rhymes like Chaucer's *proporcion : upon*, and it is to be
noted especially that the rhyming of proper names in *-on*, as *Sala-
mon, Acteon*, &c., with this class of words, which is very common in

Chaucer, does not occur in Gower's English, though we occasionally find it in his French. At the same time the possibility of
such rhymes cannot be denied, for we have *toun* : *Ylioun*, v. 7235 f.,
and *Lamedon* : *Jasoun*, v. 7197 f.

Adjectives in *-ous* do not rhyme with *-us*, as in Chaucer
Aurelius : *amorous*, *Theseüs* : *desirous*.

The terminations *-arie*, *-orie* are not used at all, but instead of
them the French forms *-aire*, *-oire*, as *adversaire*, *contraire*,
necessaire, *gloire*, *histoire*, *memoire*, *purgatoire*, *victoire*. Latin
proper names in *o* rhyme with $\bar{\rho}$, as *Cithero* (: *also*), *Leo* (: *also*), *Phito*
(: *tho*), *Juno* (: *so*, *tho*), &c., but also in several cases with *do*. There
seems no sufficient reason to suppose, as ten Brink does, that
they regularly had $\bar{o}$.

(4) CONSONANTS. The termination *-liche* (*-lich*) in adjectives
and adverbs, which Fahrenberg judging by the rhymes sets down
as very uncommon compared with *-ly*, is by far the more usual of
the two. It is true that *-ly* occurs more frequently in rhyme, but
that is due chiefly to the greater abundance of rhyme words
corresponding to it, e. g. *forthi*, *by*, *cri*, *merci*, *enemy* : we have,
however, *redely* : *properly*, Prol. 947 f. The general rule of usage
is this : *-ly* usually in rhyme (but *besiliche* : *swiche*, iv. 1235 f.),
and before a consonant in cases where the metre requires a single
syllable, as i. 2069, ' Al prively behinde his bak' (but *frendlich*,
viii. 2173), *-liche* or *-lich* before a vowel, as i. 373, 'That ronne
besiliche aboute,' cp. ii. 1695, v. 1247, and *-liche* of course where
two syllables are required, as i. 1035, 'Was thanne al openliche
schewed,' so ii. 918, iv. 57, and compare also iii. 2065 f.,

> ' Unkindely for thou hast wroght,
> Unkindeliche it schal be boght.'

But in Prol. 719 we have *only* before a vowel,

> ' Noght al only of thorient,'

though *onliche* occurs in a similar position, i. 1948, and *onlich*,
iii. 42. Again, 911,

> ' And sodeinly, er sche it wiste,'

but Prol. 503,

> ' Al sodeinliche, er it be wist,'

cp. iv. 921, compared with i. 1336.

The treatment of the O.E. spirant *h* ($=\chi$) deserves some
attention. This occurring before *t* is recognized as having in
M. E. a palatal or a guttural sound, according to the nature of the

preceding vowel, but the texts of our period usually give it as *gh* in both cases. Gower, however, makes a distinction, writing almost regularly *alihte, briht, dihte, fihte, flihte, kniht, liht, miht, mihte, niht, riht, sihte, wiht, heihte, sleihte*, &c., but *aghte, caghte, straghte, boghte, broghte, noght, oght, oghte, soghte*. Occasionally however in the first class we find *g*, as rarely *bryghte, lighte*, more frequently *heighte, sleighte*, and pretty regularly *eighte*; and there are several words in the second which have variants with *h*, but in these cases *w(u)* is inserted, as *cawhte, strawhte, dowhter (douhter), owhte* : otherwise *u* is generally absent, as we have already seen. The form referred to is commoner with the vowel *a* than with *o*.

It is hardly necessary to repeat here that *plit* is a word of Romance origin, and rhymes properly with *delit, appetit*, not with *liht, niht*, &c., being separate in etymology from O.E. *pliht*.

From the fact that there is no rhyming of *-iht* with *-it* either in Gower or Chaucer, we may certainly gather that the sounds were somewhat different ; but the fact that Gower does not usually write *gh* after *i* indicates, no doubt, that in this case the sound of the spirant was less marked than when preceded by broader vowels.

Where O.E. *h* is a final aspirate, *g* is not usually written, as *sih, hih, nih, bowh, lowh, plowh, slowh, ynowh*, except in the case of *thogh*, but very occasionally we find such forms as *drogh, plogh*. In the words which have *w(u) h* is often dropped, as in *bowes, low, slow* (preterites), *ynow*.

v. INFLEXION.—(I) SUBSTANTIVES. In a certain number of words there is variation in the matter of final *e* : thus we have *drink drinke, felawe felawh (fela), flyht flyhte, half halve, help helpe, kep kepe, lack lacke, lyf lyve, myn myne, queene queen, sor sore, wel wele, will wille, wyndou wyndowe*, to which must be added many words with the suffixes *-hede, -hode, -schipe*, and the termination *-inge*, e.g. *falshed(e), knyhthod(e), manhed(e), felaschip(e), hunting(e), know-leching(e), teching(e), wenyng(e)*. In these latter cases the presence of the *e* ending is not wholly dependent on the accent, for we have *hunting*, i. 350, but *húntynge*, iv. 2429, *techyng* and *techinge* both equally in rhyme, i. 1592, v. 611, *gládschipe*, i. 3128, *knithód*, v. 2057, *felaschíp*, ii. 1217. Accent however has some influence, and it is hardly conceivable that the final *e* should count in the metre except where the accent falls on the preceding syllable, so that where the accent is thrown back, we find that the word is regularly followed by a vowel. In the case of the (English) termination *-ere* the final *e* is usually written : such words are *beggere, forthdrawere, hindrere, ledere, lovere, makere, repere, spekere, writere*. This *-e*, however, is eithei elided or passed over in the metre (as with *janglere*, v. 526), unless an accent falls on the termination, in which case it may be sounded, as vii. 2348, ' The Sothseiere tho was lief.'

The forms *game, gamen* appear side by side both in singular and plural, as i. 347, vi. 1849, viii. 680.

As regards the oblique cases we note the following genitive forms : *cherche, herte* (also *hertes*), *hevene, ladi, soule, sterre* (pl.), *wode* (also *wodes*), to which add *dowhter* (also *dowhtres*), *fader* (also *fadres*), *moder*. In the expressions *horse side, horse heved*, &c., *horse* is genitive singular.

The *-e* termination of the dative appears in a good many pre-positional phrases : *to* (*in*) *bedde, in boke, to borwe, be* (*to*) *bote, with* (*of*) *childe, unto the chinne* (but *unto the chin*, i. 1682), *be daie, to* (*fro*) *dethe* (also *fro deth*), *of dome, on* (*under*) *fote* (but *upon the fot, at his fot*), *on fyre, to* (*upon*) *grounde, fro* (*unto*) *the grounde* (also *fro the ground*), *on hede, at* (*fro*) *home* (also *at hom*), *in* (*on, upon*) *honde, to* (*into*) *honde*, (but ' bar on *hond*,' *be the hond*), *on horse, to horse, to* (*in, of*) *house* (but *in myn hous*), *to* (*into*) *londe, be* (*in, over*) *londe, of* (*out of*) *londe, fro the londe*, (but *of his lond*, &c.), *be lyhte, to lyve, to manne, to mowthe, be mowthe, be nyhte* (also *be nyht*, and regularly *at nyht, on nyht, a nyht, to nyht*), *to rede, be* (*to, into, out of*) *schipe* (also *to schip*), *to scorne, to slepe* (also *to slep*), *to toune, to wedde, to wyve, to ʒere, be ʒere*.

In the plural we have *hors, schep* unchanged, and also with numerals, *mile, monthe, pound, ʒer* (beside *ʒeres*), *wynter*. The plural of *thing* is *thinges*, sometimes *thinge*, not *thing*. Mutation plurals, *feet, men, teeth, wommen*. Plurals in *-en, brethren, children, oxen* (also *oxes*), *ton, yhen*.

The forms in *-ere* have plurals *-ers*, as *janglers, kepers, lovers*. From *maiden* we have beside *maidens* also *maidenes* (three syllables), iv. 255, which is perhaps the true reading in Chaucer, *Leg. of G. Women*, 722. From *angel* we have plural *anglis*, iii. 2256, as well as *angles*, and *Nimphis*, v. 6932, but there are few examples of plural in *-is*.

With regard to Romance substantives Gower appears to be stricter than Chaucer in preserving their form. He gives us regularly *beste* ' beast,' *feste, requeste, tempeste*. We have however *baner* (also *banere*), *host, maner, matier* (beside *manere, matiere*), *press* (beside *presse*), *travaile, conseile* (substantives) very occasionally for *travail, conseil*.

Several distinctively feminine forms are used, as *capiteine, cham-berere, citezeine, cousine, enemie*.

In some cases the Latin inflexion is introduced, as *Tantaly, Apollinis, Centauri, in Cancro, Achillem, Esionam, Phebum*, the two last apparently introduced after the first recension.

(2) ADJECTIVES AND ADVERBS.   A few adjectives vary as regards
final *e* in the uninflected form, for example *ech eche, lich liche, low
lowe, many manye, moist moiste, old olde, other othre, such suche* (?),
trewe trew, wommanyssh wommannysshe.

In comparative forms *-e* is often dropped, as *fairer, further, longer,
rather, ʒonger*, but more often written, as *furthere, deppere, ferre,
gladdere, grettere, lengere, rathere.*   This *-e*, however, is either elided
or passed over in the metre (as ii. 503, iv. 1459, vi. 1490, 1525, 2010).
Where there is syncope of the penultimate, as after *v(u)* in *levere*, the
final *e* counts regularly as a syllable, so that in case of elision the word
is reduced to a monosyllable, which never takes place with *rathere,
furthere*, &c.

When adjectives or adverbs ending in weak *e* are combined with
a suffix or another word, *-e* is often dropped ; thus we have *everemore
evermore, furthermore, joieful joiful, hevenely hevenly, trewely, trewly*
(so also *trewman*), and so on.   In such cases a previously syncopated
penultimate ceases to be so on loss of the following *e*.

A few cases occur of *-id* for *-ed* in adjective endings, as *nakid* (also
naked), *wickid wikkid* (usually *wicked*), also *hundrid* (usually *hundred*).

The definite form is used pretty regularly in the case of English
monosyllabic adjectives, and usually also in monosyllables of French
origin.   This rule applies (1) to adjectives used after the definite
article, a demonstrative pronoun or a possessive ; (2) to those employed
as vocatives in address ; (3) to adjectives in combination with proper
names or words used as proper names[1].   Thus we have regularly (1)
' the *grete* hert,' ' the *stronge* coffre,' 'The *qwike* body with the *dede*,'
' this *proude* vice,' ' this *ʒonge* lord,' ' my *longe* wo,' ' his *lose* tunge,'
' thi *fulle* mynde,' ' whos *rihte* name,' &c.   (2) ' O *derke* ypocrisie,'
' O *goode* fader,' ' *lieve* Sone,' &c.   (3) '*grete* Rome,' ' *Blinde* Avarice,'
' *proude* Envie' (but ' *proud* Envie,' Prol. 712), ' *faire* Eole,' ' *stronge*
Sampson,' ' *wise* Tolomeüs,' &c.

We must note also the inflexions in the following expressions, ' so
hihe a love,' ii. 2425 (but *hih*, vii. 2413), ' so *grete* a wo,' v. 5737, so
grete a lust,' v. 6452, ' so *schorte* a time,' vii. 5201.

With Romance adjectives we find ' his *false* tunge,' ' the *pleine* cas,'
' *false* Nessus,' &c., and so usually in monosyllables.

In the case of English monosyllables the exceptions are few.   ' His
full answere,' i. 1629, ' hire *good* astat,' i. 2764, ' here *wrong* condicion,'
ii. 295, ' his *slyh* compas,' ii. 2341 (but 'his *slyhe* cast,' ii. 2374), 'the
ferst of hem,' iii. 27, v. 2863, cp. 5944 (usually 'the *ferste*,' as i. 580, &c.),
' my *riht* hond,' iii. 300, ' the *trew* man,' iii. 2346, ' his *hih* lignage,'
iv. 2064 (due perhaps to the usual phrase ' of hih lignage '), ' the *hih*
prouesse,' v. 6428*, ' hire *hih* astat,' v. 6597, 'the *gret* oultrage,' vii.

---

[1] This latter rule explains Chaucer's use of the inflected forms *faire,
fresshe*, &c., in ' fresshe Beaute,' ' gode, faire White,' ' fresshe May,' &c.

3413, 'hire *freissh* aray,' vii. 5000, 'hire *hol* entente,' viii. 1222, cp. viii. 1710, 2968 (but '3oure *hole* conseil ').

Among Romance adjectives the want of inflexion is more frequent in proportion to the whole number of instances, e. g. 'the *vein* honour,' Prol. 221, 'the *fals* emperour,' Prol. 739, 'Hire *clos* Envie,' ii. 684, &c.

In the case of adjectives of more than one syllable, whether English or French, the definite form is exceptional. The commonest case is that of superlatives, in which the definite form -*este* is regularly used when the accent falls on the termination, whether in rhyme or otherwise, as *faireste*, i. 767, v. 7427, *slyheste*, i. 1442, *wiseste* : *myhtieste*, i. 1097 f., *wofulleste*, vii. 5017. Even when the accent is thrown back, the definite inflexion is more usually given than not, as *faireste*, i. 1804, *hoteste*, i. 2492, *treweste*, ii. 1282, *povereste*, iv. 2238, *heyeste*, vii. 935, but sometimes dropped, as 'the *purest* Eir,' Prol. 921, 'the *3ongest* of hem,' i. 3133, ' the *lowest* of hem alle,' vii. 224 : in all cases, however, where the accent is thrown back, the adjective is followed by a word beginning with a vowel, so that the metre is not affected.

Other adjectives of which the termination is capable of accent may take the definite inflexion, when the accent is thrown on the termination, as 'the *covoitouse* flaterie,' 'this *lecherouse* pride,' this *tyrannysshe* knyht,' but on the other hand 'his fals *pitous* lokynge,' 'the *pietous* Justinian,' 'the proude *tyrannyssh* Romein,' and cases where the adjective is used as a substantive, ' the *coveitous*,' 'This *Envious*,' '*thaverous*,' &c. We have 'the *parfite* medicine,' iv. 2624 (but 'the parfit Elixir,' iv. 2522, with accent thrown back), and ' O thou *gentile* Venus,' viii. 2294 ; but perhaps *parfite*, *gentile* are to be regarded as feminine forms, as almost certainly *devolte*, i. 636.

Where the final syllable of the adjective is incapable of accent, there is ordinarily no question of a definite inflexion, except where there is syncope after *v* (*u*), as in *evele*. Such words are *croked*, *wicked*, *cruel*, *litel*, *middel*, *biter*, *dedly*, *lusti*, *sinful*(*l*), *wilful*, *woful*(*l*), *wrongful*, and we may note that comparatives in -*ere* and adjectives in -*liche* (with accent thrown back) sometimes appear in the truncated form of spelling even where a definite termination is suggested by their position, e. g. 'hire *3onger* Soster,' v. 5395, 'hir *goodlych* yhe,' ii. 2026, ' Ha, thou *ungoodlich* ypocrite,' v. 6293, 'hire *dedlich* yhe,' vii. 5089 (-*lich* in these latter cases to avoid the hiatus of 'ungoodly ypocrite,' &c.). As an exceptional instance the form *nakede* should be observed, ' his *nakede* arm,' iv. 421, given so both by F and S.

The formation of plurals in adjectives and participles used attributively is governed by the same principles. We have '*preciouse* Stones,' iv. 1354, but 'the most *principal*' (pl.), v. 1115. In the expression 'the chief flodes,' v. 1112, *chief* must be considered perhaps as a substantive, like *hed* in 'the hed planete.' Naturally words like *wicked*, *woful*, *lusti*, &c., take no plural inflexion, but we have *manye*

(*manie*) beside *many* apparently as a plural form, though *manye* also
occurs in the singular, and *enye* once as plural of *eny*.   In the expression 'som men' *som* is without inflexion in the plural, e. g. Prol. 529,
iii. 2113, but '*somme* clerkes,' Prol. 355, '*some* things,' i. 1265.

Adjectives used as predicates or in apposition are to some extent
treated according to convenience of metre or rhyme, but in the case of
monosyllables there is a decided preference for inflexion.   The following are some of the instances : 'Whan we ben *dede*,' Prol. 2, 'hem that
weren *goode*,' 42, 'my wittes ben to *smale*,' 81, 'Ther ben of suche
manie *glade*,' 299, 'become *grete*,' 303, 'ben with mannes senne *wrothe*,'
920, so *blinde*, i. 774, *smale*, 1145, *glade*, 1151, *hyhe*, *smale*, i. 1678 f.,
hore and *whyte*, i. 2045, *stronge*, iii. 1112, *dulle*, iv. 947, *whyte*, *fatte*,
grete, iv. 1310, &c.   We have also 'hise thoghtes *feinte*,' iv. 118,
'thinges . . . *veine*,' i. 2689, 'hise bedes most *devoute*,' i. 669, 'in
wordes so *coverte*,' iv. 1606, wher the men ben *coveitouse*, v. 4800.

On the other hand, 'Of hem that ben so *derk* withinne,' i. 1077,
'Hire chekes ben with teres *wet*,' i. 1680, 'Thei wexen *doumb*,' iv. 345,
'Here bodies weren *long* and *smal*,' iv. 1320, 'Thei weren *gracious*
and *wys*,' vii. 1447, 'thei weren *glad*,' viii. 881, and so frequently.

The participle used as predicate is ordinarily uninflected, but there
are a few examples of a plural form adopted for the rhyme, as *made*,
Prol. 300, *ansuerde*, i. 3246, iv. 2343, *hidde*, v. 6789.

The usage of *al*, *alle* as an adjective is in some ways peculiar, but
tolerably consistent.   In the singular before an article, a demonstrative
pronoun or a possessive, the uninflected form *al* (occasionally *all*) is
used, as 'al the baronie,' 'al the world,' 'al his welthe,' 'all his proude
fare,' 'al a mannes strengthe' (also 'the Cite all,' ii. 3473), but before
a substantive the form *alle* (dissyllable)[1], as 'alle grace,' 'alle thing,'
'alle untrouthe,' 'alle vertu,' 'in alle wise,' 'in alle haste,' 'alle wel,'
'alle charite,' but sometimes before vowels *al*, as 'al honour,' i. 879,
'al Erthe,' i. 2825, 'al Envie,' ii. 168, 'al untrowthe,' ii. 1684.   In the
plural, 'al the,' 'all these,' 'alle the,' &c. ('alle' being counted as a
monosyllable), and without the article, 'alle' (but 'al othre,' iv.
1532).

Note also the adverbial expression 'in *none* wise,' cp. '*othre* wise.'   In
cases of the combination of a French adjective with a feminine substantive of the same origin the adjective occasionally takes the French
feminine form.   Instances are as follows : '*devolte* apparantie,' i. 636,
'*veine* gloire,' i. 2677 ff., 'vertu *sovereine*,' ii. 3507, '*seinte* charite,' iv.
964, 'herbe *sovereine*,' vii. 1392, 'joie *sovereine*,' viii. 2530, and even as
predicate, 'Dame Avarice is noght *soleine*,' v. 1971.   Possibly also,

---

[1] This is a regular use in Chaucer also, e.g. *Cant. Tales*, E 1749 :

'Fulfild of alle beautee and plesaunce,'

but it has not always been clearly recognized.

'O thou *divine* pourveance,' ii. 3243, 'the *parfite* medicine,' iv. 2624, 'a *gentile* . . . on,' v. 2713, and 'O thou *gentile* Venus,' viii. 2294, may be examples of the same usage.

There is one instance of the French plural adjective in -*s*, Prol. 738, evidently introduced for the sake of the rhyme.

(3) PRONOUNS. The personal pronoun of the first person is regularly *I*, not *ich*. It is usually written *y* by the copyist of the last 235 lines of the Fairfax MS. and in the *Praise of Peace*.

The third person sing. fem. is *sche* (never written *she*), once *scheo*: the oblique case is *hire*, *hir* (never *here*), and *hire*, though usually equivalent to a monosyllable, sometimes has -*e* fully sounded, as i. 367, iv. 766, v. 1178.

The third person neuter is *it*, seldom *hit*.

In the first person plural the oblique case is *ous*, not shortened to *us* in spelling.

The possessives of the first and second persons sing., *min*, *thin*, have no plural inflexion, but the disjunctive form *thyne* pl. occurs, i. 168. On the other hand *his*, originally an uninflected form, has usually the plural *hise*, but sometimes *his*. The form *hise* is never a dissyllable.

The feminine possessive, 3rd pers., is *hire* or *hir*, freely interchanged and metrically equivalent. There is no question of a plural inflexion here, and we find '*Hire* Nase,' '*hire* browes,' '*hir* lockes,' '*Hire* Necke,' quite indifferently used, i. 1678 ff. The disjunctive is *hire*, v. 6581, and *hires*, v. 6857. .The forms *oure*, *ȝoure* are usual for the possessives of the 1st and 2nd pers. plur., and these are commonly used as monosyllables, e. g. i. 2062, 2768, and interchanged with *our*, *ȝour*; but they are also capable of being reckoned as dissyllables, e. g. Prol. 5, iii. 1087. Here again there is no plural inflexion ('*ȝour* wordes,' iii. 627). The disjunctive *ȝoures* occurs in i. 1852.

The possessive of the 3rd pers. plur. is *here*, *her*, which is practically never confused in good MSS. with *hire*, *hir* of the fem. sing.[1] We are fully justified in assuming that for Gower the distinction was absolute.

The ordinary relatives are *which* and *that*: *who* is little used as a relative except in the genitive case, *whos*. The plural *whiche* is usually pronounced as a monosyllable, as ii. 604, iv. 1496, v. 1320, and often loses -*e* in writing, as Prol. 1016, iv. 1367, 1872, v. 4041, but also sometimes counts as a dissyllable, e. g. i. 404, vii. 1256.

In combination with the definite article the singular form is 'the which,' not 'the whiche,' as Prol. 71, 975.

---

[1] In the *Praise of Peace* however the MS. has *here* for *hire*, ll. 108, 329, cp. 254. F has *hire* for *here* once accidentally, iii. 901.

**   h

(4) VERBS. In the Infinitive and Gerund, apart from the cases of *do, go, se, sle,* &c., few instances occur of the loss of final *e.* The verb *sein (sain)* has *seie* and also *say,* and beside the regular infinitive *pute* we have also *put* in several instances, the next word beginning with a vowel or mute *h.* The cases are as follows: 'And thoghte put hire in an Ile,' i. 1578, 'To put his lif,' &c., i. 3213, 'put eny lette,' ii. 93, and so also ii. 1021, iii. 1166, iv. 756, 2615, v. 273, viii. 892: but also, 'It oghte *pute* a man in fere,' i. 462, 'To *puten* Rome in full espeir,' ii. 1551, 'Theucer *pute* out of his regne,' iii. 2648, &c. In addition to the above there are a few instances of the same in other verbs, as '*get* hire a thank,' ii. 60, 'It schal noght wel *mow* be forsake,' ii. 1670, '*flitt* his herte aside,' iv. 214, '*let* it passe,' viii. 2056. (In vi. 202, 'If that sche wolde *ȝif* me leve,' we ought perhaps to read *ȝive* with S: cp. i. 1648.)

The gerund 'to done' is common, but we do not find either 'to sene' or 'to seine.'

Present Tense. In the 1st pers. sing. of the present, apart from such forms as *do, go,* &c., and *prai* beside *preie praie,* there are a few cases of apocope, as in the infinitive: 'Than cast I,' iv. 560, 'let it passe,' iv. 363, 'I put me therof in your grace,' i. 732, 'I put it al,' v. 2951, 'I red thee leve,' vi. 1359, 'Nou thenk I,' vii. 4212. In two of these instances it will be noticed that the following word begins with a consonant.

In the 3rd pers. sing. the syncopated and contracted forms are very much used by Gower. He says regularly *bit, ett, get, put, schet, set, sit* (2nd pers. *sist*), *smit, writ; arist, bint, fint, holt* (*halt*), *lest, went, wext; berth, brekth, bringth, crith, drawth, drinkth, falth, farth, forsakth, leith, lyth, preith, spekth, takth* (or *tath*), *thenkth, ȝifth,* and only occasionally *draweth, drinketh, fareth, kepeth, sitteth, waxeth,* &c. In vi. 59 the best MSS. agree in giving *sterte* for *stert,* and in viii. 2428 most have *sitte* for *sit,* but these are probably accidental variations. For the 3rd pers. plural Fahrenberg (p. 404) quotes several supposed instances of *th* ending. Of these most are expressions like 'men seith,' where 'men' is used as singular indefinite. One only is valid, viz. vii. 1107, 'Diverse sterres to him longeth': cp. vii. 536.

Preterite. With regard to the tense formation of Strong Verbs reference may be made to the Glossary, where all the characteristic forms are recorded. We confine ourselves here to a few remarks.

The following instances may be noticed of gradation between the singular and the plural of the preterite: *began,* pl. *begunne begonne, gan,* pl. *gonnen, ran,* pl. *runne, wan,* pl. *wonne, bond,* pl. *bounden, fond,* pl. *founden, song (sang),* pl. *songe sunge, sprong,* pl. *spronge sprungen, drank (dronk),* pl. *drunke, bar,* pl. *bere (beere), brak,* pl. *brieken, spak,* pl. *spieke, sat,* pl. *sete(n) siete(n) seete, bad,* pl. *bede, lay (lih),* pl. *lihe leie(n), wax,* pl. *woxen, wrot,* pl. *write(n), rod,* pl. *riden, ches*, pl. *chose*, and among preterite-presents *can*, pl. *conne, mai*, pl. *mowe, schal*, pl. *schulle schull schol, wot*, pl. *wite*.

There are some few instances in F of strong preterites with irregular -*e* termination in the 1st or 3rd pers. singular, but in no case is this authenticated by metre or rhyme. The following are examples in which F and S are agreed,' *schope* a wile,' v. 4278, ' he *bare* him,' v. 5236, 'which *sihe* his Soster,' v. 5810, ' *lete* come,' vi. 1186, ' he tho *toke* hire in his arm,' viii. 1732. These are perhaps mistakes, and they have some-times been corrected in the text on the authority of other MSS.

The 2nd pers. sing. has the -*e* termination, as *sihe* (*syhe*), iii. 2629, iv. 599, *were*, iv. 600, *knewe*, vi. 2313, *come*, viii. 2076, but *tok*, i. 2421. The 2nd pers. sing. of the preterite-present *mai* is regularly *miht* (*myht*), never 'mayest.' Occasionally the best MSS. give it as *mihte*, e. g. i. 2457, vii. 2637, 3819, but there is no metrical confirmation of this form. The preterite plural is very rarely found without -*e*, as v. 3300, 7534, vii. 3574.

Among Weak Verbs those which have the short or syncopated form keep the -*e* termination almost regularly. Such preterites are, for example, *aspide, cride, deide, leide, obeide, payde, preide, seide, teide, hadde, made, brende, sende, answerde, ferde, herde, solde, spilde, tolde, wende, betidde, dradde, fedde, fledde, hedde, gradde, ladde, radde, spedde, spradde, crepte, duelte, felte, hente, kepte, kiste, lefte, lepte, loste, mente, slepte, wente, wepte, alihte, caste, dihte, grette, knette, kutte, laste, liste, mette, plyhte, putte, schette, sette, sterte, triste, arawhte, broghte, cawhte, oghte, roghte, schryhte, soghte, strawhte, tawhte, thoghte, wroghte, cowthe, dorste, mihte, moste, scholde, wiste, wolde*.

At the same time it must be noted (as in the case of the infinitive) that with some of these forms there is an occasional tendency to drop the -*e* before a vowel at the beginning of the next word (that is, where elision would take place), and the agreement of the best MSS., especially F and S, makes it certain this was sometimes done by the author. It is impossible to trace any system, but the number of verbs affected is not large, and in nearly every case the instances of this kind of elision-apocope are largely outnumbered by the examples of normal inflexion in the same verb [1].

The following is a tolerably full list of references for these preterite forms, which are given in alphabetical order : ' *Beraft* hire,' v. 5647, ' it *betidd* upon the cas,' vii. 4381, ' Sche *cast* on me,' i. 152, ' *cast* up hire lok,' v. 5436, ' he *cast* his lok,' vi. 1035, ' *dorst* he,' ii. 1633, ' *drad* him,' viii. 1368,

---

[1] In a few cases, as Prol. 543, i. 183, 1280, v. 3393, vi. 2062, the gram-matically correct form has been printed in the text from less good MSS. and against the combined authority of F and S. On a review of the whole subject this does not now seem to me satisfactory.

'And *felt* it' (subj.), viii. 2165, 'so *ferd* I,' viii. 2445, '*had* herd hem,'
v. 5865, 'Hir bodi *hent* up,' v. 5702, '*herd* he noght sein,' iii. 2082, 'And
kept hire,' ii. 181, 'Sche *kept* al doun,' v. 1495, 'he *kest* him,' vi. 1746,
'And *kist* him,' v. 3777, 5592, 'and *knet* it,' v. 6866, 'he *kut* it,' vii. 4525,
'what him *list* he tok,' iii. 2446, 'Sche *lost* al,' ii. 2290, cp. v. 3465, 'That
mad hem,' ii. 310, and so also v. 986, 3393, 3822, 'ne *myht* I,' i. 1280, '*miht*
eschuie,' iii. 1356, and so also iii. 1440, vii. 4285, '*Put* under,' Prol. 683,
'Wan and *put* under,' Prol. 718, 'He *put* hem into,' i. 1013, 'Sche *put* hire
hand,' i. 1807, and so also ii. 3267, v. 3045, 4088, 5326, 6409, vi. 2062, vii.
4402, viii. 2702, 'thei *putt* hem,' v. 7417, 'Of ous, that *schold* ous,' Prol. 543
(so SF), '*schold* every wys man,' ii. 578, 'And *seid* hir,' i. 3188, '*Seid* ek,' v.
4309, 'And *set* hire,' ii. 2220, 'He *set* him,' v. 3691, 'he *set* an essamplaire,' vii.
4262, 'And *tawht* hem so' ('tawhte' S), iii. 176, '*told* him,' i. 3187, ii. 803,
2865 ('tolde' S), vii. 4688, '*told* hem,' v. 3883, viii. 1555, 'he *told* out,' ii. 884,
'every man *went* on his syde,' v. 7403, 'And *went* hem out' (pl.), v. 7533,
'sche *wist* it,' ii. 2010, 'thanne *wold* I,' i. 183, 'and *wold* have,' v. 4217,
'I *wold* stele,' v. 7137, '*wold* I,' viii. 2298, to which we may add '*myht* obeie,'
and '*behight* him' from the *Praise of Peace*, 39, 41.

Of these examples it is to be remembered, first that in only one case,
'I wold stele,' v. 7137, does this apocope take place before a consonant,
though in one other instance, v. 5865, the following word begins with an
aspirated *h*; and secondly, that with all these, except perhaps *put*, the full
form of the preterite is that which usually occurs before a vowel as well as
elsewhere. Even in the case of *put* we have the form *putte* frequently when
it is subject to elision, as Prol. 1069, 'And putte awey malencolie,' and so
ii. 713, 2684, iv. 399, 1368, &c., as well as regularly before a consonant, as
'With strengthe he putte kinges under,' i. 2797. The form *putt* occurs in
v. 7417, and in this case the verb is plural. The only other instances of
plurals in the list are Prol. 543 and v. 7533.

With regard to the weak verbs which form preterites with ending
-*ede*, the loss of the final *e* is somewhat more common, but it is usually
retained, and sometimes it counts as a syllable in the verse. Where
this is not the case, it is either elided in the usual way, or if it be
dropped in writing, this is only under the conditions which apply to
the verbs mentioned above, namely, before a vowel at the beginning
of the succeeding word.

It is, however, noteworthy that the use of these forms, whether in
-*ede* or -*ed*, is decidedly rare, and was avoided by our author even in
cases where the -*e* would have been subject to elision. It is evident
that he was always conscious of this ending, even if he did not always
write it, and yet he felt that the two weak syllables ought not to have
full value in the metre. The result was that he avoided the use of the
form generally, so far as it was reasonably possible to do so. The
whole number of these preterites in -*ede*, -*ed* to be found in the *Confessio
Amantis* is surprisingly small, both actually and relatively, that is,
taking account of the extent to which the verbs in question are
employed in their other tenses. The method pursued is chiefly to

substitute in narrative the present tense, or the perfect formed with
'hath,' for the 3rd person singular of the preterite, 'Conforteth' for
'Confortede,' 'Hath axed' for 'axede,' 'feigneth' for 'feignede,' and
this apparently as a matter of habit and even in cases where a vowel
follows. No doubt the use of the present tense in narrative is quite
usual apart from this, but the extremely frequent combination of strong
or syncopated preterites with the present tenses of verbs of this class
seems to me to indicate clearly how the matter stood.

The following are a few of the examples of this: 'For sche *tok* thanne
chiere on honde And *clepeth* him,' i. 1767 f., 'The king *comandeth* ben in
pes, And . . . *caste*,' 3240 f., ' *Comendeth*, and *seide* overmore,' 3361, 'he him
bethoghte, . . . And torneth to the banke ayein,' ii. 167 ff., 'for hem *sente* And
axeth hem,' 613 f., '*lay* . . . *clepeth* oute . . . *sterte*,' 848 ff., 'Sche *loketh* and
hire yhen *caste*,' 1066, 'This child he loveth kindely . . . Bot wel he. *sih* . . .
axeth . . . *seide*,' 1381 ff., 'Sche *preide* .him and *conseileth* bothe,' 1457, 'Which
semeth outward profitable And *was*,' 2201 f., 'And he himself that ilke
throwe *Abod*, and *hoveth* there stille,' iii. 1232 f., and so on.

These examples will serve to illustrate a tendency which every
reader will observe, when once his attention has been called to it.
There are indeed many narrative passages in which nearly all the strong
or syncopated verbs are used in the preterite, and all the others in the
present, and it is evident that this cannot be accidental[1].

There are, however, a certain number of instances of the use of weak
preterites, indicative or subjunctive, and a few in which the final *e*
(or *-en*) is sounded in the metre.

The following are examples of *-ede* preterites (in one instance *-ide*): ' I
wisshide after deth,' i. 120, 'he *passede* ate laste,' 142, 'he hem *stoppede* alle
faste,' 522, 'And *warnede* alle his officiers,' 2506, 'Mi ladi *lovede*, and I it wiste,'
ii. 502, 'he *axede* hem anon,' 1248, 'he *rounede* in thin Ere,' 1944, 'Bot he hire
lovede, er he wente,' 2027, 'Thogh that he *lovede* ten or tuelve,' 2063,
'*Supplantede* the worthi knyht,' 2453, 'Sche *pourede* oute,' iii. 679, so also
iii. 1631, 2556, iv. 468, 825, 842, 934, 1340, 1345, 1444, 'Lo, thus sche *deiede*
a wofull Maide,' iv. 1593, 'it *likede* ek to wende,' 2150, '*Controeveden* be sondri
wise,' 2454, ' *Translateden*. And otherwise,' 2660, 'And *foundeden* the grete
Rome,' v. 904, 'He *feignede* him,' 928, 'And *clepede* him,' 951, 'He *percede*
the harde roche,' 1678, 'Thei *faileden*, whan Crist was bore,' 1697, 'Thei
passeden the toun,' 2182, 'Alle othre *passede* of his hond,' 3258, ' *Welcomede*
him,' 3373, '*walkede* up and doun' (pl.), 3833, '*axede* him,' 5129, so also
5774, 6132, 6791, 6887, '*oppressede* al the nacion' (pl.), vi. 568, 'That
loveden longe er I was bore,' 882, 'he *usede* ay,' 1207, ' *exilede* out of londe,'
2348, '*Enformeden*,' vii. 1495, '*Devoureden*,' 3346, ' *Ensamplede* hem' (pl.),

---

[1] Prof. Lounsbury's criticism on the rhyme of vii. 5103 f., as given in
Pauli's edition, is quite sound, and Prof. Skeat's defence of it will not do.
Gower never rhymes a past participle in *-ed* with a weak preterite, though he
sometimes drops the *-e* of the preterite before a vowel. The rhyme was good
enough for Chaucer, however, as Prof. Lounsbury's examples abundantly prove.

4441, ' *Restorede* hem,' 4445, so also 4632, 4986, 4992, 4998, &c., ' *Eschuieden* to make assay,' viii. 373, 'With love *wrastlede* and was overcome,' 2240.

This list of examples, which is fairly complete up to v. 1970, will sufficiently show the manner in which *-ede* preterites are used. In more than three-fourths of the instances quoted the *-e* is subject to elision, and of those that remain nine are examples of the plural with *-eden* termination, and three only of the ending *-ede*, viz. ii. 2063, 'Thogh that he lovede ten or tuelve,' ii. 2453, ' Supplantede the worthi knyht,' and v. 1678, 'He percede the harde roche,' of which the first is really a case of syncope, ' lov'de,' as also ii. 502 (cp. vi. 882) and iv. 1593, whereas in ii. 2027 'lovede' occurs unsyncopated but with *-e* elided. It will be noted that in the plural the form *-eden* is used regularly when the syllables are to be fully pronounced, though *-ede* can be used for the sake of elision.

The *-ed* form of preterite is less frequent than the·other, and I am not aware of any clear example of its employment before a consonant or in rhyme. We have, for example, 'And *used* it,' i. 342, ' Sche *cleped* him,' i. 1535 (' *humbled* him,' i. 2065, is probably a participle, ' to have humbled himself'), ' *pryded* I me,' i. 2372, ' ne *feigned* I,' ii. 2061, ' the goddes . . . Comanded him,' iii. 2140 f., 'Thei *cleped* him,' v. 876, cp. 1057, &c. In iii. 1759, 'The Gregois *torned* fro the siege,' we have most probably a participle, 'were torned.' We may observe that the *-ed* form stands also in the plural.

Among weak preterites from originally strong verbs we may notice *abreide*, *crepte* (but past participle *crope*), *foghte*, *fledde*, *schotte*, *slepte* (also *slep*, with past participle *slepe*), *smette* (beside *smot*), *wepte*. The pret. *satte* in vii. 2282, 'He satte him thanne doun,' seems to arise from confusion of *sat* and *sette*.

Imperative. The *Confessio Amantis* is peculiarly rich in imperatives. Beside the regular imperative singular forms, e.g. *ared*, *besech*, *behold*, *ches*, *com*, *do*, *forsak*, *griet*, *help*, *hier*, *hyd*, *kep*, *lef*, *ly*, *lei*, *lest*, *lep*, *prei*, *put*, *say*, *schrif*, *spek*, *tak*, *tell*, *thenk*, *understond*, *ȝif*, &c., the MSS. give us also *hyde*, iii. 1502, *seie*, vii. 4084, *speke*, vii. 5422, *take*, iv. 2674, v. 6429, *thenke*, iii. 1083, but not in such positions as to affect the metre. The forms *axe*, *herkne*, *loke*, *wite* are regular, but *lok* also occurs (i. 1703, v. 1220).

In some instances the short form of imperative seems to be used as 3rd pers., e.g. 'hold clos the ston,' v. 3573, for 'let him hold,' 'tak in his minde,' viii. 1128, for 'let him take,' cp. viii. 1420. The singular and plural forms are often used without distinction, as v. 2333 ff., ' *Ches* . . . and *witeth* . . . *ches* and *tak* . . . *goth* . . . *taketh*,' v. 3986, 'So *help* me nou, I you beseche,' with ' *Helpeth*,' just above, several persons being addressed, and so ' *taketh* hiede And *kep* conseil,' viii. 1509 f., to one person. In the interchange of speech between the Confessor and the Lover, while sometimes the distinction is preserved, the

Confessor saying *tak, tell, understond*, and the Lover *telleth, axeth* (e. g. i. 1395, 1875), at other times the Lover says *lest, say, tell, lef*, &c. (i. 1942, 1972, ii. 2074, iii. 841, &c.) [1].

Present Participle. The form of the present participle is the most characteristic part of Gower's verb inflexion as compared (for example) with Chaucer's. Chaucer seems regularly to have used the form in *-inge* (often with apocope *-ing*) : Gower uses ordinarily the form *-ende*, and normally with the accent thrown on the termination, as i. 204, ' To me *spekende* thus began,' 236, 'Whos Prest I am *touchende* of love,' 428, ' *Stondende* as Stones hiere and there,' 633, 'So that *semende* of liht thei werke,' 1379 f., 'That for I se no sped *comende*, . . . *compleignende*,' 1682, ' *Hangende* doun unto the chin.'

Sometimes the same form is used with accent on the preceding syllable, and in this case the *-e* is systematically elided, e. g. Prol. 11, ' In tyme *comende* after this,' 259, ' *Belongende* unto the presthode,' i. 296, 'As *touchende* of my wittes fyve' (cp. 334, 742), 3025, 'And *wailende* in his bestly stevene.'

In a relatively small number of instances the form *-inge* occurs either in rhyme, as i. 524, ' So whan thei comen forth seilinge,' in rhyme with ' singe,' i. 1710, ' And liveth, as who seith, *deyinge*,' in rhyme with ' likynge ' (subst.), or with the accent thrown back, as i. 115, ' *Wisshinge* and *wepinge* al myn one,' v. 518, ' *Abidinge* in hir compaignie,' vi. 717, 'I mai go *fastinge* everemo'; rarely out of rhyme and with accent, as i. 2721, ' Mi fader, as *touchinge* of al.'

The final *e* is never lost in writing, but when the accent is thrown back it is always elided.

Past Participle. The *-id* termination of weak past participles is very rarely found in the Fairfax MS., except in the concluding passage, which is copied in a different hand from the rest. It occurs commonly in the *Praise of Peace*. Examples found elsewhere in F are *weddid*, iv. 650, *medlid*, iv. 1475.

From *setten* besides the regular past participle *set* there appears the form *sete* twice in rhyme, vii. 2864, *forȝete* : *sete*, and viii. 244, *misgete* (past partic.) : *upsete*. This seems to be formed after the analogy of *gete*. On the other hand we have *ferd*, i. 445, &c., but also *fare(n)*, iii. 2692, v. 3797, &c. The past participle of *se* is *sen, sein, seie*, but most commonly *sene*. In a few instances a final *e* is given by the MSS. in weak past participles, e. g. *herde* for *herd*, v. 4231, *schope* for *schop*, v. 4278, *sette* for *set*, vi. 10, *wiste* for *wist*, viii. 37.

The cases of weak past participles with plural inflexion (e. g. Prol. 300, i. 3246, iv. 2343, v. 6789) have already been mentioned in dealing with adjectives.

[1] Except in the case of these imperative forms the 2nd pers. plur. is quite consistently used by the Lover in his shrift, and the 2nd pers. sing. by the Confessor in reply.

There is hardly any use of the prefix *y-* (*i-*), but we have *ybore*, ii. 499.

vi. DIALECT.   Gower's language is undoubtedly in the main the English of the Court, and not a provincial dialect.   Making allowance for the influences of literary culture and for a rather marked conservatism in orthography and grammatical inflexions, we can see that it agrees on the whole with the London speech of the time, as evidenced by the contemporary documents referred to by Prof. Morsbach.   At the same time its tendencies are Southern rather than Midland, and he seems to have used Kentish forms rather more freely than Chaucer.   This is shown especially (1) in the more extensive use of the forms in which *e* stands for O. E. *y̆*, as *senne*, *kesse*, *pet*, *hell*, &c. ; (2) in the frequent employment of *ie*, both in French and English words, to represent *ē̜*, a practice which can hardly be without connexion with the Kentish *cliene*, *diepe*, *diere*, *hier*, *hield*, *niede*, &c. ; (3) in the use of *-ende* as the normal termination of the present participle. (The *Ayenbite* regularly has *-inde*.)   Probably also the preference shown by Gower for the close sound of *ē̜*, from O. E. *ǣ*, may be to some extent due to Kentish influence.   Other points of resemblance between the language of Gower and that of the *Ayenbite* (for example) are the free use of syncopated forms in the 3rd pers. sing. of verbs and the regular employment of *ous* for *us*.

vii. METRE, &c.   The smoothness and regularity of Gower's metre has been to some extent recognized.   Dr. Schipper in *Englische Metrik*, vol. i. p. 279, remarks upon the skill with which the writer, while preserving the syllabic rule, makes his verse flow always so smoothly without doing violence to the natural accentuation of the words, and giving throughout the effect of an accent verse, not one which is formed by counting syllables. Judging by the extracts printed in Morris and Skeat's *Specimens* (which are taken from MS. Harl. 3869, and therefore give practically the text of Fairfax 3), he observes that the five principal licences which he has noted generally in the English verse of the period are almost entirely absent from Gower's octosyllabics, and in particular that he neither omits the first unaccented syllable, as Chaucer so often does (e. g. 'Be it rouned, red or songe,' *Hous of Fame*, ii. 214, 'Any lettres for to rede,'

iii. 51, 'Of this hill that northward lay,' iii. 62), nor displaces the natural accent (as 'Of Decembre the tenthe day,' *Hous of Fame*, i. 111, 'Jupiter considereth wel this, ii. 134, 'Rounede everych in otheres ere,' iii. 954), nor slurs over syllables.

To say that Gower never indulges in any of these licences would be an exaggeration. Some displacement of the natural accent may be found occasionally, even apart from the case of those French words whose accent was unsettled, but it is present in a very slight degree, and the rhythm produced does not at all resemble that of the lines cited above from Chaucer : e. g. i. 2296, 'Wher that he wolde make his chace,' 2348, 'Under the grene thei begrave,' 2551, '"Drink with thi fader, Dame," he seide.' Such as it is, this licence is nearly confined to the first foot of the verse, and is not so much a displacement of the natural accent of the words as a trochaic commencement, after the fashion which has established itself as an admitted variety in the English iambic. We may, however, read long passages of the *Confessio Amantis* without finding any line in which the accent is displaced even to this extent.

Again, as to slurring of syllables, this no doubt takes place, but on regular principles and with certain words or combinations only. There are hardly more than three or four lines in the whole of the *Confessio Amantis* where a superfluous syllable stands unaccounted for in the body of the verse, as for example,

> iv. 1131, 'Som time in chambre, som time in halle,'
> v. 447, 'Of Jelousie, bot what it is,'
> v. 2914, 'And thus ful ofte aboute the hals,'
> v. 5011, 'It was fantosme, bot yit he herde.'

The writer seems to have no need of any licences. The narrative flows on in natural language, and in sentences and periods which are apparently not much affected by the exigencies of metre or rhyme, and yet the verse is always smooth and the rhyme never fails to be correct. If this is not evidence of the highest style of art, it shows at least very considerable skill.

In Gower's five-accent line, as exhibited in the Supplication of viii. 2217–2300 and in the poem *In Praise of Peace*, Schipper finds less smoothness of metre, 'owing perhaps to the greater unfamiliarity and difficulty of the stanza and verse' (*Englische Metrik*, i. 483 ff.). His examples, however, are not conclusive on this point. Some of the lines cited owe their irregularity to corruptions of text, and others prove to be quite regularly in accordance with Gower's usual metrical principles.

For instance, in viii. 2220 the true text is

'That wher so that I reste or I travaile,'

which is a metrically perfect line. Again, in the *Praise of Peace*, l. 79,   'And to the heven it ledeth ek the weie,'

it is impossible, according to Gower's usage, that 'heven' should stand as a dissyllable. He wrote always 'hevene,' and the penultimate was syncopated. So also 'levere' in l. 340, 'evere,' l. 376. Hence there is no 'epic caesura' in any of these cases. Nor again in l. 164, 'Crist is the heved,' can 'heved' be taken as a dissyllable in the verse: it is always metrically equivalent to 'hed.' The only fair instance of a superfluous syllable at the caesura is in l. 66,

'For of bataile the final ende is pees.'

It seems that the trochee occurs more commonly here than in the short line. Such examples as Schipper quotes, occurring at the beginning of the line,

'Axe of thi god, so schalt thou noght be werned,'
'Pes is the chief of al the worldes welthe,'

are of the same character as those which we find in the octo-syllabics. Perhaps, however, a difference is afforded by the more frequent occurrence of the same licence in other parts of the verse; as,

'So that undir his swerd it myht obeie,' 39.

The rhyming on words like 'manhode,' 'axinge,' &c., is in accordance with the poet's general usage.

On the whole, the combination of the syllabic and the accentual system is effected in the five-accent line of these stanzas almost as completely as in the short couplet; and in his command of the measure, in the variety of his caesura, and the ease with which he passes without pause from line to line and rounds off the stanza with the matter, the author shows himself to be as fully master of his craft upon this ground as in the more familiar measure of the *Confessio Amantis*.

As regards the treatment of weak syllables in the metre, Gower's practice, in accordance with the strict syllabic system which he adopted, is very different from Chaucer's. The rules laid down by ten Brink, *Chaucers Sprache*, § 260, as to the cases in which

weak final *e* is never counted as a syllable in the verse, except
in rhyme, require some qualification even when applied to Chaucer
(for example, 'sone' is certainly a dissyllable in *Cant. Tales*, A 1963,
Hous of Fame, i. 218), and they are almost wholly inapplicable to
Gower, as we shall see if we examine them. (*a*) Gower has the
forms *hire, oure, ȝoure*, all occasionally as dissyllables apart from
special emphasis or rhyme. (*β*) *these, some, whiche* are all sometimes dissyllables. (*γ*) The strong participles with short stems as
come, drive, write as a rule have the final *e* sounded. (*δ*) The
-*e* of the 2nd pers. sing. of the strong preterite may be sounded,
e. g. iii. 2629 (but 'Were thou,' iv. 600). (*ε*) The form *made*, both
singular and plural, regularly has -*e* sounded, *were* (pret.) usually,
and *wite* sometimes. (*ζ*) *sone, wone, schipe* (dat.), and the French
words in -*ie* (*ye*), &c., have -*e* regularly counted in the metre : so also
beste, entente, tempeste. (*η*) *before, tofore, there* are used in both ways.

Gower's usage with reference to this matter is as follows :
The personal and possessive pronouns *hire, oure, ȝoure, here* and *hise* (as
plural of *his*), written also *hir, our*, &c., are as a rule treated as monosyllables.
We have however 'Fro *hire*, which was naked al,' i. 367, 'And thenke
untoward *hire* drawe,' iv. 559, so v. 1178, 2757, vii. 1899, &c., 'In *oure* tyme
among ous hiere,' Prol. 5 (but '*Oure* king hath do this thing amis,' i. 2062),
'As ȝe be ȝoure bokes knowe,' iii. 1087, cp. v. 2951 (but 'Bot, fader, of ȝoure
lores wise,' i. 2768). Add to these *alle* (pl.) before definite article.
 In the following words also the final *e* is sometimes suppressed for
the verse : *these* (also *thes*), Prol. 900, 1037, i. 435, ii. 237, &c. (but *thesë*,
v. 813, 1127, vii. 1005, &c.) : *whiche* plur. (also *which*), ii. 604, iv. 1496, &c.
(but *whichë*, i. 404, v. 1269, vii. 822, 1256, &c.) : *eche* (also *ech*), v. 6883, according to F, cp. Prol. 516 : *there* (usually *ther*), viii. 2311, 2689 (but *therë*, iii. 1233,
&c., and often in rhyme) : *were* pret. ind. or subj. (also *wer*), iii. 1600, iv.
600, 1657, 1689 (but more usually *werë*, as Prol. 1072, iii. 762, v. 2569, vii.
4458) : *where* (usually *wher*), v. 4355 (but *wherë*, v. 2720) : *more* (also *mor*),
ii. 26, v. 2239, 6207, vii. 3237 (but *morë*, Prol. 55*, 640, iv. 2446, vii. 3287,
&c.) : *before, tofore* (also *befor, tofor*), i. 2054, 2864, iii. 2052 (but *beforë*,
Prol. 848, and often in rhyme) : *foure*, vii. 2371 (but *fourë*, ii. 1037, iv.
2464) : *fare* (wel), iii. 305, iv. 1378 (but *farëwel*, v. 4218) : *sire*, i. 2878, ii.
2995 (but *sirë*, v. 3547, 5593) : *wite*, ii. 455 (but *witë*, v. 3150, 3445) : *wole*
(also *wol*), v. 2891, 2911, &c. : *bothe*, ii. 1966, 2154, iv. 2138, &c. (but *bothë*,
Prol. 1068, i. 851, &c.) : *wolde* (also *wold*), v. 4413 (usually *woldë*) : *come*,
ii. 789, iv. 2826 (but *comë*, pp. iv. 1283, vi. 1493, vii. 4840, inf. viii. 1362) :
some, pl. subst., iii. 2112, v. 2252 (but *somë*, i. 2034 ff.) : *have*, Prol. 708,
i. 169, 2724, ii. 550, iv. 1600 (but *havë*, ii. 332, iv. 1598) : *love*, subst. iv.
930, vi. 1261 (but *lovë* much more often, e. g. i. 103, 251, 760, &c.) : *tuelve*
(also *tuelf*), iv. 1983 (but *tuelvë*, vii. 1005) : *trewe* (also *trew*), v. 2877 (but
trewë, pl., Prol. 184, def., iii. 2228) : *mowe*, inf. (also *mow*), iv. 38 : *seie*, inf.
and 1st s. pres. iii. 1737, iv. 672, v. 2616, 6428, &c. (but *seië* often) : *preie*,

1st s. pres. (also *prai*), v. 4531 (but *preië*, v. 3230) : *furthere, forthere* (also *further, forther*), iii. 81, 885 : *lengere* (also *lenger*), i. 1516, ii. 2602 : *rathere* (also *rather*), ii. 503, vii. 4161, viii. 2141 : *janglere*, v. 526 : also some isolated cases, as *aboute*, v. 2914, *Take*, v. 7169, *Minotaure*, v. 5327 (but *Minotaurë*, 5291, &c.), *Theophile*, viii. 1500.

In iv. 1131, v. 447, 5011, which we have quoted above, the superfluous syllable in each case may be connected with the pause in the sentence, as in *Mirour de l'omme*, 10623, ' L'un ad franchise, l'autre ad servage.'

Syncope (so far as regards the metre) regularly takes place in the following : *covere* (*discovere*, &c.), *delivere* (but not *deliverance*, i. 1584, v. 1657), *evene, evere, fievere, havene, hevene, levere, nevere, povere, sevene* (also *sefne*), *swevene* (also *swefne*), and some other words of a similar kind, to which add *heved, evel, devel*. In these cases a final *e* is always pronounced unless elided, and in case of elision a word like *hevene, nevere* is reduced to a monosyllable, as

'This world which evere is in balance.'

The following also are sometimes syncopated : *lovede, loveden*, ii. 502, vi. 882, but without syncope ii. 2027, *beloved*, i. 1928, *belovëd*, i. 1920 f., *behovely, behovelich*, iii. 1330, v. 4012, vii. 1949 (but *unbehovëly*, viii. 2884), *leveful*, v. 7053, *Averil*, vii. 1029, *soverein*, vii. 1776 (but usually three syllables, as Prol. 186, i. 1609, and *sovereinete*, five syllables, i. 1847), *amorous*, iii. 745 (but usually three syllables, as i. 1414), *fader*, ii. 2387, cp. *fadre*, ii. 2519 (but ordinarily a dissyllable), *unkendeli*, ii. 3124 (but *unkindëly*, iii. 2065), *comelieste, comelihiede*, v. 3048, 6734 (but *comëly*, ii. 441), *namely*, viii. 3041, also *namly*, ii. 47 (but usually three syllables, as Prol. 144, iii. 63), *Termegis*, iv. 2408. We may note, however, that this kind of syncope is less used by Gower than by Chaucer, and that *chivalerie, chivalerous, foreward, foretokne, loveday, pilegrin, surquiderie*, &c., are fully pronounced.

Unaccented *i* before weak *e* either final or in inflexions has the force of a semi-vowel, and forms no syllable of itself : so *studie, carie, tarie, chirie, merie, manye*, &c. are equivalent to dissyllables, and are reduced by elision to the value of monosyllables, as Prol. 323, 'To *studie* upon the worldes lore,' i. 452, 'To *tarie* with a mannes thoght,' i. 3238, 'And *manye* it hielden for folie,' ii. 2648, 'Thei *carie* til thei come at Kaire ' ; and so also in the other parts of the same words, e. g. i. 1645, 'And thus he *tarieth* long and late,' and in plurals like *bodies*, iv. 2463. Similarly *Mercurie* is made into a dissyllable by elision, 'And ek the god Mercurie also,' i. 422. Akin to this in treatment is the frequent combination *many a, many an*, counting as two syllables (so 'ful many untrewe,' v. 2886), but *many on, manion* as three. We may note also the case of *statue*, Prol. 891, 'As I tolde of the Statue above,' which is reduced by elision to a monosyllable.

Elision of weak final *e* takes place regularly before a vowel
or an unaspirated *h*. We must observe that several classical
proper names ending originally in *ē*, as *Alceone, Daphne, Progne,
Phebe*, have weak *e* and are subject to elision, and under this head
it may be noted that *Canace* rhymes to *place*, whereas Chaucer
(referring to Gower's story) gives the name as *Canacee*, in rhyme
with *he*. Also the combinations *byme, tome, tothe*, &c., have weak
-e and are elided before a vowel.

An aspirated *h* prevents elision as effectively as any other
consonant. We have 'min holë herte,' 'gretë hornes,' 'Cadmë
hyhte,' 'Mi Sonë, herkne,' 'proprë hous,' 'fastë holde' (and even
'othrë herbes,' iv. 3008); but there are some words in which
h is aspirated only when they are emphatic in sense or position,
as *have, hath, he, him, hire, how*, &c. For example, elision takes
place usually before *have, he, how*, but not so as a rule in cases
where they are used in rhyme or with special emphasis, e. g.
i. 2542, 'Of such werk as it scholde have,' ii. 2479, cp. v. 7766,
'Wenende that it were he,' iv. 3604, 'And al the cause hou it
wente.' On the other hand, the preterite *hadde* seems to have an
aspirated *h* even in unemphatic position, as ii. 589, 'The Sceptre
hadde forto rihte': compare vii. 2364, 'Victoire hadde upon his
fo,' with vii. 2392, 'Thogh thou victoire have nou on honde.'
Elision also takes place before *hierafter*, though not before *hiere*.

There is one instance of hiatus, viii. 110, 'That he his Sone
Isaäc,' and it may be noted that the same thing occurs with the
same name in the *Mirour*, 12241, 'De Isaak auci je lis.'

The article *the* regularly coalesces with a succeeding word beginning with
a vowel or mute *h*, as *thaffeccioun, thalemans, thamende, thapostel, thastat,
theffect, themperour, thenvious, therbage, therthe, thexperience, thonour, thother,
thunsemlieste, thyle*, &c. The exceptions, which are very few, are cases of
special emphasis, as i. 3251, 'The Erthe it is.' Similarly the negative
particle *ne* with a succeeding verb beginning with a vowel, as *nam, naproche,
nis* (but *ne have*), and also occasionally with some words beginning with
w, forming *nere, nost, not, nyle, nyste*, &c. In some few instances *to* coalesces
with the gerund, as *tacompte, teschuie*.

There is diaeresis regularly in such proper names as *Theseüs,
Peleüs, Tereüs*, and also in *Saül, Isaäc*. We have *Moïses* usually,
but *Moises* (dissyllable), iv. 648, *Thaise* usually, but *Thaïsis* in the
epitaph, viii. 1536. One example occurs affecting the *-ee* termination, viz. *Caldeë*, v. 781 (usually a dissyllable), so *Judeë, Galileë* in
Mirour, 20067, 29239. This is an essentially different case from

that of *degreës*, which is found in Chaucer. The termination *-ius* is usually dissyllabic, but vii. 2967, 'The god Mercurius and no man.' The endings *-ioun*, *-ious*, *-ien*, &c., are always fully pronounced.

As regards accent, it has been already observed that the natural accent of words is preserved far better in Gower's verse than in Chaucer's. There are, however, a number of words of French origin, of which the accent was unsettled, and also some instances of English words in which a secondary syllable was capable of receiving the principal accent, either in case of composition, as in *kingdom*, *knihthode*, *treweliche*, or with a formative termination, as that of the superlative, *fairéste*, &c., or the present participle, as *wepénde*. In such cases the accent was often determined by the metre. Many Romance words are quite freely treated in the matter of accent, as for example *folie*, *fortune*, *mercy*, *mirour*, *nature*, *parfit*, *preiere*, *resoun*, *science*, *sentence*, *tempeste*. The terminations *-hode*, *-hede*, *-inge*, *-liche*, *-ly*, *-nesse*, *-schipe* are all capable of accent, and also the penultimate syllables of *answere* and *felawe*.

Nearly all that is important about rhyme has already been said under the head of Phonology. We may here remark on some of the instances in which the form of words is accommodated to the rhyme, these being sometimes cases where variants are supplied by neighbouring dialects. Thus we have *aise* for *ese*, *ar* for *er*, *hair* for *heir*, *naght* once for *noght*, *fer* once for *fyr*, *hade*, with the original long vowel, for *hadde*, *geth* (the originally correct form) for *goth*, *fore* for *for*; and alternatives such as *moneie monoie*, *aweie awey away*, *seide saide*, *soverein soverain*, are used in accordance with the rhyme, though it is difficult to say for certain in all cases whether there was difference of sound. Thus, while we have *away* as rhyme to *day*, *awey* is found rhyming to *ey*, i. 2545, *said*, *saide* rhyming with *paid*, *Maide*, while *seide* rhymes with *alleide*, *obeide*; we find *soverein* : *aȝein*, but *brayn* : *soverain*. The form *yhe* often varies to *ȳe* when in rhyme with *-ie* termination, as *clergie* : *ȳe*, Prol. 329 f., *ȳe* : *agonie*, i. 967 f. (but also *yhe* : *pourpartie*, i. 405 f., *yhe* : *specefie*, i. 571 f.). Sometimes however the other rhyme-word is modified to correspond to it, as *pryhe* : *yhe*, v. 469 f., and there was probably no perceptible difference of pronunciation in this case. So also the preterite *lowh* is written *low* when in rhyme with *now*, Prol. 1071, and

similarly *thou* : *ynou*, vii. 2099 f. (but *bowe* : *ynowhe*, ii. 3225 f.).
We have already seen that the use of such alternative forms
as *sinne senne, wile wole, lasse lesse, hedde hidde, -ende -inge* is
sometimes determined by the rhyme.

Alliteration is used by Gower in a manner which is especially
characteristic of the new artistic style of poetry. It is sufficiently
frequent, both in formal combinations, such as 'cares colde,'
'lusty lif,' 'park and plowh,' 'swerd or spere,' 'lief and loth,'
'wel or wo,' 'dike and delve,' 'slepe softe,' 'spille . . . spede,'
and as an element of the versification :

> i. 886 f. ' For so, thei seide, al stille and softe
> God Anubus hire wolde awake.'
> iv. 2590 ' The lost is had, the lucre is lore.'
> iv. 3384 f. 'Which many a man hath mad to falle,
> Wher that he mihte nevere arise.'
> v. 3670 f. 'And thanne he gan to sighe sore,
> And sodeinliche abreide of slep.'
> vii. 3468 f. 'Sche hath hir oghne bodi feigned,
> For feere as thogh sche wolde flee.'

But it is not introduced in accordance with any fixed rules, and it
often assists the flow of the verse without in the least attracting
the attention of the reader. We do not find any examples of the
rather exaggerated popular style which Chaucer sometimes adopts
in passages of violent action, e. g. *Cant. Tales*, A 2604 ff. The
whole subject of alliteration in Gower has been carefully dealt with
by P. Höfer in his dissertation, *Alliteration bei Gower*, 1890, where
a very large number of examples are cited and classified; and to
this the reader may be referred.

viii. TEXT AND MANUSCRIPTS. About forty manuscript copies
of the *Confessio Amantis* are known to exist in public or private
libraries or in the hands of booksellers, and probably there may be
a few more in private possession, the existence of which has not
yet been recorded. As the broad lines for their classification are
necessarily laid down by the fact that the book was put forth
by the author in several different forms, it is necessary, before
proceeding further, to say something about this matter.

That the poem exists in at least two distinct forms, character-
ized by obvious differences near the beginning and at the end,
has been matter of common knowledge. Even in Berthelette's
edition of 1532 the difference at the beginning was noted, and

though the printer did not venture to deviate from the form of text
which had been made current by Caxton, yet he gave in his preface
the beginning of the poem as he found it in his manuscript.
Dr. Pauli accordingly proceeded on the assumption that there
were two normal forms, one having a dedication to Richard II
at the beginning and a form of conclusion in which mention is
made of Chaucer, and the other with a dedication to Henry of
Lancaster and a conclusion in which Chaucer is not mentioned.
Copies which do not conform to these standards are for him
simply irregular. He is aware of the additional passages in
Berthelette's edition and in the Stafford MS., and in one place he
speaks of three classes of MSS., but he does not know that there
are any written copies except the Stafford MS. which contain the
additional passages. If he had had personal knowledge of the
manuscripts at Oxford and at Cambridge, instead of being satisfied
to gather scraps of information about the former from Bodley's
Librarian and about the latter from Todd, he would have found
the passages in question also in MS. Bodley 294 at Oxford and in
the Trinity and Sidney MSS. at Cambridge.

There are then at least these three classes of manuscripts to
be recognized even by a superficial observer, and we shall find
that the more obvious differences which have been mentioned are
accompanied by a number of others of less importance. The
first recension according to our classification is that in which
the conclusion of the poem contains praises of Richard II as
a just and beneficent ruler and a presentation of the book for
his acceptance [1]. The second has the additional passages of the
fifth and seventh books, with a rearrangement of the sixth book
which has not hitherto been noticed, while the conclusion of the
poem has been rewritten so as to exclude the praises of the king,
and in some copies there is also a new preface with dedication
to Henry of Lancaster. The third exhibits a return to the form
of the first as regards the additional passages, but has the rewritten preface and epilogue. Against this merely threefold
division some objections might fairly be made. It might be
pointed out that the so-called second recension includes at least
two distinct forms, and moreover that upon further examination

---

[1] The copies which have this conclusion have also the preface in which
Richard is mentioned as the occasion of the author's undertaking, but this
preface is found also in combination with the other conclusion.

we see reason to divide the manuscripts of our first recension
into two main groups, one exhibiting an earlier and the other
a later text, this last being more in accordance generally with that
of what we call the second and third recensions than with the
earlier form of the first. For practical purposes, however, the
division which has been laid down above may fairly be adopted.
As regards the order of time, from the political tendency of the
differences between them it is clear that what we call the first
recension logically precedes the third. The intermediate position
of the second is given chiefly by the fact that one of the seven
existing manuscripts gives the earlier form of preface, and this
may also have been the case with two others, which are defective
at the beginning[1]. However, as has been said, the name is used
for convenience to cover a class of copies which, as regards the
character of their text, do not all belong to the same period, and
they must be looked upon as representing rather a concurrent
variety of the first or the third recension[2] than as a type which
is distinctly intermediate in order of time. At the same time
the smaller variations of text exhibited by these seven MSS. in
combination, as against all others[3], mark them as really a family
apart, more closely related to one another than to those that lie
outside the group.

For the sake of clearness the manuscripts are in this edition
regularly grouped according to this classification, and in the
critical notes each class is cited by itself. At the same time
it must not be assumed that the manuscripts of each recension
stand necessarily by themselves, and that no connexion is trace-
able between one class and another. On the contrary, we shall

[1] Berthelette used a manuscript (not now existing) which in this respect,
as in many others, resembled B.

[2] It may be noted that the four second recension MSS. which contain the
author's Latin note about his books ('Quia vnusquisque,' &c.), viz. BT∧P2,
agree in a form of it which is different both from that which is given by first
recension copies and that which we find in F, and is clearly intermediate
between the other two, the first form fully excusing Richard II for the
troubles of his reign and the third entirely condemning him, while this
makes no mention of his merits or demerits, but simply prays for the state
of the kingdom. It is noticeable that the second recension form definitely
substitutes Henry for Richard as the patron of the *Confessio Amantis*,
though in one at least of the copies to which it is attached this substitution
has not been made in the text of the poem.

[3] e. g. ii. 193, 365 ff., iii. 168, 1241, iv. 283, 1321, v. 1252, &c.

find that many errors in the text of the first recension appear also in some copies of the second, and even of the third. The process by which this was brought about is made clearer to us by the fact that we have an example of a manuscript which has passed from one group into another partly by erasure and partly by substitution of leaves, apparently made under the direction of the author. This is MS. Fairfax 3, which forms the basis of our text, and the handwriting of some of the substituted pages is one which may be recognized as belonging to the 'scriptorium' of the poet.

The example is a suggestive one and serves to explain several things. It makes it easy to understand, for example, how the additional matter introduced into the second recension came to be omitted in the third. The author in this instance had before him a very fully revised and corrected copy of his first edition, and this by a certain amount of rewriting over erasure and by a substitution of leaves at the beginning and end of the poem was converted into a copy of what we call the third recension, which his scribes could use at once as an authoritative exemplar. The introduction of the additional passages in the fifth and seventh books could not have been effected without a process of recopying the whole book, which would have called for much additional labour of the nature of proof-reading on the part of the author, in order to secure its correctness. This argument would apply to a book which was intended to remain in the hands of the author, or rather of the scribes whom he employed, and to be used as an archetype from which copies were to be made. If a new book had to be specially prepared for presentation, the case would be different, and it might then be worth while to incorporate the additional passages with the fully revised and re-dedicated text, as we find was done in the case of the so-called Stafford MS.

Another matter which can evidently be explained in the same way is the reappearance in some copies of the second recension of errors which belong to the first. In producing the originals of such manuscripts as these, partially revised copies of the first recension must have been used as the basis, and such errors as had not yet received correction appear in the new edition.

The assumption that a certain number of errors are original, that is to say, go back either to the author's own autograph or to the transcript first made from it, is in itself probable : we know in fact that some which appear in every copy, without exception, of the first and second recensions at length receive correction by erasure in Fairfax 3. So far as we can judge, the text of the *Confessio Amantis* during its first years exhibited a steady tendency to rid itself of error, and the process of corruption in the ordinary sense can hardly be said to have set in until after the death of the author. There are a large number of various readings in the case of which we find on the one side the great majority of first recension MSS., and on the other a small number of this same type together with practically the whole of the second and third recensions, as, for example [1] :

i. 2836 to H_1XERCLB$_2$ do AJMG, SAdBΔΛ, FWH$_3$
 2847 be *om.* H_1XGERCLB$_2$ *ins.* AJM, SAdBΔ, FWH$_3$
 2953 wele H . . . B$_2$ weie AJM, SAd BΔ, FWH$_3$
 3027 preieth H$_1$ . . . B$_2$, W braieth, AJM, S . . . ΔΛ, FH$_3$
 3374 an Erl hier H$_1$ . . . B$_2$, Λ mad a Pier AJM, SAdBΔ, FW (H$_3$ def.)
 3381 place H$_1$ . . . B$_2$, BΛ maide AJM, SAdΔ, FW (H$_3$ defective)
ii. 833 that diere H$_1$ . . . B$_2$, B that other AJ(M), SAdΔΛ, FWH$_3$
iii. 12 euermore H$_1$ . . . B$_2$ enemy AJM, SAdBTΔ, FWH$_3$
 354 I may H$_1$ . . . B$_2$ he may AJM, SAdBTΔ, FWH$_3$
iv. 109 day H$_1$ . . . B$_2$, H$_3$ lay AJM, SBTΔ, FW (Ad def.)
v. 316 thanne (than) H$_1$ . . . B$_2$, Δ hom AJM, SAdBTΔ, FWH$_3$
 368 And for no drede now wol I wonde H$_1$ . . . B$_2$, Λ In helle thou schalt understonde AJM, S . . . Δ, FWH$_3$ cp. 394, 424, 786, &c.
 2694 Whan that sche was bot of ȝong age For good ERCLB$_2$ That only for thilke avantage Of good AJMH$_1$XG, S . . . ΔΛ, FWH$_3$
 2771 nyh *om.* ERCLB$_2$ *ins.* AJMH$_1$XG, S . . . Δ, FWH$_3$
 3110 burned as the silver ERCLB$_2$ burned was as selver AJMH$_1$XG, S . . . ΔΛ, FWH$_3$ cp. 3032, 3246, &c.

We see in these examples, selected as fairly typical, that some of the variants have evidently the character of errors, while in other cases the difference of reading is due to an alternative version. The circumstances, however, of these two cases are not distinguishable, the errors are supported by as much authority as the rest, and it must be supposed that both have the same

---

[1] For the explanation of the use of letters to designate MSS. the reader is referred to the list of MSS. given later. It should be noted that AJM and FWH$_3$ represent in each case a group of about seven MSS., and H$_1$ . . . B$_2$ one of nearly twenty. We observe in the examples given that B and Λ are sometimes found either separately or together on the side of the H$_1$ . . . B$_2$ group, and that the same is true occasionally of W, while on the other hand some MSS. of the H$_1$ . . . B$_2$ group are apt to pass over to the other side in a certain part of the text and support what we call the revised reading.

origin. If then we assume that such variations as we find (for example) in i. 3396, 3416, v. 30, 47, 82, 368, 2694, &c., are due to the author, as is almost certain, there can be no doubt that the form of text which is given by the group AJM in combination with the second and third recensions is the later of the two: and if the group H1 . . . B2 represents an earlier type as regards this class of variation, it must surely do so also as regards the errors, which, as we have seen, stand upon the same ground in respcet of manuscript authority. As we cannot help believing that the author wrote originally 'To holde hir whil my lif may laste,' v. 82, and 'The more he hath the more he greedeth,' v. 394, so we may reasonably suppose that errors such as 'it' for 'hid,' i. 1755, 'that diere' for 'that other,' ii. 833, 'what' for 'war,' iii. 1065, existed in the copy which first served as an exemplar.

It may be observed here that in cases where revision seems to have taken place, we can frequently see a definite reason for the change; either the metre is made more smooth, as i. 1770, 2622, 3374, ii. 671, 751, 1763, iii. 765, 2042, 2556, iv. 234, v. 368, 1678, &c., or some name is altered into a more correct form, as where 'Element' is changed to 'Clemenee,' iv. 985, with a corresponding alteration of the rhyme, or the expression and run of the sentence is improved, as i. 368, 3416, v. 30, 1906, 6756, &c. In particular we note the tendency towards increased smoothness of metre which is shown in dealing with weak *e* terminations.

It is to be assumed on the principles which have been stated that the group ERCLB2 and the other manuscripts which agree with them represent with more or less accuracy the first form of the author's text, that H1YXG and a few more form a class in which correction and revision has taken place to some extent, but partially and unsystematically, and that AJM &c. give us the first recension text in a much more fully revised and corrected form.

It has been already said that F was originally a manuscript of the first recension. We shall find however that it did not exactly correspond to any existing first recension manuscript. Setting aside the small number of individual mistakes to be found in it, there are perhaps about eighty instances (many of a very trifling character) in which its text apparently differed originally from

that of any first recension copy which we have, and in about half
of these the text of F agrees with that of the second recension.
The manuscript which comes nearest to F in most respects
is J (St. John's Coll., Camb.), and there is a considerable number
of instances in which this MS. stands alone among first recension
copies in agreement with the Fairfax text.   In the sixth book, for
example, if J be set aside, there are at least twenty-three passages
in which F gives an apparently genuine reading unsupported
by the first recension; but in sixteen of these cases J is in agreement with F.   It must be noted, however, that this state of
things is not equally observable in the earlier part of the poem,
and indeed does not become at all marked until the fifth book.

Besides variations of reading, there are in the Fairfax MS.
a few additions to the text which are not found in any first
recension copy.   These are Prol. 495–498, 579–584 and i. 1403–
1406, two passages of four lines each and one of six, as well as
some additions to the Latin notes in the margin (at Prol. 195,
i. 2705, and v. 7725), of which the first two were evidently put in
later than the accompanying text.   Finally, there are three other
additions to the text which are found in a single copy of the first
recension, MS. Harl. 3490 (H1).   These are i. 2267–2274, where
four lines have been expanded into eight, i. 2343–2358, an interesting addition of sixteen lines to the tale of Narcissus, and
i. 2369–2372.   Thus in the matter of additions to the text H1
stands nearer to F than AJM &c., and in a few other passages
also it is found standing alone of its recension in company with
F, e. g. i. 2043, 2398, ii. 2247.   This manuscript does not belong
to the 'fully revised' group, but it gives the revised readings more
frequently perhaps than any other outside that group.

Thus notwithstanding the differences between the first recension
copies, as we have them, and the Fairfax MS. as it originally
stood, we shall have no difficulty in regarding the latter as having
been originally a revised and corrected copy of that recension,
exhibiting a text to which tolerably near approaches are made
by A, J, and H1, each in its own way, though no copy precisely
corresponding to it is known to exist.

Passing to the second recension, we must first repeat what has
already been said, that it did not supersede the first, but existed
and developed by its side, having its origin probably in the very
same year, or at latest in the next.   Its characteristic point is the

presence of considerable additions in the fifth and seventh books, together with a rearrangement of part of the sixth. There are seven manuscripts known to me, of which three are defective at the beginning. All these (except one, which is also defective at the end) have the rewritten epilogue, one in combination with the Chaucer verses and the others without them. Of the four which are perfect at the beginning, one, namely B, has the earlier form of preface, and the other three, ΛP₂ and S, the later. Of the others it is probable, but by no means certain, that T agreed with B in this respect, and practically certain that Δ agreed with S. A more satisfactory line of distinction, which divides the manuscripts of this class into two groups, is given by the general character of the text which they exhibit, and by the insertion or omission of certain of the additional passages of which we have spoken. While some of the passages, viz. v. 6395*–6438*, 7086*–7210*, vii. 3207*–3360*, are common to all the copies, as are also the transposition of vi. 665–964 and (except in case of Λ) the omission of v. 7701–7746, three of them are found in AdBTΛP₂ only, and are omitted in SΔ[1], viz. v. 7015*–7036*, vii. 2329*–2340* and 3149*–3180*. Then, as regards the text generally, the five MSS. first mentioned all have connexions of various kinds with the unrevised form of the first recension, while the last two represent a type which, except as regards variants specially characteristic of the second recension, of which there may be about sixty in all, nearly corresponds with that of the Fairfax MS.[2]

The relations of the group AdBTΛP₂ with the first recension and with one another are difficult to clear up satisfactorily. Broadly, it may be said that of these B represents an earlier type than the rest in regard to correction and Λ in regard to revision : that is to say, B retains a large number of first recension errors which do not appear in the rest (sharing some, however, with Λ), while at the same time, in cases where a line has been rewritten B almost regularly has the altered form, though with some exceptions in the first two books. On the other hand, though it often happens

---

[1] S is defective in one of these places and Ad in another, but a reckoning of the lines contained in the missing leaves proves that the facts were as stated.

[2] They do not, however, contain the additions above mentioned, at Prol. 495, 579, i. 1403, 2267, &c.

that Λ is free from original errors which appear in B, yet in many places where B has the revised form of text Λ gives us the original, in agreement with the earlier first recension type, while in others Λ agrees with B in giving the revised reading. Then again, there can be no doubt of the close connexion between B and T, but the agreement between them is not usually on those points in which B follows the first recension in error. It is as if they had been derived from the same archetype, but T (or a manuscript from which T was copied) sprang from it at a later stage than the original of B, when many of the errors noted in the first recension had been corrected, while the text of the book generally was allowed to remain as it was [1]. Finally, the text of Ad approaches very near to a fully revised and corrected type. It very occasionally reproduces the earlier first recension, as if by accident, but seems never deliberately to give an 'unrevised' reading. It should be observed that from a point towards the end of the fifth book (about v. 6280) AdBT is a group which is very frequently found in special agreement, whereas before that point we usually find BT (or BTΛ) with Ad on the other side.

Passing now to the third recension, which has the preface and epilogue as in Λ and S, but excludes the additional passages, we find it represented by eight manuscripts, with Fairfax 3 at their head. We have already seen that this manuscript was originally one of the first recension, and was altered by the author so as to substitute the new epilogue and the new preface. Besides these changes, fresh lines are in several places written over erasures, as i. 2713 f., iv. 1321 f., 1361 f., &c., the marginal date is erased at Prol. 331, and additions have been made to the marginal notes. All these alterations, as well as the points previously noted, in which F originally differed from the other copies of the first recension, are reproduced in the other MSS. of the third recension.

---

[1] It is doubtful, however, whether the special connexion between B and T extended over the whole book. It seems rather to begin about iii. 1500. The question about the relative position of these two MSS. would be easier of solution if it were not that T is defective up to ii. 2687, that is as regards the part where the connexion of B with the first recension is most apparent. The fact is that until about the middle of the third book B is found usually in accord with the ERCLB₂ group, and though it sometimes in these first books presents the characteristic second recension reading, as ii. 193, 365 ff., iii. 168, at other times it departs from it, as i. 1881, 2017.

Of these remaining MSS. one is directly copied from F, and another seems to be certainly derived from the same source, though perhaps not immediately. In the case of H₃ (MS. Harl. 7184) the question of origin is not quite so simple. Its text generally seems to suggest ultimate dependence on F, but it is very unequal as regards accuracy, and in one part it regularly follows the early first recension readings and seems to belong for the time to the ERCLB₂ group. In addition to this it has a Latin marginal note at the beginning of the Prologue, which is wanting in F. The problem is perhaps to be solved by means of the Keswick MS. This is written in several hands, varying greatly in accuracy, and exactly in that place where H₃ seems to follow a first recension copy the Keswick MS. is defective, having lost several leaves. It also contains the marginal note referred to above, and on examination we find that a whole series of corruptions are common to the two MSS. There seems to be very little doubt that K is the source of H₃, the inequality of the latter MS. being to a great extent in accordance with the change of hands in K, and the variation of H₃ in a portion of the third book to a different type of text being exactly co-incident with the gap left in K by loss of leaves, a loss which must apparently have taken place in the first forty or fifty years of its existence[1]. As to the text of K itself, in the parts which are most carefully written it reproduces that of F with scrupulous exactness, giving every detail of orthography and punctuation, and for the most part following it in such small errors as it has. It is impossible for one who places these MSS. side by side, as I have been able to do, to avoid the conviction that in some parts at least the exemplar for K was the Fairfax MS. itself. On the other hand, the Latin marginal note at the beginning was derived from some other copy, and setting aside the many mistakes, which possibly are due to mere carelessness on the part of some of the scribes, the Keswick MS. does undoubtedly contain some readings which seem to be derived from a different source. In form of text generally it corresponds exactly with F, reproducing all the additions and corrections made by erasure or otherwise, and containing the same Latin and French pieces in the same order at the end, so far at least as it is perfect. The Magdalen College MS. must be derived ultimately from the same

---

[1] K belongs to the beginning and H₃ to the middle of the fifteenth century.

source as H_3, and it has the same lapse from the third recension
to the first, coinciding with the gap in the Keswick book.   On
the other hand W, though in form of text it corresponds with
these and with F, is quite independent of the group above mentioned, and probably also of the Fairfax MS.   It is late and full of
corruptions, but in several instances it assists in the correction of
errors which appear in F, and it is apparently based on a copy which
retained some of the variants of the earlier text still uncorrected.

As for the remaining manuscript, which was formerly in the
Phillipps collection, but is now in the hands of a bookseller,
I have had so little opportunity for examining it that I ought
not to attempt a classification.

Reviewing the whole body of authorities, we can recognize
readily that two are pre-eminent as witnesses for the author's final
text, that is to say, S and F, the Stafford and the Fairfax MSS.
These are practically identical in orthography, and, except as
regards the characteristic differences, which sufficiently guarantee
their independence, exhibit essentially the same text, and one
which bears the strongest marks of authenticity.   Both are contemporary with the author, and it is perhaps difficult to say which
best represents his final judgement as to the form of his work.

The Stafford MS. seems to be the earlier in time, that is to say,
it probably precedes the final conversion of the Fairfax copy.   It
was evidently written for presentation to a member of the house
of Lancaster, perhaps to Henry himself before his accession to
the throne.   It was doubtless for some such presentation copy
that the preface was rewritten in 1392–3, with the dedication to
Henry introduced into the English text, while most of the other
copies issued during Richard's reign probably retained their
original form.   If we suppose that the new forms of preface
and epilogue were at first intended only for private circulation,
we can account for the very considerable preponderance of the
first recension in regard to the number of copies by which it is
represented, and also allow sufficient time for the gradual development of the text, first into the type which we find in A or J,
and finally into that of F, as it originally stood, a process which
can hardly be satisfactorily understood if we suppose that from
1393 onwards the Lancastrian dedication had its place in all
copies put forth by the author.   It seems on the whole probable,
for reasons to be stated afterwards, that the final conversion of

F (that is as regards the preface) did not take place until after
the deposition of Richard, and it is reasonable enough to suppose
that copies were usually issued in the original form, until after
that event occurred.

MANUSCRIPTS. The following account of the MSS. is given
on my own authority in every detail. I have been able to see
them all, and I wish here to express my thanks to the possessors
of them, and to the librarians who have them in their charge, for
the readiness with which they have given me the use of them.
I am indebted especially to the Councils of Trinity College and
St. John's College, Cambridge, and to Corpus Christi, Wadham,
Magdalen, and New College, Oxford, for allowing their MSS. to
be sent to the Bodleian Library for my use, and to remain there
for considerable periods. Except in the case of one or two, to
which my access was limited, I have examined every one carefully,
so that I am able to say (for example) to what extent, if at all, they
are imperfect. They are arranged as far as possible in accordance
with the classes and groups to which they belong, as follows :

1st Recension (*a*) AJMP₁ChN₂E₂   (*b*) H₁YXGOAd₂CathQ
(*c*) ECRLB₂SnDArHdAsh 2nd Recension (*a*) SΔ (*b*) AdTBAP₂
3rd Recension FH₂NKH₃MagdWP₃ Hn

FIRST RECENSION.

(*a*) *Revised.*

A. BODLEY 902, Bodleian Library (formerly Arch. D. 33, not in
Bernard's Catalogue, 1697). Contains *Confessio Amantis* followed
by 'Explicit iste liber' (four lines), 'Quam cinxere freta,' and 'Quia
vnusquisque.' Parchment, ff. 184, measuring 13⅝ × 9⅛ in., in quires
of 8 with catchwords. Well written in double column of 46 lines in
three different hands of early fifteenth cent., of which the first extends
to the end of the second quire (ff. 2–16), the second from thence to the
end of the tenth quire (ff. 17–80), and the third from f. 81 to the end.
The columns nearly correspond with those of the Fairfax MS. up to
f. 81, after which point some attempt is made to save space by writing
the Latin verses in the margin. Latin summaries in the margin,
except very occasionally, as on ff. 10 and 11 v⁰. Floreated half
border in fairly good style at the beginning of each book except the
fifth, and one miniature on f. 8, of the Confession, remarkable for the
fact that the figure of the Lover is evidently intended as a portrait of
the author, being that of an old man and with some resemblance in
features to the effigy on Gower's tomb. The Confessor has a red stole,

which with his right hand he is laying on the penitent's head, much as in the miniatures which we have in C and L. The note for the miniaturist still stands in the margin, ' Hic fiat confessor sedens *et* confes*sus* cora*m* se genuflectendo.'

The first leaf of the book is lost, and has been supplied in the sixteenth cent. from Berthelette's second edition. It should be noted that this is not the form of commencement which belongs properly to the MS., being that of the third recension, taken by Berthelette from Caxton. The first line of f. 2 is Prol. 144.

As to former possessors, we find written on the last leaf 'Anniballis Admiralis dominicalis,' on f. 80 'Be me Anne Russell' (?), and on f. 115 'Elyzebeth Gardnar my troust ys in god,' all apparently sixteenth cent. The first name is evidently that of Claude d'Annebaut (also called d'Hannybal), who was Admiral of France, and died in 1552. He was in England about the year 1547. The book came to the Bodleian from Gilbert Dolben, Esq., of Finedon, in Northamptonshire, in the year 1697, and not being in the Catalogue of 1697, it has to some extent escaped notice.

The text is a very good one of the revised type. It should be noted, however, that while in the earlier books AJM &c. stand very frequently together on the side of F as against the rest of the first recension, in the later, and especially in the seventh and eighth, AM &c. have an increasing tendency to stand with the first recension generally, leaving J alone in support of the corrected text. In the earlier books A sometimes stands alone in this manner, as i. 1960, ii. 961, 1356.

The orthography (especially that of the second hand) is nearly that of F. As regards final *e*, the tendency is rather to insert wrongly than to omit. Punctuation agrees generally with that of F.

J. ST. JOHN'S COLL., CAMB. B 12. Contains the same as A. Parchment, ff. 214, 12 × 9½ in., in quires of 8 with catchwords : double column of 39 lines, written in a very neat hand of the first quarter of fifteenth century. Latin summaries usually omitted, but most of them inserted up to f. 5 (Prol. 606), and a few here and there in the fifth and seventh books.

The first page has a complete border, but there are no other decorations except red and blue capitals. Old wooden binding.

The seventh leaf of quire 12 (v. 57-213) and the first of quire 14 (v. 1615-1770) are cut out, and a passage of 184 lines is omitted in the first book (i. 631-814) without loss of leaf, which shows that the manuscript from which it was copied, and which here must have lost a leaf, had the normal number of 46 lines to the column.

Various names, as Thomas Browne, Nicolas Helifax, J. Baynorde, are written in the book, and also ' John Nicholas oweth this book,' with the date 1576. At the beginning we find 'Tho. C. S.', which stands for 'Thomas Comes Southampton.' The book was in fact bought with others by Thomas Wriothesley, Earl of Southampton, from William Crashaw, Fellow of St. John's College, and presented by him to the College Library in the year 1635.

This MS. gives a text which is nearer to the type of F than that of any other first recension copy. In the later books especially it seems often to stand alone of its class in agreement with F, as v. 649, 1112, 1339, 1578, 3340, 4351, 4643, 5242, 6059, 6461, 6771, vi. 162, 442, 784, 973, 2089, vii. 445, 1027, 1666, 2424; 3235, 4336, 5348, viii. 13, 239, 747, 845, 1076, 1415, 1456 ff., 2195, 2220, 2228, 2442, 2670 ff., and it is noteworthy that this is the only first recension copy which supplies the accidental omission of 'eorum disciplina—materia' in the author's Latin account of the *Conf. Amantis* at the end. As regards individual correctness it is rather unequal. In some places it has many mistakes, as vi. 1509 ff., while in others it is very correct. The spelling is in most points like that of F, and it is usually good as regards terminations; but the scribe has some peculiarities of his own, which he introduces more or less freely, as 'ho' for 'who,' 'heo' for 'sche' (pretty regularly), 'heor' for 'her,' 'whech' for 'which.' It must also be an individual fancy which leads him regularly to substitute 'som tyme' for 'whilom' wherever it occurs. Punctuation usually agrees with that of F.

M. CAMB. UNIV. Mm. 2. 21 (Bern. Cat. ii. 9648). Contains *Conf. Amantis* only, without 'Explicit,' &c. (the last leaf being lost). Parchment, ff. 183, 14 × 9½ in. Quires of eight with catchwords and signatures : double columns of 46 lines : Latin summaries usually in margin, but occasionally in the text, as in A. Several hands, as follows, (1) ff. 1–32, 41–64, 73–88, 97–136, 145–152, 161–176 ; (2) ff. 33–40, 89–96, 137–144 ; (3) ff. 65–72 ; (4) ff. 153–160 ; (5) ff. 177–183. Finally another, different from all the above, adds sometimes a marginal note which has been dropped, as on ff. 4, 32 v°, 65, 72 v°. The first hand, in which more than two-thirds of the book is written, is fairly neat : the third much rougher than the rest, and also more inaccurate.

Floreated half border in fairly good style at the beginning of each book, except the third, fifth, and seventh, and two rather rudely painted miniatures, viz. f. 4 v°, Nebuchadnezzar's dream (the king in bed, crowned), and f. 8, the Confession, a curious little picture in the margin. The priest is laying his stole on the head of the penitent, whose features are evidently meant for a portrait. It is quite different however from that which we have in A. Below this picture we find the note, 'Hic fiat Garn*imentum*.'

The last leaf is lost, containing no doubt the 'Explicit,' 'Quam cinxere,' and 'Quia vnusquisque,' as in A

The names Stanhope and Yelverton are written on f. 39 (sixteenth cent.), and 'Margareta Straunge' on the first leaf (seventeenth cent.). Later the book belonged to Bishop Moore of Norwich (No. 462 in his library), and it passed with the rest of his books to the University of Cambridge in 1715, as a gift from the king.

M is very closely connected with A, as is shown by very many instances of special agreement, and some considerations suggest that it may be actually derived from it, as for example the writing of the Latin verses in the margin after f. 80, which in A seems to be connected with a change of hand, whereas in M it begins at the same point without any such reason. On the other hand M has a good many readings which are clearly independent, either correcting mistakes and omissions in A, as Prol. 195 *marg.*, 937, i. 673 *marg.*, 924, 1336, 3445, ii. 951, iii. 2529, vi. 620, or giving an early reading where A has a later, e.g. Prol. 869, i. 1118, 1755, ii. 961, 3516, iii. 1939, v. 3914, 5524, &c. In correctness of text and of spelling M is much inferior to A, especially as regards final *e* : for example, on f. 53 v°,

Came neu*er* ȝit to mannes ere	Cam A
Tiding | ne to mannes siȝt	Tidinge . . . sihte A
Merueil whiche so sore aflihte	Merueile which A
Aman*n*es herte as it þe dede	þo A
To hym whoche in þe same stede	him which A

P₁, formerly PHILLIPPS 2298, bought in June, 1899, by Mr. B. Quaritch, who kindly allowed me to see it. Parchment, leaf measuring about 9 × 6½ in., double column of 39 lines, in a fairly neat running hand, with many contractions because of the small size of the leaf. Latin summaries omitted. No decoration. Text agrees with AJM group, so far as I have examined it.

Ch. CHETHAM'S LIBR., MANCHESTER, A. 6. 11 (Bern. Cat. ii. 7151). Contains *Conf. Amantis* with 'Explicit' (4 lines) and 'Quam cinxere.' Parchment, ff. 126, about 15¼ × 10¾ in., quires usually of 12 or 14 leaves. Rather irregularly written in double column of 47–61 lines, late fifteenth century. No ornament. Marginal Latin almost entirely omitted, but some English notes by way of summary occasionally in margin, perhaps by later hand.

The first leaf is lost, the MS. beginning Prol. 193, and also two leaves in the second quire (i. 1092–1491) and one in the tenth (viii. 2111–2343); but besides these imperfections there are many omissions, apparently because the copyist got tired of his work, e. g. ii. 3155–3184, iii. 41–126, 817–842, 877–930, 1119–1196, iv. 17–72, 261–370, 569–704, 710–722, 915–968, 1117–1236, v. 72–112. There is also a good deal of omission and confusion in v. 6101–7082. At the end in a scroll is written 'Note-hurste,' which indicates probably that the book was copied for one of the Chethams of Nuthurst, perhaps Thomas Chetham, who died 1504. The word 'Notehurst' also occurs at the end of the Glasgow MS. of the 'Destruction of Troy,' which has in another place the names of John and Thomas Chetham of 'Notehurst' as the owners of it.

In text it belongs to the AJM group, and sometimes, as iv. 208, stands alone with J. There are many corruptions, however, and the spelling is late and bad.

N₂. NEW COLLEGE, OXFORD, 326. Contains *Conf. Amantis* only (no 'Explicit'). Parchment, ff. 207 + 4 blanks, about 13¾ × 9½ in., in quires of 8 with catchwords ; neatly written in double column of 40 lines (or 39). No Latin summaries or verses. The handwriting changes after f. 62 (at iii. 2164) and becomes rather larger and more ornamental.

Two leaves lost after f. 35, containing ii. 1066–1377, and some of the leaves of the MS. from which it was copied had been displaced, so that iv. 2501-2684 comes after 2864, then follows 3049-3232, then 2865-3048, and after these 3233 ff. (two leaves displaced in the original). Lines omitted sometimes with blanks left, as i. 1044, 2527.

From the coats of arms which it contains the book would seem to have been written for Thomas Mompesson of Bathampton, sheriff of Wilts in 1478 (K. Meyer, *John Gower's Beziehungen*, &c.). It was given to John Mompesson by Sir Giles Mompesson in 1650, and to New College by Thomas Mompesson, Fellow, in 1705.

The text is a combination of two types. It has the Lancaster dedication at the beginning, but the conclusion which belongs to the first recension. On examination it proves that the scribe who wrote the first eight quires followed a manuscript not of the F, but of the SΔ class (agreeing for example with S in i. 1881 f., 2017 ff., ii. 2387, iii. 168, 1241, and differing from F in regard to i. 2267 ff., 2343 ff., &c.), while the copyist of the remainder followed one of the revised first recension. The spelling is poor.

E₂. BIBL. EGERTON 913, Brit. Museum. A fragment, containing *Conf. Amantis* from the beginning to i. 1701. Paper, ff. 47, 11½ × 8 in., in quires of 16 with catchwords : single column, 30-37 lines on page : Latin summaries in margin. Three hands, (1) f. 1-26, 31-36; (2) 27-30; (3) 37-47.

On f. 26 vᵒ. there is an omission of i. 387-570 (one leaf of 184 lines lost in the copy). This is supplied by the insertion of four leaves after f. 26, containing i. 375-580.

The text belongs to the revised group, as shown by Prol. 6, 7, 115, 659, 869, i. 162, 278, 368, 1262, &c.

(*b*) *Intermediate.*

H₁. HARLEIAN 3490, Brit. Museum. Contains, ff. 1-6 St Edmund's *Speculum Religiosorum*, ff. 8-215 *Confessio Amantis*, left unfinished on f. 215 vᵒ. Parchment, 215 leaves, 14½ × 10 in., in quires of 8 with catchwords : double column of 34-51 lines, small neat hand of middle fifteenth cent., with some corrections, perhaps in the same hand. Latin summaries in the text, underlined with red. Blank leaf cut out after f. 6, and f. 7 left blank, so that Gower begins on the first leaf of the second quire. The text is left unfinished at viii. 3062*, part of the last page remaining blank.

Floreated pages at the beginning of the books and also at f. 11, with various coats of arms painted.

The text given by this MS. is of an intermediate type. Occasionally throughout it is found in agreement with AJM &c. rather than with ERC &c., as Prol. 6, 7, i. 162, 630, 1755, 1768 ff., 1934, &c., and in a large portion of the fifth book it passes over definitely in company with XG &c. to the revised class, but it does not contain the distinctive readings of XG. Sometimes it stands alone of the first recension in company with F &c., as iv. 2414, vii. 1749, viii. 2098, and especially in regard to the three passages, i. 2267 ff., 2343 ff., 2369 ff. In individual correctness of text and spelling the MS. does not rank high, and it is especially bad as regards insertion and omission of final *e*, as 'Wherof him ouht welle to drede,' 'Ayenste the poyntes of the beleue,' 'Of whome that he taketh eny hede.' It has *th* regularly for þ and *y* for ȝ.

Y. In the possession of the MARQUESS OF BUTE, by whose kindness I have been allowed to examine it. Contains *Confessio Amantis*, imperfect at beginning and end. Parchment, $15\frac{1}{2} \times 10\frac{3}{4}$ in., in quires of 8 with catchwords on scrolls. Very well written in double column of 50 lines, early fifteenth cent. Latin summaries in text (red). Floreated page finely illuminated at the beginning of each book, with good painting of large initials, some with figures of animals, in a style that looks earlier than the fifteenth cent. Spaces left on f. 2, apparently for two miniatures, before and after the Latin lines following i. 202.

Begins in the last Latin summary of the Prologue, 'Arion nuper citharista,' followed by Prol. 1053, 'Bot wolde god,' &c., having lost six leaves. Again, after iv. 819 nine leaves are lost, up to iv. 2490, and one leaf also which contained vi. 2367–vii. 88: the book ends with viii. 2799, two or three leaves being lost here. The book belonged to the first Marquess of Bute, who had his library at Luton. At present it is at St. John's Lodge, Regent's Park.

This is a good manuscript, carefully written and finely decorated. There are very few contractions, and in particular the termination -*oun* is generally written in full, as 'confessioun,' i. 202, 'resoun,' iii. 1111, 'devocioun,' 'contemplacioun,' v. 7125 f. &c., and *th* is written regularly for þ. As regards individual accuracy and spelling it is very fair, but the scribe adds -*e* very freely at the end of words. The type of text represented is evidently intermediate to some extent, but I have not been able to examine it sufficiently to determine its exact character. It supports the revised group in a certain number of passages, e. g. i. 264, 630, 3374, 3396, 3416, ii. 31, 1328, 1758, &c., sometimes in company with H₁ and sometimes not. In particular we may note the passage i. 3374 ff., where in some lines it is revised as above mentioned, and in others, as 3381, 3414, 3443, it keeps the earlier text. Occasionally Y seems to have a tendency to group itself with B, as i. 208, 604, and in other places we find YE or YEC forming a group in agreement with B, as i. 161, iii. 633, v. 1946, 3879.

X. SOCIETY OF ANTIQUARIES, 134. Contains, ff. 1–30 Lydgate's *Life of the Virgin* (imperfect at beginning), f. 1 begins in cap. xiii. 'Therefore quod pees,' ff. 30–249 *Confessio Amantis* with 'Explicit' (six lines), 'Quam cinxere,' and 'Quia vnusquisque,' ff. 250–283, Hoccleve's *Regement of Princes*, with 'Explicit Thomas Occlef,' ff. 283 vᵒ, metrical version of Boethius [by John Walton of Osney] with leaves

lost at the end, ends 'Amonges hem þat dwellen nyʒe present.'
Parchment, ff. 297, about 15 × 11 in., in quires of 8 without catchwords,
in a good and regular hand. The *Conf. Amantis* is in double
column of 41 lines. Latin summaries in text (red). Ornamental
borders at the beginning of books and space for miniature of Nebuchadnezzar's Dream on f. 34 vᵒ. One leaf lost between ff. 134 and 135,
containing v. 1159–1318.

The book belonged formerly to the Rev. Charles Lyttelton, LL.D.,
who notes that it came originally from the Abbey of Hales Owen.

I owe thanks to the librarian of the Society of Antiquaries for
courteously giving me access to the manuscript.

The text is of the intermediate type, passing over in a part of the fifth
book with H₁ &c. to the revised group, but not giving the revised readings
much support on other occasions. It forms however a distinct sub-group
with GOAd₂, these manuscripts having readings apparently peculiar to
themselves in several passages, e.g. v. 3688 and after v. 6848.

The spelling is not very good, and in particular final *e* is thrown in very
freely without justification : there are also many *-is*, *-id*, *-ir* terminations,
as 'servantis,' ' goodis,' ' nedis,' ' ellis,' ' crokid,' ' clepid,' ' vsid,' ' chambir,'
' aftir,' and ʒ usually for *gh* (*h*), as ' hyʒe,' ' nyʒe,' ' ouʒt,' ' lawʒe,' ' sleyʒtis,'
&c. The text however is a fair one, and the use of it by Halliwell in his
Dictionary preserved him from some of the errors of the printed editions.
The scribe was apt to drop lines occasionally and insert them at the bottom
of the column, and some, as iii. 2343, are dropped without being supplied.

G. GLASGOW, HUNTERIAN MUSEUM, S. i. 7. Contains *Confessio
Amantis*, imperfect at the end. Parchment, ff. 181 (numbered 179 by
doubling 94 and 106) with two blanks at the beginning, 16½ × 10¾ in.,
in quires of 8 with catchwords: well and regularly written in double
column of 46 lines, early fifteenth century. Latin summaries in the
text (red). Floreated page at the beginning of each book, so far as they
remain, and illuminated capitals. Many catchwords lost by cutting of
the margin : it must once have been a very large book.

The manuscript has lost about sixteen leaves at the end, and eight
altogether in various other places. In every case except one, however,
the place of the lost leaf is supplied by a new leaf inserted, one of
which has the missing portion of the text copied out from an early
edition, while the rest are blank. The leaves lost are mostly such as
would probably have had miniatures or illuminations, including the
beginning of the first, second, sixth, seventh, and eighth books. The
losses are as follows: f. 4 (containing Prol. 504–657, probably with
a miniature), text supplied by later hand, f. 7 (Prol. 984–i. 30), f. 9
(i. 199–336, probably with a miniature), f. 28 (i. 3402–ii. 108), f. 129 (131)
(v. 7718–vi. 40), f. 143 (145) (vi. 2343–vii. 60), a leaf after f. 175 (177)
(vii. 5399–viii. 126), f. 177 (179) (viii. 271–441), and all after f. 179 (181),
that is from viii. 783 to the end.

A former owner (seventeenth cent.) says, 'This Book, as I was told by the Gent: who presented it to me, did originally belong to the Abbey of Bury in Suffolk.' If so, the *Confessio Amantis* was probably read in this copy by Lydgate.

I am under great obligations to Dr. Young, Librarian of the Hunterian Museum, for the trouble he has taken to give me access to this excellent manuscript.

The Glasgow MS. is especially related to X (iv. 2773, v. 1486, 3582, 3688, 4110, 6848 ff., vi. 101, vii. 769, &c.), and belongs more generally to the group H₁X &c., which passes over to the revised class almost completely in a considerable part of the fifth book. The text, however, is on the whole much better than that of X, being both individually more correct and more frequently found on the side of the corrected readings, e.g. i. 2836, ii. 1441, 1867, v. 781, 1203, 2996, 4425, 5966, 6839, 7223, 7630, vi. 86, 746 (corrected), 1437, vii. 510, 1361, 1574, 2337, 3902, viii. 568. In at least one place, vii. 1574, it stands alone of the first recension, while in others, as v. 4425, 5966, 7630, vi. 746, 1437, &c., it is accompanied only by J. On the other hand in some passages, as v. 5802, 6019, 6257, vii. 1172 *marg.* &c., G has an earlier reading and X the later, while there is also a whole series of passages where G, sometimes in company with X, seems to show a special connexion of some kind with B (BT), as ii. 1925, iii. 733, iv. 2295, 2508, v. 4, 536, 2508, 3964, 4072, 7048, vi. 1267, 1733, vii. 3748, 4123, &c.

The book is carefully written, and corrected in the same hand, e.g. v. 3145, 5011, vi. 430, 746, vii. 4233. The spelling is pretty good, and in particular it is a contrast to X in the matter of final *e*. This is seldom wrongly inserted, and when it is omitted it is usually in places where the metre is not affected by it. Punctuation often in the course of the line, but not at the end.

O. STOWE 950, Brit. Museum. *Confessio Amantis*, imperfect at beginning and end. Parchment, ff. 175 (177 by numbering leaves of another book pasted to binding), 14¼ × 10 in., in eights with catchwords and signatures, double column of 44-46 lines; written in a small, neat hand. Latin summaries in text (red). No decorated pages.

Has lost seven leaves of the first quire, to i. 165 (incl.), and also after f. 16 one leaf (i. 2641-2991), after f. 35 one (ii. 2486-2645), after f. 44 two (iii. 673-998), after f. 97 one (v. 3714-3898), after f. 108 two (v. 5832-6184), after f. 136 two (vii. 771-1111), and at least four leaves at the end (after viii. 2549).

Formerly belonged to Lord Ashburnham.

In text this belongs to the XG group, agreeing with them, for example, at v. 3688, 6848, and in general with H₁XG, where they go together (so far as I have examined the book), e.g. in the Latin verses after v. 2858 ('Vltra testes falsos,' 'penitus') and in the readings of v. 1893, 1906, 2694, 3110, &c.

The handwriting is somewhat like that of H₁: the spelling sometimes fairly good, but unequal; bad especially at the beginning. The metre generally good.

**

k

Ad2. ADDITIONAL 22139, Brit. Museum. *Confessio Amantis*, imperfect, with the author's account of his books, 'Quia vnusquisque,' at the end, followed by Chaucer's poems, 'To you my purse,' 'The firste stok,' 'Some time this worlde,' 'Fle fro the pres.' Parchment, ff. 138, 13¾ × 10¼ in., in quires of 8 with catchwords: regularly and closely written in double column of 53 lines by two hands, the first (ff. 1–71) somewhat pointed, the second rounder and smaller. Date 1432 on a shield, f. 1. Latin summaries in text (red). Illuminated borders at beginning of books (except the eighth) and many gilt capitals: a miniature cut out on f. 4 (before Prol. 595).

The first leaves are much damaged, f. 1 having only two lines left (f. 2 begins Prol. 177), f. 3 has lost Prol. 455–478 and 505–527, &c., f. 4 has a miniature cut out, with Prol. 716–726 on the other side, f. 6 has lost Prol. 979–1061. After f. 7 there is a loss of seventeen leaves (i. 199–ii. 56), after f. 31 (originally 48) two quires (sixteen leaves) are lost and f. 32 is damaged (iii. 1150–iv. 1517), after f. 81 one leaf lost (v. 7807–vi. 154).

Bought by Brit. Museum from Thos. Kerslake of Bristol, 1857.

The text is closely connected with that of X, but not copied from that manuscript itself (see ii. 1711, vii. 92, viii. 2650). There are corrections here and there in a somewhat later hand, e. g. ii. 671, 1045, 1457, iii. 1052, iv. 2922, several of which are cases of lines supplied, which had been dropped. In v. 3688 the ordinary reading has been substituted doubtless for that of X, and in some cases the alterations are wrong, as vii. 2639, viii. 51. The manuscript has a good many individual errors and the spelling is rather poor.

Cath. ST. CATHARINE'S COLL., CAMB. *Confessio Amantis* with 'Explicit' (six lines), 'Quam cinxere' and 'Quia vnusquisque.' Parchment, ff. 188, 17¾ × 12¼ in., in quires of 8 with catchwords: well written in double column of 47 lines, afterwards 40, before the middle of fifteenth cent. Latin summaries in text (red). Floreated whole border at the beginning of each book: miniature on f. 4 v° of Nebuchadnezzar's Dream, and f. 8 v° the Confession (Priest on stool to left of picture, laying hand but not stole on penitent's head), fairly well painted.

Leaves are missing which contained i. 3089–3276, ii. 3331–3518, v. 1182–1363, 6225–6388, vi. 107–460, vii. 984–1155, and viii. 2941–3114*, and the last leaf containing 'Explicit,' &c., is placed now at the beginning of the volume. There is a confusion of the text in the third book, iii. 236–329 being repeated after 678 and 679–766 left out, also a considerable omission in the fourth (iv. 2033–3148) without loss of leaves in this MS. (The statement in the MS. that seven leaves are here lost is a mistake.) In the passage vii. 1486–2678 several leaves have been disarranged in the quire.

Given to the College in 1740 by Wm. Bohun of Beccles (Suffolk), to whose great-grandfather, Baxter Bohun, it was given in 1652 by his 'grandmother Lany.'

The text is of a rather irregular type, but often agrees with the XGO group. It has many mistakes and the spelling is poor.

Q. Belonged to the late Mr. B. Quaritch, who kindly allowed me to examine it slightly. Parchment, leaves measuring about $14 \times 8\frac{3}{4}$ in., in double column of 49 lines, well written, early fifteenth cent. Ends with the account of the author's books, 'Quia vnusquisque.' Floreated pages at the beginning of books and a good miniature of the Confession on f. 3, of a rather unusual type—the priest seated to the left of the picture and the penitent at a little distance. Latin summaries in text (red). Begins with Prol. 342, having lost two leaves here, and has lost also Prol. 529–688, Prol. 842–i. 85, and perhaps more.

The book formerly belonged to a Marquess of Hastings.

This is a good manuscript, and the spelling is fairly correct. I place it provisionally here, because its readings seem to show a tendency towards the XG group.

(c) Unrevised.

E. EGERTON 1991, Brit. Museum. *Confessio Amantis* with 'Explicit' (six lines), 'Quam cinxere,' and 'Quia vnusquisque,' after which 'Deo Gracias. And þanne ho no more.' Parchment, ff. 214, $15\frac{1}{4} \times 10$ in., in quires of 8 with catchwords: regularly written in a very good large hand in double column of 42 lines, early fifteenth cent. Latin summaries in text (red). Floreated pages at beginning of books, and a finely painted miniature of the Confession on f. 7 vº.

Two leaves lost, originally ff. 1 and 3, containing Prol. 1–134 and 454–594. The book has also suffered from damp, and parts of the first and last leaves are so discoloured as to be illegible.

A seventeenth cent. note on f. 1 vº tells us that the book was given on April 5, 1609, 'at Skarborough Castle' to the lady Eliz. Dymoke by her aunt the lady Catherine Burghe, daughter of Lord Clynton, who was afterwards earl of Lincoln and Lord High Admiral, to whom it came by her mother, the lady Eliz. Talboys. On f. 2 we find the register of the birth of Master Harry Clinton, son and heir of Lord Clinton, born at Canbery, June 6, 1542. The name Willoughby occurs also in the book (sixteenth cent.), and on a flyleaf inserted at the beginning we find 'John Brograve, 1682,' with Latin lines in the form of an acrostic about his family, signed 'Thomas Tragiscus, Bohemus.' Bought by the Brit. Mus. August 6, 1865, at Lord Charlemont's sale.

The text of this fine MS. belongs clearly to the unrevised group. At the same time its original must have had some corrections, and some also appear on the face of this MS. It stands alone of the first recension in agreement with S, F in a few passages, as v. 5438, vi. 1954, vii. 4318 *marg.*, and with J in ii. 2576, iii. 176, v. 4989 f., 7327, vii. 3484. It has also some connexion with B (BTΛ), standing in this matter either with C (or YC), as iii. 633, v. 3688, 3814, 5667, 6318, or by itself, as Prol. 169, i. 2122, ii. 1353, iv. 3401, v. 3992, 6336, vii. 323, 978, viii. 1761, 2706.

The scribe seems to have had a good ear for metre, and seldom goes wrong in any point of spelling which affects the verse, though apt to omit final *e* in case of elision. Sometimes, however, he drops words, as 'swerd,' i. 433, 'so,' v. 122, 'chaste,' v. 6277. On the whole the text of E is probably the best of its class.

C. CORPUS CHRISTI COLL., OXF. 67 (Bern. Cat. i. 2. 1534). *Confessio Amantis* with 'Explicit' (four lines), 'Quam cinxere,' and 'Quia vnusquisque,' after which 'Deo Gracias.' Parchment, large folio, ff. 209, of which three blank, in quires of 8 with catchwords: written in double column in a good hand of first quarter fifteenth cent. Latin summaries in text (red). Pages with complete borders at beginning of books (except Lib. i), and two very fair miniatures, f. 4 v° Nebuchadnezzar's Image, f. 9 v° the Confession (priest laying stole on youthful penitent's head). The book has lost four leaves, the second of the first quire (Prol. 144-301), the last of the 22nd and first of the 23rd (vii. 3137-3416), and the first of the 26th (viii. 1569-1727).

We find on the last leaf in a hand perhaps as early as the fifteenth cent.' Liber partinet Thomam Crispe Ciuem et Mercerium Londiniarum,' and on the flyleaf at the beginning a device containing the same name, and also A. Crispe, F. Crispe, W. Rawson, Anne Rawson. 'Augusten Crispe me Iure tenet' is written on the first leaf of the text, and also 'Liber Willelmi Rawson A°. Dni 1580.' Finally, 'Liber C. C. C. Oxon. 1676.' The device referred to above appears also in the decoration of the book both at the beginning and the end, but the manuscript must have been written much earlier than the time of Thomas Crispe.

This is a good copy of the unrevised group, having some connexion, as we have seen above, with E, but less good in spelling, especially as regards final *e*. For special connexion with B, see i. 2234, iv. 359, &c. CL go specially together apparently in some places, as Prol. 937 f., i. 94, 161, 165, 433, 916, but not throughout. There are some corrections by erasure of final *e*, and a line supplied by a different hand, vi. 1028. No punctuation.

R. REG. 18. C. xxii, Brit. Museum. *Confessio Amantis* with 'Explicit' (six lines), 'Quam cinxere' and 'Quia vnusquisque.' Parchment, ff. 206, $14\frac{1}{4} \times 3\frac{3}{4}$ in., in eights with catchwords: double column of 44 lines, well written, first quarter fifteenth cent. Latin in text (red). Floreated border of first page with miniature of the Confession in the initial O; also a miniature on f. 4 v° of the Image of Nebuchadnezzar's dream (hill with stone to left of picture), and half borders at beginning of books, except Lib. i.

Two blanks cut away at the end, from one of which is set off 'This boke appertayneth vnto the Right Honorable the Ladie Margaret Strange' (presumably the same whose name appears in M). The binding has 'Lady Mary Strainge.'

A very fair MS. of its class and almost absolutely typical, but gives distinctively revised readings in a few passages, as ii. 925, iv. 1342, v. 3145, viii. 1621. Omits vii. 2889-2916 and some of the Latin summaries. The words 'pope' and 'papacie' are regularly erased, see especially f. 47. Spelling and metre fairly good: no punctuation.

L. LAUD 609, Bodleian Library (Bern. Cat. 754). *Confessio Amantis* with 'Explicit' (four lines), 'Quam cinxere' and 'Quia vnusquisque.' Parchment, ff. 170, 16 × 10¾ in., in quires of 8 with catchwords: double column, first of 40 lines, then about 44, and after f. 16 of 51: well written, first quarter fifteenth cent. Latin in the text (red). Floreated border of first page and half borders at the beginning of books, well executed. Two miniatures, on f. 5 v⁰ the Image of the dream, and on f. 10 the Confession, both much like those in C and B₂, but damaged.

After f. 109 one leaf is lost (v. 5550-5739), one after f. 111 (v. 6140-6325), and eight (quire 16) after f. 118 (v. 7676-vi. 1373).

The names Symon and Thomas Elrington (sixteenth cent.) occur in the book, ff. 89, 170, and 'Liber Guilielmi Laud Archiepiscopi Cantuar. et Cancellarii Vniuersitatis Oxon. 1633' on f. 1.

In correctness of text and spelling the text is decidedly inferior to the foregoing MSS. We may note apparently good readings in the following passages, Prol. 159, i. 3023, v. 1072, vii. 374, 3040, 3639, viii. 358, 483.

B₂. BODLEY 693, Bodleian Library (Bern. Cat. 2875). *Confessio Amantis* with 'Explicit' (six lines), 'Quam cinxere' and 'Quia vnusquisque.' Parchment (gilt edged), ff. 196, 15 × 10 in., in eights with catchwords. Well written, first quarter fifteenth cent., in double column of 46 lines. Latin in text (red). Floreated border of first page and half borders at beginning of books (also on f. 8 v⁰), well executed: two small miniatures, f. 4 v⁰ the Image of the dream, f. 8 v⁰ (within an initial T) the Confession, like those in C and L, but smaller.

At the end we have 'ffrauncois Halle A⁰ MV⁰VI' (i. e. 1506), 'Garde le ffine.' In the initial on f. 1 a coat of arms is painted surrounded by the Garter and its motto. The arms are those of Charles Brandon duke of Suffolk (Brandon with quartering of Bruyn and Rokeley, see Doyle, *Official Baronage*, iii. 443), and on the same page is painted the Brandon crest (lion's head erased, crowned per pale gules and arg., langued az.). These must have been painted in later than the date of the MS. The binding is deeply stamped with the arms of Great Britain and Ireland in colours, and the letters I. R., showing that the book belonged to James I. It was presented to the Bodleian by Dr. John King, who was Dean of Ch. Ch. 1605–1611. We must suppose that James gave it to Dr. King.

The fineness of the vellum and the general style of the book seems to indicate that it was written for some distinguished person. The text is very typical of its class. In correctness and spelling it is less good than L, oftener dropping final *e* and having less regard for the metre.

Sn. ARCH. SELD. B. 11, Bodleian Library (Bern. Cat. 3357). *Confessio Amantis* with 'Explicit' (four lines), 'Quam cinxere' and 'Quia vnusquisque.' Paper (with some leaves of parchment), ff. 169, $14\frac{1}{2} \times 10\frac{3}{4}$ in. Quires with varying number of leaves, usually 12 or 16, signatures and catchwords. (No written leaves lost, but blanks cut away in quires nine and ten.) Written in double column of 44–65 lines (no ruling), in a small hand, middle fifteenth cent. Latin in text. Red and blue initials, but no other decoration.

The book has the name 'Edwarde Smythe' (sixteenth cent.) as the owner. It came into the Bodleian among John Selden's books.

The text is a poor one with a good many corruptions, from the first line of the Prologue ('To hem' for 'Of hem') onwards, many of them absurd, as 'who thoghte' for 'wo the while' (v. 6752), 'homicides' for 'houndes' (vii. 5256), and some arising from confusion between þ, ȝ, and *y*. Thus the scribe (who usually has *th* for þ and *y* for ȝ) is capable of writing 'aþen' or 'athen' for 'aȝein,' 'yer of' for 'þer of,' 'yeff' for 'þef,' 'biþete' for 'biȝete.' There are many mistakes in the coloured initials, e. g. ii. 2501, iii. 2033, 2439. Some northern forms, as 'gude,' iii. 1073, 'Qwhat,' iii. 2439. Note agreement with B in some places, as i. 365, 1479, iii. 1222, v. 2417, 6296, and a few more.

D. CAMB. UNIV. Dd. viii. 19 (Bern. Cat. ii. 9653). *Confessio Amantis* (imperfect). Parchment, ff. 127, quires of 8 with catchwords: double column of 48 (sometimes 50) lines, regularly written in a hand using very thick strokes. Latin in text (red). Spaces left for miniatures, f. 4 vᵒ, f. 8 vᵒ (the latter marked 'hic Imago'), and perhaps also f. 1. Many spaces left for illuminated capitals.

After f. 83 follows a quire of six with 5 vᵒ blank (after end of Lib. iv.) and 6 lost: then a quire of eight with 5 and 6 (also part of 4) blank, and 7, 8 lost: then, f. 94, 'Incipit liber Sextus.' So that of Lib. v. we have only about four leaves (v. 1444–2149). The leaves numbered 16, 17, 15 should stand last (in that order), and the text ends (on f. 15) with vii. 3683, the line unfinished and the rest of the page blank.

Successive owners in sixteenth cent., Magister Asshe, Thom. Carson (or Cursson), Ambr. Belson, J. Barton. It was one of Bishop Moore's books (No. 467), and came to the University in 1715.

The text shows no leaning, so far as I know, to the revised group. Perhaps somewhat akin to the MSS. which precede and follow: see Prol. 331 *marg.*, i. 110, 370.

Ar. ARUNDEL 45, College of Arms (Bern. Cat. ii. 5547). *Confessio Amantis* (imperfect). Paper, 168 leaves (numbered 167, but one dropped in numbering after f. 42) + two parchment blank at beginning, 11½ × 8¼ in. Quires of 8 (usually), with catchwords, double column of 46–51 lines, small neat writing, middle fifteenth cent. Latin in text (red) : no illumination, but spaces left for initials.

One leaf lost after f. 7 (i. 63–216), two after f. 116 (v. 5229–5594), and all after viii. 1102 (about twelve leaves gone at the end).

Former possessors, ' Thomas Goodenston, Gerdeler of London,' and (before him probably) ' Jhon Barthylmewe, Gerdyllarr and Marchant.'

Hd. At CASTLE HOWARD, the property of the Earl of Carlisle, who most kindly sent it for my use. *Confessio Amantis* with ' Explicit ' (four lines), 'Quam cinxere' and 'Quia vnusquisque.' Parchment, ff. 111 (numbered as 110) 14 × 11 in., in quires of 8 (usually), marked iiii, v, vi, &c. In double column of 60–74 lines, rather irregularly written in a small, fairly clear hand, later fifteenth cent. Latin in text. Some red and blue initials ; no other decoration.

Seventeen leaves lost at the beginning, f. 1 begins at i. 3305, and f. 8 is the first leaf of quire iiii : after f. 73 four leaves lost, containing vi. 264–1306, and in the last quire one, containing viii. 2566–2833. The leaves in the latter half of the book, from f. 66, have been much disarranged in the binding.

The name ' Tho. Martin ' is written at the beginning, in the hand-writing of the well-known Thomas Martin of Palgrave. This of course is not the book mentioned in Bern. Cat. ii. 611 as among the books collected by Lord William Howard at Naworth Castle. There seems to be at present no Gower MS. at Naworth.

Some readings seem to show a connexion of Hd with L, as iii. 1885, 2763, ' Now herkne and I þe þo,' iv. 1341, 3086, 3449, 3535, but it is not derived from it. Note also the readings of ii. 1577 'Ne,' 2825 'by,' iii. 1173 'Iupartie,' v. 3306 'Oute.' There are many corruptions in the text as well as some deliberate alterations, as ' cleped ' regularly to ' called,' and words are often dropped or inserted to the injury of the metre.

Ash. ASHMOLE 35, Bodleian Library (Bern. Cat. 6916). *Confessio Amantis* (imperfect). Paper, ff. 182, 13½ × 9½ in. Quires of 12 (usually), with catchwords, double column of 42–48 lines, fairly well written : no Latin verses or summaries, but summaries in English written in the text (red), mostly omitted in the last thirty leaves. Some initials in red, spaces left for larger capitals.

Begins with Prol. 170, having lost two leaves (one blank) at the beginning. After f. 2 one leaf is lost (Prol. 541–725), one after f. 4 (i. 1–169), one after f. 32 (ii. 1749–1927), one after f. 91 (v. 2199–2366), three after f. 181 (viii. 2505–2893), one after f. 182, which ends with viii. 3082*. Half of f. 182 is torn away, but the beginning of the

Chaucer verses remain, as well as a whole column of the early form of conclusion, in spite of the statement in the Ashmole Catalogue. Even if the conclusion were really wanting, there would be no difficulty in assigning the MS. to its proper class.

SECOND RECENSION.

(a) S. The STAFFORD MS., now in the possession of the Earl of Ellesmere, by whose kind permission I have been allowed to make use of it. Contains *Confessio Amantis* with 'Explicit' (six lines) and 'Quam cinxere.' Parchment, ff. 172 (the last three blank), 14 × 9¾ in., quires of 8 with catchwords and signatures (24 in all, the last of five leaves): written in double column of 46 lines in a good square hand of late fourteenth century type. Latin summaries in the margin. The first page has a well-executed border of geometrical pattern and a rather rudely painted miniature of Nebuchadnezzar's dream, in style resembling that of F. This page has also three heraldic shields and a crest, of which more hereafter. Floreated half borders at the beginning of books and illuminated capitals throughout, well executed and with an unusual amount of gold. On f. 56 a well painted grotesque figure of a man with legs and tail of some animal, wearing a pointed headpiece and armed with an axe. This is part of the initial decoration of Lib. iv.

The book has unfortunately lost in all seventeen leaves, as follows : one after f. 1 (Prol. 147–320), one after f. 7 (Prol. 1055–i. 106), three after f. 46 (iii. 573–1112), one after f. 68 (iv. 2351–2530), two after f. 69 (iv. 2711–3078), one after f. 70 (iv. 3262–3442), two after f. 71 (iv. 3627– v. 274), one after f. 107 (v. 6821–7000), one after f. 125 (vi. 2357–vii. 88), two after f. 139 (vii. 2641–3004), two after f. 153 (vii. 5417–viii. 336). In addition to this, one leaf, f. 50 (iii. 1665–1848), is written in a different and probably rather later hand, and seems to have been inserted to supply the place of a leaf lost in quite early times.

The question about the former owners of this fine manuscript is an interesting one. As to the devices on the first page, the first shield (within the initial O) is sable and gules per pale, a swan argent, the second (in the lower margin) sable, three ostrich feathers (argent ?) set in three scrolls or, while in the right margin there is a crest of a lion, collared with label of three points, standing on a chapeau, and below is suspended a shield quartered az. and gules, with no device. The crest is evidently meant for that of John of Gaunt, though it is not quite correct, and the three ostrich feathers (properly ermine) were used by him as a recognisance (see Sandford's *Genealogical Hist.* p. 249), while the swan is the well-known badge of Henry his son, to be seen suspended from Gower's own collar of SS on his tomb and in the miniature of the Fairfax MS. It seems probable then that the book was prepared for presentation to a member of the house of Lancaster, probably either John of Gaunt or Henry. If it be the fact that the swan badge was not adopted by Henry until 1397, this would not be the actual copy sent on the occasion of the dedication to him in 1392–93. On the other hand the absence of all royal emblems indicates that the book was prepared before Henry's accession to the throne.

In the sixteenth cent. (Queen Elizabeth's reign) the book belonged to one William Downes, whose name is written more than once on f. 170. The ornamental letters W. D. on f. 21 are probably his initials, and on f. 76 we have Phillipp Downes in a fifteenth-cent. hand. On f. 171 v° there is a note about 'the parsonages of Gwend . . . and Stythians in the county of Cornewell, percell of the possessions of the late monastary of Rewley,' and also about the 'personage of Croppreadin in the county of Oxforde,' granted for xxi years by Edward VI and paying lvi pounds a year. 'T. P. Goodwyn' is another name (seventeenth cent.). When Todd saw the MS. at the beginning of this century, it belonged to the Marquess of Stafford.

S has the Lancaster dedication and the rewritten epilogue, and with these the three additional passages, v. 6395*–6438*, 7086*–7210*, vii. 3207*–3360*, omitting v. 7701–7746, and transposing vi. 665–964. In correctness it is inferior only to F, and these two stand far above all others as primary authorities. Their independence of one another is certain, and the general agreement of their text gives it the highest guarantee of authenticity. The spelling is practically the same, as will be seen in those passages which are printed from S in this edition, e. g. vii. 3207*–3360*, indeed in most places the two texts are absolutely the same, letter for letter. As regards f. 50, which is in a different hand, it should be noted not only that it is far less correct than the rest, but also that it is copied from a different original, a MS. of the unrevised first recension, distinctive readings of which are given in iii. 1686, 1763, 1800, 1806, while no trace of such readings appears in any other part of S.

Δ. SIDNEY SUSSEX COLL., CAMB. Δ. 4. 1 (Bern. Cat. i. 3. 726). Contains *Confessio Amantis*, with 'Explicit' (six lines) and 'Quam cinxere,' (ff. 2–202 v°), and then an English version of Cato's *Disticha*. Paper, ff. 211 (of which four blank), $11\frac{1}{2} \times 8\frac{1}{2}$ in., in quires of 12 with catchwords and signatures. Written in double column of 41–48 lines in a fairly good hand, middle fifteenth century, with a good many contractions. Latin summaries usually in text, sometimes in margin. No decoration. The first leaf is lost, containing Prol. 1–140.

The book was left to the College by Samuel Ward, Master, 1643. One of the blank leaves has the word 'temsdytton' (i. e. Thames Dytton) in an early hand.

In regard to form of text this MS. agrees throughout with S, and it must no doubt have had the Lancaster preface. It is remarkable as containing the additional lines printed by Caxton at the end of the Prologue (which may have been also in S), and it has eleven Latin hexameters substituted for the prose summaries at Prol. 591 and 617, beginning,

'Dormitans statuam sublimem rex babilonis,'

and again four after the Latin prose at vii. 2891, beginning,

'Sede sedens ista iudex inflexibilis sta.'

The text has many corruptions and the spelling is not very good. Δ does not give the first recension readings on f. 50 of S, which of itself is sufficient proof that it is not derived from that manuscript, for the insertion of this leaf must be much earlier than the date of Δ.

(*b*) Ad. · ADDITIONAL 12043, British Museum. *Confessio Amantis*, imperfect at beginning and end. Parchment, ff. 156 (the last blank), 13 × 9¼ in., in quires of 8 with catchwords: well written in double column of 45-50 lines, beginning of fifteenth century. Latin summaries in the margin up to f. 16 (ii. 382), after which they are omitted. Floreated pages in good style at the beginning of each book.

More than twenty leaves are lost, viz. ten at the beginning, up to and including i. 786, one after f. 45 (iv. 1-190), two after f. 47 (iv. 559-932), two after f. 86 (v. 4605-4983), one after f. 131 (vii. 3071-3269*), one after f. 151 (viii. 1440-1632), and five or more at the end, after viii. 2403. There is also omitted without loss of leaf iii. 1665-1848, no doubt owing to loss of leaf in the copy : see below.

'Elizabeth Vernon' (fifteenth century?) on blank leaf at the end. The book belonged in the present century to Bp. Butler of Lichfield.

This MS. heads the group AdBTΔ, being nearer to the fully revised type than any of the rest, and showing only very occasional traces of the earlier readings (but iii. 254, 941, v. 6418, vii. 3298, viii. 856, 1076, &c.). It agrees with the rest, as against SΔ, in giving v. 7015*-7034*, vii. 2329*-2340*, and 3149*-3180*, but does not seem fully to join the group until the latter part of the fifth book. In connexion with this we may note the curious fact that the omitted passage, iii. 1665-1848, is precisely that contained in f. 50 of S, which apparently was supplied in place of a lost leaf. In correctness and spelling the MS. is very fair, but not good in regard to final *e*. Punctuation often where there is a pause in the line.

T. TRIN. COLL., CAMB. R. iii. 2 (Bern. Cat. i. 3. 335). Contains, ff. 1-147, *Confessio Amantis*, imperfect at the beginning, with 'Explicit' (six lines) and 'Quam cinxere,' ff. 148-152 v⁰ the French *Traitié*, with the Latin pieces 'Quis sit vel qualis,' 'Est amor in glosa,' and 'Lex docet,' f. 152 'Quia vnusquisque,' f. 152 v⁰-154 v⁰ the Latin *Carmen super multiplici viciorum pestilencia*, ending with the ten lines 'Hoc ego bis deno.' Parchment, ff. 154, 14¾ × 10 in., quires of 8 with catchwords, double column of 46 lines. Latin summaries in margin, but in some parts omitted. Well written in several hands, early fifteenth century, of which the first wrote ff. 1-8, 50-57, 74-81, 84 v⁰-89, 98-113 r⁰, the second ff. 9-32, the third ff. 33-49, 58-65, 82, 83, 84 r⁰, 90-97, the fourth ff. 66-73, 113-154. No decoration except coloured or gilt capitals.

The book has lost five whole quires at the beginning, and begins at

present with ii. 2687.   Also the second col. of f. 84 r⁰ is left blank with
omission of v. 7499-7544.   A large part of f. 33 is blank, but there is
no omission.

Presented to the College by Thomas Nevile, Master.

A good MS., with form of text in v, vi, vii, like that of AdB, and obviously
having a special connexion in its readings with B. T, however, is of a more
fully corrected type than B, and it must remain doubtful whether the preface
of the poem in T was of the earlier or the later form.   In any case the
original of the two, if (as it seems) they had a common original, was not
made up earlier than 1397, for the resemblance of the manuscripts extends
to the French and Latin poems which follow the *Conf. Amantis*, and the
last of these is dated the 20th year of king Richard.

The third and fourth hands are neater and better than the other two.
The first is rather less correct and less good in spelling than the others, and
also it omits the Latin marginal notes.   The parts written in this hand are
ii. 2687–iii. 608, v. 1415-2874, 5805-7082, v. 7545–vi. 1040, vi. 2201–vii.
2532.

With regard to the connexions within the group AdBTΛ, attention may
be drawn especially to v. 659, where Ad has the usual reading, T omits the
line, leaving a blank, while B and Λ have bad lines made up for the occasion,
to v. 4020, where Ad again has the usual text, TΛ omit, and B has a made-
up line, and to v. 7303, where AdBT omit two lines necessary to the sense
which Λ inserts.   We may note the alteration by erasure in T of v. 5936,
apparently from the reading of the unrevised text.

B. BODLEY 294, Bodleian Library (Bern. Cat. 2449).   Contents,
as in T, ff. 1–197 *Conf. Amantis*, &c., ff. 197–199 v⁰ *Traitié*, f. 199 v⁰
' Quia vnusquisque,' ff. 199 v⁰–201 *Carmen super multiplici*, &c., ending
with the lines ' Hoc ego bis deno.'   Parchment, ff. 201, 15½ × 10¾ in.,
quires of 8 with catchwords.   Well written in double column of 42-47
lines, first quarter of fifteenth cent.   Latin summaries in text (red):
' Confessor,' ' Amans,' usually omitted.   Complete border of first page
and at the beginning of each book except i and ii, painted in good
style.   Two miniatures, f. 4 v⁰ Nebuchadnezzar's dream (the king in
bed crowned), f. 9 the Confession, nearly as in E.   No leaves lost.

The name ' Edwarde Fletewoode' appears on f. 1, and the book was
probably given by him to the University in 1601.

Form of text in v, vi, vii the same as AdT.   We have in this MS. a
combination of the early preface with the rewritten conclusion, a form which
we might reasonably expect to find, and which may have been that of T,
as it certainly was of the MS. used by Berthelette.   Something has already
been said of the text of this MS., and for the rest sufficient information will
be found in the critical apparatus.   The spelling of B is exemplified in the
passages printed from it, Prol. 24*-92*, v. 7015*-7036*, vii. 2329*-2340*,
3149*-3180*.   As in the case of E, the copyist is careful of metre, and while
omitting final *e* freely before a vowel, rarely does so where it affects the
metre, and seldom adds -*e* unduly.   There is hardly any punctuation.

Λ. WOLLATON HALL, in the possession of Lord Middleton, who kindly allowed me to examine it. Contents as B. Parchment, ff. 197, $15\frac{1}{4} \times 10\frac{1}{2}$ in., in quires of 8 with catchwords and signatures. Well and regularly written in double column of 46 lines, early fifteenth century. Latin summaries in text (red) as a rule, sometimes in margin. Spaces left for miniatures at the beginning and for initials throughout, not painted. No leaves lost.

The text of this MS. is in many ways interesting. It has Lancaster dedication, but in text it often seems to belong to the unrevised first recension; for though many of the errors of this group are found to be corrected in Λ, even in cases where B retains them, as Prol. 7, 219, *Lat. Verses* after 584, 812, 844, 937 f., i. 8, 54, 264, 278, &c., ii. 671, 833, &c., and though there are also many of the revised readings, as i. 368, ii. 1758 ff. (in both of which B is unrevised), iv. 517, 766, 985 f., 2954, 3153, v. 30, 47 f., 82, 2694 f., 3110, &c., yet in many other places the original readings stand in Λ, as i. 3374 ff., iv. 2407, 2556, v. 274, 316, 394, 1893, 1906 f., &c., where BT are revised. The characteristic second recension readings are almost regularly given by Λ, which agrees with AdBT against SΔ in regard to the passages inserted; but there are some important differences between this MS. and all others of its class, viz. (1) after v. 6430* it has a combination of first and second recensions. (2) v. 7701-7746 is inserted as in the first and third recensions. (3) viii. 2941-2959 is inserted as in the first recension (with the curious corruption 'Cuther' for 'Chaucer'), the rewritten epilogue being carried on from the line 'Enclosed in a sterred skye.'

It will be observed that BTΛ often form a distinct group, as (to take only a few examples) iv. 1567, 1996, 2034, 3132, 3138, v. 654 ff., 4138, &c. We may note, however, v. 7303 f. which are inserted by Λ, though omitted in AdBT, and the reading 'she' in iv. 2973.

P₂. Phillipps 8192, at Thirlestaine House, Cheltenham. Same contents as BTΛ. Parchment, ff. 193, large fol. Well written in double col. of 46 lines, early fifteenth cent. Latin summaries in margin. Illumination on the first page and at the beginning of books, except i. and iii. On the first page a miniature of Nebuchadnezzar's Image, with a small figure in the border, and also a figure painted in the initial O. Two leaves missing and supplied in blank after f. 1 (Prol. 154-509), and one later (vii. 3199-3382). On f. 1 v° 'Joh: Finch Comitis Winchilsea filius 1700.'

A fine MS. of an early type. It has the Lancaster dedication in the Prologue and the later form of epilogue, and as regards the additional passages it agrees with AdBTΛ. In text P₂ is closely related to Λ, but it does not include v. 7701-7746 or viii. 2941-2960, nor does it agree with Λ in v. 6431* ff. As instances of their agreement we may cite Prol. 14, 'It dwelleth oft in,' 115, 'vneuened,' 127, 'ben nought diuided,' &c. In the marginal note of Prol. 22 P₂ has 'sextodecimo,' but the first three letters are over an erasure.

THIRD RECENSION.

F. FAIRFAX 3, Bodleian Library (Bern. Cat. 3883). Contains, ff. 2–186, *Confessio Amantis*, with 'Explicit' and 'Quam cinxere,' ff. 186 vº–190 vº *Traitié*, &c., ff. 190 vº–194 *Carmen de multiplici viciorum pestilencia*, ending with the lines 'Hoc ego bis deno,' &c., f. 194 'Quia vnusquisque,' f. 194 vº sixteen Latin lines by 'a certain philosopher' in praise of the author, beginning 'Eneidos Bucolis que Georgica,' f. 195 a leaf of a Latin moral treatise from the old binding. Parchment, ff. 195 (including one blank flyleaf at the beginning and one of another book at the end), $13\frac{1}{2} \times 9\frac{1}{4}$ in., in quires of 8 with catchwords; the first quire begins at f. 2, the twenty-fourth quire has six leaves and the twenty-fifth (last) three. The leaves of the seventh quire are disarranged and should be read in the following order, 50, 52, 53, 51, 56, 54, 55, 57. The *Confessio Amantis* is written in double column of 46 lines, in a very good hand of the end of the fourteenth cent. Latin summaries in the margin. Half borders, some with animal figures, at the beginning of each book, and two miniatures, one at the beginning, rather large, of Nebuchadnezzar's dream, and the other on f. 8 of the Confession, in which the priest is dressed in green and has a wreath of roses on his head, while the penitent, whose features are damaged, wears a hood and a collar of SS with a badge, probably a swan, dependent from it. This was no doubt intended as a portrait of the author: the collar and badge have somewhat the appearance of having been added after the original painting was made. The size of the illuminated capitals indicates precisely the nature of the various divisions of the work.

On f. 2 is written 'The Ladie Isabell Fairfax daughter and hare of Thwats hir bouk,' on f. 8 'This boke belongeth to my lady farfax off Steton,' and on f. 1 'Sʳ Thomas fayrfax of Denton Knighte true owner of this booke, 1588.' This Lady Isabell Fairfax was the granddaughter and heiress of John Thwaites of Denton, who died in 1511, and was married to Sir William Fairfax of Steeton. Sir Thomas Fairfax of Denton, whose name appears in the book, was her grandson. The book no doubt came from the Thwaites family, and we are thus able to trace it back as far as John Thwaites of Denton, who died in old age not much more than a hundred years after the death of the author. It was bequeathed with other MSS. to the University of Oxford by Sir Thomas Fairfax the parliamentary general, grandson of the above Sir Thomas Fairfax of Denton, and was placed in the Bodleian Library in 1675.

The first leaf of the text, up to Prol. 146, is written in a second hand which has also written ff. 186–194, including the last lines of the *Conf. Amantis* from viii. 3147. A third hand (with very different orthography) has written viii. 2938–3146, being the last 29 lines of f. 41 vº (over an erasure) and the whole of f. 185, which is a leaf inserted in the place of one cut away (the last of quire 23). At viii. 2938 there is visible a note, 'now haue, etc.,' for the guidance of the scribe after the erasure had been made. From the fact that two hands have been employed in the transformation of the MS. at the beginning and end it seems probable that the changes were made at two separate times (as we also know by the dates that the rewritten epilogue preceded the rewritten preface), and that what I have called the third hand was really the second in order of time, being employed to substitute the later epilogue for the former, while the other hand, doing its work probably after the accession of Henry IV, replaced the first leaf by one containing the Lancaster dedication, which had been in existence since 1392–3, but perhaps only in private circulation, and added also the *Traitié* and the Latin poems, with the account of the author's books, 'Quia vnus-quisque,' in its revised form. I say after the accession of Henry IV, because the reference in the third recension account of the books to Richard's fall, 'ab alto corruens in foueam quam fecit finaliter proiectus est,' seems to require as late a date as this. It should be noted that this hand is the same as that which has made somewhat similar additions to the All Souls and Glasgow MSS. of the *Vox Clamantis.* Other examples of alteration of first recension readings by erasure in F are Prol. 331 *marg.*, 336, i. 2713 f., iv. 1321 f., 1361 f., *Lat. Verses after* vii. 1640, *Lat. Verses after* vii. 1984.

As this edition prints the text of the Fairfax MS. and its relations have already been discussed, little more need be said here except as to the manner in which the text is dealt with in the printing. It should be noted then that *i* and *j*, *u* and *v* are used in accordance with modern practice, that no distinction is made between the two forms of *s*, that *th* is used for *þ*, and *y* for *ʒ* in *ʒe, ʒit, ʒiue, aʒein, beʒete,* &c. (this last rather against my judgement, for no good MS. has it). It should be observed also that the Fairfax scribe frequently uses *v* for *u* at the end of a word, as 'nov,' 'hov' (often ' hou '), 'þov' (usually ' þou '), 'ʒov' (also 'ʒou'), 'auov,' 'windov,' 'blev,' 'knev,' &c., and sometimes in other positions, either for the sake of distinction from *n* or merely for ornament, as ' comvne,' ' retenve,' ' rvnne,' ' þvrgh,' ' havk,' ' fovl,' ' hovndes,' ' movþ,' ' rovnede,' ' slovh,' ' trovþe,' ' ynovh,' &c., beside ' comune,' ' runne,' ' þurgh,' ' hauk,' ' foul,' &c. In all these cases *v* is given in the text as *u*. The termination '-on̄' is regularly printed as '-oun.' French words with this ending appear in F with -ou or -on̄, usually the latter (but 'resoun' in full, Prol. 151), and sometimes we have ' ton̄' for ' toun,' as vii. 5313, viii. 2523. So also 'stonde : wounde,' i. 1425 f., 'gronde' for 'grounde,' i. 2051, 'expon̄de : founde,' i. 2867 f., 'branche : staunche,' i. 2837 f., 'chance,' i. 3203, 'granteþ,' ii. 1463, 'supplante,' ii. 2369, 'sklandre,' v. 5536 ('sclaundre,' v. 712), 'comande : launde,' vii. 2159.

The contraction ꝑ as a separate word is in this edition almost regularly given as 'per.' It is hardly ever written fully in F, but we have ' Per aunter,' v. 3351, ' Per chaunce,' v. 7816, and J regularly gives ' per chance,' ' per cas,' &c., without contraction. Other MSS., as A and B, incline rather to ' par.' F has 'perceive,' ' aperceive,' but ' parfit.'

With regard to the use of capitals, this edition in the main follows the MS. Some letters, however, as *k, v, w, y,* can hardly be said to have any difference of form, and others are used rather rarely as capitals, while in the case of some, and especially *s*, the capital form is used with excessive freedom. It has seemed desirable therefore to introduce a greater degree of consistency, while preserving the general usage of the MS. Proper names are regularly given in this edition with capitals (usually so in the MS., but not always), and sentences are begun with capital letters after a full stop. On the other hand the *I* (or *J*), which is often used as an initial, has frequently been suppressed, and occasionally this has been done in the case of other letters. It may be observed, however, that capital letters are on the whole used very systematically in the MS., and other good MSS., especially S, agree with F in the main principles. Certain substantives as ' Ere,' ' Erthe,' ' Schip,' ' Sone,' ' Ston,' are almost invariably used with capitals, and names of animals, as 'Cat,' 'Hare,' 'Hound,' ' Leoun,' ' Mous,' 'Oxe,' ' Pie,' 'Ro,' ' Schep,' ' Tigre,' of some parts of the body, as ' Arm,' ' Hiele,' ' Lippes,' ' Nase,' ' Pappes,' ' Skulle,' and many other concrete substantives, are apt to be written with capitals, sometimes apparently in order to give them more importance. Capitals are seldom thus used except in the case of substantives and some numerals, as ' Nyne,' 'Seconde,' 'Sexte,' ' Tenthe,' and in many cases it is pretty evident that a distinction is intended, e. g. between ' Sone' and 'sone' (adv.), 'Se' (= sea) and 'se' (verb), ' Dore' and 'dore' (verb), see iv. 2825 f., ' More' and 'more,' 'Pype' and ' pipe' (verb), iv. 3342 f., ' Myn' and 'myn' (poss. pron.), 'Mone' and 'mone' (verb), but see v. 5804, 5808, ' In' and 'in,' vii. 4921 f., viii. 1169 f., 1285 f. That some importance was attached to the matter is shown by the cases where careful alterations of small letters into capitals have been made in the MS., as Prol. 949, i. 1687, v. 1435, 3206, 4019, vii. 2785, &c.

Many corrections were made by the first hand, and some of these are noteworthy, especially the cases where a final *e* seems to be deliberately erased for the sake of the metre or before a vowel, as i. 60 'get' for 'gete,' iii. 2346 'trew' for 'trewe,' vi. 1359 'I red' for ' I rede,' vii. 1706 'ffyf' for ' ffyue,' or where an *e* has been added afterwards, as ii. 3399 ' deþe,' iii. 449 ' bowe,' v. 1269, 3726, 5265, 'whiche.'

It remains only to speak of the punctuation of the MS., which is evidently carried out carefully. The frequent stops at the ends of lines are for the most part meaningless, but those elsewhere are of importance and usually may be taken as a guide to the sense. They are sometimes certainly wrong (e. g. i. 1102 Togedre· 1284 will· 2965 fro· ii. 1104 wille· 1397 name· 2354 astat· iii. 2638 be· iv. 497 grace· 1751 besinesse· 1985 hardi· 2502 alle· 3354 Slep· 3635 lif· v. 4 good· 231 herte· 444 wynd· 1342 See· 1630 only· 2318 bord· &c), but the proportion of error is small, and the punctuation of F generally must be treated with respect. There is usually a stop wherever a marked pause comes in the line, and this punctuation occurs on an average about once in ten lines. The following record of the punctuation of iv. 1301–1600 will serve as an illustration of its nature and extent : 1303 loue· 1307 ladis· 1316 cloþed· 1369 seide· 1374 seiþ· 1376 loue· 1388 slow· 1409 wepe· 1412 Dame· 1415 loue· 1439 hirself· 1457 is· 1459 peine· 1461 haltres· 1466 told· 1470 *pa*ramours· 1471 lawe· 1474 ianglinge· 1489 take· 1490 loue· 1491 herte· 1492 mariage· 1496 children· 1497 mai· 1499 tarie· 1501 let· 1512 god· seide· 1532 oþre· 1534 ferste· 1535 dovht*er*· 1536 cloþes· 1547 Tohewe· 1560 seiþ· 1561 point· 1566 maidenhod· 1567 had· 1591 come· 1592 deþ.

H₂. HARLEIAN 3869, Brit. Museum. Contains the same as F, with some religious poems in a different hand on blanks at the beginning and end. Paper, except outer leaves of each quire, ff. 368 (including four leaves at the beginning and two at the end with religious poems as above mentioned), $11\frac{1}{4} \times 7\frac{1}{2}$ in., in quires of 16 (usually), with signatures, first quire beginning f. 5 and having 14 leaves. Written in single column of 38–50 lines, rather irregularly. Latin summaries in margin (red). On f. 5 at the beginning of the *Confessio Amantis* a large picture of Nebuchadnezzar's dream, like that in F, on f. 8 an ill-painted picture of the Confession.

On f. 1 we find written 'London yᵉ 28 Janʸ. 1628, George Cogiluy,' and on f. 2 'Jan. 22. 1721 Oxford' (i.e. Harley). On the same page is the date, '1445 yᵉ 23 of May.'

This MS. appears to be copied directly from F, and gives an excellent text, reproducing that of the Fairfax MS. with considerable accuracy, and for the most part copying also its mistakes and peculiarities, as Prol. 80 officie, 249 wich, 419 com, 588 sende, 592 befalle, 668 *marg.* diminuntur, 723 chiualrie, 1078 waxed, i. 120 wisshide, 160 scheo, 227 beleft, 234 sone sone, 335 whilon, 1626 vnsemylieste, 2511 Embroudred, ii. 352 Ennvie, *Lat. after* 382 infamen, 710 hiere, 949 þong, 1169 no, 1441 keste, 1539 *om.* the, and so on. Some obvious mistakes are corrected, however, as Prol. 370, i. 1257, 2105, 3357, ii. 117.

N. NEW COLLEGE, OXF. 266 (Bern. Cat. i. 2. 1230). *Confessio Amantis* with 'Explicit' (six lines) and 'Quam cinxere.' Parchment, ff. 183 (originally 187), $13\frac{1}{4} \times 9$ in., quires of 8 (one of 10 and the last 9) with catchwords. Well written in double column of 46 lines usually, sometimes more, first quarter fifteenth cent. Latin summaries in margin. Many floreated pages (half borders) and illuminated capitals, well executed. Also a large number of miniatures, of which some have been cut out and others much damaged.

The first two leaves are damaged, and four leaves have been cut out, viz. the original f. 7 (Prol. 1066–i. 106), f. 35 (ii. 1521–1704), f. 74 (iv. 2229–2397) and f. 113 (v. 5505–5662), also the outer half of f. 171 (viii. 271–318) and several miniatures with text at the back.

The name of John Cutt of Schenley, Hertfordshire, appears in the book (late fifteenth cent.), and on the first leaf 'Thomæ Martin Liber,' perhaps the Thomas Martin who was Fellow of New College 1538–1553, and died in 1584. The binding of old black leather has stamped upon it the letters W. D., with a double-headed eagle crowned.

This book seems to be derived from F, though perhaps not immediately. The orthography is like that of F, but differs in some points, as 'shal,' 'she,' &c, for 'schal,' 'sche,' 'noht' for 'noght,' besides being very uncertain about final *e*, often to the destruction of the metre. As examples of particular correspondence with F we may note Prol. 370 argumeten, 588 send, 592 befalle, 723 chiualrie, 957 mistormeth, i. 120 wisshide, 227 beleft, 234 sone

sone, 1036 be shrewed, 3357 seled, ii. 318 ff. fela, felaw, felawh (varying as F), *after* 382 infamen, &c., but sometimes F is corrected in small matters, as Prol. 201 erthly, 249 which, 280 pacience, i. 110 to fare, &c.

The feature of the book is the series of miniatures, illustrating it throughout. In this respect it is unique, so far as I know, though other copies similarly illustrated must once have existed. The following is a complete list of the subjects (leaves cited by original number) : f. 15 (i. 1417) Florent and the old woman, f. 18 (i. 2021) man blowing trumpet, lord, wife, and five children looking out of a castle, f. 23 (i. 2785) *cut out*, f. 24 (i. 3067) *cut out and sewn in, much damaged*, f. 30 (ii. 587) *cut out*, f. 44 (ii. 3187) mothers bringing babies to Constantine, f. 56 (iii. 1885) Clytemnestra torn by horses, two crowned persons conversing in the foreground, f. 59 (iii. 2363) Pirate brought before Alexander, f. 61 (iv. 1) Dido killing herself, Eneas riding away, f. 68 (iv. 1245) lady with halters and red bridle questioned by Rosiphelee, f. 71 (iv. 1815) *cut out*, f. 72 (iv. 2045) fight between Hercules and Achelous, f. 77 (iv. 2927) Alceone in bed dreaming, body of king in the water, f. 83 (v. 141) Midas at table, f. 93 (v. 2031) Crassus having gold poured down his throat, f. 94 (v. 2273) king opening coffers, f. 95 (v. 2391) *cut out*, f. 96 (v. 2643) *cut out*, f. 98 (v. 2961) *almost defaced*, f. 100 (v. 3247) *cut out*, f. 109 (v. 4937) Bardus pulling Adrian out of the pit, f. 111 (v. 5231) Ariadne left sleeping, ship sailing away, f. 117 (v. 6225) a procession of naked nymphs to bathe, f. 120 (v. 6807) *cut out*, f. 133 (vi. 1391) Telegonus supporting his father's head, guards lying dead, f. 136 (vi. 1789) *cut out*, f. 150 (vii. 1783) *cut out*, f. 158 (vii. 3417) *cut out*, f. 159 (vii. 3627) Gideon and his men blowing trumpets, &c., enemy asleep in a tent, f. 165 (vii. 4593) *cut out*, f. 171 (viii. 271 ff.) half the page cut away, with probably three miniatures, for only 52 lines are gone, whereas there was space for 92.

K. KESWICK HALL, near Norwich, in the possession of J. H. Gurney, Esq., who most kindly sent it to Oxford for my use. Contains the same as F, but is slightly imperfect at the end. Parchment, ff. 189, 13 × 9¾ in., quires of 8 with catchwords. Well written in double column of 46 lines (corresponding column for column with F throughout), apparently in six different hands, of which the first wrote quires 1, 2, 6, 8–11, 21, the second 3 and perhaps 7, the third 4, 5, 16, 17, the fourth 12–15, 19, the fifth 18, and the sixth 20, 22–24. Latin summaries in the margin (sometimes omitted). Three leaves are lost in the seventh quire (iii. 1087–1632), and one at the end, containing the last thirteen lines of the Latin *Carmen de multiplici*, &c., with probably the account of the books and the piece 'Eneidos, Bucolis.' A floreated initial to each book, and space left for miniatures on ff. 1 and 7. Old stamped leather binding.

Former possessors, Thomas Stone 'of Bromsberrowe in the County of Glouc.', Henry Harman, William Mallowes (Q. Elizabeth's reign?), John Feynton.

The various hands differ very much from one another in correctness. The first and the fourth give a text so closely corresponding to that of F, that it is almost impossible not to believe that it is copied from it. In the case of

**

some of the other hands this exact correspondence in details of spelling and punctuation disappears, and a much less correct text is given, but this seems chiefly due to carelessness (the third hand, for example, is evidently inaccurate and much neglects the metre). At the same time it must be noted that K has the marginal note at the beginning of the Prologue, which is wanting in F, ' Hic in principio,' &c., and there are some readings which seem to be derived from another source, as iii. 778, 906, 921, 1732, 1832 (all in the seventh quire), where there is agreement with AM. On the whole the question of the dependence of K upon F must be left doubtful.

We can trace to this MS. a good many of the mistakes which appear in H₃ and the Magdalen MS., and found their way sometimes thus into printed editions, e.g. Prol. 160 bothe, 260 to make manhode, i. 3170 *om.* his, ii. 78 fader, 101 hem wolde, 103 all hys cause, 126 he, 135 pore, 138 wich, 162 In (*originally* The). The cause of the great increase of error about the beginning of the second book is the appearance on the scene of the careless third hand, which on f. 40 (for example) in its last ten lines has at least twenty variations in spelling, &c., from the text of F, while the first hand resuming has not a single one in its first eighteen lines. Indeed, whole columns may be found in the parts copied by the first or the fourth hand which do not differ from F in the smallest particular, either of spelling or punctuation.

H₃. HARLEIAN 7184, Brit. Museum. *Confessio Amantis*, imperfect. Parchment, ff. 134, 21½ × 14½ in., in quires of 12 with catchwords: regularly written in double column of 49 lines, in a large pointed hand of the middle fifteenth cent. Latin summaries in the text (red). Large capitals finely illuminated and pages bordered at the beginning of the books (the first page especially is richly decorated, but has suffered damage), also illuminated titles, ' Liber Primus,' &c., at the head of each page.

The book has lost more than fifty leaves, viz. one leaf after each of the following, f. 25 (i. 3322–ii. 46), f. 55 (iii. 1908–2103), f. 61 (iv. 400–576), f. 78 (iv. 3701–v. 161), f. 110 (v. 6183–6360), and f. 118 (vi. *Latin Verses* i. 4–182), twelve leaves after f. 126 (vi. 1571–vii. 1405), four after f. 131 (vii. 2354–3088), and thirty or more after f. 134, from vii. 3594 to the end of the book.

On the first page ' Oxford B. H.'

This is a very large and magnificent volume, written on fine parchment, doubtless for some distinguished person. The text, however, is late and not very good. It is almost certain that it is derived ultimately from the Keswick MS. The evidence of this is as follows: (1) Mistakes made in that MS. are nearly regularly reproduced in H₃. Some instances have been referred to in the account of K : we may add here that where K omits the Latin summaries in a part of the seventh book, e.g. vii. 1641–1884, 1917–2765, H₃ does the same, and where variants apparently from the AM group appear in K, as iii. 778, 906, 921, 1732, they are found also in H₃. (2) The inequality which is to be observed in the text of H₃, some parts being much less correct than others, corresponds in the main with the difference of hands in K. Thus we find that a great crop of error springs up in H₃ from the point where the third hand of K begins, the preceding portion of the text being very fairly correct, and so to some extent elsewhere. For example, in v. 917-1017 (a part written in K by the first hand) there are about eight metrical faults in a hundred lines, while in vi. 183-283 (written in K by the third hand), there are at least twenty-five. (3) In a certain part of the third book H₃ suddenly ceases to follow the third recension text, and almost regularly gives the readings of the ERCLB₂ group. This appears first in iii. 1088 and ceases to be the case after iii. 1686, thus remarkably corresponding with the gap caused in K by the loss of three leaves after iii. 1086. It is difficult not to believe that this very marked change was caused by the following of another MS. in a place where K was defective.

The spelling of H₃ is rather late: there is no use of $\flat$, and y is used for $\jmath$ in 'ye,' 'yiue,' &c.

Magd. MAGDALEN COLLEGE, OXF. 213 (Bern. Cat. i. 2. 2354). *Confessio Amantis* with 'Explicit' (six lines) and Table of Contents in English (on two fly-leaves at the beginning and one at the end). Parchment, ff. 180 + 3 (as above), 18¾ × 13¼ in., in quires of 8 with catchwords: written in double column of 48 lines in a large hand of the middle fifteenth cent. something like that of H₃. Table of contents and columns 2, 3, 4 of f. 2 in a different hand. Latin summaries in text (red). Fine coloured letters with floreated half borders at the beginning of each book, and some neat drawing in connexion with the scrolls of the catchwords.

The book has lost one leaf after f. 22 (ii. 409-586) and eight after f. 88 (v. 701-2163). On f. 155 v⁰ the MS. omits vii. 2519-2695 without loss of leaf or blank.

Presented to the College by Marchadin Hunnis in 1620. A note by the present Librarian states that he was elected a demy of the College in 1606, appointed second master of the College Grammar School in 1610, and dismissed from that office as 'insufficiens' in Dec. 1611. The book is reported missing in Coxe's catalogue.

This MS. is in many points like H₃ in its text, and must certainly have the same origin, both being perhaps derived from a MS. dependent on K. It reproduces most of the corruptions which we find in H₃, adding many others of its own, and it has the same readings in the third book which we have already noted in H₃.

A point of interest about this MS. is its apparent connexion with Caxton's edition. It seems evident that among the MSS. from which Caxton worked (and he had three at least) was either this very copy or one so like it as to be practically undistinguishable. Of this we shall say more when we speak of Caxton's edition.

W. WADHAM COLL., OXF. 13. *Confessio Amantis* with 'Explicit' (six lines) and 'Quam cinxere,' then the *Traitié*, slightly imperfect at the end, ending 'un amie soulain,' xvii. 9. Paper, ff. 450, including two original blanks at the beginning, 11½ × 8¼ in., in quires of 8 with catchwords : written in column of 30–48 lines (without ruling) in two hands, of which the first wrote up to iv. 2132, and the other from thence to the end. Latin summaries in margin, but sometimes omitted or cut short. Some decoration of the first page of the text in black and red ; capitals, titles, &c. in red.

Three leaves are lost in the *Conf. Amantis*, containing Prol. 728–794, iv. 2386–2473, and v. 1–78, and several also at the end of the volume. There is great confusion in the text of the Prologue, which goes as follows : 1–92, 499–860 (with loss as above), 93–144, 861–1044, 145–498, and then 1045 ff. This is not produced by any disarrangement of leaves in the present MS., but a considerable dislocation of quires has taken place in a later part of the volume, seven quires of the fourth and fifth books having been taken out of their proper place and bound up between vi. 2132 and 2133.

This book was evidently written for one John Dedwood, since his name and device, a piece of the trunk of a dead tree, occur as part of the decorations of the first page. The two blanks at the beginning are written over with a list of Mayors and Sheriffs for a series of years, and these prove to be those of the city of Chester from the year 1469–1499 (see Ormerod's *Hist. of Cheshire*, i. 211 f.). The name of John Dedwood occurs among these as Sheriff in the year 1481 and as Mayor in 1483 (but the record in the MS. is here damaged). He had also been Mayor in 1468. We may therefore suppose that the MS. dates from about 1470. The name Troutbecke occurs several times (with other names) in the book, and later (1765) it belonged to Rich. Warner of Woodford Row, Essex.

The first hand of this MS. is cramped and ugly, varying a good deal in size, the second is neat and uniform. The text is late and full of mistakes, and the spelling bad, even such forms as ' loves,' ' beres,' ' gos ' being quite common for ' loveth,' &c., and often *-et* or *-ut* as a participle termination, ' despeyret,' ' resignet,' ' weddut,' ' cleput,' &c. A certain interest attaches to the MS. however from the fact that it seems to be clearly independent of F as well as of the KH₃ group. While agreeing with F completely in form of text, and supporting it also as a rule against the mistakes of KH₃, it has a considerable number of readings which belong to the first recension uncorrected type, and in other cases it agrees specially with B. Instances of the former are to be found in Prol. 159, i. 8, 1839, 2423, 2801, 3027, ii. 961, 1200, 1441, 3306, 3516, iii. 68, 626, 2056, v. 1698, 2500, 3376, vi. 543, 1151, 1631, vii. 1490, *Latin verses after* 1640 and 1984, 5104, viii. 510, 2342, 2925, &c. These, with others of a similar kind, scattered through the whole book, seem to be of the nature of accidental survivals, a first recension copy (the remote ancestor of W) having been altered by collation with one resembling F. W agrees with apparent mistakes of F and the rest of the third recension in some passages, as iii. 446, iv. 2867, 2973, vii. 5135, viii. 1069, 1999, but supports what is apparently the true reading against them in Prol. 1078, i. 1068, ii. 2299, 2537,

iii. 1605, v. 2906, &c. In most of these last instances W merely remains in agreement with the first recension, where F, &c. depart from it, therefore its testimony may be of an accidental character.

The list of Mayors and Sheriffs of Chester on the first pages has perhaps some local interest, as it is contemporary and probably made by a responsible person. Comparing it with that given in Ormerod's *Hist. of Cheshire*, we find several differences, as 'Ric. Sadler' for 'Rich. Smith' as one of the Sheriffs of 1475, 'John Monkesfelde, Rob. Pleche,' Sheriffs for 1478, 'Mathewe Hewse' for 'Mathew Johnson,' 1479, 'Rychard Kir e' for 'Rich. Barker,' 1492. The same pages have some notes about current historical events, as (under 1469), 'The which yere were hedet the lorde Wellybe and the lorde Well. his son for the grete insurreccion and rysing of the Comyns of the Counte of Lyncolne. Also the same yere entred our Souereyne and moste noble Prince Kynge Edward now reynynge,' &c. Under 1470 is a note of the battles of Barnet and Tewkesbury, and at 1476 the record of a visit to Chester of 'our Souereigne lorde Prince,' who stayed there from Christmas to Easter.

P₃. Formerly PHILLIPPS 8942, bought in March, 1895, by Messrs. H. S. Nichols & Co., and afterwards in the possession of Messrs. Maggs, Booksellers. *Confessio Amantis*, imperfect, ending viii. 3119, 'As Tullius som tyme wrot.' Parchment, rather roughly written, middle of fifteenth century. From the Towneley Collection.

Hn. HATTON 51, Bodleian Library (Bern. Cat. 4099). *Confessio Amantis*, imperfect. Parchment, ff. 206, 12 × 9 in., in quires first of 6 and then usually of 8 (lettered); double column of 42–48 lines, untidy writing. Has lost *k* 4 (iii. 1314–1475), *n* 2 (iv. 2118–2268), *s* 2 (v. 5169–5333), *t* 2 (v. 6774–6914), and five or six at the end (after viii. 2408). Copied from Caxton's edition, including the Table of Contents and the confusion in leaf numbering.

Besides these, there are several MSS. which contain selections from the *Confessio Amantis*, as

HARL. 7333, Brit. Museum, which, besides the *Canterbury Tales* and other things, has seven stories from the *Conf. Amantis*, viz. f. 120 Tereus (v. 5551 ff.), f. 122 Constance (ii. 587 ff.), f. 126 The Three Questions (i. 3067 ff.), f. 127 vº The Travellers and the Angel (ii. 291 ff.), f. 127 vº Virgil's Mirror, f. 128 vº The Two Coffers, f. 129 The Beggars and the Pasties, &c. (v. 2031–2498). Parchment, large folio, column of 66 lines, no Latin. These stories are in the same hand as the *Cant. Tales*, which go before, and the *Parlement of Foules*, which follows them. The text is that of the first recension unrevised : a very poor copy.

CAMB. UNIV. Ee. ii. 15. Paper, ff. 95, end of fifteenth or beginning of sixteenth cent., much mutilated. Contains ff. 30–32, a fragment of The Three Questions (i. 3124–3315), and ff. 33–35, a fragment of the Trump of Death (i. 2083 ff.).

CAMB. UNIV. Ff. i. 6. Paper, ff. 159, 8½ × 6 in., written in various hands. Contains, ff. 3–5, part of the tale of Tereus (v. 5920–6052), ff. 5–10, iv. 1114–1466 including the tale of Rosiphelee, ff. 45–51, The Three Questions (i. 3067–3425), ff. 81–84, iv. 2746–2926, ff. 84 v⁰–95, viii. 271–846. The text of iv. 1321 agrees with that of the second recension.

BALL. COLL., OXF. 354. Paper, ff. 253, 11½ × 4¼ in. Contains a miscellaneous collection of verse and prose, with memoranda &c., all, or nearly all, apparently in the hand of the owner of the book, one Richard Hill of Langley, Herts, who has registered on f. 21 (25) the birth of his seven children, from the year 1518 to 1526, and has kept a short journal of public events which ends with the year 1536. Among the extracts are several stories from the *Confessio Amantis*, neatly written, about 54–60 lines to the page, with no Latin. These extend over about 46 leaves of the book and are as follows (leaves by old numbering): ff. 55–70 v⁰ Tale of Appolinus, viii. 271–2028, ff. 70 v⁰–81 v⁰ Tales of Constance and of Perseus, ii. 587–1865, ff. 81 v⁰–83 v⁰ Adrian and Bardus, v. 4937–5162, ff. 83 v⁰–84 v⁰, vi. 485–595, ff. 84 v⁰–86 v⁰ Dives and Lazarus &c., vi. 975–1238, ff. 86 v⁰–89 v⁰ Constantine, ii. 3187–3507, ff. 89 v⁰–91 v⁰ Nebuchadnezzar, i. 2785–3066, ff. 91 v⁰–94 v⁰ Tales of Diogenes and of Pyramus, iii. 1201–1502 and 1655–1672, ff. 94 v⁰–96 Midas (unfinished), v. 141–312, ff. 171 v⁰–175, The Three Questions, i. 3067–3402. The text is copied not from Caxton's edition but from a MS. of the first recension (*b*) or (*c*). It is not very correct, and short passages or couplets are omitted here and there, as i. 3051–3054, viii. 1763–1766, 1945 f., &c.

RAWLINSON D. 82, Bodleian Library. Contains on ff. 25–33 *Conf. Amantis*, viii. 2377–2970. Paper, written in single column of 33 lines, no Latin. Copied from a MS. resembling B, but not apparently either from B itself or from Berthelette's MS.

PHILLIPPS 22914 is reported as a fragment (four leaves) containing *Confessio Amantis*, v. 775–1542.

Nine good miniatures cut out of a MS. of the *Conf. Amantis* are in the possession of Mr. A. H. Frere, who kindly allowed me to see them. They are as follows. (1) Tereus, (2) Codrus, (3) Socrates and his wife, (4) Dives and Lazarus, (5) Roman Triumph, (6) Ulysses and Telegonus, (7) The Three Questions, (8) Lycurgus taking an oath from the Athenians (?), (9) King on a quay with bales and gold vessels, apparently landed from a ship near, perhaps Apollonius landing at Tarsis. Several of the pictures represent more than one scene of the

story, as that of Tereus, in which we have the king at meat presented
with the head of his son, while there are three birds in the background
and the scene of the outrage on Philomene on the left; and again in
(4), where the rich man and his wife are sitting at table and refusing
food to the beggar, while in the background on the right an angel is
receiving the soul of the dying Lazarus.

These miniatures are supposed to have belonged to Sir John Fenn,
editor of the Paston Letters. The MS. from which they were cut
seems to have been of the middle of the fifteenth cent.

Evidence is afforded of one other large and well written MS. of the
Conf. Amantis by a fragment of parchment in the Shrewsbury School
Library, of which a photograph has most kindly been sent to me by
Dr. Calvert of Shrewsbury. It contains about 70 lines of the Prologue,
viz. 189-195 (with the Latin), 224-244, 274-294, 323-343. The leaf
to which it belonged must have measured at least $15\frac{1}{2} \times 11\frac{1}{2}$ in., and
was written in double column of 50 lines.

Three other MSS. are mentioned in the Catalogue of 1697 (vol. ii.
pt. 1), viz. 611 'John Gower's Old English Poems' with 'S. Anselmi
Speculum Religiosorum,' at Naworth Castle, which I strongly suspect
is identical with Harl. 3490 (H_1), 4035, 'Goweri Confessio Amantis,
Fol. magn.,' belonging to Ric. Brideoake, Esq., of Ledwell, Oxon., and
6974, 'Jo. Gower's Poems, fol.,' belonging to Sir Henry Langley of the
County of Salop (i. e. of the Abbey, Shrewsbury).

The average excellence of the Gower MSS. stands high, and there
is a surprisingly large proportion of well written and finely decorated
copies, which attain to more than a respectable tandard of correctness. Manuscripts such as L or B₂, which stand in the third rank
among copies of the Confessio Amantis, would take a very different place
among the authorities for any of Chaucer's works, second only to the
Ellesmere MS. if they were copies of the Canterbury Tales, and easily
in the first place if it were a question of the Legend of Good Women or
the Hous of Fame. It is evident not only that Gower was careful about
the text of his writings, but also that there was some organized system
of reproduction, which was wanting in the case of Chaucer.

VERSION. It remains to say something of the Spanish prose version
of the Confessio Amantis, which exists in manuscript in the Library
of the Escorial (g. ii. 19). Information about this was first given me
by Mr. J. Fitzmaurice-Kelly, and since then by the learned Librarian
of the Escorial, Fr. Guillermo Antolin, O.S.A., who most obligingly sent
me an account of it. The Catalogue (1858) thus describes the book:
' Confision del amante, libro así intitulado compuesto por Juan Goer
natural del Reyno de Englaterra, e tornado en lengua Portuguesa por
Roberto Payn ó Payna canónigo de la ciudad de Lisboa, e despues
fué puesto en lenguaje castellano por Juan de Cuenca natural de Huete.

Cod. escrito en papel el año de 1400, fol. menor. pasta.' The statement about the author and the translators is taken from the beginning of
the translation itself. It seems to be rather implied that the Castilian
version made by Juan de Cuenca was based upon the Portuguese of
Robert Payn, no doubt an Englishman. The present Librarian adds
that it is a book of 411 leaves, and of the end of the fourteenth or
beginning of the fifteenth cent.

The translation was made from a copy of the first recension. So
far as I can judge by the extracts with which the Librarian has
furnished me, it is a tolerably close version. For example, Prol. 22 ff.
' e por que pocos escriven en lenguaje yngles yo entiendo de componer
en el un lybro a onrra del Rey rricardo cuyo sugebto yo so en todo
obedescimiento de mi coraçon, como dicho sugebto puede y deue a su
dicho señor, . . . asy fue que un tiempo acaescio como avía de ser que
yo yendo en un batel a rremos por el rrio de atenas que va a la cibdad
de noua troya . . . y yo estonces falle por ventura a este mi señor e luego
como me vido mando que fuese a una barca en que el venia, y entre
otras cosas que me dixo,' &c. And again viii. 2941 ff. (the Chaucer
greeting), ' Saluda de mi parte a caucer mi disciplo e mi poeta, quando
con el to_pares, el qual por mi en la su mancibia fiso toda su diligencia
para componer y escreuir desyres e cantares de diversas maneras de
los quales toda la tierra es llena, por la qual cosa en especial le soy
mucho tenido mas que a ninguno de los otros. Por ende dile que le
enbio desir que tal esta en su postrimera hedad por dar fyn a todas
sus obras se travaje de fáser su testamento de amor, asi como tu has
fecho agora en tu confision.'

EDITIONS. The *Confessio Amantis* has been already six times
printed, viz. by Caxton, by Berthelette (twice), in Chalmers' English
Poets, by Pauli, and by Prof. Henry Morley. All the later editions
are dependent, directly or indirectly, on Berthelette.

CAXTON printed the *Conf. Amantis* in 1483. His text is a composite
one, taken from at least three MSS. At first he follows a copy of the third
recension, either the Magdalen MS. itself or one remarkably like it,
and he continues this for more than half the book, up to about v. 4500.
Then for a time he seems to follow a second recension copy, either alone
or in combination with the other, but from about v. 6400 to the end he
prints from a manuscript of the unrevised first recension, inserting
however the additional passages in the seventh book and the conclusion
(after the Chaucer greeting) from one of his other MSS. The account
of the books ' Quia vnusquisque ' at the end is from a first recension
MS. The principle, no doubt, was to include as much as possible, but
two of the additional passages, v. 7015*-7036* and 7086*-7210*, were
omitted, probably by oversight, while a first recension copy was being

followed. The later form of epilogue was perhaps printed rather than the other because it is longer. Caxton prints the lines at the end of the Prologue, which are given only by Δ, and there are some other indications that he had a MS. of this type ; but he had also one of the AdBT group, which alone contain vii. 2329*-2340* and 3149*-3180*

On f. cxvi vᵒ Caxton still agrees with Magd. almost regularly, e.g. v. 4450 And myn hap 4454 is not trouble 4465 But for that 4467 ne shall yeue and lene 4484 doo 4503 A good word, whereas on f. cxvii he differs repeatedly, e.g. 4528, 4532, 4543, 4555, 4560, 4572, and seems never to be in full agreement after this. That he is following a first recension copy after about v. 6400 is clear from the unbroken series of readings belonging to this class which he exhibits. The text generally is very poor and the metre extremely bad.

BERTHELETTE in 1532 printed the *Conf. Amantis* from a MS. very closely resembling B. He did not venture, however, to substitute the preface which he found in his copy for that to which Caxton had given currency, but merely expressed surprise that the printed copies should deviate so much from the MSS., and printed separately that which his manuscript gave. He also takes from Caxton the lines at the end of the Prologue, the additional third recension passages, Prol. 495-498, 579-584, i. 1403-1406, 2267-2274, 2343-2358, 2369-2372 [1], and also the Chaucer greeting, viii. 2941-2960*, but he has overlooked v. 7701-7746. He inserts of course all the additional passages in v. and vii, as he found them in his MS., loudly protesting against Caxton for omitting 'lynes and columnes, ye and sometyme holle padges.'

Berthelette's text is better than Caxton's, but his manuscript must have been decidedly inferior in correctness to B.

The second edition, 1554, is a reprint of the first, column for column, in different type. A few mistakes are corrected, and the spelling is somewhat changed, especially by substitution in many cases of *i* for *y*.

CHALMERS published the *Conf. Amantis* in vol. ii. of the collection of British Poets, 1810, taking the text from Berthelette's edition of 1554.

PAULI professed to follow Berthelette's first edition with collation throughout of MSS. Harl. 7184 and 3869, and occasional reference to Harl. 3490 and the Stafford MS. It is almost impossible that this full collation can really have been made, for by it nearly all Berthelette's errors might have been corrected, whereas we find them as a matter

---

[1] In the case of most of these passages the text proves them to be taken from Caxton's edition. Thus in Prol. 497 both editions omit ' to,' Prol. 583 both omit ' propre,' i. 2248 both have 'Vnder graue' for 'Vnder the grene,' in 2354 ' other' for ' thilke,' and in 2372 ' in me' for ' I me.'

of fact on every page of Pauli's edition. As to the critical judgement of the editor, it is enough to say that he regarded Harl. 7184 as a better authority for the text and spelling than either Harl. 3869 or the Stafford MS. (being attracted apparently by the external magnificence of the volume), and that he actually pronounced it to be of the fourteenth cent. His diligence may be measured by the fact that because Harl. 3490 stops short at viii. 3062* (in the middle of a sentence), being left unfinished by the scribe, therefore Pauli's edition omits the remainder of this conclusion, 3063*–3114* [1], though he had the MS. in the Royal Library (R) within his reach, by means of which he might have completed his copy. He is also seriously inaccurate in the statements which he makes about the Stafford MS. as regards the additional passages.

A certain number of the errors in Berthelette's edition are corrected, but very many remain, and in some cases further corruption has been introduced by the editor, either from Harl. 7184 or otherwise. The orthography has been ' restored,' but hardly with success.

MORLEY (1889) followed Pauli's text, with conjectural alterations of his own, and a few corrections from Berthelette, as i. 773. Often the changes are quite wrong, e. g. Prol. 82, 608, i. 777, 1675 f., 2957 f., the most extraordinary perhaps being iv. 2408 f. The editor professes to omit iii. 142–338 and a few lines here and there in other places. The omissions, however, are much more extensive than this seems to imply. In the fourth book alone they are as follows, 401–408, 428–436, 443–506, 516–523, 1467–1475, 1490–1594, 2131–2182, 2754–2770, 2858–2862, 2883–2888, 3181–3302, and in some cases it is impossible even to conjecture on what principle they are made.

THE PRESENT EDITION. The text follows the Bodleian Fairfax MS. and every deviation from this is noted. The critical apparatus is constructed upon the following principles.

Three manuscripts have been collated throughout with the text of F, viz. Bodley 902 (A), Corpus Christi Coll. 67 (C), and Bodley 294 (B). These are selected to represent respectively the first recension revised, the first recension unrevised, and the second recension texts. A is an excellent copy, the best of its class, C is a carefully written MS., the best of the group to which it belongs, with the exception of Egerton 1991, and B, besides being a good copy

---

[1] These lines have never been printed in any edition before the present, though published separately by K. Meyer in his *John Gower's Beziehungen*, &c., 1889, and by Prof. Easton of the University of Pennsylvania in his *Readings in Gower*, 1895. There are a large number of sound emendations from the Brit. Museum MSS. suggested in this latter book, but the author had no clear idea of the principles on which the text should be constructed.

and almost the only second recension MS. which is not imperfect, has perhaps a special claim to attention because its text is of the type which all the editions except that of Caxton have followed. In all cases where variation has been found, except where it is merely of form and spelling or of a very trifling and accidental kind, the readings of at least fourteen other selected copies have been ascertained, and by this procedure those variations which are merely individual have been distinguished from those which are shared by a class or a group. The result is given in the critical notes, all the variations of A and B being there cited except those that are very trifling [1], while the readings of C are usually given only when shared by some other manuscript.

It is important that it should be observed which the manuscripts are which have thus been referred to and how their evidence is cited. They are divided always according to their recension, first, second or third, and they are cited in an unvarying order, as follows : AJMH₁ X(G)ERCLB₂, SAdBTΔ, FWH₃ (or K), so that A . . . B₂ means the whole series of the first class, and S . . . Δ that of the second, while H₁ . . . B₂ stands for H₁X(G)ERCLB₂, and E . . . B₂ for ERCLB₂. These nineteen (or eighteen) manuscripts are present as witnesses throughout, whether named or not; for when the manuscripts are named which give a variation, it is to be assumed that the remainder have the reading of the text. Thus the note

' 1295 wisdom] wordes H₁ . . . B₂, H₃ '

must be taken to imply that ' wisdom ' is the reading of AJM, SAdBTΔ, FW and ' wordes ' of H₁XGERCLB₂, H₃ :

' 1296 gostly B '

means that the reading of the text, ' goodly,' is given by every one of the nineteen except B :

' 1318 How þer(e) H₁G . . . B₂ '

means that the reading of the text is that of AJMX, SAdBTΔ, FWH₃ and that of the note belongs to H₁GERCLB₂ :

' 1330 for to] þat þou SAdBTΔ '

indicates a reading of the second recension only :

[1] The following will serve as examples of those omitted : iii. 367 tawh B
422 vngood lieste A   618 is (for it) A   652 softe softe B   658 sely
sely B   739 marg. litigabant B   864 artow B   923 he (for
hem) B   iv. 635 f. betake . . . þurghsott A   650 wedde A   1105 no
wol no B   1229 herte B   1239 þo (for þou) A, &c.

'3340 tho] þe AM ... B₂'

stands for the fact that all the first recension copies except J vary
from F, while the rest agree. Occasionally readings of other MSS.
are cited besides those mentioned above, as Y, Λ or Magd., but the
absence of such citation must not be taken to imply anything.

It must be observed, however, that in some cases a more limited
reference seemed desirable, especially on matters of form and
spelling, points about which it would be idle to adduce any
evidence but that of a few copies. Where selection of this kind
is employed, the manuscripts on both sides are cited : thus such
notes as

'3691 set AJ, S, F   sette C, B,'
'4307 all S, F   alle AJ, B'

must not be taken to imply the reading of any copy except those
mentioned. In a few cases this form is used to avoid misunderstanding in passages where the record of readings is for some
reason incomplete, as i. 2300, viii. 566, 1713, 1927.

In citing a variation as given by a class or group of MSS. no
attempt is made to give the spelling of each one separately. The
form cited is that given either by the majority or by a leading MS.
with variations sometimes added in parentheses.

Attention should be paid also to the following points : (1) It was not
found possible to complete the collation of the Glasgow MS. (G) before
the text was printed, and consequently its readings must not be taken
as implied, when not mentioned, any further than v. 1970. The collation has since been completed and some of the results are noted in the
account of the MS. (2) K takes the place of H₃ in vi. 1671–vii. 1405,
and vii. 3594 to the end, where H₃ is defective. (3) Before assuming
the evidence of any MS. *ex silentio* it is necessary that the reader
should assure himself that it is not defective in the part concerned.
The means of doing this are fully afforded by the accounts given of the
separate MSS., where their imperfections are noted, and it must be
remembered that J and Ad are for the most part defective as regards
the Latin summaries, and that this is the case with T also in certain
parts. The readings of S on f. 50 are for the most part passed over,
as not originally belonging to that MS. (4) A few abbreviated Latin
terms are used in the critical notes, as *in ras.* to indicate that the text
is written over an erasure, or *p. m.* to denote the reading of the first
hand.

The lines are numbered in each book (for the first time), and
the numbers with an asterisk attached are those of the lines in
other recensions than that of the text. In addition to this it

should be observed that as nearly all references to Gower for the last forty years have been made by Pauli's edition, it has been thought advisable to place in the margin of this text indications of the volumes and pages of that edition: thus **P. I. 153** stands for 'Pauli, vol. i. p. 153.'

Setting aside matters of spelling, punctuation and grammatical form, we may note that the material differences of reading between the text of this edition and that of Pauli are in number about two thousand.

OTHER ENGLISH WORKS. With regard to the text of the poem *In Praise of Peace* all that need be said will be found in the notes upon it. The Trentham MS., which contains it, has already been fully described in the volume of 'French Works.'

A poem in five seven-line stanzas, beginning 'Passe forthe þou pilgryme and bridel wele þy beste,' occurs in (Shirley's) MS. Ashmole 59, f. 17 vᵒ (Bodl. Libr.), with the title 'Balade moral of gode counseyle made by Gower.' The same without the final stanza (owing to loss of a leaf) occurs in MS. Rawlinson C. 86, but with no title or ascription of authorship, and both texts have been printed (not quite correctly) by Dr. Karl Meyer in his *John Gower's Beziehungen*, &c., 1889. In addition to these copies there is one in the British Museum MS. Addit. 29729, which has been published by Dr. Max Förster in the *Archiv für das Studium der neueren Sprachen*, vol. 102, p. 50. In this MS. the piece is ascribed to Benedict Burgh, and it is called 'A leson to kepe well the tonge.'

It is almost impossible that these verses can have been written by Gower, but out of deference to Shirley's authority (which is not very weighty however), and in order that the reader may judge, it is printed here, all deviations from the Ashmole text being noted, except in the case of 'th' for 'þ,' and some readings of the Rawlinson copy (R) being added in parentheses.

BALADE MORAL OF GODE COUNSEYLE MADE BY GOWER.

Passe forth, thou pilgryme, and bridel wel thy beeste;
Loke not agein for thing that may betyde;
Thenke what thou wilt, but speke ay with the leeste;
Avyse thee wel who stondeth thee besyde;
Let not thyne herte beo with thy tonge bewryde;
Trust not to muche in fayre visayginge,
For peynted cheere shapeth efft to stynge.

1 forþe wele   2 ageine   4 weele   stondeþe   7 shapeþe (efft] her R)

Byholde thy selff, or that thou other deme;
Ne beo not glad whane other done amyss ;
Sey never al that which wolde the sothe seme,   10
Thou maist not wite what thy fortune is:
For there is no wight on lyve iwyss
That stondeth sure, ther fore I rede beware,
And looke aboute for stumbling in the snare.

Reporte not muche on other mennes sawe ;
Be ay adrad to here a wicked fame ;
For man shal dye by dome of goddes lawe,
That here enpeyreth any mannes name.
Avyse thee wel ther fore or thow attame
Suche as thou mayst never revoke ageyn ;   20
A good name leste is leste for ay certain.

Pley not with pecus ne ffawvel to thy feere ;
Chese thou hem never, yif thou do affter me ;
The hande is hurt that bourdeth with the bere ;
Fawvel fareth even right as doth a bee ;
Hony mowthed, ful of swetnesse is she,
But loke behinde and ware thee from hir stonge,
Thow shalt have hurt yf thou play with hir longe.

Dispreyse no wight but if effte thou may him preyse,
Ne preyse no firre but thou may discomende :   30
Weyghe thy wordes and hem by mesure peyse ;
Thenke that the gilty may by grace amende,
And eke the gode may happen to offende :
Remember eke that what man doth amiss,
Thou hast or art or may be suche as he is.

This is full of lines that Gower would not have written, with superfluous syllables in the metre, as ll. 1, 5, 10, 17, 29, 33, 35 (omitting those that might pass with amended spelling), accent on weak syllables, as ll. 20, 25, 26, 31, defective rhyme, as 'besyde' : 'bewryde' (participle), and 'feere' (companion) : 'bere,' or suppression of syllable at the beginning, as in l. 12. The form 'mayst' (maist) for 'miht' is not found in any respectable Gower MS. Moreover the style is not that of Gower, but evidently imitated from Chaucer's poem 'Fle from the pres.'

9 gladde (glad R)   amysse   10 þee   11 wit (witte R)   12 ewysse
13 stondeþe   15 mens (mennys R)   16 adradde   18 enpeyreþe   mans
(mannes R)   19 wele   þowe   20 ageyne   21 gode (good R)
certaine   22 (Playe not pecus R)   24 hurte   bourdeþe
(a brere R)   25 fareþe   doþe   26 right ful (full R)   27 frome   28 þowe
shalt kache hareme to pley wᵗ þeos beestis longe (Thow shalt haue hurt yf
þou play with her longe R)   34 Remembre doþe amisse   35 haste arte

CORRIGENDA

p. 464, note on 745 ff., *add* The authority here followed is the *Trésor* of Brunetto Latini, pp. 84–88 (ed. 1863).

p. 468, note on 463 ff., *add* The authority for this is perhaps the *Trésor*, p. 191.

p. 489, note on 2459 ff., *for* I am unable . . . form of it. *read* The name Geta was taken by Gower from the *Geta* of Vitalis Blesensis, a dramatic piece in Latin elegiacs founded on Plautus, in which Geta takes the place of Sosia: see Wright's *Early Mysteries*, &c., pp. 79–90.

CONFESSIO AMANTIS

i. *Torpor, ebes sensus, scola parua labor minimusque*
Causant quo minimus ipse minora canam :
Qua tamen Engisti lingua canit Insula Bruti
Anglica Carmente metra iuuante loquar.
Ossibus ergo carens que conterit ossa loquelis
Absit, et interpres stet procul oro malus.

Incipit Prologus

Of hem that writen ous tofore
The bokes duelle, and we therfore
Ben tawht of that was write tho :
Forthi good is that we also
In oure tyme among ous hiere
Do wryte of newe som matiere,
Essampled of these olde wyse
So that it myhte in such a wyse,

The text is that of F (Fairfax 3). The MSS. most commonly cited are the following :—

Of the first recension, A (Bodley 902), J (St. John's Coll. Camb. B 12), M (Camb. Univ. Mm. 2. 21), E₂ (Egerton 913), H₁ (Harleian 3490), Y (Marquess of Bute's), X (Soc. of Antiquaries 134), G (Glasgow, Hunterian Mus. S i. 7), E (Egerton 1991), R (Reg. 18 C xxii.), C (Corpus Christi Coll. Oxf. 67), L (Laud 609), B₂ (Bodley 693).

Of the second, S (Stafford), Ad. (Brit. Mus. Addit. 12043), B (Bodley 294), T (Trin. Coll. Camb. R 3. 2), Δ (Sidney Coll. Camb. Δ 4. 1).

Of the third, F (Fairfax 3), W (Wadham Coll. 13), K (Keswick Hall), H₃ (Harl. 7184), Magd. (Magdalen Coll. Oxf. 213).

5 ff. time, write, wise, &c., S   6 Do ME₂H₁, SΛ, FWKH₃
So JXGRB₂, B   To CL   7 Essampled (Ensampled) JME₂H₁, SΛ,
FWKH₃ Ensamples X ... B₂ &c., B   8 awyse F   a wise S

** B

[DESIGN OF THE
BOOK.]

Whan we ben dede and elleswhere,
Beleve to the worldes eere   10
In tyme comende after this.
Bot for men sein, and soth it is,
That who that al of wisdom writ
It dulleth ofte a mannes wit
To him that schal it aldai rede,   P. i. 2
For thilke cause, if that ye rede,
I wolde go the middel weie
And wryte a bok betwen the tweie,
Somwhat of lust, somewhat of lore,
That of the lasse or of the more   20
Som man mai lyke of that I wryte :
And for that fewe men endite
In oure englissh, I thenke make
*A bok for Engelondes sake,
The yer sextenthe of kyng Richard.   P. i. 3
What schal befalle hierafterward
God wot, for now upon this tyde
Men se the world on every syde
In sondry wyse so diversed,
That it welnyh stant al reversed,   30
As forto speke of tyme ago.

Hic in principio
declarat qualiter in
anno Regis Ricardi
secundi sexto decimo
Iohannes Gower pre-
sentem libellum com-
posuit et finaliter com-
pleuit, quem strenu-
issimo domino suo
domino Henrico de
Lancastria tunc Der-
beie Comiti cum omni
reuerencia specialiter
destinauit.

---

*A bok for king Richardes sake,
To whom belongeth my ligeance
With al myn hertes obeissance
In al that evere a liege man
Unto his king may doon or can :
So ferforth I me recomande
To him which al me may comande,   30*
Preyende unto the hihe regne

15 rede *om.* B   23 Englisch S   24-92 *These lines are found in
copies of the third recension* (FH2NKH3Magd.W &c.) *and also in* SΛ. *The
rest have* 24*-92*. *The marginal note,* ' Hic in principio—destinauit,' *is
found only in* ΛP2, KH3Magd. *Of these,* Magd. *has* in principio
libri *for* in principio, *and* Λ *gives* quarto *for* sexto.   28 on] in S
29, 30 *Two lines omitted in* S
    24*-92* *All variations from* B *are noted.*   24* book B
25* bilongeþ B   27* euer B   29* f. recomaunde . . . comaunde B
31* Prayend B

The cause whi it changeth so
It needeth nought to specifie,
The thing so open is at ẙe
That every man it mai beholde: **P. i. 4**
And natheles be daies olde,
Whan that the bokes weren levere,
Wrytinge was beloved evere
Of hem that weren vertuous;
For hier in erthe amonges ous,   40
If noman write hou that it stode,
The pris of hem that weren goode
Scholde, as who seith, a gret partie
Be lost: so for to magnifie
The worthi princes that tho were,
The bokes schewen hiere and there,
Wherof the world ensampled is;

Which causeth every king to regne,
That his corone longe stonde.
I thenke and have it understonde,
As it bifel upon a tyde,
As thing which scholde tho betyde,—
Under the toun of newe Troye,
Which tok of Brut his ferste joye,
In Temse whan it was flowende
As I be bote cam rowende,
So as fortune hir tyme sette,
My liege lord par chaunce I mette;
And so befel, as I cam nyh,
Out of my bot, whan he me syh,
He bad me come in to his barge.
And whan I was with him at large,
Amonges othre thinges seid

Hic declarat in primis qualiter ob reuerenciam serenissimi principis domini sui Regis Anglie Ricardi secundi totus suus humilis Iohannes Gower, licet graui infirmitate a diu multipliciter fatigatus, huius opusculi labores suscipere non recusauit, set tanquam fauum ex variis floribus recollectum, presentem libellum ex variis cronicis, historiis, poetarum phi-

40*

33 nouȝt S, F   38 Writing . . . belouyd S   41 no man S
46 schiewe S   47 essampled S
    36* bityde B   37* *margin* Regis Anglie Ricardi secundi
erased in B *leaving blank*   38* took B   39* Themese G
Themse R   40* by B   42* *margin* sed B   43* bifel B
43* f. neigh . . . seigh B   45* *margin* Cronicarum historiis XG
47* seyde B

[DESIGN OF THE
BOOK.]

And tho that deden thanne amis
Thurgh tirannie and crualte,   **P. i. 5**
Right as thei stoden in degre,   50
So was the wrytinge of here werk.
Thus I, which am a burel clerk,
Purpose forto wryte a bok
After the world that whilom tok
Long tyme in olde daies passed :
Bot for men sein it is now lassed,
In worse plit than it was tho,
I thenke forto touche also
The world which neweth every dai,
So as I can, so as I mai.   60
Thogh I seknesse have upon honde
And longe have had, yit woll I fonde
To wryte and do my bisinesse,
That in som part, so as I gesse,

---

losophorumque dictis,
quatenus sibi infirm-
itas permisit, studiosis-
sime compilauit.

He hath this charge upon me leid,
And bad me doo my besynesse
That to his hihe worthinesse   50*
Som newe thing I scholde boke,
That he himself it mihte loke
After the forme of my writynge.
And thus upon his comandynge
Myn herte is wel the more glad
To write so as he me bad ;
And eek my fere is wel the lasse
That non envye schal compasse
Withoute a resonable wite
To feyne and blame that I write.   60*
A gentil herte his tunge stilleth,
That it malice non distilleth,
But preyseth that is to be preised ;
But he that hath his word unpeysed

49 tirantie S   51 is þe writing S   52 bural S
63 Tho write S
48* leyde B   49* busynesse B   51* booke B   52* mightc
looke B   53* f. writyng . . . comaundyng B   55* hert B
59* Wiþout B   62* noon B

The wyse man mai ben avised.
For this prologe is so assised
That it to wisdom al belongeth :
What wysman that it underfongeth,
He schal drawe into remembrance
The fortune of this worldes chance, 70
The which noman in his persone
Mai knowe, bot the god al one.
Whan the prologe is so despended,
This bok schal afterward ben ended
Of love, which doth many a wonder
And many a wys man hath put under.
And in this wyse I thenke trete
Towardes hem that now be grete,
Betwen the vertu and the vice P. i. 6
Which longeth unto this office. 80

And handleth ⟨onwrong⟩ every thing,
I preye un to the hevene king
Fro suche tunges he me schilde.
And natheles this world is wilde
Of such jangling, and what befalle,
My kinges heste schal nought falle, 70*
That I, in hope to deserve
His thonk, ne schal his wil observe ;
And elles were I nought excused,
For that thing may nought be refused
Which that a king himselve bit.
Forthi the symplesce of my wit
I thenke if that it myhte avayle
In his service to travaile :
Though I seknesse have upon honde,
And longe have had, yit wol I fonde, 80*

68 wise man S   71 no man S   72 allone S   75 awonder F.
76 awys man F   a wise man S.   80 officie F
   65* handeleþ B   onkrong euery H₁ outkrong euery JME₂XGR
CL   outkroud euery B₂   outtrong euery Ar   outkrong eny B   out
wronge ony Cath.   66* pray B   heuene GR   heuen B
69* bifalle B   75* Which JME₂XGCL   What H₁RB₂, B   byt B
76* ffor þy B   77* it might (it myht) JME₂CL   it may GRB₂, B
I may H₁ Sn   it XCath.   78* to do trauayle G   80* long B

[DEDICATION.]

Bot for my wittes ben to smale
To tellen every man his tale,
This bok, upon amendment
To stonde at his commandement,
With whom myn herte is of accord,
I sende unto myn oghne lord,
Which of Lancastre is Henri named :
The hyhe god him hath proclamed
Ful of knyhthode and alle grace.
So woll I now this werk embrace   90
With hol trust and with hol believe ;
God grante I mot it wel achieve.

[THE FORMER TIME BETTER THAN THIS.]

ii. *Tempus preteritum presens fortuna beatum*
*   Linquit, et antiquas vertit in orbe vias.*
Progenuit veterem concors dileccio pacem,
*   Dum facies hominis nuncia mentis erat :*
Legibus vnicolor tunc temporis aura refulsit,
*   Iusticie plane tuncque fuere vie.*
Nuncque latens odium vultum depingit amoris,
*   Paceque sub ficta tempus ad arma tegit ;*
Instar et ex variis mutabile Cameliontis
*   Lex gerit, et regnis sunt noua iura nouis :*   (10)

So as I made my beheste,
To make a bok after his heste,
And write in such a maner wise,
Which may be wisdom to the wise
And pley to hem that lust to pleye.
But in proverbe I have herd seye
That who that wel his werk begynneth
The rather a good ende he wynneth ;
And thus the prologe of my bok
After the world that whilom tok,   90*
And eek somdel after the newe,
I wol begynne for to newe.

Latin Verses ii. 2 antūnas . . . vrbe S   6 ff. tunc que . . . Nunc que . . . Pace que . . . sic que F   8 subficta S
  81* byheste B   82* book B   87* bygynneþ B
89* f. book . . . took B   92* bygynne B   for to newe
JME₂H₁XGR, B   for the newe D Ar.   for to schewe CLB₂

Climata que fuerant solidissima sicque per orbem
Soluuntur, nec eo centra quietis habent.

If I schal drawe in to my mynde
The tyme passed, thanne I fynde
The world stod thanne in al his welthe :
Tho was the lif of man in helthe,
Tho was plente, tho was richesse,
Tho was the fortune of prouesse,
Tho was knyhthode in pris be name,
Wherof the wyde worldes fame   100
Write in Cronique is yit withholde ;   **P. i. 7**
Justice of lawe tho was holde,
The privilege of regalie
Was sauf, and al the baronie
Worschiped was in his astat ;
The citees knewen no debat,
The poeple stod in obeissance
Under the reule of governance,
And pes, which ryhtwisnesse keste,
With charite tho stod in reste :   110
Of mannes herte the corage
Was schewed thanne in the visage ;
The word was lich to the conceite
Withoute semblant of deceite :
Tho was ther unenvied love,
Tho was the vertu sett above
And vice was put under fote.
Now stant the crop under the rote,
The world is changed overal,
And therof most in special   120
That love is falle into discord.

De statu regnorum,
vt dicunt, secundum
temporalia, videlicet
tempore regis Ricardi
secundi anno regni
sui sexto decimo.

96 *margin* videlicet—sexto decimo *inserted only in* MSS. *of the third*
recension, FWKH₃ &c.   S *has instead of it (after space of one line),* Nota
quod tempore creacionis huius libri fuerunt guerre et opiniones guer-
rarum tam in sancta Cristi ecclesia quam per singula mundi regna
quasi vniuersaliter diuulgate.   Quapropter in hoc presenti prologo
euentus tam graues scriptor per singulos gradus specialiter deplangit.
So Λ *without space and with* dei *for* Cristi   109 which
JME₂CL, FKH₃   wiþ H₁XGRB₂, SBΛ, W   113 word JME₂B₂, Λ,
FWK &c.   world H₁XGRCL &c., SB   115 vnenuied JME₂, S,
FWK &c.   vneuened Λ   noon enuyed (non enuied) H₁ . . . B₂, B

[TEMPORAL RULERS.]

And that I take to record
Of every lond for his partie
The comun vois, which mai noght lie;
Noght upon on, bot upon alle
It is that men now clepe and calle,
And sein the regnes ben divided,
In stede of love is hate guided,
The werre wol no pes purchace,
And lawe hath take hire double face,   130
So that justice out of the weie   P. i. 8
With ryhtwisnesse is gon aweie:
And thus to loke on every halve,
Men sen the sor withoute salve,
Which al the world hath overtake.
Ther is no regne of alle outtake,
For every climat hath his diel
After the tornynge of the whiel,
Which blinde fortune overthroweth;
Wherof the certain noman knoweth: 140
The hevene wot what is to done,
Bot we that duelle under the mone
Stonde in this world upon a weer,
And namely bot the pouer
Of hem that ben the worldes guides
With good consail on alle sides
Be kept upriht in such a wyse,
That hate breke noght thassise
Of love, which is al the chief
To kepe a regne out of meschief.   150
For alle resoun wolde this,

Apostolus. Regem honorificate.

That unto him which the heved is
The membres buxom scholden bowe,
And he scholde ek her trowthe allowe,
With al his herte and make hem chiere,

Salomon. Omnia fac cum consilio.

For good consail is good to hiere.
Althogh a man be wys himselve,

124 comun GC, S   comune B, F   127 the] þat H₁RB₂, B
143 a weer S   a wer B   aweer F   144 A *begins here*
147 S *has lost a leaf*, ll. 147–320   149 which A, B   whiche F
155 his *om.* B   157 aman F

Yit is the wisdom more of tuelve ;
And if thei stoden bothe in on,
To hope it were thanne anon   160
That god his grace wolde sende   **P. i. 9**
To make of thilke werre an ende,
Which every day now groweth newe :
And that is gretly forto rewe
In special for Cristes sake,
Which wolde his oghne lif forsake
Among the men to yeve pes.
But now men tellen natheles
That love is fro the world departed,
So stant the pes unevene parted   170
With hem that liven now adaies.
Bot forto loke at alle assaies,
To him that wolde resoun seche
After the comun worldes speche
It is to wondre of thilke werre,
In which non wot who hath the werre ;
For every lond himself deceyveth
And of desese his part receyveth,
And yet ne take men no kepe.
Bot thilke lord which al may kepe,   180
To whom no consail may ben hid,
Upon the world which is betid,
Amende that wherof men pleigne
With trewe hertes and with pleine,
And reconcile love ayeyn,
As he which is king sovereign
Of al the worldes governaunce,
And of his hyhe porveaunce
Afferme pes betwen the londes
And take her cause into hise hondes,   190
So that the world may stonde appesed **P. i. 10**
And his godhede also be plesed.

iii. *Quas coluit Moises vetus aut nouus ipse Iohannes,*
    Hesternas leges vix colit ista dies.

159 stoden AJME₂L, Δ, FKH₃   stonden H₁ . . . RB₂ &c., BΛ, W
169 loue AJME₂XL, FWKH₃ it E, B *om.* H₁RB₂Sn

Sic prius ecclesia bina virtute polita
Nunc magis inculta pallet vtraque via.
Pacificam Petri vaginam mucro resumens
Horruit ad Cristi verba cruoris iter;
Nunc tamen assiduo gladium de sanguine tinctum
Vibrat auaricia, lege tepente sacra.
Sic lupus est pastor, pater hostis, mors miserator,
Predoque largitor, pax et in orbe timor.   (10)

De statu cleri, vt
dicunt, secundum spi-
ritualia, videlicet tem-
pore Roberti Gibbon-
ensis, qui nomen Clem-
entis sibi sortitus est,
tunc antipape.

To thenke upon the daies olde,
The lif of clerkes to beholde,
Men sein how that thei weren tho
Ensample and reule of alle tho
Whiche of wisdom the vertu soughten.
Unto the god ferst thei besoughten
As to the substaunce of her Scole,
That thei ne scholden noght befole   200
Her wit upon none erthly werkes,
Which were ayein thestat of clerkes,
And that thei myhten fle the vice
Which Simon hath in his office,
Wherof he takth the gold in honde.
For thilke tyme I understonde
The Lumbard made non eschange
The bisschopriches forto change,
Ne yet a lettre for to sende
For dignite ne for Provende,   210
Or cured or withoute cure.
The cherche keye in aventure
Of armes and of brygantaille   **P. i. 11**
Stod nothing thanne upon bataille;
To fyhte or for to make cheste
It thoghte hem thanne noght honeste;
Bot of simplesce and pacience
Thei maden thanne no defence:
The Court of worldly regalie

Latin Verses iii. 8 tepente JE₂, ΔΛ, FWKH₃   repente AMH₁ ... B₂
B, Magd.   10 Predo que F
194 ff. *margin* De statu—antipape *om.* AE₂   videlicet—antipape
inserted in third recension only (different hand in F)   201 ertly F
205 an honde R, B   anhonde H₁B₂   210 prebende A, Λ   215 for
om. XGLB₂, WH₃   219 worþy(-i) H₁ERLB₂, B   worlde W

To hem was thanne no baillie;   220
The vein honour was noght desired,
Which hath the proude herte fyred;
Humilite was tho withholde,
And Pride was a vice holde.
Of holy cherche the largesse
Yaf thanne and dede gret almesse
To povere men that hadden nede:
Thei were ek chaste in word and dede,
Wherof the poeple ensample tok;
Her lust was al upon the bok,   230
Or forto preche or forto preie,
To wisse men the ryhte weie
Of suche as stode of trowthe unliered.
Lo, thus was Petres barge stiered
Of hem that thilke tyme were,
And thus cam ferst to mannes Ere
The feith of Crist and alle goode
Thurgh hem that thanne weren goode
And sobre and chaste and large and wyse.
Bot now men sein is otherwise,   240
Simon the cause hath undertake,
The worldes swerd on honde is take;
And that is wonder natheles,   **P. i. 12**
Whan Crist him self hath bode pes
And set it in his testament,
How now that holy cherche is went,
Of that here lawe positif
Hath set to make werre and strif
For worldes good, which may noght laste.
God wot the cause to the laste   250
Of every right and wrong also;
But whil the lawe is reuled so
That clerkes to the werre entende,
I not how that thei scholde amende
The woful world in othre thinges,
To make pes betwen the kynges
After the lawe of charite,
Which is the propre duete

234 Petrus H₁E . . . B₂, W   Petris XG   249 wich F

Belongende unto the presthode.
Bot as it thenkth to the manhode,   260
The hevene is ferr, the world is nyh,
And veine gloire is ek so slyh,
Which coveitise hath now withholde,
That thei non other thing beholde,
Bot only that thei myhten winne.
And thus the werres thei beginne,
Wherof the holi cherche is taxed,
That in the point as it is axed
The disme goth to the bataille,
As thogh Crist myhte noght availe   270
To don hem riht be other weie.
In to the swerd the cherche keie
Is torned, and the holy bede   P. i. 13
Into cursinge, and every stede
Which scholde stonde upon the feith
And to this cause an Ere leyth,
Astoned is of the querele.
That scholde be the worldes hele
Is now, men sein, the pestilence
Which hath exiled pacience   280
Fro the clergie in special :
And that is schewed overal,
In eny thing whan thei ben grieved.
Bot if Gregoire be believed,
As it is in the bokes write,
He doth ous somdel forto wite
The cause of thilke prelacie,
Wher god is noght of compaignie :
For every werk as it is founded
Schal stonde or elles be confounded ;   290
Who that only for Cristes sake
Desireth cure forto take,
And noght for pride of thilke astat,
To bere a name of a prelat,
He schal be resoun do profit

260 to þe manhod(e) AJME2, ΔΛ, FW   to m. H1 ... B2, B   to make
m. KH3   267 þe FKH3Magd.   þat A ... B2 &c., BΔΛ   om. W
280 paciencie F

In holy cherche upon the plit
That he hath set his conscience;
Bot in the worldes reverence
Ther ben of suche manie glade,
Whan thei to thilke astat ben made,
Noght for the merite of the charge,
Bot for thei wolde hemself descharge
Of poverte and become grete;
And thus for Pompe and for beyete
The Scribe and ek the Pharisee
Of Moïses upon the See
In the chaiere on hyh ben set;
Wherof the feith is ofte let,
Which is betaken hem to kepe.
In Cristes cause alday thei slepe,
Bot of the world is noght foryete;
For wel is him that now may gete
Office in Court to ben honoured.
The stronge coffre hath al devoured
Under the keye of avarice
The tresor of the benefice,
Wherof the povere schulden clothe
And ete and drinke and house bothe;
The charite goth al unknowe,
For thei no grein of Pite sowe:
And slouthe kepeth the libraire
Which longeth to the Saintuaire;
To studie upon the worldes lore
Sufficeth now withoute more;
Delicacie his swete toth
Hath fostred so that it fordoth
Of abstinence al that ther is.
And forto loken over this,
If Ethna brenne in the clergie,
Al openly to mannes yё
At Avynoun thexperience

[The Church.]

Gregorius. Terrenis
lucris inhiant, honore
prelacie gaudent, et
300 non vt prosint, set vt
presint, episcopatum
desiderant.

P. i. 14

310

320

330

317 povere] pore þei (þai) CL, W (pouere þey)   321 S *resumes*
331 *Copies of first and second recensions have here, in margin* Anno
domini Millesimo CCC° Nonagesimo. S *gives this with the addition* quia
tunc erat ecclesia diuisa *and so also* RSnDAr, Δ F *has an erasure in
the margin.*

Therof hath yove an evidence,
Of that men sen hem so divided.   **P. i. 15**
And yit the cause is noght decided ;
Bot it is seid and evere schal,
Betwen tuo Stoles lyth the fal,
Whan that men wenen best to sitte :
In holy cherche of such a slitte
Is for to rewe un to ous alle ;
God grante it mote wel befalle   340
Towardes him which hath the trowthe.
Bot ofte is sen that mochel slowthe,
Whan men ben drunken of the cuppe,
Doth mochel harm, whan fyr is uppe,
Bot if somwho the flamme stanche ;
And so to speke upon this branche,
Which proud Envie hath mad to springe,
Of Scisme, causeth forto bringe
This newe Secte of Lollardie,
And also many an heresie   350
Among the clerkes in hemselve.
It were betre dike and delve
And stonde upon the ryhte feith,
Than knowe al that the bible seith
And erre as somme clerkes do.
Upon the hond to were a Schoo
And sette upon the fot a Glove
Acordeth noght to the behove
Of resonable mannes us :
If men behielden the vertus   360
That Crist in Erthe taghte here,
Thei scholden noght in such manere,
Among hem that ben holden wise,   **P. i. 16**
The Papacie so desguise
Upon diverse eleccioun,
Which stant after thaffeccioun
Of sondry londes al aboute :
Bot whan god wole, it schal were oute,

336 lyþ F (*in ras.*) KH₃Magd.   is A ... B₂ &c., SBΔΛ   338 flitte
AXGCL   341 whiche F   347 proud A, SB   proude C, F
354 that] what EB₂, B

For trowthe mot stonde ate laste.
Bot yet thei argumenten faste   370
Upon the Pope and his astat,
Wherof thei falle in gret debat;
This clerk seith yee, that other nay,
And thus thei dryve forth the day,
And ech of hem himself amendeth
Of worldes good, bot non entendeth
To that which comun profit were.
Thei sein that god is myhti there,
And schal ordeine what he wile,
Ther make thei non other skile   380
Where is the peril of the feith,
Bot every clerk his herte leith
To kepe his world in special,
And of the cause general,
Which unto holy cherche longeth,
Is non of hem that underfongeth
To schapen eny resistence:
And thus the riht hath no defence,
Bot ther I love, ther I holde.
Lo, thus tobroke is Cristes folde,   390
Wherof the flock withoute guide
Devoured is on every side,
In lacke of hem that ben unware   **P. i. 17**
Schepherdes, whiche her wit beware
Upon the world in other halve.
The scharpe pricke in stede of salve
Thei usen now, wherof the hele
Thei hurte of that thei scholden hele;
And what Schep that is full of wulle
Upon his back, thei toose and pulle,   400
Whil ther is eny thing to pile:
And thogh ther be non other skile
Bot only for thei wolden wynne,
Thei leve noght, whan thei begynne,
Upon her acte to procede,
Which is no good schepherdes dede.

370 argumeten F   373 This . . . þat AJM, SΛ, F &c.   This . . .
þis E₂X . . . B₂, B   The . . . this H₁   396 pricke *om.* A

And upon this also men sein,
That fro the leese which is plein
Into the breres thei forcacche
Her Orf, for that thei wolden lacche   410
With such duresce, and so bereve
That schal upon the thornes leve
Of wulle, which the brere hath tore ;
Wherof the Schep ben al totore
Of that the hierdes make hem lese.
Lo, how thei feignen chalk for chese,
For though thei speke and teche wel,
Thei don hemself therof no del :
For if the wolf come in the weie,
Her gostly Staf is thanne aweie,   420
Wherof thei scholde her flock defende ;
Bot if the povere Schep offende
In eny thing, thogh it be lyte,   **P. i. 18**
They ben al redy forto smyte ;
And thus, how evere that thei tale,
The strokes falle upon the smale,
And upon othre that ben grete
Hem lacketh herte forto bete.
So that under the clerkes lawe
Men sen the Merel al mysdrawe,   430
I wol noght seie in general,
For ther ben somme in special
In whom that alle vertu duelleth,

Qui vocatur a deo
tanquam Aaron.

And tho ben, as thapostel telleth,
That god of his eleccioun
Hath cleped to perfeccioun
In the manere as Aaron was :
Thei ben nothing in thilke cas
Of Simon, which the foldes gate
Hath lete, and goth in othergate,   440
Bot thei gon in the rihte weie.
Ther ben also somme, as men seie,
That folwen Simon ate hieles,

409 forcacche AME2, SΛΛ, FWKH3   forþ cacche H1 . . . B2, B
for tacche (?) J   410 Her Orf] Herof (Here of) RCSn, Δ
Wheorof H1   Therof Λ   419 com FK   421 folk EC, W

Whos carte goth upon the whieles [The Church.]
Of coveitise and worldes Pride,
And holy cherche goth beside,
Which scheweth outward a visage
Of that is noght in the corage.
For if men loke in holy cherche,
Betwen the word and that thei werche 450
Ther is a full gret difference :
Thei prechen ous in audience
That noman schal his soule empeire, **P. i. 19**
For al is bot a chirie feire
This worldes good, so as thei telle ;
Also thei sein ther is an helle,
Which unto mannes sinne is due,
And bidden ous therfore eschue
That wikkid is, and do the goode.
Who that here wordes understode, 460
It thenkth thei wolden do the same ;
Bot yet betwen ernest and game
Ful ofte it torneth other wise.
With holy tales thei devise
How meritoire is thilke dede
Of charite, to clothe and fede
The povere folk and forto parte
The worldes good, bot thei departe
Ne thenken noght fro that thei have.
Also thei sein, good is to save 470
With penance and with abstinence
Of chastite the continence ;
Bot pleinly forto speke of that,
I not how thilke body fat,
Which thei with deynte metes kepe
And leyn it softe forto slepe,
Whan it hath elles al his wille,
With chastite schal stonde stille :
And natheles I can noght seie,
In aunter if that I misseye. 480
Touchende of this, how evere it stonde,

450 thei] men B   453 apeyre AM   457 vnto mannes soule is
AME₂ is to mannes synne B
**   C

[THE CHURCH.]

I here and wol noght understonde,
For therof have I noght to done :   P. i. 20
Bot he that made ferst the Mone,
The hyhe god, of his goodnesse,
If ther be cause, he it redresce.
Bot what as eny man accuse,
This mai reson of trowthe excuse ;
The vice of hem that ben ungoode
Is no reproef unto the goode :   490
For every man hise oghne werkes
Schal bere, and thus as of the clerkes
The goode men ben to comende,
And alle these othre god amende :
For thei ben to the worldes ÿe
The Mirour of ensamplerie,
To reulen and to taken hiede
Betwen the men and the godhiede.

[THE COMMONS.]

iv. *Vulgaris populus regali lege subactus*
Dum iacet, vt mitis agna subibit onus.
Si caput extollat et lex sua frena relaxet,
Vt sibi velle iubet, Tigridis instar habet.
Ignis, aqua dominans duo sunt pietate carentes,
Ira tamen plebis est violenta magis.

De statu plebis, vt
dicunt, secundum ac-
cidencium mutabilia.

Now forto speke of the comune,
It is to drede of that fortune   500
Which hath befalle in sondri londes :
Bot often for defalte of bondes
Al sodeinliche, er it be wist,
A Tonne, whanne his lye arist,
Tobrekth and renneth al aboute,
Which elles scholde noght gon oute ;
And ek fulofte a litel Skar
Upon a Banke, er men be war,
Let in the Strem, which with gret peine, P. i. 21
If evere man it schal restreigne.   510

486 he *om.* AM   487 as AJME₂, SΔ, FKH₃   þat H₁ . . . B₂, B
is W   495-498 *Four lines found only in third recension copies*
FWKH₃ &c.   501 *margin* mutabilia accidencium H₁RB₂, B
accidencia mutabilia X   510 euere (euer) AME₂X, SΔΛ, FKH₃
euery JH₁RB₂, W   eny CL, B

Wher lawe lacketh, errour groweth,
He is noght wys who that ne troweth,
For it hath proeved ofte er this ;
And thus the comun clamour is
In every lond wher poeple dwelleth,
And eche in his compleignte telleth
How that the world is al miswent,
And ther upon his jugement
Yifth every man in sondry wise.
Bot what man wolde himself avise,   520
His conscience and noght misuse,
He may wel ate ferste excuse
His god, which evere stant in on :
In him ther is defalte non,
So moste it stonde upon ousselve   [MAN THE CAUSE OF
Nought only upon ten ne twelve,   EVIL.]
Bot plenerliche upon ous alle,
For man is cause of that schal falle.

    And natheles yet som men wryte
And sein that fortune is to wyte,   530   Nota contra hoc,
And som men holde oppinion   quod aliqui sortem for-
That it is constellacion,   tune, aliqui influen-
Which causeth al that a man doth :   ciam planetarum po-
                                                     nunt, per quod, vt
God wot of bothe which is soth.   dicitur, rerum euentus
The world as of his propre kynde   necessario contingit.
Was evere untrewe, and as the blynde   Set pocius dicendum
Improprelich he demeth fame,   est, quod ea que nos
                                                     prospera et aduersa
He blameth that is noght to blame   in hoc mundo voca-
And preiseth that is noght to preise : P. i. 22   mus, secundum merita
                                                     et demerita hominum
Thus whan he schal the thinges peise,   540   digno dei iudicio pro-
Ther is deceipte in his balance,   veniunt.
And al is that the variance
Of ous, that scholde ous betre avise ;
For after that we falle and rise,
The world arist and falth withal,
So that the man is overal
His oghne cause of wel and wo.
That we fortune clepe so

518 argument B   543 scholde A, B, K   schold S, F

[MAN THE CAUSE OF EVIL.]

Out of the man himself it groweth ;
And who that other wise troweth,   550
Behold the poeple of Irael :
For evere whil thei deden wel, .
Fortune was hem debonaire,
And whan thei deden the contraire,
Fortune was contrariende.
So that it proeveth wel at ende
Why that the world is wonderfull
And may no while stonde full,
Though that it seme wel besein ;
For every worldes thing is vein,   560
And evere goth the whiel aboute,
And evere stant a man in doute,
Fortune stant no while stille,
So hath ther noman al his wille.
Als fer as evere a man may knowe,
Ther lasteth nothing bot a throwe ;
The world stant evere upon debat,
So may be seker non astat,

Boicius. O quàm
dulcedo humane vite
multa amaritudine a-
spersa est !

Now hier now ther, now to now fro,   **P. i. 23**
Now up now down, this world goth so,   570
And evere hath don and evere schal :
Wherof I finde in special
A tale writen in the Bible,
Which moste nedes be credible ;
And that as in conclusioun
Seith that upon divisioun
Stant, why no worldes thing mai laste,
Til it be drive to the laste.
And fro the ferste regne of alle
Into this day, hou so befalle,   580
Of that the regnes be muable
The man himself hath be coupable,
Which of his propre governance
Fortuneth al the worldes chance.

551 Irael JM, S, FH₂N : *the rest* Israel   565 aman F   579-584
Six lines found only in third recension : cp. 495

v.   *Prosper et aduersus obliquo tramite versus*   [Nebuchadnezzar's
      Immundus mundus decipit omne genus.   Dream.]
    Mundus in euentu versatur vt alea casu,
      Quam celer in ludis iactat auara manus.
    Sicut ymago viri variantur tempora mundi,
      Statque nichil firmum preter amare deum.

    The hyhe almyhti pourveance,
    In whos eterne remembrance
    Fro ferst was every thing present,
    He hath his prophecie sent,
    In such a wise as thou schalt hiere,
    To Daniel of this matiere,   590
    Hou that this world schal torne and wende,   Hic in prologo
    Till it be falle to his ende ;   tractat de Statua illa,
    Wherof the tale telle I schal,   quam Rex Nabugodo-
                                                   nosor viderat in somp-
    In which it is betokned al.   nis, cuius caput au-
        As Nabugodonosor slepte,   P. i. 24   reum, pectus argen-
    A swevene him tok, the which he kepte   teum, venter eneus, ti-
                                                   bie ferree, pedum vero
    Til on the morwe he was arise,   quedam pars ferrea,
    For he therof was sore agrise.   quedam fictilis videba-
    To Daniel his drem he tolde,   tur, sub qua membror-
                                                   um diuersitate secun-
    And preide him faire that he wolde   600   dum Danielis exposi-
    Arede what it tokne may ;   cionem huius mundi
    And seide : ' Abedde wher I lay,   variacio figurabatur.
    Me thoghte I syh upon a Stage
    Wher stod a wonder strange ymage.
    His hed with al the necke also
    Thei were of fin gold bothe tuo ;
    His brest, his schuldres and his armes
    Were al of selver, bot the tharmes,
    The wombe and al doun to the kne,
    Of bras thei were upon to se ;   610
    The legges were al mad of Stiel,
    So were his feet also somdiel,
    And somdiel part to hem was take
    Of Erthe which men Pottes make ;

Latin Verses v. 3 vesatur vt H₁RB₂, B   vesatur et CL   4 ictat
H₁R, B   6 *line om.* H₁RB₂Sn, B
  588 send F   592 befalle F   608 the tharmes] þe armes M, Λ
tharmes B₂, H₃Magd.   610 weren on AX   611 made al AMH₁

[NEBUCHADNEZZAR'S
DREAM.]

Hic narrat vlterius
de quodam lapide
grandi, qui, vt in
dicto sompnio vide-
batur, ab excelso
monte super statuam
corruens ipsam quasi
in nichilum penitus
contriuit.

Hic loquitur de
interpretacione som-
pnii, et primo dicit de
significacione capitis
aurei.

De pectore ar-
genteo.

De ventre eneo.

De tibeis ferreis.

De significacione
pedum, qui ex duabus
materiis discordanti-
bus adinuicem diuisi
extiterant.

De lapidis statuam
confringentis signifi-
cacione.

The fieble meynd was with the stronge,
So myhte it wel noght stonde longe.
And tho me thoghte that I sih
A gret ston from an hull on hyh
Fel doun of sodein aventure
Upon the feet of this figure,   620
With which Ston al tobroke was
Gold, Selver, Erthe, Stiel and Bras,
That al was in to pouldre broght,
And so forth torned into noght.'
This was the swevene which he hadde, **P. i. 25**
That Daniel anon aradde,
And seide him that figure strange
Betokneth how the world schal change
And waxe lasse worth and lasse,
Til it to noght al overpasse.   630
The necke and hed, that weren golde,
He seide how that betokne scholde
A worthi world, a noble, a riche,
To which non after schal be liche.
Of Selver that was overforth
Schal ben a world of lasse worth ;
And after that the wombe of Bras
Tokne of a werse world it was.
The Stiel which he syh afterward
A world betokneth more hard :   640
Bot yet the werste of everydel
Is last, whan that of Erthe and Stiel
He syh the feet departed so,
For that betokneth mochel wo.
Whan that the world divided is,
It moste algate fare amis,
For Erthe which is meynd with Stiel
Togedre may noght laste wiel,
Bot if that on that other waste ;
So mot it nedes faile in haste.   650
The Ston, which fro the hully Stage

616 nought wel KH₃   nought (*om.* wel) AM, W (nat)   618 on]
an B   618 *margin* grandi] gracia dei (grā dī) RB₂Sn
627 *margin* dicit *om.* B

He syh doun falle on that ymage,
And hath it into pouldre broke,
That swevene hath Daniel unloke,
And seide how that is goddes myht,   **P. i. 26**
Which whan men wene most upryht
To stonde, schal hem overcaste.
And that is of this world the laste,
And thanne a newe schal beginne,
Fro which a man schal nevere twinne ;   660
Or al to peine or al to pes
That world schal lasten endeles.
        Lo thus expondeth Daniel
The kynges swevene faire and wel
In Babiloyne the Cite,
Wher that the wiseste of Caldee
Ne cowthen wite what it mente ;
Bot he tolde al the hol entente,
As in partie it is befalle.
Of gold the ferste regne of alle   670
Was in that kinges time tho,
And laste manye daies so,
Therwhiles that the Monarchie
Of al the world in that partie
To Babiloyne was soubgit ;
And hield him stille in such a plit,
Til that the world began diverse :
And that was whan the king of Perse,
Which Cirus hyhte, ayein the pes
Forth with his Sone Cambises   680
Of Babiloine al that Empire,
Ryht as thei wolde hemself desire,
Put under in subjeccioun
And tok it in possessioun,
And slayn was Baltazar the king,   **P. i. 27**
Which loste his regne and al his thing.
And thus whan thei it hadde wonne,
The world of Selver was begonne

[NEBUCHADNEZZAR'S
DREAM.]

[THE EMPIRES OF
THE WORLD.]

Hic consequenter
scribit qualiter huius
seculi regna variis mu-
tacionibus, prout in dic-
ta statua figurabatur,
secundum temporum
distincciones sencibil-
iter hactenus diminu-
untur.

De seculo aureo,
quod in capite statue
designatum est, a
tempore ipsius Nabu-
godonosor Regis Cal-
dee vsque in regnum
Ciri Regis Persarum.

De seculo argenteo,
quod in pectore desig-

[THE EMPIRES OF
THE WORLD.]
natum est, a tempore
ipsius Regis Ciri
vsque in regnum Alex-
andri Regis Mace-
donie.

And that of gold was passed oute :
And in this wise it goth aboute   690
In to the Regne of Darius ;
And thanne it fell to Perse thus,
That Alisaundre put hem under,
Which wroghte of armes many a wonder,
So that the Monarchie lefte
With Grecs, and here astat uplefte,
And Persiens gon under fote,
So soffre thei that nedes mote.

De seculo eneo,
quod in ventre desig-
natum est, a tempore
ipsius Alexandri vs-
que in regnum Iulii
Romanorum Impara-
toris.

And tho the world began of Bras,
And that of selver ended was ;   700
Bot for the time thus it laste,
Til it befell that ate laste
This king, whan that his day was come,
With strengthe of deth was overcome.
And natheles yet er he dyde,
He schop his Regnes to divide
To knyhtes whiche him hadde served,
And after that thei have deserved
Yaf the conquestes that he wan ;
Wherof gret werre tho began   710
Among hem that the Regnes hadde,
Thurgh proud Envie which hem ladde,
Til it befell ayein hem thus :
The noble Cesar Julius,
Which tho was king of Rome lond,   **P. i. 28**
With gret bataille and with strong hond
Al Grece, Perse and ek Caldee
Wan and put under, so that he
Noght al only of thorient
Bot al the Marche of thoccident   720
Governeth under his empire,
As he that was hol lord and Sire,
And hield thurgh his chivalerie
Of al this world the Monarchie,
And was the ferste of that honour
Which tok the name of Emperour.

Wher Rome thanne wolde assaille,
Ther myhte nothing contrevaille,
Bot every contre moste obeie :
Tho goth the Regne of Bras aweie,
And comen is the world of Stiel,
And stod above upon the whiel.
As Stiel is hardest in his kynde
Above alle othre that men finde
Of Metals, such was Rome tho
The myhtieste, and laste so
Long time amonges the Romeins
Til thei become so vileins,
That the fals Emperour Leo
With Constantin his Sone also
The patrimoine and the richesse,
Which to Silvestre in pure almesse
The ferste Constantinus lefte,
Fro holy cherche thei berefte.
Bot Adrian, which Pope was,
And syh the meschief of this cas,
Goth in to France forto pleigne,
And preith the grete Charlemeine,
For Cristes sake and Soule hele
That he wol take the querele
Of holy cherche in his defence.
And Charles for the reverence
Of god the cause hath undertake,
And with his host the weie take
Over the Montz of Lombardie ;
Of Rome and al the tirandie
With blodi swerd he overcom,
And the Cite with strengthe nom ;
In such a wise and there he wroghte,
That holy cherche ayein he broghte
Into franchise, and doth restore
The Popes lost, and yaf him more :

[THE EMPIRES OF
THE WORLD.]
De seculo ferreo,
quod in tibeis desig-
730 natum est, a tempore
Iulii vsque in regnum
Karoli magni Regis
Francorum.

740

P. i. 29

750

760

730 *margin* vsque ad H₁ . . . B₂, B   732 stant H₁ . . . B₂, B
margin Francie H₁ . . . B₂, B   739 þe fals Emperour AJMXGCL, SΔ,
FKH₃ þe Emp. fals H₁ERB₂   þe emperour B   745 Bot] Good (God)
GCL And H₁   750 wolde MH₁XGCL, Δ   754 haþ take B   did take Δ

[The Empires of
the World.]

And thus whan he his god hath served,
He tok, as he wel hath deserved,
The Diademe and was coroned.
Of Rome and thus was abandoned
Thempire, which cam nevere ayein
Into the hond of no Romein;
Bot a long time it stod so stille
Under the Frensche kynges wille,   770
Til that fortune hir whiel so ladde,
That afterward Lombardz it hadde,
Noght be the swerd, bot be soffrance
Of him that tho was kyng of France,
Which Karle Calvus cleped was;   **P. i. 30**
And he resigneth in this cas
Thempire of Rome unto Lowis
His Cousin, which a Lombard is.
And so hit laste into the yeer
Of Albert and of Berenger;   780
Bot thanne upon dissencioun
Thei felle, and in divisioun
Among hemself that were grete,
So that thei loste the beyete
Of worschipe and of worldes pes.
Bot in proverbe natheles
Men sein, ful selden is that welthe
Can soffre his oghne astat in helthe;
And that was on the Lombardz sene,
Such comun strif was hem betwene   790
Thurgh coveitise and thurgh Envie,
That every man drowh his partie,
Which myhte leden eny route,
Withinne Burgh and ek withoute:
The comun ryht hath no felawe,
So that the governance of lawe
Was lost, and for necessite,
Of that thei stode in such degre
Al only thurgh divisioun,

De seculo nouissimis iam temporibus ad similitudinem pedum in discordiam lapso et diuiso, quod post decessum ipsius Karoli, cum imperium Romanorum in manus Longobardorum peruenerat, tempore Alberti et Berengarii incepit: nam ob eorum diuisionem contigit, vt Almanni imperatoriam adepti sunt maiestatem. In cuius solium quendam principem theotonicum Othonem nomine sublimari primitus constituerunt. Et ab illo regno incipiente diuisio per vniuersum orbem in posteros concreuit, vnde nos ad alterutrum diuisi huius seculi consummacionem iam vltimi expectamus.

Hem nedeth in conclusioun
Of strange londes help beside.
    And thus for thei hemself divide
And stonden out of reule unevene,
Of Alemaine Princes sevene
Thei chose in this condicioun,   **P. i. 31**
That upon here eleccioun
Thempire of Rome scholde stonde.
And thus thei lefte it out of honde
For lacke of grace, and it forsoke,
That Alemans upon hem toke :   810
And to confermen here astat,
Of that thei founden in debat
Thei token the possessioun
After the composicioun
Among hemself, and therupon
Thei made an Emperour anon,
Whos name as the Cronique telleth
Was Othes; and so forth it duelleth,
Fro thilke day yit unto this
Thempire of Rome hath ben and is   820
To thalemans. And in this wise,   [THE LATEST TIME.]
As ye tofore have herd divise
How Daniel the swevene expondeth
Of that ymage, on whom he foundeth
The world which after scholde falle,
Come is the laste tokne of alle ;
Upon the feet of Erthe and Stiel
So stant this world now everydiel
Departed ; which began riht tho,
Whan Rome was divided so :   830
And that is forto rewe sore,
For alway siththe more and more
The world empeireth every day.
Wherof the sothe schewe may,
At Rome ferst if we beginne :   **P. i. 32**

[THE LATEST TIME.]

The wall and al the Cit withinne
Stant in ruine and in decas,
The feld is wher the Paleis was,
The toun is wast; and overthat,
If we beholde thilke astat   840
Which whilom was of the Romeins,
Of knyhthode and of Citezeins,
To peise now with that beforn,
The chaf is take for the corn,
As forto speke of Romes myht:
Unethes stant ther oght upryht
Of worschipe or of worldes good,
As it before tyme stod.
And why the worschipe is aweie,
If that a man the sothe seie,   850

[DIVISION THE CAUSE OF EVIL.]

The cause hath ben divisioun,
Which moder of confusioun
Is wher sche cometh overal,
Noght only of the temporal
Bot of the spirital also.
The dede proeveth it is so,
And hath do many day er this,
Thurgh venym which that medled is
In holy cherche of erthly thing:
For Crist himself makth knowleching   860
That noman may togedre serve
God and the world, bot if he swerve
Froward that on and stonde unstable;
And Cristes word may noght be fable.
The thing so open is at ÿe,   P. i. 33
It nedeth noght to specefie
Or speke oght more in this matiere;
Bot in this wise a man mai lere
Hou that the world is gon aboute,

---

836 al þe Cit S, F   al þe cite (citee) A...B₂, BΔΛ, KH₃   the cite W
Magd.   al the toune H₁   837 f. deces...wes ECL, B   deues...
was H₁Sn   deues . . . wes RB₂   838 wher] þer AME₂H₁
844 fro (from) H₁ERB₂, B, WMagd.   845 And for to Λ, Magd.
And so to H₁EB₂, B   And so R   As to L   850 soþe XGSn,
FWKH₃   soþ schal AJMH₁ERCLB₂, SBΔΛ   865 line om. B
869 þis world MH₁ ... B₂, B

The which welnyh is wered oute,
After the forme of that figure
Which Daniel in his scripture
Expondeth, as tofore is told.
Of Bras, of Selver and of Gold
The world is passed and agon,
And now upon his olde ton
It stant of brutel Erthe and Stiel,
The whiche acorden nevere a diel;
So mot it nedes swerve aside
As thing the which men sen divide.   880
    Thapostel writ unto ous alle
And seith that upon ous is falle   Hic dicit secundum
Thende of the world; so may we knowe,   apostolum, quod nos
This ymage is nyh overthrowe,   sumus in quos fines
Be which this world was signified,   seculi deuenerunt.
That whilom was so magnefied,
And now is old and fieble and vil,
Full of meschief and of peril,
And stant divided ek also
Lich to the feet that were so,   89c
As I tolde of the Statue above.
And this men sen, thurgh lacke of love
Where as the lond divided is,
It mot algate fare amis:
And now to loke on every side,   **P. i. 34**
A man may se the world divide,
The werres ben so general
Among the cristene overal,
That every man now secheth wreche,
And yet these clerkes alday preche   900
And sein, good dede may non be
Which stant noght upon charite:
I not hou charite may stonde,
Wher dedly werre is take on honde.
Bot al this wo is cause of man,
The which that wit and reson can,
And that in tokne and in witnesse

873 Expondeþ S, FK   892 this] þus AMH₁X, H₃   900 these]
þis AM ... E, B, W

[Division the Cause of Evil.]

That ilke ymage bar liknesse
Of man and of non other beste.
For ferst unto the mannes heste   910
Was every creature ordeined,
Bot afterward it was restreigned:
Whan that he fell, thei fellen eke,
Whan he wax sek, thei woxen seke;
For as the man hath passioun
Of seknesse, in comparisoun
So soffren othre creatures.

Hic scribit quod ex diuisionis passione singula creata detrimentum corruptibile paciuntur.

Lo, ferst the hevenly figures,
The Sonne and Mone eclipsen bothe.
And ben with mannes senne wrothe;   920
The purest Eir for Senne alofte
Hath ben and is corrupt fulofte,
Right now the hyhe wyndes blowe,
And anon after thei ben lowe,
Now clowdy and now clier it is: **P. i. 35**
So may it proeven wel be this,
A mannes Senne is forto hate,
Which makth the welkne to debate.
And forto se the proprete
Of every thyng in his degree,   930
Benethe forth among ous hiere
Al stant aliche in this matiere:
The See now ebbeth, now it floweth,
The lond now welketh, now it groweth,
Now be the Trees with leves grene,
Now thei be bare and nothing sene,
Now be the lusti somer floures,
Now be the stormy wynter shoures,
Now be the daies, now the nyhtes,
So stant ther nothing al upryhtes,   940
Now it is lyht, now it is derk;
And thus stant al the worldes werk

912 Bot] ffor H₁ERB₂, B   923 hyhe] while H₁ERB₂, B
934 welweþ AJM, W (weloweth)   937 f. the...the] þei...þei
(þay...þay) AH₁ERB₂, B þer...þer CL þese...þey X þe...
þey G   939 þei (þay) daies H₁...R, B   now the nyhtes]
now be þe n. MCB₂, Δ   now be þey (thei) n. H₁XG

After the disposicioun
Of man and his condicioun.

Forthi Gregoire in his Moral
Seith that a man in special
The lasse world is properly :
And that he proeveth redely ;
For man of Soule resonable
Is to an Angel resemblable,   950
And lich to beste he hath fielinge,
And lich to Trees he hath growinge ;
The Stones ben and so is he :
Thus of his propre qualite
The man, as telleth the clergie,   **P. i. 36**
Is as a world in his partie,
And whan this litel world mistorneth,
The grete world al overtorneth.
The Lond, the See, the firmament,
Thei axen alle jugement   960
Ayein the man and make him werre :
Therwhile himself stant out of herre,
The remenant wol noght acorde :
And in this wise, as I recorde,
The man is cause of alle wo,
Why this world is divided so.

  Division, the gospell seith,
On hous upon another leith,
Til that the Regne al overthrowe :
And thus may every man wel knowe,   970
Division aboven alle
Is thing which makth the world to falle,
And evere hath do sith it began.

It may ferst proeve upon a man ;
The which, for his complexioun
Is mad upon divisioun
Of cold, of hot, of moist, of drye,
He mot be verray kynde dye :
For the contraire of his astat

Hic dicit secundum
euangelium, quod om-
ne regnum in se diui-
sum desolabitur.

Quod ex sue com-
plexionis materia di-
uisus homo mortalis
existat.

946 aman F   950 Is to an] It is an H₁ERB₂, B   957
mistormeþ FKH₃   963 stant out of acord(e) H₁ERB₂, B   966
Why] Wiþ RCLB₂   967 as þe g. s. AG, W   976 *margin* existit A

[Division the Cause
of Evil.]

Stant evermore in such debat,   980
Til that o part be overcome,
Ther may no final pes be nome.
Bot other wise, if a man were
Mad al togedre of o matiere
Withouten interrupcioun,   **P. i. 37**
Ther scholde no corrupcioun
Engendre upon that unite :
Bot for ther is diversite
Withinne himself, he may noght laste,
That he ne deieth ate laste.   990
Bot in a man yit over this
Full gret divisioun ther is,
Thurgh which that he is evere in strif,
Whil that him lasteth eny lif :
The bodi and the Soule also
Among hem ben divided so,
That what thing that the body hateth
The soule loveth and debateth ;
Bot natheles fulofte is sene
Of werre which is hem betwene   1000
The fieble hath wonne the victoire.
And who so drawth into memoire
What hath befalle of old and newe,
He may that werre sore rewe,
Which ferst began in Paradis :
For ther was proeved what it is,
And what desese there it wroghte ;
For thilke werre tho forth broghte
The vice of alle dedly Sinne,
Thurgh which division cam inne   1010
Among the men in erthe hiere,
And was the cause and the matiere
Why god the grete flodes sende,
Of al the world and made an ende
Bot Noë with his felaschipe,   **P. i. 38**
Which only weren saulf be Schipe.
And over that thurgh Senne it com

Quod homo ex corporis et anime condicione diuisus, sicut saluacionis ita et dampnacionis aptitudinem ingreditur.

Qualiter Adam a statu innocencie diuisus a paradiso voluptatis in terram laboris peccator proiectus est.

Qualiter populi per vniuersum orbem a cultura dei diuisi, Noe cum sua sequela dumtaxat exceptis, diluuio interierunt.

982 be nome] benome FKH₃

That Nembrot such emprise nom,
Whan he the Tour Babel on heihte
Let make, as he that wolde feihte
Ayein the hihe goddes myht,
Wherof divided anon ryht
Was the langage in such entente,
Ther wiste non what other mente,
So that thei myhten noght procede.
And thus it stant of every dede,
Wher Senne takth the cause on honde,
It may upriht noght longe stonde ;
For Senne of his condicioun
Is moder of divisioun
And tokne whan the world schal faile.
For so seith Crist withoute faile,
That nyh upon the worldes ende
Pes and acord awey schol wende
And alle charite schal cesse,
Among the men and hate encresce ;
And whan these toknes ben befalle,
Al sodeinly the Ston schal falle,
As Daniel it hath beknowe,
Which al this world schal overthrowe,
And every man schal thanne arise
To Joie or elles to Juise,
Wher that he schal for evere dwelle,
Or straght to hevene or straght to helle.
In hevene is pes and al acord,   **P. i. 39**
Bot helle is full of such descord
That ther may be no loveday :
Forthi good is, whil a man may,
Echon to sette pes with other
And loven as his oghne brother ;
So may he winne worldes welthe
And afterward his soule helthe.
　　Bot wolde god that now were on
An other such as Arion,

[DIVISION THE CAUSE
OF EVIL.]

1020 Qualiter in edifica-
cione turris Babel,
quam in dei contemp-
tum Nembrot erexit,
lingua prius hebraica
in varias linguas ce-
lica vindicta diuide-
batur.

1030

Qualiter mundus,
qui in statu diuisionis
quasi cotidianis pre-
senti tempore vexatur
flagellis, a lapide superueniente, id est a di-
uina potencia vsque ad
resolucionem omnis
carnis subito conter-
etur.

1040

1050

Hic narrat exem-
plum de concordia et
vnitate inter homines

1018 suche prise H₁ERB₂, B   1019 he om. RLB₂, B, W   that H₁
1029 condicion F   1033 margin vexat H₁ERB₂, B   1038 And A
1055 S has lost a leaf (1055 —i. 106)

[DIVISION THE CAUSE
OF EVIL.]

prouocanda ; et dicit
qualiter quidam Arion
nuper Citharista ex
sui cantus cithareque
consona melodia tante
virtutis extiterat, vt
ipse non solum virum
cum viro, set eciam
leonem cum cerua, lup-
um cum agna, canem
cum lepore, ipsum
audientes vnanimiter
absque vlla discordia
adinuicem pacificauit.

Which hadde an harpe of such temprure,
And therto of so good mesure
He song, that he the bestes wilde
Made of his note tame and milde,
The Hinde in pes with the Leoun,
The Wolf in pes with the Moltoun,   1060
The Hare in pees stod with the Hound ;
And every man upon this ground
Which Arion that time herde,
Als wel the lord as the schepherde,
He broghte hem alle in good acord ;
So that the comun with the lord,
And lord with the comun also,
He sette in love bothe tuo
And putte awey malencolie.
That was a lusti melodie,   1070
Whan every man with other low ;
And if ther were such on now,
Which cowthe harpe as he tho dede,
He myhte availe in many a stede
To make pes wher now is hate ;   **P. i. 40**
For whan men thenken to debate,
I not what other thing is good.
Bot wher that wisdom waxeth wod,
And reson torneth into rage,
So that mesure upon oultrage   1080
Hath set his world, it is to drede ;
For that bringth in the comun drede,
Which stant at every mannes Dore :
Bot whan the scharpnesse of the spore
The horse side smit to sore,
It grieveth ofte. And now nomore,
As forto speke of this matiere,
Which non bot only god may stiere.

Explicit Prologus

1078 waxed FK   1087 As] And YERSn, B *om.* B₂ 1088 god
only may H₁ER, B god may only B₂

P. i. 41

Incipit Liber Primus

i. *Naturatus amor nature legibus orbem*
Subdit, et vnanimes concitat esse feras:
Huius enim mundi Princeps amor esse videtur,
Cuius eget diues, pauper et omnis ope.
Sunt in agone pares amor et fortuna, que cecas
Plebis ad insidias vertit vterque rotas.
Est amor egra salus, vexata quies, pius error,
Bellica pax, vulnus dulce, suaue malum.

I may noght strecche up to the hevene
Min hand, ne setten al in evene
This world, which evere is in balance:
It stant noght in my sufficance
So grete thinges to compasse,
Bot I mot lete it overpasse
And treten upon othre thinges.
Forthi the Stile of my writinges
Fro this day forth I thenke change
And speke of thing is noght so strange,   10
Which every kinde hath upon honde,   P. i. 42
And wherupon the world mot stonde,
And hath don sithen it began,
And schal whil ther is any man ;
And that is love, of which I mene
To trete, as after schal be sene.
In which ther can noman him reule,
For loves lawe is out of reule,
That of tomoche or of tolite
Welnyh is every man to wyte,   20

Postquam in Pro-
logo tractatum hac-
tenus existit, qualiter
hodierne condicionis
diuisio caritatis di-
leccionem superauit,
intendit auctor ad
presens suum libel-
lum, cuius nomen Con-
fessio Amantis nun-
cupatur, componere de
illo amore, a quo non
solum humanum ge-
nus, sed eciam cuncta
animancia naturaliter
subiciuntur. Et quia
nonnulli amantes ultra

1 strecchen vp to h. EC, Δ   strecche vp to h. XB₂ (vt)   8 fforþi
(ffor þy) AJME₂E, ΔΛ, FKH₃   ffor H₁YXR ... B₂, B, W   10 thing is]
þinges E₂H₁Y ... B₂, B   noght so] more YX   13 *margin*
intendit] intendit eciam ERCL   intendit et H₁B₂

D 2

[LOVE RULES THE
    WORLD.]
quam expedit desi-
derii passionibus cre-
bro stimulantur, ma-
teria libri per totum
super hiis specialius
diffunditur.

And natheles ther is noman
In al this world so wys, that can
Of love tempre the mesure,
Bot as it falth in aventure :
For wit ne strengthe may noght helpe,
And he which elles wolde him yelpe
Is rathest throwen under fote,
Ther can no wiht therof do bote.
For yet was nevere such covine,
That couthe ordeine a medicine   30
To thing which god in lawe of kinde
Hath set, for ther may noman finde
The rihte salve of such a Sor.
It hath and schal ben everemor
That love is maister wher he wile,
Ther can no lif make other skile ;
For wher as evere him lest to sette,
Ther is no myht which him may lette.
Bot what schal fallen ate laste,
The sothe can no wisdom caste,   40
Bot as it falleth upon chance ;   **P. i. 43**
For if ther evere was balance
Which of fortune stant governed,
I may wel lieve as I am lerned
That love hath that balance on honde,
Which wol no reson understonde.
For love is blind and may noght se,
Forthi may no certeinete
Be set upon his jugement,
Bot as the whiel aboute went   50
He yifth his graces undeserved,
And fro that man which hath him served
Fulofte he takth aweye his fees,
As he that pleieth ate Dees,
And therupon what schal befalle
He not, til that the chance falle,
Wher he schal lese or he schal winne.

23 *margin* crebre H₁E ... B₂   26 *margin* diffundetur B   37 evere
him lest] himself lest (list) H₁YERB₂, B (lust)   50 aboute is went ACL
is aboute went Δ   51 grace H₁XGERB₂, BΔ   54 And H₁YERB₂, B

And thus fulofte men beginne,
That if thei wisten what it mente,
Thei wolde change al here entente.
  And forto proven it is so,
I am miselven on of tho,
Which to this Scole am underfonge.
For it is siththe go noght longe,
As forto speke of this matiere,
I may you telle, if ye woll hiere,
A wonder hap which me befell,
That was to me bothe hard and fell,
Touchende of love and his fortune,
The which me liketh to comune
And pleinly forto telle it oute.
To hem that ben lovers aboute
Fro point to point I wol declare
And wryten of my woful care,
Mi wofull day, my wofull chance,
That men mowe take remembrance
Of that thei schall hierafter rede:
For in good feith this wolde I rede,
That every man ensample take
Of wisdom which him is betake,
And that he wot of good aprise
To teche it forth, for such emprise
Is forto preise; and therfore I
Woll wryte and schewe al openly
How love and I togedre mette,
Wherof the world ensample fette
Mai after this, whan I am go,
Of thilke unsely jolif wo,
Whos reule stant out of the weie,
Nou glad and nou gladnesse aweie,
And yet it may noght be withstonde
For oght that men may understonde.

P. i. 44

70

80

90

[EXAMPLE OF THE AUTHOR.]

60 Hic quasi in persona aliorum, quos amor alligat, fingens se auctor esse Amantem, varias eorum passiones variis huius libri distinccionibus per singula scribere proponit.

ii. *Non ego Sampsonis vires, non Herculis arma*
   Vinco, sum sed vt hii victus amore pari.
  Vt discant alii, docet experiencia facti,
   Rebus in ambiguis que sit habenda via.

[HIS WOFUL CASE.]

    76 now B.   80 is him AG

[His woful case.]

Deuius ordo ducis temptata pericla sequentem
Instruit a tergo, ne simul ille cadat.
Me quibus ergo Venus, casus, laqueauit amantem,
Orbis in exemplum scribere tendo palam.

Upon the point that is befalle
Of love, in which that I am falle,
I thenke telle my matiere: P. i. 45
Now herkne, who that wol it hiere,
Of my fortune how that it ferde.

Hic declarat mate-
riam, dicens qualiter
Cupido quodam ignito
iaculo sui cordis mem-
oriam graui vlcere per-
forauit, quod Venus
percipiens ipsum, vt
dicit, quasi in mortis
articulo spasmatum,
ad confitendum se
Genio sacerdoti super
amoris causa sic semi-
uiuum specialiter com-
mendauit.

This enderday, as I forthferde
To walke, as I yow telle may,—
And that was in the Monthe of Maii,   100
Whan every brid hath chose his make
And thenkth his merthes forto make
Of love that he hath achieved;
Bot so was I nothing relieved,
For I was further fro my love
Than Erthe is fro the hevene above,
As forto speke of eny sped:
So wiste I me non other red,
Bot as it were a man forfare
Unto the wode I gan to fare,   110
Noght forto singe with the briddes,
For whanne I was the wode amiddes,
I fond a swote grene pleine,
And ther I gan my wo compleigne
Wisshinge and wepinge al myn one,
For other merthes made I none.
So hard me was that ilke throwe,
That ofte sithes overthrowe
To grounde I was withoute breth;
And evere I wisshide after deth,   120
Whanne I out of my peine awok,

Latin Verses ii. 5 Deuius AJME₂, ΔΛ, FKH₃   Denuus (?) H₁Y
Demum XGEC, B   Deinq*ue* L   Deui B₂Sn   Veni R   7 Me] Aere
H₁Y*p.m.*ERB₂, B
      102 take CL, B   107 S *resumes*   109 forsake B   110 Vnto...
I gan tofare F   And to ... forth is he fare CL   And to ... gan I to
fare Y   To ... I gan fare R   To ... I made me ȝare B₂   Vnto ...
my way gan take B   *line om.* SnD   116 oþere A   120 wisshide
FK · wisschide S   wisshid H₃   *al.* wissched

And caste up many a pitous lok
Unto the hevene, and seide thus :
'O thou Cupide, O thou Venus,
Thou god of love and thou goddesse,   **P. i. 46**
Wher is pite? wher is meknesse?
Now doth me pleinly live or dye,
For certes such a maladie
As I now have and longe have hadd,
It myhte make a wisman madd,   130
If that it scholde longe endure.
O Venus, queene of loves cure,
Thou lif, thou lust, thou mannes hele,
Behold my cause and my querele,
And yif me som part of thi grace,
So that I may finde in this place
If thou be gracious or non.'
And with that word I sawh anon
The kyng of love and qweene bothe;
Bot he that kyng with yhen wrothe   140
His chiere aweiward fro me caste,
And forth he passede ate laste.

Bot natheles er he forth wente   [THE FIERY DART.]
A firy Dart me thoghte he hente
And threw it thurgh myn herte rote :
In him fond I non other bote,
For lenger list him noght to duelle.

Bot sche that is the Source and Welle   [VENUS QUEEN OF
Of wel or wo, that schal betide   LOVE.]
To hem that loven, at that tide   150
Abod, bot forto tellen hiere
Sche cast on me no goodly chiere :
Thus natheles to me sche seide,
'What art thou, Sone?' and I abreide
Riht as a man doth out of slep,   **P. i. 47**
And therof tok sche riht good kep
And bad me nothing ben adrad :
Bot for al that I was noght glad,
For I ne sawh no cause why.
And eft scheo asketh, what was I :   160

130 wismam FK   160 scheo FK   *al.* sche

[HIS COMPLAINT TO
CUPID AND VENUS.]

[VENUS QUEEN OF
LOVE.]

I seide, 'A Caitif that lith hiere:
What wolde ye, my Ladi diere?
Schal I ben hol or elles dye?'
Sche seide, 'Tell thi maladie:
What is thi Sor of which thou pleignest?
Ne hyd it noght, for if thou feignest,
I can do the no medicine.'
'Ma dame, I am a man of thyne,
That in thi Court have longe served,
And aske that I have deserved,   170
Som wele after my longe wo.'
And sche began to loure tho,
And seide, 'Ther is manye of yow
Faitours, and so may be that thow
Art riht such on, and be feintise
Seist that thou hast me do servise.'
And natheles sche wiste wel,
Mi world stod on an other whiel
Withouten eny faiterie:
Bot algate of my maladie   180
Sche bad me telle and seie hir trowthe.
'Ma dame, if ye wolde have rowthe,'
Quod I, 'than wolde I telle yow.'
'Sey forth,' quod sche, 'and tell me how;
Schew me thi seknesse everydiel.'   P. i. 48
'Ma dame, that can I do wel,
Be so my lif therto wol laste.'
With that hir lok on me sche caste,
And seide: 'In aunter if thou live,
Mi will is ferst that thou be schrive;   190
And natheles how that it is
I wot miself, bot for al this

[GENIUS, THE PRIEST
OF LOVE.]

Unto my prest, which comth anon,
I woll thou telle it on and on,
Bothe all thi thoght and al thi werk.

161 Ma dame I sayde Iohn Gowere E, B   And I answerde wiþ drery
chiere C   And I answerd wiþ ful myld chere L   *line om.* RB₂SnD
162 What wolde ȝe wiþ me my l. d. ERLB₂   What wolde ȝe wiþ
me l. d. XGC, B   163 or elles] or schal I C   or L   164 tell
(telle) me H₁YE ... B₂, BΛ, W   165 of which] which þat CL
where of W   183 þan wolde C   þan wold A, B   þanne wold S, FK

O Genius myn oghne Clerk,   [GENIUS, THE PRIEST
Com forth and hier this mannes schrifte,'   OF LOVE.]
Quod Venus tho; and I uplifte
Min hefd with that, and gan beholde
The selve Prest, which as sche wolde   2co
Was redy there and sette him doun
To hiere my confessioun.

iii. *Confessus Genio si sit medicina salutis*
    Experiar morbis, quos tulit ipsa Venus.
    Lesa quidem ferro medicantur membra saluti,
    Raro tamen medicum vulnus amoris habet.

    This worthi Prest, this holy man   [THE LOVER'S
To me spekende thus began,   SHRIFT.]
And seide: 'Benedicite,
Mi Sone, of the felicite
Of love and ek of all the wo
Thou schalt thee schrive of bothe tuo.
What thou er this for loves sake   Hic dicit qualiter
Hast felt, let nothing be forsake,   210 Genio pro Confessore
Tell pleinliche as it is befalle.'   sedenti   prouolutus
    P. i. 49 Amans ad confiten-
And with that word I gan doun falle   dum se flexis genibus
On knees, and with devocioun   incuruatur, supplicans
And with full gret contricioun   tamen, vt ad sui sen-
                                       sus   informacionem
I seide thanne: 'Dominus,   confessor ille in dicen-
Min holi fader Genius,   dis opponere sibi be-
So as thou hast experience   nignius dignaretur.
Of love, for whos reverence
Thou schalt me schriven at this time,
I prai the let me noght mistime   220
Mi schrifte, for I am destourbed
In al myn herte, and so contourbed,
That I ne may my wittes gete,
So schal I moche thing foryete:
Bot if thou wolt my schrifte oppose
Fro point to point, thanne I suppose,
Ther schal nothing be left behinde.
Bot now my wittes ben so blinde,
That I ne can miselven teche.'

200 Prest *om.* B   208 thee] be Y, B, Magd.   213 and with]
wiþ good B   wiþ XC   as wiþ Λ   224 schal] þat A   227 beleft FK

[THE LOVER'S
    SHRIFT.]

Sermo Genii sacer-
dotis super confes-
sione ad Amantem.

Tho he began anon to preche,   230
And with his wordes debonaire
He seide tome softe and faire:
'Thi schrifte to oppose and hiere,
My Sone, I am assigned hiere
Be Venus the godesse above,
Whos Prest I am touchende of love.
Bot natheles for certein skile
I mot algate and nedes wile
Noght only make my spekynges
Of love, bot of othre thinges,   240
That touchen to the cause of vice.   **P. i. 50**
For that belongeth to thoffice
Of Prest, whos ordre that I bere,
So that I wol nothing forbere,
That I the vices on and on
Ne schal thee schewen everychon;
Wherof thou myht take evidence
To reule with thi conscience.
Bot of conclusion final
Conclude I wol in special   250
For love, whos servant I am,
And why the cause is that I cam.
So thenke I to don bothe tuo,
Ferst that myn ordre longeth to,
The vices forto telle arewe,
Bot next above alle othre schewe
Of love I wol the propretes,
How that thei stonde be degrees
After the disposicioun
Of Venus, whos condicioun   260
I moste folwe, as I am holde.
For I with love am al withholde,
So that the lasse I am to wyte,
Thogh I ne conne bot a lyte
Of othre thinges that ben wise:
I am noght tawht in such a wise;

232 tome F   *al.* to me   234 sone sone F   am *om.* B   264 I ne
conne] I now can (conne) ECLB₂, B   I ne now can XR   ne can
nowe H₁   266 awise FK

For it is noght my comun us
To speke of vices and vertus,
Bot al of love and of his lore,
For Venus bokes of nomore   270
Me techen nowther text ne glose.   **P. i. 51**
Bot for als moche as I suppose
It sit a prest to be wel thewed,
And schame it is if he be lewed,
Of my Presthode after the forme
I wol thi schrifte so enforme,
That ate leste thou schalt hiere
The vices, and to thi matiere
Of love I schal hem so remene,
That thou schalt knowe what thei mene.   280
For what a man schal axe or sein
Touchende of schrifte, it mot be plein,
It nedeth noght to make it queinte,
For trowthe hise wordes wol noght peinte :
That I wole axe of the forthi,
My Sone, it schal be so pleinly,
That thou schalt knowe and understonde
The pointz of schrifte how that thei stonde.'

iv. *Visus et auditus fragilis sunt ostia mentis,*
    Que viciosa manus claudere nulla potest.
    Est ibi larga via, graditur qua cordis ad antrum
    Hostis, et ingrediens fossa talenta rapit.
    Hec michi confessor Genius primordia profert,
    Dum sit in extremis vita remorsa malis.
    Nunc tamen vt poterit semiviua loquela fateri,
    Verba per os timide conscia mentis agam.

[THE FIVE SENSES.]

Betwen the lif and deth I herde
This Prestes tale er I answerde,   290
And thanne I preide him forto seie
His will, and I it wolde obeie
After the forme of his apprise.
Tho spak he tome in such a wise,
And bad me that I scholde schrive   **P. i. 52**

Hic incipit confes-
sio Amantis, cui de

277 laste (last) JYRCL,BΔΛ   278 vice H₁ ... B₂, B   281 aman F
288 The] þo B   293 the] þer F   294 tome FK   *al.* to me
awise F   wise AEC, B   295 scholde (schuld) me H₁ ... B₂, B

[THE FIVE SENSES.]
duobus precipue quin-
que sensuum, hoc est
de visu et auditu, con-
fessor pre ceteris op-
ponit.

As touchende of my wittes fyve,
And schape that thei were amended
Of that I hadde hem misdispended.
For tho be proprely the gates,
Thurgh whiche as to the herte algates   300
Comth alle thing unto the feire,
Which may the mannes Soule empeire.
And now this matiere is broght inne,
Mi Sone, I thenke ferst beginne
To wite how that thin yhe hath stonde,
The which is, as I understonde,
The moste principal of alle,
Thurgh whom that peril mai befalle.
    And forto speke in loves kinde,
Ful manye suche a man mai finde,   310
Whiche evere caste aboute here yhe,
To loke if that thei myhte aspie
Fulofte thing which hem ne toucheth,
Bot only that here herte soucheth
In hindringe of an other wiht;
And thus ful many a worthi knyht
And many a lusti lady bothe
Have be fulofte sythe wrothe.
So that an yhe is as a thief
To love, and doth ful gret meschief;   320
And also for his oghne part
Fulofte thilke firy Dart
Of love, which that evere brenneth,
Thurgh him into the herte renneth:
And thus a mannes yhe ferst   **P. i. 53**
Himselve grieveth alther werst,
And many a time that he knoweth
Unto his oghne harm it groweth.
Mi Sone, herkne now forthi
A tale, to be war therby   330
Thin yhe forto kepe and warde,
So that it passe noght his warde.

[SEEING.]

298 mispended XR, FWKH₃   so myspended B₂   310
manye suche S   manye such F   many suche AC   318 Haþ
M ... RLB₂, B

Ovide telleth in his bok
Ensample touchende of mislok,
And seith hou whilom ther was on,
A worthi lord, which Acteon
Was hote, and he was cousin nyh
To him that Thebes ferst on hyh
Up sette, which king Cadme hyhte.
This Acteon, as he wel myhte,
Above alle othre caste his chiere,
And used it fro yer to yere,
With Houndes and with grete Hornes
Among the wodes and the thornes
To make his hunting and his chace :
Where him best thoghte in every place
To finde gamen in his weie,
Ther rod he forto hunte and pleie.
So him befell upon a tide
On his hunting as he cam ride,
In a Forest al one he was :
He syh upon the grene gras
The faire freisshe floures springe,
He herde among the leves singe
The Throstle with the nyhtingale :   **P. i. 54**
Thus er he wiste into a Dale
He cam, wher was a litel plein,
All round aboute wel besein
With buisshes grene and Cedres hyhe ;
And ther withinne he caste his yhe.   360
Amidd the plein he syh a welle,
So fair ther myhte noman telle,
In which Diana naked stod
To bathe and pleie hire in the flod
With many a Nimphe, which hire serveth.
Bot he his yhe awey ne swerveth
Fro hire, which was naked al,

[TALE OF ACTEON.]
Hic narrat Confessor exemplum de visu ab illicitis preseruando, dicens qualiter Acteon Cadmi Regis Thebarum nepos, dum in quadam Foresta venacionis causa spaciaretur, accidit vt ipse quendam fontem nemorosa arborum pulcritudine circumuentum superueniens, vidit ibi Dianam cum suis Nimphis nudam in flumine balneantem ; quam diligencius intuens oculos suos a muliebri nuditate nullatenus auertere volebat. Vnde indignata Diana ipsum in cerui figuram transformauit ; quem canes proprii apprehendentes mortiferis dentibus penitus dilaniarunt.

334 *margin* exemplum *om.* AM   335 whilon FK   339 Vp sette
S, F   Vpsette AC, B   *margin* spaciaret B   349 atide FK
353 floures freische H₁ . . . B₂, B   355 Trostle FK   357 wher was]
in to (into) H₁ . . . B₂, B   365 many nimphes Sn, B   many Nimphe
YEC   many simphe RLB₂   mani a maiden Δ

[Tale of Acteon.]

And sche was wonder wroth withal,
And him, as sche which was godesse,
Forschop anon, and the liknesse 370
Sche made him taken of an Hert,
Which was tofore hise houndes stert,
That ronne besiliche aboute
With many an horn and many a route,
That maden mochel noise and cry:
And ate laste unhappely
This Hert his oghne houndes slowhe
And him for vengance al todrowhe.

Confessor.

Lo now, my Sone, what it is
A man to caste his yhe amis, 380
Which Acteon hath dere aboght;
Be war forthi and do it noght.
For ofte, who that hiede toke,
Betre is to winke than to loke.
And forto proven it is so, **P. i. 55**
Ovide the Poete also
A tale which to this matiere
Acordeth seith, as thou schalt hiere.

[Tale of Medusa.]

In Metamor it telleth thus,
How that a lord which Phorceüs 390
Was hote, hadde dowhtres thre.
Bot upon here nativite
Such was the constellacion,
That out of mannes nacion
Fro kynde thei be so miswent,
That to the liknesse of Serpent
Thei were bore, and so that on
Of hem was cleped Stellibon,
That other soster Suriale,
The thridde, as telleth in the tale, 400
Medusa hihte, and natheles
Of comun name Gorgones

Hic ponit aliud ex-
emplum de eodem,
vbi dicit quod quidam
princeps nomine Phor-
ceus tres progenuit
filias, Gorgones a vul-
go nuncupatas, que
uno partu exorte de-
formitatem Monstro-
rum serpentinam ob-
tinuerunt; quibus, cum
in etatem peruenerant,
talis destinata fuerat
natura, quod quicum-
que in eas aspiceret
in lapidem subito mu-
tabatur. Et sic quam
plures incaute respi-

368 for anger þerof swal(l) H₁EXG, B   for anger þerfor swal YR
for anger þerof schall CLB₂   therefore for anger schall DAr   370 and
the] in to CL   in þe B₂   371 taken] in fourme L   om. B₂
374 aroute F   377 hondes FK   388 and seiþ RCLB₂   and says W
391 and hadde CLB₂, W   397 bore] boþe FWKH₃Magd.

In every contre ther aboute,
As Monstres whiche that men doute,
Men clepen hem; and bot on yhe
Among hem thre in pourpartie
Thei hadde, of which thei myhte se,
Now hath it this, now hath it sche;
After that cause and nede it ladde,
Be throwes ech of hem it hadde.   410
A wonder thing yet more amis
Ther was, wherof I telle al this :
What man on hem his chiere caste
And hem behield, he was als faste
Out of a man into a Ston   **P. i. 56**
Forschape, and thus ful manyon
Deceived were, of that thei wolde
Misloke, wher that thei ne scholde.
Bot Perseüs that worthi knyht,
Whom Pallas of hir grete myht   420
Halp, and tok him a Schield therto,
And ek the god Mercurie also
Lente him a swerd, he, as it fell,
Beyende Athlans the hihe hell
These Monstres soghte, and there he fond
Diverse men of thilke lond
Thurgh sihte of hem mistorned were,
Stondende as Stones hiere and there.
Bot he, which wisdom and prouesse
Hadde of the god and the godesse,   430
The Schield of Pallas gan enbrace,
With which he covereth sauf his face,
Mercuries Swerd and out he drowh,
And so he bar him that he slowh
These dredful Monstres alle thre.

   Lo now, my Sone, avise the,
That thou thi sihte noght misuse :
Cast noght thin yhe upon Meduse,
That thou be torned into Ston :
For so wys man was nevere non,   440

[TALE OF MEDUSA.]
cientes visis illis peri-
erunt.   Set Perseus
miles clipeo Palladis
gladioque   Mercurii
munitus   eas   extra
montem Athlantis co-
habitantes animo au-
daci absque sui peri-
culo interfecit.

Confessor.

423 he, as it fell] as it befel (*om.* he) C   as it fel L, W   425 These]
þis A   430 Haþ B, W

Bot if he wel his yhe kepe
And take of fol delit no kepe,
That he with lust nys ofte nome,
Thurgh strengthe of love and overcome.
Of mislokynge how it hath ferd,   **P. i. 57**
As I have told, now hast thou herd,
My goode Sone, and tak good hiede.

[HEARING.]

And overthis yet I thee rede
That thou be war of thin heringe,
Which to the Herte the tidinge   450
Of many a vanite hath broght,
To tarie with a mannes thoght.
And natheles good is to hiere
Such thing wherof a man may lere
That to vertu is acordant,
And toward al the remenant
Good is to torne his Ere fro ;
For elles, bot a man do so,
Him may fulofte mysbefalle.
I rede ensample amonges alle,   460
Wherof to kepe wel an Ere
It oghte pute a man in fere.

[THE PRUDENCE OF
THE SERPENT.]

A Serpent, which that Aspidis
Is cleped, of his kynde hath this,
That he the Ston noblest of alle,
The which that men Carbuncle calle,
Berth in his hed above on heihte.
For which whan that a man be sleyhte,
The Ston to winne and him to daunte,
With his carecte him wolde enchaunte,   470
Anon as he perceiveth that,
He leith doun his on Ere al plat
Unto the ground, and halt it faste,
And ek that other Ere als faste
He stoppeth with his tail so sore,   **P. i. 58**
That he the wordes lasse or more

Hic narrat Confes-
sor exemplum, vt non
ab auris exaudicione
fatua animus deceptus
inuoluatur. Et dicit
qualiter ille serpens,
qui aspis vocatur,
quendam preciosissi-
mum lapidem nomine
Carbunculum in sue
frontis medio gestans,
contra verba incan-
tantis aurem vnam
terre affigendo premit,
et aliam sue caude
stimulo firmissime ob-
turat.

441 wel AJE₂C, S, FKH₃ wil (wille) YXGERLB₂, BΔ, W   wol(e)
MH₁, Magd.   447 and *om.* B.   454, 458 aman FK   470 *margin*
aspidis B   476 *margin* firmissimo H₁GRCLB₂

Of his enchantement ne hiereth;
And in this wise himself he skiereth,
So that he hath the wordes weyved
And thurgh his Ere is noght deceived.   480

  An othre thing, who that recordeth,
Lich unto this ensample acordeth,
Which in the tale of Troie I finde.
Sirenes of a wonder kynde
Ben Monstres, as the bokes tellen,
And in the grete Se thei duellen :
Of body bothe and of visage
Lik unto wommen of yong age
Up fro the Navele on hih thei be,
And doun benethe, as men mai se,   490
Thei bere of fisshes the figure.
And overthis of such nature
Thei ben, that with so swete a stevene
Lik to the melodie of hevene
In wommanysshe vois thei singe,
With notes of so gret likinge,
Of such mesure, of such musike,
Wherof the Schipes thei beswike
That passen be the costes there.
For whan the Schipmen leie an Ere   500
Unto the vois, in here avys
Thei wene it be a Paradys,
Which after is to hem an helle.
For reson may noght with hem duelle,
Whan thei tho grete lustes hiere ;   **P. i. 59**
Thei conne noght here Schipes stiere,
So besiliche upon the note
Thei herkne, and in such wise assote,
That thei here rihte cours and weie
Foryete, and to here Ere obeie,   510
And seilen til it so befalle
That thei into the peril falle,

[TALE OF THE
SIRENS.]

Aliud exemplum
super eodem, qualiter
rex Vluxes cum a
bello Troiano versus
Greciam nauigio re-
mearet, et prope illa
Monstra marina, Si-
renes nuncupata, an-
gelica voce canoras,
ipsum ventorum ad-
uersitate nauigare o-
porteret, omnium nau-
tarum suorum aures
obturari coegit. Et sic
salutari prouidencia
prefultus absque peri-
culo saluus cum sua
classe Vluxes per-
transiuit.

481 oþre SB, F *rest* oþer   488 womman A a womman
MXGGLB₂   491 bereþ XRCLB₂, B   505 tho] þe JE₂H₁ ... B₂,
B, W H₃Magd. so ΔΛ
**   E

[TALE OF THE SIRENS.]

Where as the Schipes be todrawe,
And thei ben with the Monstres slawe.
Bot fro this peril natheles
With his wisdom king Uluxes
Ascapeth and it overpasseth;
For he tofor the hond compasseth
That noman of his compaignie
Hath pouer unto that folie   520
His Ere for no lust to caste;
For he hem stoppede alle faste,
That non of hem mai hiere hem singe.
So whan they comen forth seilinge,
Ther was such governance on honde,
That thei the Monstres have withstonde
And slain of hem a gret partie.
Thus was he sauf with his navie,
This wise king, thurgh governance.

Confessor.

[THE SINS OF THE
EYE AND THE EAR.]

Wherof, my Sone, in remembrance   530
Thou myht ensample taken hiere,
As I have told, and what thou hiere
Be wel war, and yif no credence,
Bot if thou se more evidence.
For if thou woldest take kepe   **P. i. 60**
And wisly cowthest warde and kepe
Thin yhe and Ere, as I have spoke,
Than haddest thou the gates stoke
Fro such Sotie as comth to winne
Thin hertes wit, which is withinne,   540
Wherof that now thi love excedeth
Mesure, and many a peine bredeth.
Bot if thou cowthest sette in reule
Tho tuo, the thre were eth to reule:
Forthi as of thi wittes five
I wole as now nomore schryve,
Bot only of these ilke tuo.
Tell me therfore if it be so,
Hast thou thin yhen oght misthrowe?

Amans.

Mi fader, ye, I am beknowe,   550

522 atte (at) laste XEC, B   531 myht S   might AC, B
myhte F   549 yhe B

I have hem cast upon Meduse,
Therof I may me noght excuse :
Min herte is growen into Ston,
So that my lady therupon
Hath such a priente of love grave,
That I can noght miselve save.

    What seist thou, Sone, as of thin Ere ?

Opponit Confessor.
Respondet Amans.

    Mi fader, I am gultyf there ;
For whanne I may my lady hiere,
Mi wit with that hath lost his Stiere :   560
I do noght as Uluxes dede,
Bot falle anon upon the stede,
Wher as I se my lady stonde ;
And there, I do yow understonde,
I am topulled in my thoght,   **P. i. 61**
So that of reson leveth noght,
Wherof that I me mai defende.

    My goode Sone, god thamende :

Confessor.

For as me thenketh be thi speche
Thi wittes ben riht feer to seche.   570
As of thin Ere and of thin yhe
I woll nomore specefie,
Bot I woll axen overthis
Of othre thing how that it is.

v. *Celsior est Aquila que Leone ferocior ille,*
  Quem tumor elati cordis ad alta mouet.
Sunt species quinque, quibus esse Superbia ductrix
  Clamat, et in multis mundus adheret eis.
Laruando faciem ficto pallore subornat
  Fraudibus Ypocrisis mellea verba suis.
Sicque pios animos quamsepe ruit muliebres
  Ex humili verbo sub latitante dolo.

[THE SEVEN DEADLY SINS. PRIDE.]

    Mi Sone, as I thee schal enforme,
Ther ben yet of an other forme
Of dedly vices sevene applied,
Wherof the herte is ofte plied
To thing which after schal him grieve.
The ferste of hem thou schalt believe   580

Hic loquitur quod septem sunt peccata mortalia, quorum caput Superbia varias species habet, et earum prima Ypocrisis dicitur, cuius proprieta-

Latin Verses v. 1 Aquila*que* F   8 sub latitante J, S, F   sublatitante AC, B   580 ferste C, S ferst A, F first B

tem secundum vicium
simpliciter Confessor
Amanti declarat.

[FIVE MINISTERS OF
PRIDE.
i. HYPOCRISY.]

Amans.

Confessor.

Ipocrisis Religiosa.

Is Pride, which is principal,
And hath with him in special
Ministres five ful diverse,
Of whiche, as I the schal reherse,
The ferste is seid Ypocrisie.
If thou art of his compaignie,
Tell forth, my Sone, and schrif the clene.
 I wot noght, fader, what ye mene:
Bot this I wolde you beseche,   **P. i. 62**
That ye me be som weie teche   590
What is to ben an ypocrite;
And thanne if I be forto wyte,
I wol beknowen, as it is.
 Mi Sone, an ypocrite is this,—
A man which feigneth conscience,
As thogh it were al innocence,
Withoute, and is noght so withinne;
And doth so for he wolde winne
Of his desir the vein astat.
And whanne he comth anon therat,   600
He scheweth thanne what he was,
The corn is torned into gras,
That was a Rose is thanne a thorn,
And he that was a Lomb beforn
Is thanne a Wolf, and thus malice
Under the colour of justice
Is hid; and as the poeple telleth,
These ordres witen where he duelleth,
As he that of here conseil is,
And thilke world which thei er this   610
Forsoken, he drawth in ayein:
He clotheth richesse, as men sein,
Under the simplesce of poverte,
And doth to seme of gret decerte
Thing which is litel worth withinne:
He seith in open, fy! to Sinne,
And in secre ther is no vice

582 *margin* primitus declarat A . . . B₂, S . . . Δ 584 I *om.* FKH₃
593 be knowen FK 604 toforn Y, B, W 608 *margin*
Ipocrisis Relig. *om.* AM, B 610 word L, B

Of, which that he nis a Norrice :
And evere his chiere is sobre and softe, **P. i. 63**
And where he goth he blesseth ofte,   620
Wherof the blinde world he dreccheth.
Bot yet al only he ne streccheth
His reule upon religioun,
Bot next to that condicioun
In suche as clepe hem holy cherche
It scheweth ek how he can werche   Ipocrisis ecclesiastica.
Among tho wyde furred hodes,
To geten hem the worldes goodes.
And thei hemself ben thilke same
That setten most the world in blame,   630
Bot yet in contraire of her lore
Ther is nothing thei loven more ;
So that semende of liht thei werke
The dedes whiche are inward derke.
And thus this double Ypocrisie
With his devolte apparantie
A viser set upon his face,
Wherof toward this worldes grace
He semeth to be riht wel thewed,
And yit his herte is al beschrewed.   640
Bot natheles he stant believed,
And hath his pourpos ofte achieved
Of worschipe and of worldes welthe,
And takth it, as who seith, be stelthe
Thurgh coverture of his fallas.
And riht so in semblable cas
This vice hath ek his officers
Among these othre seculers   Ipocrisis secularis.
Of grete men, for of the smale   **P. i. 64**
As for tacompte he set no tale,   650
Bot thei that passen the comune
With suche him liketh to comune,
And where he seith he wol socoure
The poeple, there he woll devoure ;
For now aday is manyon

626 gan AM   schal R   *margin* Ipocr. eccles. *om.* A   627 þe
JE₂H₁ . . . B₂, B, W   630 That] þay (þai) X . . . B₂, B

[HYPOCRISY.]

Which spekth of Peter and of John
And thenketh Judas in his herte.
Ther schal no worldes good asterte
His hond, and yit he yifth almesse
And fasteth ofte and hiereth Messe :   660
With *mea culpa*, which he seith,
Upon his brest fullofte he leith
His hond, and cast upward his yhe,
As thogh he Cristes face syhe ;
So that it seemeth ate syhte,
As he al one alle othre myhte
Rescoue with his holy bede.
Bot yet his herte in other stede
Among hise bedes most devoute
Goth in the worldes cause aboute,   670
How that he myhte his warisoun
Encresce.

[HYPOCRISY OF
LOVERS.]
Hic tractat Confes-
sor cum Amante su-
per illa presertim Ipo-
crisia, que sub amoris
facie fraudulenter la-
titando mulieres ipsius
ficticiis credulas se-
pissime decipit inno-
centes.

                    And in comparisoun
Ther ben lovers of such a sort,
That feignen hem an humble port,
And al is bot Ypocrisie,
Which with deceipte and flaterie
Hath many a worthi wif beguiled.
For whanne he hath his tunge affiled,
With softe speche and with lesinge,   **P. i. 65**
Forth with his fals pitous lokynge,   680
He wolde make a womman wene
To gon upon the faire grene,
Whan that sche falleth in the Mir.
For if he may have his desir,
How so falle of the remenant,
He halt no word of covenant ;
Bot er the time that he spede,
Ther is no sleihte at thilke nede,
Which eny loves faitour mai,
That he ne put it in assai,   690
As him belongeth forto done.
The colour of the reyni Mone

656 and of] and AM   and seynt Hı   674 *margin* Hic tractat
—innocentes *om.* A.

With medicine upon his face
He set, and thanne he axeth grace,
As he which hath sieknesse feigned.
Whan his visage is so desteigned,
With yhe upcast on hire he siketh,
And many a contenance he piketh,
To bringen hire in to believe
Of thing which that he wolde achieve,   700
Wherof he berth the pale hewe ;
And for he wolde seme trewe,
He makth him siek, whan he is heil.
Bot whanne he berth lowest the Seil,
Thanne is he swiftest to beguile
The womman, which that ilke while
Set upon him feith or credence.

Mi Sone, if thou thi conscience
Entamed hast in such a wise,
In schrifte thou thee myht avise   710
And telle it me, if it be so.
Min holy fader, certes no.
As forto feigne such sieknesse
It nedeth noght, for this witnesse
I take of god, that my corage
Hath ben mor siek than my visage.
And ek this mai I wel avowe,
So lowe cowthe I nevere bowe
To feigne humilite withoute,
That me ne leste betre loute   720
With alle the thoghtes of myn herte ;
For that thing schal me nevere asterte,
I speke as to my lady diere,
To make hire eny feigned chiere.
God wot wel there I lye noght,
Mi chiere hath be such as my thoght ;
For in good feith, this lieveth wel,
Mi will was betre a thousendel
Than eny chiere that I cowthe.
Bot, Sire, if I have in my yowthe   730
Don other wise in other place,

[HYPOCRISY OF LOVERS.]

P. i. 66

Opponit Confessor.

Respondet Amans.

704 bereþ (berþ) lowest seil AH₁ . . . B₂, B, Magd.   723 tomy F

[Hypocrisy of Lovers.]

I put me therof in your grace:
For this excusen I ne schal,
That I have elles overal
To love and to his compaignie
Be plein withoute Ypocrisie;
Bot ther is on the which I serve,
Althogh I may no thonk deserve,
To whom yet nevere into this day   P. i. 67
I seide onlyche or ye or nay,   740
Bot if it so were in my thoght.
As touchende othre seie I noght
That I nam somdel forto wyte
Of that ye clepe an ypocrite.

Confessor.

    Mi Sone, it sit wel every wiht
To kepe his word in trowthe upryht
Towardes love in alle wise.
For who that wolde him wel avise
What hath befalle in this matiere,
He scholde noght with feigned chiere   750
Deceive Love in no degre.
To love is every herte fre,
Bot in deceipte if that thou feignest
And therupon thi lust atteignest,
That thow hast wonne with thi wyle,
Thogh it thee like for a whyle,
Thou schalt it afterward repente.
And forto prove myn entente,
I finde ensample in a Croniqe
Of hem that love so beswike.   760

[Tale of Mundus and Paulina.]

Quod Ipocrisia sit in amore periculosa, narrat exemplum qualiter sub regno Tiberii Imperatoris quidam miles nomine Mundus, qui Romanorum dux milicie tunc prefuit, dominam Paulinam

    It fell be olde daies thus,
Whil themperour Tiberius
The Monarchie of Rome ladde,
Ther was a worthi Romein hadde
A wif, and sche Pauline hihte,
Which was to every mannes sihte
Of al the Cite the faireste,
And as men seiden, ek the beste.

732 put A, SB, F   putte C   756 the hit like W   it be like H₁L
it be liking C

It is and hath ben evere yit,
That so strong is no mannes wit,
Which thurgh beaute ne mai be drawe
To love, and stonde under the lawe
Of thilke bore frele kinde,
Which makth the hertes yhen blinde,
Wher no reson mai be comuned :
And in this wise stod fortuned
This tale, of which I wolde mene ;
This wif, which in hire lustes grene
Was fair and freissh and tendre of age,
Sche may noght lette the corage
Of him that wole on hire assote.

 Ther was a Duck, and he was hote
Mundus, which hadde in his baillie
To lede the chivalerie
Of Rome, and was a worthi knyht ;
Bot yet he was noght of such myht
The strengthe of love to withstonde,
That he ne was so broght to honde,
That malgre wher he wole or no,
This yonge wif he loveth so,
That he hath put al his assay
To wynne thing which he ne may
Gete of hire graunt in no manere,
Be yifte of gold ne be preiere.
And whanne he syh that be no mede
Toward hir love he myhte spede,
Be sleyhte feigned thanne he wroghte ;
And therupon he him bethoghte
How that ther was in the Cite
A temple of such auctorite,
To which with gret Devocioun
The noble wommen of the toun
Most comunliche a pelrinage
Gon forto preie thilke ymage
Which the godesse of childinge is,

P. i. 68 [Tale of Mundus
770   and Paulina.]
pulcherrimam castita-
tisque famosissimam
mediantibus duobus
falsis presbiteris in
templo Ysis deum se
esse fingens sub ficte
sanctitatis ypocrisi
nocturno tempore vi-
ciauit. Vnde idem dux
in exilium, presbiteri
in mortem ob sui cri-
minis enormitatem
dampnati extiterant,
ymagoque dee Ysis a
780 templo euulsa vniuer-
so conclamante populo
in flumen Tiberiadis
proiecta mergebatur.

790

P. i. 69
800

773 *margin* do*mini* se esse fingens ME₂   do*mini* se esse fingentes A
775 Ther(e) AM   776 stonde RCLB₂   stant H₁GE   782 Duck
A, F   Duk (duk) SB   Duke C

And cleped was be name Ysis :
And in hire temple thanne were,
To reule and to ministre there
After the lawe which was tho,
Above alle othre Prestes tuo.   810
This Duck, which thoghte his love gete,
Upon a day hem tuo to mete
Hath bede, and thei come at his heste ;
Wher that thei hadde a riche feste,
And after mete in prive place
This lord, which wolde his thonk pourchace,
To ech of hem yaf thanne a yifte,
And spak so that be weie of schrifte
He drowh hem unto his covine,
To helpe and schape how he Pauline   820
After his lust deceive myhte.
And thei here trowthes bothe plyhte,
That thei be nyhte hire scholden wynne
Into the temple, and he therinne
Schal have of hire al his entente :
And thus acorded forth thei wente.
   Now lest thurgh which ypocrisie
Ordeigned was the tricherie,
Wherof this ladi was deceived. ~   **P. i. 70**
These Prestes hadden wel conceived   830
That sche was of gret holinesse ;
And with a contrefet simplesse,
Which hid was in a fals corage,
Feignende an hevenely message
Thei come and seide unto hir thus :
' Pauline, the god Anubus
Hath sent ous bothe Prestes hiere,
And seith he woll to thee appiere
Be nyhtes time himself alone,
For love he hath to thi persone :   840
And therupon he hath ous bede,
That we in Ysis temple a stede

820 he] the B, W   that H₁   834 ffeigned AMH₁XLB₂, W
(ffeignet) þey feigned C   837 seyt vs B *p.m.*   Prestes]
present B

Honestely for thee pourveie,
Wher thou be nyhte, as we thee seie,
Of him schalt take avisioun.
For upon thi condicioun,
The which is chaste and ful of feith,
Such pris, as he ous tolde, he leith,
That he wol stonde of thin acord ;
And forto bere hierof record   850
He sende ous hider bothe tuo.'
Glad was hire innocence tho
Of suche wordes as sche herde,
With humble chiere and thus answerde,
And seide that the goddes wille
Sche was al redy to fulfille,
That be hire housebondes leve
Sche wolde in Ysis temple at eve
Upon hire goddes grace abide,   **P. i. 71**
To serven him the nyhtes tide.   860
The Prestes tho gon hom ayein,
And sche goth to hire sovereign,
Of goddes wille and as it was
Sche tolde him al the pleine cas,
Wherof he was deceived eke,
And bad that sche hire scholde meke
Al hol unto the goddes heste.
And thus sche, which was al honeste
To godward after hire entente,
At nyht unto the temple wente,   870
Wher that the false Prestes were ;
And thei receiven hire there
With such a tokne of holinesse,
As thogh thei syhen a godesse,
And al withinne in prive place
A softe bedd of large space
Thei hadde mad and encourtined,
Wher sche was afterward engined.
Bot sche, which al honour supposeth,
The false Prestes thanne opposeth,   880
And axeth be what observance

876 lofte H₁ ... B₂

Sche myhte most to the plesance
Of godd that nyhtes reule kepe :
And thei hire bidden forto slepe
Liggende upon the bedd alofte,
For so, thei seide, al stille and softe
God Anubus hire wolde awake.
The conseil in this wise take,
The Prestes fro this lady gon;   P. i. 72
And sche, that wiste of guile non,   890
In the manere as it was seid
To slepe upon the bedd is leid,
In hope that sche scholde achieve
Thing which stod thanne upon bilieve,
Fulfild of alle holinesse.
Bot sche hath failed, as I gesse,
For in a closet faste by
The Duck was hid so prively
That sche him myhte noght perceive ;
And he, that thoghte to deceive,   900
Hath such arrai upon him nome,
That whanne he wolde unto hir come,
It scholde semen at hire yhe
As thogh sche verrailiche syhe
God Anubus, and in such wise
This ypocrite of his queintise
Awaiteth evere til sche slepte.
And thanne out of his place he crepte
So stille that sche nothing herde,
And to the bedd stalkende he ferde,   910
And sodeinly, er sche it wiste,
Beclipt in armes he hire kiste :
Wherof in wommanysshe drede
Sche wok and nyste what to rede;
Bot he with softe wordes milde
Conforteth hire and seith, with childe
He wolde hire make in such a kynde
That al the world schal have in mynde
The worschipe of that ilke Sone ;   P. i. 73

884 biddeþ B   886 al *om.* B   893 wolde AM   896 hath]
þat B   903 to H₁ ... L vnto B₂

For he schal with the goddes wone,   920
And ben himself a godd also.
With suche wordes and with mo,
The whiche he feigneth in his speche,
This lady wit was al to seche,
As sche which alle trowthe weneth:
Bot he, that alle untrowthe meneth,
With blinde tales so hire ladde,
That all his wille of hire he hadde.
And whan him thoghte it was ynowh,
Ayein the day he him withdrowh   930
So prively that sche ne wiste
Wher he becom, bot as him liste
Out of the temple he goth his weie.
And sche began to bidde and preie
Upon the bare ground knelende,
And after that made hire offrende,
And to the Prestes yiftes grete
Sche yaf, and homward be the Strete.
The Duck hire mette and seide thus:
'The myhti godd which Anubus   940
Is hote, he save the, Pauline,
For thou art of his discipline
So holy, that no mannes myht
Mai do that he hath do to nyht
Of thing which thou hast evere eschuied.
Bot I his grace have so poursuied,
That I was mad his lieutenant:
Forthi be weie of covenant
Fro this day forth I am al thin,   P. i. 74
And if thee like to be myn,   950
That stant upon thin oghne wille.'
    Sche herde his tale and bar it stille,
And hom sche wente, as it befell,
Into hir chambre, and ther sche fell
Upon hire bedd to wepe and crie,
And seide: 'O derke ypocrisie,
Thurgh whos dissimilacion
Of fals ymaginacion

                924 al to] for to A

I am thus wickedly deceived!
Bot that I have it aperceived   960
I thonke unto the goddes alle;
For thogh it ones be befalle,
It schal nevere eft whil that I live,
And thilke avou to godd I yive.'
And thus wepende sche compleigneth,
Hire faire face and al desteigneth
With wofull teres of hire ȳe,
So that upon this agonie
Hire housebonde is inne come,
And syh how sche was overcome   970
With sorwe, and axeth what hire eileth.
And sche with that hirself beweileth
Welmore than sche dede afore,
And seide, 'Helas, wifhode is lore
In me, which whilom was honeste,
I am non other than a beste,
Now I defouled am of tuo.'
And as sche myhte speke tho,
Aschamed with a pitous onde   **P. i. 75**
Sche tolde unto hir housebonde   980
The sothe of al the hole tale,
And in hire speche ded and pale
Sche swouneth welnyh to the laste.
And he hire in hise armes faste
Uphield, and ofte swor his oth
That he with hire is nothing wroth,
For wel he wot sche may ther noght:
Bot natheles withinne his thoght
His herte stod in sori plit,
And seide he wolde of that despit   990
Be venged, how so evere it falle,
And sende unto hise frendes alle.
And whan thei weren come in fere,
He tolde hem upon this matiere,
And axeth hem what was to done:
And thei avised were sone,
And seide it thoghte hem for the beste

975 me *om.* B

To sette ferst his wif in reste,
And after pleigne to the king
Upon the matiere of this thing.   1000
Tho was this wofull wif conforted
Be alle weies and desported,
Til that sche was somdiel amended;
And thus a day or tuo despended,
The thridde day sche goth to pleigne
With many a worthi Citezeine,
And he with many a Citezein.

Whan themperour it herde sein,
And knew the falshed of the vice,   **P. i. 76**
He seide he wolde do justice: 1010
And ferst he let the Prestes take,
And for thei scholde it noght forsake,
He put hem into questioun;
Bot thei of the suggestioun
Ne couthen noght a word refuse,
Bot for thei wolde hemself excuse,
The blame upon the Duck thei leide.
Bot therayein the conseil seide
That thei be noght excused so,
For he is on and thei ben tuo,   1020
And tuo han more wit then on,
So thilke excusement was non.
And over that was seid hem eke,
That whan men wolden vertu seke,
Men scholde it in the Prestes finde;
Here ordre is of so hyh a kinde,
That thei be Duistres of the weie:
Forthi, if eny man forsueie
Thurgh hem, thei be noght excusable.
And thus be lawe resonable   1030
Among the wise jugges there
The Prestes bothe dampned were,
So that the prive tricherie
Hid under fals Ipocrisie
Was thanne al openliche schewed,

1013 put SB, F putte AC   1015 a] o C, B   1023 seid
A, S seyd B seide F   1027 diustres A

[TALE OF MUNDUS
AND PAULINA.]

That many a man hem hath beschrewed.
And whan the Prestes weren dede,
The temple of thilke horrible dede
Thei thoghten purge, and thilke ymage, **P. i. 77**
Whos cause was the pelrinage,   1040
Thei drowen out and als so faste
Fer into Tibre thei it caste,
Wher the Rivere it hath defied :
And thus the temple purified
Thei have of thilke horrible Sinne,
Which was that time do therinne.
Of this point such was the juise,
Bot of the Duck was other wise :
For he with love was bestad,
His dom was noght so harde lad ;   1050
For Love put reson aweie
And can noght se the rihte weie.
And be this cause he was respited,
So that the deth him was acquited,
Bot for al that he was exiled,
For he his love hath so beguiled,
That he schal nevere come ayein :
For who that is to trowthe unplein,
He may noght failen of vengance.

    And ek to take remembrance   1060
Of that Ypocrisie hath wroght
On other half, men scholde noght
To lihtly lieve al that thei hiere,
Bot thanne scholde a wisman stiere
The Schip, whan suche wyndes blowe :
For ferst thogh thei beginne lowe,
At ende thei be noght menable,
Bot al tobreken Mast and Cable,
So that the Schip with sodein blast,   **P. i. 78**
Whan men lest wene, is overcast ;   1070

1036 haþ hem AME₂H₁L, W (has hem)   be schrewed FK
1059 veniance XRCLB₂   1067 menable AJYXG, SAdΔ, F meuable
(moeuable) ELB₂, B, WH₃ *doubtful* MH₁RC, Magd. 1068 al
tobroken (al to broke &c.) AMERCB₂, Ad, FH₃Magd.   alto
brosten E₂L

As now fulofte a man mai se :
And of old time how it hath be
I finde a gret experience,
Wherof to take an evidence
Good is, and to be war also
Of the peril, er him be wo.

Of hem that ben so derk withinne,
At Troie also if we beginne,
Ipocrisie it hath betraied :
For whan the Greks hadde al assaied,   1080
And founde that be no bataille
Ne be no Siege it myhte availe
The toun to winne thurgh prouesse,
This vice feigned of simplesce
Thurgh sleyhte of Calcas and of Crise
It wan be such a maner wise.
An Hors of Bras thei let do forge
Of such entaile, of such a forge,
That in this world was nevere man
That such an other werk began.   1090
The crafti werkman Epius
It made, and forto telle thus,
The Greks, that thoghten to beguile
The kyng of Troie, in thilke while
With Anthenor and with Enee,
That were bothe of the Cite
And of the conseil the wiseste,
The richeste and the myhtieste,
In prive place so thei trete   **P. i. 79**
With fair beheste and yiftes grete   1100
Of gold, that thei hem have engined ;
Togedre and whan thei be covined,
Thei feignen forto make a pes,
And under that yit natheles
Thei schopen the destruccioun
Bothe of the kyng and of the toun.

[THE TROJAN HORSE.]

Hic vlterius ponit exemplum de illa eciam Ypocrisia, que inter virum et virum decipiens periculosissima consistit. Et narrat, qualiter Greci in obsidione ciuitatis Troie, cum ipsam vi comprehendere nullatenus potuerunt, fallaci animo cum Troianis pacem vt dicunt pro perpetuo statuebant : et super hoc quendam eouum mire grossitudinis de ere fabricatum ad sacrificandum in templo Minerue confingentes, sub tali sanctitatis ypocrisi dictam Ciuitatem intrarunt, et ipsam cum inhabitantibus gladio et igne comminuentes pro perpetuo penitus deuastarunt.

1079 it] hem H₁ . . . ECLB₂, B   he R   1083 *margin* inter virum
et virum] inter virum H₁E . . . B₂   inter viros XG   1090 *margin* hoc
om. AM   1093 *margin* in templo *om.* H₁ . . . B₂   1099 *margin*
deuastarunt] demonstrarunt A
**   F

And thus the false pees was take
Of hem of Grece and undertake,
And therupon thei founde a weie,
Wher strengthe myhte noght aweie,   1110
That sleihte scholde helpe thanne;
And of an ynche a large spanne
Be colour of the pees thei made,
And tolden how thei weren glade
Of that thei stoden in acord;
And for it schal ben of record,
Unto the kyng the Gregois seiden,
Be weie of love and this thei preiden,
As thei that wolde his thonk deserve,
A Sacrifice unto Minerve,   1120
The pes to kepe in good entente,
Thei mosten offre er that thei wente.
The kyng conseiled in this cas
Be Anthenor and Eneas
Therto hath yoven his assent:
So was the pleine trowthe blent
Thurgh contrefet Ipocrisie
Of that thei scholden sacrifie.

The Greks under the holinesse   P. i. 80
Anon with alle besinesse   1130
Here Hors of Bras let faire dihte,
Which was to sen a wonder sihte;
For it was trapped of himselve,
And hadde of smale whieles twelve,
Upon the whiche men ynowe
With craft toward the toun it drowe,
And goth glistrende ayein the Sunne.
Tho was ther joie ynowh begunne,
For Troie in gret devocioun
Cam also with processioun   1140
Ayein this noble Sacrifise
With gret honour, and in this wise
Unto the gates thei it broghte.
Bot of here entre whan thei soghte,

1115 stood in a cord B   1118 þus M ... R, BAd, WH₃Magd.
1125 ȝiuen A

The gates weren al to smale ;
And therupon was many a tale,
Bot for the worschipe of Minerve,
To whom thei comen forto serve,
Thei of the toun, whiche understode
That al this thing was do for goode,   1150
For pes, wherof that thei ben glade.
The gates that Neptunus made
A thousend wynter ther tofore,
Thei have anon tobroke and tore ;
The stronge walles doun thei bete,
So that in to the large strete
This Hors with gret solempnite
Was broght withinne the Cite,
And offred with gret reverence,   **P. i. 81**
Which was to Troie an evidence   1160
Of love and pes for everemo.
The Gregois token leve tho
With al the hole felaschipe,
And forth thei wenten into Schipe
And crossen seil and made hem yare,
Anon as thogh thei wolden fare :
Bot whan the blake wynter nyht
Withoute Mone or Sterre lyht
Bederked hath the water Stronde,
Al prively thei gon to londe   1170
Ful armed out of the navie.
Synon, which mad was here aspie
Withinne Troie, as was conspired,
Whan time was a tokne hath fired ;
And thei with that here weie holden,
And comen in riht as thei wolden,
Ther as the gate was tobroke.
The pourpos was full take and spoke :
Er eny man may take kepe,
Whil that the Cite was aslepe,   1180
Thei slowen al that was withinne,

1145 tosmale F   1162 token] toke(n) her(e) CLB₂   1165 trossen
ECL trussen H₁R tuossen B₂   1172 Symon H₁CLB₂, FWH₃Magd.
mad *om.* AM

[THE TROJAN HORSE.]

And token what thei myhten wynne
Of such good as was sufficant,
And brenden up the remenant.
And thus cam out the tricherie,
Which under fals Ypocrisie
Was hid, and thei that wende pees
Tho myhten finde no reles
Of thilke swerd which al devoureth.   P. i. 82

[HYPOCRISY IN LOVE.]

Fulofte and thus the swete soureth,   1190
Whan it is knowe to the tast:
He spilleth many a word in wast
That schal with such a poeple trete;
For whan he weneth most beyete,
Thanne is he schape most to lese.
And riht so if a womman chese
Upon the wordes that sche hiereth
Som man, whan he most trewe appiereth,
Thanne is he forthest fro the trowthe:
Bot yit fulofte, and that is rowthe,   1200
Thei speden that ben most untrewe
And loven every day a newe,
Wherof the lief is after loth
And love hath cause to be wroth.
Bot what man that his lust desireth
Of love, and therupon conspireth
With wordes feigned to deceive,
He schal noght faile to receive
His peine, as it is ofte sene.

Confessor.

Forthi, my Sone, as I thee mene,   1210
It sit the wel to taken hiede
That thou eschuie of thi manhiede
Ipocrisie and his semblant,
That thou ne be noght deceivant,
To make a womman to believe
Thing which is noght in thi bilieve:
For in such feint Ipocrisie
Of love is al the tricherie,
Thurgh which love is deceived ofte;   P. i. 83

1197 the wordes that] þe which B   1210 *margin* Confessor
om. A   1216 thi] þe XR, B

For feigned semblant is so softe,
Unethes love may be war.
Forthi, my Sone, as I wel dar,
I charge thee to fle that vice,
That many a womman hath mad nice;
Bot lok thou dele noght withal.
    Iwiss, fader, nomor I schal.   Amans.
    Now, Sone, kep that thou hast swore: Confessor.
For this that thou hast herd before
Is seid the ferste point of Pride:
And next upon that other side,   1230
To schryve and speken overthis
Touchende of Pride, yit ther is
The point seconde, I thee behote,
Which Inobedience is hote.

vi. *Flectere quam frangi melius reputatur, et olle*
   Fictilis ad cacabum pugna valere nequit.
Quem neque lex hominum, neque lex diuina valebit
   Flectere, multociens corde reflectit amor.
Quem non flectit amor, non est flectendus ab vllo,
   Set rigor illius plus Elephante riget.
Dedignatur amor poterit quos scire rebelles,
   Et rudibus sortem prestat habere rudem;
Set qui sponte sui subicit se cordis amore,
   Frangit in aduersis omnia fata pius.   (10)

    This vice of Inobedience
Ayein the reule of conscience
Al that is humble he desalloweth,
That he toward his god ne boweth
After the lawes of his heste.
Noght as a man bot as a beste,   1240   Hic loquitur de se-
Which goth upon his lustes wilde,   **P. i. 84** cunda specie Superbie,
So goth this proude vice unmylde,   que Inobediencia dici-
That he desdeigneth alle lawe: tur: et primo illius
He not what is to be felawe,   vicii naturam simpli-
And serve may he noght for pride;   citer declarat, et trac-
So is he badde on every side,   tat consequenter su-
And is that selve of whom men speke,   per illa precipue Ino-
Which wol noght bowe er that he breke.   bediencia, que in curia
                                               Cupidinis exosa amo-
                                               ris causam ex sua im-
                                               becillitate sepissime
                                               retardat. In cuius

Latin Verses vi. 4 reflectat H₁ . . . CB₂   ne flectat L

materia Confessor A-
manti specialius oppo-
nit.

I not if love him myhte plie,
For elles forto justefie   1250
His herte, I not what mihte availe.

Confessor.

   Forthi, my Sone, of such entaile
If that thin herte be disposed,
Tell out and let it noght be glosed :
For if that thou unbuxom be
To love, I not in what degree
Thou schalt thi goode world achieve.

Amans.

   Mi fader, ye schul wel believe,
The yonge whelp which is affaited
Hath noght his Maister betre awaited,   1260
To couche, whan he seith 'Go lowe,'
That I, anon as I may knowe
Mi ladi will, ne bowe more.
Bot other while I grucche sore
Of some thinges that sche doth,
Wherof that I woll telle soth :
For of tuo pointz I am bethoght,
That, thogh I wolde, I myhte noght
Obeie unto my ladi heste ;
Bot I dar make this beheste,   1270
Save only of that ilke tuo   **P. i. 85**
I am unbuxom of no mo.

Opponit Confessor.
Respondet Amans.

   What ben tho tuo? tell on, quod he.
   Mi fader, this is on, that sche
Comandeth me my mowth to close,
And that I scholde hir noght oppose
In love, of which I ofte preche,
Bot plenerliche of such a speche
Forbere, and soffren hire in pes.
Bot that ne myhte I natheles   1280
For al this world obeie ywiss ;
For whanne I am ther as sche is,
Though sche my tales noght alowe,
Ayein hir will yit mot I bowe,
To seche if that I myhte have grace :

1252 *margin* Confessor *om.* S, F   1257 schat F   1263 ne]
me H₁ . . . B₂, B^Λ   (l. 1263 *om.* Ad)   1273 f. *margin* Opp. Conf.
Resp. Am. *om.* A   1280 myhte A   myht S, F

Bot that thing may I noght enbrace
For ought that I can speke or do ;
And yit fulofte I speke so,
That sche is wroth and seith, ' Be stille.'
If I that heste schal fulfille   1290
And therto ben obedient,
Thanne is my cause fully schent,
For specheles may noman spede.
So wot I noght what is to rede ; ·
Bot certes I may noght obeie,
That I ne mot algate seie
Somwhat of that I wolde mene ;
For evere it is aliche grene,
The grete love which I have,
Wherof I can noght bothe save   1300
My speche and this obedience :   **P. i. 86**
And thus fulofte my silence
I breke, and is the ferste point
Wherof that I am out of point
In this, and yit it is no pride.
    Now thanne upon that other side
To telle my desobeissance,
Ful sore it stant to my grevance
And may noght sinke into my wit ;
For ofte time sche me bit   1310
To leven hire and chese a newe,
And seith, if I the sothe knewe
How ferr I stonde from hir grace,
I scholde love in other place.
Bot therof woll I desobeie ;
For also wel sche myhte seie,
' Go tak the Mone ther it sit,'
As bringe that into my wit :
For ther was nevere rooted tre,
That stod so faste in his degre,   1320
That I ne stonde more faste
Upon hire love, and mai noght caste

1286 pourchace A   1303 is] þis AME₂, þis is ∆, W   1304 point]
ioint GCLB₂, W   1310 For ofte] fful ofte (ffulofte) H₁ . . . B₂, B
1314 other] anoþer (an oþer) H₁XRLB₂, B∆

Min herte awey, althogh I wolde.
For god wot, thogh I nevere scholde
Sen hir with yhe after this day,
Yit stant it so that I ne may
Hir love out of my brest remue.
This is a wonder retenue,
That malgre wher sche wole or non
Min herte is everemore in on, 1330
So that I can non other chese, P. i. 87
Bot whether that I winne or lese,
I moste hire loven til I deie;
And thus I breke as be that weie
Hire hestes and hir comandinges,
Bot trewliche in non othre thinges.
Forthi, my fader, what is more
Touchende to this ilke lore
I you beseche, after the forme
That ye pleinly me wolde enforme, 1340
So that I may myn herte reule
In loves cause after the reule.

[Murmur and Complaint.]

vii. *Murmur in aduersis ita concipit ille superbus,*
Pena quod ex bina sorte peru. get eum.
Obuia fortune cum spes in amore resistit,
Non sine mentali murmure plangit amans.

Hic loquitur de Murmure et Planctu, qui super omnes alios Inobediencie secreciores vt ministri illi deseruiunt.

Toward this vice of which we trete
Ther ben yit tweie of thilke estrete,
Here name is Murmur and Compleignte:
Ther can noman here chiere peinte,
To sette a glad semblant therinne,
For thogh fortune make hem wynne,
Yit grucchen thei, and if thei lese,
Ther is no weie forto chese, 1350
Wherof thei myhten stonde appesed.
So ben thei comunly desesed;
Ther may no welthe ne poverte
Attempren hem to the decerte

1336 treweliche in oþre A   1338 Touchend vnto H1 . . . B2, B
Touchende of (Touchand of) SAdΔ, H3
Latin Verses vii. 4 munere B
1345 compleingte F   1347 *margin* deseruiunt A, SB deseruiant FK

Of buxomnesse be no wise:
For ofte time thei despise
The goode fortune as the badde,   **P. i. 88**
As thei no mannes reson hadde,
Thurgh pride, wherof thei be blinde.

   And ryht of such a maner kinde   1360
Ther be lovers, that thogh thei have
Of love al that thei wolde crave,
Yit wol thei grucche be som weie,
That thei wol noght to love obeie
Upon the trowthe, as thei do scholde;
And if hem lacketh that thei wolde,
Anon thei falle in such a peine,
That evere unbuxomly thei pleigne
Upon fortune, and curse and crie,
That thei wol noght here hertes plie   1370
To soffre til it betre falle.
Forthi if thou amonges alle
Hast used this condicioun,
Mi Sone, in thi Confessioun
Now tell me pleinly what thou art.

   Mi fader, I beknowe a part,   *Amans.*
So as ye tolden hier above
Of Murmur and Compleignte of love,
That for I se no sped comende,
Ayein fortune compleignende   1380
I am, as who seith, everemo:
And ek fulofte tyme also,
Whan so is that I se and hiere
Or hevy word or hevy chiere
Of my lady, I grucche anon;
Bot wordes dar I speke non,
Wherof sche myhte be desplesed,   **P. i. 89**
Bot in myn herte I am desesed:
With many a Murmur, god it wot,
Thus drinke I in myn oghne swot,   1390
And thogh I make no semblant,
Min herte is al desobeissant;

1376 *margin* Amans *om.* A   1378 Compleingte F   1384 Of
. . . of YXE . . . L, B   Of: . . or GB₂   . . . and (*om.* Or) H₁

[MURMUR AND
COMPLAINT.]

Confessor.

And in this wise I me confesse
Of that ye clepe unbuxomnesse.
Now telleth what youre conseil is.
    Mi Sone, and I thee rede this,
What so befalle of other weie,
That thou to loves heste obeie
Als ferr as thou it myht suffise:
For ofte sithe in such a wise   1400
Obedience in love availeth,
Wher al a mannes strengthe faileth;
Wherof, if that the list to wite
In a Cronique as it is write,
A gret ensample thou myht fynde,
Which now is come to my mynde.

[TALE OF FLORENT.]

Hic contra amori
inobedientes ad com-
mendacionem Obedi-
encie Confessor super
eodem exemplum po-
nit; vbi dicit quod,
cum quedam Regis Ci-
zilie filia in sue iuuen-
tutis floribus pulcher-
rima ex eius Nouerce
incantacionibus in ve-
tulam   turpissimam
transformata extitit,
Florencius tunc Im-
paratoris Claudi Ne-
pos, miles in armis
strenuissimus amoro-
sisque legibus inten-
dens, ipsam ex sua
obediencia in pulcri-
tudinem pristinam mi-
rabiliter reformauit.

    Ther was whilom be daies olde
A worthi knyht, and as men tolde
He was Nevoeu to themperour
And of his Court a Courteour: 1410
Wifles he was, Florent he hihte,
He was a man that mochel myhte,
Of armes he was desirous,
Chivalerous and amorous,
And for the fame of worldes speche,
Strange aventures forto seche,
He rod the Marches al aboute.   P. i. 90
And fell a time, as he was oute,
Fortune, which may every thred
Tobreke and knette of mannes sped,   1420
Schop, as this knyht rod in a pas,
That he be strengthe take was,
And to a Castell thei him ladde,
Wher that he fewe frendes hadde:
For so it fell that ilke stounde

1396 and] as B   1396 *margin* Confessor *om.* A   1403–6 *These
four lines in third recension only: the others have two, given thus in* A,
                And in ensample of þis matiere
                A tale I fynde, as þou schalt hiere.
Below this in A, Exemplum super eodem.
    1408 knyht *om.* A   1416 for to] wold he B   1417 *margin*
amoris *que* A . . . B₂, Λ   1420 *margin* transformauit A

That he hath with a dedly wounde
Feihtende his oghne hondes slain
Branchus, which to the Capitain
Was Sone and Heir, wherof ben wrothe
The fader and the moder bothe.   1430
That knyht Branchus was of his hond
The worthieste of al his lond,
And fain thei wolden do vengance
Upon Florent, bot remembrance
That thei toke of his worthinesse
Of knyhthod and of gentilesse,
And how he stod of cousinage
To themperour, made hem assuage,
And dorsten noght slen him for fere :
In gret desputeisoun thei were   1440
Among hemself, what was the beste.
Ther was a lady, the slyheste
Of alle that men knewe tho,
So old sche myhte unethes go,
And was grantdame unto the dede :
And sche with that began to rede,
And seide how sche wol bringe him inne, P. i. 91
That sche schal him to dethe winne
Al only of his oghne grant,
Thurgh strengthe of verray covenant   1450
Withoute blame of eny wiht.
Anon sche sende for this kniht,
And of hire Sone sche alleide
The deth, and thus to him sche seide :
' Florent, how so thou be to wyte
Of Branchus deth, men schal respite
As now to take vengement,
Be so thou stonde in juggement
Upon certein condicioun,
That thou unto a questioun   1460
Which I schal axe schalt ansuere ;
And over this thou schalt ek swere,
That if thou of the sothe faile,
Ther schal non other thing availe,

1440 despitesoun A   1464 *line om.* B

That thou ne schalt thi deth receive.
And for men schal thee noght deceive,
That thou therof myht ben avised,
Thou schalt have day and tyme assised
And leve saufly forto wende,
Be so that at thi daies ende   1470
Thou come ayein with thin avys.

   This knyht, which worthi was and wys,
This lady preith that he may wite,
And have it under Seales write,
What questioun it scholde be
For which he schal in that degree
Stonde of his lif in jeupartie.   **P. i. 92**
With that sche feigneth compaignie,
And seith : ‘Florent, on love it hongeth
Al that to myn axinge longeth :   1480
What alle wommen most desire
This wole I axe, and in thempire
Wher as thou hast most knowlechinge
Tak conseil upon this axinge.’

   Florent this thing hath undertake,
The day was set, the time take,
Under his seal he wrot his oth,
In such a wise and forth he goth
Hom to his Emes court ayein ;
To whom his aventure plein   1490
He tolde, of that him is befalle.
And upon that thei weren alle
The wiseste of the lond asent,
Bot natheles of on assent
Thei myhte noght acorde plat,
On seide this, an othre that.
After the disposicioun
Of naturel complexioun
To som womman it is plesance,
That to an other is grevance ;   1500
Bot such a thing in special,
Which to hem alle in general

[TALE OF FLORENT.]

Is most plesant, and most desired
Above alle othre and most conspired,
Such o thing conne thei noght finde
Be Constellacion ne kinde:
And thus Florent withoute cure   P. i. 93
Mot stonde upon his aventure,
And is al schape unto the lere,
As in defalte of his answere.   1510
This knyht hath levere forto dye
Than breke his trowthe and forto lye
In place ther as he was swore,
And schapth him gon ayein therfore.
Whan time cam he tok his leve,
That lengere wolde he noght beleve,
And preith his Em he be noght wroth,
For that is a point of his oth,
He seith, that noman schal him wreke,
Thogh afterward men hiere speke   1520
That he par aventure deie.
And thus he wente forth his weie
Alone as knyht aventurous,
And in his thoght was curious
To wite what was best to do:
And as he rod al one so,
And cam nyh ther he wolde be,
In a forest under a tre
He syh wher sat a creature,
A lothly wommannysch figure,   1530
That forto speke of fleisch and bon
So foul yit syh he nevere non.
This knyht behield hir redely,
And as he wolde have passed by,
Sche cleped him and bad abide;
And he his horse heved aside
Tho torneth, and to hire he rod,   P. i. 94
And there he hoveth and abod,
To wite what sche wolde mene.
And sche began him to bemene,   1540

1505. Such o þing ME2, S, FH3   Suiche one þing Δ   Such a þing
AJH1 . . . B2, BAd, W   1509 in to E . . . B2, B   to H3

And seide : 'Florent be thi name,
Thou hast on honde such a game,
That bot thou be the betre avised,
Thi deth. is schapen and devised,
That al the world ne mai the save,
Bot if that thou my conseil have.'
　　Florent, whan he this tale herde,
Unto this olde wyht answerde
And of hir conseil he hir preide.
And sche ayein to him thus seide :　　　　1550
'Florent, if I for the so schape,
That thou thurgh me thi deth ascape
And take worschipe of thi dede,
What schal I have to my mede ? '
'What thing,' quod he, 'that thou wolt axe.'
'I bidde nevere a betre taxe,'
Quod sche, 'bot ferst, er thou be sped,
Thou schalt me leve such a wedd,
That I wol have thi trowthe in honde
That thou schalt be myn housebonde.'　　　1560
'Nay,' seith Florent, 'that may noght be.'
'Ryd thanne forth thi wey,' quod sche,
'And if thou go withoute red,
Thou schalt be sekerliche ded.'
Florent behihte hire good ynowh
Of lond, of rente, of park, of plowh,
Bot al that compteth sche at noght.　　P. i. 95
Tho fell this knyht in mochel thoght,
Now goth he forth, now comth ayein,
He wot noght what is best to sein,　　　　1570
And thoghte, as he rod to and fro,
That chese he mot on of the tuo,
Or forto take hire to his wif
Or elles forto lese his lif.
And thanne he caste his avantage,
That sche was of so gret an age,
That sche mai live bot a while,
And thoghte put hire in an Ile,

Wher that noman hire scholde knowe,
Til sche with deth were overthrowe.   1580
And thus this yonge lusti knyht
Unto this olde lothly wiht
Tho seide : 'If that non other chance
Mai make my deliverance,
Bot only thilke same speche
Which, as thou seist, thou schalt me teche,
Have hier myn hond, I schal thee wedde.'
And thus his trowthe he leith to wedde.
With that sche frounceth up the browe :
'This covenant I wol allowe,'   1590
Sche seith : 'if eny other thing
Bot that thou hast of my techyng
Fro deth thi body mai respite,
I woll thee of thi trowthe acquite,
And elles be non other weie.
Now herkne me what I schal seie.
Whan thou art come into the place,   P. i. 96
Wher now thei maken gret manace
And upon thi comynge abyde,
Thei wole anon the same tide   1600
Oppose thee of thin answere.
I wot thou wolt nothing forbere
Of that thou wenest be thi beste,
And if thou myht so finde reste,
Wel is, for thanne is ther nomore.
And elles this schal be my lore,
That thou schalt seie, upon this Molde
That alle wommen lievest wolde
Be soverein of mannes love :
For what womman is so above,   1610
Sche hath, as who seith, al hire wille ;
And elles may sche noght fulfille
What thing hir were lievest have.
With this answere thou schalt save
Thiself, and other wise noght.
And whan thou hast thin ende wroght,
Com hier ayein, thou schalt me finde,
And let nothing out of thi minde.'

He goth him forth with hevy chiere,
As he that not in what manere   1620
He mai this worldes joie atteigne:
For if he deie, he hath a peine,
And if he live, he mot him binde
To such on which of alle kinde
Of wommen is thunsemlieste:
Thus wot he noght what is the beste:
Bot be him lief or be him loth,   **P. i. 97**
Unto the Castell forth he goth
His full answere forto yive,
Or forto deie or forto live.   1630
Forth with his conseil cam the lord,
The thinges stoden of record,
He sende up for the lady sone,
And forth sche cam, that olde Mone.
In presence of the remenant
The strengthe of al the covenant
Tho was reherced openly,
And to Florent sche bad forthi
That he schal tellen his avis,
As he that woot what is the pris.   1640
Florent seith al that evere he couthe,
Bot such word cam ther non to mowthe,
That he for yifte or for beheste
Mihte eny wise his deth areste.
And thus he tarieth longe and late,
Til that this lady bad algate
That he schal for the dom final
Yive his answere in special
Of that sche hadde him ferst opposed:
And thanne he hath trewly supposed   1650
That he him may of nothing yelpe,
Bot if so be tho wordes helpe,
Whiche as the womman hath him tawht;
Wherof he hath an hope cawht
That he schal ben excused so,
And tolde out plein his wille tho.

1626 þunsemylieste FK   þunsemelieste B   1632 acord B
1648 ȝiue AC, B   ȝif F   1652 þe AMH₁, Ad, H₃

P. i. 98 [TALE OF FLORENT.]

And whan that this Matrone herde
The manere how this knyht ansuerde,
Sche seide : ' Ha treson, wo thee be,
That hast thus told the privite,   1660
Which alle wommen most desire !
I wolde that thou were afire.'
Bot natheles in such a plit
Florent of his answere is quit :
And tho began his sorwe newe,
For he mot gon, or ben untrewe,
To hire which his trowthe hadde.
Bot he, which alle schame dradde,
Goth forth in stede of his penance,
And takth the fortune of his chance,   1670
As he that was with trowthe affaited.
    This olde wyht him hath awaited
In place wher as he hire lefte :
Florent his wofull heved uplefte
And syh this vecke wher sche sat,
Which was the lothlieste what
That evere man caste on his yhe :
Hire Nase bass, hire browes hyhe,
Hire yhen smale and depe set,
Hire chekes ben with teres wet,   1680
And rivelen as an emty skyn
Hangende doun unto the chin,
Hire Lippes schrunken ben for age,
Ther was no grace in the visage,
Hir front was nargh, hir lockes hore,
Sche loketh forth as doth a More,
Hire Necke is schort, hir schuldres courbe, **P. i. 99**
That myhte a mannes lust destourbe,
Hire body gret and nothing smal,
And schortly to descrive hire al,   1690
Sche hath no lith withoute a lak ;
Bot lich unto the wollesak
Sche proferth hire unto this knyht,
And bad him, as he hath behyht,
So as sche hath ben his warant,

1693 proferþ H₁, Ad, F   profurt W   rest profreþ, profereþ

**   G

That he hire holde covenant,
And be the bridel sche him seseth.
Bot godd wot how that sche him pleseth
Of suche wordes as sche spekth:
Him thenkth welnyh his herte brekth   1700
For sorwe that he may noght fle,
Bot if he wolde untrewe be.
  Loke, how a sek man for his hele
Takth baldemoine with Canele,
And with the Mirre takth the Sucre,
Ryht upon such a maner lucre
Stant Florent, as in this diete:
He drinkth the bitre with the swete,
He medleth sorwe with likynge,
And liveth, as who seith, deyinge;   1710
His youthe schal be cast aweie
Upon such on which as the weie
Is old and lothly overal.
Bot nede he mot that nede schal:
He wolde algate his trowthe holde,
As every knyht therto is holde,
What happ so evere him is befalle: **P. i. 100**
Thogh sche be the fouleste of alle,
Yet to thonour of wommanhiede
Him thoghte he scholde taken hiede;   1720
So that for pure gentilesse,
As he hire couthe best adresce,
In ragges, as sche was totore,
He set hire on his hors tofore
And forth he takth his weie softe;
No wonder thogh he siketh ofte.
Bot as an oule fleth be nyhte
Out of alle othre briddes syhte,
Riht so this knyht on daies brode
In clos him hield, and schop his rode   1730
On nyhtes time, til the tyde
That he cam there he wolde abide;
And prively withoute noise
He bringth this foule grete Coise

To his Castell in such a wise
That noman myhte hire schappe avise,
Til sche into the chambre cam :
Wher he his prive conseil nam
Of suche men as he most troste,
And tolde hem that he nedes moste   1740
This beste wedde to his wif,
For elles hadde he lost his lif.
 The prive wommen were asent,
That scholden ben of his assent :
Hire ragges thei anon of drawe,
And, as it was that time lawe,
She hadde bath, sche hadde reste,   **P. i. 101**
And was arraied to the beste.
Bot with no craft of combes brode
Thei myhte hire hore lockes schode,   1750
And sche ne wolde noght be schore
For no conseil, and thei therfore,
With such atyr as tho was used,
Ordeinen that it was excused,
And hid so crafteliche aboute,
That noman myhte sen hem oute.
Bot when sche was fulliche arraied
And hire atyr was al assaied,
Tho was sche foulere on to se :
Bot yit it may non other be,   1760
Thei were wedded in the nyht ;
So wo begon was nevere knyht
As he was thanne of mariage.
And sche began to pleie and rage,
As who seith, I am wel ynowh ;
Bot he therof nothing ne lowh,
For sche tok thanne chiere on honde
And clepeth him hire housebonde,
And seith, ' My lord, go we to bedde,
For I to that entente wedde,   1770
That thou schalt be my worldes blisse : '

1755 hid] it MYX ... CB₂, B diȝt L   1768 cleped X ... B₂, B
cleput W   1770 entent(e) þe wedde X ... CB₂, BΛ   entent was
wedde I , Λ, W

G 2

[TALE OF FLORENT.]

And profreth him with that to kisse,
As sche a lusti Lady were.
His body myhte wel be there,
Bot as of thoght and of memoire
His herte was in purgatoire.
Bot yit for strengthe of matrimoine   **P. i. 102**
He myhte make non essoine,
That he ne mot algates plie
To gon to bedde of compaignie: 1780
And whan thei were abedde naked,
Withoute slep he was awaked;
He torneth on that other side,
For that he wolde hise yhen hyde
Fro lokynge on that foule wyht.
The chambre was al full of lyht,
The courtins were of cendal thinne,
This newe bryd which lay withinne,
Thogh it be noght with his acord,
In armes sche beclipte hire lord,   1790
And preide, as he was torned fro,
He wolde him torne ayeinward tho;
'For now,' sche seith, 'we ben bothe on.'
And he lay stille as eny ston,
Bot evere in on sche spak and preide,
And bad him thenke on that he seide,
Whan that he tok hire be the hond.

     He herde and understod the bond,
How he was set to his penance,
And as it were a man in trance   1800
He torneth him al sodeinly,
And syh a lady lay him by
Of eyhtetiene wynter age,
Which was the faireste of visage
That evere in al this world he syh:
And as he wolde have take hire nyh,
Sche put hire hand and be his leve   **P. i. 103**
Besoghte him that he wolde leve,
And seith that forto wynne or lese

1785 on] of X ... B₂, BΛ   fole F   1793 ben] beþ RCLB₁
buþ AM   1809 seide (sayde) for to X ... B₂, B   saide þat for to W

He mot on of tuo thinges chese,   1810 [TALE OF FLORENT.]
Wher he wol have hire such on nyht,
Or elles upon daies lyht,
For he schal noght have bothe tuo.
And he began to sorwe tho,
In many a wise and caste his thoght,
Bot for al that yit cowthe he noght
Devise himself which was the beste.
And sche, that wolde his hertes reste,
Preith that he scholde chese algate,
Til ate laste longe and late   1820
He seide: 'O ye, my lyves hele,
Sey what you list in my querele,
I not what ansuere I schal yive:
Bot evere whil that I may live,
I wol that ye be my maistresse,
For I can noght miselve gesse
Which is the beste unto my chois.
Thus grante I yow myn hole vois,
Ches for ous bothen, I you preie;
And what as evere that ye seie,   1830
Riht as ye wole so wol I.'
    'Mi lord,' sche seide, 'grant merci,
For of this word that ye now sein,
That ye have mad me soverein,
Mi destine is overpassed,
That nevere hierafter schal be lassed
Mi beaute, which that I now have,   **P. i. 104**
Til I be take into my grave;
Bot nyht and day as I am now
I schal alwey be such to yow.   1840
The kinges dowhter of Cizile
I am, and fell bot siththe awhile,
As I was with my fader late,
That my Stepmoder for an hate,
Which toward me sche hath begonne,
Forschop me, til I hadde wonne
The love and sovereinete

1822 ȝe lust AM   thu liste H₁   þou list Δ   ȝe wyl Sn, W (wille)
1839 Bot] Boþ(e) H₁ . . . B₂, BΔΛ, W

[TALE OF FLORENT.]

Of what knyht that in his degre
Alle othre passeth of good name:
And, as men sein, ye ben the same,   1850
The dede proeveth it is so;
Thus am I youres evermo.'
Tho was plesance and joye ynowh,
Echon with other pleide and lowh;
Thei live longe and wel thei ferde,
And clerkes that this chance herde
Thei writen it in evidence,
To teche how that obedience
Mai wel fortune a man to love
And sette him in his lust above,   1860
As it befell unto this knyht.

Confessor.

    Forthi, my Sone, if thou do. ryht,
Thou schalt unto thi love obeie,
And folwe hir will be alle weie.

Amans.

    Min holy fader, so I wile:
For ye have told me such a skile
Of this ensample now tofore,   **P. i. 105**
That I schal evermo therfore
Hierafterward myn observance
To love and to his obeissance   1870
The betre kepe: and over this
Of pride if ther oght elles is,
Wherof that I me schryve schal,
What thing it is in special,
Mi fader, axeth, I you preie.

Confessor.

    Now lest, my Sone, and I schal seie:
For yit ther is Surquiderie,
Which stant with Pride of compaignie;
Wherof that thou schalt hiere anon,
To knowe if thou have gult or non   1880
Upon the forme as thou schalt hiere:
Now understond wel the matiere.

viii. *Omnia scire putat, set se Presumpcio nescit,*
    Nec sibi consimilem quem putat esse parem.

1881 f. *om.* SAdΔΛ

Qui magis astutus reputat se vincere bellum,
  In laqueos Veneris forcius ipse cadit.
Sepe Cupido virum sibi qui presumit amantem
  Fallit, et in vacuas spes redit ipsa vias.

[iii. Surquidry or
Presumption.]

Surquiderie is thilke vice
Of Pride, which the thridde office
Hath in his Court, and wol noght knowe
The trowthe til it overthrowe.
Upon his fortune and his grace
Comth 'Hadde I wist' fulofte aplace;
For he doth al his thing be gesse,
And voideth alle sikernesse.
Non other conseil good him siemeth
Bot such as he himselve diemeth;
For in such wise as he compasseth,   P. i. 106
His wit al one alle othre passeth;
And is with pride so thurghsoght,
That he alle othre set at noght,
And weneth of himselven so,
That such as he ther be nomo,
So fair, so semly, ne so wis;
And thus he wolde bere a pris   1900
Above alle othre, and noght forthi
He seith noght ones 'grant mercy'
To godd, which alle grace sendeth,
So that his wittes he despendeth
Upon himself, as thogh ther were
No godd which myhte availe there:
Bot al upon his oghne witt
He stant, til he falle in the pitt
So ferr that he mai noght arise.
    And riht thus in the same wise   1910
This vice upon the cause of love
So proudly set the herte above,
And doth him pleinly forto wene
That he to loven eny qwene
Hath worthinesse and sufficance;
And so withoute pourveance

Hic loquitur de ter-
cia specie Superbie,
que Presumpcio dici-
tur, cuius naturam
1890 primo secundum vi-
cium Confessor sim-
pliciter declarat.

Hic tractat Confes-
sor cum Amante super
illa saltem presump-
cione, ex cuius super-
bia quam plures fatui
amantes, cum maioris
certitudinis in amore
spem sibi promittunt,

1889 alle þing B, W   al þis þing M   1891 him] it AM
1895 þurghsoght S   þurgh-soght F   1906 good YXERCB₂, H₃

[iii. Surquidry or
Presumption.]
inexpediti cicius desti-
tuuntur.

Fulofte he heweth up so hihe,
That chippes fallen in his yhe;
And ek ful ofte he weneth this,
Ther as he noght beloved is,   1920
To be beloved alther best.
Now, Sone, tell what so thee lest
Of this that I have told thee hier.   P. i. 107

Amans.

   Ha, fader, be noght in a wer:
I trowe ther be noman lesse,
Of eny maner worthinesse,
That halt him lasse worth thanne I
To be beloved; and noght forthi
I seie in excusinge of me,
To alle men that love is fre.   1930
And certes that mai noman werne;
For love is of himself so derne,
It luteth in a mannes herte:
Bot that ne schal me noght asterte,
To wene forto be worthi
To loven, bot in hir mercy.
Bot, Sire, of that ye wolden mene,
That I scholde otherwise wene
To be beloved thanne I was,
I am beknowe as in that cas.   1940

Confessor.
Amans.

   Mi goode Sone, tell me how.
   Now lest, and I wol telle yow,
Mi goode fader, how it is.
Fulofte it hath befalle or this
Thurgh hope that was noght certein,
Mi wenynge hath be set in vein
To triste in thing that halp me noght,
Bot onliche of myn oughne thoght.
For as it semeth that a belle
Lik to the wordes that men telle   1950
Answerth, riht so ne mor ne lesse,
To yow, my fader, I confesse,
Such will my wit hath overset,   P. i. 108
That what so hope me behet,

1931 noman] no womman YXGERB₂, B   1934 me noght] not
(nouȝt) me X . . . B₂, BΔ   1940 þis cas B

Ful many a time I wene it soth,
Bot finali no spied it doth.
Thus may I tellen, as I can,
Wenyng beguileth many a man;
So hath it me, riht wel I wot:
For if a man wole in a Bot   1960
Which is withoute botme rowe,
He moste nedes overthrowe.
Riht so wenyng hath ferd be me:
For whanne I wende next have be,
As I be my wenynge caste,
Thanne was I furthest ate laste,
And as a foll my bowe unbende,
Whan al was failed that I wende.
Forthi, my fader, as of this,
That my wenynge hath gon amis   1970
Touchende to Surquiderie,
Yif me my penance er I die.
Bot if ye wolde in eny forme
Of this matiere a tale enforme,
Which were ayein this vice set,
I scholde fare wel the bet.

    Mi Sone, in alle maner wise
Surquiderie is to despise,
Wherof I finde write thus.
The proude knyht Capaneüs
He was of such Surquiderie,
That he thurgh his chivalerie
Upon himself so mochel triste,
That to the goddes him ne liste
In no querele to beseche,
Bot seide it was an ydel speche,
Which caused was of pure drede,
For lack of herte and for no nede.
And upon such presumpcioun
He hield this proude opinioun,
Til ate laste upon a dai,

[iii. SURQUIDRY OR
   PRESUMPTION.]

[TALE OF CAPANEUS.]
   Hic ponit Confes-
sor exemplum contra
illos, qui de suis viri-
1980 bus presumentes de-
biliores efficiuntur. Et
narrat qualiter ille
Capaneus, miles in ar-
P. i. 109 mis probatissimus, de
sua presumens auda-
cia inuocacionem ad
superos tempore ne-
cessitatis ex vecordia
tantum et non aliter
primitus prouenisse
asseruit. Vnde in ob-
sidione Ciuitatis The-
barum, cum ipse quo-
dam die coram suis
1990 hostibus ad debellandum se obtulit, ignis

1958 a *om.* MGERCB₂, B   1960 For] But B   wold(e)
JX . . . B₂, B   1966 Than*ne* F   Than AC, B

[TALE OF CAPANEUS.]
de celo·subito super-
veniens ipsum arma-
tum totaliter in cine-
res combussit.

Aboute Thebes wher he lay,
Whan it of Siege was belein,
This knyht, as the Croniqes sein,
In alle mennes sihte there,
Whan he was proudest in his gere,
And thoghte how nothing myhte him dere,
Ful armed with his schield and spere
As he the Cite wolde assaile,
Godd tok himselve the bataille   2000
Ayein his Pride, and fro the sky
A firy thonder sodeinly
He sende, and him to pouldre smot.
And thus the Pride which was hot,
Whan he most in his strengthe wende,
Was brent and lost withouten ende :
So that it proeveth wel therfore,
The strengthe of man is sone lore,
Bot if that he it wel governe.
And over this a man mai lerne   2010
That ek fulofte time it grieveth,
Whan that a man himself believeth,
As thogh it scholde him wel beseme   **P. i. 110**
That he alle othre men can deme,
And hath foryete his oghne vice.
A tale of hem that ben so nyce,
And feigne hemself to be so wise,
I schal thee telle in such a wise,
Wherof thou schalt ensample take
That thou no such thing undertake.   2020

I finde upon Surquiderie,
How that whilom of Hungarie
Be olde daies was a King
Wys and honeste in alle thing :
And so befell upon a dai,
And that was in the Monthe of Maii,

2005 strengthe] triste (truste) X . . . B₂, B   2009 wil B
2017-20 *For these four lines* SAdΔ *have two,—*
     Wherof þou miht þiselue lere,
     I þenke telle, as þou schalt hiere.
2026 moone (mone) XGR, B

As thilke time it was usance,
This kyng with noble pourveance
Hath for himself his Charr araied,
Wher inne he wolde ride amaied
Out of the Cite forto pleie,
With lordes and with gret nobleie
Of lusti folk that were yonge:
Wher some pleide and some songe,
And some gon and some ryde,
And some prike here hors aside
And bridlen hem now in now oute.
The kyng his yhe caste aboute,
Til he was ate laste war
And syh comende ayein his char
Two pilegrins of so gret age,
That lich unto a dreie ymage
Thei weren pale and fade hewed,
And as a bussh which is besnewed,
Here berdes weren hore and whyte;
Ther was of kinde bot a lite,
That thei ne semen fulli dede.
Thei comen to the kyng and bede
Som of his good par charite;
And he with gret humilite
Out of his Char to grounde lepte,
And hem in bothe hise armes kepte
And keste hem bothe fot and hond
Before the lordes of his lond,
And yaf hem of his good therto:
And whanne he hath this dede do,
He goth into his char ayein.
Tho was Murmur, tho was desdeign,
Tho was compleignte on every side,
Thei seiden of here oghne Pride
Eche until othre: 'What is this?
Oure king hath do this thing amis,
So to abesse his realte

[THE TRUMP OF
DEATH.]

2030 Hic loquitur Confessor contra illos, qui de sua sciencia presumentes aliorum condiciones diiudicantes indiscrete redarguunt. Et narrat exemplum de quodam principe Regis Hungarie germano, qui cum fratrem suum pauperibus in publico vidit humiliatum, ipsum redarguendo in contrarium edocere presumebat: 2040 set Rex omni sapiencia prepollens ipsum sic incaute presumentem ad humilitatis memoriam terribili prouidencia micius castigauit.

P. i. III

2050

2060

2041 pilgrimis (pilgrims &c.) AJMXRLB₂ peregrins B pilgrins H₁
2043 Thei] That H₁, FWKH₃Magd. 2049 pur charite MX ...
B₂, BΔ, W 2054 his lordes XGECB₂, B

That every man it myhte se,
And humbled him in such a wise
To hem that were of non emprise.'
Thus was it spoken to and fro
Of hem that were with him tho
Al prively behinde his bak;
Bot to himselven noman spak.　　　　2070
The kinges brother in presence
Was thilke time, and gret offence
He tok therof, and was the same　　**P. i. 112**
Above alle othre which most blame
Upon his liege lord hath leid,
And hath unto the lordes seid,
Anon as he mai time finde,
Ther schal nothing be left behinde,
That he wol speke unto the king.

Now lest what fell upon this thing.　　2080
The day was merie and fair ynowh,
Echon with othre pleide and lowh,
And fellen into tales newe,
How that the freisshe floures grewe,
And how the grene leves spronge,
And how that love among the yonge
Began the hertes thanne awake,
And every bridd hath chose hire make:
And thus the Maies day to thende
Thei lede, and hom ayein thei wende.　　2090
The king was noght so sone come,
That whanne he hadde his chambre nome,
His brother ne was redi there,
And broghte a tale unto his Ere
Of that he dede such a schame
In hindringe of his oghne name,
Whan he himself so wolde drecche,
That to so vil a povere wrecche
Him deigneth schewe such simplesce
Ayein thastat of his noblesce:　　2100
And seith he schal it nomor use,
And that he mot himself excuse

2078 beleft FK　belefte A　　2088 hire] his H₁ . . . B₂, B, W

Toward hise lordes everychon.   **P. i. 113**   [The Trump of
The king stod stille as eny ston,   Death.]
And to his tale an Ere he leide,
And thoghte more than he seide :
Bot natheles to that he herde
Wel cortaisly the king answerde,
And tolde it scholde be amended.
And thus whan that her tale is ended,   2110
Al redy was the bord and cloth,
The king unto his Souper goth
Among the lordes to the halle ;
And whan thei hadden souped alle,
Thei token leve and forth thei go.
The king bethoghte himselve tho
How he his brother mai chastie,
That he thurgh his Surquiderie
Tok upon honde to despreise
Humilite, which is to preise,   2120
And therupon yaf such conseil
Toward his king that was noght heil ;
Wherof to be the betre lered,
He thenkth to maken him afered.
  It fell so that in thilke dawe
Ther was ordeined be the lawe
A trompe with a sterne breth,
Which cleped was the Trompe of deth :
And in the Court wher the king was
A certein man this Trompe of bras   2130
Hath in kepinge, and therof serveth,
That whan a lord his deth deserveth,
He schal this dredful trompe blowe   **P. i. 114**
Tofore his gate, and make it knowe
How that the jugement is yove
Of deth, which schal noght be foryove.
The king, whan it was nyht, anon
This man asente and bad him gon
To trompen at his brother gate ;
And he, which mot so don algate,   2140
Goth forth and doth the kynges heste.

2105 An F   2122 which was E, B which is G and was L

This lord, which herde of this tempeste
That he tofore his gate blew,
Tho wiste he be the lawe and knew
That he was sikerliche ded:
And as of help he wot no red,
Bot sende for hise frendes alle
And tolde hem how it is befalle.
And thei him axe cause why;
Bot he the sothe noght forthi   2150
Ne wiste, and ther was sorwe tho:
For it stod thilke tyme so,
This trompe was of such sentence,
That therayein no resistence
Thei couthe ordeine be no weie,
That he ne mot algate deie,
Bot if so that he may pourchace
To gete his liege lordes grace.
Here wittes therupon thei caste,
And ben apointed ate laste.   2160
    This lord a worthi ladi hadde
Unto his wif, which also dradde
Hire lordes deth, and children five   **P. i. 115**
Betwen hem two thei hadde alyve,
That weren yonge and tendre of age,
And of stature and of visage
Riht faire and lusty on to se.
Tho casten thei that he and sche
Forth with here children on the morwe,
As thei that were full of sorwe,   2170
Al naked bot of smok and scherte,
To tendre with the kynges herte,
His grace scholden go to seche
And pardoun of the deth beseche.
Thus passen thei that wofull nyht,
And erly, whan thei sihe it lyht,
Thei gon hem forth in such a wise
As thou tofore hast herd devise,
Al naked bot here schortes one.

2159 Hire FK   2171 Sherte F   2173 go biseche B
2179 schortes M, FK   *rest* schertes (shirtes &c.)

Thei wepte and made mochel mone,   2180
Here Her hangende aboute here Eres;
With sobbinge and with sory teres
This lord goth thanne an humble pas,
That whilom proud and noble was;
Wherof the Cite sore afflyhte,
Of hem that sihen thilke syhte:
And natheles al openly
With such wepinge and with such cri
Forth with hise children and his wif
He goth to preie for his lif.   2190
Unto the court whan thei be come,
And men therinne have hiede nome,
Ther was no wiht, if he hem syhe,   P. i. 116
Fro water mihte kepe his yhe
For sorwe which thei maden tho.
The king supposeth of this wo,
And feigneth as he noght ne wiste;
Bot natheles at his upriste
Men tolden him how that it ferde:
And whan that he this wonder herde,   2200
In haste he goth into the halle,
And alle at ones doun thei falle,
If eny pite may be founde.
The king, which seth hem go to grounde,
Hath axed hem what is the fere,
Why thei be so despuiled there.
His brother seide: 'Ha lord, mercy!
I wot non other cause why,
Bot only that this nyht ful late
The trompe of deth was at my gate   2210
In tokne that I scholde deie;
Thus be we come forto preie
That ye mi worldes deth respite.'
    'Ha fol, how thou art forto wyte,'
The king unto his brother seith,
'That thou art of so litel feith,
That only for a trompes soun

2181 hanged(e) AMH1, Δ, W (honget)   2191 become FK
2208 wot] not AM

Hast gon despuiled thurgh the toun,
Thou and thi wif in such manere
Forth with thi children that ben here,   2220
In sihte of alle men aboute,
For that thou seist thou art in doute
Of deth, which stant under the lawe   P. i. 117
Of man, and man it mai withdrawe,
So that it mai par chance faile.
Now schalt thou noght forthi mervaile
That I doun fro my Charr alihte,
Whanne I behield tofore my sihte
In hem that were of so gret age
Min oghne deth thurgh here ymage,   2230
Which god hath set be lawe of kynde,
Wherof I mai no bote finde:
For wel I wot, such as thei be,
Riht such am I in my degree,
Of fleissh and blod, and so schal deie.
And thus, thogh I that lawe obeie
Of which the kinges ben put under,
It oghte ben wel lasse wonder
Than thou, which art withoute nede
For lawe of londe in such a drede,   2240
Which for tacompte is bot a jape,
As thing which thou miht overscape.
Forthi, mi brother, after this
I rede, sithen that so is
That thou canst drede a man so sore,
Dred god with al thin herte more:
For al schal deie and al schal passe,
Als wel a Leoun as an asse,
Als wel a beggere as a lord,
Towardes deth in on acord   2250
Thei schullen stonde.' And in this wise
The king hath with hise wordes wise
His brother tawht and al foryive.   P. i. 118

Confessor.

Forthi, mi Sone, if thou wolt live
In vertu, thou most vice eschuie,

And with low herte humblesce suie,   [THE TRUMP OF
So that thou be noght surquidous.   DEATH.]

   Mi fader, I am amorous,   Amans.
Wherof I wolde you beseche
That ye me som ensample teche,   2260
Which mihte in loves cause stonde.

   Mi Sone, thou schalt understonde,   Confessor.
In love and othre thinges alle
If that Surquiderie falle,
It may to him noght wel betide
Which useth thilke vice of Pride,
Which torneth wisdom to wenynge
And Sothfastnesse into lesynge
Thurgh fol ymaginacion.
And for thin enformacion,   2270
That thou this vice as I the rede
Eschuie schalt, a tale I rede,
Which fell whilom be daies olde,
So as the clerk Ovide tolde.

   Ther was whilom a lordes Sone,   [TALE OF NARCISSUS.]
Which of his Pride a nyce wone
Hath cawht, that worthi to his liche,
To sechen al the worldes riche,
Ther was no womman forto love.   Hic in speciali trac-
So hihe he sette himselve above   2280 tat Confessor cum A-
Of stature and of beaute bothe,   mante contra illos, qui
That him thoghte alle wommen lothe: de propria formositate
                           presumentes amorem
So was ther no comparisoun   **P. i. 119** mulieris dedignantur.
As toward his condicioun.   Et narrat exemplum,
                           qualiter cuiusdam Prin-

2260 som ensample] by som weie B   2261 in *om.* XE . . . B₂
2265 f.   To man in any maner side
           He may wel nowher þan abide R
           To man in eny maner side
           It may to him nouȝt wel betide B₂
CL *combine the above with the reading of the text.*
   2267–74 *Eight lines found thus in copies of the third recension,*
FWKH₃ &c., *and also in* H₁. *The rest have four, given as follows by* S,
        fforþi eschuie it I þe rede
        ffor in Ouide a tale I rede
        How þat a man was ouertake
        Wherof þou myht ensample take.

**   H

[TALE OF NARCISSUS.]

cipis filius nomine Nar-
cizus estiuo tempore,
cum ipse venacionis
causa quendam ceruum
solus cum suis canibus
exagitaret, in grauem
sitim incurrens neces-
sitate compulsus ad
bibendum de quodam
fonte pronus se incli-
nauit; vbi ipse faciem
suam pulcherrimam in
aqua percipiens, puta-
bat se per hoc illam
Nimpham, quam Poete
Ekko vocant, in flu-
mine coram suis ocu-
lis pocius conspexisse;
de cuius amore con-
festim laqueatus, vt ip-
sam ad se de fonte ex-
traheret, pluribus blan-
diciis adulabatur. Set
cum illud perficere nul-
latenus potuit, pre nim-
io languore deficiens
contra lapides ibidem
adiacentes caput ex-
uerberans cerebrum ef-
fudit. Et sic de propria
pulcritudine qui fuerat
presumptuosus, de pro-
pria pulcritudine fat-
uatus interiit.

This yonge lord Narcizus hihte:
No strengthe of love bowe mihte
His herte, which is unaffiled;
Bot ate laste he was beguiled:
For of the goddes pourveance
It fell him on a dai par chance,   2290
That he in all his proude fare
Unto the forest gan to fare,
Amonges othre that ther were
To hunte and to desporte him there.
And whanne he cam into the place
Wher that he wolde make his chace,
The houndes weren in a throwe
Uncoupled and the hornes blowe:
The grete hert anon was founde,
Which swifte feet sette upon grounde,   2300
And he with spore in horse side
Him hasteth faste forto ride,
Til alle men be left behinde.
And as he rod, under a linde
Beside a roche, as I thee telle,
He syh wher sprong a lusty welle:
The day was wonder hot withalle,
And such a thurst was on him falle,
That he moste owther deie or drinke;
And doun he lihte and be the brinke   2310
He teide his Hors unto a braunche,
And leide him lowe forto staunche
His thurst: and as he caste his lok   **P. i. 120**
Into the welle and hiede tok,
He sih the like of his visage,
And wende ther were an ymage
Of such a Nimphe as tho was faie,
Wherof that love his herte assaie
Began, as it was after sene,
Of his sotie and made him wene   2320
It were a womman that he syh.

2293 *margin* pronus] proulis XE . . . B₂   2294 to
om. B, W   2299 The grete] A grete AM, W   2300 vpon AJ, Ad,
FH₃ on þe XERC, B vpon the H₁   2302 *margin* poterat B

The more he cam the welle nyh,
The nerr cam sche to him ayein;
So wiste he nevere what to sein;
For whanne he wepte, he sih hire wepe,
And whanne he cride, he tok good kepe,
The same word sche cride also:
And thus began the newe wo,
That whilom was to him so strange;
Tho made him love an hard eschange,   2330
To sette his herte and to beginne
Thing which he mihte nevere winne.
And evere among he gan to loute,
And preith that sche to him come oute;
And otherwhile he goth a ferr,
And otherwhile he draweth nerr,
And evere he fond hire in o place.
He wepth, he crith, he axeth grace,
There as he mihte gete non;
So that ayein a Roche of Ston,   2340
As he that knew non other red,
He smot himself til he was ded.
Wherof the Nimphes of the welles,   **P. i. 121**
And othre that ther weren elles
Unto the wodes belongende,
The body, which was ded ligende,
For pure pite that thei have
Under the grene thei begrave.
And thanne out of his sepulture
Ther sprong anon par aventure   2350
Of floures such a wonder syhte,
That men ensample take myhte
Upon the dedes whiche he dede,
As tho was sene in thilke stede;
For in the wynter freysshe and faire
The floures ben, which is contraire
To kynde, and so was the folie
Which fell of his Surquiderie.
    Thus he, which love hadde in desdeign,   Confessor.

2332 neuer mighte B   2335 a ferr J, SB, F   aferr A   2343-58
Sixteen lines found only in third recension copies, FWKH3 &c., *and in* H1

H 2

Worste of all othre was besein,   2360
And as he sette his pris most hyhe,
He was lest worth in loves yhe
And most bejaped in his wit :
Wherof the remembrance is yit,
So that thou myht ensample take,
And ek alle othre for his sake.

Amans.

    Mi fader, as touchende of me,
This vice I thenke forto fle,
Which of his wenynge overtroweth ;
And nameliche of thing which groweth   2370
In loves cause or wel or wo
Yit pryded I me nevere so.
Bot wolde god that grace sende,   **P. i. 122**
That toward me my lady wende
As I towardes hire wene !
Mi love scholde so be sene,
Ther scholde go no pride a place.
Bot I am ferr fro thilke grace,
As forto speke of tyme now ;
So mot I soffre, and preie yow   2380
That ye wole axe on other side
If ther be eny point of Pride,
Wherof it nedeth to be schrive.

Confessor.

    Mi Sone, godd it thee foryive,
If thou have eny thing misdo
Touchende of this, bot overmo
Ther is an other yit of Pride,
Which nevere cowthe hise wordes hide,
That he ne wole himself avaunte ;
Ther mai nothing his tunge daunte,   2390
That he ne clappeth as a Belle :
Wherof if thou wolt that I telle,
It is behovely forto hiere,
So that thou myht thi tunge stiere,
Toward the world and stonde in grace,
Which lacketh ofte in many place

2369-72 *third recension and* H₁ *only*   2379 And X . . . B₂, B
2380 and preie]I preie (prey) XGECLB₂, B   I seigh R   2386
euermo JMH₁XGRLB₂, BΔ, W   2396 aplace AM

To him that can noght sitte stille,
Which elles scholde have al his wille.

ix. *Magniloque propriam minuit iactancia lingue*   [iv. AVANTANCE OR
    Famam, quam stabilem firmat honore cilens.   BOASTING.]
    Ipse sui laudem meriti non percipit, vnde
    Se sua per verba iactat in orbe palam.
    Estque viri culpa iactancia, que rubefactas
    In muliere reas causat habere genas.

The vice cleped Avantance   **P. i. 123**
With Pride hath take his aqueintance,   2400
So that his oghne pris he lasseth,
When he such mesure overpasseth
That he his oghne Herald is.
That ferst was wel is thanne mis,
That was thankworth is thanne blame,   Hic loquitur de quar-
And thus the worschipe of his name   ta specie Superbie, que
Thurgh pride of his avantarie   Iactancia dicitur, ex
He torneth into vilenie.   cuius natura causatur,
                                               vt homo de seipso tes-
I rede how that this proude vice   timonium perhibens su-
Hath thilke wynd in his office,   2410 arum virtutum merita
Which thurgh the blastes that he bloweth   de laude in culpam
The mannes fame he overthroweth   transfert, et suam fa-
Of vertu, which scholde elles springe   mam cum ipse extol-
Into the worldes knowlechinge;   lere vellet, illam pro-
                                               prio ore subvertit. Set
Bot he fordoth it alto sore.   et Venus in amoris cau-
And riht of such a maner lore   sa de isto vicio macu-
Ther ben lovers: forthi if thow   latos a sua Curia super
Art on of hem, tell and sei how.   omnes alios abhorrens
Whan thou hast taken eny thing   expellit, et eorum mul-
Of loves yifte, or Nouche or ring,   2420 tiloquium verecunda
Or tok upon thee for the cold   detestatur. Vnde Con-
Som goodly word that thee was told,   fessor Amanti oppo-
Or frendly chiere or tokne or lettre,   nens materiam plenius
Wherof thin herte was the bettre,   declarat.
Or that sche sende the grietinge,
Hast thou for Pride of thi likinge
Mad thin avant wher as the liste?

2398 al *om.* H₁, FH₃   2410 wynd] hunt(e) H₁YX ... L, B
haunt B₂   2416 *margin* verecundia M ... B₂, Ad   vecundia W
2421 tok (took) J, B, F   toke AC   2423 Of JX ... B₂, B, W

I wolde, fader, that ye wiste,
Mi conscience lith noght hiere :   **P. i. 124**
Yit hadde I nevere such matiere,   2430
Wherof min herte myhte amende,
Noght of so mochel that sche sende
Be mowthe and seide, 'Griet him wel :'
And thus for that ther is no diel
Wherof to make myn avant,
It is to reson acordant
That I mai nevere, bot I lye,
Of love make avanterie.
I wot noght what I scholde have do,
If that I hadde encheson so,   2440
As ye have seid hier manyon ;
Bot I fond cause nevere non :
Bot daunger, which welnyh me slowh,
Therof I cowthe telle ynowh,
And of non other Avantancè :
Thus nedeth me no repentance.
Now axeth furthere of my lif,
For hierof am I noght gultif.

    Mi Sone, I am wel paid withal ;
For wite it wel in special   2450
That love of his verrai justice
Above alle othre ayein this vice
At alle times most debateth,
With al his herte and most it hateth.
And ek in alle maner wise
Avantarie is to despise,
As be ensample thou myht wite,
Which I finde in the bokes write.

    Of hem that we Lombars now calle **P. i. 125**
Albinus was the ferste of alle   2460
Which bar corone of Lombardie,
And was of gret chivalerie
In werre ayein diverse kinges.
So fell amonges othre thinges,
That he that time a werre hadde

2457 myht (might) JC, B   myhte A, S, F   2460 ferste S   ferst A, B, F

With Gurmond, which the Geptes ladde,
And was a myhti kyng also:
Bot natheles it fell him so,
Albinus slowh him in the feld,
Ther halp him nowther swerd ne scheld,   2470
That he ne smot his hed of thanne,
Wherof he tok awey the Panne,
Of which he seide he wolde make
A Cuppe for Gurmoundes sake,
To kepe and drawe into memoire
Of his bataille the victoire.
And thus whan he he the feld hath wonne,
The lond anon was overronne
And sesed in his oghne hond,
Wher he Gurmondes dowhter fond,   2480
Which Maide Rosemounde hihte,
And was in every mannes sihte
A fair, a freissh, a lusti on.
His herte fell to hire anon,
And such a love on hire he caste,
That he hire weddeth ate laste;
And after that long time in reste
With hire he duelte, and to the beste
Thei love ech other wonder wel.   P. i. 126
Bot sche which kepth the blinde whel,   2490
Venus, whan thei be most above,
In al the hoteste of here love,
Hire whiel sche torneth, and thei felle
In the manere as I schal telle.
   This king, which stod in al his welthe
Of pes, of worschipe and of helthe,
And felte him on no side grieved,
As he that hath his world achieved,
Tho thoghte he wolde a feste make;
And that was for his wyves sake,   2500
That sche the lordes ate feste,
That were obeissant to his heste,

[TALE OF ALBINUS
AND ROSEMUND.]
desiderio completo se
iactant. Et narrat qual-
iter Albinus primus
Rex Longobardorum,
cum ipse quendam a-
lium Regem nomine
Gurmundum in bello
morientem triumphas-
set, testam capitis de-
functi auferens ci-
phum ex ea gemmis et
auro circumligatum in
sue victorie memoriam
fabricari constituit: in-
super et ipsius Gur-
mundi filiam Rose-
mundam rapiens, mar-
itali thoro in coniugem
sibi copulauit. Vnde
ipso Albino postea cor-
am sui Regni nobili-
bus in suo regali con-
uiuio sedente, dicti
Gurmundi ciphum in-
fuso vino ad se inter
epulas afferri iussit;
quem sumptum vxori
sue Regine porrexit
dicens, 'Bibe cum patre
tuo.' Quod et ipsa hu-
iusmodi operis ignara
fecit. Quo facto Rex
statim super hiis que
per prius gesta fue-
rant cunctis audienti-
bus per singula se iac-
tauit. Regina vero cum
talia audisset, celato
animo factum abhor-
rens in mortem domini
sui Regis circumspec-
ta industria conspira-
uit; ipsumque auxiliant-
ibus Glodesida et Hel-
mege breui subsecuto
tempore interfecit: cu-
ius mortem Dux Ra-
uennensis tam in cor-
pus dicte Regine quam
suorum fautorum post
ea vindicauit. Set et
huius tocius infortunii

2473 *margin* testum H₁ . . . B₂ (E *corr.* testam)   2488 dwelled
JMEB₂, Δ, W (dwellet) duelleþ XGRCL   2489 *margin* statim]
statum G   statutum XE . . . B₂   2497 agrieued B   2501 ate] of þe B

[TALE OF ALBINUS
AND ROSEMUND.]
sola superbie iactancia
fomitem ministrabat.

Mai knowe : and so forth therupon
He let ordeine, and sende anon
Be lettres and be messagiers,
And warnede alle hise officiers
That every thing be wel arraied :
The grete Stiedes were assaied
For joustinge and for tornement,
And many a perled garnement　　　　　　2510
Embroudred was ayein the dai.
The lordes in here beste arrai
Be comen ate time set,
On jousteth wel, an other bet,
And otherwhile thei torneie,
And thus thei casten care aweie
And token lustes upon honde.
And after, thou schalt understonde,
To mete into the kinges halle　　　　　**P. i. 127**
Thei come, as thei be beden alle :　　　　2520
And whan thei were set and served,
Thanne after, as it was deserved,
To hem that worthi knyhtes were,
So as thei seten hiere and there,
The pris was yove and spoken oute
Among the heraldz al aboute.
And thus benethe and ek above
Al was of armes and of love,
Wherof abouten ate bordes
Men hadde manye sondri wordes,　　　　2530
That of the merthe which thei made
The king himself began to glade
Withinne his herte and tok a pride,
And sih the Cuppe stonde aside,
Which mad was of Gurmoundes hed,
As ye have herd, whan he was ded,
And was with gold and riche Stones
Beset and bounde for the nones,
And stod upon a fot on heihte
Of burned gold, and with gret sleihte　　　2540
Of werkmanschipe it was begrave

2511 Embroudred F　*rest* Embrowded (Embroudid &c.)

Of such werk as it scholde have,
And was policed ek so clene
That no signe of the Skulle is sene,
Bot as it were a Gripes Ey.
The king bad bere his Cuppe awey,
Which stod tofore him on the bord,
And fette thilke. Upon his word
This Skulle is fet and wyn therinne,   **P. i. 128**
Wherof he bad his wif beginne: 2550
'Drink with thi fader, Dame,' he seide.
And sche to his biddinge obeide,
And tok the Skulle, and what hire liste
Sche drank, as sche which nothing wiste
What Cuppe it was: and thanne al oute
The kyng in audience aboute
Hath told it was hire fader Skulle,
So that the lordes knowe schulle
Of his bataille a soth witnesse,
And made avant thurgh what prouesse   2560
He hath his wyves love wonne, ·
Which of the Skulle hath so begonne.
Tho was ther mochel Pride alofte,
Thei speken alle, and sche was softe,
Thenkende on thilke unkynde Pride,
Of that hire lord so nyh hire side
Avanteth him that he hath slain
And piked out hire fader brain,
And of the Skulle had mad a Cuppe.
Sche soffreth al til thei were uppe,   2570
And tho sche hath seknesse feigned,
And goth to chambre and hath compleigned
Unto a Maide which sche triste,
So that non other wyht it wiste.
This Mayde Glodeside is hote,
To whom this lady hath behote
Of ladischipe al that sche can,
To vengen hire upon this man,
Which dede hire drinke in such a plit **P. i. 129**
Among hem alle for despit   2580

Of hire and of hire fader bothe;
Wherof hire thoghtes ben so wrothe,
Sche seith, that sche schal noght be glad,
Til that sche se him so bestad
That he nomore make avant.
And thus thei felle in covenant,
That thei acorden ate laste,
With suche wiles as thei caste
That thei wol gete of here acord
Som orped knyht to sle this lord: 2590
And with this sleihte thei beginne,
How thei Helmege myhten winne,
Which was the kinges Boteler,
A proud a lusti Bacheler,
And Glodeside he loveth hote.
And sche, to make him more assote,
Hire love granteth, and be nyhte
Thei schape how thei togedre myhte
Abedde meete: and don it was
This same nyht; and in this cas   2600
The qwene hirself the nyht secounde
Wente in hire stede, and there hath founde
A chambre derk withoute liht,
And goth to bedde to this knyht.
And he, to kepe his observance,
To love doth his obeissance,
And weneth it be Glodeside;
And sche thanne after lay aside,
And axeth him what he hath do,   **P. i. 130**
And who sche was sche tolde him tho,   2610
And seide: 'Helmege, I am thi qwene,
Now schal thi love wel be sene
Of that thou hast thi wille wroght:
Or it schal sore ben aboght,
Or thou schalt worche as I thee seie.
And if thou wolt be such a weie
Do my plesance and holde it stille,
For evere I schal ben at thi wille,
Bothe I and al myn heritage.'

2611 thi] þe JH₁ . . . B₂, BΛ

Anon the wylde loves rage,   2620 [TALE OF ALBINUS
In which noman him can governe,   AND ROSEMUND.]
Hath mad him that he can noght werne,
Bot fell al hol to hire assent:
And thus the whiel is al miswent,
The which fortune hath upon honde;
For how that evere it after stonde,
Thei schope among hem such a wyle,
The king was ded withinne a whyle.
So slihly cam it noght aboute
That thei ne ben descoevered oute, ,   2630
So that it thoghte hem for the beste
To fle, for there was no reste:
And thus the tresor of the king
Thei trusse and mochel other thing,
And with a certein felaschipe
Thei fledde and wente awey be schipe,
And hielde here rihte cours fro thenne,
Til that thei come to Ravenne,
Wher thei the Dukes helpe soghte.   **P. i. 131**
And he, so as thei him besoghte,   2640
A place granteth forto duelle;
Bot after, whan he herde telle
Of the manere how thei have do,
This Duk let schape for hem so,
That of a puison which thei drunke
Thei hadden that thei have beswunke.
    And al this made avant of Pride:
Good is therfore a man to hide
His oghne pris, for if he speke,
He mai lihtliche his thonk tobreke.   2650
In armes lith non avantance
To him which thenkth his name avance
And be renomed of his dede:
And also who that thenkth to spede
Of love, he mai him noght avaunte;
For what man thilke vice haunte,
His pourpos schal fulofte faile.
    In armes he that wol travaile

2622 Hath mad] Made H₁ ... B₂, B   2658 he] who AM

Or elles loves grace atteigne,
His lose tunge he mot restreigne, 2660
Which berth of his honour the keie.

Forthi, my Sone, in alle weie
Tak riht good hiede of this matiere.

I thonke you, my fader diere,
This scole is of a gentil lore;
And if ther be oght elles more
Of Pride, which I schal eschuie,
Now axeth forth, and I wol suie
What thing that ye me wole enforme. **P. i. 132**

Mi Sone, yit in other forme 2670
Ther is a vice of Prides lore,
Which lich an hauk whan he wol sore,
Fleith upon heihte in his delices
After the likynge of his vices,
And wol no mannes resoun knowe,
Till he doun falle and overthrowe.
This vice veine gloire is hote,
Wherof, my Sone, I thee behote
To trete and speke in such a wise,
That thou thee myht the betre avise. 2680

x. *Gloria perpetuos pregnat mundana dolores,*
Qui tamen est vanus gaudia vana cupit.
Eius amiciciam, quem gloria tollit inanis,
Non sine blandiciis planus habebit homo:
Verbis compositis qui scit strigilare fauellum,
Scandere sellata iura valebit eques.
Sic in amore magis qui blanda subornat in ore
Verba, per hoc brauium quod nequit alter habet.
Et tamen ornatos cantus variosque paratus
Letaque corda suis legibus optat amor. (10)

The proude vice of veine gloire
Remembreth noght of purgatoire,
Hise worldes joyes ben so grete,
Him thenkth of hevene no beyete;
This lives Pompe is al his pes:
Yit schal he deie natheles,

And therof thenkth he bot a lite,   [v. VAIN-GLORY.]
For al his lust is to delite   sorAmanti consequen-
In newe thinges, proude and veine,   ter opponit.
Als ferforth as he mai atteigne.   2690
I trowe, if that he myhte make   **P. i. 133**
His body newe, he wolde take
A newe forme and leve his olde :
For what thing that he mai beholde,
The which to comun us is strange,
Anon his olde guise change
He wole and falle therupon,
Lich unto the Camelion,
Which upon every sondri hewe
That he beholt he moste newe   2700
His colour, and thus unavised
Fulofte time he stant desguised.
Mor jolif than the brid in Maii
He makth him evere freissh and gay,
And doth al his array desguise,   Salomon. Amictus eius
So that of him the newe guise   annunciat de eo.
Of lusti folk alle othre take ;
And ek he can carolles make,
Rondeal, balade and virelai.
And with al this, if that he may   2710
Of love gete him avantage,
Anon he wext of his corage
So overglad, that of his ende
Him thenkth ther is no deth comende :
For he hath thanne at alle tide
Of love such a maner pride,
Him thenkth his joie is endeles.
 Now schrif thee, Sone, in godes pes,   Confessor.
And of thi love tell me plein
If that thi gloire hath be so vein.   2720
 Mi fader, as touchinge of al   **P. i. 134**   Amans.

2687 Þerfor AM, W Þer on Ad alite A, SB, F, &c. 2705 *margin*
Salomon. Amictus—eo *in third recension only.* 2713 f. *This text*
only in copies of third recension, F(*in ras.*)WKH₃ &c. *The rest have,*
     So ouerglad Þat purgatoire
    Ne myhte abregge his veine gloire

I may noght wel ne noght ne schal
Of veine gloire excuse me,
That I ne have for love be
The betre adresced and arraied;
And also I have ofte assaied
Rondeal, balade and virelai
For hire on whom myn herte lai
To make, and also forto peinte
Caroles with my wordes qweinte,　　　　　2730
To sette my pourpos alofte;
And thus I sang hem forth fulofte
In halle and ek in chambre aboute,
And made merie among the route,
Bot yit ne ferde I noght the bet.
Thus was my gloire in vein beset
Of al the joie that I made;
For whanne I wolde with hire glade,
And of hire love songes make,
Sche saide it was noght for hir sake,　　　　　2740
And liste noght my songes hiere
Ne witen what the wordes were.
So forto speke of myn arrai,
Yit couthe I nevere be so gay
Ne so wel make a songe of love,
Wherof I myhte ben above
And have encheson to be glad;
Bot rathere I am ofte adrad
For sorwe that sche seith me nay.
And natheles I wol noght say,　　　　　2750
That I nam glad on other side;　　　　**P. i. 135**
For fame, that can nothing hide,
Alday wol bringe unto myn Ere
Of that men speken hier and there,
How that my ladi berth the pris,
How sche is fair, how sche is wis,
How sche is wommanlich of chiere;
Of al this thing whanne I mai hiere,
What wonder is thogh I be fain?
And ek whanne I may hiere sain　　　　　2760

2751 nam] am H₁ ... B₂, W   on] an AJ

Tidinges of my ladi hele,

Althogh I may noght with hir dele,
Yit am I wonder glad of that;
For whanne I wot hire good astat,
As for that time I dar wel swere,
Non other sorwe mai me dere,
Thus am I gladed in this wise.
Bot, fader, of youre lores wise,
Of whiche ye be fully tawht,
Now tell me if yow thenketh awht   2770
That I therof am forto wyte.

Of that ther is I thee acquite,

Confessor.

Mi sone, he seide, and for thi goode
I wolde that thou understode:
For I thenke upon this matiere
To telle a tale, as thou schalt hiere,
How that ayein this proude vice
The hihe god of his justice
Is wroth and gret vengance doth.
Now herkne a tale that is soth: 2780
Thogh it be noght of loves kinde,   **P. i. 136**
A gret ensample thou schalt finde
This veine gloire forto fle,
Which is so full of vanite.

xi. *Humani generis cum sit sibi gloria maior,*
   Sepe subesse solet proximus ille dolor :
   Mens elata graues descensus sepe subibit,
   Mens humilis stabile molleque firmat iter.
   Motibus innumeris volutat fortuna per orbem ;
   Cum magis alta petis, inferiora time.

Ther was a king that mochel myhte,
Which Nabugodonosor hihte,
Of whom that I spak hier tofore.

Hic ponit Confessor
exemplum contra vi-
cium inanis glorie,
narrans qualiter Na-
bugodonosor Rex Cal-
deorum, cum ipse in

Yit in the bible his name is bore,
For al the world in Orient
Was hol at his comandement: 2790

2770 þou þenkeþ (þenkþ) AXRCLB₂   þou þenke M   ȝe þenke
(þinke) H₁Sn, Δ   ȝe thenketh (ye þinketh) Ad, W
Latin Verses xi. 5 immunis H₁XGECLB₂, B
2789 in the orient Δ, WH₃

[NEBUCHADNEZZAR'S
PUNISHMENT.]

omni sue maiestatis
gloria celsior extitis-
set, deus eius super-
biam castigare volens
ipsum extra formam
hominis in bestiam
fenum comedentem
transmutauit. Et sic
per septennium peni-
tens, cum ipse po-
tenciorem se agnouit,
misertus deus ipsum in
sui regni solium resti-
tuta sanitate emenda-
tum graciosius collo-
cauit.

As thanne of kinges to his liche
Was non so myhty ne so riche;
To his Empire and to his lawes,
As who seith, alle in thilke dawes
Were obeissant and tribut bere,
As thogh he godd of Erthe were.
With strengthe he putte kinges under,
And wroghte of Pride many a wonder;
He was so full of veine gloire,
That he ne hadde no memoire   2800
That ther was eny good bot he,
For pride of his prosperite;
Til that the hihe king of kinges,
Which seth and knoweth alle thinges,
Whos yhe mai nothing asterte,—
The privetes of mannes herte
Thei speke and sounen in his Ere   P. i. 137
As thogh thei lowde wyndes were,—
He tok vengance upon this pride.
Bot for he wolde awhile abide   2810
To loke if he him wolde amende,
To him a foretokne he sende,
And that was in his slep be nyhte.
This proude kyng a wonder syhte
Hadde in his swevene, ther he lay:
Him thoghte, upon a merie day
As he behield the world aboute,
A tree fulgrowe he syh theroute,
Which stod the world amiddes evene,
Whos heihte straghte up to the hevene;   2820
The leves weren faire and large,
Of fruit it bar so ripe a charge,
That alle men it myhte fede:
He sih also the bowes spriede
Above al Erthe, in whiche were
The kinde of alle briddes there;

2796 *margin* subito transmutauit A . . . B₂, S . . . Δ   2801 good
FKH₃   godd (god) A . . . B₂, S . . . Δ, W   2812 a foretokene K
a fortoken W   aforetokne S, F   afortokene R   a fore tokne (token)
JXEC, H₃   afore tokne (-en) AMH₁GLB₂, BAdΔ

And eke him thoghte he syh also
The kinde of alle bestes go
Under this tre aboute round
And fedden hem upon the ground.   2830
As he this wonder stod and syh,
Him thoghte he herde a vois on hih
Criende, and seide aboven alle:
'Hew doun this tree and lett it falle,
The leves let defoule in haste
And do the fruit destruie and waste,
And let of schreden every braunche,   **P. i. 138**
Bot ate Rote let it staunche.
Whan al his Pride is cast to grounde,
The rote schal be faste bounde,   2840
And schal no mannes herte bere,
Bot every lust he schal forbere
Of man, and lich an Oxe his mete
Of gras he schal pourchace and ete,
Til that the water of the hevene
Have waisshen him be times sevene,
So that he be thurghknowe ariht
What is the heveneliche myht,
And be mad humble to the wille
Of him which al mai save and spille.'   2850
    This king out of his swefne abreide,
And he upon the morwe it seide
Unto the clerkes whiche he hadde:
Bot non of hem the sothe aradde,
Was non his swevene cowthe undo.
And it stod thilke time so,
This king hadde in subjeccioun
Judee, and of affeccioun
Above alle othre on Daniel
He loveth, for he cowthe wel   2860
Divine that non other cowthe:
To him were alle thinges cowthe,

2835 defoule] do foule X . . . B₂   doune falle H₁   2836 do]
to H₁XE . . . B₂   2839 his Pride] þis pride H₁ . . . CB₂
þis tre L   2847 be *om.* H₁ . . . B₂, H₃   þurghknowe A, F þurgh
knowe J, SB

**   I

As he it hadde of goddes grace.
He was before the kinges face
Asent, and bode that he scholde
Upon the point the king of tolde
The fortune of his swevene expounde, **P. i. 139**
As it scholde afterward be founde.
Whan Daniel this swevene herde,
He stod long time er he ansuerde,   2870
And made a wonder hevy chiere.
The king tok hiede of his manere,
And bad him telle that he wiste,
As he to whom he mochel triste,
And seide he wolde noght be wroth.
Bot Daniel was wonder loth,
And seide: 'Upon thi fomen alle,
Sire king, thi swevene mote falle;
And natheles touchende of this
I wol the tellen how it is,   2880
And what desese is to thee schape:
God wot if thou it schalt ascape.

    The hihe tree, which thou hast sein
With lef and fruit so wel besein,
The which stod in the world amiddes,
So that the bestes and the briddes
Governed were of him al one,
Sire king, betokneth thi persone,
Which stant above all erthli thinges.
Thus regnen under the the kinges,   2890
And al the poeple unto thee louteth,
And al the world thi pouer doubteth,
So that with vein honour deceived
Thou hast the reverence weyved
Fro him which is thi king above,
That thou for drede ne for love
Wolt nothing knowen of thi godd;   **P. i. 140**
Which now for thee hath mad a rodd,
Thi veine gloire and thi folie

2863 it *om.* H₁XERCB₂   that L, W   2869 his B   þe MX
2874 As] And H₁ . . . L   2885 wode B   2891 al] of
H₁ . . . B₂ (ofte R)   2898 a rodd AJ, B   arodd S, FK

With grete peines to chastie.
And of the vois thou herdest speke,
Which bad the bowes forto breke
And hewe and felle doun the tree,
That word belongeth unto thee;
Thi regne schal ben overthrowe,
And thou despuiled for a throwe:
Bot that the Rote scholde stonde,
Be that thou schalt wel understonde,
Ther schal abyden of thi regne
A time ayein whan thou schalt regne.   2910
And ek of that thou herdest seie,
To take a mannes herte aweie
And sette there a bestial,
So that he lich an Oxe schal
Pasture, and that he be bereined
Be times sefne and sore peined,
Til that he knowe his goddes mihtes,
Than scholde he stonde ayein uprihtes,—
Al this betokneth thin astat,
Which now with god is in debat: 2920
Thi mannes forme schal be lassed,
Til sevene yer ben overpassed,
And in the liknesse of a beste
Of gras schal be thi real feste,
The weder schal upon thee reine.
And understond that al this peine,
Which thou schalt soffre thilke tide,   **P. i. 141**
Is schape al only for thi pride
Of veine gloire, and of the sinne
Which thou hast longe stonden inne.   2930
  So upon this condicioun
Thi swevene hath exposicioun.
Bot er this thing befalle in dede,
Amende thee, this wolde I rede:
Yif and departe thin almesse,
Do mercy forth with rihtwisnesse,
Besech and prei the hihe grace,
For so thou myht thi pes pourchace

2903 falle H₁ . . . B₂, W   2905 The A
I 2

[NEBUCHADNEZZAR'S
PUNISHMENT.]

With godd, and stonde in good acord.'
 Bot Pride is loth to leve his lord,   2940
And wol noght soffre humilite
With him to stonde in no degree;
And whan a schip hath lost his stiere,
Is non so wys that mai him stiere
Ayein the wawes in a rage.
This proude king in his corage
Humilite hath so forlore,
That for no swevene he sih tofore,
Ne yit for al that Daniel
Him hath conseiled everydel,   2950
He let it passe out of his mynde,
Thurgh veine gloire, and as the blinde,
He seth no weie, er him be wo.
And fell withinne a time so,
As he in Babiloine wente,
The vanite of Pride him hente;
His herte aros of veine gloire,   **P. i. 142**
So that he drowh into memoire
His lordschipe and his regalie
With wordes of Surquiderie.   2960
And whan that he him most avaunteth,
That lord which veine gloire daunteth,
Al sodeinliche, as who seith treis,
Wher that he stod in his Paleis,
He tok him fro the mennes sihte:
Was non of hem so war that mihte
Sette yhe wher that he becom.
And thus was he from his kingdom
Into the wilde Forest drawe,
Wher that the myhti goddes lawe   2970
Thurgh his pouer dede him transforme
Fro man into a bestes forme;
And lich an Oxe under the fot
He graseth, as he nedes mot,
To geten him his lives fode.
Tho thoghte him colde grases goode,
That whilom eet the hote spices,

Thus was he torned fro delices:
The wyn which he was wont to drinke
He tok thanne of the welles brinke   2980
Or of the pet or of the slowh,
It thoghte him thanne good ynowh:
In stede of chambres wel arraied
He was thanne of a buissh wel paied,
The harde ground he lay upon,
For othre pilwes hath he non;
The stormes and the Reines falle,   **P. i. 143**
The wyndes blowe upon him alle,
He was tormented day and nyht,
Such was the hihe goddes myht,'   2990
Til sevene yer an ende toke.
Upon himself tho gan he loke;
In stede of mete gras and stres,
In stede of handes longe cles,
In stede of man a bestes lyke
He syh; and thanne he gan to syke
For cloth of gold and for perrie,
Which him was wont to magnefie.
Whan he behield his Cote of heres,
He wepte and with fulwoful teres   3000
Up to the hevene he caste his chiere
Wepende, and thoghte in this manere;
Thogh he no wordes myhte winne,
Thus seide his herte and spak withinne:
'O mihti godd, that al hast wroght
And al myht bringe ayein to noght,
Now knowe I wel, bot al of thee,
This world hath no prosperite:
In thin aspect ben alle liche,
The povere man and ek the riche,   3010
Withoute thee ther mai no wight,
And thou above alle othre miht.
O mihti lord, toward my vice
Thi merci medle with justice;

2988 blew(e) M, B   2990 Such] Which H₁ ... B₂   2997 for]
þe H₁ ... B₂   of KH₃   om.W   3000 fulwoful A, F   ful woful J, B
3010 the riche   om. B   3011 wight B, F   wiht AJ, S

[Nebuchadnezzar's
Punishment.]

And I woll make a covenant,
That of my lif the remenant
I schal it be thi grace amende,   **P. i. 144**
And in thi lawe so despende
That veine gloire I schal eschuie,
And bowe unto thin heste and suie   3020
Humilite, and that I vowe.'
And so thenkende he gan doun bowe,
And thogh him lacke vois and speche,
He gan up with his feet areche,
And wailende in his bestly stevene
He made his pleignte unto the hevene.
He kneleth in his wise and braieth,
To seche merci and assaieth
His god, which made him nothing strange,
Whan that he sih his pride change.   3030
Anon as he was humble and tame,
He fond toward his god the same,
And in a twinklinge of a lok
His mannes forme ayein he tok,
And was reformed to the regne
In which that he was wont to regne;
So that the Pride of veine gloire
Evere afterward out of memoire
He let it passe. And thus is schewed
What is to ben of Pride unthewed   3040
Ayein the hihe goddes lawe,
To whom noman mai be felawe.

Confessor.

     Forthi, my Sone, tak good hiede
So forto lede thi manhiede,
That thou ne be noght lich a beste.
Bot if thi lif schal ben honeste,
Thou most humblesce take on honde,   **P. i. 145**
For thanne myht thou siker stonde:
And forto speke it otherwise,
A proud man can no love assise;   3050
For thogh a womman wolde him plese,
His Pride can noght ben at ese.

3023 and speche JH₁L, FWH₃   of speche AM ... CB₂, S ... Δ
3027 braieth] preieþ (prayeþ) H₁ ... B₂, W

Ther mai noman to mochel blame
A vice which is forto blame;
Forthi men scholde nothing hide
That mihte falle in blame of Pride,
Which is the werste vice of alle:
Wherof, so as it was befalle,
The tale I thenke of a Cronique
To telle, if that it mai thee like,   3060
So that thou myht humblesce suie
And ek the vice of Pride eschuie,
Wherof the gloire is fals and vein;
Which god himself hath in desdeign,
That thogh it mounte for a throwe,
It schal doun falle and overthrowe.

xii. *Est virtus humilis, per quam deus altus ad yma*
  Se tulit et nostre viscera carnis habet.
Sic humilis superest, et amor sibi subditur omnis,
  Cuius habet nulla sorte superbus opem :
Odit eum terra, celum deiecit et ipsum,
  Sedibus inferni statque receptus ibi.

A king whilom was yong and wys,   [TALE OF THE THREE QUESTIONS.]
The which sette of his wit gret pris.
Of depe ymaginaciouns   Hic narrat Confes-
And strange interpretaciouns,   sor exemplum simpli-
                                            3070 citer contra Superbi-
Problemes and demandes eke,   P. i. 146 am; et dicit quod nup-
His wisdom was to finde and seke;   er quidam Rex famose
Wherof he wolde in sondri wise   prudencie cuidam mil-
                                                 iti suo super tribus
Opposen hem that weren wise.   questionibus, vt inde
Bot non of hem it myhte bere   certitudinis responsio-
Upon his word to yeve answere,   nem daret, sub pena
                                                 capitalis sentencie ter-
Outaken on, which was a knyht;   minum prefixit. Pri-
To him was every thing so liht,   mo, quid minoris in-
                                                 digencie ab inhabi-
That also sone as he hem herde,   tantibus orbem auxi-
                                                 lium maius obtinuit.
The kinges wordes he answerde;   3080 Secundo, quid maioris
What thing the king him axe wolde,   valencie meritum con-
                                                 tinens minoris expen-
Therof anon the trowthe he tolde.   se reprisas exiguit.

Latin Verses xii. 5 eum] eni*m* B
3078 *margin* habitantibus H₁ . . . B₂, BΛ   3080 *margin* valencie
meritum] meriti H₁ . . . B₂, BΛ

[TALE OF THE THREE
QUESTIONS.]

Tercio, quid omnia
bona diminuens ex sui
proprietate nichil pe-
nitus valuit. Quarum
vero questionum que-
dam virgo dicti mili-
tis filia sapientissima
nomine patris sui so-
lucionem aggrediens
taliter Regi respondit.
Ad primam dixit, quod
terra nullius indiget,
quam tamen adiuuare
cotidianis laboribus
omnes intendunt. Ad
secundam dixit, quod
humilitas omnibus vir-
tutibus prevalet, que
tamen nullius prode-
galitatis expensis men-
suram excedit. Ad ter-
ciam dixit, quod su-
perbia omnia tam cor-
poris quam anime bona
deuastans maiores ex-
pensarum excessus in-
ducit. Et tamen nul-
lius valoris, ymmo to-
cius perdicionis, caus-
am sua culpa minis-
trat.

The king somdiel hadde an Envie,
And thoghte he wolde his wittes plie
To sette som conclusioun,
Which scholde be confusioun
Unto this knyht, so that the name
And of wisdom the hihe fame
Toward himself he wolde winne.
And thus of al his wit withinne   3090
This king began to studie and muse,
What strange matiere he myhte use
The knyhtes wittes to confounde;
And ate laste he hath it founde,
And for the knyht anon he sente,
That he schal telle what he mente.
Upon thre pointz stod the matiere
Of questions, as thou schalt hiere.

The ferste point of alle thre   iᵃ questio.
Was this: 'What thing in his degre   3100
Of al this world hath nede lest,   **P. i. 147**
And yet men helpe it althermest?'

The secounde is: 'What most is worth,   iiᵃ questio.
And of costage is lest put forth?'

The thridde is: 'Which is of most cost,   iiiᵃ questio.
And lest is worth and goth to lost?'

The king thes thre demandes axeth,
And to the knyht this lawe he taxeth,
That he schal gon and come ayein
The thridde weke, and telle him plein   3110
To every point, what it amonteth.
And if so be that he misconteth,
To make in his answere a faile,
Ther schal non other thing availe,
The king seith, bot he schal be ded
And lese hise goodes and his hed.
The knyht was sori of this thing
And wolde excuse him to the king,
Bot he ne wolde him noght forbere,
And thus the knyht of his ansuere   3120

3108 he *om.* KH₃   3120 his] þis X . . . B₂

[TALE OF THE THREE QUESTIONS.]

Goth hom to take avisement:
Bot after his entendement
The more he caste his wit aboute,
The more he stant therof in doute.
Tho wiste he wel the kinges herte,
That he the deth ne scholde asterte,
And such a sorwe hath to him take,
That gladschipe he hath al forsake.
He thoghte ferst upon his lif,
And after that upon his wif,   3130
Upon his children ek also,   P. i. 148
Of whiche he hadde dowhtres tuo;
The yongest of hem hadde of age
Fourtiene yer, and of visage
Sche was riht fair, and of stature
Lich to an hevenely figure,
And of manere and goodli speche,
Thogh men wolde alle Londes seche,
Thei scholden noght have founde hir like.
Sche sih hire fader sorwe and sike,   3140
And wiste noght the cause why;
So cam sche to him prively,
And that was where he made his mone
Withinne a Gardin al him one;
Upon hire knes sche gan doun falle
With humble herte and to him calle,
And seide: 'O goode fader diere,
Why make ye thus hevy chiere,
And I wot nothing how it is?
And wel ye knowen, fader, this,   3150
What aventure that you felle
Ye myhte it saufly to me telle,
For I have ofte herd you seid,
That ye such trust have on me leid,
That to my soster ne my brother,
In al this world ne to non other,
Ye dorste telle a privite
So wel, my fader, as to me.

3126 schal AM   3155 ne my] ne to my GRB2, AdΔΛ,
W (nor to my)   and my H1

[TALE OF THE THREE
QUESTIONS.]

Forthi, my fader, I you preie,
Ne casteth noght that herte aweie,　　　3160
For I am sche that wolde kepe　　**P. i. 149**
Youre honour.'　And with that to wepe
Hire yhe mai noght be forbore,
Sche wissheth forto ben unbore,
Er that hire fader so mistriste
To tellen hire of that he wiste :
And evere among merci sche cride,
That he ne scholde his conseil hide
From hire that so wolde him good
And was so nyh his fleissh and blod.　　3170
So that with wepinge ate laste
His chiere upon his child he caste,
And sorwfulli to that sche preide
He tolde his tale and thus he seide :
' The sorwe, dowhter, which I make
Is noght al only for my sake,
Bot for thee bothe and for you alle :
For such a chance is me befalle,
That I schal er this thridde day
Lese al that evere I lese may,　　　3180
Mi lif and al my good therto :
Therfore it is I sorwe so.'
' What is the cause, helas !' quod sche,
' Mi fader, that ye scholden be
Ded and destruid in such a wise ?'
And he began the pointz devise,
Whiche as the king told him be mowthe,
And seid hir pleinly that he cowthe
Ansuere unto no point of this.
And sche, that hiereth how it is,　　　3190
Hire conseil yaf and seide tho :　　**P. i. 150**
' Mi fader, sithen it is so,
That ye can se non other weie,
Bot that ye moste nedes deie,
I wolde preie of you a thing :

3183 helas A, S, F　　A las J　allas B &c.　　3185 a *om.* E, B
3187 told SB, F　tolde AJ　　3188 seid (seyd) B, F　seide AJ
he ne cowþe H₁XGRCLB₂　　3195 pray yow of BΔ　　o þing B

Let me go with you to the king,
And ye schull make him understonde
How ye, my wittes forto fonde,
Have leid your ansuere upon me;
And telleth him, in such degre   3200
Upon my word ye wole abide
To lif or deth, what so betide.
For yit par chaunce I may pourchace
With som good word the kinges grace,
Your lif and ek your good to save;
For ofte schal a womman have
Thing which a man mai noght areche.'
The fader herde his dowhter speche,
And thoghte ther was resoun inne,
And sih his oghne lif to winne   3210
He cowthe don himself no cure;
So betre him thoghte in aventure
To put his lif and al his good,
Than in the maner as it stod
His lif in certein forto lese.
And thus thenkende he gan to chese
To do the conseil of this Maide,
And tok the pourpos which sche saide.
    The dai was come and forth thei gon,
Unto the Court thei come anon,   3220
Wher as the king in juggement   P. i. 151
Was set and hath this knyht assent.
Arraied in hire beste wise
This Maiden with hire wordes wise
Hire fader ladde be the hond
Into the place, wher he fond
The king with othre whiche he wolde,
And to the king kneiende he tolde
As he enformed was tofore,
And preith the king that he therfore   3230
His dowhtres wordes wolde take,
And seith that he wol undertake
Upon hire wordes forto stonde.
    Tho was ther gret merveile on honde,

3201 I wole XERCB₂   3209 þought þat þer was XGRCLB₂

That he, which was so wys a knyht,
His lif upon so yong a wyht
Besette wolde in jeupartie,
And manye it hielden for folie:
Bot ate laste natheles
The king comandeth ben in pes,   3240
And to this Maide he caste his chiere,
And seide he wolde hire tale hiere,
He bad hire speke, and sche began:
'Mi liege lord, so as I can,'
Quod sche, 'the pointz of whiche I herde,
Thei schul of reson ben ansuerde.
    The ferste I understonde is this,
What thing of al the world it is,
Which men most helpe and hath lest nede.
Mi liege lord, this wolde I rede: 3250
The Erthe it is, which everemo   **P. i. 152**
With mannes labour is bego;
Als wel in wynter as in Maii
The mannes hond doth what he mai
To helpe it forth and make it riche,
And forthi men it delve and dyche
And eren it with strengthe of plowh,
Wher it hath of himself ynowh,
So that his nede is ate leste.
For every man and bridd and beste,   3260
And flour and gras and rote and rinde,
And every thing be weie of kynde
Schal sterve, and Erthe it schal become;
As it was out of Erthe nome,
It schal to therthe torne ayein:
And thus I mai be resoun sein
That Erthe is the most nedeles,
And most men helpe it natheles.
So that, my lord, touchende of this
I have ansuerd hou that it is.   3270

3245 pointes (pointz) which(e) H₁ ... B₂, B, WKH₃ (pointes
which as L)   3249 hath lest nede] haþ most nede R han most
nede XEC han lest nede B₂   3261 And] Of H₁ ... B₂, B   3264 of
þe erþe AMB₂, Δ

That other point I understod,
Which most is worth and most is good,
And costeth lest a man to kepe:
Mi lord, if ye woll take kepe,
I seie it is Humilite,
Thurgh which the hihe trinite
As for decerte of pure love
Unto Marie from above,
Of that he knew hire humble entente,
His oghne Sone adoun he sente,   3280
Above alle othre and hire he ches   **P. i. 153**
For that vertu which bodeth pes:
So that I may be resoun calle
Humilite most worth of alle.
And lest it costeth to maintiene,
In al the world as it is sene;
For who that hath humblesce on honde,
He bringth no werres into londe,
For he desireth for the beste
To setten every man in reste.   3290
Thus with your hihe reverence
Me thenketh that this evidence
As to this point is sufficant.

And touchende of the remenant,
Which is the thridde of youre axinges,
What leste is worth of alle thinges,
And costeth most, I telle it, Pride;
Which mai noght in the hevene abide,
For Lucifer with hem that felle
Bar Pride with him into helle.   3300
Ther was Pride of to gret a cost,
Whan he for Pride hath hevene lost;
And after that in Paradis
Adam for Pride loste his pris:
In Midelerthe and ek also
Pride is the cause of alle wo,
That al the world ne may suffise
To stanche of Pride the reprise:

3285 to] in AM   3300 into] to AM   3301 grete (gret) cost
MH₁G, B

Pride is the heved of alle Sinne,
Which wasteth al and mai noght winne; 3310
Pride is of every mis the pricke, **P. i. 154**
Pride is the werste of alle wicke,
And costneth most and lest is worth
In place where he hath his forth.
Thus have I seid that I wol seie
Of myn answere, and to you preie,
Mi liege lord, of youre office
That ye such grace and such justice
Ordeigne for mi fader hiere,
That after this, whan men it hiere, 3320
The world therof mai speke good.'
    The king, which reson understod
And hath al herd how sche hath said,
Was inly glad and so wel paid
That al his wraththe is overgo:
And he began to loke tho
Upon this Maiden in the face,
In which he fond so mochel grace,
That al his pris on hire he leide,
In. audience and thus he seide: 3330
'Mi faire Maide, wel thee be!
Of thin ansuere and ek of thee
Me liketh wel, and as thou wilt,
Foryive be thi fader gilt.
And if thou were of such lignage,
That thou to me were of parage,
And that thi fader were a Pier,
As he is now a Bachilier,
So seker as I have a lif,
Thou scholdest thanne be my wif. 3340
Bot this I seie natheles, **P. i. 155**
That I wol schape thin encress;
What worldes good that thou wolt crave,
Axe of my yifte and thou schalt have.'
And sche the king with wordes wise
Knelende thonketh in this wise:
'Mi liege lord, god mot you quite!

3313 costeþ H₁XLB₂, BΔ, H₃   costs W

Mi fader hier hath bot a lite
Of warison, and that he wende
Hadde al be lost; bot now amende   3350
He mai wel thurgh your noble grace.'
With that the king riht in his place
Anon forth in that freisshe hete
An Erldom, which thanne of eschete
Was late falle into his hond,
Unto this knyht with rente and lond
Hath yove and with his chartre sesed;
And thus was all the noise appesed.

   This Maiden, which sat on hire knes
Tofore the king, hise charitees   3360
Comendeth, and seide overmore:
'Mi liege lord, riht now tofore
Ye seide, as it is of record,
That if my fader were a lord
And Pier unto these othre grete,
Ye wolden for noght elles lete,
That I ne scholde be your wif;
And this wot every worthi lif,
A kinges word it mot ben holde.
Forthi, my lord, if that ye wolde   3370
So gret a charite fulfille,   **P. i. 156**
God wot it were wel my wille:
For he which was a Bacheler,
Mi fader, is now mad a Pier;
So whenne as evere that I cam,
An Erles dowhter now I am.'

   This yonge king, which peised al,
Hire beaute and hir wit withal,
As he that was with love hent,
Anon therto yaf his assent.   3380
He myhte noght the maide asterte,
That sche nis ladi of his herte;

3357 seled F   3361 euermore MX . . . B₂, B, W   3363 as]
and H₁ . . . B₂, B   3369 it mot ben] mot (mote) nede be
H₁ . . . B₂, BΛ   3374 mad a Pier] an Erl(e) hier H₁ . . .
B₂, Λ   3379 that] which H₁ . . . B₂, B   3381 maide] place
H₁ . . . B₂, BΛ

So that he tok hire to his wif,
To holde whyl that he hath lif:
And thus the king toward his knyht
Acordeth him, as it is riht.

And over this good is to wite,
In the Cronique as it is write,
This noble king of whom I tolde
Of Spaine be tho daies olde   3390
The kingdom hadde in governance,
And as the bok makth remembrance,
Alphonse was his propre name:
The knyht also, if I schal name,
Danz Petro hihte, and as men telle,
His dowhter wyse Peronelle
Was cleped, which was full of grace:
And that was sene in thilke place,
Wher sche hir fader out of teene
Hath broght and mad hirself a qweene,   3400
Of that sche hath so wel desclosed   **P. i. 157**
The pointz wherof sche was opposed.

[HUMILITY.]
Gonfessor.

Lo now, my Sone, as thou myht hiere,
Of al this thing to my matiere
Bot on I take, and that is Pride,
To whom no grace mai betide:
In hevene he fell out of his stede,
And Paradis him was forbede,
The goode men in Erthe him hate,
So that to helle he mot algate,   3410
Where every vertu schal be weyved
And every vice be received.
Bot Humblesce is al otherwise,
Which most is worth, and no reprise
It takth ayein, bot softe and faire,
If eny thing stond in contraire,

3396 His doughtres (doghter) name Peronelle H₁ . . . B₂, Λ
3398 sene (seene) A, B   scene S, F   schene (*om.* was) J   3403
myht] may H₁ . . . B₂   3412 be] schal be H₁ . . . B₂   3414
worþy and no prise X . . . CB₂   worth and no prise H₁   worþy
and of no prise LSn, Λ   worth and of no reprise W   3416 And
it is alway debonaire H₁ . . . B₂, Λ   stond J, S, F   stonde A, B

With humble speche it is redresced:
Thus was this yonge Maiden blessed,
The which I spak of now tofore,
Hire fader lif sche gat therfore,   3420
And wan with al the kinges love.
Forthi, my Sone, if thou wolt love,
It sit thee wel to leve Pride
And take Humblesce upon thi side;
The more of grace thou schalt gete.

  Mi fader, I woll noght foryete   Amans.
Of this that ye have told me hiere,
And if that eny such manere
Of humble port mai love appaie,
Hierafterward I thenke assaie: 3430
Bot now forth over I beseche   **P. i. 158**
That ye more of my schrifte seche.   Confessor.

  Mi goode Sone, it schal be do:
Now herkne and ley an Ere to;
For as touchende of Prides fare,
Als ferforth as I can declare
In cause of vice, in cause of love,
That hast thou pleinly herd above,
So that ther is nomor to seie
Touchende of that; bot other weie   3440
Touchende Envie I thenke telle,
Which hath the propre kinde of helle,
Withoute cause to misdo
Toward himself and othre also,
Hierafterward as understonde
Thou schalt the spieces, as thei stonde.

Explicit Liber Primus.

3443 to misdo] of þing misdo H₁ . . . CB₂   of nothing mysdo L
3445 as] as I AJL, Λ, W

**   K

[ENVY.]

i. *Inuidie culpa magis est attrita dolore,*
 Nam sua mens nullo tempore leta manet :
Quo gaudent alii, dolet ille, nec vnus amicus
 Est, cui de puro comoda velle facit.
Proximitatis honor sua corda veretur, et omnis
 Est sibi leticia sic aliena dolor.
Hoc etenim vicium quam sepe repugnat amanti,
 Non sibi, set reliquis, dum fauet ipsa Venus.
Est amor ex proprio motu fantasticus, et que
 Gaudia fert alius, credit obesse sibi. (10)

Hic in secundo li-
bro tractat de Inuidia
et eius speciebus, qua-
rum dolor alterius
gaudii prima nuncupa-
tur, cuius condicionem
secundum vicium Con-
fessor primitus descri-
bens, Amanti, quatenus
amorem concernit, su-
per eodem consequen-
ter opponit.

  Now after Pride the secounde
Ther is, which many a woful stounde
Towardes othre berth aboute
Withinne himself and noght withoute ;
For in his thoght he brenneth evere,
Whan that he wot an other levere
Or more vertuous than he,
Which passeth him in his degre ;
Therof he takth his maladie :
That vice is cleped hot Envie. 10
  Forthi, my Sone, if it be so
Thou art or hast ben on of tho,
As forto speke in loves cas,
If evere yit thin herte was
Sek of an other mannes hele ? P. i. 160
  So god avance my querele,
Mi fader, ye, a thousend sithe :
Whanne I have sen an other blithe
Of love, and hadde a goodly chiere,

[i. SORROW FOR AN-
OTHER MAN'S JOY.]

  Latin Verses i. 10 aliis H₁ . . . B₂, BΛ, W

Ethna, which brenneth yer be yere,   20 [SORROW FOR AN-
OTHER MAN'S JOY.]
Was thanne noght so hot as I
Of thilke Sor which prively
Min hertes thoght withinne brenneth.
The Schip which on the wawes renneth,
And is forstormed and forblowe,
Is noght more peined for a throwe
Than I am thanne, whanne I se
An other which that passeth me
In that fortune of loves yifte.
Bot, fader, this I telle in schrifte,   30
That is nowher bot in o place;
For who that lese or finde grace
In other stede, it mai noght grieve:
Bot this ye mai riht wel believe,
Toward mi ladi that I serve,
Thogh that I wiste forto sterve,
Min herte is full of such sotie,
That I myself mai noght chastie.
Whan I the Court se of Cupide
Aproche unto my ladi side   40
Of hem that lusti ben and freisshe,—
Thogh it availe hem noght a reisshe,
Bot only that thei ben in speche,—
My sorwe is thanne noght to seche:
Bot whan thei rounen in hire Ere,   **P. i. 161**
Than groweth al my moste fere,
And namly whan thei talen longe;
My sorwes thanne be so stronge
Of that I se hem wel at ese,
I can noght telle my desese.   50
Bot, Sire, as of my ladi selve,
Thogh sche have wowers ten or twelve,
For no mistrust I have of hire
Me grieveth noght, for certes, Sire,
I trowe, in al this world to seche,
Nis womman that in dede and speche
Woll betre avise hire what sche doth,

31 nowher] now heer (here) MX . . . B₂

Ne betre, forto seie a soth,
Kepe hire honour ate alle tide,
And yit get hire a thank beside.   60
Bot natheles I am beknowe,
That whanne I se at eny throwe,
Or elles if I mai it hiere,
That sche make eny man good chiere,
Thogh I therof have noght to done,
Mi thought wol entermette him sone.
For thogh I be miselve strange,
Envie makth myn herte change,
That I am sorghfully bestad
Of that I se an other glad   70
With hire; bot of other alle,
Of love what so mai befalle,
Or that he faile or that he spede,
Therof take I bot litel heede.
Now have I seid, my fader, al   **P. i. 162**
As of this point in special,
Als ferforthli as I have wist.
Now axeth further what you list.

Confessor.

　Mi Sone, er I axe eny more,
I thenke somdiel for thi lore   80
Telle an ensample of this matiere
Touchende Envie, as thou schalt hiere.
Write in Civile this I finde:
Thogh it be noght the houndes kinde
To ete chaf, yit wol he werne
An Oxe which comth to the berne,
Therof to taken eny fode.
And thus, who that it understode,
It stant of love in many place:
Who that is out of loves grace   90
And mai himselven noght availe,
He wolde an other scholde faile;
And if he may put eny lette,
He doth al that he mai to lette.

59 ate A, S, F at J, B   60 get J, S, F   gete AC, B   71 oþer
(othir) MH₁, AdΔ, H₃ oþre AJEC, SB, F   78 further] fader KH₃
92 wolde] þought(e) XEC þough H₁RLB₂

Wherof I finde, as thou schalt wite,
To this pourpos a tale write.

Ther ben of suche mo than twelve,
That ben noght able as of hemselve
To gete love, and for Envie
Upon alle othre thei aspie;   100
And for hem lacketh that thei wolde,
Thei kepte that non other scholde
Touchende of love his cause spede:
Wherof a gret ensample I rede,
Which unto this matiere acordeth,   P. i. 163
As Ovide in his bok recordeth,
How Poliphemus whilom wroghte,
Whan that he Galathee besoghte
Of love, which he mai noght lacche.
That made him forto waite and wacche   110
Be alle weies how it ferde,
Til ate laste he knew and herde
How that an other hadde leve
To love there as he mot leve,
As forto speke of eny sped:
So that he knew non other red,
Bot forto wayten upon alle,
Til he may se the chance falle
That he hire love myhte grieve,
Which he himself mai noght achieve.   120
This Galathee, seith the Poete,
Above alle othre was unmete
Of beaute, that men thanne knewe,
And hadde a lusti love and trewe,
A Bacheler in his degree,
Riht such an other as was sche,
On whom sche hath hire herte set,
So that it myhte noght be let
For yifte ne for no beheste,
That sche ne was al at his heste.   130

Hic ponit Confessor
exemplum saltem con-
tra istos qui in amoris
causa aliorum gaudiis
inuidentes nequaquam
per hoc sibi ipsis pro-
ficiunt. Et narrat,
qualiter quidam iuue-
nis miles nomine Acis,
quem Galathea Nim-
pha pulcherrima toto
corde peramauit, cum
ipsi sub quadam rupe
iuxta litus maris col-
loquium adinuicem
habuerunt, Poliphe-
mus Gigas concussa
rupe magnam inde
partem super caput
Acis ab alto proiciens
ipsum per inuidiam
interfecit. Et cum ipse
super hoc dictam Gala-
theam rapere voluis-
set, Neptunus Giganti
obsistens ipsam inuio-
latam salua custodia
preseruauit. Set et
dii miserti corpus Acis
defuncti in fontem
aque dulcissime subito
transmutarunt.

96 write] I write AM   116 *margin* capere H₁ ... B₂, B
117 Bot] Bo F   119 *margin* et *om.* B   123 that men thanne
knewe] þat men þat (*om.* knewe) A   þat men þat knew M   that than
men knewe Ad   of men that knewe H₃   129 no *om.* AM

[TALE OF ACIS AND GALATEA.]

This yonge knyht Acis was hote,
Which hire ayeinward als so hote
Al only loveth and nomo.
Hierof was Poliphemus wo
Thurgh pure Envie, and evere aspide, **P. i. 164**
And waiteth upon every side,
Whan he togedre myhte se
This yonge Acis with Galathe.

So longe he waiteth to and fro,
Til ate laste he fond hem tuo, 140
In prive place wher thei stode
To speke and have here wordes goode.
The place wher as he hem syh,
It was under a banke nyh
The grete See, and he above
Stod and behield the lusti love
Which ech of hem to other made
With goodly chiere and wordes glade,
That al his herte hath set afyre
Of pure Envie: and as a fyre 150
Which fleth out of a myhti bowe,
Aweie he fledde for a throwe,
As he that was for love wod,
Whan that he sih how that it stod.
This Polipheme a Geant was;
And whan he sih the sothe cas,
How Galathee him hath forsake
And Acis to hire love take,
His herte mai it noght forbere
That he ne roreth lich a Bere; 160
And as it were a wilde beste,
The whom no reson mihte areste,
He ran Ethna the hell aboute,
Wher nevere yit the fyr was oute,
Fulfild of sorghe and gret desese, **P. i. 165**
That he syh Acis wel at ese.

136 tyde B   149 set J, SB   sette A, F   150 vyre (vire) H₁ ... L,
B, W   160 lich] as B, KH₃   162 The whom AX, SAd, F   Tho
whome M   To whom J H₁ G ... B₂, Λ   In whom K *in ras.* H₃   The
which B, W   Hom *om.* The) Δ   areste] haue reste J

[TALE OF ACIS AND
GALATEA.]

Til ate laste he him bethoghte,
As he which al Envie soghte,
And torneth to the banke ayein,
Wher he with Galathee hath seyn   170
Acis, whom that he thoghte grieve,
Thogh he himself mai noght relieve.
This Geant with his ruide myht
Part of the banke he schof doun riht,
The which evene upon Acis fell,
So that with fallinge of this hell
This Poliphemus Acis slowh,
Wherof sche made sorwe ynowh.
And as sche fledde fro the londe,
Neptunus tok hire into honde   180
And kept hire in so sauf a place
Fro Polipheme and his manace,
That he with al his false Envie
Ne mihte atteigne hir compaignie.
This Galathee of whom I speke,
That of hirself mai noght be wreke,
Withouten eny semblant feigned
Sche hath hire loves deth compleigned,
And with hire sorwe and with hire wo
Sche hath the goddes moeved so,   190
That thei of pite and of grace
Have Acis in the same place,
Ther he lai ded, into a welle
Transformed, as the bokes telle,
With freisshe stremes and with cliere, **P. i. 166**
As he whilom with lusti chiere
Was freissh his love forto qweme.
And with this ruide Polipheme
For his Envie and for his hate
Thei were wrothe.

        And thus algate,   200   Confessor.
Mi Sone, thou myht understonde,
That if thou wolt in grace stonde
With love, thou most leve Envie:
And as thou wolt for thi partie

176 þe helle AM (hille)   181 kept J, SB, F   kepte A   193 Wher SAdBΔ

[TALE OF ACIS AND
GALATEA.]

Toward thi love stonde fre,
So most thou soffre an other be,
What so befalle upon the chaunce :
For it is an unwys vengance,
Which to non other man is lief,
And is unto himselve grief.   210

Amans.

     Mi fader, this ensample is good ;
Bot how so evere that it stod
With Poliphemes love as tho,
It schal noght stonde with me so,
To worchen eny felonie
In love for no such Envie.
Forthi if ther oght elles be,
Now axeth forth, in what degre
It is, and I me schal confesse
With schrifte unto youre holinesse.   220

[ii. JOY FOR ANOTHER
MAN'S GRIEF.]

ii. *Orta sibi solito mentalia gaudia liuor*
     Dum videt alterius, dampna doloris agit.
Inuidus obridet hodie fletus aliorum,
     Fletus cui proprios crastina fata parant.
Sic in amore pari stat sorte iocosus, amantes   **P. i. 167**
     Cum videt illusos, inuidus ille quasi.
Sit licet in vacuum, sperat tamen ipse leuamen
     Alterius casu, lapsus et ipse simul.

     Mi goode Sone, yit ther is
A vice revers unto this,
Which envious takth his gladnesse
Of that he seth the hevinesse

Hic loquitur Confessor de secunda specie Inuidie, que gaudium alterius doloris dicitur, et primo eiusdem vicii materiam tractans amantis conscienciam super eodem vlterius inuestigat.

Of othre men : for his welfare
Is whanne he wot an other care :
Of that an other hath a fall,
He thenkth himself arist withal.
Such is the gladschipe of Envie
In worldes thing, and in partie   230
Fulofte times ek also
In loves cause it stant riht so.

Latin Verses ii. 1 Orta] Vita H₁ . . . B₂, B   5 sorte] forte
H₁XGRCLB₂
228 He] Him E, KH₃

If thou, my Sone, hast joie had,
Whan thou an other sihe unglad,
Schrif the therof.

           Mi fader, yis:

Amans.

I am beknowe unto you this.
Of these lovers that loven streyte,
And for that point which thei coveite
Ben poursuiantz fro yeer to yere
In loves Court, whan I may hiere   240
How that thei clymbe upon the whel,
And whan thei wene al schal be wel,
Thei ben doun throwen ate laste,
Thanne am I fedd of that thei faste,
And lawhe of that I se hem loure;
And thus of that thei brewe soure
I drinke swete, and am wel esed   P. i. 168
Of that I wot thei ben desesed.
Bot this which I you telle hiere
Is only for my lady diere;   250
That for non other that I knowe
Me reccheth noght who overthrowe,
Ne who that stonde in love upriht:
Bot be he squier, be he knyht,
Which to my ladiward poursuieth,
The more he lest of that he suieth,
The mor me thenketh that I winne,
And am the more glad withinne
Of that I wot him sorwe endure.
For evere upon such aventure   260
It is a confort, as men sein,

Boicius. Consola-
cio miserorum est
habere consortem in
pena.

To him the which is wo besein
To sen an other in his peine,
So that thei bothe mai compleigne.
Wher I miself mai noght availe
To sen an other man travaile,
I am riht glad if he be let;
And thogh I fare noght the bet,
His sorwe is to myn herte a game:
Whan that I knowe it is the same   270
Which to mi ladi stant enclined,

[JOY FOR ANOTHER MAN'S GRIEF.]

And hath his love noght termined,
I am riht joifull in my thoght.
If such Envie grieveth oght,
As I beknowe me coupable,
Ye that be wys and resonable,
Mi fader, telleth youre avis.   **P. i. 169**

Confessor.

   Mi Sone, Envie into no pris
Of such a forme, I understonde,
Ne mihte be no resoun stonde   280
For this Envie hath such a kinde,
That he wole sette himself behinde
To hindre with an othre wyht,
And gladly lese his oghne riht
To make an other lesen his.
And forto knowe how it so is,
A tale lich to this matiere
I thenke telle, if thou wolt hiere,
To schewe proprely the vice
Of this Envie and the malice.   290

[THE TRAVELLERS AND THE ANGEL.]

Hic ponit Confessor exemplum presertim contra illum, qui sponte sui ipsius detrimentum in alterius penam maiorem patitur. Et narrat quod, cum Iupiter angelum suum in forma hominis, vt hominum condiciones exploraret, ab excelso in terram misit, contigit quod ipse angelus duos homines, quorum vnus cupidus, alter inuidus erat, itinerando spacio quasi vnius diei comitabatur. Et cum sero factum esset, angelus eorum noticie seipsum tunc manifestans dixit, quod quicquid alter eorum ab ipso donari sibi pecierit, illud statim obtine-

   Of Jupiter this finde I write,
How whilom that he wolde wite
Upon the pleigntes whiche he herde,
Among the men how that it ferde,
As of here wrong condicion
To do justificacion :
And for that cause doun he sente
An Angel, which aboute wente,
That he the sothe knowe mai.
So it befell upon a dai   300
This Angel, which him scholde enforme,
Was clothed in a mannes forme,
And overtok, I understonde,
Tuo men that wenten over londe,
Thurgh whiche he thoghte to aspie
His cause, and goth in compaignie.
This Angel with hise wordes wise   **P. i. 170**
Opposeth hem in sondri wise,
Now lowde wordes and now softe,

That mad hem to desputen ofte,
And ech of hem his reson hadde.
And thus with tales he hem ladde
With good examinacioun,
Til he knew the condicioun,
What men thei were bothe tuo ;
And sih wel ate laste tho,
That on of hem was coveitous,
And his fela was envious.
And thus, whan he hath knowlechinge,
Anon he feigneth departinge,
And seide he mot algate wende.
Bot herkne now what fell at ende :
For thanne he made hem understonde
That he was there of goddes sonde,
And seide hem, for the kindeschipe
That thei have don him felaschipe,
He wole hem do som grace ayein,
And bad that on of hem schal sein
What thing him is lievest to crave,
And he it schal of yifte have ;
And over that ek forth withal
He seith that other have schal
The double of that his felaw axeth ;
And thus to hem his grace he taxeth.
   The coveitous was wonder glad,
And to that other man he bad
And seith that he ferst axe scholde :
For he supposeth that he wolde
Make his axinge of worldes good ;
For thanne he knew wel how it stod,
That he himself be double weyhte
Schal after take, and thus be sleyhte,
Be cause that he wolde winne,
He bad his fela ferst beginne.
This Envious, thogh it be late,
Whan that he syh he mot algate

310 [THE TRAVELLERS AND
          THE ANGEL.]

bit, quod et socio suo
secum comitanti affir-
mat duplicandum. Su-
per quo cupidus im-
peditus auaricia, sper-
ans sibi diuicias car-
pere duplicatas, pri-
mo petere recusauit.
Quod cum inuidus an-
imaduerteret, naturam
sui vicii concernens,
ita vt socius suus vtro-
que lumine priuaretur,
320 seipsum monoculum
fieri constanter pri-
mus ab angelo postu-
labat. Et sic vnius
inuidia alterius auari-
ciam maculauit.

330

P. i. 171

340

310 mad S, F   made AJ, B   315 *margin* igitur (gⁱ) diuicias
carpere XER, B   sibi diuicias capere MH₁, W   igitur diuicias capere
CI.   346 What]at B   What Ad

[The Travellers and
the Angel.]

Make his axinge ferst, he thoghte,
If he worschipe or profit soghte,
It schal be doubled to his fiere:
That wolde he chese in no manere.   350
Bot thanne he scheweth what he was
Toward Envie, and in this cas
Unto this Angel thus he seide
And for his yifte this he preide,
To make him blind of his on yhe,
So that his fela nothing syhe.
This word was noght so sone spoke,
That his on yhe anon was loke,
And his felawh forthwith also
Was blind of bothe his yhen tuo.   360
Tho was that other glad ynowh,
That on wepte, and that other lowh,
He sette his on yhe at no cost,
Wherof that other two hath lost.

Of thilke ensample which fell tho,
Men tellen now fulofte so,
The world empeireth comunly: P. i. 172
And yit wot non the cause why;
For it acordeth noght to kinde
Min oghne harm to seche and finde   370
Of that I schal my brother grieve;
It myhte nevere wel achieve.

Confessor.   What seist thou, Sone, of this folie?
Amans.   Mi fader, bot I scholde lie,
Upon the point which ye have seid
Yit was myn herte nevere leid,
Bot in the wise as I you tolde.
Bot overmore, if that ye wolde
Oght elles to my schrifte seie
Touchende Envie, I wolde preie.   380
Confessor.   Mi Sone, that schal wel be do:
Now herkne and ley thin Ere to.

352 Ennvie F   354 thus] þis A   and thus W   365-72 *Eight*
lines om. SAdBΔΛ   377 the wise] þis wise B   378 *euermore*
AJMG . . . B₂, Magd   forthermore W

iii. *Inuidie pars est detraccio pessima, pestem*
    Que magis infamem flatibus oris agit.
  Lingua venenato sermone repercutit auras,
    Sic ut in alterius scandala fama volat.
  Morsibus a tergo quos inficit ipsa fideles,
    Vulneris ignoti sepe salute carent.
  Set generosus amor linguam conseruat, vt eius
    Verbum quod loquitur nulla sinistra gerat.

[iii. DETRACTION.]

Touchende as of Envious brod
I wot noght on of alle good;
Bot natheles, suche as thei be,
Yit is ther on, and that is he
Which cleped is Detraccioun.
And to conferme his accioun,
He hath withholde Malebouche,
Whos tunge neither pyl ne crouche
Mai hyre, so that he pronounce   **P. i. 173**
A plein good word withoute frounce
Awher behinde a mannes bak.
For thogh he preise, he fint som lak,
Which of his tale is ay the laste,
That al the pris schal overcaste:
And thogh ther be no cause why,
Yit wole he jangle noght forthi,
As he which hath the heraldie
Of hem that usen forto lye.   400
For as the Netle which up renneth
The freisshe rede Roses brenneth
And makth hem fade and pale of hewe,
Riht so this fals Envious hewe,
In every place wher he duelleth,
With false wordes whiche he telleth
He torneth preisinge into blame
And worschipe into worldes schame.
Of such lesinge as he compasseth,
Is non so good that he ne passeth   410
Betwen his teeth and is bacbited,
And thurgh his false tunge endited:

Hic tractat Confessor de tercia specie Inuidie, que Detraccio dicitur, cuius morsus vipereos lesa quamsepe fama de-390 plangit.

Latin Verses iii. 2 infamen F
  401 the *om.* AM   409 suche F

[DETRACTION.]

Lich to the Scharnebudes kinde,
Of whos nature this I finde,
That in the hoteste of the dai,
Whan comen is the merie Maii,
He sprat his wynge and up he fleth:
And under al aboute he seth
The faire lusti floures springe,
Bot therof hath he no likinge;　　　　　420
Bot where he seth of eny beste　　　**P. i. 174**
The felthe, ther he makth his feste,
And therupon he wole alyhte,
Ther liketh him non other sihte.
Riht so this janglere Envious,
Thogh he a man se vertuous
And full of good condicioun,
Therof makth he no mencioun:
Bot elles, be it noght so lyte,
Wherof that he mai sette a wyte,　　　　430
Ther renneth he with open mouth,
Behinde a man and makth it couth.
Bot al the vertu which he can,
That wole he hide of every man,
And openly the vice telle,
As he which of the Scole of helle
Is tawht, and fostred with Envie
Of houshold and of compaignie,
Wher that he hath his propre office
To sette on every man a vice.　　　　440
How so his mouth be comely,
His word sit evermore awry
And seith the worste that he may.

[DETRACTION OF LOVERS.]

　　And in this wise now a day
In loves Court a man mai hiere
Fulofte pleigne of this matiere,
That many envious tale is stered,
Wher that it mai noght ben ansuered;
Bot yit fulofte it is believed,
And many a worthi love is grieved　　　450
Thurgh bacbitinge of fals Envie.　　　**P. i. 175**
　　If thou have mad such janglerie

In loves Court, mi Sone, er this,
Schrif thee therof.
          Mi fader, yis :
Bot wite ye how ? noght openly,
Bot otherwhile prively,
Whan I my diere ladi mete,
And thenke how that I am noght mete
Unto hire hihe worthinesse,
And ek I se the besinesse   460
Of al this yonge lusty route,
Whiche alday pressen hire aboute,
And ech of hem his time awaiteth,
And ech of hem his tale affaiteth,
Al to deceive an innocent,
Which woll noght ben of here assent ;
And for men sein unknowe unkest,
Hire thombe sche holt in hire fest
So clos withinne hire oghne hond,
That there winneth noman lond ;   470
Sche lieveth noght al that sche hiereth,
And thus fulofte hirself sche skiereth
And is al war of 'hadde I wist' :—
Bot for al that myn herte arist,
Whanne I thes comun lovers se,
That woll noght holden hem to thre,
Bot welnyh loven overal,
Min herte is Envious withal,
And evere I am adrad of guile,
In aunter if with eny wyle   480
Thei mihte hire innocence enchaunte. **P. i. 176**
Forthi my wordes ofte I haunte
Behynden hem, so as I dar,
Wherof my ladi may be war :
I sai what evere comth to mowthe,
And worse I wolde, if that I cowthe ;
For whanne I come unto hir speche,
Al that I may enquere and seche

[DETRACTION OF
LOVERS.]

Hic in amoris causa
huius vicii crimen ad
memoriam reducens
Confessor Amanti su-
per eodem plenius op-
ponit.

467 vnknowen vnkost R   vnknowen gest AM   473 hadde
I wist] hadde (had) wist XRC   haddy wist(e) H₁ELB₂   haddiwist
M, H₃   haddy I wist Ad

Of such deceipte, I telle it al,
And ay the werste in special.　　　　　　490
So fayn I wolde that sche wiste
How litel thei ben forto triste,
And what thei wolde and what thei mente,
So as thei be of double entente :
Thus toward hem that wicke mene
My wicked word was evere grene.
And natheles, the soth to telle,
In certain if it so befelle
That althertrewest man ybore,
To chese among a thousend score,　　　　　500
Which were alfulli forto triste,
Mi ladi lovede, and I it wiste,
Yit rathere thanne he scholde spede,
I wolde swiche tales sprede
To my ladi, if that I myhte,
That I scholde al his love unrihte,
And therto wolde I do mi peine.
For certes thogh I scholde feigne,
And telle that was nevere thoght,
For al this world I myhte noght　　　　　510
To soffre an othre fully winne,　　　　　**P. i. 177**
Ther as I am yit to beginne.
For be thei goode, or be thei badde,
I wolde non my ladi hadde ;
And that me makth fulofte aspie
And usen wordes of Envie,
Al forto make hem bere a blame.
And that is bot of thilke same,
The whiche unto my ladi drawe,
For evere on hem I rounge and gknawe　　　520
And hindre hem al that evere I mai ;
And that is, sothly forto say,
Bot only to my lady selve :
I telle it noght to ten ne tuelve,
Therof I wol me wel avise,
To speke or jangle in eny wise
That toucheth to my ladi name,

517 Al] And H₁ . . . B₂, H₃

The which in ernest and in game
I wolde save into my deth;
For me were levere lacke breth   530
Than speken of hire name amis.
Now have ye herd touchende of this,
Mi fader, in confessioun:
And therfor of Detraccioun
In love, of that I have mispoke,
Tel how ye wole it schal be wroke.
I am al redy forto bere
Mi peine, and also to forbere
What thing that ye wol noght allowe;
For who is bounden, he mot bowe.   540
So wol I bowe unto youre heste,   P. i. 178
For I dar make this beheste,
That I to yow have nothing hid,
Bot told riht as it is betid;
And otherwise of no mispeche,
Mi conscience forto seche,
I can noght of Envie finde,
That I mispoke have oght behinde
Wherof love owhte be mispaid.
Now have ye herd and I have said;   550
What wol ye, fader, that I do?

   Mi Sone, do nomore so,
Bot evere kep thi tunge stille,
Thou miht the more have of thi wille.
For as thou saist thiselven here,
Thi ladi is of such manere,
So wys, so war in alle thinge,
It nedeth of no bakbitinge
That thou thi ladi mis enforme:
For whan sche knoweth al the forme,   560
How that thiself art envious,
Thou schalt noght be so gracious
As thou peraunter scholdest elles.
Ther wol noman drinke of tho welles
Whiche as he wot is puyson inne;
And ofte swich as men beginne

       554 of om. J ... B₂, B, W

* *

[Detraction of
Lovers.]

Towardes othre, swich thei finde,
That set hem ofte fer behinde,
Whan that thei wene be before.
Mi goode Sone, and thou therfore 570
Bewar and lef thi wicke speche, **P. i. 179**
Wherof hath fallen ofte wreche
To many a man befor this time.
For who so wole his handes lime,
Thei mosten be the more unclene;
For many a mote schal be sene,
That wolde noght cleve elles there;
And that schold every wys man fere:
For who so wol an other blame,
He secheth ofte his oghne schame, 580
Which elles myhte be riht stille.
Forthi if that it be thi wille
To stonde upon amendement,
A tale of gret entendement
I thenke telle for thi sake,
Wherof thou miht ensample take.

[Tale of Constance.]

Hic loquitur Con-
fessor contra istos in
amoris causa detra-
hentes, qui suis oblo-
quiis aliena solacia
perturbant. Et narrat
exemplum de Constan-
cia Tiberii Rome Im-
paratoris filia, omnium
virtutum famosissima,
ob cuius amorem Sol-
danus tunc Persie, vt
eam in vxorem ducere
posset, Cristianum se
fieri promisit; cuius
accepta caucione con-
silio Pelagii tunc pape
dicta filia vna cum
duobus Cardinalibus
aliisque Rome proceri-
bus in Persiam mari-
tagii causa nauigio

A worthi kniht in Cristes lawe
Of grete Rome, as is the sawe,
The Sceptre hadde forto rihte;
Tiberie Constantin he hihte, 590
Whos wif was cleped Ytalie:
Bot thei togedre of progenie
No children hadde bot a Maide;
And sche the god so wel apaide,
That al the wide worldes fame
Spak worschipe of hire goode name.
Constance, as the Cronique seith,
Sche hihte, and was so ful of feith,
That the greteste of Barbarie,
Of hem whiche usen marchandie, 600
Sche hath converted, as thei come **P. i. 180**
To hire upon a time in Rome,
To schewen such thing· as thei broghte;
Whiche worthili of hem sche boghte,

And over that in such a wise
Sche hath hem with hire wordes wise
Of Cristes feith so full enformed,
That thei therto ben all conformed,
So-that baptesme thei receiven
And alle here false goddes weyven.
Whan thei ben of the feith certein,
Thei gon to Barbarie ayein,
And ther the Souldan for hem sente
And axeth hem to what entente
Thei have here ferste feith forsake.
And thei, whiche hadden undertake
The rihte feith to kepe and holde,
The matiere of here tale tolde
With al the hole circumstance.
And whan the Souldan of Constance   620
Upon the point that thei ansuerde
The beaute and the grace herde,
As he which thanne was to wedde,
In alle haste his cause spedde
To sende for the mariage.
And furthermor with good corage
He seith, be so he mai hire have,
That Crist, which cam this world to save,
He woll believe : and this recorded,
Thei ben on either side acorded,   630
And therupon to make an ende   **P. i. 181**
The Souldan hise hostages sende
To Rome, of Princes Sones tuelve :
Wherof the fader in himselve
Was glad, and with the Pope avised
Tuo Cardinals he hath assissed
With othre lordes many mo,
That with his doghter scholden go,
To se the Souldan be converted.
    Bot that which nevere was wel herted,
Envie, tho began travaile   640
In destourbance of this spousaile
So prively that non was war.

606 *margin* fuit] fiunt XERCL, B   fu*er*it B2

L 2

[TALE OF CONSTANCE.]
honorifice destinata
fuit : que tamen oblo-
quencium postea de-
traccionibus variis mo-
dis, prout inferius ar-
ticulatur, absque sui
610 culpa dolorosa fata
multipliciter passa est.

Qualiter adueniente
Constancia in Barba-
riam Mater Soldani,
huiusmodi   nupcias

[Tale of Constance.]

perturbare volens, fi-
lium suum vna cum
dicta Constancia Car-
dinalibusque et aliis
Romanis primo die ad
conuiuium inuitauit :
et conuescentibus illis
in mensa ipsum Sol-
danum omnesque ibi-
dem preter Constan-
ciam Romanos ab in-
sidiis latitantibus sub-
dola detraccione inter-
fici procurauit. Ipsam-
que Constanciam in
quadam naui absque
gubernaculo positam
per altum mare vento-
rum flatibus agitan-
dam in exilium dirigi
solam constituit.

The Moder which this Souldan bar
Was thanne alyve, and thoghte this
Unto hirself : ' If it so is
Mi Sone him wedde in this manere,
Than have I lost my joies hiere,
For myn astat schal so be lassed.'
Thenkende thus sche hath compassed   650
Be sleihte how that sche may beguile
Hire Sone ; and fell withinne a while,
Betwen hem two whan that thei were,
Sche feigneth wordes in his Ere,
And in this wise gan to seie :
' Mi Sone, I am be double weie
With al myn herte glad and blithe,
For that miself have ofte sithe
Desired thou wolt, as men seith,
Receive and take a newe feith,   660
Which schal be forthringe of thi lif :   **P. i. 182**
And ek so worschipful a wif,
The doughter of an Emperour,
To wedde it schal be gret honour.
Forthi, mi Sone, I you beseche
That I such grace mihte areche,
Whan that my doughter come schal,
That I mai thanne in special,
So as me thenkth it is honeste,
Be thilke which the ferste feste   670
Schal make unto hire welcominge.'
The Souldan granteth hire axinge,
And sche therof was glad ynowh :
For under that anon she drowh
With false wordes that sche spak
Covine of deth behinde his bak.
And therupon hire ordinance
She made so, that whan Constance
Was come forth with the Romeins,
Of clerkes and of Citezeins,   680

649 be so AM   sone be X   658 *margin* in exilium] et in
exilium X, B   et exilium H₁ERLB₂   671 welcominge] comyng(e)
H₁ . . . B₂, B

A riche feste sche hem made:
And most whan that thei weren glade,
With fals covine which sche hadde
Hire clos Envie tho sche spradde,
And alle tho that hadden be
Or in apert or in prive
Of conseil to the mariage,
Sche slowh hem in a sodein rage
Endlong the bord as thei be set,
So that it myhte noght be let;   690
Hire oghne Sone was noght quit,   **P. i. 183**
Bot deide upon the same plit.
Bot what the hihe god wol spare
It mai for no peril misfare:
This worthi Maiden which was there
Stod thanne, as who seith, ded for feere,
To se the feste how that it stod,
Which al was torned into blod:
The Dissh forthwith the Coppe and al
Bebled thei weren overal;   700
Sche sih hem deie on every side;
No wonder thogh sche wepte and cride
Makende many a wofull mone.
Whan al was slain bot sche al one,
This olde fend, this Sarazine,
Let take anon this Constantine
With al the good sche thider broghte,
And hath ordeined, as sche thoghte,
A nakid Schip withoute stiere,
In which the good and hire in fiere,   710
Vitailed full for yeres fyve,
Wher that the wynd it wolde dryve,
Sche putte upon the wawes wilde.
    Bot he which alle thing mai schilde,
Thre yer, til that sche cam to londe,
Hire Schip to stiere hath take in honde,
And in Northumberlond aryveth;
And happeth thanne that sche dryveth
Under a Castel with the flod,

Qualiter nauis cum
Constancia in partes
Anglie, que tunc pa-
gana fuit, prope Hum-
ber sub quodam cas-
tello Regis, qui tunc
Allee vocabatur, post

710 hiere F   716 *margin* ad partes H₁ . . . RLB₂, B

[TALE OF CONSTANCE.]
triennium applicuit,
quam quidam miles
nomine Elda, dicti
castelli tunc custos, e
naui lete suscipiens
vxori sue Hermyng-
helde in custodiam ho-
norifice commendauit.

Which upon Humber banke stod   720
And was the kynges oghne also,   P. i. 184
The which Allee was cleped tho,
A Saxon and a worthi knyht,
Bot he believeth noght ariht.
Of this Castell was Chastellein
Elda the kinges Chamberlein,
A knyhtly man after his lawe;
And whan he sih upon the wawe
The Schip drivende al one so,
He bad anon men scholden go   730
To se what it betokne mai.
This was upon a Somer dai,
The Schip was loked and sche founde;
Elda withinne a litel stounde
It wiste, and with his wif anon
Toward this yonge ladi gon,
Wher that thei founden gret richesse;
Bot sche hire wolde noght confesse,
Whan thei hire axen what sche was.
And natheles upon the cas   740
Out of the Schip with gret worschipe
Thei toke hire into felaschipe,
As thei that weren of hir glade:
Bot sche no maner joie made,
Bot sorweth sore of that sche fond
No cristendom in thilke lond;
Bot elles sche hath al hire wille,
And thus with hem sche duelleth stille.
    Dame Hermyngheld, which was the wif
Of Elda, lich hire oghne lif   750

Qualiter Constancia
Eldam cum vxore sua
Hermynghelda, qui
antea Cristiani non ex-
titerant, ad fidem Cristi
miraculose conuertit.

Constance loveth; and fell so,   P. i. 185
Spekende alday betwen hem two,
Thurgh grace of goddes pourveance
This maiden tawhte the creance
Unto this wif so parfitly,
Upon a dai that faste by
In presence of hire housebonde,
Wher thei go walkende on the Stronde,

751 and] and it H₁ ... B₂, B   *margin* Elda H₁G ... B₂, B

A blind man, which cam there lad,
Unto this wif criende he bad,   760
With bothe hise hondes up and preide
To hire, and in this wise he seide:
'O Hermyngeld, which Cristes feith,
Enformed as Constance seith,
Received hast, yif me my sihte.'
  Upon his word hire herte afflihte
Thenkende what was best to done,
Bot natheles sche herde his bone
And seide, 'In trust of Cristes lawe,
Which don was on the crois and slawe,   770
Thou bysne man, behold and se.'
With that to god upon his kne
Thonkende he tok his sihte anon,
Wherof thei merveile everychon,
Bot Elda wondreth most of alle:
This open thing which is befalle
Concludeth him be such a weie,
That he the feith mot nede obeie.
  Now lest what fell upon this thing.
This Elda forth unto the king   780
A morwe tok his weie and rod,   **P. i. 186**
And Hermyngeld at home abod
Forth with Constance wel at ese.
Elda, which thoghte his king to plese,
As he that thanne unwedded was,
Of Constance al the pleine cas
Als goodliche as he cowthe tolde.
The king was glad and seide he wolde
Come thider upon such a wise
That he him mihte of hire avise,   790
The time apointed forth withal.
This Elda triste in special
Upon a knyht, whom fro childhode
He hadde updrawe into manhode:
To him he tolde al that he thoghte,
Wherof that after him forthoghte;
And natheles at thilke tide

Qualiter quidam mi-
les iuuenis in amorem
Constancie exardes-
cens, pro eo quod ipsa
assentire noluit, eam
de morte Hermyng-
helde, quam ipsemet
noctanter interfecit,
verbis detractoriis ac-
cusauit. Set Angelus
domini ipsum sic de-
trahentem in maxilla
subito percuciens non
solum pro mendace
comprobauit, set ictu
mortali post ipsius
confessionem penitus
interfecit.

782 *margin* ipsa sibi A . . . B₂, BΔ

Unto his wif he bad him ride
To make redi alle thing
Ayein the cominge of the king,   800
And seith that he himself tofore
Thenkth forto come, and bad therfore
That he him kepe, and told him whanne.
This knyht rod forth his weie thanne;
And soth was that of time passed
He hadde in al his wit compassed
How he Constance myhte winne;
Bot he sih tho no sped therinne,
Wherof his lust began tabate,
And that was love is thanne hate;   810
Of hire honour he hadde Envie,   **P. i. 187**
So that upon his tricherie
A lesinge in his herte he caste.
Til he cam home he hieth faste,
And doth his ladi tunderstonde
The Message of hire housebonde:
And therupon the longe dai
Thei setten thinges in arrai,
That al was as it scholde be
Of every thing in his degree;   820
And whan it cam into the nyht,
This wif hire hath to bedde dyht,
Wher that this Maiden with hire lay.
This false knyht upon delay
Hath taried til thei were aslepe,
As he that wolde his time kepe
His dedly werkes to fulfille;
And to the bed he stalketh stille,
Wher that he wiste was the wif,
And in his hond a rasour knif   830
He bar, with which hire throte he cutte,
And prively the knif he putte
Under that other beddes side,

Wher that Constance lai beside.
Elda cam hom the same nyht,
And stille with a prive lyht,
As he that wolde noght awake
His wif, he hath his weie take
Into the chambre, and ther liggende
He fond his dede wif bledende,   840
Wher that Constance faste by   **P. i. 188**
Was falle aslepe; and sodeinly
He cride alowd, and sche awok,
And forth withal sche caste a lok
And sih this ladi blede there,
Wherof swounende ded for fere
Sche was, and stille as eny Ston
She lay, and Elda therupon
Into the Castell clepeth oute,
And up sterte every man aboute,   850
Into the chambre and forth thei wente.
Bot he, which alle untrouthe mente,
This false knyht, among hem alle
Upon this thing which is befalle
Seith that Constance hath don this dede;
And to the bed with that he yede
After the falshed of his speche,
And made him there forto seche,
And fond the knif, wher he it leide,
And thanne he cride and thanne he seide,   860
'Lo, seth the knif al blody hiere!
What nedeth more in this matiere
To axe?' And thus hire innocence
He sclaundreth there in audience
With false wordes whiche he feigneth.
Bot yit for al that evere he pleigneth,
Elda no full credence tok:
And happeth that ther lay a bok,
Upon the which, whan he it sih,
This knyht hath swore and seid on hih,   870
That alle men it mihte wite,   **P. i. 189**

'Now be this bok, which hier is write,
Constance is gultif, wel I wot.'
With that the hond of hevene him smot
In tokne of that he was forswore,
That he hath bothe hise yhen lore,
Out of his hed the same stounde
Thei sterte, and so thei weren founde.
A vois was herd, whan that they felle,
Which seide, 'O dampned man to helle,   880
Lo, thus hath god the sclaundre wroke
That thou ayein Constance hast spoke:
Beknow the sothe er that thou dye.'
And he told out his felonie,
And starf forth with his tale anon.
Into the ground, wher alle gon,
This dede lady was begrave:
Elda, which thoghte his honour save,
Al that he mai restreigneth sorwe.
        For the seconde day a morwe   890
The king cam, as thei were acorded;
And whan it was to him recorded
What god hath wroght upon this chaunce,
He tok it into remembrance
And thoghte more than he seide.
For al his hole herte he leide
Upon Constance, and seide he scholde
For love of hire, if that sche wolde,
Baptesme take and Cristes feith
Believe, and over that he seith   900
He wol hire wedde, and upon this   **P. i. 190**
Asseured ech til other is.
And forto make schorte tales,
Ther cam a Bisschop out of Wales
Fro Bangor, and Lucie he hihte,
Which thurgh the grace of god almihte
The king with many an other mo
Hath cristned, and betwen hem tuo
He hath fulfild the mariage.
Bot for no lust ne for no rage   910

Qualiter Rex Allee
ad fidem Cristi conuer-
sus baptismum recepit
et Constanciam super
hoc leto animo despon-
sauit; que tamen qua-
lis vel vnde fuit alicui
nullo modo fatebatur.
Et cum infra breue pos-
tea a domino suo im-
pregnata fuisset, ipse
ad debellandum cum
Scotis iter arripuit, et
ibidem super guerras
aliquamdiu permansit.

882 hast] has C, Δ   haþ RLB2, AdB, **W**   884 told J, SB, F   tolde AC

Sche tolde hem nevere what sche was ;   [TALE OF CONSTANCE.]
And natheles upon the cas
The king was glad, how so it stod,
For wel he wiste and understod
Sche was a noble creature.
The hihe makere of nature
Hire hath visited in a throwe,
That it was openliche knowe
Sche was with childe be the king,
Wherof above al other thing   920
He thonketh god and was riht glad.
And fell that time he was bestad
Upon a werre and moste ride ;
And whil he scholde there abide,
He lefte at hom to kepe his wif
Suche as he knew of holi lif,
Elda forth with the Bisschop eke ;
And he with pouer goth to seke
Ayein the Scottes forto fonde
The werre which he tok on honde.   930
    The time set of kinde is come,   **P. i. 191**
This lady hath hire chambre nome,
And of a Sone bore full,   Qualiter Regina Con-
Wherof that sche was joiefull,   stancia infantem mas-
Sche was delivered sauf and sone.   culum, quem in bap-
The bisshop, as it was to done,   tismo Mauricium vo-
Yaf him baptesme and Moris calleth ;   cant, Rege absente
And therupon, as it befalleth,   enixa est. Set inuida
With lettres writen of record   Regis mater Domilda
Thei sende unto here liege lord,   super isto facto condo-
That kepers weren of the qweene :   lens litteris mendaci-
And he that scholde go betwene,   bus Regi certificauit
The Messager, to Knaresburgh,   quod vxor sua demo-
Which toun he scholde passe thurgh, niaci et non humani
Ridende cam the ferste day.   940 generisquoddam mon-
The kinges Moder there lay,   strosum fantasma loco
Whos rihte name was Domilde,   geniture ad ortum pro-
                                                            duxit ; huiusmodique
                                                            detraccionibus aduer-
                                                            sus Constanciam in
                                                            tanto procurauit, quod
                                                            ipsa in nauim, qua
                                                            prius venerat, iterum
                                                            ad exilium vna cum
                                                            suo partu remissa de-
                                                            solabatur.

912 the] þis H₁ ... B₂, B, H₃   925 He] And H₁YXGECLB₂, B
938 *margin* quod] quia H₁ ... B₂, B   939 *margin* non *om.* B
947 *margin* desolabitur YRCL, B, W

[TALE OF CONSTANCE.]

Which after al the cause spilde :
For he, which thonk deserve wolde,
Unto this ladi goth and tolde   950
Of his Message al how it ferde.
And sche with feigned joie it herde
And yaf him yiftes largely,
Bot in the nyht al prively
Sche tok the lettres whiche he hadde,
Fro point to point and overradde,
As sche that was thurghout untrewe,
And let do wryten othre newe
In stede of hem, and thus thei spieke :

'Oure liege lord, we thee beseke   960
That thou with ous ne be noght wroth,   P. i. 192
Though we such thing as is thee loth
Upon oure trowthe certefie.

Prima littera in commendacionem Constancie ab Episcopo Regi missa per Domildam in contrarium falsata.

Thi wif, which is of faierie,
Of such a child delivered is
Fro kinde which stant al amis :
Bot for it scholde noght be seie,
We have it kept out of the weie
For drede of pure worldes schame,
A povere child and in the name   970
Of thilke which is so misbore
We toke, and therto we be swore,
That non bot only thou and we
Schal knowen of this privete :
Moris it hatte, and thus men wene
That it was boren of the qweene
And of thin oghne bodi gete.
Bot this thing mai noght be foryete,
That thou ne sende ous word anon
What is thi wille therupon.'   980

This lettre, as thou hast herd devise,
Was contrefet in such a wise
That noman scholde it aperceive :
And sche, which thoghte to deceive,
It leith wher sche that other tok.

949 þong F   951 his] þis AB₂   957 As] And C, H₃
961 ne om. J . . . B₂, B, W   962 as] þat ERCB₂

This Messager, whan he awok,
And wiste nothing how it was,
Aros and rod the grete pas
And tok this lettre to the king.
And whan he sih this wonder thing,   990
He makth the Messager no chiere,   P. i. **193**
Bot natheles in wys manere
He wrot ayein, and yaf hem charge
That thei ne soffre noght at large
His wif to go, bot kepe hire stille,
Til thei have herd mor of his wille.
This Messager was yifteles,
Bot with this lettre natheles,
Or be him lief or be him loth,
In alle haste ayein he goth   1000
Be Knaresburgh, and as he wente,
Unto the Moder his entente
Of that he fond toward the king
He tolde ; and sche upon this thing
Seith that he scholde abide al nyht
And made him feste and chiere ariht,
Feignende as thogh sche cowthe him thonk.
Bot he with strong wyn which he dronk
Forth with the travail of the day
Was drunke, aslepe and while he lay,   1010
Sche hath hise lettres overseie
And formed in an other weie.

Ther was a newe lettre write,
Which seith : 'I do you forto wite,   *Secunda littera per*
That thurgh the conseil of you tuo   *Regem Episcopo re-*
I stonde in point to ben undo,   *missa a Domilda ite-*
As he which is a king deposed.   *rum falsata.*
For every man it hath supposed,
How that my wif Constance is faie ;
And if that I, thei sein, delaie   1020
To put hire out of compaignie,   P. i. **194**
The worschipe of my Regalie

993 him H₁ . . . CB₂, B   1009 ffor wiþ RLB₂   1020 I, thei
sein, delaie] I seie (se) eny delaie H₁ . . . B₂, B   thei seine d.
(*om.* I) H₃   1021 put AJ, S, F   putte C, B

Is lore ; and over this thei telle,
Hire child schal noght among hem duelle,
To cleymen eny heritage.
So can I se non avantage,
Bot al is lost, if sche abide :
Forthi to loke on every side
Toward the meschief as it is,
I charge you and bidde this,   1030
That ye the same Schip vitaile,
In which that sche tok arivaile,
Therinne and putteth bothe tuo,
Hireself forthwith hire child also,
And so forth broght unto the depe
Betaketh hire the See to kepe.
Of foure daies time I sette,
That ye this thing no longer lette,
So that your lif be noght forsfet.'
And thus this lettre contrefet   1040
The Messager, which was unwar,
Upon the kingeshalve bar,
And where he scholde it hath betake.
Bot whan that thei have hiede take,
And rad that writen is withinne,
So gret a sorwe thei beginne,
As thei here oghne Moder sihen
Brent in a fyr before here yhen :
Ther was wepinge and ther was wo,
Bot finaly the thing is do.   1050
 Upon the See thei have hire broght, **P. i. 195**
Bot sche the cause wiste noght,
And thus upon the flod thei wone,
This ladi with hire yonge Sone :
And thanne hire handes to the hevene
Sche strawhte, and with a milde stevene
Knelende upon hire bare kne
Sche seide, ' O hihe mageste,
Which sest the point of every trowthe,
Tak of thi wofull womman rowthe   1060

1045 that writen is] þe writen is AM þat writen was B₂, B, W
þat wryten (*om.* is) X 1048 tofore B, W

And of this child that I schal kepe.'
And with that word sche gan to wepe,
Swounende as ded, and ther sche lay;
Bot he which alle thinges may
Conforteth hire, and ate laste
Sche loketh and hire yhen caste
Upon hire child and seide this :
'Of me no maner charge it is
What sorwe I soffre, bot of thee
Me thenkth it is a gret pite,   1070
For if I sterve thou schalt deie :
So mot I nedes be that weie
For Moderhed and for tendresse
With al myn hole besinesse
Ordeigne me for thilke office,
As sche which schal be thi Norrice.'
Thus was sche strengthed forto stonde ;
And tho sche tok hire child in honde
And yaf it sowke, and evere among
Sche wepte, and otherwhile song   1080
To rocke with hire child aslepe :   **P. i. 196**
And thus hire oghne child to kepe
Sche hath under the goddes cure.

And so fell upon aventure,
Whan thilke yer hath mad his ende,
Hire Schip, so as it moste wende
Thurgh strengthe of wynd which god hath yive,
Estward was into Spaigne drive
Riht faste under a Castell wall,
Wher that an hethen Amirall   1090
Was lord, and he a Stieward hadde,
Oon Theloüs, which al was badde,
A fals knyht and a renegat.
He goth to loke in what astat
The Schip was come, and there he fond
Forth with a child upon hire hond
This lady, wher sche was al one.

Qualiter Nauis Constancie post biennium in partes Hispanie superioris inter Sarazenos iactabatur, a quorum manibus deus ipsam conseruans graciosissime liberauit.

1063 Sownend(e) A, B   1066 yhe A . . . B₂, SAdB   1070 þenkeþ
it is gret E, B, H₃   1071 schalt] most B   1085 ff. *margin*
Qualiter—liberauit *om.* AM(*p.m.*)

He tok good hiede of the persone,
And sih sche was a worthi wiht,
And thoghte he wolde upon the nyht   1100
Demene hire at his oghne wille,
And let hire be therinne stille,
That mo men sih sche noght that dai.
At goddes wille and thus sche lai,
Unknowe what hire schal betide ;
And fell so that be nyhtes tide
This knyht withoute felaschipe
Hath take a bot and cam to Schipe,
And thoghte of hire his lust to take,
And swor, if sche him daunger make,   1110
That certeinly sche scholde deie.   P. i. 197
Sche sih ther was non other weie,
And seide he scholde hire wel conforte,
That he ferst loke out ate porte,
That noman were nyh the stede,
Which myhte knowe what thei dede,
And thanne he mai do what he wolde.
He was riht glad that sche so tolde,
And to the porte anon he ferde :
Sche preide god, and he hire herde,   1120
And sodeinliche he was out throwe
And dreynt, and tho began to blowe
A wynd menable fro the lond,
And thus the myhti goddes hond
Hire hath conveied and defended.

And whan thre yer be full despended,
Hire Schip was drive upon a dai,
Wher that a gret Navye lay
Of Schipes, al the world at ones :
And as god wolde for the nones,   1130
Hire Schip goth in among hem alle,

Qualiter   nauicula
Constancie   quodam
die per altum mare
vagans inter copiosam
Nauium multitudinem
dilapsa est, quarum
Arcennus   Romano-

1101 at] as AM   1103 mo men sih sche] AM (sighe), SAdΔ
(saw), F   no men seih (sigh) sche G . . . B₂, B, H₃   no man s. she
H₁X, W   no men sie hire J   noght *om.* W   1120 preide]
preide to L   preieþ to C   praieth Δ   preith H₃   1123 menable
M, Δ, F   meuable GRCLB₂, B   *doubtful* AJH₁YXE, SAd, H₃
meveable W   1127 ff. *margin* Qualiter—educauit *om.* AM(*p.m.*)
1129 *margin* vagans] nauigans B

And stinte noght, er it be falle
And hath the vessell undergete,
Which Maister was of al the Flete,
Bot there it resteth and abod.
This grete Schip on Anker rod;
The Lord cam forth, and whan he sih
That other ligge abord so nyh,
He wondreth what it myhte be,
And bad men to gon in and se.   1140
This ladi tho was crope aside,   **P. i. 198**
As sche that wolde hireselven hide,
For sche ne wiste what thei were :
Thei soghte aboute and founde hir there
And broghten up hire child and hire;
And therupon this lord to spire
Began, fro whenne that sche cam,
And what sche was. Quod sche, 'I am
A womman wofully bestad.
I hadde a lord, and thus he bad,   1150
That I forth with my litel Sone
Upon the wawes scholden wone,
Bot why the cause was, I not :
Bot he which alle thinges wot
Yit hath, I thonke him, of his miht
Mi child and me so kept upriht,
That we be save bothe tuo.'
This lord hire axeth overmo
How sche believeth, and sche seith,
'I lieve and triste in Cristes feith,   1160
Which deide upon the Rode tree.'
'What is thi name?' tho quod he.
'Mi name is Couste,' sche him seide :
Bot forthermor for noght he preide
Of hire astat to knowe plein,
Sche wolde him nothing elles sein
Bot of hir name, which sche feigneth;
Alle othre thinges sche restreigneth,

[TALE OF CONSTANCE.]
rum Consul, Dux et
Capitaneus ipsam ig-
notam suscipiens vs-
que ad Romam secum
perduxit; vbi equalem
vxori sue Helene per-
mansuram reuerenter
associauit, necnon et
eiusdem filium Mauri-
cium in omni habun-
dancia quasi proprium
educauit.

1132 be falle J, S, F   befalle AC, B   1133 the] þat A ... B₂, SAdBΔ
1140 to go in] go in AM, Δ   to gon L   to go doun G   gone (to se) W
1151 forþ wiþ J, SB   forþwiþ A, F   1158 euermo H₁ ... CB₂, W
**   M

That a word more sche ne tolde.
This lord thanne axeth if sche wolde   1170
With him abide in compaignie,   **P. i. 199**
And seide he cam fro Barbarie
To Romeward, and hom he wente.
Tho sche supposeth what it mente,
And seith sche wolde with him wende
And duelle unto hire lyves ende,
Be so it be to his plesance.
And thus upon here aqueintance
He tolde hire pleinly as it stod,
Of Rome how that the gentil blod   1180
In Barbarie was betraied,
And therupon he hath assaied
Be werre, and taken such vengance,
That non of al thilke alliance,
Be whom the tresoun was compassed,
Is from the swerd alyve passed;
Bot of Constance hou it was,
That cowthe he knowe be no cas,
Wher sche becam, so as he seide.

Hire Ere unto his word sche leide,   1190
Bot forther made sche no chiere.
And natheles in this matiere
It happeth thilke time so:
This Lord, with whom sche scholde go,
Of Rome was the Senatour,
And of hir fader themperour
His brother doughter hath to wyve,
Which hath hir fader ek alyve,
And was Salustes cleped tho;
This wif Heleine hihte also,   1200
To whom Constance was Cousine.   **P. i. 200**
Thus to the sike a medicine
Hath god ordeined of his grace,
That forthwith in the same place

1169 o word H₁ECB₂, B   ne] no F   1178 hire (hir) JMX . . .
B₂, AdB   hys W   1184 al *om.* H₁Sn, H₃   1189 becam GEC, AdB,
W   be cam (bi cam &c.) A . . . XRLB₂, F   1191 forther] for þat H₁ . . .
B₂, B   1193 happed H₁ . . . RLB₂, B   1200 This] His H₁ . . . B₂, B, W

This Senatour his trowthe plihte,
For evere, whil he live mihte,
To kepe in worschipe and in welthe,
Be so that god wol yive hire helthe,
This ladi, which fortune him sende.
And thus be Schipe forth sailende   1210
Hire and hir child to Rome he broghte,
And to his wif tho he besoghte
To take hire into compaignie:
And sche, which cowthe of courtesie
Al that a good wif scholde konne,
Was inly glad that sche hath wonne
The felaschip of so good on.
Til tuelve yeres were agon,
This Emperoures dowhter Custe
Forth with the dowhter of Saluste   1220
Was kept, bot noman redily
Knew what sche was, and noght forthi
Thei thoghten wel sche hadde be
In hire astat of hih degre,
And every lif hire loveth wel.
Now herke how thilke unstable whel,
Which evere torneth, wente aboute.
The king Allee, whil he was oute,
As thou tofore hast herd this cas,
Deceived thurgh his Moder was: 1230
Bot whan that he cam hom ayein,
He axeth of his Chamberlein
And of the Bisschop ek also,
Wher thei the qweene hadden do.
And thei answerde, there he bad,
And have him thilke lettre rad,
Which he hem sende for warant,
And tolde him pleinli as it stant,
And sein, it thoghte hem gret pite
To se so worthi on as sche,   1240
With such a child as ther was bore,
So sodeinly to be forlore.

[TALE OF CONSTANCE.]

Qualiter Rex Allee inita pace cum Scotis a guerris rediens et non inuenta vxore sua causam exilii diligencius perscrutans, cum Matrem suam Domildam inde culpabilem sciuisset, ipsam in igne **P. i. 201** proiciens comburi fecit.

1217 felaschip J, S, F   felaschipe A   1226 herkne SAdΔ   herkene X, H₃   herken B₂, W   1237 he *om.* B

M 2

[TALE OF CONSTANCE.]

He axeth hem what child that were;
And thei him seiden, that naghere,
In al the world thogh men it soghte,
Was nevere womman that forth broghte
A fairer child than it was on.
And thanne he axede hem anon,
Whi thei ne hadden write so:
Thei tolden, so thei hadden do.　　　　　　1250
He seide, 'Nay.' Thei seiden, 'Yis.'
The lettre schewed rad it is,
Which thei forsoken everidel.
Tho was it understonde wel
That ther is tresoun in the thing:
The Messager tofore the king
Was broght and sodeinliche opposed;
And he, which nothing hath supposed
Bot alle wel, began to seie
That he nagher upon the weie　　　　　　1260
Abod, bot only in a stede;
And cause why that he so dede
Was, as he wente to and fro,　　　　　**P. i. 202**
At Knaresburgh be nyhtes tuo
The kinges Moder made him duelle.
And whan the king it herde telle,
Withinne his herte he wiste als faste
The treson which his Moder caste;
And thoghte he wolde noght abide,
Bot forth riht in the same tide　　　　　1270
He tok his hors and rod anon.
With him ther riden manion,
To Knaresburgh and forth thei wente,
And lich the fyr which tunder hente,
In such a rage, as seith the bok,
His Moder sodeinliche he tok
And seide unto hir in this wise:
'O beste of helle, in what juise
Hast thou deserved forto deie,

1245 it] him YX . . . B₂, B　*om.* H₁Sn　　　1258 And he which
noþing haþ supposed A J M, SAdΔ　As he wh. n. haþ supposed FWKH₃
And he noþing haþ ȝit supposed H₁ . . . B₂, B

That hast so falsly put aweie   1280 [TALE OF CONSTANCE.]
With tresoun of thi bacbitinge
The treweste at my knowlechinge
Of wyves and the most honeste?
Bot I wol make this beheste,
I schal be venged er I go.'
And let a fyr do make tho,
And bad men forto caste hire inne:
Bot ferst sche tolde out al the sinne,
And dede hem alle forto wite
How sche the lettres hadde write,   1290
Fro point to point as it was wroght.
And tho sche was to dethe broght
And brent tofore hire Sones yhe: **P. i. 203**
Wherof these othre, whiche it sihe
And herden how the cause stod,
Sein that the juggement is good,
Of that hir Sone hire hath so served;
For sche it hadde wel deserved
Thurgh tresoun of hire false tunge,
Which thurgh the lond was after sunge,   1300
Constance and every wiht compleigneth.
Bot he, whom alle wo distreigneth,
This sorghfull king, was so bestad,
That he schal nevermor be glad,
He seith, eftsone forto wedde,
Til that he wiste how that sche spedde,
Which hadde ben his ferste wif:
And thus his yonge unlusti lif
He dryveth forth so as he mai.

    Til it befell upon a dai,   1310
Whan he hise werres hadde achieved,   Qualiter post lap-
And thoghte he wolde be relieved   sum xii. annorum Rex
Of Soule hele upon the feith   Allee   absolucionis
Which he hath take, thanne he seith   causa Romam profi-
That he to Rome in pelrinage   ciscens vxorem suam
Wol go, wher Pope was Pelage,   Constanciam vna cum
To take his absolucioun.   filio suo diuina proui-
                                                 dencia ibidem letus
                                                 inuenit.

1285 I schal FWKH₃   It schal A . . . B₂, SAdB△   1303 so]
þo AM   wo Ad

And upon this condicioun
He made Edwyn his lieutenant,
Which heir to him was apparant,   1320
That he the lond in his absence
Schal reule : and thus be providence
Of alle thinges wel begon   **P. i. 204**
He tok his leve and forth is gon.
Elda, which tho was with him there,
Er thei fulliche at Rome were,
Was sent tofore to pourveie ;
And he his guide upon the weie,
In help to ben his herbergour,
Hath axed who was Senatour,   1330
That he his name myhte kenne.
Of Capadoce, he seide, Arcenne
He hihte, and was a worthi kniht.
To him goth Elda tho forth riht
And tolde him of his lord tidinge,
And preide that for his comynge
He wolde assigne him herbergage ;
And he so dede of good corage.
    Whan al is do that was to done,
The king himself cam after sone.   1340
This Senatour, whan that he com,
To Couste and to his wif at hom
Hath told how such a king Allee
Of gret array to the Citee
Was come, and Couste upon his tale
With herte clos and colour pale
Aswoune fell, and he merveileth
So sodeinly what thing hire eyleth,
And cawhte hire up, and whan sche wok,
Sche syketh with a pitous lok   1350
And feigneth seknesse of the See ;
Bot it was for the king Allee,
For joie which fell in hire thoght   **P. i. 205**
That god him hath to toune broght.

1328 his guide] is guide H₁XGECLB₂, B   1343 how] how þat AM
1353 fell] was E, B   is G   *om.* XRCLB₂   (that she hadde in here
thouht H₁)

[TALE OF CONSTANCE.]

This king hath spoke with the Pope
And told al that he cowthe agrope,
What grieveth in his conscience ;
And thanne he thoghte in reverence
Of his astat, er that he wente,
To make a feste, and thus he sente   1360
Unto the Senatour to come
Upon the morwe and othre some,
To sitte with him at the mete.
This tale hath Couste noght foryete,
Bot to Moris hire Sone tolde
That he upon the morwe scholde
In al that evere he cowthe and mihte
Be present in the kinges sihte,
So that the king him ofte sihe.
Moris tofore the kinges yhe   1370
Upon the morwe, wher he sat,
Fulofte stod, and upon that
The king his chiere upon him caste,
And in his face him thoghte als faste
He sih his oghne wif Constance ;
For nature as in resemblance
Of face hem liketh so to clothe,
That thei were of a suite bothe.
The king was moeved in his thoght
Of that he seth, and knoweth it noght ;   1380
This child he loveth kindely,
And yit he wot no cause why.
Bot wel he sih and understod   **P. i. 206**
That he toward Arcenne stod,
And axeth him anon riht there,
If that this child his Sone were.
He seide, 'Yee, so I him calle,
And wolde it were so befalle,
Bot it is al in other wise.'
And tho began he to devise   1390
How he the childes Moder fond
Upon the See from every lond

1356 agrope A, SAd, F   grope J ... B₂, BΔ, WH₃   1363 at
þe J, S, F   atte A, B   1378 a suite] o suite AM

[TALE OF CONSTANCE.]

Withinne a Schip was stiereles,
And how this ladi helpeles
Forth with hir child he hath forthdrawe.
The king hath understonde his sawe,
The childes name and axeth tho,
And what the Moder hihte also
That he him wolde telle he preide.
'Moris this child is hote,' he seide,   1400
'His Moder hatte Couste, and this
I not what maner name it is.'
But Allee wiste wel ynowh,
Wherof somdiel smylende he lowh ;
For Couste in Saxoun is to sein
Constance upon the word Romein.
Bot who that cowthe specefie
What tho fell in his fantasie,
And how his wit aboute renneth
Upon the love in which he brenneth,   1410
It were a wonder forto hiere :
For he was nouther ther ne hiere,
Bot clene out of himself aweie,   **P. i. 207**
That he not what to thenke or seie,
So fain he wolde it were sche.
Wherof his hertes privete
Began the werre of yee and nay,
The which in such balance lay,
That contenance for a throwe
He loste, til he mihte knowe   1420
The sothe : bot in his memoire
The man which lith in purgatoire
Desireth noght the hevene more,
That he ne longeth al so sore
To wite what him schal betide.
And whan the bordes were aside
And every man was rise aboute,
The king hath weyved al the route,
And with the Senatour al one
He spak and preide him of a bone,   1430
To se this Couste, wher sche duelleth

1412 nouther] nowher LSn   neuer H₃   (now þer now here X)

[TALE OF CONSTANCE.]

At hom with him, so as he telleth.
The Senatour was wel appaied,
This thing no lengere is delaied,
To se this Couste goth the king;
And sche was warned of the thing,
And with Heleine forth sche cam
Ayein the king, and he tho nam
Good hiede, and whan he sih his wif,
Anon with al his hertes lif   1440
He cawhte hire in his arm and kiste.
Was nevere wiht that sih ne wiste
A man that more joie made,   **P. i. 208**
Wherof thei weren alle glade
Whiche herde tellen of this chance.
    This king tho with his wif Constance,
Which hadde a gret part of his wille,
In Rome for a time stille
Abod and made him wel at ese:
Bot so yit cowthe he nevere plese   1450
His wif, that sche him wolde sein
Of hire astat the trowthe plein,
Of what contre that sche was bore,
Ne what sche was, and yit therfore
With al his wit he hath don sieke.
Thus as they lihe abedde and spieke,
Sche preide him and conseileth bothe,
That for the worschipe of hem bothe,
So as hire thoghte it were honeste,
He wolde an honourable feste   1460
Make, er he wente, in the Cite,
Wher themperour himself schal be:
He graunteth al that sche him preide.
Bot as men in that time seide,
This Emperour fro thilke day
That ferst his dowhter wente away
He was thanne after nevere glad;

1434 is] was G, B   1441 armes H₁XRCLB₂, AdΔ, W
kiste] keste F   1445 this] his AM   the W   1447 agret F
1457 preiþ him AM   preith (*om.* him) H₁   1458 worshipe F
1461 the] þat B

Bot what that eny man him bad
Of grace for his dowhter sake,
That grace wolde he noght forsake ;　　1470
And thus ful gret almesse he dede,
Wherof sche hadde many a bede.

　　This Emperour out of the toun　　**P. i. 209**
Withinne a ten mile enviroun,
Where as it thoghte him for the beste,
Hath sondry places forto reste ;
And as fortune wolde tho,
He was duellende at on of tho.
The king Allee forth with thassent
Of Couste his wif hath thider sent　　1480
Moris his Sone, as he was taght,
To themperour and he goth straght,
And in his fader half besoghte,
As he which his lordschipe soghte,
That of his hihe worthinesse
He wolde do so gret meknesse,
His oghne toun to come and se,
And yive a time in the cite,
So that his fader mihte him gete
That he wolde ones with him ete.　　1490
This lord hath granted his requeste ;
And whan the dai was of the feste,
In worschipe of here Emperour
The king and ek the Senatour
Forth with here wyves bothe tuo,
With many a lord and lady mo,
On horse riden him ayein ;
Til it befell, upon a plein
Thei sihen wher he was comende.
With that Constance anon preiende　　1500
Spak to hir lord that he abyde,
So that sche mai tofore ryde,
To ben upon his bienvenue　　**P. i. 210**

Qualiter Constancia, que antea per totum tempus exilii sui penes omnes incognitam se celauit, tunc demum patri suo Imperatori seipsam per omnia manifestauit : quod cum Rex Allee sciuisset, vna cum vniuersa Romanorum multitudine inestimabili gaudio admirantes cunctipotentem laudarunt.

1468 eny] euery H₁ ... L, B　　euer eny B₂　　1472 he H₁, B
1479 forþ wiþ AJ, SB　forþwiþ F　　1483 fader half J, B, F　faderhalt
A, S　　1484 Wiþ due reuerence as he oughte H₁ ... B₂　　1495 fforþ
wiþ J, SB　fforþwiþ A, F

The ferste which schal him salue ;
And thus after hire lordes graunt
Upon a Mule whyt amblaunt
Forth with a fewe rod this qweene.
Thei wondren what sche wolde mene,
And riden after softe pas ;
Bot whan this ladi come was   1510
To themperour, in his presence
Sche seide alowd in audience,
'Mi lord, mi fader, wel you be !
And of this time that I se
Youre honour and your goode hele,
Which is the helpe of my querele,
I thonke unto the goddes myht.'
For joie his herte was affliht
Of that sche tolde in remembrance ;
And whanne he wiste it was Constance,   1520
Was nevere fader half so blithe.
Wepende he keste hire ofte sithe,
So was his herte al overcome ;
For thogh his Moder were come
Fro deth to lyve out of the grave,
He mihte nomor wonder have
Than he hath whan that he hire sih.
With that hire oghne lord cam nyh
And is to themperour obeied ;
Bot whan the fortune is bewreied,   1530
How that Constance is come aboute,
So hard an herte was non oute,
That he for pite tho ne wepte.   **P. i. 211**

   Arcennus, which hire fond and kepte,
Was thanne glad of that is falle,
So that with joie among hem alle
Thei riden in at Rome gate.
This Emperour thoghte al to late,
Til that the Pope were come,
And of the lordes sende some   1540
To preie him that he wolde haste :
And he cam forth in alle haste,

     1539 the *om.* F

[TALE OF CONSTANCE.]

And whan that he the tale herde,
How wonderly this chance ferde,
He thonketh god of his miracle,
To whos miht mai be non obstacle :
The king a noble feste hem made,
And thus thei weren alle glade.
A parlement, er that thei wente,
Thei setten unto this entente,   1550
To puten Rome in full espeir
That Moris was apparant heir
And scholde abide with hem stille,
For such was al the londes wille.

     Whan every thing was fulli spoke,
Of sorwe and queint was al the smoke,
Tho tok his leve Allee the king,
And with full many a riche thing,
Which themperour him hadde yive,
He goth a glad lif forto live ;   1560
For he Constance hath in his hond,
Which was the confort of his lond.
For whan that he cam hom ayein,   **P. i. 212**
Ther is no tunge it mihte sein
What joie was that ilke stounde
Of that he hath his qweene founde,
Which ferst was sent of goddes sonde,
Whan sche was drive upon the Stronde,
Be whom the misbelieve of Sinne
Was left, and Cristes feith cam inne   1570
To hem that whilom were blinde.

     Bot he which hindreth every kinde
And for no gold mai be forboght,
The deth comende er he be soght,
Tok with this king such aqueintance,
That he with al his retenance
Ne mihte noght defende his lif ;
And thus he parteth from his wif,
Which thanne made sorwe ynowh.
And therupon hire herte drowh   1580

Qualiter Mauricius cum Imperatore vt heres Imperii remansit, et Rex Allee cum Constancia in Angliam regressi sunt.

Qualiter Rex Allee post biennium in Anglia humane carnis resolucionem subiens nature debitum persoluit, post cuius obitum Constancia cum patre suo Rome se transtulit moraturam.

To leven Engelond for evere
And go wher that sche hadde levere,
To Rome, whenne that sche cam :
And thus of al the lond sche nam
Hir leve, and goth to Rome ayein.
And after that the bokes sein,
She was noght there bot a throwe,
Whan deth of kinde hath overthrowe
Hir worthi fader, which men seide
That he betwen hire armes deide.
And afterward the yer suiende
The god hath mad of hire an ende,
And fro this worldes faierie
Hath take hire into compaignie.
Moris hir Sone was corouned,
Which so ferforth was abandouned
To Cristes feith, that men him calle
Moris the cristeneste of alle.
    And thus the wel meninge of love
Was ate laste set above ;
And so as thou hast herd tofore,
The false tunges weren lore,
Whiche upon love wolden lie.
Forthi touchende of this Envie
Which longeth unto bacbitinge,
Be war thou make no lesinge
In hindringe of an other wiht :
And if thou wolt be tawht ariht
What meschief bakbitinge doth
Be other weie, a tale soth
Now miht thou hiere next suiende,
Which to this vice is acordende.

    In a Cronique, as thou schalt wite,
A gret ensample I finde write,
Which I schal telle upon this thing.
Philippe of Macedoyne kyng

[TALE OF CONSTANCE.]

De morte Impera-
toris.
1590

De morte Constan-
cie.
P. i. 213

De   coronacione
Mauricii, qui adhuc
in Cronicis Mauricius
Imperator Cristianis-
simus nuncupatus est.

1600

1610

[DEMETRIUS AND
PERSEUS.]
Hic ponit Confessor
exemplum contra istos
detractores, qui in

1582 wher that] where (wher) H₁ . . . B₂, BΔ, W   1599 wel
meninge (meuinge) AMRLB₂, SAd, F welle menyng H₁X whele
meneng Δ   whel meuynge J   whele mevinge W   whiel (whele)
moeuyng YGEC, B, H₃

[DEMETRIUS AND
PERSEUS.]

alterius 'vituperium
mendacia confingen-
tes diffamacionem fieri
procurant. Et narrat
qualiter Perseus, Phi-
lippi Regis Macedonie
filius, Demetrio fratri
suo ob eius probitatem
inuidens, composito
detraccionis mendacio
ipsum apud patrem
suum mortaliter accu-
sauit, dicens quod ipse
non solum patrem set
et totum Macedonie
regnum Romanis hos-
tibus proditorie ven-
didisset : quem super
hoc in iudicium pro-
ducens, testibus que
iudicibus auro subor-
natis, quamuis falsis-
sime morte condemp-
natum euicit : quo de-
functo eciam et pater
infra breue postea
mortuus est. Et sic
Perseo successiue reg-
nante deus huiusmodi
detraccionis inuidiam
abhorrens ipsum cum
vniuersa suorum pug-
natorum multitudine
extra Danubii fluuium
ab Emilio tunc Roman-
orum Consule euentu
bellico interfici fortu-
nauit. Ita quod ab
illo die Macedonie
potestas penitus de-
structa Romano Im-
perio subiugata deser-
uiuit, et eius detraccio,
quam contra alium
conspirauerat, in sui
ipsius diffamacionem
pro perpetuo diuulga-
ta consistit.

Two Sones hadde be his wif,
Whos fame is yit in Grece rif :
Demetrius the ferste brother
Was hote, and Perseüs that other.   1620
Demetrius men seiden tho
The betre knyht was of the tuo,
To whom the lond was entendant,   **P. i. 214**
As he which heir was apparant
To regne after his fader dai :
Bot that thing which no water mai
Quenche in this world, bot evere brenneth,
Into his brother herte it renneth,
The proude Envie of that he sih
His brother scholde clymbe on hih,   1630
And he to him mot thanne obeie :
That may he soffre be no weie.
With strengthe dorst he nothing fonde,
So tok he lesinge upon honde,
Whan he sih time and spak therto.
For it befell that time so,
His fader grete werres hadde
With Rome, whiche he streite ladde
Thurgh mihty hond of his manhode,
As he which hath ynowh knihthode,   1640
And ofte hem hadde sore grieved.
Bot er the werre were achieved,
As he was upon ordinance
At hom in Grece, it fell per chance,
Demetrius, which ofte aboute
Ridende was, stod that time oute,
So that this Perse in his absence,
Which bar the tunge of pestilence,
With false wordes whiche he feigneth
Upon his oghne brother pleigneth   1650
In privete behinde his bak,
And to his fader thus he spak :
'Mi diere fader, I am holde   **P. i. 215**

1618 ȝit is in G. rif H₁XGRCLB₂   ȝit in G. is rif E, B, H₃
1623 attendant B   1631 þanne mot e) AM   þan mot W   1640 hath
ynowh] haþ Inowh of LB₂   inow had of Δ   knihthode J
knithode (knythode) A, F   1644 p chance A, B, F   perchaunce J

[DEMETRIUS AND
PERSEUS.]

Be weie of kinde, as resoun wolde,
That I fro yow schal nothing hide,
Which mihte torne in eny side
Of youre astat into grevance:
Forthi myn hertes obeissance
Towardes you I thenke kepe;
For it is good ye take kepe   1660
Upon a thing which is me told.
Mi brother hath ous alle sold
To hem of Rome, and you also;
For thanne they behote him so,
That he with hem schal regne in pes.
Thus hath he cast for his encress
That youre astat schal go to noght;
And this to proeve schal be broght
So forforth, that I undertake
It schal noght wel mow be forsake.'   1670
    The king upon this tale ansuerde
And seide, if this thing which he herde
Be soth and mai be broght to prove,
'It schal noght be to his behove,
Which so hath schapen ous the werste,
For he himself schal be the ferste
That schal be ded, if that I mai.'
    Thus afterward upon a dai,
Whan that Demetrius was come,
Anon his fader hath him nome,   1680
And bad unto his brother Perse
That he his tale schal reherse
Of thilke tresoun which he tolde.   P. i. 216
And he, which al untrowthe wolde,
Conseileth that so hih a nede
Be treted wher as it mai spede,
In comun place of juggement.
The king therto yaf his assent,
Demetrius was put in hold,
Wherof that Perseüs was bold.   1690

1669 Soferforþ F   1675 Which so haþ YGER, SAdΔΛ   Which
so as AJMH₁XCB₂, B, F   Whych so has W   Which so L   Which
tho as H₃   1678 adai F

Thus stod the trowthe under the charge,
And the falshede goth at large,
Which thurgh beheste hath overcome
The greteste of the lordes some,
That privelich of his acord
Thei stonde as witnesse of record:
The jugge was mad favorable:
Thus was the lawe deceivable
So ferforth that the trowthe fond
Rescousse non, and thus the lond   1700
Forth with the king deceived were.
  The gulteles was dampned there
And deide upon accusement:
Bot such a fals conspirement,
Thogh it be prive for a throwe,
Godd wolde noght it were unknowe;
And that was afterward wel proved
In him which hath the deth controved.
Of that his brother was so slain
This Perseüs was wonder fain,   1710
As he that tho was apparant,
Upon the Regne and expectant;
Wherof he wax so proud and vein,   **P. i. 217**
That he his fader in desdeign
Hath take and set of non acompte,
As he which thoghte him to surmonte;
That wher he was ferst debonaire,
He was tho rebell and contraire,
And noght as heir bot as a king
He tok upon him alle thing   1720
Of malice and of tirannie
In contempt of the Regalie,
Livende his fader, and so wroghte,
That whan the fader him bethoghte
And sih to whether side it drowh,
Anon he wiste well ynowh
How Perse after his false tunge

1706 it were noght AM   1707 that] þus H₁ . . . L, B   þis B₂
1711 that tho was] which þo was SAdΔ   þat was heir H₁YG . . .
B₂, B   which heyr was X

Hath so thenvious belle runge,
That he hath slain his oghne brother.
Wherof as thanne he knew non other,   1730
Bot sodeinly the jugge he nom,
Which corrupt sat upon the dom,
In such a·wise and hath him pressed,
That he the sothe him hath confessed
Of al that hath be spoke and do.

    Mor sori than the king was tho
Was nevere man upon this Molde,
And thoghte in certein that he wolde
Vengance take upon this wrong.
Bot thother parti was so strong,   1740
That for the lawe of no statut
Ther mai no riht ben execut;
And upon this division   **P. i. 218**
The lond was torned up so doun:
Wherof his herte is so distraght,
That he for pure sorwe hath caght
The maladie of which nature
Is queint in every creature.

    And whan this king was passed thus,
This false tunged Perseüs   1750
The regiment hath underfonge.
Bot ther mai nothing stonde longe
Which is noght upon trowthe grounded;
For god, which alle thing hath bounded
And sih the falshod of his guile,
Hath set him bot a litel while,
That he schal regne upon depos;
For sodeinliche as he aros
So sodeinliche doun he fell.

    In thilke time it so befell,   1760
This newe king of newe Pride
With strengthe schop him forto ride,
And seide he wolde Rome waste,
Wherof he made a besi haste,

1728 belles B   1743 diuision J, F   diuisioun A, B   1758 as he
aros] right as he ros (aros) H₁ . . . B₂, B   1763 wold(e) to Rome
faste H₁ . . . B₂, B

**   N

And hath assembled him an host
In al that evere he mihte most:
What man that mihte wepne bere
Of alle he wolde non forbere;
So that it mihte noght be nombred,
The folk which after was encombred   1770
Thurgh him, that god wolde overthrowe.
    Anon it was at Rome knowe,
The pompe which that Perse ladde;   P. i. 219
And the Romeins that time hadde
A Consul, which was cleped thus
Be name, Paul Emilius,
A noble, a worthi kniht withalle;
And he, which chief was of hem alle,
This werre on honde hath undertake.
And whanne he scholde his leve take   1780
Of a yong dowhter which was his,
Sche wepte, and he what cause it is
Hire axeth, and sche him ansuerde
That Perse is ded; and he it herde,
And wondreth what sche meene wolde:
And sche upon childhode him tolde
That Perse hir litel hound is ded.
With that he pulleth up his hed
And made riht a glad visage,
And seide how that was a presage   1790
Touchende unto that other Perse,
Of that fortune him scholde adverse,
He seith, for such a prenostik
Most of an hound was to him lik:
For as it is an houndes kinde
To berke upon a man behinde,
Riht so behinde his brother bak
With false wordes whiche he spak
He hath do slain, and that is rowthe.
'Bot he which hateth alle untrowthe,   1800
The hihe god, it schal redresse;
For so my dowhter prophetesse

1770 after were B   was efter H₃   afterward was Δ   1778 As he
FWH₃   1780 whanne om. AM   1788 is hed F

Forth with hir litel houndes deth   **P. i. 220**
Betokneth.' And thus forth he geth
Conforted of this evidence,
With the Romeins in his defence
Ayein the Greks that ben comende.
   This Perseüs, as noght seende
This meschief which that him abod,
With al his multitude rod,   1810
And prided him upon the thing,
Of that he was become a king,
And how he hadde his regne gete;
Bot he hath al the riht foryete
Which longeth unto governance.
Wherof thurgh goddes ordinance
It fell, upon the wynter tide
That with his host he scholde ride
Over Danubie thilke flod,
Which al befrose thanne stod   1820
So harde, that he wende wel
To passe: bot the blinde whiel,
Which torneth ofte er men be war,
Thilke ys which that the horsmen bar
Tobrak, so that a gret partie
Was dreint; of the chivalerie
The rerewarde it tok aweie,
Cam non of hem to londe dreie.
   Paulus the worthi kniht Romein
Be his aspie it herde sein,   1830
And hasteth him al that he may,
So that upon that other day
He cam wher he this host beheld,   **P. i. 221**
And that was in a large feld,
Wher the Baneres ben desplaied.
He hath anon hise men arraied,
And whan that he was embatailled,
He goth and hath the feld assailed,
And slowh and tok al that he fond;
Wherof the Macedoyne lond,   1840

1803 fforþ wiþ A, SB fforwiþ F   1804 goþ B   1808 sende A J
1809 This] The A ... B₂, S ... Δ   1811 the] þis X ... B₂, B, W
1829 the] þis H₁, B

N 2

Which thurgh king Alisandre honoured
Long time stod, was tho devoured.
To Perse and al that infortune
Thei wyte, so that the comune
Of al the lond his heir exile;
And he despeired for the while
Desguised in a povere wede
To Rome goth, and ther for nede
The craft which thilke time was,
To worche in latoun and in bras,   1850
He lerneth for his sustienance.
Such was the Sones pourveance,
And of his fader it is seid,
In strong prisoun that he was leid
In Albe, wher that he was ded
For hunger and defalte of bred.
The hound was tokne and prophecie
That lich an hound he scholde die,
Which lich was of condicioun,
Whan he with his detraccioun   1860
Bark on his brother so behinde.

Confessor.

   Lo, what profit a man mai finde,
Which hindre wole an other wiht.   **P. i. 222**
Forthi with al thin hole miht,
Mi Sone, eschuie thilke vice.

Amans.

   Mi fader, elles were I nyce:
For ye therof so wel have spoke,
That it is in myn herte loke
And evere schal: bot of Envie,
If ther be more in his baillie   1870
Towardes love, sai me what.

Confessor.

   Mi Sone, as guile under the hat
With sleyhtes of a tregetour
Is hidd, Envie of such colour
Hath yit the ferthe deceivant,
The which is cleped Falssemblant,
Wherof the matiere and the forme
Now herkne and I thee schal enforme.

1856 hunger G, SB   hungre AJE, F   1867 þerfor(e) H₁XE
. . . B₂, B   1869 of] if (ȝif) X . . . B₂   om. W

iv. *Nil bilinguis aget, nisi duplo concinat ore,*   [iv.FALSE-SEMBLANT.]
    Dumque diem loquitur, nox sua vota tegit.
  Vultus habet lucem, tenebras mens, sermo salutem,
  Actus set morbum dat suus esse grauem.
  Pax tibi quam spondet, magis est prenostica guerre;
    Comoda si dederit, disce subesse dolum.
  Quod patet esse fides in eo fraus est, que politi
    Principium pacti finis habere negat.
  O quam condicio talis deformat amantem,
    Qui magis apparens est in amore nichil.   10

    Of Falssemblant if I schal telle,
    Above alle othre it is the welle   1880
    Out of the which deceipte floweth.
    Ther is noman so wys that knoweth
    Of thilke flod which is the tyde,
    Ne how he scholde himselven guide

    To take sauf passage there.   **P. i. 223**
    And yit the wynd to mannes Ere
    Is softe, and as it semeth oute
    It makth clier weder al aboute;
    Bot thogh it seme, it is noght so.
    For Falssemblant hath everemo   1890
    Of his conseil in compaignie
    The derke untrewe Ypocrisie,
    Whos word descordeth to his thoght:
    Forthi thei ben togedre broght
    Of o covine, of on houshold,
    As it schal after this be told.

    Of Falssemblant it nedeth noght
    To telle of olde ensamples oght;
    For al dai in experience
    A man mai se thilke evidence   1900
    Of faire wordes whiche he hiereth;
    Bot yit the barge Envie stiereth
    And halt it evere fro the londe,
    Wher Falssemblant with Ore on honde
    It roweth, and wol noght arive,
    Bot let it on the wawes dryve

Hic tractat Confessor super quarta specie Inuidie, que dissimilacio dicitur, cuius vultus quanto maioris amicicie apparenciam ostendit, tanto subtilioris doli fallacias ad decipiendum mens ymaginatur.

1895 a couine H₁XRCLB₂   1896 be told J, B   betold A, S, F
1902 Envie] of Enuie LB₂, H₃

[FALSE-SEMBLANT.]

In gret tempeste and gret debat,
Wherof that love and his astat
Empeireth.   And therfore I rede,
Mi Sone, that thou fle and drede   1910
This vice, and what that othre sein,
Let thi Semblant be trewe and plein.
For Falssemblant is thilke vice,
Which nevere was withoute office:
Wher that Envie thenkth to guile,   **P. i. 224**
He schal be for that ilke while
Of prive conseil Messagier.
For whan his semblant is most clier,
Thanne is he most derk in his thoght,
Thogh men him se, thei knowe him noght;   1920
Bot as it scheweth in the glas
Thing which therinne nevere was,
So scheweth it in his visage
That nevere was in his corage:
Thus doth he al his thing with sleyhte.

Hic in amoris causa
Confessor super isto
vicio Amanti opponit.

Now ley thi conscience in weyhte,
Mi goode Sone, and schrif the hier,
If thou were evere Custummer
To Falssemblant in eny wise.

Confessio Amantis.

For ought I can me yit avise,   1930
Mi goode fader, certes no.
If I for love have oght do so,
Now asketh, I wol praie yow:
For elles I wot nevere how
Of Falssemblant that I have gilt.

Confessor.

Mi Sone, and sithen that thou wilt
That I schal axe, gabbe noght,
Bot tell if evere was thi thoght
With Falssemblant and coverture
To wite of eny creature   1940
How that he was with love lad;
So were he sori, were he glad,
Whan that thou wistest how it were,
Al that he rounede in thin Ere

1907 and] and in AM   in H1   1916 be for] before RCLB2, ∆, H3
1925 with] by (be) XG, B   1944 rowneth B   rownet L

Thou toldest forth in other place,   **P. i. 225**   [FALSE-SEMBLANT.]
To setten him fro loves grace
Of what womman that thee best liste,
Ther as noman his conseil wiste
Bot thou, be whom he was deceived
Of love, and from his pourpos weyved ;   1950
And thoghtest that his destourbance
Thin oghne cause scholde avance,
As who saith, ' I am so celee,
Ther mai no mannes privete
Be heled half so wel as myn.'
Art thou, mi Sone, of such engin ?
Tell on.
      Mi goode fader, nay   Amans.
As for the more part I say ;
Bot of somdiel I am beknowe,
That I mai stonde in thilke rowe   1960
Amonges hem that Saundres use.
I wol me noght therof excuse,
That I with such colour ne steyne,
Whan I my beste Semblant feigne
To my felawh, til that I wot
Al his conseil bothe cold and hot :
For be that cause I make him chiere,
Til I his love knowe and hiere ;
And if so be myn herte soucheth
That oght unto my ladi toucheth   1970
Of love that he wol me telle,
Anon I renne unto the welle
And caste water in the fyr,
So that his carte amidd the Myr,
Be that I have his conseil knowe,   **P. i. 226**
Fulofte sithe I overthrowe,
Whan that he weneth best to stonde.
Bot this I do you understonde,
If that a man love elles where,
So that my ladi be noght there,   1980
And he me telle, I wole it hide,
Ther schal no word ascape aside,

    1960 in] on B   1971 to me telle B

For with deceipte of no semblant
To him breke I no covenant;
Me liketh noght in other place
To lette noman of his grace,
Ne forto ben inquisitif
To knowe an other mannes lif:
Wher that he love or love noght,
That toucheth nothing to my thoght,   1990
Bot al it passeth thurgh myn Ere
Riht as a thing that nevere were,
And is foryete and leid beside.
Bot if it touche on eny side
Mi ladi, as I have er spoken,
Myn Eres ben noght thanne loken;
For certes, whanne that betitt,
My will, myn herte and al my witt
Ben fully set to herkne and spire
What eny man wol speke of hire.   2000
Thus have I feigned compaignie
Fulofte, for I wolde aspie
What thing it is that eny man
Telle of mi worthi lady can:
And for tuo causes I do this,   **P. i. 227**
The ferste cause wherof is,—
If that I myhte ofherkne and seke
That eny man of hire mispeke,
I wolde excuse hire so fully,
That whan sche wist it inderly,   2010
Min hope scholde be the more
To have hir thank for everemore.
    That other cause, I you assure,
Is, why that I be coverture
Have feigned semblant ofte time
To hem that passen alday byme
And ben lovers als wel as I,
For this I weene trewely,
That ther is of hem alle non,
That thei ne loven everich on   2020

1990 to] of AM   2003 eny] euery Hı ... B₂   2010 wist
SB, F   wiste AJ

Mi ladi: for sothliche I lieve
And durste setten it in prieve,
Is non so wys that scholde asterte,
Bot he were lustles in his herte,
Forwhy and he my ladi sihe,
Hir visage and hir goodlych yhe,
Bot he hire lovede, er he wente.
And for that such is myn entente,
That is the cause of myn aspie,
Why that I feigne compaignie   2030
And make felawe overal;
For gladly wolde I knowen al
And holde me covert alway,
That I fulofte ye or nay
Ne liste ansuere in eny wise,   P. i. 228
Bot feigne semblant as the wise
And herkne tales, til I knowe
Mi ladi lovers al arowe.
And whanne I hiere how thei have wroght,
I fare as thogh I herde it noght   2040
And as I no word understode;
Bot that is nothing for here goode:
For lieveth wel, the sothe is this,
That whanne I knowe al how it is,
I wol bot forthren hem a lite,
Bot al the worste I can endite
I telle it to my ladi plat
In forthringe of myn oghne astat,
And hindre hem al that evere I may.
Bot for al that yit dar I say,   2050
I finde unto miself no bote,
Althogh myn herte nedes mote
Thurgh strengthe of love al that I hiere
Discovere unto my ladi diere:
For in good feith I have no miht
To hele fro that swete wiht,
If that it touche hire eny thing.
Bot this wot wel the hevene king,
That sithen ferst this world began,

2040 it *om.* B   2043 the sothe] and soþ B   2045 alite A, B, F, &c.

Unto non other strange man   2060
Ne feigned I semblant ne chiere,
To wite or axe of his matiere,
Thogh that he lovede ten or tuelve,
Whanne it was noght my ladi selve:
Bot if he wolde axe eny red   **P. i. 229**
Al onlich of his oghne hed,
How he with other love ferde,
His tales with myn Ere I herde,
Bot to myn herte cam it noght
Ne sank no deppere in my thoght,   2070
Bot hield conseil, as I was bede,
And tolde it nevere in other stede,
Bot let it passen as it com.
Now, fader, say what is thi dom,
And hou thou wolt that I be peined
For such Semblant as I have feigned.

Confessor.

  Mi Sone, if reson be wel peised,
Ther mai no vertu ben unpreised
Ne vice non be set in pris.
Forthi, my Sone, if thou be wys,   2080
Do no viser upon thi face,
Which as wol noght thin herte embrace:
For if thou do, withinne a throwe
To othre men it schal be knowe,
So miht thou lihtli falle in blame
And lese a gret part of thi name.
And natheles in this degree
Fulofte time thou myht se
Of suche men that now aday
This vice setten in a say: 2090
I speke it for no mannes blame,
Bot forto warne thee the same.
Mi Sone, as I mai hiere talke
In every place where I walke,
I not if it be so or non,   **P. i. 230**
Bot it is manye daies gon
That I ferst herde telle this,

2072 tolde AJ, S told B, F   2090 a say M, SAd, FH⸳
asay AJ   assay(e) H₁ . . . B₂, B, W

How Falssemblant hath ben and is   [FALSE-SEMBLANT.]
Most comunly fro yer to yere
With hem that duelle among ous here,   2100
Of suche as we Lombardes calle.
For thei ben the slyeste of alle,
So as men sein in toune aboute,
To feigne and schewe thing withoute
Which is revers to that withinne :
Wherof that thei fulofte winne,
Whan thei be reson scholden lese ;
Thei ben the laste and yit thei chese,
And we the ferste, and yit behinde
We gon, there as we scholden finde   2110
The profit of oure oghne lond :
Thus gon thei fre withoute bond
To don her profit al at large,
And othre men bere al the charge.
Of Lombardz unto this covine,
Whiche alle londes conne engine,
Mai Falssemblant in special
Be likned, for thei overal,
Wher as they thenken forto duelle,
Among hemself, so as thei telle,   2120
Ferst ben enformed forto lere
A craft which cleped is Fa crere :
For if Fa crere come aboute,
Thanne afterward hem stant no doute
To voide with a soubtil hond   **P. i. 231**
The beste goodes of the lond
And bringe chaf and take corn.
Where as Fa crere goth toforn,
In all his weie he fynt no lette ;
That Dore can non huissher schette   2130
In which him list to take entre :
And thus the conseil most secre
Of every thing Fa crere knoweth,
Which into strange place he bloweth,
Where as he wot it mai most grieve.

2111 The profit] To profit XE ... B₂   2122 ffa crere AJ, S, F
al. ffacrere   2128 biforn (be forn) B₂, B

And thus Fa crere makth believe,
So that fulofte he hath deceived,
Er that he mai ben aperceived.
Thus is this vice forto drede;
For who these olde bokes rede   2140
Of suche ensamples as were ar,
Him oghte be the more war
Of alle tho that feigne chiere,
Wherof thou schalt a tale hiere.

[DEIANIRA AND
NESSUS.]

Of Falssemblant which is believed
Ful many a worthi wiht is grieved,
And was long time er we wer bore.
To thee, my Sone, I wol therfore
A tale telle of Falssemblant,
Which falseth many a covenant,   2150
And many a fraude of fals conseil
Ther ben hangende upon his Seil:
And that aboghten gulteles
Bothe Deianire and Hercules,
The whiche in gret desese felle   **P. i. 232**
Thurgh Falssemblant, as I schal telle.
Whan Hercules withinne a throwe
Al only hath his herte throwe
Upon this faire Deianire,
It fell him on a dai desire,   2160
Upon a Rivere as he stod,
That passe he wolde over the flod
Withoute bot, and with him lede
His love, bot he was in drede
For tendresce of that swete wiht,
For he knew noght the forde ariht.
Ther was a Geant thanne nyh,
Which Nessus hihte, and whanne he sih
This Hercules and Deianyre,
Withinne his herte he gan conspire,   2170
As he which thurgh his tricherie
Hath Hercules in gret envie,

Hic ponit Confessor
exemplum contra is-
tos, qui sub dissimil-
ate beneuolencie spe-
culo alios in amore
defraudant. Et nar-
rat qualiter Hercules,
cum ipse quoddam
fluuium, cuius vada non
nouit, cum Deianira
transmeare proposuit,
superueniens Nessus
Gigas ob amiciciam
Herculis, vt dixit, Dei-
aniram in vlnas suas
suscipiens trans ripam
salvo perduxit. Et
statim cum ad litus
peruenisset, quamci-
to currere potuit, ip-
sam tanquam propri-
am in preiudicium
Herculis asportare fu-
giens conabatur: per
quod non solum ipsi
set eciam Herculi mor-
tis euentum fortuna
postmodum causauit.

2139 þe vice H₁ ... B₂   his v. H₃   2150 *margin* speculo *om.*
AM (*p. m.*)   2170 conspire] spire XGRCLB₂ to spire (spere) H₁, Ad

Which he bar in his herte loke,
And thanne he thoghte it schal be wroke.
Bot he ne dorste natheles
Ayein this worthi Hercules
Falle in debat as forto feihte;
Bot feigneth Semblant al be sleihte
Of frendschipe and of alle goode,
And comth where as thei bothe stode,   2180
And makth hem al the chiere he can,
And seith that as here oghne man
He is al redy forto do
What thing he mai; and it fell so
That thei upon his Semblant triste,   P. i. 233
And axen him if that he wiste
What thing hem were best to done,
So that thei mihten sauf and sone
The water passe, he and sche.
And whan Nessus the privete   2190
Knew of here herte what it mente,
As he that was of double entente,
He made hem riht a glad visage;
And whanne he herde of the passage
Of him and hire, he thoghte guile,
And feigneth Semblant for a while
To don hem plesance and servise,
Bot he thoghte al an other wise.
This Nessus with hise wordes slyhe
Yaf such conseil tofore here yhe   2200
Which semeth outward profitable
And was withinne deceivable.
He bad hem of the Stremes depe
That thei be war and take kepe,
So as thei knowe noght the pas;
Bot forto helpe in such a cas,
He seith himself that for here ese
He wolde, if that it mihte hem plese,
The passage of the water take,
And for this ladi undertake   2210

2178 al] as H₁ . . B₂   2191 hire A   2198 *line om.* B
on oþer JCLB₂, W   2207 seigh (seih) EC   sih(e) LB₂

To bere unto that other stronde
And sauf to sette hire up alonde,
And Hercules may thanne also
The weie knowe how he schal go:
And herto thei acorden alle.   P. i. 234
Bot what as after schal befalle,
Wel payd was Hercules of this,
And this Geant also glad is,
And tok this ladi up alofte
And set hire on his schuldre softe,   2220
And in the flod began to wade,
As he which no grucchinge made,
And bar hire over sauf and sound.
Bot whanne he stod on dreie ground
And Hercules was fer behinde,
He sette his trowthe al out of mynde,
Who so therof be lief or loth,
With Deianyre and forth he goth,
As he that thoghte to dissevere
The compaignie of hem for evere.   2230
Whan Hercules therof tok hiede,
Als faste as evere he mihte him spiede
He hyeth after in a throwe;
And hapneth that he hadde a bowe,
The which in alle haste he bende,
As he that wolde an Arwe sende,
Which he tofore hadde envenimed.
He hath so wel his schote timed,
That he him thurgh the bodi smette,
And thus the false wiht he lette.   2240
    Bot lest now such a felonie:
Whan Nessus wiste he scholde die,
He tok to Deianyre his scherte,
Which with the blod was of his herte
Thurghout desteigned overal,   P. i. 235
And tolde how sche it kepe schal
Al prively to this entente,

2214 Thei F   2218 glad also H₁ . . . B₂   2220 set A, S, F
sette JC, B   2221 began] he gan GCL   2228 and] þo H₁XE
. . . B₂ *om.* YG, H₃   2247 Al] And H₁, FWH₃

That if hire lord his herte wente
To love in eny other place,
The scherte, he seith, hath such a grace,   2250
That if sche mai so mochel make
That he the scherte upon him take,
He schal alle othre lete in vein
And torne unto hire love ayein.
Who was tho glad bot Deianyre?
Hire thoghte hire herte was afyre
Til it was in hire cofre loke,
So that no word therof was spoke.
    The daies gon, the yeres passe,
The hertes waxen lasse and lasse   2260
Of hem that ben to love untrewe:
This Hercules with herte newe
His love hath set on Eolen,
And therof spieken alle men.
This Eolen, this faire maide,
Was, as men thilke time saide,
The kinges dowhter of Eurice;
And sche made Hercules so nyce
Upon hir Love and so assote,
That he him clotheth in hire cote,   2270
And sche in his was clothed ofte;
And thus fieblesce is set alofte,
And strengthe was put under fote,
Ther can noman therof do bote.
Whan Deianyre hath herd this speche, **P. i. 236**
Ther was no sorwe forto seche:
Of other helpe wot sche non,
Bot goth unto hire cofre anon;
With wepende yhe and woful herte
Sche tok out thilke unhappi scherte,   2280
As sche that wende wel to do,
And broghte hire werk aboute so
That Hercules this scherte on dede,
To such entente as she was bede

2248 lord his] lordes H₁ . . . B₂, Ad   2251 mykel (mekyl &c.)
H₁G . . . B₂, W   2270 he *om.* B   sche H₁   2271 clad fulofte B
2272 fieblest MX . . . C   þe fieblest LB₂   the febleste H₁   feblenes Δ

Of Nessus, so as I seide er.
Bot therof was sche noght the ner,
As no fortune may be weyved;
With Falssemblant sche was deceived,
That whan sche wende best have wonne,
Sche lost al that sche hath begonne.   2290
For thilke scherte unto the bon
His body sette afyre anon,
And cleveth so, it mai noght twinne,
For the venym that was therinne.
And he thanne as a wilde man
Unto the hihe wode he ran,
And as the Clerk Ovide telleth,
The grete tres to grounde he felleth
With strengthe al of his oghne myght,
And made an huge fyr upriht,   2300
And lepte himself therinne at ones
And brende him bothe fleissh and bones.
Which thing cam al thurgh Falssemblant,
That false Nessus the Geant
Made unto him and to his wif;   **P. i. 237**
Wherof that he hath lost his lif,
And sche sori for everemo.

Confessor.

    Forthi, my Sone, er thee be wo,
I rede, be wel war therfore;
For whan so gret a man was lore,   2310
It oghte yive a gret conceipte
To warne alle othre of such deceipte.

Amans.

    Grant mercy, fader, I am war
So fer that I nomore dar
Of Falssemblant take aqueintance;
Bot rathere I wol do penance
That I have feigned chiere er this.
Now axeth forth, what so ther is
Of that belongeth to my schrifte.

Confessor.

    Mi Sone, yit ther is the fifte   2320
Which is conceived of Envie,
And cleped is Supplantarie,
Thurgh whos compassement and guile

Ful many a man hath lost his while
In love als wel as otherwise,
Hierafter as I schal devise.

v. *Inuidus alterius est Supplantator honoris,*
    Et tua quo vertat culmina subtus arat.
Est opus occultum, quasi que latet anguis in herba,
    Quod facit, et subita sorte nociuus adest.
Sic subtilis amans alium supplantat amantem,
    Et capit occulte, quod nequit ipse palam;
Sepeque supplantans in plantam plantat amoris,
    Quod putat in propriis alter habere bonis.

The vice of Supplantacioun
With many a fals collacioun,
Which he conspireth al unknowe,   **P. i. 238**
Full ofte time hath overthrowe   2330
The worschipe of an other man.
So wel no lif awayte can
Ayein his sleyhte forto caste,
That he his pourpos ate laste
Ne hath, er that it be withset.
Bot most of alle his herte is set
In court upon these grete Offices
Of dignitees and benefices:
Thus goth he with his sleyhte aboute
To hindre and schowve an other oute   2340
And stonden with his slyh compas
In stede there an other was;
And so to sette himselven inne,
He reccheth noght, be so he winne,
Of that an other man schal lese,
And thus fulofte chalk for chese
He changeth with ful litel cost,
Wherof an other hath the lost
And he the profit schal receive.
For his fortune is to deceive   2350
And forto change upon the whel
His wo with othre mennes wel:

Hic tractat Confes-
sor de quinta specie
Inuidie, que Supplan-
tacio dicitur, cuius
cultor, priusquam per-
cipiatur, aliene digni-
tatis et officii multo-
ciens intrusor existit.

Latin Verses v. 1 Supplantacio AM   supplantare H₃   3 linguis
AM   ignis H₁   8 Quam B
    2328 manye A, S, F   2337 þis AMG . . L, W   the H₁, Δ
        **   O

Of that an other man avaleth,
His oghne astat thus up he haleth,
And takth the bridd to his beyete,
Wher othre men the buisshes bete.
    Mi Sone, and in the same wise
Ther ben lovers of such emprise,
That schapen hem to be relieved   P. i. 239
Where it is wrong to ben achieved :   2360
For it is other mannes riht,
Which he hath taken dai and niht
To kepe for his oghne Stor
Toward himself for everemor,
And is his propre be the lawe,
Which thing that axeth no felawe,
If love holde his covenant.
Bot thei that worchen be supplaunt,
Yit wolden thei a man supplaunte,
And take a part of thilke plaunte   2370
Which he hath for himselve set :
And so fulofte is al unknet,
That som man weneth be riht fast.
For Supplant with his slyhe cast
Fulofte happneth forto mowe
Thing which an other man hath sowe,
And makth comun of proprete
With sleihte and with soubtilite,
As men mai se fro yer to yere.
Thus cleymeth he the bot to stiere,   2380
Of which an other maister is.

Hic in amoris causa opponit Confessor Amanti super eodem.

    Forthi, my Sone, if thou er this
Hast ben of such professioun,
Discovere thi confessioun :
Hast thou supplanted eny man?

Confessio Amantis.

    For oght that I you telle can,
Min holi fader, as of the dede
I am withouten eny drede

2354 vp he haleþ ∆, FWH₃Magd   he vp haleþ (vphaleþ) A ... B₂,
SAdB   2369 thei] such(e) A ... B₂, SAdB∆   *line om.* WMagd
2373 men H₁ ... B₂   2382 *margin* Hic in amoris ... eodem]
Confessor B   2387 as of dede SAdB∆

Al gulteles; bot of my thoght   **P. i. 240**   [SUPPLANTATION.]
Mi conscience excuse I noght.   2390
For were it wrong or were it riht,
Me lakketh nothing bote myht,
That I ne wolde longe er this
Of other mannes love ywiss
Be weie of Supplantacioun
Have mad apropriacioun
And holde that I nevere boghte,
Thogh it an other man forthoghte.
And al this speke I bot of on,
For whom I lete alle othre gon;   2400
Bot hire I mai noght overpasse,
That I ne mot alwey compasse,
Me roghte noght be what queintise,
So that I mihte in eny wise
Fro suche that mi ladi serve
Hire herte make forto swerve
Withouten eny part of love.
For be the goddes alle above
I wolde it mihte so befalle,
That I al one scholde hem alle   2410
Supplante, and welde hire at mi wille.
And that thing mai I noght fulfille,
Bot if I scholde strengthe make;
And that I dar noght undertake,
Thogh I were as was Alisaundre,
For therof mihte arise sklaundre;
And certes that schal I do nevere,
For in good feith yit hadde I levere
In my simplesce forto die,   **P. i. 241**
Than worche such Supplantarie.   2420
Of otherwise I wol noght seie
That if I founde a seker weie,
I wolde as for conclusioun
Worche after Supplantacioun,
So hihe a love forto winne.

2392 lakked(e) (lacked) X . . . L   lakket W   bote J, S, F
the rest bot *or* but   2408 the] þo B   2414 I dar A, FWH₃
dar I J . . . B₂, SAdBΔ   2425 hihe AC, S, F   hih GE, B

O 2

[SUPPLANTATION.]

Confessor.

Now, fader, if that this be Sinne,
I am al redy to redresce
The gilt of which I me confesse.
    Mi goode Sone, as of Supplant
Thee thar noght drede tant ne quant,   2430
As for nothing that I have herd,
Bot only that thou hast misferd
Thenkende, and that me liketh noght,
For godd beholt a mannes thoght.
And if thou understode in soth
In loves cause what it doth,
A man to ben a Supplantour,
Thou woldest for thin oghne honour
Be double weie take kepe :
Ferst for thin oghne astat to kepe,   2440
To be thiself so wel bethoght
That thou supplanted were noght,
And ek for worschipe of thi name
Towardes othre do the same,
And soffren every man have his.
Bot natheles it was and is,
That in a wayt at alle assaies
Supplant of love in oure daies
The lief fulofte for the levere   **P. i. 242**
Forsakth, and so it hath don evere.   2450
    Ensample I finde therupon,

Qualiter Agamenon de amore Brexeide Achillem, et Diomedes de amore Criseide Troilum supplantauit.

At Troie how that Agamenon
Supplantede the worthi knyht
Achilles of that swete wiht,
Which named was Brexeïda ;
And also of Criseïda,
Whom Troilus to love ches,
Supplanted hath Diomedes.

[GETA AND AMPHI-TRION.]

Qualiter Amphitri-on socium suum Ge-tam, qui Almeenam

    Of Geta and Amphitrion,
That whilom weren bothe as on   2460
Of frendschipe and of compaignie,
I rede how that Supplantarie

2427 al *om.* B   2434 godd *om.* AM   2447 a wayt
(a wait) J, S, F   awayt (await) AC, B   2461 *margin* socrum
H₁ . . . B₂

In love, as it betidde tho,
Beguiled hath on of hem tuo.
For this Geta that I of meene,
To whom the lusti faire Almeene
Assured was be weie of love,
Whan he best wende have ben above
And sikerest of that he hadde,
Cupido so the cause ladde,   2470
That whil he was out of the weie,
Amphitrion hire love aweie
Hath take, and in this forme he wroghte.
Be nyhte unto the chambre he soghte,
Wher that sche lay, and with a wyle
He contrefeteth for the whyle
The vois of Gete in such a wise,
That made hire of hire bedd arise,
Wenende that it were he,   **P. i. 243**
And let him in, and whan thei be   2480
Togedre abedde in armes faste,
This Geta cam thanne ate laste
Unto the Dore and seide, 'Undo.'
And sche ansuerde and bad him go,
And seide how that abedde al warm
Hir lief lay naked in hir arm ;
Sche wende that it were soth.
Lo, what Supplant of love doth :
This Geta forth bejaped wente,
And yit ne wiste he what it mente ;   2490
Amphitrion him hath supplanted
With sleyhte of love and hire enchaunted :
And thus put every man out other,
The Schip of love hath lost his Rother,
So that he can no reson stiere.
And forto speke of this matiere
Touchende love and his Supplant,
A tale which is acordant
Unto thin Ere I thenke enforme.

[GETA AND AMPHI-
TRION.]
peramauit, seipsum
loco alterius cautelosa
supplantacione sub-
stituit.

2473 in this forme he] in thys forme W   þis infortune YGEC
in þis fortune H₁XRLB₂   2477 a wise J, SB   awise A, F
2497 þis AM

Now herkne, for this is the forme.   2500

[TALE OF THE FALSE
BACHELOR.]

Hic in amoris causa
contra fraudem detrac-
cionis ponit Confessor
exemplum. Et narrat
de quodam Romani
Imparatoris filio, qui
probitates armorum
super omnia excer-
cere affectans nesci-
ente patre vltra mare
in partes Persie ad
deseruiendum Solda-
no super guerras cum
solo milite tanquam
socio suo ignotus se
transtulit. Et cum ip-
sius milicie fama super
alios ibidem celsior
accreuisset, contigit ut
in quodam bello contra
Caliphum Egipti inito
Soldanus a sagitta mor-
taliter vulneratus, pri-
usquam moreretur,
quendam anulum filie
sue secretissimum isti
nobili Romano tradi-
dit, dicens qualiter
filia sua sub paterne
benediccionis vinculo
adiurata est, quod qui-
cumque dictum anu-
lum ei afferret, ipsam in
coniugem pre omnibus
susciperet. Defuncto
autem Soldano, versus
Ciuitatem que Kaire
dicitur itinerantes, iste
Romanus commilitoni
suo huius misterii se-
cretum reuelauit; qui
noctanter a bursa do-
mini sui anulum furto
surripiens, hec que
audiuit usui proprio
falsissima Supplanta-
cione applicauit. Et
sic seruus pro domino
desponsata sibi Sol-
dani filia coronatus
Persie regnauit.

Of thilke Cite chief of alle
Which men the noble Rome calle,
Er it was set to Cristes feith,
Ther was, as the Cronique seith,
An Emperour, the which it ladde
In pes, that he no werres hadde :
Ther was nothing desobeissant
Which was to Rome appourtenant,
Bot al was torned into reste.   **P. i. 244**
To some it thoghte for the beste,   2510
To some it thoghte nothing so,
And that was only unto tho
Whos herte stod upon knyhthode :
Bot most of alle of his manhode
The worthi Sone of themperour,
Which wolde ben a werreiour,
As he that was chivalerous
Of worldes fame and desirous,
Began his fadre to beseche
That he the werres mihte seche,   2520
In strange Marches forto ride.
His fader seide he scholde abide,
And wolde granten him no leve :
Bot he, which wolde noght beleve,
A kniht of his to whom he triste,
So that his fader nothing wiste,
He tok and tolde him his corage,
That he pourposeth a viage.
If that fortune with him stonde,
He seide how that he wolde fonde   2530
The grete See to passe unknowe,
And there abyde for a throwe
Upon the werres to travaile.
And to this point withoute faile
This kniht, whan he hath herd his lord,
Is swore, and stant of his acord,

2510 þought hem for B   2519 for to seche X ... B₂   2520]o
werres G ... B₂   2523 hem B   2530 how that] how H₁ þat B

As thei that bothe yonge were;
So that in prive conseil there
Thei ben assented forto wende.   **P. i. 245**
And therupon to make an ende,   2540
Tresor ynowh with hem thei token,
And whan the time is best thei loken,
That sodeinliche in a Galeie
Fro Romelond thei wente here weie
And londe upon that other side.
The world fell so that ilke tide,
Which evere hise happes hath diverse,
The grete Soldan thanne of Perse
Ayein the Caliphe of Egipte
A werre, which that him beclipte,   2550
Hath in a Marche costeiant.
And he, which was a poursuiant
Worschipe of armes to atteigne,
This Romein, let anon ordeigne,
That he was redi everydel:
And whan he was arraied wel
Of every thing which him belongeth,
Straght unto Kaire his weie he fongeth,
Wher he the Soldan thanne fond,
And axeth that withinne his lond   2560
He mihte him for the werre serve,
As he which wolde his thonk deserve.
   The Soldan was riht glad with al,
And wel the more in special
Whan that he wiste he was Romein;
Bot what was elles in certein,
That mihte he wite be no weie.
And thus the kniht of whom I seie
Toward the Soldan is beleft,   **P. i. 246**
And in the Marches now and eft,   2570
Wher that the dedli werres were,
He wroghte such knihthode there,
That every man spak of him good.
And thilke time so it stod,

2537 As H₁, W   And AJMYX . . . B₂, SAdBΔΛ, FH₃Magd
2559 he *om.* AM   2562 þong F   2573 That] And B

[Tale of the false
Bachelor.]

This mihti Soldan be his wif
A Dowhter hath, that in this lif
Men seiden ther was non so fair.
Sche scholde ben hir fader hair,
And was of yeres ripe ynowh :
Hire beaute many an herte drowh   2580
To bowe unto that ilke lawe
Fro which no lif mai be withdrawe,
And that is love, whos nature
Set lif and deth in aventure
Of hem that knyhthode undertake.
   This lusti peine hath overtake
The herte of this Romein so sore,
That to knihthode more and more
Prouesce avanceth his corage.
Lich to the Leoun in his rage,   2590
Fro whom that alle bestes fle,
Such was the knyht in his degre :
Wher he was armed in the feld,
Ther dorste non abide his scheld ;
Gret pris upon the werre he hadde.
Bot sche which al the chance ladde,
Fortune, schop the Marches so,
That be thassent of bothe tuo,
The Soldan and the Caliphe eke,   **P. i. 247**
Bataille upon a dai thei seke,   2600
Which was in such a wise set
That lengere scholde it noght be let.
Thei made hem stronge on every side,
And whan it drowh toward the tide
That the bataille scholde be,
The Soldan in gret privete
A goldring of his dowhter tok,
And made hire swere upon a bok
And ek upon the goddes alle,
That if fortune so befalle   2610
In the bataille that he deie,

2576 this] his AMXR ... B₂, H₃W   hire G   here H₁   2581 that
ilke] þilke AM   2586 Thus AM   2592 þe H₁ ... B₂, FWH₃
þis AJM, SAdB△

That sche schal thilke man obeie
And take him to hire housebonde,
Which thilke same Ring to honde
Hire scholde bringe after his deth.
This hath sche swore, and forth he geth
With al the pouer of his lond
Unto the Marche, where he fond
His enemy full embatailled.

The Soldan hath the feld assailed :   2620
Thei that ben hardy sone assemblen,
Wherof the dredfull hertes tremblen :
That on sleth, and that other sterveth,
Bot above alle his pris deserveth
This knihtly Romein ; where he rod,
His dedly swerd noman abod,
Ayein the which was no defence ;
Egipte fledde in his presence,
And thei of Perse upon the chace   **P. i. 248**
Poursuien : bot I not what grace   2630
Befell, an Arwe out of a bowe
Al sodeinly that ilke throwe
The Soldan smot, and ther he lay :
The chace is left for thilke day,
And he was bore into a tente.

The Soldan sih how that it wente,
And that he scholde algate die ;
And to this knyht of Romanie,
As unto him whom he most triste,
His Dowhter Ring, that non it wiste,   2640
He tok, and tolde him al the cas,
Upon hire oth what tokne it was
Of that sche scholde ben his wif.
Whan this was seid, the hertes lif
Of this Soldan departeth sone ;
And therupon, as was to done,
The dede body wel and faire
Thei carie til thei come at Kaire,
Wher he was worthily begrave.

The lordes, whiche as wolden save   2650

2632 that ilke] wiþinne a B   2649 Wher] Ther B

The Regne which was desolat,
To bringe it into good astat
A parlement thei sette anon.
Now herkne what fell therupon:
This yonge lord, this worthi kniht
Of Rome, upon the same niht
That thei amorwe trete scholde,
Unto his Bacheler he tolde
His conseil, and the Ring with al   P. i. 249
He scheweth, thurgh which that he schal, 2660
He seith, the kinges Dowhter wedde,
For so the Ring was leid to wedde,
He tolde, into hir fader hond,
That with what man that sche it fond
She scholde him take to hire lord.
And this, he seith, stant of record,
Bot noman wot who hath this Ring.

   This Bacheler upon this thing
His Ere and his entente leide,
And thoghte more thanne he seide,   2670
And feigneth with a fals visage
That he was glad, bot his corage
Was al set in an other wise.
These olde Philosophres wise
Thei writen upon thilke while,
That he mai best a man beguile
In whom the man hath most credence;
And this befell in evidence
Toward this yonge lord of Rome.
His Bacheler, which hadde tome,   2680
Whan that his lord be nihte slepte,
This Ring, the which his maister kepte,
Out of his Pours awey he dede,
And putte an other in the stede.

   Amorwe, whan the Court is set,
The yonge ladi was forth fet,
To whom the lordes don homage,

2654 herkneþ XE . . . B₂   2661 kinges] soldans X . . . B₂
Souldan H₁   2678 þus AM   2680 tome AJYGECB₃,
SAdB∆Λ, FWKH₃ thome L come MH₁XR

And after that of Mariage
Thei trete and axen of hir wille.   **P. i. 250**
Bot sche, which thoghte to fulfille   2690
Hire fader heste in this matiere,
Seide openly, that men mai hiere,
The charge which hire fader bad.
   Tho was this Lord of Rome glad
And drowh toward his Pours anon,
Bot al for noght, it was agon :
His Bacheler it hath forthdrawe,
And axeth ther upon the lawe
That sche him holde covenant.
The tokne was so sufficant   2700
That it ne mihte be forsake,
And natheles his lord hath take
Querelle ayein his oghne man ;
Bot for nothing that evere he can
He mihte as thanne noght ben herd,
So that his cleym is unansuerd,
And he hath of his pourpos failed.
   This Bacheler was tho consailed
And wedded, and of thilke Empire
He was coroned Lord and Sire,   2710
And al the lond him hath received ;
Wherof his lord, which was deceived,
A seknesse er the thridde morwe
Conceived hath of dedly sorwe :
And as he lay upon his deth,
Therwhile him lasteth speche and breth,
He sende for the worthieste
Of al the lond and ek the beste,
And tolde hem al the sothe tho,   **P. i. 251**
That he was Sone and Heir also   2720
Of themperour of grete Rome,
And how that thei togedre come,
This kniht and he ; riht as it was,
He tolde hem al the pleine cas,
And for that he his conseil tolde,

[TALE OF THE FALSE
BACHELOR.]

2698 þer vpon J, SB   þervpon A, F   2708 þo was Hₜ . . . Bⱼ
was so H₃   hath so T

That other hath al that he wolde,
And he hath failed of his mede :
As for the good he takth non hiede,
He seith, bot only of the love,
Of which he wende have ben above.　　　2730
And therupon be lettre write
He doth his fader forto wite
Of al this matiere as it stod ;
And thanne with an hertly mod
Unto the lordes he besoghte
To telle his ladi how he boghte
Hire love, of which an other gladeth ;
And with that word his hewe fadeth,
And seide, 'A dieu, my ladi swete.'
The lif hath lost his kindly hete,　　　2740
And he lay ded as eny ston ;
Wherof was sory manyon,
Bot non of alle so as sche.

This false knyht in his degree
Arested was and put in hold :
For openly whan it was told
Of the tresoun which is befalle,
Thurghout the lond thei seiden alle,
If it be soth that men suppose,　　　**P. i. 252**
His oghne untrowthe him schal depose.　　2750
And forto seche an evidence,
With honour and gret reverence,
Wherof they mihten knowe an ende,
To themperour anon thei sende
The lettre which his Sone wrot.
And whan that he the sothe wot,
To telle his sorwe is endeles,
Bot yit in haste natheles
Upon the tale which he herde
His Stieward into Perse ferde　　　2760
With many a worthi Romein eke,
His liege tretour forto seke ;
And whan thei thider come were,

2733 this] þe A...B₂, SAdBTΔ　　2741 ded] stille B　　2752 and
gret] and with gret LB₂, W

This kniht him hath confessed there
How falsly that he hath him bore,
Wherof his worthi lord was lore.
Tho seiden some he scholde deie,
Bot yit thei founden such a weie
That he schal noght be ded in Perse;
And thus the skiles ben diverse.   2770
Be cause that he was coroned,
And that the lond was abandoned
To him, althogh it were unriht,
Ther is no peine for him diht;
Bot to this point and to this ende
Thei granten wel that he schal wende
With the Romeins to Rome ayein.
And thus acorded ful and plein,
The qwike body with the dede   **P. i. 253**
With leve take forth thei lede,   2780
Wher that Supplant hath his juise.
    Wherof that thou thee miht avise
Upon this enformacioun
Touchende of Supplantacioun,
That thou, my Sone, do noght so:
And forto take hiede also
What Supplant doth in other halve,
Ther is noman can finde a salve
Pleinly to helen such a Sor;
It hath and schal ben everemor,   2790
Whan Pride is with Envie joint,
He soffreth noman in good point,
Wher that he mai his honour lette.
And therupon if I schal sette
Ensample, in holy cherche I finde
How that Supplant is noght behinde;
God wot if that it now be so:
For in Cronique of time ago
I finde a tale concordable
Of Supplant, which that is no fable,   2800
In the manere as I schal telle,
So as whilom the thinges felle.

.2775 þe point H₁ . . . B₂

[POPE BONIFACE.]

Hic ponit Confessor exemplum contra istos in causa dignitatis adquirende supplantatores. Et narrat qualiter Papa Bonefacius predecessorem suum Celestinum a papatu coniectata circumuencione fraudulenter supplantauit. Set qui potentes a sede deponit, huiusmodi supplantacionis fraudem non sustinens, ipsum sic in sublime exaltatum postea in profundi carceris miseriam proici, fame que siti cruciari, necnon et ab huius vite gaudiis dolorosa morte explantari finali conclusione permisit.

At Rome, as it hath ofte falle,
The vicair general of alle
Of hem that lieven Cristes feith
His laste day, which non withseith,
Hath schet as to the worldes ÿe,
Whos name if I schal specefie,
He hihte Pope Nicolas.   P. i. 254
And thus whan that he passed was,   2810
The Cardinals, that wolden save
The forme of lawe, in the conclave
Gon forto chese a newe Pope,
And after that thei cowthe agrope
Hath ech of hem seid his entente :
Til ate laste thei assente
Upon an holy clerk reclus,
Which full was of gostli vertus ;
His pacience and his simplesse
Hath set him into hih noblesse.   2820
Thus was he Pope canonized,
With gret honour and intronized,
And upon chance as it is falle,
His name Celestin men calle ;
Which notefied was be bulle
To holi cherche and to the fulle
In alle londes magnified.
Bot every worschipe is envied,
And that was thilke time sene :
For whan this Pope of whom I meene   2830
Was chose, and othre set beside,
A Cardinal was thilke tide
Which the papat longe hath desired
And therupon gretli conspired ;
Bot whan he sih fortune is failed,
For which long time he hath travailed,
That ilke fyr which Ethna brenneth
Thurghout his wofull herte renneth,

Which is resembled to Envie,   **P. i. 255** [POPE BONIFACE.]
Wherof Supplant and tricherie   2840
Engendred is; and natheles
He feigneth love, he feigneth pes,
Outward he doth the reverence,
Bot al withinne his conscience
Thurgh fals ymaginacioun
He thoghte Supplantacioun.
And therupon a wonder wyle
He wroghte: for at thilke whyle
It fell so that of his lignage
He hadde a clergoun of yong age,   2850
Whom he hath in his chambre affaited.
This Cardinal his time hath waited,
And with his wordes slyhe and queinte,
The whiche he cowthe wysly peinte,
He schop this clerk of which I telle
Toward the Pope forto duelle,
So that withinne his chambre anyht
He lai, and was a prive wyht
Toward the Pope on nyhtes tide.
      Mai noman fle that schal betide.   2860
This Cardinal, which thoghte guile,
Upon a day whan he hath while
This yonge clerc unto him tok,
And made him swere upon a bok,
And told him what his wille was.
And forth withal a Trompe of bras
He hath him take, and bad him this:
'Thou schalt,' he seide, 'whan time is
Awaite, and take riht good kepe,   **P. i. 256**
Whan that the Pope is fast aslepe   2870
And that non other man be nyh;
And thanne that thou be so slyh
Thurghout the Trompe into his Ere,
Fro hevene as thogh a vois it were,
To soune of such prolacioun
That he his meditacioun

2852] is tyme B   2865 told A, B, F   tolde J   2870 on slepe
H₁XGRCL ... B₂, Ad, W   2875 The sone AM

Therof mai take and understonde,
As thogh it were of goddes sonde.
And in this wise thou schalt seie,
That he do thilke astat aweie 2880
Of Pope, in which he stant honoured,
So schal his Soule be socoured
Of thilke worschipe ate laste
In hevene which schal evere laste.'

    This clerc, whan he hath herd the forme
How he the Pope scholde enforme,
Tok of the Cardinal his leve,
And goth him hom, til it was Eve,
And prively the trompe he hedde,
Til that the Pope was abedde. 2890
And at the Midnyht, whan he knewh
The Pope slepte, thanne he blewh
Withinne his trompe thurgh the wal,
And tolde in what manere he schal
His Papacie leve, and take
His ferste astat: and thus awake
This holi Pope he made thries,
Wherof diverse fantasies
Upon his grete holinesse **P. i. 257**
Withinne his herte he gan impresse. 2900
The Pope ful of innocence
Conceiveth in his conscience
That it is goddes wille he cesse;
Bot in what wise he may relesse
His hihe astat, that wot he noght.
And thus withinne himself bethoght,
He bar it stille in his memoire,
Til he cam to the Consistoire;
And there in presence of hem alle
He axeth, if it so befalle 2910
That eny Pope cesse wolde,
How that the lawe it soffre scholde.
Thei seten alle stille and herde,
Was non which to the point ansuerde,

2881 of which M, B   which E (*p. m.*)   2903 is *om.* F
2906 bethoght] he þought H₁ ... B₂, B, W

For to what pourpos that it mente
Ther was noman knew his entente,
Bot only he which schop the guile.
 This Cardinal the same while
Al openly with wordes pleine
Seith, if the Pope wolde ordeigne   2920
That ther be such a lawe wroght,
Than mihte he cesse, and elles noght.
And as he seide, don it was;
The Pope anon upon the cas
Of his Papal Autorite
Hath mad and yove the decre:
And whan that lawe was confermed
In due forme and al affermed,
This innocent, which was deceived,   **P. i. 258**
His Papacie anon hath weyved,   2930
Renounced and resigned eke.
That other was nothing to seke,
Bot undernethe such a jape
He hath so for himselve schape,
That how as evere it him beseme,
The Mitre with the Diademe
He hath thurgh Supplantacion:
And in his confirmacion
Upon the fortune of his grace
His name is cleped Boneface.   2940
 Under the viser of Envie,
Lo, thus was hid the tricherie,
Which hath beguiled manyon.
Bot such conseil ther mai be non,
With treson whan it is conspired,
That it nys lich the Sparke fyred
Up in the Rof, which for a throwe
Lith hidd, til whan the wyndes blowe
It blaseth out on every side.
This Bonefas, which can noght hyde   2950
The tricherie of his Supplant,
Hath openly mad his avant
How he the Papacie hath wonne.
Bot thing which is with wrong begonne

**   P

[POPE BONIFACE.]

Mai nevere stonde wel at ende ;
Wher Pride schal the bowe bende,
He schet fulofte out of the weie :
And thus the Pope of whom I seie,
Whan that he stod on hih the whiel,   **P. i. 259**
He can noght soffre himself be wel.   2960
Envie, which is loveles,
And Pride, which is laweles,
With such tempeste made him erre,
That charite goth out of herre :
So that upon misgovernance
Ayein Lowyz the king of France
He tok querelle of his oultrage,
And seide he scholde don hommage
Unto the cherche bodily.
Bot he, that wiste nothing why   2970
He scholde do so gret servise
After the world in such a wise,
Withstod the wrong of that demande ;
For noght the Pope mai comande
The king wol noght the Pope obeie.
This Pope tho be alle weie
That he mai worche of violence
Hath sent the bulle of his sentence
With cursinge and with enterdit.
    The king upon this wrongful plyt,   2980
To kepe his regne fro servage,
Conseiled was of his Barnage
That miht with miht schal be withstonde.
Thus was the cause take on honde,
And seiden that the Papacie
Thei wolde honoure and magnefie
In al that evere is spirital ;
Bot thilke Pride temporal
Of Boneface in his persone,   **P. i. 260**
Ayein that ilke wrong al one   2990
Thei wolde stonden in debat :
And thus the man and noght the stat

2959 on þe hih(e) whiel LB₂   opon the whele W   2964 out of
þe herre AM   out of herte J

The Frensche schopen be her miht
To grieve. And fell ther was a kniht,
Sire Guilliam de Langharet,
Which was upon this cause set;
And therupon he tok a route
Of men of Armes and rod oute,
So longe and in a wayt he lay,
That he aspide upon a day   3000
The Pope was at Avinoun,
And scholde ryde out of the toun
Unto Pontsorge, the which is
A Castell in Provence of his.
Upon the weie and as he rod,
This kniht, which hoved and abod
Embuisshed upon horse bak,
Al sodeinliche upon him brak
And hath him be the bridel sesed,
And seide: 'O thou, which hast desesed 3010
The Court of France be thi wrong,
Now schalt thou singe an other song:
Thin enterdit and thi sentence
Ayein thin oghne conscience
Hierafter thou schalt fiele and grope.
We pleigne noght ayein the Pope,
For thilke name is honourable,
Bot thou, which hast be deceivable
And tricherous in al thi werk,   **P. i. 261**
Thou Bonefas, thou proude clerk,   3020
Misledere of the Papacie,
Thi false bodi schal abye
And soffre that it hath deserved.'
    Lo, thus the Supplantour was served;
For thei him ladden into France
And setten him to his penance
Withinne a tour in harde bondes,
Wher he for hunger bothe hise hondes
Eet of and deide, god wot how:

2993 schapen H₁ ... B₂, BTΛ   2999 a wayt F a wait J awayt
AC, B   3003 Poursorge H₁ ... B₂, B   3012 an other] a
newe H₁, B   3021 the] þi H₁ ... B₂, B, Magd

Cronica Bonefacii.
Intrasti ut vulpis, reg-
nasti ut leo, et mor-
tuus es ut canis.

Of whom the wrytinge is yit now　　3030
Registred, as a man mai hiere,
Which spekth and seith in this manere:
　Thin entre lich the fox was slyh,
Thi regne also with pride on hih
Was lich the Leon in his rage;
Bot ate laste of thi passage
Thi deth was to the houndes like.
　Such is the lettre of his Cronique
Proclamed in the Court of Rome,
Wherof the wise ensample nome.　　3040
And yit, als ferforth as I dar,
I rede alle othre men be war,
And that thei loke wel algate
That non his oghne astat translate
Of holi cherche in no degree
Be fraude ne soubtilite:
For thilke honour which Aaron tok
Schal non receive, as seith the bok,
Bot he be cleped as he was.　　**P. i. 262**
What I schal thenken in this cas　　3050
Of that I hiere now aday,
I not: bot he which can and may,
Be reson bothe and be nature
The help of every mannes cure,
He kepe Simon fro the folde.
For Joachim thilke Abbot tolde
How suche daies scholden falle,
That comunliche in places alle
The Chapmen of such mercerie
With fraude and with Supplantarie　　3060
So manye scholden beie and selle,
That he ne may for schame telle
So foul a Senne in mannes Ere.
Bot god forbiede that it were
In oure daies that he seith:
For if the Clerc beware his feith

Nota de prophecia
Ioachim Abbatis.

Quanti Mercenarii
erunt in ouile dei, tuas
aures meis narracion-
ibus fedare nolo.

3055 He kepe] He helpe H₁ . . . B₂, B　He kepte T　To kepe
SAdΔ　　3058 ff *margin* Quanti . . . nolo SΔ, FH₃Magd　*om.* A . . .
B₂, B (S *has* qui sic ait Quanti Mercenarii tunc erunt &c.)

In chapmanhod at such a feire,
The remenant mot nede empeire
Of al that to the world belongeth;
For whan that holi cherche wrongeth,   3070
I not what other thing schal rihte.
And natheles at mannes sihte
Envie forto be preferred
Hath conscience so differred,
That noman loketh to the vice
Which is the Moder of malice,
And that is thilke false Envie,
Which causeth many a tricherie;
For wher he may an other se   **P. i. 263**
That is mor gracious than he,   3080
It schal noght stonden in his miht
Bot if he hindre such a wiht:
And that is welnyh overal,
This vice is now so general.

Envie thilke unhapp indrowh,   [JOAB. AHITOPHEL.]
Whan Joab be deceipte slowh   Qualiter Ioab prin-
Abner, for drede he scholde be   ceps milicie Dauid
                                         inuidie causa Abner
With king David such as was he.   subdole interfecit. Et
And thurgh Envie also it fell   qualiter eciam Achito-
                                         fell ob hoc quod Cusy
Of thilke false Achitofell,   3090 in consilio Absolon
For his conseil was noght achieved,   preferebatur, accen-
Bot that he sih Cusy believed   sus inuidia laqueo se
                                         suspendit.
With Absolon and him forsake,
He heng himself upon a stake.

Senec witnesseth openly   [NATURE OF ENVY.]
How that Envie proprely
Is of the Court the comun wenche,
And halt taverne forto schenche
That drink which makth the herte brenne,
And doth the wit aboute renne,   3100
Be every weie to compasse
How that he mihte alle othre passe,
As he which thurgh unkindeschipe
Envieth every felaschipe;
So that thou miht wel knowe and se,

3085 indrowh AJ, F   in drowh (in drough) C, SB

Ther is no vice such as he,
Ferst toward godd abhominable,
And to mankinde unprofitable :
And that be wordes bot a fewe   **P. i. 294**
I schal be reson prove and schewe.   3110

vi. *Inuidie stimulus sine causa ledit abortus,*
     Nam sine temptante crimine crimen habet.
     Non est huius opus temptare Cupidinis archum,
     Dumque faces Veneris ethnica flamma vorat.
     Absque rubore gene, pallor quas fuscus obumbrat,
     Frigida nature cetera membra docent.

Envie if that I schal descrive,
He is noght schaply forto wyve
In Erthe among the wommen hiere ;
For ther is in him no matiere
Wherof he mihte do plesance.
Ferst for his hevy continance
Of that he semeth evere unglad,
He is noght able to ben had ;
And ek he brenneth so withinne,
That kinde mai no profit winne,   3120
Wherof he scholde his love plese :
For thilke blod which scholde have ese
To regne among the moiste veines,
Is drye of thilke unkendeli peines
Thurgh whiche Envie is fyred ay.
And thus be reson prove I may
That toward love Envie is noght ;
And otherwise if it be soght,
Upon what side as evere it falle,
It is the werste vice of alle,   3130
Which of himself hath most malice.
For understond that every vice
Som cause hath, wherof it groweth,
Bot of Envie noman knoweth
Fro whenne he cam bot out of helle. **P. i. 265**
For thus the wise clerkes telle,
That no spirit bot of malice

Hic describit Con-
fessor naturam Inui-
die tam in amore quam
aliter secundum pro-
prietatem vicii sub
compendio.

3112 schapli noght AM   3119 An F

Be weie of kinde upon a vice
Is tempted, and be such a weie
Envie hath kinde put aweie   3140
And of malice hath his steringe,
Wherof he makth his bakbitinge,
And is himself therof desesed.
So mai ther be no kinde plesed;
For ay the mor that he envieth,
The more ayein himself he plieth.
Thus stant Envie in good espeir
To ben himself the develes heir,
As he which is his nexte liche
And forthest fro the heveneriche,   3150
For there mai he nevere wone.

   Forthi, my goode diere Sone,   Confessor.
If thou wolt finde a siker weie
To love, put Envie aweie.

   Min holy fader, reson wolde   Amans.
That I this vice eschuie scholde:
Bot yit to strengthe mi corage,
If that ye wolde in avantage
Therof sette a recoverir,
It were tome a gret desir,   3160
That I this vice mihte flee.

   Nou understond, my Sone, and se,   Confessor.
Ther is phisique for the seke,
And vertus for the vices eke.
Who that the vices wolde eschuie,   **P. i. 266**
He mot be resoun thanne suie
The vertus; for be thilke weie
He mai the vices don aweie,
For thei togedre mai noght duelle:
For as the water of a welle   3170
Of fyr abateth the malice,
Riht so vertu fordoth the vice.
Ayein Envie is Charite,
Which is the Moder of Pite,
That makth a mannes herte tendre,

3160 tome A, F   to me JC, SB   3170 þe welle H₁ . . .
B₂, B

[CHARITY AND PITY.]

That it mai no malice engendre
In him that is enclin therto.
For his corage is tempred so,
That thogh he mihte himself relieve,
Yit wolde he noght an other grieve,   3180
Bot rather forto do plesance
He berth himselven the grevance,
So fain he wolde an other ese.
Wherof, mi Sone, for thin ese
Now herkne a tale which I rede,
And understond it wel, I rede.

[TALE OF CONSTAN-
TINE AND SILVESTER.]

    Among the bokes of latin
I finde write of Constantin
The worthi Emperour of Rome,
Suche infortunes to him come,   3190
Whan he was in his lusti age,
The lepre cawhte in his visage
And so forth overal aboute,
That he ne mihte ryden oute:
So lefte he bothe Schield and spere,   **P. i. 267**
As he that mihte him noght bestere,
And hield him in his chambre clos.
Thurgh al the world the fame aros,
The grete clerkes ben asent
And come at his comandement   3200
To trete upon this lordes hele.
So longe thei togedre dele,
That thei upon this medicine
Apointen hem, and determine
That in the maner as it stod
Thei wolde him bathe in childes blod
Withinne sevene wynter age:
For, as thei sein, that scholde assuage
The lepre and al the violence,
Which that thei knewe of Accidence   3210
And noght be weie of kinde is falle.
And therto thei acorden alle

Hic ponit Confessor exemplum de virtute caritatis contra Inuidiam. Et narrat de Constantino Helene filio, qui cum Imperii Romani dignitatem optinuerat, a morbo lepre infectus, medici pro sanitate recuperanda ipsum in sanguine puerorum masculorum balneare proposuerunt. Set cum innumera multitudo matrum cum filiis huiusmodi medicine causa in circuitu palacii affuisset, Imparatorque eorum gemitus et clamores percepisset, caritate motus ingemiscens sic ait: 'O vere ipse est dominus, qui se facit seruum pietatis.' Et hiis dictis statum suum cunctipotentis medele committens, sui ipsius morbum pocius quam infancium mortem benignus elegit. Vnde ipse, qui antea Paganus et leprosus exti-

3177 enclynd (enclined) H₁...B₂, BT, W   inclinand Δ   3199
ben] were B   3204 margin est ipse A...B₂, SBΔ   3207
margin medele] indele H₁...B₂, B   3209 margin benignius A, SBΔ

As for final conclusioun,
And tolden here opinioun
To themperour: and he anon
His conseil tok, and therupon
With lettres and with scales oute
Thei sende in every lond aboute
The yonge children forto seche,
Whos blod, thei seiden, schal be leche   3220
For themperoures maladie.
Ther was ynowh to wepe and crie
Among the Modres, whan thei herde
Hou wofully this cause ferde,
Bot natheles thei moten bowe ;   **P. i. 268**
And thus wommen ther come ynowhe
With children soukende on the Tete.
Tho was ther manye teres lete,
Bot were hem lieve or were hem lothe,
The wommen and the children bothe   3230
Into the Paleis forth be broght
With many a sory hertes thoght
Of hem whiche of here bodi bore
The children hadde, and so forlore
Withinne a while scholden se.
The Modres wepe in here degre,
And manye of hem aswoune falle,
The yonge babes criden alle :
This noyse aros, the lord it herde,
And loked out, and how it ferde   3240
He sih, and as who seith abreide
Out of his slep, and thus he seide :
' O thou divine pourveance,
Which every man in the balance
Of kinde hast formed to be liche,
The povere is bore as is the riche
And deieth in the same wise,
Upon the fol, upon the wise
Siknesse and hele entrecomune ;
Mai non eschuie that fortune   3250

[TALE OF CONSTAN-
TINE AND SILVESTER.]
terat, ex vnda baptis-
matis renatus vtrius-
que materie, tam cor-
poris quam anime, di-
uino miraculo conse-
cutus est salutem.

3214 *margin* ex vnda baptismatis *om.* H₁ . . . B₂, BΔ   3220 scholde
AM, TΔ, W   3231 be] he AM   3237 on swowne H₁ . . . B₂, B

Which kinde hath in hire lawe set;
Hire strengthe and beaute ben beset
To every man aliche fre,
That sche preferreth no degre
As in the disposicioun   **P. i. 269**
Of bodili complexioun :
And ek of Soule resonable
The povere child is bore als able
To vertu as the kinges Sone ;
For every man his oghne wone   3260
After the lust of his assay
The vice or vertu chese may.
Thus stonden alle men franchised,
Bot in astat thei ben divised ;

Nota.

To some worschipe and richesse,
To some poverte and distresse,
On lordeth and an other serveth ;
Bot yit as every man deserveth
The world yifth noght his yiftes hiere.
Bot certes he hath gret matiere   3270
To ben of good condicioun,
Which hath in his subjeccioun
The men that ben of his semblance.'
And ek he tok a remembrance
How he that made lawe of kinde
Wolde every man to lawe binde,
And bad a man, such as he wolde
Toward himself, riht such he scholde
Toward an other don also.
And thus this worthi lord as tho   3280
Sette in balance his oghne astat
And with himself stod in debat,
And thoghte hou that it was noght good
To se so mochel mannes blod
Be spilt for cause of him alone.   **P. i. 270**
He sih also the grete mone,
Of that the Modres were unglade,
And of the wo the children made,

3265 *margin* Nota AJ, F *om.* C, B   3283 hou that] how MI.,
Δ, W   3285 for] by (be) H₁ . . . B₂, H₃

Wherof that al his herte tendreth,
And such pite withinne engendreth,
That him was levere forto chese
His oghne bodi forto lese,
Than se so gret a moerdre wroght
Upon the blod which gulteth noght.
Thus for the pite which he tok
Alle othre leches he forsok,
And put him out of aventure
Al only into goddes cure ;
And seith, 'Who that woll maister be,
He mot be servant to pite.'
So ferforth he was overcome
With charite, that he hath nome
His conseil and hise officers,
And bad unto hise tresorers
That thei his tresour al aboute
Departe among that povere route
Of wommen and of children bothe,
Wherof thei mihte hem fede and clothe
And saufli tornen hom ayein
Withoute lost of eny grein.
Thurgh charite thus he despendeth
His good, wherof that he amendeth
The povere poeple, and contrevaileth
The harm, that he hem so travaileth :
And thus the woful nyhtes sorwe
To joie is torned on the morwe ;
Al was thonkinge, al was blessinge,
Which erst was wepinge and cursinge ;
Thes wommen gon hom glade ynowh,
Echon for joie on other lowh,
And preiden for this lordes hele,
Which hath relessed the querele,
And hath his oghne will forsake
In charite for goddes sake.
    Bot now hierafter thou schalt hiere
What god hath wroght in this matiere,

[Tale of Constan-
tine and Silvester.]

3290

3300

3310

P. i. 271

3320

3290 gendreþ AM, W   3306 that] þe M . . . B₂, SAdBΔ, W
3314 so om. H₁ . . . B₂

As he which doth al equite.
To him that wroghte charite
He was ayeinward charitous,
And to pite he was pitous :   3330
For it was nevere knowe yit
That charite goth unaquit.
The nyht, whan he was leid to slepe,
The hihe god, which wolde him kepe,
Seint Peter and seint Poul him sende,
Be whom he wolde his lepre amende.
Thei tuo to him slepende appiere
Fro god, and seide in this manere :
'O Constantin, for thou hast served
Pite, thou hast pite deserved :   3340
Forthi thou schalt such pite have
That god thurgh pite woll thee save.
So schalt thou double hele finde,
Ferst for thi bodiliche kinde,
And for thi wofull Soule also,   **P. i. 272**
Thou schalt ben hol of bothe tuo.
And for thou schalt thee noght despeire,
Thi lepre schal nomore empeire
Til thou wolt sende therupon
Unto the Mont of Celion,   3350
Wher that Silvestre and his clergie
Togedre duelle in compaignie
For drede of thee, which many day
Hast ben a fo to Cristes lay,
And hast destruid to mochel schame
The prechours of his holy name.
Bot now thou hast somdiel appesed
Thi god, and with good dede plesed,
That thou thi pite hast bewared
Upon the blod which thou hast spared. 3360
Forthi to thi salvacion
Thou schalt have enformacioun,
Such as Silvestre schal the teche :
The nedeth of non other leche.'
   This Emperour, which al this herde,
'Grant merci lordes,' he ansuerde,

[TALE OF CONSTAN-
TINE AND SILVESTER.]

'I wol do so as ye me seie.
Bot of o thing I wolde preie:
What schal I telle unto Silvestre
Or of youre name or of youre estre?'   3370
And thei him tolden what thei hihte,
And forth withal out of his sihte
Thei passen up into the hevene.
And he awok out of his swevene,
And clepeth, and men come anon: **P. i. 273**
He tolde his drem, and therupon
In such a wise as he hem telleth
The Mont wher that Silvestre duelleth
Thei have in alle haste soght,
And founde he was and with hem broght 3380
To themperour, which to him tolde
His swevene and elles what he wolde.
And whan Silvestre hath herd the king,
He was riht joiful of this thing,
And him began with al his wit
To techen upon holi writ
Ferst how mankinde was forlore,
And how the hihe god therfore
His Sone sende from above,
Which bore was for mannes love,   3390
And after of his oghne chois
He tok his deth upon the crois;
And how in grave he was beloke,
And how that he hath helle broke,
And tok hem out that were him lieve;
And forto make ous full believe
That he was verrai goddes Sone,
Ayein the kinde of mannes wone
Fro dethe he ros the thridde day,
And whanne he wolde, as he wel may,   3400
He styh up to his fader evene
With fleissh and blod into the hevene;
And riht so in the same forme
In fleissh and blod he schal reforme,
Whan time comth, the qwike and dede **P. i. 274**

3395 were hem B   3402 into heuene AMR, Δ, W

[TALE OF CONSTAN-
TINE AND SILVESTER.]

At thilke woful dai of drede,
Where every man schal take his dom,
Als wel the Maister as the grom.
The mihti kinges retenue
That dai may stonde of no value   3410
With worldes strengthe to defende ;
For every man mot thanne entende
To stonde upon his oghne dedes
And leve alle othre mennes nedes.
That dai mai no consail availe,
The pledour and the plee schal faile,
The sentence of that ilke day
Mai non appell sette in delay ;
Ther mai no gold the Jugge plie,
That he ne schal the sothe trie   3420
And setten every man upriht,
Als wel the plowman as the kniht :
The lewed man, the grete clerk
Schal stonde upon his oghne werk,
And such as he is founde tho,
Such schal he be for everemo.
Ther mai no peine be relessed,
Ther mai no joie ben encressed,
Bot endeles, as thei have do,
He schal receive on of the tuo.   3430
And thus Silvestre with his sawe
The ground of al the newe lawe
With gret devocion he precheth,
Fro point to point and pleinly techeth
Unto this hethen Emperour ;   **P. i. 275**
And seith, the hihe creatour
Hath underfonge his charite,
Of that he wroghte such pite,
Whan he the children hadde on honde.
Thus whan this lord hath understonde   3440
Of al this thing how that it ferde,
Unto Silvestre he thanne ansuerde,
With al his hole herte and seith

3406 On H₁ ... B₂ And H₃ (That ilke W)   3430 He schal] Thei
schul (schal) H₁ ... B₂   3431 And þis H₁ERC, W And þus þis L

That he is redi to the feith.

And so the vessel which for blod
Was mad, Silvestre, ther it stod,
With clene water of the welle
In alle haste he let do felle,
And sette Constantin therinne
Al naked up unto the chinne.   3450
And in the while it was begunne,
A liht, as thogh it were a Sunne,
Fro hevene into the place com
Wher that he tok his cristendom ;
And evere among the holi tales
Lich as thei weren fisshes skales
Ther fellen from him now and eft,
Til that ther was nothing beleft
Of al his grete maladie.
For he that wolde him purefie,   3460
The hihe god hath mad him clene,
So that ther lefte nothing sene ;
He hath him clensed bothe tuo,
The bodi and the Soule also.
   Tho knew this Emperour in dede   **P. i. 276**
That Cristes feith was forto drede,
And sende anon hise lettres oute
And let do crien al aboute,
Up peine of deth that noman weyve
That he baptesme ne receive :   3470
After his Moder qweene Heleine
He sende, and so betwen hem tweine
Thei treten, that the Cite all
Was cristned, and sche forth withall.
This Emperour, which hele hath founde,
Withinne Rome anon let founde
Tuo cherches, whiche he dede make
For Peter and for Poules sake,
Of whom he hadde avisioun ;
And yaf therto possessioun   3480
Of lordschipe and of worldes good.

3458 Til that ... beleft] Til ... him beleft (be lefte &c.) H₁ ... B₂
3470 ne *om.* AM   3476 he let(e) founde AM   3479 Of hem B

[TALE OF CONSTAN-
TINE AND SILVESTER.]

Bot how so that his will was good
Toward the Pope and his Franchise,
Yit hath it proved other wise,
To se the worchinge of the dede:
For in Cronique this I rede;
Anon as he hath mad the yifte,
A vois was herd on hih the lifte,
Of which al Rome was adrad,
And seith: 'To day is venym schad   3490
In holi cherche of temporal,
Which medleth with the spirital.'
And hou it stant of that degree
Yit mai a man the sothe se:
God mai amende it, whan he wile,   **P. i. 277**
I can ther to non other skile.

Confessor.

Bot forto go ther I began,
How charite mai helpe a man
To bothe worldes, I have seid:
And if thou have an Ere leid,   3500
Mi Sone, thou miht understonde,
If charite be take on honde,
Ther folweth after mochel grace.
Forthi, if that thou wolt pourchace
How that thou miht Envie flee,
Aqueinte thee with charite,
Which is the vertu sovereine.

Amans.

Mi fader, I schal do my peine:
For this ensample which ye tolde
With al myn herte I have withholde,   3510
So that I schal for everemore
Eschuie Envie wel the more:
And that I have er this misdo,
Yif me my penance er I go.
And over that to mi matiere
Of schrifte, why we sitten hiere
In privete betwen ous tweie,
Now axeth what ther is, I preie.

Confessor.

Mi goode Sone, and for thi lore

3486 For] ffro F   3487 so as AM   3492 Wich F
3516 why] whil(e) M . . . B₂, W

I woll thee telle what is more,   3520
So that thou schalt the vices knowe:
For whan thei be to thee full knowe,
Thou miht hem wel the betre eschuie.
And for this cause I thenke suie
The forme bothe and the matiere,   **P. i. 278**
As now suiende thou schalt hiere
Which vice stant next after this:
And whan thou wost how that it is,
As thou schalt hiere me devise,
Thow miht thiself the betre avise.   3530

Explicit Liber Secundus.

Incipit Liber Tercius.

[IRE OR WRATH.]

i. *Ira suis paribus est par furiis Acherontis,*   **P. i. 279**
   Quo furor ad tempus nil pietatis habet.
Ira malencolicos animos perturbat, vt equo
   Iure sui pondus nulla statera tenet.
Omnibus in causis grauat Ira, set inter amantes.
   Illa magis facili sorte grauamen agit:
Est vbi vir discors leuiterque repugnat amori,
   Sepe loco ludi fletus ad ora venit.

     IF thou the vices lest to knowe,
Mi Sone, it hath noght ben unknowe,
Fro ferst that men the swerdes grounde,
That ther nis on upon this grounde,
A vice forein fro the lawe,
Wherof that many a good felawe
Hath be distraght be sodein chance;
And yit to kinde no plesance
It doth, bot wher he most achieveth
His pourpos, most to kinde he grieveth,   10
As he which out of conscience
Is enemy to pacience:
And is be name on of the Sevene,
Which ofte hath set this world unevene,
And cleped is the cruel Ire,   **P. i. 280**
Whos herte is everemore on fyre
To speke amis and to do bothe,
For his servantz ben evere wrothe.
     Mi goode fader, tell me this:
What thing is Ire?
               Sone, it is   20
That in oure englissh Wrathe is hote,

Hic in tercio libro tractat super quinque speciebus Ire, quarum prima Malencolia dicitur, cuius vicium Confessor primo describens Amanti super eodem consequenter opponit.

7 *margin* primo] prima H₁XERCL   primum B₂ *om.* G   9 f. he ... he] it ... it XRC. W   it ... he H₁GELB₂   12 enemy] euermore (euer more) H₁ ... B₂

Which hath hise wordes ay so hote,
That all a mannes pacience
Is fyred of the violence.
For he with him hath evere fyve
Servantz that helpen him to stryve :
The ferst of hem Malencolie   [i. MELANCHOLY.]
Is cleped, which in compaignie
An hundred times in an houre
Wol as an angri beste loure,   30
And noman wot the cause why.
Mi Sone, schrif thee now forthi :
Hast thou be Malencolien ?

    Ye, fader, be seint Julien,   Confessio Amantis.
Bot I untrewe wordes use,
I mai me noght therof excuse :
And al makth love, wel I wot,
Of which myn herte is evere hot,
So that I brenne as doth a glede
For Wrathe that I mai noght spede.   40
And thus fulofte a day for noght
Save onlich of myn oghne thoght
I am so with miselven wroth,
That how so that the game goth
With othre men, I am noght glad ;   P. i. 281
Bot I am wel the more unglad,
For that is othre mennes game
It torneth me to pure grame.
Thus am I with miself oppressed
Of thoght, the which I have impressed,   50
That al wakende I dreme and meete
That I with hire al one meete
And preie hire of som good ansuere :
Bot for sche wol noght gladly swere,
Sche seith me nay withouten oth ;
And thus wexe I withinne wroth,
That outward I am al affraied,
And so distempred and esmaied.
A thousand times on a day
Ther souneth in myn Eres nay,   60

49 mi seluen A   51 walkend(e) H₁ ... CB₂, B   wawende L

Q 2

[MELANCHOLY.]

The which sche seide me tofore:
Thus be my wittes as forlore;
And namely whan I beginne
To rekne with miself withinne
How many yeres ben agon,
Siththe I have trewly loved on
And nevere tok of other hede,
And evere aliche fer to spede
I am, the more I with hir dele,
So that myn happ and al myn hele   70
Me thenkth is ay the leng the ferre,
That bringth my gladschip out of herre,
Wherof my wittes ben empeired,
And I, as who seith, al despeired.
For finaly, whan that I muse   P. i. 282
And thenke how sche me wol refuse,
I am with anger so bestad,
For al this world mihte I be glad:
And for the while that it lasteth
Al up so doun my joie it casteth,   80
And ay the furthere that I be,
Whan I ne may my ladi se,
The more I am redy to wraththe,
That for the touchinge of a laththe
Or for the torninge of a stree
I wode as doth the wylde Se,
And am so malencolious,
That ther nys servant in myn hous
Ne non of tho that ben aboute,
That ech of hem ne stant in doute,   90
And wenen that I scholde rave
For Anger that thei se me have;
And so thei wondre more and lasse,
Til that thei sen it overpasse.
Bot, fader, if it so betide,
That I aproche at eny tide
The place wher my ladi is,
And thanne that hire like ywiss

62 al forlore (alle for lore) H₁, B, H₃   68 fer AJ, STΔΛ, FH₃
for M . . . B₂, AdB, W   86 wolde AM

To speke a goodli word untome,
For al the gold that is in Rome   100
Ne cowthe I after that be wroth,
Bot al myn Anger overgoth ;
So glad I am of the presence
Of hire, that I all offence
Foryete, as thogh it were noght,   P. i. 283
So overgladed is my thoght.
And natheles, the soth to telle,
Ayeinward if it so befelle
That I at thilke time sihe
On me that sche miscaste hire yhe,   110
Or that sche liste noght to loke,
And I therof good hiede toke,
Anon into my ferste astat
I torne, and am with al so mat,
That evere it is aliche wicke.
And thus myn hand ayein the pricke
I hurte and have do many day,
And go so forth as I go may,
Fulofte bitinge on my lippe,
And make unto miself a whippe,   120
With which in many a chele and hete
Mi wofull herte is so tobete,
That all my wittes ben unsofte
And I am wroth, I not how ofte ;
And al it is Malencolie,
Which groweth of the fantasie
Of love, that me wol noght loute :
So bere I forth an angri snoute
Ful manye times in a yer.
Bot, fader, now ye sitten hier   130
In loves stede, I yow beseche,
That som ensample ye me teche,
Wherof I mai miself appese.

   Mi Sone, for thin hertes ese   Confessor.
I schal fulfille thi preiere,   P. i. 284
So that thou miht the betre lere
What mischief that this vice stereth,

109 þat þilke AM

Which in his Anger noght forbereth,
Wherof that after him forthenketh,
Whan he is sobre and that he thenketh   140
Upon the folie of his dede ;
And of this point a tale I rede.

[TALE OF CANACE
AND MACHAIRE.]

Hic ponit Confes-
sor exemplum contra
istos, qui cum vires
amoris non sunt reali-
ter experti. contra
alios amantes malen-
colica seueritate ad
iracundiam vindicte
prouocantur. Et nar-
rat qualiter Rex Eolus
filium nomine Macha-
rium et filiam nomine
Canacem habuit, qui
cum ab infancia vsque
ad pubertatem inui-
cem educati fuerant,
Cupido tandem ignito
iaculo amborum cordis
desideria   amorose
penetrauit, ita quod
Canacis natura coope-
rante a fratre suo
inpregnata parturit :
super quo pater, intol-
lerabilem iuuentutis
concupiscenciam ig-
norans nimiaque furo-
ris malencolia preuen-
tus, dictam filiam cum
partu dolorosissimo
casu interfici adiudi-
cauit.

Ther was a king which Eolus
Was hote, and it befell him thus,
That he tuo children hadde faire,
The Sone cleped was Machaire,
The dowhter ek Canace hihte.
Be daie bothe and ek be nyhte,
Whil thei be yonge, of comun wone
In chambre thei togedre wone,   150
And as thei scholden pleide hem ofte,
Til thei be growen up alofte   '
Into the youthe of lusti age,
Whan kinde assaileth the corage
With love and doth him forto bowe,
That he no reson can allowe,
Bot halt the lawes of nature :
For whom that love hath under cure,
As he is blind himself, riht so
He makth his client blind also.   160
In such manere as I you telle
As thei al day togedre duelle,
This brother mihte it noght asterte
That he with al his hole herte
His love upon his Soster caste :   **P. i. 285**
And so it fell hem ate laste,
That this Machaire with Canace
Whan thei were in a prive place,
Cupide bad hem ferst to kesse,
And after sche which is Maistresse   170
In kinde and techeth every lif
Withoute lawe positif,
Of which sche takth nomaner charge,

148 *margin* malencolia H₁ . . . B₂   162 *margin* concupiscencia
H₁XR . . . B₂   168 Whan . . . in a] Whan þat . . . in SAdBTΔ
Whenne . . . in W

Bot kepth hire lawes al at large,
Nature, tok hem into lore
And tawht hem so, that overmore
Sche hath hem in such wise daunted,
That thei were, as who seith, enchaunted.
And as the blinde an other ledeth
And til thei falle nothing dredeth,   180
Riht so thei hadde non insihte ;
Bot as the bridd which wole alihte
And seth the mete and noght the net,
Which in deceipte of him is set,
This yonge folk no peril sihe,
Bot that was likinge in here yhe,
So that thei felle upon the chance
Where witt hath lore his remembrance.
So longe thei togedre assemble,
The wombe aros, and sche gan tremble,   190
And hield hire in hire chambre clos
For drede it scholde be disclos
And come to hire fader Ere :
Wherof the Sone hadde also fere,
And feigneth cause forto ryde ;   **P. i. 286**
For longe dorste he noght abyde,
In aunter if men wolde sein
That he his Soster hath forlein :
For yit sche hadde it noght beknowe
Whos was the child at thilke throwe.   200
Machaire goth, Canace abit,
The which was noght delivered yit,
Bot riht sone after that sche was.
    Now lest and herkne a woful cas.
The sothe, which mai noght ben hid,
Was ate laste knowe and kid
Unto the king, how that it stod.
And whan that he it understod,
Anon into Malencolie,
As thogh it were a frenesie,   210

176 tawht (taught) AJ, B, F   tawhte S   overmore] euermore
AMH₁XGRCLB₂, TΔ, W   181 in sihte (in siht) AJM   186
that] al B   200 drowe AM

He fell, as he which nothing cowthe
How maistrefull love is in yowthe:
And for he was to love strange,
He wolde noght his herte change
To be benigne and favorable
To love, bot unmerciable
Betwen the wawe of wod and wroth
Into his dowhtres chambre he goth,
And sih the child was late bore,
Wherof he hath hise othes swore   220
That sche it schal ful sore abye.
And sche began merci to crie,
Upon hire bare knes and preide,
And to hire fader thus sche seide:
'Ha mercy! fader, thenk I am   **P. i. 287**
Thi child, and of thi blod I cam.
That I misdede yowthe it made,
And in the flodes bad me wade,
Wher that I sih no peril tho:
Bot now it is befalle so,   230
Merci, my fader, do no wreche!'
And with that word sche loste speche
And fell doun swounende at his fot,
As sche for sorwe nedes mot.
Bot his horrible crualte
Ther mihte attempre no pite:
Out of hire chambre forth he wente
Al full of wraththe in his entente,
And tok the conseil in his herte
That sche schal noght the deth asterte,   240
As he which Malencolien
Of pacience hath no lien,
Wherof his wraththe he mai restreigne.
And in this wilde wode peine,
Whanne al his resoun was untame,
A kniht he clepeth be his name,
And tok him as be weie of sonde
A naked swerd to bere on honde,
And seide him that he scholde go
And telle unto his dowhter so   250

In the manere as he him bad,
How sche that scharpe swerdes blad
Receive scholde and do withal
So as sche wot wherto it schal.
Forth in message goth this kniht   **P. i. 288**
Unto this wofull yonge wiht,
This scharpe swerd to hire he tok:
Wherof that al hire bodi qwok,
For wel sche wiste what it mente,
And that it was to thilke entente   260
That sche hireselven scholde slee.
And to the kniht sche seide: 'Yee,
Now that I wot my fadres wille,
That I schal in this wise spille,
I wole obeie me therto,
And as he wole it schal be do.
Bot now this thing mai be non other,
I wole a lettre unto mi brother,
So as my fieble hand may wryte,
With al my wofull herte endite.'   270
Sche tok a Penne on honde tho,
Fro point to point and al the wo,
Als ferforth as hireself it wot,
Unto hire dedly frend sche wrot,
And tolde how that hire fader grace
Sche mihte for nothing pourchace;
And overthat, as thou schalt hiere,
Sche wrot and seide in this manere:
'O thou my sorwe and my gladnesse,
O thou myn hele and my siknesse,   280
O my wanhope and al my trust,
O my desese and al my lust,
O thou my wele, o thou my wo,
O thou my frend, o thou my fo,
O thou my love, o thou myn hate,   **P. i. 289**
For thee mot I be ded algate.
Thilke ende may I noght asterte,
And yit with al myn hole herte,
Whil that me lasteth eny breth,

254 it schal] sche schal H₁ ... B₂, Ad   286 For thee] ffor þi B

I wol the love into my deth.   290
Bot of o thing I schal thee preie,
If that my litel Sone deie,
Let him be beried in my grave
Beside me, so schalt thou have
Upon ous bothe remembrance.
For thus it stant of my grevance;
Now at this time, as thou schalt wite,
With teres and with enke write
This lettre I have in cares colde:
In my riht hond my Penne I holde,   300
And in my left the swerd I kepe,
And in my barm ther lith to wepe
Thi child and myn, which sobbeth faste.
Now am I come unto my laste:
Fare wel, for I schal sone deie,
And thenk how I thi love abeie.'
The pomel of the swerd to grounde
Sche sette, and with the point a wounde
Thurghout hire herte anon sche made,
And forth with that al pale and fade   310
Sche fell doun ded fro ther sche stod.
The child lay bathende in hire blod
Out rolled fro the moder barm,
And for the blod was hot and warm,
He basketh him aboute thrinne.   **P. i. 290**
Ther was no bote forto winne,
For he, which can no pite knowe,
The king cam in the same throwe,
And sih how that his dowhter dieth
And how this Babe al blody crieth;   320
Bot al that mihte him noght suffise,
That he ne bad to do juise
Upon the child, and bere him oute,
And seche in the Forest aboute
Som wilde place, what it were,
To caste him out of honde there,
So that som beste him mai devoure,

290 vnto H₁ . . . B₂   313 modres (moderis, moders) H₁ . . . B₂, Δ
315 baskleþ AMH₁Sn, SΔΛ   basked C

Where as noman him schal socoure.
Al that he bad was don in dede:
Ha, who herde evere singe or rede   330
Of such a thing as that was do?
Bot he which ladde his wraththe so
Hath knowe of love bot a lite;
Bot for al that he was to wyte,
Thurgh his sodein Malencolie
To do so gret a felonie.
    Forthi, my Sone, how so it stonde,
Be this cas thou miht understonde
That if thou evere in cause of love
Schalt deme, and thou be so above   340
That thou miht lede it at thi wille,
Let nevere thurgh thi Wraththe spille
Which every kinde scholde save.
For it sit every man to have
Reward to love and to his miht,
Ayein whos strengthe mai no wiht:
And siththe an herte is so constreigned,
The reddour oghte be restreigned
To him that mai no bet aweie,
Whan he mot to nature obeie.   350
For it is seid thus overal,
That nedes mot that nede schal
Of that a lif doth after kinde,
Wherof he mai no bote finde.
What nature hath set in hir lawe
Ther mai no mannes miht withdrawe,
And who that worcheth therayein,
Fulofte time it hath be sein,
Ther hath befalle gret vengance,
Wherof I finde a remembrance.   360

    Ovide after the time tho
Tolde an ensample and seide so,
How that whilom Tiresias,
As he walkende goth per cas,

[TALE OF CANACE
AND MACHAIRE.]

Confessor.

P. i. 291

[TIRESIAS AND THE
SNAKES.]

331 that] þo AM, Ad, Magd hyt W   354 I may H₁ ... B₂
355 What þing nature haþ set in lawe A ... B₂, S ... Δ

[TIRESIAS AND THE
SNAKES.]

Hic narrat qualiter
Tiresias in quodam
monte duos serpentes
inuenit pariter com-
miscentes, quos cum
virga percussit. Irati
dii ob hoc quod natu-
ram impediuit, ipsum
contra naturam a for-
ma virili in muliebrem
transmutarunt.

Upon an hih Montaine he sih
Tuo Serpentz in his weie nyh,
And thei, so as nature hem tawhte,
Assembled were, and he tho cawhte
A yerde which he bar on honde,
And thoghte that he wolde fonde   370
To letten hem, and smot hem bothe :
Wherof the goddes weren wrothe ;
And for he hath destourbed kinde
And was so to nature unkinde,
Unkindeliche he was transformed,   **P. i. 292**
That he which erst a man was formed
Into a womman was forschape.
That was to him an angri jape ;
Bot for that he with Angre wroghte,
Hise Angres angreliche he boghte.   380

Confessor.

Lo thus, my Sone, Ovide hath write,
Wherof thou miht be reson wite,
More is a man than such a beste :
So mihte it nevere ben honeste
A man to wraththen him to sore
Of that an other doth the lore
Of kinde, in which is no malice,
Bot only that it is a vice :
And thogh a man be resonable,
Yit after kinde he is menable   390
To love, wher he wole or non.
Thenk thou, my Sone, therupon
And do Malencolie aweie ;
For love hath evere his lust to pleie,
As he which wolde no lif grieve.

Amans.

Mi fader, that I mai wel lieve ;
Al that ye tellen it is skile :
Let every man love as he wile,
Be so it be noght my ladi,
For I schal noght be wroth therby.   400
Bot that I wraththe and fare amis,

390 menable H₁XG, AdΔ, F   menabe J   meuable (?)
AMB₂, ST, H₃   mevable R   moeuable EC, B   mouable
(movable) L, W

Al one upon miself it is,
That I with bothe love and kinde
Am so bestad, that I can finde
No weie how I it mai asterte: **P. i. 293**
Which stant upon myn oghne herte
And toucheth to non other lif,
Save only to that swete wif
For whom, bot if it be amended,
Mi glade daies ben despended,   410
That I miself schal noght forbere
The Wraththe which that I now bere,
For therof is non other leche.
Now axeth forth, I yow beseche,
Of Wraththe if ther oght elles is,
Wherof to schryve.
   Sone, yis.

ii. *Ira mouet litem, que lingue frena resoluens*   [ii. CHESTE.]
 Laxa per infames currit vbique vias.
 Rixarum nutrix quos educat ista loquaces,
 Hos Venus a latere linquit habere vagos.
 Set pacienter agens taciturno qui celet ore,
 Vincit, et optati carpit amoris iter.

Of Wraththe the secounde is Cheste,
Which hath the wyndes of tempeste
To kepe, and many a sodein blast
He bloweth, wherof ben agast   420
Thei that desiren pes and reste.
He is that ilke ungoodlieste   Hic tractat Confes-
Which many a lusti love hath twinned;   sor super secunda
For he berth evere his mowth unpinned,   specie Ire, que Lis
                                                    dicitur, ex cuius con-
So that his lippes ben unloke   tumeliis innumerosa
And his corage is al tobroke,   dolorum occasio tam
That every thing which he can telle,   in amoris causa quam
It springeth up as doth a welle,   aliter in quampluribus
Which mai non of his stremes hyde,   sepissime exorta est.
Bot renneth out on every syde.   430
So buillen up the foule sawes   **P. i. 294**

402 Al one] Along(e) H₁G ... B₂ All longe X   408 Save] Saufly B
Latin Verses ii. 6 Vincit] Viuat H₁ ... CB₂ Viuit L

That Cheste wot of his felawes:
For as a Sive kepeth Ale,
Riht so can Cheste kepe a tale;
Al that he wot he wol desclose,
And speke er eny man oppose.
As a Cite withoute wal,
Wher men mai gon out overal
Withouten eny resistence,
So with his croked eloquence   440
He spekth al that he wot withinne:
Wherof men lese mor than winne,
For ofte time of his chidinge
He bringth to house such tidinge,
That makth werre ate beddeshed.
He is the levein of the bred,
Which soureth al the past aboute:
Men oghte wel such on to doute,
For evere his bowe is redi bent,
And whom he hit I telle him schent,   450
If he mai perce him with his tunge.
And ek so lowde his belle is runge,
That of the noise and of the soun
Men feeren hem in al the toun
Welmore than thei don of thonder.
For that is cause of more wonder;
For with the wyndes whiche he bloweth
Fulofte sythe he overthroweth
The Cites and the policie,
That I have herd the poeple crie,   460
And echon seide in his degre,   **P. i. 295**
'Ha wicke tunge, wo thee be!'
For men sein that the harde bon,
Althogh himselven have non,
A tunge brekth it al to pieces.
He hath so manye sondri spieces
Of vice, that I mai noght wel
Descrive hem be a thousendel:
Bot whan that he to Cheste falleth,

445 makeþ ... at H₁ ... B₂, BΔ   446 He] His FWKH₃
It Magd

Ful many a wonder thing befalleth,   470
For he ne can nothing forbere.
   Now tell me, Sone, thin ansuere,   Opponit Confessor.
If it hath evere so betidd,
That thou at eny time hast chidd
Toward thi love.
             Fader, nay ;   Confessio Amantis.
Such Cheste yit unto this day
Ne made I nevere, god forbede :
For er I sunge such a crede,
I hadde levere to be lewed ;
For thanne were I al beschrewed   480
And worthi to be put abak
With al the sorwe upon my bak
That eny man ordeigne cowthe.
Bot I spak nevere yit be mowthe
That unto Chestè mihte touche,
And that I durste riht wel vouche
Upon hirself as for witnesse ;
For I wot, of hir gentilesse
That sche me wolde wel excuse,
That I no suche thinges use.   490
And if it scholde so betide   **P. i. 296**
That I algates moste chide,
It myhte noght be to my love :
For so yit was I nevere above,
For al this wyde world to winne
That I dorste eny word beginne,
Be which sche mihte have ben amoeved
And I of Cheste also reproeved.
Bot rathere, if it mihte hir like,
The beste wordes wolde I pike   500
Whiche I cowthe in myn herte chese,
And serve hem forth in stede of chese,
For that is helplich to defie ;
And so wolde I my wordes plie,
That mihten Wraththe and Cheste avale

---

476 yit *om.* AM   478 synge (sing) H₁XECB₂, AdBΛ, H₃
480 be schrewed FK   490 no þinges suche H₁XGRCB₂   no thynge
suche W   504 wolde I] wolde (*om.* I) FKH₃   wolle I W

With tellinge of my softe tale.
Thus dar I make a foreward,
That nevere unto my ladiward
Yit spak I word in such a wise,
Wherof that Cheste scholde arise.   510
This seie I noght, that I fulofte
Ne have, whanne I spak most softe,
Per cas seid more thanne ynowh ;
Bot so wel halt noman the plowh
That he ne balketh otherwhile,
Ne so wel can noman affile
His tunge, that som time in rape
Him mai som liht word overscape,
And yit ne meneth he no Cheste.
Bot that I have ayein hir heste   520
Fulofte spoke, I am beknowe ;   **P. i. 297**
And how my will is, that ye knowe :
For whan my time comth aboute,
That I dar speke and seie al oute
Mi longe love, of which sche wot
That evere in on aliche hot
Me grieveth, thanne al my desese
I telle, and though it hir desplese,
I speke it forth and noght ne leve :
And thogh it be beside hire leve,   530
I hope and trowe natheles
That I do noght ayein the pes ;
For thogh I telle hire al my thoght,
Sche wot wel that I chyde noght.
Men mai the hihe god beseche,
And he wol hiere a mannes speche
And be noght wroth of that he seith ;
So yifth it me the more feith
And makth me hardi, soth to seie,
That I dar wel the betre preie   540
Mi ladi, which a womman is.
For thogh I telle hire that or this
Of love, which me grieveth sore,

519 meueþ (?) JMXELB₂, W   moeueþ GC   532 the] hir (hire) H₁
. . . B₂   536 hire B

Hire oghte noght be wroth the more,
For I withoute noise or cri
Mi pleignte make al buxomly
To puten alle wraththe away.
Thus dar I seie unto this day
Of Cheste in ernest or in game
Mi ladi schal me nothing blame.   550
   Bot ofte time it hath betidd   **P. i. 298**
That with miselven I have chidd,
That noman couthe betre chide:
And that hath ben at every tide,
Whanne I cam to misef al one;
For thanne I made a prive mone,
And every tale by and by,
Which as I spak to my ladi,
I thenke and peise in my balance
And drawe into my remembrance;   560
And thanne, if that I finde a lak
Of eny word that I mispak,
Which was to moche in eny wise,
Anon my wittes I despise
And make a chidinge in myn herte,
That eny word me scholde asterte
Which as I scholde have holden inne.
And so forth after I beginne
And loke if ther was elles oght
To speke, and I ne spak it noght: 570
And thanne, if I mai seche and finde
That eny word be left behinde,
Which as I scholde more have spoke,
I wolde upon miself be wroke,
And chyde with miselven so
That al my wit is overgo.
For noman mai his time lore
Recovere, and thus I am therfore
So overwroth in al my thoght,
That I myself chide al to noght: 580
Thus for to moche or for to lite   **P. i. 299**
Fulofte I am miself to wyte.

573 S *has lost three leaves* (ll. 573-1112)   581 Thus] That B
**
R

[CHESTE.]

Bot al that mai me noght availe,
With cheste thogh I me travaile:
Bot Oule on Stock and Stock on Oule;
The more that a man defoule,
Men witen wel which hath the werse;
And so to me nys worth a kerse,
Bot torneth on myn oghne hed,
Thogh I, til that I were ded,   590
Wolde evere chyde in such a wise
Of love as I to you devise.
Bot, fader, now ye have al herd
In this manere how I have ferd
Of Cheste and of dissencioun,
Yif me youre absolucioun.

Confessor.

Mi Sone, if that thou wistest al,
What Cheste doth in special
To love and to his welwillinge,
Thou woldest flen his knowlechinge   600
And lerne to be debonaire.
For who that most can speke faire
Is most acordende unto love:
Fair speche hath ofte brought above
Ful many a man, as it is knowe,
Which elles scholde have be riht lowe
And failed mochel of his wille.
Forthi hold thou thi tunge stille
And let thi witt thi wille areste,
So that thou falle noght in Cheste,   610
Which is the source of gret destance: **P. i. 300**
And tak into thi remembrance
If thou miht gete pacience,
Which is the leche of alle offence,
As tellen ous these olde wise:

Seneca. Paciencia
est vindicta omnium
iniuriarum.

For whan noght elles mai suffise
Be strengthe ne be mannes wit,
Than pacience it oversit
And overcomth it ate laste;
Bot he mai nevere longe laste,   620

611 destrance AM   612 vnto H₁ ... B₂   619 overcomth
t] ouercomeþ C

Which wol noght bowe er that he breke.
Tak hiede, Sone, of that I speke.

   Mi fader, of your goodli speche
And of the witt which ye me teche
I thonke you with al myn herte :
For that world schal me nevere asterte,
That I ne schal your wordes holde,
Of Pacience as ye me tolde,
Als ferforth as myn herte thenketh;
And of my wraththe it me forthenketh.   630
Bot, fader, if ye forth withal
Som good ensample in special
Me wolden telle of som Cronique,
It scholde wel myn herte like
Of pacience forto hiere,
So that I mihte in mi matiere
The more unto my love obeie
And puten mi desese aweie.

   Mi Sone, a man to beie him pes   [PATIENCE OF
Behoveth soffre as Socrates   640   SOCRATES.]
Ensample lefte, which is write :   **P. i. 301**
And for thou schalt the sothe wite,
Of this ensample what I mene,
Althogh it be now litel sene   Hic ponit Confessor
Among the men thilke evidence,   exemplum de pacien-
Yit he was upon pacience   cia in amore contra
                    lites habenda. Et nar-
So sett, that he himself assaie   rat qualiter vxor So-
In thing which mihte him most mispaie   cratis ipsum quodam
                    die multis sermonibus
Desireth, and a wickid wif   litigauit ; set cum ipse
He weddeth, which in sorwe and strif   absque vlla respon-
                    sione omnia probra
Ayein his ese was contraire.   650 pacienter sustulit, in-
                    dignata vxor quan-
Bot he spak evere softe and faire,   dam ydriam plenam
                    aque, quam in manu
Til it befell, as it is told,   tenebat, super caput
In wynter, whan the dai is cold,   viri sui subito effudit,
                    dicens, 'Euigila et lo-
This wif was fro the welle come,   quere': qui respon-
Wher that a pot with water nome   dens tunc ait, 'O vere
                    iam scio et expertus

624 wich F   626 world (worlde) AM, AdTΔ, FH₃   word JH₁
. . . B₂, BΛ, W   633 teche YEC, B   of] in AM, H₃   639
a man to] for to B   647 assaie *om.* A (*p. m.*)   to assaie M, H₃
assayed X   did assai Δ

R 2

[PATIENCE OF
SOCRATES.]

sum quia post vento-
rum rabiem sequun-
tur ymbres ' : et isto
modo litis contume-
liam sua paciencia de-
uicit.

Sche hath, and broghte it into house,
And sih how that hire seli spouse
Was sett and loked on a bok
Nyh to the fyr, as he which tok   660
His ese for a man of age.
And sche began the wode rage,
And axeth him what devel he thoghte,
And bar on hond that him ne roghte
What labour that sche toke on honde,
And seith that such an Housebonde
Was to a wif noght worth a Stre.
He seide nowther nay ne ye,
Bot hield him stille and let hire chyde ;
And sche, which mai hirself noght hyde,   670
Began withinne forto swelle,   **P. i. 302**
And that sche broghte in fro the welle,
The waterpot sche hente alofte
And bad him speke, and he al softe
Sat stille and noght a word ansuerde ;
And sche was wroth that he so ferde,
And axeth him if he be ded ;
And al the water on his hed
Sche pourede oute and bad awake.
Bot he, which wolde noght forsake   680
His Pacience, thanne spak,
And seide how that he fond no lak
In nothing which sche hadde do :
For it was wynter time tho,
And wynter, as be weie of kinde
Which stormy is, as men it finde,
Ferst makth the wyndes forto blowe,
And after that withinne a throwe
He reyneth and the watergates
Undoth ; 'and thus my wif algates,   690
Which is with reson wel besein,
Hath mad me bothe wynd and rein
After the Sesoun of the yer.'
And thanne he sette him nerr the fer,

663 axex F   679 bad] bad him AM, H₃

And as he mihte hise clothes dreide,
That he nomore o word ne seide ;
Wherof he gat him somdel reste,
For that him thoghte was the beste.
   I not if thilke ensample yit   Confessor.
Acordeth with a mannes wit,   700
To soffre as Socrates tho dede :   P. i. 303
And if it falle in eny stede
A man to lese so his galle,
Him oghte among the wommen alle
In loves Court be juggement
The name bere of Pacient,
To yive ensample to the goode
Of pacience how that it stode,
That othre men it mihte knowe.
And, Sone, if thou at eny throwe   710
Be tempted ayein Pacience,
Tak hiede upon this evidence ;
It schal per cas the lasse grieve.
   Mi fader, so as I believe,   Amans.
Of that schal be no maner nede,
For I wol take so good hiede,
That er I falle in such assai,
I thenke eschuie it, if I mai.
Bot if ther be oght elles more
Wherof I mihte take lore,   720
I preie you, so as I dar,
Now telleth, that I mai be war,
Som other tale in this matiere.
   Sone, it is evere good to lere,   Confessor.
Wherof thou miht thi word restreigne,
Er that thou falle in eny peine.
For who that can no conseil hyde,
He mai noght faile of wo beside,
Which schal befalle er he it wite,
As I finde in the bokes write.   730

   Yit cam ther nevere good of strif,   P. i. 304
To seche in all a mannes lif :

704 Him] He H₁... B₂   732 teche XERCB₂

[JUPITER, JUNO AND TIRESIAS.]

Hic ponit Confessor exemplum, quod de alterius lite intromittere cauendum est. Et narrat qualiter Iupiter cum Iunone super quadam questione litigabat, videlicet vtrum vir an mulier in amoris concupiscencia feruencius ardebat; super quo Tiresiam eorum iudicem constituebant. Et quia ille contra Iunonem in dicte litis causa sentenciam diffiniuit, irata dea ipsum amborum oculorum lumine claritatis absque remissione priuauit.

Thogh it beginne on pure game,
Fulofte it torneth into grame
And doth grevance upon som side.
Wherof the grete Clerk Ovide
After the lawe which was tho
Of Jupiter and of Juno
Makth in his bokes mencioun
How thei felle at dissencioun   740
In manere as it were a borde,
As thei begunne forto worde
Among hemself in privete :
And that was upon this degree,
Which of the tuo more amorous is,
Or man or wif. And upon this
Thei mihten noght acorde in on,
And toke a jugge therupon,
Which cleped is Tiresias,
And bede him demen in the cas ;   750
And he withoute avisement
Ayein Juno yaf juggement.
This goddesse upon his ansuere
Was wroth and wolde noght forbere,
Bot tok awey for everemo
The liht fro bothe hise yhen tuo.
Whan Jupiter this harm hath sein,
An other bienfait therayein
He yaf, and such a grace him doth,
That for he wiste he seide soth,   760
A Sothseiere he was for evere :   **P. i. 305**
Bot yit that other were levere,
Have had the lokinge of his yhe,
Than of his word the prophecie ;
Bot how so that the sothe wente,
Strif was the cause of that he hente
So gret a peine bodily.

Confessor.
    Mi Sone, be thou war ther by,

733 on] in H₁XE . . . B₂, AdΔ, W   of G, B   741 aborde A, FK
743 *margin* constituebat H₁ . . . B₂   750 the cas] þis cas BΛ, W
756 hise] her B   762 were him leuere H₁ . . . B₂   hadde leuer W
765 Bot] Lo H₁ . . . B₂

And hold thi tunge stille clos:
For who that hath his word desclos   770
Er that he wite what he mene,
He is fulofte nyh his tene
And lest ful many time grace,
Wher that he wolde his thonk pourchace.
And over this, my Sone diere,
Of othre men, if thou miht hiere
In privete what thei have wroght,
Hold conseil and descoevere it noght,
For Cheste can no conseil hele,
Or be it wo or be it wele: 780
And tak a tale into thi mynde,
The which of olde ensample I finde.

    Phebus, which makth the daies lihte,   [PHEBUS AND
A love he hadde, which tho hihte·   CORNIDE.]
Cornide, whom aboven alle   Quia litigantes ora
He pleseth: bot what schal befalle   sua cohibere nequiunt,
Of love ther is noman knoweth,   hic ponit Confessor
                                             exemplum contra illos
Bot as fortune hire happes throweth.   qui in amoris causa
So it befell upon a chaunce,   alterius consilium re-
A yong kniht tok hire aqueintance   790   uelare presumunt. Et
And hadde of hire al that he wolde: **P. i. 306** narrat qualiter que-
                                             dam auis tunc albis-
Bot a fals bridd, which sche hath holde   sima nomine coruus
And kept in chambre of pure yowthe,   consilium domine sue
Discoevereth all that evere he cowthe.   Cornide Phebo denu-
                                             dauit; vnde contigit non
This briddes name was as tho   solum ipsam Cornidem
Corvus, the which was thanne also   interfici, set et coruum,
Welmore whyt than eny Swan,   qui antea tanquam nix
And he that schrewe al that he can   albus fuit, in piceum
                                             colorem pro perpetuo
Of his ladi to Phebus seide;   transmutari.
And he for wraththe his swerd outbreide,   800
With which Cornide anon he slowh.
Bot after him was wo ynowh,
And tok a full gret repentance,
Wherof in tokne and remembrance

773 many a time CL, B, W   778 it *om.* AJM, KH₃   hem Δ
784 *margin* Quia] Qualiter H₁ . . . B₂   788 happe (hap) H₁ . . .
CB₂, W   happeþ L   795 *margin* fuerit H₁XRCLB₂   fuerat GE
798 that] þe H₁ . . . B₂, B

Of hem whiche usen wicke speche,
Upon this bridd he tok this wreche,
That ther he was snow whyt tofore,
Evere afterward colblak therfore
He was transformed, as it scheweth,
And many a man yit him beschreweth,   810
And clepen him into this day
A Raven, be whom yit men mai
Take evidence, whan he crieth,
That som mishapp it signefieth.
Be war therfore and sei the beste,
If thou wolt be thiself in reste,
Mi goode Sone, as I the rede.

For in an other place I rede
Of thilke Nimphe which Laar hihte:
For sche the privete be nyhte,   820
How Jupiter lay be Jutorne,   **P. i. 307**
Hath told, god made hire overtorne:
Hire tunge he kutte, and into helle
For evere he sende hir forto duelle,
As sche that was noght worthi hiere
To ben of love a Chamberere,
For sche no conseil cowthe hele.
And suche adaies be now fele
In loves Court, as it is seid,
That lete here tunges gon unteid.   830

Mi Sone, be thou non of tho,
To jangle and telle tales so,
And namely that thou ne chyde,
For Cheste can no conseil hide,
For Wraththe seide nevere wel.

Mi fader, soth is everydel
That ye me teche, and I wol holde
The reule to which I am holde,
To fle the Cheste, as ye me bidde,
For wel is him that nevere chidde.   840

Now tell me forth if ther be more
As touchende unto Wraththes lore.

[iii. HATE.]

iii.   *Demonis est odium quasi Scriba, cui dabit Ira*
    Materiam scripti cordis ad antra sui.
    Non laxabit amor odii quem frena restringunt,
    Nec secreta sui iuris adire sinit.

Of Wraththe yit ther is an other,
Which is to Cheste his oghne brother,
And is be name cleped Hate,
That soffreth noght withinne his gate
That ther come owther love or pes,   **P. i. 308**
For he wol make no reles
Of no debat which is befalle.

   Now spek, if thou art on of alle,   850
That with this vice hast ben withholde.

   As yit for oght that ye me tolde,
Mi fader, I not what it is.

   In good feith, Sone, I trowe yis.

   Mi fader, nay, bot ye me lere.

   Now lest, my Sone, and thou schalt here.
Hate is a wraththe noght schewende,
Bot of long time gaderende,
And duelleth in the herte loken,
Til he se time to be wroken ;   860
And thanne he scheweth his tempeste
Mor sodein than the wilde beste,
Which wot nothing what merci is.
Mi Sone, art thou knowende of this ?

   My goode fader, as I wene,
Now wot I somdel what ye mene ;
Bot I dar saufly make an oth,
Mi ladi was me nevere loth.
I wol noght swere natheles
That I of hate am gulteles ;   870
For whanne I to my ladi plie
Fro dai to dai and merci crie,
And sche no merci on me leith
Bot schorte wordes to me seith,
Thogh I my ladi love algate,

Hic tractat Confessor de tercia specie Ire, que Odium dicitur, cuius natura omnes Ire inimicicias ad mentem reducens, illas vsque ad tempus vindicte velut Scriba demonis in cordis papiro commemorandas inserit.

Confessio Amantis.

848 *margin* velud B, F   858 gadarende F   868 me] mo AM

Tho wordes moste I nedes hate;
And wolde thei were al despent,   **P. i. 309**
Or so ferr oute of londe went
That I nevere after scholde hem hiere;
And yit love I my ladi diere.   880
Thus is ther Hate, as ye mai se,
Betwen my ladi word and me;
The word I hate and hire I love,
What so me schal betide of love.

Bot forthere mor I wol me schryve,
That I have hated al my lyve
These janglers, whiche of here Envie
Ben evere redi forto lie;
For with here fals compassement
Fuloften thei have mad me schent   890
And hindred me fulofte time,
Whan thei no cause wisten bime,
Bot onliche of here oghne thoght:
And thus fuloften have I boght
The lie, and drank noght of the wyn.
I wolde here happ were such as myn:
For how so that I be now schrive,
To hem ne mai I noght foryive,
Til that I se hem at debat
With love, and thanne myn astat   900
Thei mihten be here oghne deme,
And loke how wel it scholde hem qweme
To hindre a man that loveth sore.
And thus I hate hem everemore,
Til love on hem wol don his wreche:
For that schal I alway beseche
Unto the mihti Cupido,   **P. i. 310**
That he so mochel wolde do,
So as he is of love a godd,
To smyte hem with the same rodd   910
With which I am of love smite;
So that thei mihten knowe and wite
How hindringe is a wofull peine

900 thanne] þan wiþ H₁XGECLB₂, B þan in R   901 hire F
906 I schal AM, KH₃Magd

[HATE.]

To him that love wolde atteigne.
Thus evere on hem I wayte and hope,
Til I mai sen hem lepe a lope,
And halten on the same Sor
Which I do now: for overmor
I wolde thanne do my myht
So forto stonden in here lyht,   920
That thei ne scholden finde a weie
To that thei wolde, bot aweie
I wolde hem putte out of the stede
Fro love, riht as thei me dede
With that thei speke of me be mowthe.
So wolde I do, if that I cowthe,
Of hem, and this, so god me save,
Is al the hate that I have,
Toward these janglers everydiel;
I wolde alle othre ferde wel.   930
Thus have I, fader, said mi wille;
Say ye now forth, for I am stille.

　　Mi Sone, of that thou hast me said   Confessor.
I holde me noght fulli paid:
That thou wolt haten eny man,
To that acorden I ne can,
Thogh he have hindred thee tofore.   **P. i. 311**
Bot this I telle thee therfore,
Thou miht upon my beneicoun
Wel haten the condicioun   940
Of tho janglers, as thou me toldest,
Bot furthermor, of that thou woldest
Hem hindre in eny other wise,
Such Hate is evere to despise.
Forthi, mi Sone, I wol thee rede,
That thou drawe in be frendlihede
That thou ne miht noght do be hate;
So miht thou gete love algate
And sette thee, my Sone, in reste,
For thou schalt finde it for the beste.   950

918 ouermor F   eueremore (euer mor etc.) A . . . B₂, AdBTᴅ,
WKH₃   921 finde] haue AM, KH₃Magd   be put L   941 tho] ᴊe
H₁ . . . B₂, AdB, W

And over this, so as I dar,
I rede that thou be riht war
Of othre mennes hate aboute,
Which every wysman scholde doute:
For Hate is evere upon await,
And as the fisshere on his bait
Sleth, whan he seth the fisshes faste,
So, whan he seth time ate laste,
That he mai worche an other wo,
Schal noman tornen him therfro,　　　　　960
That Hate nyle his felonie
Fulfille and feigne compaignie
Yit natheles, for fals Semblant
Is toward him of covenant
Withholde, so that under bothe
The prive wraththe can him clothe,
That he schal seme of gret believe.　　**P. i. 312**
Bot war thee wel that thou ne lieve
Al that thou sest tofore thin yhe,
So as the Gregois whilom syhe:　　　　　970
The bok of Troie who so rede,
Ther mai he finde ensample in dede.

[KING NAMPLUS AND
THE GREEKS.]

Hic ponit Confessor
exemplum contra illos
qui, cum Ire sue odium
aperte vindicare non
possint, ficta dissimi-
lacione vindictam sub-
dole assequuntur. Et
narrat quod cum Pala-
mades princeps Gre-
corum in obsidione
Troie a quibusdam suis
emulis proditorie in-
terfectus fuisset, pa-
terque suus Rex Nam-
plus in patria sua tunc
existens huiusmodi
euentus certitudinem

Sone after the destruccioun,
Whan Troie was al bete doun
And slain was Priamus the king,
The Gregois, whiche of al this thing
Ben cause, tornen hom ayein.
Ther mai noman his happ withsein;
It hath be sen and felt fulofte,
The harde time after the softe:　　　980
Be See as thei forth homward wente,
A rage of gret tempeste hem hente;
Juno let bende hire parti bowe,
The Sky wax derk, the wynd gan blowe,
The firy welkne gan to thondre,
As thogh the world scholde al to sondre;

970 þe whilom H₁XGCL　　　973 destruccioun AJ, B destruccion
F　　979 *margin* assequentur A　　　982 *margin* proditorum
H₁XRCLB₂　　983 *margin* patroque X . . . B₂　　　pater Δ

Fro hevene out of the watergates
The reyni Storm fell doun algates
And al here takel made unwelde,
That noman mihte himself bewelde.
Ther mai men hiere Schipmen crie,
That stode in aunter forto die :
He that behinde sat to stiere
Mai noght the forestempne hiere ;
The Schip aros ayein the wawes,
The lodesman hath lost his lawes,
The See bet in on every side :
Thei nysten what fortune abide,
Bot sette hem al in goddes wille,
Wher he hem wolde save or spille.

And it fell thilke time thus :
Ther was a king, the which Namplus
Was hote, and he a Sone hadde,
At Troie which the Gregois ladde,
As he that was mad Prince of alle,
Til that fortune let him falle :
His name was Palamades.
Bot thurgh an hate natheles
Of some of hem his deth was cast
And he be tresoun overcast.
His fader, whan he herde it telle,
He swor, if evere his time felle,
He wolde him venge, if that he mihte,
And therto his avou behihte :
And thus this king thurgh prive hate
Abod upon await algate,
For he was noght of such emprise
To vengen him in open wise.
The fame, which goth wyde where,
Makth knowe how that the Gregois were
Homward with al the felaschipe
Fro Troie upon the See be Schipe.
Namplus, whan he this understod,
And knew the tydes of the flod,

⌊KING NAMPLUS AND
    THE GREEKS.⌋

sciuisset, Grecos in sui
cordis odium super om-
990 nia recollegit. Vnde
contigit quod, cum
Greci deuicta Troia
per altum mare versus
Greciam nauigio re-
meantes obscurissimo
noctis tempore nimia
ventorum tempestate
iactabantur, Rex Nam-
plus in terra sua con-
P. i. 313   tra litus maris, vbi ma-
iora saxorum emine-
bant pericula, super
cacumina montium
grandissimos noctan-
1000 ter fecit ignes : quos
Greci aspicientes sal-
uum portum ibidem
inuenire certissime
putabant, et terram ap-
proximantes diruptis
nauibus magna pars
Grecorum periclitaba-
tur. Et sic, quod Nam-
plus viribus nequiit,
odio latitante per dis-
similacionis fraudem
vindicauit.

1010

1020

1000 wolde hem AM, Δ, WH₃   1005 *margin* Et sic quoq*ue* H₁ . . . B₂
1007 *margin* latitantem B   1014 behihte] he hight(e) GCL, W

And sih the wynd blew to the lond,
A gret deceipte anon he fond
Of prive hate, as thou schalt hiere,   P. i. 314
Wherof I telle al this matiere.
This king the weder gan beholde,
And wiste wel thei moten holde   1030
Here cours endlong his marche riht,
And made upon the derke nyht
Of grete Schydes and of blockes
Gret fyr ayein the grete rockes,
To schewe upon the helles hihe,
So that the Flete of Grece it sihe.
And so it fell riht as he thoghte:
This Flete, which an havene soghte,
The bryghte fyres sih a ferr,
And thei hem drowen nerr and nerr,   1040
And wende wel and understode
How al that fyr was mad for goode,
To schewe wher men scholde aryve,
And thiderward thei hasten blyve.
In Semblant, as men sein, is guile,
And that was proved thilke while;
The Schip, which wende his helpe acroche,
Drof al to pieces on the roche,
And so ther deden ten or twelve;
Ther mihte noman helpe himselve,   1050
For ther thei wenden deth ascape,
Withouten help here deth was schape.
Thus thei that comen ferst tofore
Upon the Rockes be forlore,
Bot thurgh the noise and thurgh the cri
These othre were al war therby;
And whan the dai began to rowe,   P. i. 315
Tho mihten thei the sothe knowe,
That wher they wenden frendes finde,
Thei founden frenschipe al behinde.   1060
The lond was thanne sone weyved,

1028 this] my B   1029 The king B   1031 Here] His
AM, H₃   Hir(e) J, T   1044 afterward B   1047 This schip
H₁ ... B₂, B   1060 frenschipe A, F   frenschip J   frendschip B

Wher that thei hadden be deceived,
Therto thei seiden alle yee,
Fro that dai forth and war thei were
Of that thei hadde assaied there.

   Mi Sone, hierof thou miht avise   Confessor.
How fraude stant in many wise
Amonges hem that guile thenke ;
Ther is no Scrivein with his enke   1070
Which half the fraude wryte can
That stant in such a maner man :
Forthi the wise men ne demen
The thinges after that thei semen,
Bot after that thei knowe and finde.
The Mirour scheweth- in his kinde
As he hadde al the world withinne,
And is in soth nothing therinne ;
And so farth Hate for a throwe :
Til he a man hath overthrowe,   1080
Schal noman knowe be his chere
Which is avant, ne which arere.
Forthi, mi Sone, thenke on this.

   Mi fader, so I wole ywiss ;   Amans.
And if ther more of Wraththe be,
Now axeth forth per charite,
As ye be youre bokes knowe,   **P. i. 316**
And I the sothe schal beknowe.

iv. *Qui cohibere manum nequit, et sit spiritus eius*
Sepius in luctum Venus et sua gaudia transfert,
   Cumque suis thalamis talis amicus adest.
Est amor amplexu non ictibus alliciendus,
   Frangit amicicias impetuosa manus.

    Mi Sone, thou schalt understonde
That yit towardes Wraththe stonde   1090
Of dedly vices othre tuo :

1065 dai] tyme H₁ ... B₂, B   war] what X ... B₂, B   what
that H₁
Latin Verses iv. 1 sit] sic H₁ ... B₂, B, WH₃

[CONTEK AND HOMI-
CIDE.]

Hic tractat Confes-
sor super quarta et
quinta specie Ire, que
impetuositas et homi-
cidium dicuntur. Set
primo de impetuosi-
tate specialius tractare
intendit, cuius natura
spiritum in naribus
gestando ad omnes Ire
mociones in vindictam
parata pacienciam nul-
latenus obseruat.

And forto telle here names so,
It is Contek and Homicide,
That ben to drede on every side.
Contek, so as the bokes sein,
Folhast hath to his Chamberlein,
Be whos conseil al unavised
Is Pacience most despised,
Til Homicide with hem meete.
Fro merci thei ben al unmeete,   1100
And thus ben thei the worste of alle
Of hem whiche unto wraththe falle,
In dede bothe and ek in thoght :
For thei acompte here wraththe at noght,
Bot if ther be schedinge of blod ;
And thus lich to a beste wod
Thei knowe noght the god of lif.
Be so thei have or swerd or knif
Here dedly wraththe forto wreke,
Of Pite list hem noght to speke ;   1110
Non other reson thei ne fonge,
Bot that thei ben of mihtes stronge.
Bot war hem wel in other place,   **P. i. 317**
Where every man behoveth grace,
Bot ther I trowe it schal hem faile,
To whom no merci mihte availe,
Bot wroghten upon tiraundie,
That no pite ne mihte hem plie.

Opponit Confessor.

Now tell, my Sone.

                  Fader, what ?
If thou hast be coupable of that.   1120

Confessio Amantis.

    Mi fader, nay, Crist me forbiede :
I speke onliche as of the dede,
Of which I nevere was coupable
Withoute cause resonable.
    Bot this is noght to mi matiere
Of schrifte, why we sitten hiere ;

1094 to drede] togidre B   to geder H₁   1108 thei] þe F
1112 Bot that] But (Bot) at H₁XCLB₂   1113 S *resumes*   1118
ne *om.* MH₁L, Δ, WH₃   1119 my] me EL, W me my H₁
1122 as of] as for M, Ad   of L   1123 was neuer(e) H₁, Ad, WH₃

For we ben sett to schryve of love,
As we begunne ferst above :
And natheles I am beknowe
That as touchende of loves throwe,   1130
Whan I my wittes overwende,
Min hertes contek hath non ende,
Bot evere it stant upon debat
To gret desese of myn astat
As for the time that it lasteth.
For whan mi fortune overcasteth
Hire whiel and is to me so strange,
And that I se sche wol noght change,
Than caste I al the world aboute,
And thenke hou I at home and oute   1140
Have al my time in vein despended,
And se noght how to ben amended,
Bot rathere forto be empeired,   **P. i. 318**
As he that is welnyh despeired :
For I ne mai no thonk deserve,
And evere I love and evere I serve,
And evere I am aliche nerr.
Thus, for I stonde in such a wer,
I am, as who seith, out of herre ;
And thus upon miself the werre   1150
I bringe, and putte out alle pes,
That I fulofte in such a res
Am wery of myn oghne lif.
So that of Contek and of strif
I am beknowe and have ansuerd,
As ye, my fader, now have herd.
Min herte is wonderly begon
With conseil, wherof witt is on,
Which hath resoun in compaignie ;
Ayein the whiche stant partie   1160
Will, which hath hope of his acord,
And thus thei bringen up descord.
Witt and resoun conseilen ofte
That I myn herte scholde softe,
And that I scholde will remue

1145 þong J, F   þing BΛ, W   1164 I *om.* H₁XRCLB₂, H₃
**   S

[CONTEK WITHIN THE
HEART.]

And put him out of retenue,
Or elles holde him under fote:
For as thei sein, if that he mote
His oghne rewle have upon honde,
Ther schal no witt ben understonde.   1170
Of hope also thei tellen this,
That overal, wher that he is,
He set the herte in jeupartie   **P. i. 319**
With wihssinge and with fantasie,
And is noght trewe of that he seith,
So that in him ther is no feith:
Thus with reson and wit avised
Is will and hope aldai despised.
Reson seith that I scholde leve
To love, wher ther is no leve   1180
To spede, and will seith therayein
That such an herte is to vilein,
Which dar noght love and til he spede,
Let hope serve at such a nede:
He seith ek, where an herte sit
Al hol governed upon wit,
He hath this lyves lust forlore.
And thus myn herte is al totore
Of such a Contek as thei make:
Bot yit I mai noght will forsake,   1190
That he nys Maister of my thoght,
Or that I spede, or spede noght.

Confessor.   Thou dost, my Sone, ayein the riht;
Bot love is of so gret a miht,
His lawe mai noman refuse,
So miht thou thee the betre excuse.
And natheles thou schalt be lerned
That will scholde evere be governed
Of reson more than of kinde,
Wherof a tale write I finde.   1200
    A Philosophre of which men tolde

1166 put AJ, F   putte C, B   1171 thei tellen] to telle B   1173
jeupartie] champartie H₁ ... B₂   1174 wihssinge AJ, F   wissching
(wisshing) C, B   1179 I] it AM   1187 this] his H₁ ... B₂, WH₃
1190 will] wel H₁ ... B₂, WH₃   1198 evere *om.* H₁ ... B₂, H₃

Ther was whilom be daies olde,
And Diogenes thanne he hihte.   P. i. 320
So old he was that he ne mihte
The world travaile, and for the beste
He schop him forto take his reste,
And duelte at hom in such a wise,
That nyh his hous he let devise
Endlong upon an Axeltre
To sette a tonne in such degre,   1210
That he it mihte torne aboute ;
Wherof on hed was taken oute,
For he therinne sitte scholde
And torne himself so as he wolde,
To take their and se the hevene
And deme of the planetes sevene,
As he which cowthe mochel what.
And thus fulofte there he sat
To muse in his philosophie
Solein withoute compaignie :   1220
So that upon a morwetyde,
As thing which scholde so betyde,
Whan he was set ther as him liste
To loke upon the Sonne ariste,
Wherof the propretes he sih,
It fell ther cam ridende nyh
King Alisandre with a route ;
And as he caste his yhe aboute,
He sih this Tonne, and what it mente
He wolde wite, and thider sente   1230
A knyht, be whom he mihte it knowe,
And he himself that ilke throwe
Abod, and hoveth there stille.   P. i. 321
This kniht after the kinges wille
With spore made his hors to gon
And to the tonne he cam anon,
Wher that he fond a man of Age,
And he him tolde the message,
Such as the king him hadde bede,

[TALE OF DIOGENES
AND ALEXANDER.]

Hic ponit Confessor
exemplum, quod ho-
minis impetuosa vo-
luntas sit discrecionis
moderamine guber-
nanda. Et narrat qua-
liter Diogenes, qui
motus animi sui ra-
cioni subiugarat, Re-
gem Alexandrum su-
per isto facto sibi op-
ponentem plenius in-
formauit.

[TALE OF DIOGENES
AND ALEXANDER.]

And axeth why in thilke stede　　　　1240
The Tonne stod, and what it was.
And he, which understod the cas,
Sat stille and spak no word ayein.
The kniht bad speke and seith, 'Vilein,
Thou schalt me telle, er that I go;
It is thi king which axeth so.'
'Mi king,' quod he, 'that were unriht.'
'What is he thanne?' seith the kniht,
'Is he thi man?' 'That seie I noght,'
Quod he, 'bot this I am bethoght,　　　1250
Mi mannes man hou that he is.'
'Thou lyest, false cherl, ywiss,'
The kniht him seith, and was riht wroth,
And to the king ayein he goth
And tolde him how this man ansuerde.
The king, whan he this tale herde,
Bad that thei scholden alle abyde,
For he himself wol thider ryde.
And whan he cam tofore the tonne,
He hath his tale thus begonne:　　　1260
'Alheil,' he seith, 'what man art thou?'
Quod he, 'Such on as thou sest now.'
The king, which hadde wordes wise,　　**P. i. 322**
His age wolde noght despise,
Bot seith, 'Mi fader, I thee preie
That thou me wolt the cause seie,
How that I am thi mannes man.'
'Sire king,' quod he, 'and that I can,
If that thou wolt.' 'Yis,' seith the king.
Quod he, 'This is the sothe thing:　　　1270
Sith I ferst resoun understod,
And knew what thing was evel and good,
The will which of my bodi moeveth,
Whos werkes that the god reproeveth,
I have restreigned everemore,
As him which stant under the lore
Of reson, whos soubgit he is,

1241 he was SAdBTΔ　　　1253 king B　　　1258 wold(e)
M . . . CB2, AdTΔ, WH2　　　1276 As] Of B　And W

[TALE OF DIOGENES
AND ALEXANDER.]

So that he mai noght don amis :
And thus be weie of covenant
Will is my man and my servant,   1280
And evere hath ben and evere schal.
And thi will is thi principal,
And hath the lordschipe of thi witt,
So that thou cowthest nevere yit
Take o dai reste of thi labour ;
Bot forto ben a conquerour
Of worldes good, which mai noght laste,
Thou hiest evere aliche faste,
Wher thou no reson hast to winne :
And thus thi will is cause of Sinne,   1290
And is thi lord, to whom thou servest,
Wherof thou litel thonk deservest.'
The king of that he thus answerde   **P. i. 323**
Was nothing wroth, bot whanne he herde
The hihe wisdom which he seide,
With goodly wordes this he preide,
That he him wolde telle his name.
'I am,' quod he, 'that ilke same,
The which men Diogenes calle.'
Tho was the king riht glad withalle,   1300
For he hadde often herd tofore
What man he was, so that therfore
He seide, 'O wise Diogene,
Now schal thi grete witt be sene ;
For thou schalt of my yifte have
What worldes thing that thou wolt crave.'
Quod he, 'Thanne hove out of mi Sonne,
And let it schyne into mi Tonne ;
For thou benymst me thilke yifte,
Which lith noght in thi miht to schifte :   1310
Non other good of thee me nedeth.'
    This king, whom every contre dredeth,
Lo, thus he was enformed there :
Wherof, my Sone, thou miht lere
How that thi will schal noght be lieved,

1295 wisdom] wordes H₁ . . . B₂, H₃   1296 gostly B   1307 mi]
ʃe A   1312 This] The B

Where it is noght of wit relieved.
And thou hast seid thiself er this
How that thi will thi maister is;
Thurgh which thin hertes thoght withinne
Is evere of Contek to beginne,   1320
So that it is gretli to drede
That it non homicide brede.
For love is of a wonder kinde,   **P. i. 324**
And hath hise wittes ofte blinde,
That thei fro mannes reson falle;
Bot whan that it is so befalle
That will schal the corage lede,
In loves cause it is to drede:
Wherof I finde ensample write,
Which is behovely forto wite.   1330

I rede a tale, and telleth this:
The Cite which Semiramis
Enclosed hath with wall aboute,
Of worthi folk with many a route
Was enhabited here and there;
Among the whiche tuo ther were
Above alle othre noble and grete,
Dwellende tho withinne a Strete
So nyh togedre, as it was sene,
That ther was nothing hem betwene,   1340
Bot wow to wow and wall to wall.
This o lord hadde in special
A Sone, a lusti Bacheler,
In al the toun was non his pier:
That other hadde a dowhter eke,
In al the lond that forto seke
Men wisten non so faire as sche.
And fell so, as it scholde be,
This faire dowhter nyh this Sone
As thei togedre thanne wone,   1350
Cupide hath so the thinges schape,
That thei ne mihte his hand ascape,

1318 How þer(e) H₁G ... B₂, H₃   1330 forto] þat þou SAdBTΔ
1331 this] þus H₁E ... B₂, H₃   1332 Semiranus E ... B₂, H₃   1336
margin ipsos H₁ ... B₂, H₃, *om.* Δ

That he his fyr on hem ne caste :   P. i. 325
Wherof her herte he overcaste
To folwe thilke lore and suie
Which nevere man yit miht eschuie ;
And that was love, as it is happed,
Which hath here hertes so betrapped,
That thei be alle weies seche ·
How that thei mihten winne a speche,   1360
Here wofull peine forto lisse.

   Who loveth wel, it mai noght misse,
And namely whan ther be tuo
Of on acord, how so it go,
Bot if that thei som weie finde ;
For love is evere of such a kinde
And hath his folk so wel affaited,
That howso that it be awaited,
Ther mai noman the pourpos lette :
And thus betwen hem tuo thei sette   1370
An hole upon a wall to make,
Thurgh which thei have her conseil take
At alle times, whan thei myhte.
This faire Maiden Tisbee hihte,
And he whom that sche loveth hote
Was Piramus be name hote.
So longe here lecoun thei recorden,
Til ate laste thei acorden
Be nihtes time forto wende
Al one out fro the tounes ende,   1380
Wher was a welle under a Tree ;
And who cam ferst, or sche or he,
He scholde stille there abide.   **P. i. 326**
So it befell the nyhtes tide
This maiden, which desguised was,
Al prively the softe pas
Goth thurgh the large toun unknowe,
Til that sche cam withinne a throwe
Wher that sche liketh forto duelle,
At thilke unhappi freisshe welle,   1390
Which was also the Forest nyh.

1358 so *om.* AM   1384 the] by (be) H₁ ... B₂, H₃ a W

Wher sche comende a Leoun syh
Into the feld to take his preie,
In haste and sche tho fledde aweie,
So as fortune scholde falle,
For feere and let hire wympel falle
Nyh to the welle upon therbage.
This Leoun in his wilde rage
A beste, which that he fond oute,
Hath slain, and with his blodi snoute,   1400
Whan he hath eten what he wolde,
To drynke of thilke stremes colde
Cam to the welle, where he fond
The wympel, which out of hire hond
Was falle, and he it hath todrawe,
Bebled aboute and al forgnawe;
And thanne he strawhte him forto drinke
Upon the freisshe welles brinke,
And after that out of the plein
He torneth to the wode ayein.   1410
And Tisbee dorste noght remue,
Bot as a bridd which were in Mue
Withinne a buissh sche kepte hire clos **P. i. 327**
So stille that sche noght aros;
Unto hirself and pleigneth ay.
    And fell, whil that sche there lay,
This Piramus cam after sone
Unto the welle, and be the Mone
He fond hire wimpel blodi there.
Cam nevere yit to mannes Ere   1420
Tidinge, ne to mannes sihte
Merveile, which so sore aflihte
A mannes herte, as it tho dede
To him, which in the same stede
With many a wofull compleignynge
Began his handes forto wringe,
As he which demeth sikerly
That sche be ded: and sodeinly

1394 fleigh (fleih &c.) H₁G ... B₂, H₃ flew X   1406 al fordrawe
(al for drawe) H₁XRCB₂, H₃   alto gnawe L   1422 afrighte
(afriht &c.) H₁G ... B₂, H₃

His swerd al nakid out he breide
In his folhaste, and thus he seide :   1430
' I am cause of this felonie,
So it is resoun that I die,
As sche is ded be cause of me.'
And with that word upon his kne
He fell, and to the goddes alle
Up to the hevene he gan to calle,
And preide, sithen it was so
That he may noght his love as tho
Have in this world, that of her grace
He miht hire have in other place,   1440
For hiere wolde he noght abide,
He seith : bot as it schal betide,
The Pomel of his swerd to grounde   **P. i. 328**
He sette, and thurgh his herte a wounde
He made up to the bare hilte :
And in this wise himself he spilte
With his folhaste and deth he nam ;
For sche withinne a while cam,
Wher he lai ded upon his knif.
So wofull yit was nevere lif   1450
As Tisbee was, whan sche him sih :
Sche mihte noght o word on hih
Speke oute, for hire herte schette,
That of hir lif no pris sche sette,
Bot ded swounende doun sche fell.
Til after, whanne it so befell
That sche out of hire traunce awok,
With many a wofull pitous lok
Hire yhe alwei among sche caste
Upon hir love, and ate laste   1460
Sche cawhte breth and seide thus :
' O thou which cleped art Venus,
Goddesse of love, and thou, Cupide,
Which loves cause hast forto guide,
I wot now wel that ye be blinde,

1430 fulhast (fulle haste &c.) AMH₁XCLB₂, Ad, W   foule haste Δ
1433 As] And H₁ ... B₂, H₃   1440 miht (might) J, B, F   mihte A   1448
fforþ sche X ... B₂, Δ, WH₃   And sche T   1462 art cleped L, AdBTΔ

[PYRAMUS AND
THISBE.]

Of thilke unhapp which I now finde
Only betwen my love and me.
This Piramus, which hiere I se
Bledende, what hath he deserved?
For he youre heste hath kept and served,   1470
And was yong and I bothe also:
Helas, why do ye with ous so?
Ye sette oure herte bothe afyre,   P. i. 329
And maden ous such thing desire
Wherof that we no skile cowthe;
Bot thus oure freisshe lusti yowthe
Withoute joie is al despended,
Which thing mai nevere ben amended:
For as of me this wol I seie,
That me is levere forto deie   1480
Than live after this sorghful day.'
And with this word, where as he lay,
Hire love in armes sche embraseth,
Hire oghne deth and so pourchaseth
That now sche wepte and nou sche kiste,
Til ate laste, er sche it wiste,
So gret a sorwe is to hire falle,
Which overgoth hire wittes alle.
As sche which mihte it noght asterte,
The swerdes point ayein hire herte   1490
Sche sette, and fell doun therupon,
Wherof that sche was ded anon:
And thus bothe on o swerd bledende
Thei weren founde ded liggende.

Confessor.

Now thou, mi Sone, hast herd this tale,
Bewar that of thin oghne bale
Thou be noght cause in thi folhaste,
And kep that thou thi witt ne waste
Upon thi thoght in aventure,
Wherof thi lyves forfeture   1500
Mai falle: and if thou have so thoght
Er this, tell on and hyde it noght.

1473 hertes H₁ ... B₂,SAdBTΔ, WH₃   1479 as for me H₁ ... B₂,
H₃   1487 gret EC, SB   grete AJ, F   1489 And sche H₁ ... B₂, H₃
1496 that of] of þat H₁XE ... B₂

Mi fader, upon loves side
Mi conscience I woll noght hyde,
How that for love of pure wo
I have ben ofte moeved so,
That with my wisshes if I myhte,
A thousand times, I yow plyhte,
I hadde storven in a day ;
And therof I me schryve may,
Though love fully me ne slowh,
Mi will to deie was ynowh,
So am I of my will coupable :
And yit is sche noght merciable,
Which mai me yive lif and hele.
Bot that hir list noght with me dele,
I wot be whos conseil it is,
And him wolde I long time er this,
And yit I wolde and evere schal,
Slen and destruie in special.
The gold of nyne kinges londes
Ne scholde him save fro myn hondes,
In my pouer if that he were ;
Bot yit him stant of me no fere
For noght that evere I can manace.
He is the hindrere of mi grace,
Til he be ded I mai noght spede ;
So mot I nedes taken hiede
And schape how that he were aweie,
If I therto mai finde a weie.
    Mi Sone, tell me now forthi,
Which is that mortiel enemy
That thou manacest to be ded.
    Mi fader, it is such a qwed,
That wher I come, he is tofore,
And doth so, that mi cause is lore.
    What is his name ?
                    It is Daunger,
Which is mi ladi consailer :
For I was nevere yit so slyh,
To come in eny place nyh

P. i. 330 [The Lover's Confession. Danger.]

Confessio Amantis.

1510

1520

1530

Confessor.

P. i. 331

Confessio Amantis.

1540

1503 loue F   1512 was] is BT

Wher as sche was be nyht or day,
That Danger ne was redy ay,
With whom for speche ne for mede
Yit mihte I nevere of love spede;
For evere this I finde soth,
Al that my ladi seith or doth
To me, Daunger schal make an ende,
And that makth al mi world miswende:
And evere I axe his help, bot he
Mai wel be cleped sanz pite;   1550
For ay the more I to him bowe,
The lasse he wol my tale alowe.
He hath mi ladi so englued,
Sche wol noght that he be remued;
For evere he hangeth on hire Seil,
And is so prive of conseil,
That evere whanne I have oght bede,
I finde Danger in hire stede
And myn ansuere of him I have;
Bot for no merci that I crave,   1560
Of merci nevere a point I hadde.
I finde his ansuere ay so badde,
That werse mihte it nevere be: **P. i. 332**
And thus betwen Danger and me
Is evere werre til he dye.
Bot mihte I ben of such maistrie,
That I Danger hadde overcome,
With that were al my joie come.
Thus wolde I wonde for no Sinne,
Ne yit for al this world to winne;   1570
If that I mihte finde a sleyhte,
To leie al myn astat in weyhte,
I wolde him fro the Court dissevere,
So that he come ayeinward nevere.
Therfore I wisshe and wolde fain
That he were in som wise slain;
For while he stant in thilke place,
Ne gete I noght my ladi grace.

1562 And þus daunger my fortune ladde H₁ ... B₂, H₃ (chaunce
for fortune E)

Thus hate I dedly thilke vice,
And wolde he stode in non office   1580
In place wher mi ladi is;
For if he do, I wot wel this,
That owther schal he deie or I
Withinne a while; and noght forthi
On my ladi fulofte I muse,
How that sche mai hirself excuse,
If that I deie in such a plit.
Me thenkth sche mihte noght be qwyt
That sche ne were an homicide:
And if it scholde so betide,   1590
As god forbiede it scholde be,
Be double weie it is pite.
For I, which al my will and witt   **P. i. 333**
Have yove and served evere yit,
And thanne I scholde in such a wise
In rewardinge of my servise
Be ded, me thenkth it were a rowthe:
And furthermor, to telle trowthe,
Sche, that hath evere be wel named,
Were worthi thanne to be blamed   1600
And of reson to ben appeled,
Whan with o word sche mihte have heled
A man, and soffreth him so deie.
Ha, who sawh evere such a weie?
Ha, who sawh evere such destresse?
Withoute pite gentilesse,
Withoute mercy wommanhede,
That wol so quyte a man his mede,
Which evere hath be to love trewe.
Mi goode fader, if ye rewe   1610
Upon mi tale, tell me now,
And I wol stinte and herkne yow.
    Mi Sone, attempre thi corage   Confessor.
Fro Wraththe, and let thin herte assuage:
For who so wole him underfonge,

[MORE HASTE WORSE
SPEED.]

He mai his grace abide longe,
Er he of love be received;
And ek also, bot it be weyved,
Ther mihte mochel thing befalle,
That scholde make a man to falle　　　　　1620
Fro love, that nevere afterward
Ne durste he loke thiderward.
In harde weies men gon softe,　　　　P. i. 334
And er thei clymbe avise hem ofte:
Men sen alday that rape reweth;
And who so wicked Ale breweth,
Fulofte he mot the werse drinke:
Betre is to flete than to sincke;
Betre is upon the bridel chiewe
Thanne if he felle and overthrewe,　　　　1630
The hors and stikede in the Myr:
To caste water in the fyr
Betre is than brenne up al the hous:
The man which is malicious
And folhastif, fulofte he falleth,
And selden is whan love him calleth.
Forthi betre is to soffre a throwe
Than be to wilde and overthrowe;
Suffrance hath evere be the beste
To wissen him that secheth reste:　　　　1640
And thus, if thou wolt love and spede,
Mi Sone, soffre, as I the rede.
What mai the Mous ayein the Cat?
And for this cause I axe that,
Who mai to love make a werre,
That he ne hath himself the werre?
Love axeth pes and evere schal,
And who that fihteth most withal
Schal lest conquere of his emprise:
For this thei tellen that ben wise,　　　　1650
Wicke is to stryve and have the werse;
To hasten is noght worth a kerse;
Thing that a man mai noght achieve, P. i. 335

1641 and _om._ H₁, B　　　1649 Schal best B　Lest schal
H₁ ... B₂, H₃

That mai noght wel be don at Eve,   [MORE HASTE WORSE SPEED.]
It mot abide til the morwe.
Ne haste noght thin oghne sorwe,
Mi Sone, and tak this in thi witt,
He hath noght lost that wel abitt.
  Ensample that it falleth thus,
Thou miht wel take of Piramus,   1660
Whan he in haste his swerd outdrowh
And on the point himselve slowh
For love of Tisbee pitously,
For he hire wympel fond blody
And wende a beste hire hadde slain;
Wher as him oghte have be riht fain,
For sche was there al sauf beside:
Bot for he wolde noght abide,
This meschief fell. Forthi be war,
Mi Sone, as I the warne dar,   1670
Do thou nothing in such a res,
For suffrance is the welle of Pes.
Thogh thou to loves Court poursuie,
Yit sit it wel that thou eschuie
That thou the Court noght overhaste,
For so miht thou thi time waste;
Bot if thin happ therto be schape,
It mai noght helpe forto rape.
Therfore attempre thi corage;
Folhaste doth non avantage,   1680
Bot ofte it set a man behinde
In cause of love, and that I finde
Be olde ensample, as thou schalt hiere, **P. i. 336**
Touchende of love in this matiere.

  A Maiden whilom ther was on,   [TALE OF PHEBUS AND DAPHNE.]
Which Daphne hihte, and such was non
Of beaute thanne, as it was seid.
Phebus his love hath on hire leid,   Hic ponit Confessor
And therupon to hire he soghte   exemplum contra il-
In his folhaste, and so besoghte,   los qui in amoris causa
                    1690 nimia festinacione con-

1661 outdrowh F out drowh (drough) AJ, B   1671 a res
GEC, B ares AJ, S, F   1686 such was] þer was H₁ ... B₂, H₃

cupiscentes tardius expediunt. Et narrat qualiter pro eo quod Phebus quamdam virginem pulcherimam nomine Daphnem nimia amoris acceleracione insequebatur, iratus Cupido cor Phebi sagitta aurea ignita ardencius vulnerauit : et econtra cor Daphne quadam sagitta plumbea, que frigidissima fuit, sobrius perforauit. Et sic quanto magis Phebus ardencior in amore Daphnem prosecutus est, tanto magis ipsa frigidior Phebi concupiscenciam toto corde fugitiua dedignabatur.

That sche with him no reste hadde;
For evere upon hire love he gradde,
And sche seide evere unto him nay.
So it befell upon a dai,
Cupide, which hath every chance
Of love under his governance,
Syh Phebus hasten him so sore :
And for he scholde him haste more,
And yit noght speden ate laste,
A dart thurghout his herte he caste,   1700
Which was of gold and al afyre,
That made him manyfold desire
Of love more thanne he dede.
To Daphne ek in the same stede
A dart of Led he caste and smot,
Which was al cold and nothing hot.
And thus Phebus in love brenneth,
And in his haste aboute renneth,
To loke if that he mihte winne ;
Bot he was evere to beginne,   1710
For evere awei fro him sche fledde,
So that he nevere his love spedde.
And forto make him full believe   **P. i. 337**
That no Folhaste mihte achieve
To gete love in such degree,
This Daphne into a lorer tre
Was torned, which is evere grene,
In tokne, as yit it mai be sene,
That sche schal duelle a maiden stille,
And Phebus failen of his wille.   1720

  Be suche ensamples, as thei stonde,
Mi Sone, thou miht understonde,
To hasten love is thing in vein,
Whan that fortune is therayein.
To take where a man hath leve
Good is, and elles he mot leve ;
For whan a mannes happes failen,
Ther is non haste mai availen.

  Mi fader, grant merci of this :

1704 *margin* prosecutus T, F persecutus AC, B, W

Bot while I se mi ladi is   1730   [Fool-haste.]
No tre, but halt hire oghne forme,
Ther mai me noman so enforme,
To whether part fortune wende,
That I unto mi lyves ende
Ne wol hire serven everemo.

    Mi Sone, sithen it is so,   Confessor.
I seie nomor; bot in this cas
Bewar how it with Phebus was.
Noght only upon loves chance,
Bot upon every governance   1740
Which falleth unto mannes dede,
Folhaste is evere forto drede,
And that a man good consail take,   **P. i. 338**
Er he his pourpos undertake,
For consail put Folhaste aweie.

    Now goode fader, I you preie,   Amans.
That forto wisse me the more,
Som good ensample upon this lore
Ye wolden telle of that is write,
That I the betre mihte wite   1750
How I Folhaste scholde eschuie,
And the wisdom of conseil suie.

    Mi Sone, that thou miht enforme   Confessor.
Thi pacience upon the forme
Of olde essamples, as thei felle,
Now understond what I schal telle.

    Whan noble Troie was belein   [Athemas and
And overcome, and hom ayein   Demephon.]
The Gregois torned fro the siege,
The kinges founde here oghne liege
In manye places, as men seide,   1760   Hic ponit Confessor
That hem forsoke and desobeide.   exemplum contra il-
Among the whiche fell this cas   los qui nimio furore
To Demephon and Athemas,   accensi vindictam Ire
That weren kinges bothe tuo,   sue vltra quam decet
And bothe weren served so: consequi affectant. Et
                                  narrat qualiter Athe-
                                  mas et Demephon Re-
                                  ges, cum ipsi de bello
                                  Troiano ad propria

1732 me *om.* AML, KH₃Magd   (no man so me W)   1763 þe
cas H₁ . . . B₂
 **
                     T

[ATHEMAS AND
DEMEPHON.]

remeassent et a suis
ibidem pacifice recep-
ti non fuissent, con-
gregato aliunde pug-
natorum excercitu, re-
giones suas non solum
incendio vastare set
et omnes in eisdem
habitantes a minimo
vsque ad maiorem in
perpetuam vindicte
memoriam gladio in-
terficere feruore ira-
cundie proposuerunt.
Set Rex Nestor, qui
senex et sapiens fuit,
ex paciencia tractatus
inter ipsos Reges et
eorum Regna inita
pace et concordia hu-
iusmodi impetuosita-
tem micius pacifica-
uit.

Here lieges wolde hem noght receive,
So that thei mote algates weyve
To seche lond in other place,
For there founde thei no grace.   1770
Wherof they token hem to rede,
And soghten frendes ate nede,
And ech of hem asseureth other   **P. i. 339**
To helpe as to his oghne brother,
To vengen hem of thilke oultrage
And winne ayein here heritage.
And thus thei ryde aboute faste
To gete hem help, and ate laste
Thei hadden pouer sufficant,
And maden thanne a covenant,   1780
That thei ne scholden no lif save,
Ne prest, ne clerc, ne lord, ne knave,
Ne wif, ne child, of that thei finde,
Which berth visage of mannes kinde,
So that no lif schal be socoured,
Bot with the dedly swerd devoured:
In such Folhaste here ordinance
Thei schapen forto do vengance.
Whan this pourpos was wist and knowe
Among here host, tho was ther blowe   1790
Of wordes many a speche aboute:
Of yonge men the lusti route
Were of this tale glad ynowh,
Ther was no care for the plowh;
As thei that weren Folhastif,
Thei ben acorded to the strif,
And sein it mai noght be to gret
To vengen hem of such forfet:
Thus seith the wilde unwise tonge
Of hem that there weren yonge.   1800
Bot Nestor, which was old and hor,
The salve sih tofore the sor,
As he that was of conseil wys: **P. i. 340**
So that anon be his avis

1767 liege B   1777 *margin* feruore*m* AM   1783 *margin* micius]
inicius H₁GECL   1800 weren þer(e) H₁XE ... B₂   weren þanne G

Ther was a prive conseil nome.
This Demephon and Athemas
Here pourpos tolden, as it was;
Thei sieten alle stille and herde,
Was non bot Nestor hem ansuerde.   1810
He bad hem, if thei wolde winne,
They scholden se, er thei beginne,
Here ende, and sette here ferste entente,
That thei hem after ne repente:
And axeth hem this questioun,
To what final conclusioun
Thei wolde regne Kinges there,
If that no poeple in londe were;
And seith, it were a wonder wierde
To sen a king become an hierde,   1820
Wher no lif is bot only beste
Under the liegance of his heste;
For who that is of man no king,
The remenant is as no thing.
He seith ek, if the pourpos holde
To sle the poeple, as thei tuo wolde,
Whan thei it mihte noght restore,
Al Grece it scholde abegge sore,
To se the wilde beste wone
Wher whilom duelte a mannes Sone: 1830
And for that cause he bad hem trete,
And stinte of the manaces grete.
Betre is to winne be fair speche,   **P. i. 341**
He seith, than such vengance seche;
For whanne a man is most above,   Nota.
Him nedeth most to gete him love.
    Whan Nestor hath his tale seid,
Ayein him was no word withseid;
It thoghte hem alle he seide wel:
And thus fortune hire dedly whiel   1840
Fro werre torneth into pes.
Bot forth thei wenten natheles;

And whan the Contres herde sein
How that here kinges be besein
Of such a pouer as thei ladde,
Was non so bold that hem ne dradde,
And forto seche pes and grith
Thei sende and preide anon forthwith,
So that the kinges ben appesed,
And every mannes herte is esed ;   1850
Al was foryete and noght recorded.
And thus thei ben togedre acorded ;
The kinges were ayein received,
And pes was take and wraththe weived,
And al thurgh conseil which was good
Of him that reson understod.

Confessor.

Be this ensample, Sone, attempre
Thin herte and let no will distempre

Nota.

Thi wit, and do nothing be myht
Which mai be do be love and riht.   1860
Folhaste is cause of mochel wo ;
Forthi, mi Sone, do noght so.

[HOMICIDE.]

And as touchende of Homicide   **P. i. 342**
Which toucheth unto loves side,
Fulofte it falleth unavised
Thurgh will, which is noght wel assised,
Whan wit and reson ben aweie
And that Folhaste is in the weie,
Wherof hath falle gret vengance.
Forthi tak into remembrance   1870
To love in such a maner wise
That thou deserve no juise :
For wel I wot, thou miht noght lette,
That thou ne schalt thin herte sette
To love, wher thou wolt or non ;
Bot if thi wit be overgon,
So that it torne into malice,
Ther wot noman of thilke vice,
What peril that ther mai befalle :
Wherof a tale amonges alle,   1880
Which is gret pite forto hiere,

1859 *margin* Nota F *om.* A, B   1866 Thourgh F

I thenke forto tellen hiere,
That thou such moerdre miht withstonde,
Whan thou the tale hast understonde.

Of Troie at thilke noble toun,
Whos fame stant yit of renoun
And evere schal to mannes Ere,
The Siege laste longe there,
Er that the Greks it mihten winne,
Whil Priamus was king therinne;
Bot of the Greks that lyhe aboute
Agamenon ladde al the route.
This thing is knowen overal,
Bot yit I thenke in special
To my matiere therupon
Telle in what wise Agamenon,
Thurgh chance which mai noght be weived,
Of love untrewe was deceived.
An old sawe is, 'Who that is slyh
In place where he mai be nyh,
He makth the ferre Lieve loth':
Of love and thus fulofte it goth.
Ther while Agamenon batailleth
To winne Troie, and it assailleth,
Fro home and was long time ferr,
Egistus drowh his qweene nerr,
And with the leiser which he hadde
This ladi at his wille he ladde:
Climestre was hire rihte name,
Sche was therof gretli to blame,
To love there it mai noght laste.
Bot fell to meschief ate laste;
For whan this noble worthi kniht
Fro Troie cam, the ferste nyht
That he at home abedde lay,
Egistus, longe er it was day,

[TALE OF ORESTES.]

Hic ponit Confessor exemplum contra illos qui ob sue concupiscencie desiderium homicide efficiuntur. Et narrat qualiter Climestra vxor Regis Agamenontis, cum ipse a bello Troiano domi redisset, consilio Egisti, quem adultera peramauit, sponsum suum in cubili dormientem sub noctis silencio trucidabat; cuius mortem filius eius Horestes tunc minoris etatis postea diis admonitus seueritate crudelissima vindicauit.

P. i. 343

1890

1900

1910

1885 at thilke] þilke B, H₃   þat ilke W   of þilke L   1893 thing]
king ERL, BT   1899 *margin* crudelissima seueritate A ... B₂, BT &c.
1908 hadde B   1913 worþi noble AM   1914 ferste (firste) AJ, B
ferst F

As this Climestre him hadde asent,
And weren bothe of on assent,
Be treson slowh him in his bedd.
Bot moerdre, which mai noght ben hedd,   1920
Sprong out to every mannes Ere,
Wherof the lond was full of fere.

    Agamenon hath be this qweene   **P. i.** 344
A Sone, and that was after sene;
Bot yit as thanne he was of yowthe,
A babe, which no reson cowthe,
And as godd wolde, it fell him thus.
A worthi kniht Taltabius
This yonge child hath in kepinge,
And whan he herde of this tidinge,   1930
Of this treson, of this misdede,
He gan withinne himself to drede,
In aunter if this false Egiste
Upon him come, er he it wiste,
To take and moerdre of his malice
This child, which he hath to norrice :
And for that cause in alle haste
Out of the lond he gan him haste
And to the king of Crete he strawhte
And him this yonge lord betawhte,   1940
And preide him for his fader sake
That he this child wolde undertake
And kepe him til he be of Age,
So as he was of his lignage;
And tolde him over al the cas,
How that his fadre moerdred was,
And hou Egistus, as men seide,
Was king, to whom the lond obeide.
And whanne Ydomeneux the king
Hath understondinge of this thing,   1950
Which that this kniht him hadde told,
He made sorwe manyfold,
And tok this child into his warde,   **P. i.** 345
And seide he wolde him kepe and warde,

Til that he were of such a myht   [TALE OF ORESTES.]
To handle a swerd and ben a knyht,
To venge him at his oghne wille.
And thus Horestes duelleth stille,
Such was the childes rihte name,
Which after wroghte mochel schame   1960
In vengance of his fader deth.
    The time of yeres overgeth,
That he was man of brede and lengthe,
Of wit, of manhod and of strengthe,
A fair persone amonges alle.
And he began to clepe and calle,
As he which come was to manne,
Unto the King of Crete thanne,
Preiende that he wolde him make
A kniht and pouer with him take,   1970
For lengere wolde he noght beleve,
He seith, bot preith the king of leve
To gon and cleyme his heritage
And vengen him of thilke oultrage
Which was unto his fader do.
The king assenteth wel therto,
With gret honour and knyht him makth,
And gret pouer to him betakth,
And gan his journe forto caste:
So that Horestes ate laste   1980
His leve tok and forth he goth.
As he that was in herte wroth,
His ferste pleinte to bemene,   **P. i. 346**
Unto the Cite of Athene
He goth him forth and was received,
So there was he noght deceived.
The Duc and tho that weren wise
Thei profren hem to his servise;
And he hem thonketh of here profre
And seith himself he wol gon offre   1990
Unto the goddes for his sped,

1968 Unto] Vnto to F   Grece M . . . B₂ (*except* EC)   1979 gan
his journe] gan his money XGE   gaue his money H₁RCLB₂   1989
he *om.* B

[Tale of Orestes.]

As alle men him yeven red.
So goth he to the temple forth :
Of yiftes that be mochel worth
His sacrifice and his offringe
He made ; and after his axinge
He was ansuerd, if that he wolde
His stat recovere, thanne he scholde
Upon his Moder do vengance
So cruel, that the remembrance   2000
Therof mihte everemore abide,
As sche that was an homicide
And of hire oghne lord Moerdrice.
Horestes, which of thilke office
Was nothing glad, as thanne he preide
Unto the goddes there and seide
That thei the juggement devise,
How sche schal take the juise.
And therupon he hadde ansuere,
That he hire Pappes scholde of tere   2010
Out of hire brest his oghne hondes,
And for ensample of alle londes
With hors sche scholde be todrawe,   **P. i. 347**
Til houndes hadde hire bones gnawe
Withouten eny sepulture :
This was a wofull aventure.
And whan Horestes hath al herd,
How that the goddes have ansuerd,
Forth with the strengthe which he ladde
The Duc and his pouer he hadde,   2020
And to a Cite forth thei gon,
The which was cleped Cropheon,
Where as Phoieus was lord and Sire,
Which profreth him withouten hyre
His help and al that he mai do,
As he that was riht glad therto,
To grieve his mortiel enemy :
And tolde hem certein cause why,
How that Egiste in Mariage

2003 of] þus B   2005 and þan (þanne) GL, BT   2023 Phogeus
H₁ ... B₂   Phoreus TΔ   Florence W

His dowhter whilom of full Age   2030 [Tale of Orestes.]
Forlai, and afterward forsok,
Whan he Horestes Moder tok.
   Men sein, 'Old Senne newe schame':
Thus more and more aros the blame
Ayein Egiste on every side.
Horestes with his host to ride
Began, and Phoieus with hem wente;
I trowe Egiste him schal repente.
Thei riden forth unto Micene,
Wher lay Climestre thilke qweene,   2040
The which Horestes moder is:
And whan sche herde telle of this,
The gates weren faste schet,   **P. i. 348**
And thei were of here entre let.
Anon this Cite was withoute
Belein and sieged al aboute,
And evere among thei it assaile,
Fro day to nyht and so travaile,
Til ate laste thei it wonne;
Tho was ther sorwe ynowh begonne.   2050
   Horestes dede his moder calle
Anon tofore the lordes alle
And ek tofor the poeple also,
To hire and tolde his tale tho,
And seide, 'O cruel beste unkinde,
How mihtest thou thin herte finde,
For eny lust of loves drawhte,
That thou acordest to the slawhte
Of him which was thin oghne lord?
Thi treson stant of such record,   2060
Thou miht thi werkes noght forsake;
So mot I for mi fader sake
Vengance upon thi bodi do,
As I comanded am therto.
Unkindely for thou hast wroght,
Unkindeliche it schal be boght,

2041 is] was H₁ . . . B₂   2042 herd telle of þis cas H₁ . . . B₂
2044 entre] purpos H₁ . . . B₂   2046 lieged AM   2056 þou þin
(þi) AJM, SAdΛ, F   þou in þin (þi) H₁ . . . B₂, BΛ, W   in thyn T

[TALE OF ORESTES.]

The Sone schal the Moder sle,
For that whilom thou seidest yee
To that thou scholdest nay have seid.'
And he with that his hond hath leid   2070
Upon his Moder brest anon,
And rente out fro the bare bon
Hire Pappes bothe and caste aweie   **P. i. 349**
Amiddes in the carte weie,
And after tok the dede cors
And let it drawe awey with hors
Unto the hound and to the raven;
Sche was non other wise graven.

    Egistus, which was elles where,
Tidinges comen to his Ere   2080
How that Micenes was belein,
Bot what was more herd he noght sein;
With gret manace and mochel bost
He drowh pouer and made an host
And cam in rescousse of the toun.
Bot al the sleyhte of his tresoun
Horestes wiste it be aspie,
And of his men a gret partie
He made in buisshement abide,
To waite on him in such a tide   2090
That he ne mihte here hond ascape:
And in this wise as he hath schape
The thing befell, so that Egiste
Was take, er he himself it wiste,
And was forth broght hise hondes bounde,
As whan men han a tretour founde.
And tho that weren with him take,
Whiche of tresoun were overtake,
Togedre in o sentence falle;
Bot false Egiste above hem alle   2100
Was demed to diverse peine,
The worste that men cowthe ordeigne,
And so forth after be the lawe   **P. i. 350**
He was unto the gibet drawe,

2077 and to] vnto BΔΛ   2082 herd J, SB, F   herde A   2100 false
AJ, S, F   fals C, B

Where he above alle othre hongeth,
As to a tretour it belongeth.
  Tho fame with hire swifte wynges
Aboute flyh and bar tidinges,
And made it cowth in alle londes
How that Horestes with hise hondes   2110
Climestre his oghne Moder slowh.
Some sein he dede wel ynowh,
And som men sein he dede amis,
Diverse opinion ther is:
That sche is ded thei speken alle,
Bot pleinli hou it is befalle,
The matiere in so litel throwe
In soth ther mihte noman knowe
Bot thei that weren ate dede:
And comunliche in every nede   2120
The worste speche is rathest herd
And lieved, til it be ansuerd.
The kinges and the lordes grete
Begonne Horestes forto threte
To puten him out of his regne:
'He is noght worthi forto regne,
The child which slowh his moder so,'
Thei saide; and therupon also
The lordes of comun assent
A time sette of parlement,   2130
And to Athenes king and lord
Togedre come of on acord,
To knowe hou that the sothe was: **P. i. 351**
So that Horestes in this cas
Thei senden after, and he com.
King Menelay the wordes nom
And axeth him of this matiere:
And he, that alle it mihten hiere,
Ansuerde and tolde his tale alarge,
And hou the goddes in his charge   2140
Comanded him in such a wise
His oghne hond to do juise.

2107 Tho AJM, ST, F The H₁ ... B₂, AdBΔΛ, WH₃   hire]
his C the H₁ *om.* AM   2139 at large H₁XGECL, B, W

And with this tale a Duc aros,
Which was a worthi kniht of los,
His name was Menesteüs,
And seide unto the lordes thus:
'The wreeche which Horestes dede,
It was thing of the goddes bede,
And nothing of his crualte;
And if ther were of mi degree   2150
In al this place such a kniht
That wolde sein it was no riht,
I wole it with my bodi prove.'
And therupon he caste his glove,
And ek this noble Duc alleide
Ful many an other skile, and seide
Sche hadde wel deserved wreche,
Ferst for the cause of Spousebreche,
And after wroghte in such a wise
That al the world it oghte agrise,   2160
Whan that sche for so foul a vice
Was of hire oghne lord moerdrice.
Thei seten alle stille and herde,   **P. i. 352**
Bot therto was noman ansuerde,
It thoghte hem alle he seide skile,
Ther is noman withseie it wile;
Whan thei upon the reson musen,
Horestes alle thei excusen:
So that with gret solempnete
He was unto his dignete   2170
Received, and coroned king.
And tho befell a wonder thing:
Egiona, whan sche this wiste,
Which was the dowhter of Egiste
And Soster on the moder side
To this Horeste, at thilke tide,
Whan sche herde how hir brother spedde,
For pure sorwe, which hire ledde,
That he ne hadde ben exiled,

2166 wiþsatt his wille X . . . B₂   withsit hit wille H₁   with seith
hys wille Δ, W   2168 þei alle X . . . B₂   2177 herde AJ, B
herd F

Sche hath hire oghne lif beguiled 2180 [TALE OF ORESTES.]
Anon and hyng hireselve tho.
It hath and schal ben everemo,
To moerdre who that wole assente,
He mai noght faille to repente:
This false Egiona was on,
Which forto moerdre Agamenon
Yaf hire acord and hire assent,
So that be goddes juggement,
Thogh that non other man it wolde,
Sche tok hire juise as sche scholde; 2190
And as sche to an other wroghte,
Vengance upon hireself sche soghte,
And hath of hire unhappi wit **P. i. 353**
A moerdre with a moerdre quit.
Such is of moerdre the vengance.
    Forthi, mi Sone, in remembrance   Confessor.
Of this ensample tak good hiede:
For who that thenkth his love spiede
With moerdre, he schal with worldes schame
Himself and ek his love schame. 2200
    Mi fader, of this aventure   Amans.
Which ye have told, I you assure
Min herte is sory forto hiere,
Bot only for I wolde lere
What is to done, and what to leve.
    And over this now be your leve,   Hic queritur qui-
That ye me wolden telle I preie,   bus de causis licet
If ther be lieffull eny weie   hominem occidere.
Withoute Senne a man to sle.
    Mi Sone, in sondri wise ye. 2210   Confessor.
What man that is of traiterie,
Of moerdre or elles robberie
Atteint, the jugge schal noght lette,
Bot he schal slen of pure dette,
And doth gret Senne, if that he wonde.
For who that lawe hath upon honde,

2206f. *margin* Hic queritur—occidere *om.* B   2207 *margin*
hominem FWH₃   homini hominem A ... B₂, STΔΛ   2209 to]
may B *om.* AM

[Lawful Homicide.]

And spareth forto do justice
For merci, doth noght his office,
That he his mercy so bewareth,

Seneca. Iudex qui
parcit vlcisci, multos
improbos facit.

Whan for o schrewe which he spareth   2220
A thousand goode men he grieveth :
With such merci who that believeth
To plese god, he is deceived,   **P. i. 354**
Or elles resoun mot be weyved.

Apostolus.   Non
sine causa   Iudex
gladium portat.

The lawe stod er we were bore,
How that a kinges swerd is bore
In signe that he schal defende
His trewe poeple and make an ende
Of suche as wolden hem devoure.

Pugna pro patria.

Lo thus, my Sone, to socoure   2230
The lawe and comun riht to winne,
A man mai sle withoute Sinne,
And do therof a gret almesse,
So forto kepe rihtwisnesse.

And over this for his contre
In time of werre a man is fre
Himself, his hous and ek his lond
Defende with his oghne hond,
And slen, if that he mai no bet,
After the lawe which is set.   2240

Amans.

      Now, fader, thanne I you beseche
Of hem that dedly werres seche
In worldes cause and scheden blod,
If such an homicide is good.

Confessor.

      Mi Sone, upon thi question
The trowthe of myn opinion,
Als ferforth as my wit arecheth
And as the pleine lawe techeth,
I woll thee telle in evidence,
To rewle with thi conscience.   2250

2220 *margin* Seneca *om.* B   2221 *margin* parcit] parat
H₁G . . . B₂   2225 *margin* Apostolus—portat *om.* H₁ . . . B₂
2235 *margin* Pugna pro patria] Pugna pro patria · licitum est vim
vi repellere SBT Pro patria pugna &c. Λ *om.* H₁   2244 Is
such an homicide good H₁ . . . B₂ (In *for* Is R)   2248 techeþ
FWH₃Magd · it techeþ A . . . B₂, S . . . ΔΛ

v. *Quod creat ipse deus, necat hoc homicida creatum,*   [EVIL OF WAR.]
  Vltor et humano sanguine spargit humum.
  Vt pecoris sic est hominis cruor, heu, modo fusus, **P. i. 355**
  Victa iacet pietas, et furor vrget opus.
  Angelus 'In terra pax' dixit, et vltima Cristi
  Verba sonant pacem, quam modo guerra fugat.

    The hihe god of his justice
  That ilke foule horrible vice
  Of homicide he hath forbede,
  Be Moïses as it was bede.
  Whan goddes Sone also was bore,
  He sende hise anglis doun therfore,
  Whom the Schepherdes herden singe,
  Pes to the men of welwillinge
  In erthe be among ous here.
  So forto speke in this matiere   2260
  After the lawe of charite,
  Ther schal no dedly werre be :
  And ek nature it hath defended
  And in hir lawe pes comended,
  Which is the chief of mannes welthe,
  Of mannes lif, of mannes helthe.
  Bot dedly werre hath his covine
  Of pestilence and of famine,
  Of poverte and of alle wo,
  Wherof this world we blamen so,   2270
  Which now the werre hath under fote,
  Til god himself therof do bote.
  For alle thing which god hath wroght
  In Erthe, werre it bringth to noght :
  The cherche is brent, the priest is slain,
  The wif, the maide is ek forlain,
  The lawe is lore and god unserved :
  I not what mede he hath deserved
  That suche werres ledeth inne.   **P. i. 356**
  If that he do it forto winne,   2280
  Ferst to acompte his grete cost
  Forth with the folk that he hath lost,
  As to the worldes rekeninge

Hic loquitur contra motores guerre, que non solum homicidii set vniversi mundi desolacionis mater existit.

2256 anglis C, F angelis AJ aungels B   2259 be *om.* AM

[EVIL OF WAR.]

Ther schal he finde no winnynge;
And if he do it to pourchace
The hevene mede, of such a grace
I can noght speke, and natheles
Crist hath comanded love and pes,
And who that worcheth the revers,
I trowe his mede is ful divers.   2290
And sithen thanne that we finde
That werres in here oghne kinde
Ben toward god of no decerte,
And ek thei bringen in poverte
Of worldes good, it is merveile
Among the men what it mai eyle,
That thei a pes ne conne sette.
I trowe Senne be the lette,

Apostolus. Stipen-
dium peccati mors est.

And every mede of Senne is deth;
So wot I nevere hou that it geth: 2300
Bot we that ben of o believe
Among ousself, this wolde I lieve,
That betre it were pes to chese,
Than so be double weie lese.
    I not if that it now so stonde,
Bot this a man mai understonde,
Who that these olde bokes redeth,
That coveitise is on which ledeth,
And broghte ferst the werres inne.   **P. i. 357**
At Grece if that I schal beginne,   2310
Ther was it proved hou it stod:
To Perce, which was ful of good,
Thei maden werre in special,
And so thei deden overal,
Wher gret richesse was in londe,
So that thei leften nothing stonde
Unwerred, bot onliche Archade.

Nota, quod Greci
omnem terram fer-
tilem debellabant, set
tantum Archadiam,
pro eo quod pauper et

For there thei no werres made,
Be cause it was bareigne and povere,
Wherof thei mihten noght recovere;   2320
And thus poverte was forbore,

2287 and *om.* B   2293 of] in AM   2299 *margin* Apostolus
—mors est *om.* B   2318 werre H₁ ... B₂, T

He that noght hadde noght hath lore.
Bot yit it is a wonder thing,   sterilis fuit, pacifice
Whan that a riche worthi king,   dimiserunt.
Or other lord, what so he be,
Wol axe and cleyme proprete
In thing to which he hath no riht,
Bot onliche of his grete miht :
For this mai every man wel wite,
That bothe kinde and lawe write   2330
Expressly stonden therayein.
Bot he mot nedes somwhat sein,
Althogh ther be no reson inne,
Which secheth cause forto winne :
For wit that is with will oppressed,
Whan coveitise him hath adressed,
And alle resoun put aweie,
He can wel finde such a weie
To werre, where as evere him liketh,   **P. i. 358**
Wherof that he the world entriketh,   2340
That many a man of him compleigneth :
Bot yit alwei som cause he feigneth,
And of his wrongful herte he demeth
That al is wel, what evere him semeth,
Be so that he mai winne ynowh.
For as the trew man to the plowh
Only to the gaignage entendeth,
Riht so the werreiour despendeth
His time and hath no conscience.
And in this point for evidence   2350
Of hem that suche werres make,
Thou miht a gret ensample take,
How thei her tirannie excusen
Of that thei wrongfull werres usen,
And how thei stonde of on acord,
The Souldeour forth with the lord,
The povere man forth with the riche,
As of corage thei ben liche,
To make werres and to pile

2343 herte] cause H₁ . . . B₂ (*line om.* X)   2346 trew S, F
trewe AJ, B
**   U

For lucre and for non other skyle :   2360
Wherof a propre tale I rede,
As it whilom befell in dede.

    Of him whom al this Erthe dradde,
Whan he the world so overladde
Thurgh werre, as it fortuned is,
King Alisandre, I rede this ;
How in a Marche, where he lay,
It fell per chance upon a day
A Rovere of the See was nome,   **P. i. 359**
Which many a man hadde overcome   2370
And slain and take here good aweie :
This Pilour, as the bokes seie,
A famous man in sondri stede
Was of the werkes whiche he dede.
This Prisoner tofor the king
Was broght, and there upon this thing
In audience he was accused :
And he his dede hath noght excused,
Bot preith the king to don him riht,
And seith, 'Sire, if I were of miht,   2380
I have an herte lich to thin ;
For if the pouer were myn,
Mi will is most in special
To rifle and geten overal
The large worldes good aboute.
Bot for I lede a povere route
And am, as who seith, at meschief,
The name of Pilour and of thief
I bere ; and thou, which routes grete
Miht lede and take thi beyete,   2390
And dost riht as I wolde do,
Thi name is nothing cleped so,
Bot thou art named Emperour.
Oure dedes ben of o colour
And in effect of o decerte,
Bot thi richesse and my poverte
Tho ben noght taken evene liche.

Hic declarat per ex-
emplum contra istos
Principes seu alios
quoscumque illicite
guerre motores. Et
narrat de quodam pi-
rata in partibus mari-
nis spoliatore notissi-
mo, qui cum captus
fuisset, et in iudicium
coram Rege Alexan-
dro productus et de
latrocinio accusatus,
dixit, 'O Alexander,
vere quia cum paucis
sociis spoliorum causa
naues tantum exploro,
ego latrunculus vo-
cor; tu autem, quia
cum infinita bellato-
rum multitudine vni-
uersam terram subiu-
gando spoliasti, Impe-
rator diceris. Itaquod
status tuus a statu meo
differt, set eodem
animo condicionem
parilem habemus. '
Alexander vero eius
audaciam in respon-
sione comprobans, ip-
sum penes se familia-
rem retinuit; et sic
bellicosus bellatori
complacuit.

2379 *margin* cum *om.* H₁ . . . B₂, B   2382 the] þy (thi) XL

And natheles he that is riche
This dai, tomorwe he mai be povere; **P. i. 360**
And in contraire also recovere   2400
A povere man to gret richesse
Men sen : forthi let rihtwisnesse
Be peised evene in the balance.
  The king his hardi contienance
Behield, and herde hise wordes wise,
And seide unto him in this wise :
'Thin ansuere I have understonde,
Wherof my will is, that thou stonde
In mi service and stille abide.'
And forth withal the same tide   2410
He hath him terme of lif withholde,
The mor and for he schal ben holde,
He made him kniht and yaf him lond,
Which afterward was of his hond
An orped kniht in many a stede,
And gret prouesce of armes dede,
As the Croniqes it recorden.
  And in this wise thei acorden,
The whiche of o condicioun
Be set upon destruccioun :   2420
Such Capitein such retenue.
Bot forto se to what issue
The thing befalleth ate laste,
It is gret wonder that men caste
Here herte upon such wrong to winne,
Wher no beyete mai ben inne,
And doth desese on every side :
Bot whan reson is put aside
And will governeth the corage,   **P. i. 361**
The faucon which that fleth ramage   2430
And soeffreth nothing in the weie,
Wherof that he mai take his preie,
Is noght mor set upon ravine,
Than thilke man which his covine
Hath set in such a maner wise :

2402 rihtwisne F   2406 to him JH₁ . . . B₂   2412 schulde
(sholde) BT   2434 is couine JMCLB₂, Ad
U 2

For al the world ne mai suffise
To will which is noght resonable.
  Wherof ensample concordable

[WARS AND DEATH
OF ALEXANDER.]
  Hic secundum ges-
ta Regis Alexandri de
guerris illicitis ponit
Confessor exemplum,
dicens quod quamuis
Alexander sua poten-
cia tocius mundi victor
sibi subiugarat im-
perium, ipse tandem
mortis victoria subiu-
gatus cunctipotentis
sentenciam euadere
non potuit.

Lich to this point of which I meene,
Was upon Alisandre sene,   2440
Which hadde set al his entente,
So as fortune with him wente,
That reson mihte him non governe,
Bot of his will he was so sterne,
That al the world he overran
And what him list he tok and wan.
In Ynde the superiour
Whan that he was ful conquerour,
And hadde his wilful pourpos wonne
Of al this Erthe under the Sonne,   2450
This king homward to Macedoine,
Whan that he cam to Babiloine,
And wende most in his Empire,
As he which was hol lord and Sire,
In honour forto be received,
Most sodeinliche he was deceived,
And with strong puison envenimed.
And as he hath the world mistimed
Noght as he scholde with his wit,   **P. i. 362**
Noght as he wolde it was aquit.   2460
  Thus was he slain that whilom slowh,
And he which riche was ynowh
This dai, tomorwe he hadde noght:
And in such wise as he hath wroght
In destorbance of worldes pes,
His werre he fond thanne endeles,
In which for evere desconfit
He was. Lo now, for what profit
Of werre it helpeth forto ryde,
For coveitise and worldes pride   2470
To sle the worldes men aboute,

2436 ne mai] may nought (not &c) A. . . B₂, S . . . Δ   2437 To
will] To him H₁ . . . B₂   2443 non] nought (not) JMCB₂, B, W
2444 *margin* subiugauerat H₁ . . . B₂,SΔ   2449 wilsful F   2460 it was
quit (quite &c) H₁ . . . B₂, TΔ   was hyt quyt W   he was aquit M

As bestes whiche gon theroute.
For every lif which reson can
Oghth wel to knowe that a man
Ne scholde thurgh no tirannie
Lich to these othre bestes die,
Til kinde wolde for him sende.
I not hou he it mihte amende,
Which takth awei for everemore
The lif that he mai noght restore.   2480

     Forthi, mi Sone, in alle weie
Be wel avised, I thee preie,
Of slawhte er that thou be coupable
Withoute cause resonable.

     Mi fader, understonde it is,
That ye have seid; bot over this
I prei you tell me nay or yee,
To passe over the grete See
To werre and sle the Sarazin,   **P. i. 363**
Is that the lawe?

                    Sone myn,   2490
To preche and soffre for the feith,
That have I herd the gospell seith;
Bot forto slee, that hiere I noght.
Crist with his oghne deth hath boght
Alle othre men, and made hem fre,
In tokne of parfit charite;
And after that he tawhte himselve,
Whan he was ded, these othre tuelve
Of hise Apostles wente aboute
The holi feith to prechen oute,   2500
Wherof the deth in sondri place
Thei soffre, and so god of his grace
The feith of Crist hath mad aryse:
Bot if thei wolde in other wise
Be werre have broght in the creance,

[WARS AND DEATH
OF ALEXANDER.]

Confessor.

Amans.

[ARE CRUSADES
LAWFUL?]

Confessor.

Nota.

2474 Oghþ SAdT, F   Oght (Ought &c.) AMGC, Δ, W
Oweþ JH₁XERLB₂, B, H₃   2476 othre] olde B   2478 mihte
(myght) FWH₃   mai (may) A . . . B₂, S . . . Δ   2491 fei SΔ
feie Ad2492   sei SΔ   seie Ad   2505 *margin* Nota AJ, F
om. B

[ARE CRUSADES
LAWFUL?]

It hadde yit stonde in balance.
And that mai proven in the dede ;
For what man the Croniqes rede,
Fro ferst that holi cherche hath weyved
To preche, and hath the swerd received,　　2510
Wherof the werres ben begonne,
A gret partie of that was wonne
To Cristes feith stant now miswent :
Godd do therof amendement,
So as he wot what is the beste.

[GUILT OF HOMI-
CIDE.]

Bot, Sone, if thou wolt live in reste
Of conscience wel assised,
Er that thou sle, be wel avised :
For man, as tellen ous the clerkes,　　**P. i. 364**
Hath god above alle ertheli werkes　　2520
Ordeined to be principal,
And ek of Soule in special
He is mad lich to the godhiede.
So sit it wel to taken hiede
And forto loke on every side,
Er that thou falle in homicide,
Which Senne is now so general,
That it welnyh stant overal,
In holi cherche and elles where.
Bot al the while it stant so there,　　2530
The world mot nede fare amis :
For whan the welle of pite is
Thurgh coveitise of worldes good
Defouled with schedinge of blod,
The remenant of folk aboute
Unethe stonden eny doute
To werre ech other and to slee.
So is it all noght worth a Stree,
The charite wherof we prechen,
For we do nothing as we techen :　　2540
And thus the blinde conscience
Of pes hath lost thilke evidence
Which Crist upon this Erthe tawhte.
Now mai men se moerdre and manslawhte

2529 and] as AJX . . . B₂, BT　　　2544 manslawte F

Lich as it was be daies olde,
Whan men the Sennes boghte and solde.
  In Grece afore Cristes feith,
I rede, as the Cronique seith,
Touchende of this matiere thus,   **P. i. 365**
In thilke time hou Peleüs   2550
His oghne brother Phocus slowh;
Bot for he hadde gold ynowh
To yive, his Senne was despensed
With gold, wherof it was compensed:
Achastus, which with Venus was
Hire Priest, assoilede in that cas,
Al were ther no repentance.
And as the bok makth remembrance,
It telleth of Medee also;
Of that sche slowh her Sones tuo,   2560
Egeüs in the same plit
Hath mad hire of hire Senne quit.
The Sone ek of Amphioras,
Whos rihte name Almeüs was,
His Moder slowh, Eriphile;
Bot Achilo the Priest and he,
So as the bokes it recorden,
For certein Somme of gold acorden
That thilke horrible sinfull dede
Assoiled was.   And thus for mede   2570
Of worldes good it falleth ofte
That homicide is set alofte
Hiere in this lif; bot after this
Ther schal be knowe how that it is
Of hem that suche thinges werche,
And hou also that holi cherche
Let suche Sennes passe quyte,
And how thei wole hemself aquite
Of dedly werres that thei make.   **P. i. 366**
For who that wolde ensample take,   2580
The lawe which is naturel
Be weie of kinde scheweth wel

[GUILT OF HOMI-
CIDE.]

Facilitas venie oc-
casionem prebet delin-
quendi.

2556 assoiled him H₁XE . . . B₂   assoileþ him G   2568 For]
Of A . . . B₂   2573 lif] world B   2578 wold M, B

[GUILT OF HOMI-
CIDE.]

That homicide in no degree,
Which werreth ayein charite,
Among the men ne scholde duelle.
For after that the bokes telle,
To seche in al this worldesriche,
Men schal noght finde upon his liche
A beste forto take his preie:
And sithen kinde hath such a weie,   2590
Thanne is it wonder of a man,
Which kynde hath and resoun can,
That he wol owther more or lasse
His kinde and resoun overpasse,
And sle that is to him semblable.
So is the man noght resonable
Ne kinde, and that is noght honeste,
Whan he is worse than a beste.

[A STRANGE BIRD.]
Nota secundum So-
linum contra homici-
das de natura cuius-
dam Auis faciem ad
similitudinem huma-
nam habentis, que cum
de preda sua hominem
juxta fluuium occiderit
videritque in aqua si-
milem sibi occisum,
statim pre dolore mo-
ritur.

Among the bokes whiche I finde
Solyns spekth of a wonder kinde,   2600
And seith of fowhles ther is on,
Which hath a face of blod and bon
Lich to a man in resemblance.
And if it falle him so per chance,
As he which is a fowhl of preie,
That he a man finde in his weie,
He wol him slen, if that he mai:
Bot afterward the same dai,
Whan he hath eten al his felle,   **P. i. 367**
And that schal be beside a welle,   2610
In which whan he wol drinke take,
Of his visage and seth the make
That he hath slain, anon he thenketh
Of his misdede, and it forthenketh
So gretly, that for pure sorwe
He liveth noght til on the morwe.
Be this ensample it mai well suie
That man schal homicide eschuie,
For evere is merci good to take,
Bot if the lawe it hath forsake   2620
And that justice is therayein.

2587 *Paragraph here* AJ, F   2591 it is G . . . B₂, Δ

For ofte time I have herd sein
Amonges hem that werres hadden,
That thei som while here cause ladden
Be merci, whan thei mihte have slain,
Wherof that thei were after fain :
And, Sone, if that thou wolt recorde   [MERCY.]
The vertu of Misericorde,
Thou sihe nevere thilke place,
Where it was used, lacke grace.   2630
For every lawe and every kinde
The mannes wit to merci binde ;
And namely the worthi knihtes,
Whan that thei stonden most uprihtes
And ben most mihti forto grieve,
Thei scholden thanne most relieve
Him whom thei mihten overthrowe,
As be ensample a man mai knowe.

He mai noght failen of his mede   P. i. 368 [TALE OF TELAPHUS
That hath merci : for this I rede,   2640   AND TEUCER.]
In a Cronique and finde thus.
Whan Achilles with Telaphus   Hic ponit Confessor
His Sone toward Troie were,   exemplum de pietate
It fell hem, er thei comen there,   contra homicidium in
Ayein Theucer the king of Mese   guerris habenda. Et
To make werre and forto sese   narrat qualiter Achil-
His lond, as thei that wolden regne   les vna cum Thelapho
And Theucer pute out of his regne.   filio suo contra Regem
And thus the Marches thei assaile,   Mesee, qui tunc Theu-
                                               cer vocabatur, bel-
                                               lum inierunt ; et cum
                                               Achilles dictum Re-
Bot Theucer yaf to hem bataille ;   2650 gem in bello prostra-
Thei foghte on bothe sides faste,   tum occidere voluis-
Bot so it hapneth ate laste,   set, Thelaphus pietate
This worthi Grek, this Achilles,   motus ipsum clipeo
The king among alle othre ches :   suo cooperiens veniam
As he that was cruel and fell,   pro Rege a patre pos-
With swerd in honde on him he fell,   tulauit : pro quo facto
And smot him with a dethes wounde,   ipse Rex adhuc viuens
That he unhorsed fell to grounde.   Thephalum Regni sui
                                               heredem libera volun-
                                               tate constituit.

2624 That] But BT   2638 And BT   2642 Telaphus J, F
Thelaphus A, SB   2650 Bot] That H₁ . . . B₂

[TALE OF TELAPHUS AND TEUCER.]

Achilles upon him alyhte,
And wolde anon, as he wel mihte,   2660
Have slain him fullich in the place;
Bot Thelaphus his fader grace
For him besoghte, and for pite
Preith that he wolde lete him be,
And caste his Schield betwen hem tuo.
Achilles axeth him why so,
And Thelaphus his cause tolde,
And seith that he is mochel holde,
For whilom Theucer in a stede   **P. i. 369**
Gret grace and socour to him dede,   2670
And seith that he him wolde aquite,
And preith his fader to respite.
Achilles tho withdrowh his hond;
Bot al the pouer of the lond,
Whan that thei sihe here king thus take,
Thei fledde and han the feld forsake:
The Grecs unto the chace falle,
And for the moste part of alle
Of that contre the lordes grete
Thei toke, and wonne a gret beyete.   2680
And anon after this victoire
The king, which hadde good memoire,
Upon the grete merci thoghte,
Which Telaphus toward him wroghte,
And in presence of al the lond
He tok him faire be the hond,
And in this wise he gan to seie:
'Mi Sone, I mot be double weie
Love and desire thin encress;
Ferst for thi fader Achilles   2690
Whilom ful many dai er this,
Whan that I scholde have fare amis,
Rescousse dede in mi querele
And kepte al myn astat in hele:
How so ther falle now distance
Amonges ous, yit remembrance

2671 wol B   2684 Telaphus F Thelaphus AJ, SB
2696 remembrance] in remembrance AM

I have of merci which he dede   [TALE OF TELAPHUS
As thanne : and thou now in this stede   AND TEUCER.]
Of gentilesce and of franchise   **P. i. 370**
Hast do mercy the same wise.   2700
So wol I noght that eny time
Be lost of that thou hast do byme ;
For hou so this fortune falle,
Yit stant mi trust aboven alle,
For the mercy which I now finde,
That thou wolt after this be kinde :
And for that such is myn espeir,
As for my Sone and for myn Eir
I thee receive, and al my lond
I yive and sese into thin hond.'   2710
And in this wise thei acorde,
The cause was Misericorde :
The lordes dede here obeissance
To Thelaphus, and pourveance
Was mad so that he was coroned :
And thus was merci reguerdoned,
Which he to Theucer dede afore.
   Lo, this ensample is mad therfore,   Confessor.
That thou miht take remembrance,
Mi Sone ; and whan thou sest a chaunce, 2720
Of other mennes passioun
Tak pite and compassioun,
And let nothing to thee be lief,
Which to an other man is grief.
And after this if thou desire
To stonde ayein the vice of Ire,
Consaile thee with Pacience,
And tak into thi conscience
Merci to be thi governour.   **P. i. 371**
So schalt thou fiele no rancour,   2730
Wherof thin herte schal debate
With homicide ne with hate
For Cheste or for Malencolie :
Thou schalt be soft in compaignie
Withoute Contek or Folhaste :
For elles miht thou longe waste

2723 belief FK

Thi time, er that thou have thi wille
Of love; for the weder stille
Men preise, and blame the tempestes.

Amans.

    Mi fader, I wol do youre hestes, 2740
And of this point ye have me tawht,
Toward miself the betre sawht
I thenke be, whil that I live.
Bot for als moche as I am schrive
Of Wraththe and al his circumstance,
Yif what you list to my penance,
And asketh forthere of my lif,
If otherwise I be gultif
Of eny thing that toucheth Sinne.

Confessor.

    Mi Sone, er we departe atwinne, 2750
I schal behinde nothing leve.

Amans.

    Mi goode fader, be your leve
Thanne axeth forth what so you list,
For I have in you such a trist,
As ye that be my Soule hele,
That ye fro me wol nothing hele,
For I schal telle you the trowthe.

Confessor.

    Mi Sone, art thou coupable of Slowthe
In eny point which to him longeth? **P. i. 372**

Amans.

    My fader, of tho pointz me longeth 2760
To wite pleinly what thei meene,
So that I mai me schrive cleene.

Confessor.

    Now herkne, I schal the pointz devise;
And understond wel myn aprise:
For schrifte stant of no value
To him that wol him noght vertue
To leve of vice the folie:
For word is wynd, bot the maistrie
Is that a man himself defende
Of thing which is noght to comende, 2770
Wherof ben fewe now aday.
And natheles, so as I may
Make unto thi memoire knowe,
The pointz of Slowthe thou schalt knowe.

Explicit Liber Tercius.

2763 the] þo AJG ... B₂, SBTΔ   2764 myn] þis B

Incipit Liber Quartus.

i. *Dicunt accidiam fore nutricem viciorum,*   **P. ii.** 1   [SLOTH.]
  Torpet et in cunctis tarda que lenta bonis:
Que fieri possent hodie transfert piger in cras,
  Furatoque prius ostia claudit equo.
Poscenti tardo negat emolumenta Cupido,
  Set Venus in celeri ludit amore viri.

UPON the vices to procede   [i. LACHESSE.]
After the cause of mannes dede,
The ferste point of Slowthe I calle
Lachesce, and is the chief of alle,   Hic in quarto libro
And hath this propreliche of kinde,   loquitur Confessor de
                                             speciebus Accidie, qua-
To leven alle thing behinde.   rum primam Tardacio-
Of that he mihte do now hier   nem vocat, cuius con-
He tarieth al the longe yer,   dicionem pertractans
                                             Amanti super hoc con-
And everemore he seith, 'Tomorwe';   sequenter opponit.
And so he wol his time borwe,   10
And wissheth after 'God me sende,'   **P. ii, 2**
That whan he weneth have an ende,
Thanne is he ferthest to beginne.
Thus bringth he many a meschief inne
Unwar, til that he be meschieved,
And may noght thanne be relieved.
    And riht so nowther mor ne lesse
It stant of love and of lachesce:
Som time he slowtheth in a day
That he nevere after gete mai.   20
Now, Sone, as of this ilke thing,
If thou have eny knowleching,
That thou to love hast don er this,
Tell on.
        Mi goode fader, yis.   Confessio Amantis.

Latin Verses i. 6 ludet H₁ ... B₂
12 to haue H₁XGRCLB₂

As of lachesce I am beknowe
That I mai stonde upon his rowe,
As I that am clad of his suite:
For whanne I thoghte mi poursuite
To make, and therto sette a day
To speke unto the swete May,   30
Lachesce bad abide yit,
And bar on hond it was no wit
Ne time forto speke as tho.
Thus with his tales to and fro
Mi time in tariinge he drowh:
Whan ther was time good ynowh,
He seide, 'An other time is bettre;
Thou schalt mowe senden hire a lettre,
And per cas wryte more plein
Than thou be Mowthe durstest sein.'   40
Thus have I lete time slyde   **P. ii. 3**
For Slowthe, and kepte noght my tide,
So that lachesce with his vice
Fulofte hath mad my wit so nyce,
That what I thoghte speke or do
With tariinge he hield me so,
Til whanne I wolde and mihte noght.
I not what thing was in my thoght,
Or it was drede, or it was schame;
Bot evere in ernest and in game   50
I wot ther is long time passed.
Bot yit is noght the love lassed,
Which I unto mi ladi have;
For thogh my tunge is slowh to crave
At alle time, as I have bede,
Min herte stant evere in o stede
And axeth besiliche grace,
The which I mai noght yit embrace.
And god wot that is malgre myn;
For this I wot riht wel a fin,   60
Mi grace comth so selde aboute,
That is the Slowthe of which I doute

Mor than of al the remenant
Which is to love appourtenant.
And thus as touchende of lachesce,
As I have told, I me confesse
To you, mi fader, and beseche
That furthermor ye wol me teche;
And if ther be to this matiere
Som goodly tale forto liere   70
How I mai do lachesce aweie,   **P. ii. 4**
That ye it wolden telle I preie.

   To wisse thee, my Sone, and rede,   Confessor.
Among the tales whiche I rede,
An old ensample therupon
Now herkne, and I wol tellen on.

   Ayein Lachesce in loves cas   [ENEAS AND DIDO.]
I finde how whilom Eneas,
Whom Anchises to Sone hadde,
With gret navie, which he ladde   80 Hic ponit Confessor
Fro Troie, aryveth at Cartage,   exemplum contra istos
Wher for a while his herbergage   qui in amoris causa
He tok; and it betidde so,   tardantes delinquunt.
With hire which was qweene tho   Et narrat qualiter Di-
Of the Cite his aqueintance   do Regina Cartaginis
He wan, whos name in remembrance   Eneam ab incendiis
Is yit, and Dido sche was hote;   Troie fugitiuum in
Which loveth Eneas so hote   amorem suum gauisa
Upon the wordes whiche he seide,   suscepit: qui cum post-
That al hire herte on him sche leide   ea in partes Ytalie a
And dede al holi what he wolde.   Cartagine bellaturum
                                              se transtulit, nimiam-
   Bot after that, as it be scholde,   que ibidem moram fa-
Fro thenne he goth toward Ytaile   ciens tempus reditus
Be Schipe, and there his arivaile   90 sui ad Didonem vltra
Hath take, and schop him forto ryde.   modum tardauit, ipsa
Bot sche, which mai noght longe abide   intollerabili dolore con-
The hote peine of loves throwe,   cussa sui cordis intima
Anon withinne a litel throwe   mortali gladio trans-
A lettre unto hir kniht hath write,   fodit.
And dede him pleinly forto wite,   100

69 to this] to my B   of this H₃   70 liere] hiere (here &c.)
H₁ ... B₂, BTΛ   84 qweene] a queene BTΛ

[ENEAS AND DIDO.]

If he made eny tariinge,   P. ii. 5
To drecche of his ayeincomynge,
That sche ne mihte him fiele and se,
Sche scholde stonde in such degre
As whilom stod a Swan tofore,
Of that sche hadde hire make lore;
For sorwe a fethere into hire brain
She schof and hath hireselve slain;
As king Menander in a lay
The sothe hath founde, wher sche lay   110
Sprantlende with hire wynges tweie,
As sche which scholde thanne deie
For love of him which was hire make.
     'And so schal I do for thi sake,'
This qweene seide, 'wel I wot.'
Lo, to Enee thus sche wrot
With many an other word of pleinte:
Bot he, which hadde hise thoghtes feinte
Towardes love and full of Slowthe,
His time lette, and that was rowthe: 120
For sche, which loveth him tofore,
Desireth evere more and more,
And whan sche sih him tarie so,
Hire herte was so full of wo,
That compleignende manyfold
Sche hath hire oghne tale told,
Unto hirself and thus sche spak:
'Ha, who fond evere such a lak
Of Slowthe in eny worthi kniht?
Now wot I wel my deth is diht   130
Thurgh him which scholde have be mi lif.' P. ii. 6
Bot forto stinten al this strif,
Thus whan sche sih non other bote,
Riht evene unto hire herte rote
A naked swerd anon sche threste,
And thus sche gat hireselve reste
In remembrance of alle slowe.

Confessor.   Wherof, my Sone, thou miht knowe

109 day H₁ . . . B₂, H₃   111 Spraulende (Sprawland) M, WKH₃
138 miht (myht) J, S   mihte A, F

How tariinge upon the nede

[ENEAS AND DIDO.]

In loves cause is forto drede;   140
And that hath Dido sore aboght,
Whos deth schal evere be bethoght.
And overmore if I schal seche
In this matiere an other spieche,
In a Cronique I finde write
A tale which is good to wite.

At Troie whan king Ulixes

[ULYSSES AND
PENELOPE.]

Upon the Siege among the pres
Of hem that worthi knihtes were
Abod long time stille there,   150
In thilke time a man mai se
How goodli that Penolope,

Hic loquitur super
eodem qualiter Peno-
lope Vlixem maritum
suum, in obsidione
Troie diucius moran-
tem, ob ipsius ibidem
tardacionem Epistola
sua redarguit.

Which was to him his trewe wif,
Of his lachesce was pleintif;
Wherof to Troie sche him sende
Hire will be lettre, thus spekende:
'Mi worthi love and lord also,
It is and hath ben evere so,
That wher a womman is al one,
It makth a man in his persone   160
The more hardi forto wowe,   **P. ii. 7**
In hope that sche wolde bowe
To such thing as his wille were,
Whil that hire lord were elleswhere.
And of miself I telle this;
For it so longe passed is,
Sithe ferst than ye fro home wente,
That welnyh every man his wente
To there I am, whil ye ben oute,
Hath mad, and ech of hem aboute,   170
Which love can, my love secheth,
With gret preiere and me besecheth:
And some maken gret manace,
That if thei mihten come in place,
Wher that thei mihte here wille have,

143 euermore AM, Δ, WH₃   168 is went(e) ML, ΔΛ, WH₃
170 Had AMJXGERLB₂, BΛ, FH₃
* *   X

Ther is nothing me scholde save,
That thei ne wolde werche thinges;
And some tellen me tidynges
That ye ben ded, and some sein
That certeinly ye ben besein   180
To love a newe and leve me.
Bot hou as evere that it be,
I thonke unto the goddes alle,
As yit for oght that is befalle
Mai noman do my chekes rede:
Bot natheles it is to drede,
That Lachesse in continuance
Fortune mihte such a chance,
Which noman after scholde amende.'
Lo, thus this ladi compleignende   190
A lettre unto hire lord hath write,   **P. ii. 8**
And preyde him that he wolde wite
And thenke hou that sche was al his,
And that he tarie noght in this,
Bot that he wolde his love aquite,
To hire ayeinward and noght wryte,
Bot come himself in alle haste,
That he non other paper waste;
So that he kepe and holde his trowthe
Withoute lette of eny Slowthe.   200
     Unto hire lord and love liege
To Troie, wher the grete Siege
Was leid, this lettre was conveied.
And he, which wisdom hath pourveied
Of al that to reson belongeth,
With gentil herte it underfongeth:
And whan he hath it overrad,
In part he was riht inly glad,
And ek in part he was desesed:
Bot love his herte hath so thorghsesed   210
With pure ymaginacioun,

184 foroght A, F   189 after noman AM   205 resoun to
H₁ ... B₂   208 In part he was inly glad AM   In partie (party)
he was inly glad H₁ ... B₂   In parti he was riht inly glad J   In parti
was inli riht glad Δ

That for non occupacioun
Which he can take on other side,
He mai noght flitt his herte aside
Fro that his wif him hadde enformed;
Wherof he hath himself conformed
With al the wille of his corage
To schape and take the viage
Homward, what time that he mai·:
So that him thenketh of a day   220
A thousand yer, til he mai se   **P. ii. 9**
The visage of Penolope,
Which he desireth most of alle.
And whan the time is so befalle
That Troie was destruid and brent,
He made non delaiement,
Bot goth him home in alle hihe,
Wher that he fond tofore his yhe
His worthi wif in good astat:
And thus was cessed the debat   230
Of love, and Slowthe was excused,
Which doth gret harm, where it is used,
And hindreth many a cause honeste.

   For of the grete Clerc Grosteste
I rede how besy that he was
Upon clergie an Hed of bras
To forge, and make it forto telle
Of suche thinges as befelle.
And sevene yeres besinesse
He leyde, bot for the lachesse   240
Of half a Minut of an houre,
Fro ferst that he began laboure
He loste all that he hadde do.

   And otherwhile it fareth so,
In loves cause who is slow,
That he withoute under the wow
Be nyhte stant fulofte acold,
Which mihte, if that he hadde wold

[ULYSSES AND
PENELOPE.]

[GROSTESTE.]
   Nota adhuc super
eodem de quodam
Astrologo, qui quod-
dam opus ingeniosum
quasi ad complemen-
tum septennio perdu-
cens, vnius momenti
tardacione omnem sui
operis diligenciam
penitus frustrauit.

214 flitt AJ, S, F   flitte B   215 Fro] ffor L, BΛ, WH₂   hadde
him H₁ . . . B₂   226 no H₁ . . . CB₂, BTΔ, W   234 Lo of
H₁ . . . B₂ (of *om.* R)   242 ffor ferst B

                    X 2

His time kept, have be withinne.

[THE FOOLISH
VIRGINS.]

Nota adhuc contra
tardacionem de v. vir-
ginibus fatuis, que
nimiam moram facien-
tes intrante sponso ad
nupcias cum ipso non
introierunt.

Bot Slowthe mai no profit winne,   250
Bot he mai singe in his karole   **P. ii. 10**
How Latewar cam to the Dole,
Wher he no good receive mihte.
And that was proved wel be nyhte
Whilom of the Maidenes fyve,
Whan thilke lord cam forto wyve :
For that here oyle was aweie
To lihte here lampes in his weie,
Here Slowthe broghte it so aboute,
Fro him that thei ben schet withoute.   260

Confessor.

Wherof, my Sone, be thou war,
Als ferforth as I telle dar.
For love moste ben awaited :
And if thou be noght wel affaited
In love to eschuie Slowthe,
Mi Sone, forto telle trowthe,
Thou miht noght of thiself ben able
To winne love or make it stable,
All thogh thou mihtest love achieve.

Confessio Amantis

Mi fader, that I mai wel lieve.   270
Bot me was nevere assigned place,
Wher yit to geten eny grace,
Ne me was non such time apointed ;
For thanne I wolde I were unjoynted
Of every lime that I have,
If I ne scholde kepe and save
Min houre bothe and ek my stede,
If my ladi it hadde bede.
Bot sche is otherwise avised
Than grante such a time assised ;   280
And natheles of mi lachesse   **P. ii. 11**
Ther hath be no defalte I gesse
Of time lost, if that I mihte :
Bot yit hire liketh noght alyhte

Upon no lure which I caste ;
For ay the more I crie faste,
The lasse hire liketh forto hiere.
So forto speke of this matiere,
I seche that I mai noght finde,
I haste and evere I am behinde,   290
And wot noght what it mai amounte.
Bot, fader, upon myn acompte,
Which ye be sett to examine
Of Schrifte after the discipline,
Sey what your beste conseil is.
   Mi Sone, my conseil is this :   Confessor.
Hou so it stonde of time go,
Do forth thi besinesse so,
That no Lachesce in the be founde :
For Slowthe is mihti to confounde   300
The spied of every mannes werk.
For many a vice, as seith the clerk,
Ther hongen upon Slowthes lappe
Of suche as make a man mishappe,
To pleigne and telle of hadde I wist.
And therupon if that thee list
To knowe of Slowthes cause more,
In special yit overmore
Ther is a vice full grevable
To him which is therof coupable,   310
And stant of alle vertu bare,   **P. ii. 12**
Hierafter as I schal declare.

ii. *Qui nichil attemptat, nichil expedit, oreque muto*
   Munus Amicicie vir sibi raro capit.
  Est modus in verbis, set ei qui parcit amori
   Verba referre sua, non fauet vllus amor.

    Touchende of Slowthe in his degre,
Ther is yit Pusillamite,
Which is to seie in this langage,
He that hath litel of corage   Hic loquitur Con-
And dar no mannes werk beginne :   fessor de quadam
                            specie Accidie, que

296 this *om.* AM   297 go AJ, S, F ago B   310 To] Of B
Latin Verses ii. 3 parcat H₁ . . . B₂ parat H₃   4 refert H₁ . . . B₂

[PUSILLANIMITY.]
pusillanimitas dicta
est, cuius ymaginatiua
formido neque virtutes
aggredi neque vicia
fugere audet; sicque
vtriusque vite, tam ac-
tiue quam contempla-
tiue, premium non at-
tingit.

So mai he noght be resoun winne;
For who that noght dar undertake,
Be riht he schal no profit take.   320
Bot of this vice the nature
Dar nothing sette in aventure,
Him lacketh bothe word and dede,
Wherof he scholde his cause spede:
He woll no manhed understonde,
For evere he hath drede upon honde:
Al is peril that he schal seie,
Him thenkth the wolf is in the weie,
And of ymaginacioun
He makth his excusacioun   330
And feigneth cause of pure drede,
And evere he faileth ate nede,
Til al be spilt that he with deleth.
He hath the sor which noman heleth,
The which is cleped lack of herte;
Thogh every grace aboute him sterte,
He wol noght ones stere his fot;   **P. ii. 13**
So that be resoun lese he mot,
That wol noght auntre forto winne.

Confessor.

   And so forth, Sone, if we beginne   340
To speke of love and his servise,
Ther ben truantz in such a wise,
That lacken herte, whan best were
To speke of love, and riht for fere
Thei wexen doumb and dar noght telle,
Withoute soun as doth the belle,
Which hath no claper forto chyme;
And riht so thei as for the tyme
Ben herteles withoute speche
Of love, and dar nothing beseche;   350
And thus thei lese and winne noght.
Forthi, my Sone, if thou art oght
Coupable as touchende of this Slowthe,
Schrif thee therof and tell me trowthe.

Amans.

   Mi fader, I am al beknowe

328 the] his H₁ . . . B₂, Ad   342 tyrauntz (tirauntis &c.)
YCB₂, B

That I have ben on of tho slowe,   [PUSILLANIMITY.]
As forto telle in loves cas.
Min herte is yit and evere was,
As thogh the world scholde al tobreke,
So ferful, that I dar noght speke   360
Of what pourpos that I have nome,
Whan I toward mi ladi come,
Bot let it passe and overgo.
    Mi Sone, do nomore so: Confessor.
For after that a man poursuieth
To love, so fortune suieth,
Fulofte and yifth hire happi chance   **P. ii. 14**
To him which makth continuance
To preie love and to beseche;
As be ensample I schal thee teche.   370

    I finde hou whilom ther was on,
Whos name was Pymaleon,
Which was a lusti man of yowthe: [PYGMALEON AND THE
The werkes of entaile he cowthe   STATUE.]
Above alle othre men as tho;   Hic in amoris causa
And thurgh fortune it fell him so,   loquitur contra pusil-
As he whom love schal travaile,   lanimes, et dicit quod
He made an ymage of entaile   Amans pre timore
Lich to a womman in semblance   verbis obmutescere
Of feture and of contienance,   non debet, set contin-
So fair yit nevere was figure.   uando preces sui
Riht as a lyves creature   amoris expedicionem
Sche semeth, for of yvor whyt   tucius prosequatur.
He hath hire wroght of such delit,   380 Et ponit Confessor
That sche was rody on the cheke   exemplum, qualiter
And red on bothe hire lippes eke;   Pigmaleon, pro eo
Wherof that he himself beguileth.   quod preces continu-
For with a goodly lok sche smyleth,   auit, quandam ymagi-
So that thurgh pure impression   nem eburneam, cuius
Of his ymaginacion   390   pulcritudinis concu-
With al the herte of his corage   piscencia illaqueatus
                                  extitit, in carnem et
                                  sanguinem ad latus
                                  suum transformatam
                                  senciit.

356 þo J, T, F   þe AM . . . B₂, SAdBΔ, WH₃   359 Al þough
C, B   363 let AJ, S, F   lete (lette) C, B   372 Pymaleon
AJ, S, F   Pigmaleon EC, B, H₃   384 hire] it B

His love upon this faire ymage
He sette, and hire of love preide ;
Bot sche no word ayeinward seide.
The longe day, what thing he dede,
This ymage in the same stede
Was evere bi, that ate mete   **P. ii. 15**
He wolde hire serve and preide hire ete,
And putte unto hire mowth the cuppe ;
And whan the bord was taken uppe,   400
He hath hire into chambre nome,
And after, whan the nyht was come,
He leide hire in his bed al nakid.
He was forwept, he was forwakid,
He keste hire colde lippes ofte,
And wissheth that thei weren softe,
And ofte he rouneth in hire Ere,
And ofte his arm now hier now there
He leide, as he hir wolde embrace,
And evere among he axeth grace,   410
As thogh sche wiste what he mente :
And thus himself he gan tormente
With such desese of loves peine,
That noman mihte him more peine.
Bot how it were, of his penance
He made such continuance
Fro dai to nyht, and preith so longe,
That his preiere is underfonge,
Which Venus of hire grace herde ;
Be nyhte and whan that he worst ferde,   420
And it lay in his nakede arm,
The colde ymage he fieleth warm
Of fleissh and bon and full of lif.
    Lo, thus he wan a lusti wif,
Which obeissant was at his wille ;
And if he wolde have holde him stille
And nothing spoke, he scholde have failed : **P. ii. 16**
Bot for he hath his word travailed
And dorste speke, his love he spedde,

401 into his chambre H₁ ... B₂ (*except* E)   403 He] And AM
411 he] it H₁, B

And hadde al that he wolde abedde.
For er thei wente thanne atwo,
A knave child betwen hem two
Thei gete, which was after hote
Paphus, of whom yit hath the note
A certein yle, which Paphos
Men clepe, and of his name it ros.

   Be this ensample thou miht finde
That word mai worche above kinde.
Forthi, my Sone, if that thou spare
To speke, lost is al thi fare,
For Slowthe bringth in alle wo.
And over this to loke also,
The god of love is favorable
To hem that ben of love stable,
And many a wonder hath befalle:
Wherof to speke amonges alle,
If that thee list to taken hede,
Therof a solein tale I rede,
Which I schal telle in remembraunce
Upon the sort of loves chaunce.

   The king Ligdus upon a strif
Spak unto Thelacuse his wif,
Which thanne was with childe grete;
He swor it scholde noght be lete,
That if sche have a dowhter bore,
That it ne scholde be forlore
And slain, wherof sche sory was.
So it befell upon this cas,
Whan sche delivered scholde be,
Isis be nyhte in privete,
Which of childinge is the goddesse,
Cam forto helpe in that destresse,
Til that this lady was al smal,
And hadde a dowhter forth withal;
Which the goddesse in alle weie
Bad kepe, and that thei scholden seie

430 [PYGMALEON AND THE STATUE.]

Confessor.

440

450

[TALE OF IPHIS.]

P. ii. 17

Hic ponit exem-
plum super eodem,
qualiter Rex Ligdus
vxori sue Thelacuse
pregnanti minabatur,
quod si filiam pareret,
infans occideretur:
460 que tamen postea cum
filiam ediderat, Isis
dea partus tunc pre-
sens filiam nomine
filii Yphim appellari
ipsamque more mas-
culi educari admonuit:
quam pater filium cre-
dens, ipsam in mari-
tagium filie cuiusdam

453 f. grete : lete AJ, S, F   gret : let B   458 *margin* Isus H₁G
RCLB₂, T

[TALE OF IPHIS.]

principis etate solita
copulauit. Set cum
Yphis debitum sue
coniugi vnde soluere
non habuit, deos in
sui adiutorium inter-
pellabat; qui super hoc
miserti femininum ge-
nus in masculinum ob
affectum nature in Y-
phe per omnia trans-
mutarunt.

It were a Sone: and thus Iphis
Thei namede him, and upon this
The fader was mad so to wene.
And thus in chambre with the qweene   470
This Iphis was forthdrawe tho,
And clothed and arraied so
Riht as a kinges Sone scholde.
Til after, as fortune it wolde,
Whan it was of a ten yer age,
Him was betake in mariage
A Duckes dowhter forto wedde,
Which Iante hihte, and ofte abedde
These children leien, sche and sche,
Whiche of on age bothe be.   480
So that withinne time of yeeres,
Togedre as thei ben pleiefieres,
Liggende abedde upon a nyht,
Nature, which doth every wiht
Upon hire lawe forto muse,
Constreigneth hem, so that thei use
Thing which to hem was al unknowe;   **P. ii. 18**
Wherof Cupide thilke throwe
Tok pite for the grete love,
And let do sette kinde above,   490
So that hir lawe mai ben used,
And thei upon here lust excused.
For love hateth nothing more
Than thing which stant ayein the lore
Of that nature in kinde hath sett:
Forthi Cupide hath so besett
His grace upon this aventure,
That he acordant to nature,
Whan that he syh the time best,
That ech of hem hath other kest,   500
Transformeth Iphe into a man,
Wherof the kinde love he wan
Of lusti yonge Iante his wif;

470 *line om.* B   479 he and sche H1 ... B2 sche and he B
481 a tyme B   497 Hir B   498 he] be BT   499 the]
his AdB *om.* L

And tho thei ladde a merie lif,   [TALE OF IPHIS.]
Which was to kinde non offence.
    And thus to take an evidence,   Confessor.
It semeth love is welwillende
To hem that ben continuende
With besy herte to poursuie
Thing which that is to love due.   510
Wherof, my Sone, in this matiere
Thou miht ensample taken hiere,
That with thi grete besinesse
Thou miht atteigne the richesse
Of love, if that ther be no Slowthe.
    I dar wel seie be mi trowthe,   Amans.
Als fer as I my witt can seche,   **P. ii. 19**
Mi fader, as for lacke of speche,
Bot so as I me schrof tofore,
Ther is non other time lore,   520
Wherof ther mihte ben obstacle
To lette love of his miracle,
Which I beseche day and nyht.
Bot, fader, so as it is riht
In forme of schrifte to beknowe
What thing belongeth to the slowe,
Your faderhode I wolde preie,
If ther be forthere eny weie
Touchende unto this ilke vice.
    Mi Sone, ye, of this office   530   Confessor.
Ther serveth on in special,
Which lost hath his memorial,
So that he can no wit withholde
In thing which he to kepe is holde,
Wherof fulofte himself he grieveth :
And who that most upon him lieveth,
Whan that hise wittes ben so weyved,
He mai full lihtly be deceived.

---

514 myht (might) J, B   mihte A, S, F   the] þi H₁ . . . B₂
to T   515 that *om.* B   517 Also fer as my E . . . B₂   As (Als
fer as my H₁XG   521 mihte ben] might(e) be non H₁ . . . B₂
535 himself fulofte A . . . B₂ (fulle of M), W

iii. *Mentibus oblitus alienis labitur ille,*
   Quem probat accidia non meminisse sui.
   Sic amor incautus, qui non memoratur ad horas,
   Perdit et offendit, quod cuperare nequit.

To serve Accidie in his office,
Ther is of Slowthe an other vice,   540
Which cleped is Foryetelnesse;
That noght mai in his herte impresse
Of vertu which reson hath sett,   **P. ii. 20**
So clene his wittes he foryet.
For in the tellinge of his tale
Nomore his herte thanne his male
Hath remembrance of thilke forme,
Wherof he scholde his wit enforme
As thanne, and yit ne wot he why.
Thus is his pourpos noght forthi   550
Forlore of that he wolde bidde,
And skarsly if he seith the thridde
To love of that he hadde ment:
Thus many a lovere hath be schent.
Tell on therfore, hast thou be oon
Of hem that Slowthe hath so begon?
   Ye, fader, ofte it hath be so,
That whanne I am mi ladi fro
And thenke untoward hire drawe,
Than cast I many a newe lawe   560
And al the world torne up so doun,
And so recorde I mi lecoun
And wryte in my memorial
What I to hire telle schal,
Riht al the matiere of mi tale:
Bot al nys worth a note schale;
For whanne I come ther sche is,
I have it al foryete ywiss;
Of that I thoghte forto telle
I can noght thanne unethes spelle   570
That I wende altherbest have rad,

Latin Verses iii. 3 morabatur AM
546 *margin* se constituit B   548 wit] herte A . . . B₂
therfore] forþer(e) BT   560 cast J, SB, F   caste A   555

So sore I am of hire adrad.
For as a man that sodeinli   P. ii. 21
A gost behelde, so fare I ;
So that for feere I can noght gete
Mi witt, bot I miself foryete,
That I wot nevere what I am,
Ne whider I schal, ne whenne I cam,
Bot muse as he that were amased.
Lich to the bok in which is rased   580
The lettre, and mai nothing be rad,
So ben my wittes overlad,
That what as evere I thoghte have spoken,
It is out fro myn herte stoken,
And stonde, as who seith, doumb and def,
That all nys worth an yvy lef,
Of that I wende wel have seid.
And ate laste I make abreid,
Caste up myn hed and loke aboute,
Riht as a man that were in doute   590
And wot noght wher he schal become.
Thus am I ofte al overcome,
Ther as I wende best to stonde :
Bot after, whanne I understonde,
And am in other place al one,
I make many a wofull mone
Unto miself, and speke so :
'Ha fol, wher was thin herte tho,
Whan thou thi worthi ladi syhe?
Were thou afered of hire yhe?   600
For of hire hand ther is no drede :
So wel I knowe hir wommanhede,
That in hire is nomore oultrage   P. ii. 22
Than in a child of thre yeer age.
Whi hast thou drede of so good on,
Whom alle vertu hath begon,
That in hire is no violence
Bot goodlihiede and innocence
Withouten spot of eny blame?

574 be holde R   beholdeþ BT, W   584 ouht fro F   out of
H₁ . . . B₂, B   588 abreid (abreide) A, F   a breid JEC, B

Ha, nyce herte, fy for schame!⠀⠀⠀⠀⠀⠀610
Ha, couard herte of love unlered,
Wherof art thou so sore afered,
That thou thi tunge soffrest frese,
And wolt thi goode wordes lese,
Whan thou hast founde time and space?
How scholdest thou deserve grace,
Whan thou thiself darst axe non,
Bot al thou hast foryete anon?'
And thus despute I loves lore,
Bot help ne finde I noght the more,⠀⠀⠀620
Bot stomble upon myn oghne treine
And make an ekinge of my peine.
For evere whan I thenke among
How al is on miself along,
I seie, 'O fol of alle foles,
Thou farst as he betwen tuo stoles
That wolde sitte and goth to grounde.
It was ne nevere schal be founde,
Betwen foryetelnesse and drede
That man scholde any cause spede.'⠀⠀⠀630
And thus, myn holi fader diere,
Toward miself, as ye mai hiere,
I pleigne of my foryetelnesse;⠀⠀⠀**P. ii. 23**
Bot elles al the besinesse,
That mai be take of mannes thoght,
Min herte takth, and is thorghsoght
To thenken evere upon that swete
Withoute Slowthe, I you behete.
For what so falle, or wel or wo,
That thoght foryete I neveremo,⠀⠀⠀640
Wher so I lawhe or so I loure:
Noght half the Minut of an houre
Ne mihte I lete out of my mende,
Bot if I thoghte upon that hende.
Therof me schal no Slowthe lette,
Til deth out of this world me fette,

618 And B⠀⠀⠀624 is] þis XCL⠀⠀⠀627 Thow (þou) AM⠀⠀⠀628 schal]
it schal AJH₁ . . . CB₂⠀⠀⠀⠀⠀⠀641 or wher (wheþer) I H₁G . . . B₂
or where so I X⠀⠀or elles T⠀⠀or Δ⠀⠀⠀642 a mynut (minute) X, BΔ, W

Althogh I hadde on such a Ring,
As Moises thurgh his enchanting
Som time in Ethiope made,
Whan that he Tharbis weddid hade.   650
Which Ring bar of Oblivion
The name, and that was be resoun
That where it on a finger sat,
Anon his love he so foryat,
As thogh he hadde it nevere knowe:
And so it fell that ilke throwe,
Whan Tharbis hadde it on hire hond,
No knowlechinge of him sche fond,
Bot al was clene out of memoire,
As men mai rede in his histoire;   660
And thus he wente quit away,
That nevere after that ilke day
Sche thoghte that ther was such on;   **P. ii. 24**
Al was foryete and overgon.
Bot in good feith so mai noght I :
For sche is evere faste by,
So nyh that sche myn herte toucheth,
That for nothing that Slowthe voucheth
I mai foryete hire, lief ne loth ;
For overal, where as sche goth,   670
Min herte folwith hire aboute.
Thus mai I seie withoute doute,
For bet, for wers, for oght, for noght,
Sche passeth nevere fro my thoght;
Bot whanne I am ther as sche is,
Min herte, as I you saide er this,
Som time of hire is sore adrad,
And som time it is overglad,
Al out of reule and out of space.
For whan I se hir goodli face   680
And thenke upon hire hihe pris,
As thogh I were in Paradis,
I am so ravisht of the syhte,
That speke unto hire I ne myhte

672 seie A, S, F   sey (say) J, B   676 erþis F   684 That]
To FWKII₃

[FORGETFULNESS.]

As for the time, thogh I wolde :
For I ne mai my wit unfolde
To finde o word of that I mene,
Bot al it is foryete clene ;
And thogh I stonde there a myle,
Al is foryete for the while,　　　　690
A tunge I have and wordes none.
And thus I stonde and thenke al one
Of thing that helpeth ofte noght ;　　**P. ii. 25**
Bot what I hadde afore thoght
To speke, whanne I come there,
It is foryete, as noght ne were,
And stonde amased and assoted,
That of nothing which I have noted
I can noght thanne a note singe,
Bot al is out of knowlechinge :　　　　700
Thus, what for joie and what for drede,
Al is foryeten ate nede.
So that, mi fader, of this Slowthe
I have you said the pleine trowthe ;
Ye mai it as you list redresce :
For thus stant my foryetelnesse
And ek my pusillamite.
Sey now forth what you list to me,
For I wol only do be you.

Confessor.

　　Mi Sone, I have wel herd how thou　710
Hast seid, and that thou most amende :
For love his grace wol noght sende
To that man which dar axe non.
For this we knowen everichon,
A mannes thoght withoute speche
God wot, and yit that men beseche
His will is ; for withoute bedes
He doth his grace in fewe stedes :
And what man that foryet himselve,
Among a thousand be noght tuelve,　　720
That wol him take in remembraunce,
Bot lete him falle and take his chaunce.

Forthi pull up a besi herte,   P. ii. 26 [Forgetfulness.]
Mi Sone, and let nothing asterte
Of love fro thi besinesse :
For touchinge of foryetelnesse,
Which many a love hath set behinde,
A tale of gret ensample I finde,
Wherof it is pite to wite
In the manere as it is write.   730

King Demephon, whan he be Schipe   [Demephon and
To Troieward with felaschipe   Phillis.]
Sailende goth, upon his weie
It hapneth him at Rodopeie,   Hic in amoris causa
As Eolus him hadde blowe,   contra obliuiosos po-
To londe, and rested for a throwe.   nit Confessor exem-
And fell that ilke time thus,   plum, qualiter Deme-
The dowhter of Ligurgius,   phon versus bellum
Which qweene was of the contre,   Troianum itinerando
Was sojournende in that Cite   740 a Phillide Rodopeie
Withinne a Castell nyh the stronde,   Regina non tantum in
Wher Demephon cam up to londe.   hospicium, set eciam
                                             in amorem, gaudio
Phillis sche hihte, and of yong age   magno susceptus est :
And of stature and of visage   qui postea ab ipsa
Sche hadde al that hire best besemeth.   Troie discedens redi-
Of Demephon riht wel hire qwemeth,   turum infra certum
Whan he was come, and made him chiere ;   tempus fidelissime se
And he, that was of his manere   compromisit. Set quia
A lusti knyht, ne myhte asterte   huiusmodi promissi-
That he ne sette on hire his herte ;   750 onis diem statutum
So that withinne a day or tuo   postmodum   oblitus
He thoghte, how evere that it go,   est, Phillis obliuionem
He wolde assaie the fortune,   Demephontis lacrimis
                                        P. ii. 27 primo deplangens,tan-
And gan his herte to commune   dem cordula collo suo
With goodly wordes in hire Ere ;   circumligata in qua-
And forto put hire out of fere,   dam corulo pre dolore
He swor and hath his trowthe pliht   750 se mortuam suspendit.
To be for evere hire oghne knyht.
And thus with hire he stille abod,
Ther while his Schip on Anker rod,   760

740 margin ob ipsa H₁XE . . . B₂   760 Ther while] The while
BT, W þat while M   Theke while J
**   Y

And hadde ynowh of time and space
To speke of love and seche grace.
      This ladi herde al that he seide,
And hou he swor and hou he preide,
Which was as an enchantement
To hire, that was innocent :
As thogh it were trowthe and feith,
Sche lieveth al that evere he seith,
And as hire infortune scholde,
Sche granteth him al that he wolde.   770
Thus was he for the time in joie,
Til that he scholde go to Troie ;
Bot tho sche made mochel sorwe,
And he his trowthe leith to borwe
To come, if that he live may,
Ayein withinne a Monthe day,
And therupon thei kisten bothe :
Bot were hem lieve or were hem lothe,
To Schipe he goth and forth he wente
To Troie, as was his ferste entente.   780
      The daies gon, the Monthe passeth,
Hire love encresceth and his lasseth,
For him sche lefte slep and mete,   **P. ii. 28**
And he his time hath al foryete ;
So that this wofull yonge qweene,
Which wot noght what it mihte meene,
A lettre sende and preide him come,
And seith how sche is overcome
With strengthe of love in such a wise,
That sche noght longe mai suffise   790
To liven out of his presence ;
And putte upon his conscience
The trowthe which he hath behote,
Wherof sche loveth him so hote,
Sche seith, that if he lengere lette
Of such a day as sche him sette,
Sche scholde sterven in his Slowthe,

766 al Innocent H₁ ... B₂   an Innocent M   790 longe may not
(nought) X ... B₂   longe nouht may H₁   797 wold(e) AM
wolde hym W

Which were a schame unto his trowthe.
This lettre is forth upon hire sonde,
Wherof somdiel confort on honde 800
Sche tok, as sche that wolde abide
And waite upon that ilke tyde
Which sche hath in hire lettre write.
  Bot now is pite forto wite,
As he dede erst, so he foryat
His time eftsone and oversat.
Bot sche, which mihte noght do so,
The tyde awayteth everemo,
And caste hire yhe upon the See:
Somtime nay, somtime yee, 810
Somtime he cam, somtime noght,
Thus sche desputeth in hire thoght
And wot noght what sche thenke mai; **P. ii. 29**
Bot fastende al the longe day
Sche was into the derke nyht,
And tho sche hath do set up lyht
In a lanterne on hih alofte
Upon a Tour, wher sche goth ofte,
In hope that in his cominge
He scholde se the liht brenninge, 820
Wherof he mihte his weies rihte
To come wher sche was be nyhte.
Bot al for noght, sche was deceived,
For Venus hath hire hope weyved,
And schewede hire upon the Sky
How that the day was faste by,
So that withinne a litel throwe
The daies lyht sche mihte knowe.
Tho sche behield the See at large;
And whan sche sih ther was no barge 830
Ne Schip, als ferr as sche may kenne,
Doun fro the Tour sche gan to renne
Into an Herber all hire one,
Wher many a wonder woful mone
Sche made, that no lif it wiste,
As sche which all hire joie miste,
That now sche swouneth, now sche pleigneth,

And al hire face sche desteigneth
With teres, whiche, as of a welle
The stremes, from hire yhen felle ;   840
So as sche mihte and evere in on
Sche clepede upon Demephon,
And seide, 'Helas, thou slowe wiht,   **P. ii. 30**
Wher was ther evere such a knyht,
That so thurgh his ungentilesce
Of Slowthe and of foryetelnesse
Ayein his trowthe brak his stevene?'
And tho hire yhe up to the hevene
Sche caste, and seide, 'O thou unkinde,
Hier schalt thou thurgh thi Slowthe finde,   850
If that thee list to come and se,
A ladi ded for love of thee,
So as I schal myselve spille;
Whom, if it hadde be thi wille,
Thou mihtest save wel ynowh.'
With that upon a grene bowh
A Ceinte of Selk, which sche ther hadde,
Sche knette, and so hireself sche ladde,
That sche aboute hire whyte swere
It dede, and hyng hirselven there.   860
Wherof the goddes were amoeved,
And Demephon was so reproeved,
That of the goddes providence
Was schape such an evidence
Evere afterward ayein the slowe,
That Phillis in the same throwe
Was schape into a Notetre,
That alle men it mihte se,
And after Phillis Philliberd
This tre was cleped in the yerd,   870
And yit for Demephon to schame
Into this dai it berth the name.
This wofull chance how that it ferde   **P. ii. 31**
Anon as Demephon it herde,
And every man it hadde in speche,
His sorwe was noght tho to seche;
He gan his Slowthe forto banne,

Bot it was al to late thanne.
    Lo thus, my Sone, miht thou wite Confessor.
Ayein this vice how it is write ;   880
For noman mai the harmes gesse,
That fallen thurgh foryetelnesse,
Wherof that I thi schrifte have herd.
Bot yit of Slowthe hou it hath ferd
In other wise I thenke oppose,
If thou have gult, as I suppose.

iv.   Dum plantare licet, cultor qui necgligit ortum, [iv. NEGLIGENCE.]
    Si desint fructus, imputet ipse sibi.
  Preterit ista dies bona, nec valet illa secunda,
    Hoc caret exemplo lentus amore suo.

    Fulfild of Slowthes essamplaire
Ther is yit on, his Secretaire,
And he is cleped Negligence :
Which wol noght loke his evidence,   890 Hic tractat Confes-
Wherof he mai be war tofore ;   sor de vicio Necgligen-
                          cie, cuius condicio Ac-
Bot whanne he hath his cause lore,   cidiam amplectens om-
Thanne is he wys after the hond :   nes artes sciencie, tam
                          in amoris causa quam
Whanne helpe may no maner bond,   aliter,   ignominiosa
Thanne ate ferste wolde he binde :   pretermittens,   cum
Thus everemore he stant behinde.   nullum poterit emin-
                          ere remedium, sui mi-
Whanne he the thing mai noght amende, nisterii   diligenciam
Thanne is he war, and seith at ende,   expostfacto in vacuum
'Ha, wolde god I hadde knowe !'   **P. ii. 32** attemptare presumit.
Wherof bejaped with a mowe   900
He goth, for whan the grete Stiede
Is stole, thanne he taketh hiede,
And makth the stable dore fast :
Thus evere he pleith an aftercast
Of al that he schal seie or do.
He hath a manere eke also,
Him list noght lerne to be wys,
For he set of no vertu pris
Bot as him liketh for the while ;
So fieleth he fulofte guile,   910
Whan that he weneth siker stonde.

      Latin verses iv. 2 ipse] esse AM, **W**

And thus thou miht wel understonde,
Mi Sone, if thou art such in love,
Thou miht noght come at thin above
Of that thou woldest wel achieve.

Confessio Amantis.

    Mi holi fader, as I lieve,
I mai wel with sauf conscience
Excuse me of necgligence
Towardes love in alle wise :
For thogh I be non of the wise,   920
I am so trewly amerous,
That I am evere curious
Of hem that conne best enforme
To knowe and witen al the forme,
What falleth unto loves craft.
Bot yit ne fond I noght the haft,
Which mihte unto that bladd acorde ;
For nevere herde I man recorde
What thing it is that myhte availe   **P. ii. 33**
To winne love withoute faile.   930
Yit so fer cowthe I nevere finde
Man that be resoun ne be kinde
Me cowthe teche such an art,
That he ne failede of a part ;
And as toward myn oghne wit,
Controeve cowthe I nevere yit
To finden eny sikernesse,
That me myhte outher more or lesse
Of love make forto spede :
For lieveth wel withoute drede,   940
If that ther were such a weie,
As certeinliche as I schal deie
I hadde it lerned longe ago.
Bot I wot wel ther is non so :
And natheles it may wel be,
I am so rude in my degree
And ek mi wittes ben so dulle,
That I ne mai noght to the fulle
Atteigne to so hih a lore.
Bot this I dar seie overmore,   950

927 þe blad (blade) M, BTΔ, WH₃

Althogh mi wit ne be noght strong,
It is noght on mi will along,
For that is besi nyht and day
To lerne al that he lerne may,
How that I mihte love winne :
Bot yit I am as to beginne
Of that I wolde make an ende,
And for I not how it schal wende,
That is to me mi moste sorwe.   P. ii. 34
Bot I dar take god to borwe,   960
As after min entendement,
Non other wise necgligent
Thanne I yow seie have I noght be :
Forthi per seinte charite
Tell me, mi fader, what you semeth.

   In good feith, Sone, wel me qwemeth,   Confessor.
That thou thiself hast thus aquit
Toward this vice, in which no wit
Abide mai, for in an houre
He lest al that he mai laboure   970
The longe yer, so that men sein,
What evere he doth it is in vein.
For thurgh the Slowthe of Negligence
Ther was yit nevere such science
Ne vertu, which was bodely,
That nys destruid and lost therby.
Ensample that it hath be so
In boke I finde write also.

   Phebus, which is the Sonne hote,   [TALE OF PHAETON.]
That schyneth upon Erthe hote   980
And causeth every lyves helthe,
He hadde a Sone in al his welthe,
Which Pheton hihte, and he desireth   Hic contra vicium
And with his Moder he conspireth,   necgligencie   ponit
The which was cleped Clemenee,   Confessor exemplum;
For help and conseil, so that he   et narrat quod cum
                                           Pheton filius Solis
                                           currum patris sui per
                                           aera regere debuerat,

955 mihte] may hir B   may T   968 vice om. BT   974 neuere
ȝit AM   984 margin cum om. BT   985 Clemenee] Element
ERC   Olement H₁XG   Clement LB₂   Clemencee T   Clemente M
986 so that he] þat he sent H₁ . . . B₂

[TALE OF PHAETON.]

admonitus a patre
vt equos ne deuiarent
equa manu diligen-
cius refrenaret. ipse
consilium patris sua
negligencia preteri-
ens, equos cum curru
nimis basse errare per-
misit; vnde non solum
incendio orbem in-
flammauit, set et seip-
sum de curru caden-
tem in quoddam flu-
uium demergi ad in-
teritum causauit.

His fader carte lede myhte
Upon the faire daies brihte.
And for this thing thei bothe preide   P. ii. 35
Unto the fader, and he seide   990
He wolde wel, bot forth withal
Thre pointz he bad in special
Unto his Sone in alle wise,
That he him scholde wel avise
And take it as be weie of lore.
Ferst was, that he his hors to sore
Ne prike, and over that he tolde
That he the renes faste holde;
And also that he be riht war
In what manere he lede his charr,   1000
That he mistake noght his gate,
Bot up avisement algate
He scholde bere a siker yhe,
That he to lowe ne to hyhe
His carte dryve at eny throwe,
Wherof that he mihte overthrowe.
And thus be Phebus ordinance
Tok Pheton into governance
The Sonnes carte, which he ladde :
Bot he such veine gloire hadde   1010
Of that he was set upon hyh,
That he his oghne astat ne syh
Thurgh negligence and tok non hiede;
So mihte he wel noght longe spede.
For he the hors withoute lawe
The carte let aboute drawe
Wher as hem liketh wantounly,
That ate laste sodeinly,
For he no reson wolde knowe,   P. ii. 36
This fyri carte he drof to lowe,   1020
And fyreth al the world aboute;
Wherof thei weren alle in doubte,
And to the god for helpe criden

988 brihte] nyhte (niȝt) AM   1002 up] vpon BT   vp an Ad
om. M   1014 wel noght longe] nought longe wel C   not
longe W

Of suche unhappes as betyden.   [TALE OF PHAETON.]
Phebus, which syh the necgligence,
How Pheton ayein his defence
His charr hath drive out of the weie,
Ordeigneth that he fell aweie
Out of the carte into a flod
And dreynte. Lo now, hou it stod   1030
With him that was so necgligent,
That fro the hyhe firmament,
For that he wolde go to lowe,
He was anon doun overthrowe.

 In hih astat it is a vice   [TALE OF ICARUS.]
To go to lowe, and in service
It grieveth forto go to hye,
Wherof a tale in poesie   Exemplum super
I finde, how whilom Dedalus,   eodem de Icharo De-
Which hadde a Sone, and Icharus   1040 dali filio in carcere
                                             Minotauri existente,
He hihte, and thogh hem thoghte lothe,   cui Dedalus, vt inde
In such prison thei weren bothe   euolaret, alas com-
With Minotaurus, that aboute   ponens, firmiter in-
                                             iunxit ne nimis alte
Thei mihten nawher wenden oute ;   propter Solis ardorem
So thei begonne forto schape   ascenderet : quod Ich-
How thei the prison mihte ascape.   arus sua negligencia
This Dedalus, which fro his yowthe   postponens, cum alc-
                                             ius sublimatus fuisset,
Was tawht and manye craftes cowthe,   subito ad terram cor-
Of fetheres and of othre thinges   P. ii. 37 ruens expirauit.
Hath mad to fle diverse wynges   1050
For him and for his Sone also ;
To whom he yaf in charge tho
And bad him thenke therupon,
How that his wynges ben set on
With wex, and if he toke his flyhte
To hyhe, al sodeinliche he mihte
Make it to melte with the Sonne.
And thus thei have her flyht begonne
Out of the prison faire and softe ;
And whan thei weren bothe alofte,   1060
This Icharus began to monte,

1029 þe flod (flood) E, B   1035 *Paragr. in* MSS. *begins at*
l. 1039

[TALE OF ICARUS.]

And of the conseil non accompte
He sette, which his fader tawhte,
Til that the Sonne his wynges cawhte,
Wherof it malt, and fro the heihte
Withouten help of eny sleihte
He fell to his destruccion.
And lich to that condicion
Ther fallen ofte times fele
For lacke of governance in wele,   1070
Als wel in love as other weie.

Amans.

Now goode fader, I you preie,
If ther be more in the matiere
Of Slowthe, that I mihte it hiere.

Confessor.

Mi Sone, and for thi diligence,
Which every mannes conscience
Be resoun scholde reule and kepe,
If that thee list to taken kepe,
I wol thee telle, aboven alle   P. ii. 38
In whom no vertu mai befalle,   1080
Which yifth unto the vices reste
And is of slowe the sloweste.

[v. IDLENESS.]

v. *Absque labore vagus vir inutilis ocia plectens,*
    Nescio quid presens vita valebit ei.
    Non amor in tali misero viget, immo valoris
    Qui faciunt opera clamat habere suos.

Among these othre of Slowthes kinde,
Which alle labour set behinde,
And hateth alle besinesse,
Ther is yit on, which Ydelnesse

Hic loquitur Confessor super illa specie Accidie, que Ocium dicitur, cuius condicio in virtutum cultura nullius occupacionis diligenciam admittens, cuiuscumque expedicionem cause non attingit.

Is cleped, and is the Norrice
In mannes kinde of every vice,
Which secheth eases manyfold.
In Wynter doth he noght for cold,   1090
In Somer mai he noght for hete;
So whether that he frese or swete,

1073 þis matiere B₂, BΛ   1074 it *om.* H₁, B   1075 and]
as BT   1082 slowe AJM, F   slouþe H₁ . . . B₂, S . . . ΔΛ, WH₃
1086 yit on, which] on ȝit which A, W   on ȝit *þat* M   on which þat
H₁ . . . B₂

Or he be inne, or he be oute,
He wol ben ydel al aboute,
Bot if he pleie oght ate Dees.
For who as evere take fees
And thenkth worschipe to deserve,
Ther is no lord whom he wol serve,
As forto duelle in his servise,
Bot if it were in such a wise,   1100
Of that he seth per aventure
That be lordschipe and coverture
He mai the more stonde stille,
And use his ydelnesse at wille.
For he ne wol no travail take   **P. ii. 39**
To ryde for his ladi sake,
Bot liveth al upon his wisshes;
And as a cat wolde ete fisshes
Withoute wetinge of his cles,
So wolde he do, bot natheles   1110
He faileth ofte of that he wolde.

   Mi Sone, if thou of such a molde   Confessor.
Art mad, now tell me plein thi schrifte.

   Nay, fader, god I yive a yifte,   Amans.
That toward love, as be mi wit,
Al ydel was I nevere yit,
Ne nevere schal, whil I mai go.

   Now, Sone, tell me thanne so,   Confessor.
What hast thou don of besischipe
To love and to the ladischipe   1120
Of hire which thi ladi is?

   Mi fader, evere yit er this   Confessio Amantis.
In every place, in every stede,
What so mi lady hath me bede,
With al myn herte obedient
I have therto be diligent.
And if so is sche bidde noght,
What thing that thanne into my thoght
Comth ferst of that I mai suffise,
I bowe and profre my servise,   1130
Somtime in chambre, somtime in halle,

1093 be he ... be he C, BΔ, H₃ be ... be he H₁   1095 oght *om.* B

Riht as I se the times falle.
And whan sche goth to hiere masse,
That time schal noght overpasse,
That I naproche hir ladihede,　　　　　**P. ii. 40**
In aunter if I mai hire lede
Unto the chapelle and ayein.
Thanne is noght al mi weie in vein,
Somdiel I mai the betre fare,
Whan I, that mai noght fiele hir bare,　　　1140
Mai lede hire clothed in myn arm :
Bot afterward it doth me harm
Of pure ymaginacioun ;
For thanne this collacioun
I make unto miselven ofte,
And seie, 'Ha lord, hou sche is softe,
How sche is round, hou sche is smal !
Now wolde god I hadde hire al
Withoute danger at mi wille !'
And thanne I sike and sitte stille,　　　　1150
Of that I se mi besi thoght
Is torned ydel into noght.
Bot for al that lete I ne mai,
Whanne I se time an other dai,
That I ne do my besinesse
Unto mi ladi worthinesse.
For I therto mi wit afaite
To se the times and awaite
What is to done and what to leve :
And so, whan time is, be hir leve,　　　　1160
What thing sche bit me don, I do,
And wher sche bidt me gon, I go,
And whanne hir list to clepe, I come.
Thus hath sche fulliche overcome
Min ydelnesse til I sterve,　　　　　　**P. ii. 41**
So that I mot hire nedes serve,
For as men sein, nede hath no lawe.
Thus mot I nedly to hire drawe,

1133 to hire (hir) masse AMH₁, Ad　to huyre masse B　toward
hir masse X . . . B₂　　1162 bidt F (cp. l. 2802) bit J, SB
biddeþ A

I serve, I bowe, I loke, I loute,
Min yhe folweth hire aboute,   1170
What so sche wole so wol I,
Whan sche wol sitte, I knele by,
And whan sche stant, than wol I stonde :
Bot whan sche takth hir werk on honde
Of wevinge or enbrouderie,
Thau can I noght bot muse and prie
Upon hir fingres longe and smale,
And now I thenke, and now I tale,
And now I singe, and now I sike,
And thus mi contienance I pike.   1180
And if it falle, as for a time
Hir liketh noght abide bime,
Bot besien hire on other thinges,
Than make I othre tariinges
To dreche forth the longe dai,
For me is loth departe away.
And thanne I am so simple of port,
That forto feigne som desport
I pleie with hire litel hound
Now on the bedd, now on the ground,   1190
Now with hir briddes in the cage ;
For ther is non so litel page,
Ne yit so simple a chamberere,
That I ne make hem alle chere,
Al for thei scholde speke wel :   **P. ii. 42**
Thus mow ye sen mi besi whiel,
That goth noght ydeliche aboute.
And if hir list to riden oute
On pelrinage or other stede,
I come, thogh I be noght bede,   1200
And take hire in min arm alofte
And sette hire in hire sadel softe,
And so forth lede hire be the bridel,
For that I wolde noght ben ydel.
And if hire list to ride in Char,
And thanne I mai therof be war,

1174 And B   1183 oþer JGC, S, F   oþre AE, AdB, H₃
othere T

Anon I schape me to ryde
Riht evene be the Chares side ;
And as I mai, I speke among,
And otherwhile I singe a song,   1210
Which Ovide in his bokes made,
And seide, 'O whiche sorwes glade,
O which wofull prosperite
Belongeth to the proprete
Of love, who so wole him serve !
And yit therfro mai noman swerve,
That he ne mot his lawe obeie.'
And thus I ryde forth mi weie,
And am riht besi overal
With herte and with mi body al,   1220
As I have said you hier tofore.
My goode fader, tell therfore,
Of Ydelnesse if I have gilt.

Confessor.

    Mi Sone, bot thou telle wilt
Oght elles than I mai now hiere,   **P. ii. 43**
Thou schalt have no penance hiere.
And natheles a man mai se,
How now adayes that ther be
Ful manye of suche hertes slowe,
That wol noght besien hem to knowe   1230
What thing love is, til ate laste,
That he with strengthe hem overcaste,
That malgre hem thei mote obeie
And don al ydelschipe aweie,
To serve wel and besiliche.
Bot, Sone, thou art non of swiche,
For love schal the wel excuse :
Bot otherwise, if thou refuse
To love, thou miht so per cas
Ben ydel, as somtime was   1240
A kinges dowhter unavised,
Til that Cupide hire hath chastised :
Wherof thou schalt a tale hiere
Acordant unto this matiere.

Of Armenye, I rede thus,
Ther was a king, which Herupus
Was hote, and he a lusti Maide
To dowhter hadde, and as men saide
Hire name was Rosiphelee ;
Which tho was of gret renomee,   1250
For sche was bothe wys and fair
And scholde ben hire fader hair.
Bot sche hadde o defalte of Slowthe
Towardes love, and that was rowthe ;
For so wel cowde noman seie,   P. ii. 44
Which mihte sette hire in the weie
Of loves occupacion
Thurgh non ymaginacion ;
That scole wolde sche noght knowe.
And thus sche was on of the slowe   1260
As of such hertes besinesse,
Til whanne Venus the goddesse,
Which loves court hath forto reule,
Hath broght hire into betre reule,
Forth with Cupide and with his miht :
For thei merveille how such a wiht,
Which tho was in hir lusti age,
Desireth nother Mariage
Ne yit the love of paramours,
Which evere hath be the comun cours   1270
Amonges hem that lusti were.
So was it schewed after there :
For he that hihe hertes loweth
With fyri Dartes whiche he throweth,
Cupide, which of love is godd,
In chastisinge hath mad a rodd
To dryve awei hir wantounesse ;
So that withinne a while, I gesse,
Sche hadde on such a chance sporned,
That al hire mod was overtorned,   1280
Which ferst sche hadde of slow manere :

[TALE OF ROSIPHE-
LEE.]

Hic ponit Confessor
exemplum contra is-
tos qui amoris occu-
pacionem omittentes,
grauioris infortunii
casus expectant. Et
narrat de quadam
Armenie Regis filia,
que huiusmodi condi-
cionis in principio
iuuentutis ociosa per-
sistens, mirabili postea
visione castigata in
amoris obsequium
pre ceteris diligencior
efficitur.

1249 *margin* amoris] in amoris AC, H₃ in Amoris *causa* W   1251
margin expectaret H₁ ... B₂   1257 *margin* diligencior *om.* B   1266
how] of B   1272 schrewed A   1275 Cupide AJ, F Cupido SBT

For thus it fell, as thou schalt hiere.
Whan come was the Monthe of Maii,
Sche wolde walke upon a dai,
And that was er the Sonne Ariste;   **P. ii. 45**
Of wommen bot a fewe it wiste,
And forth sche wente prively
Unto the Park was faste by,
Al softe walkende on the gras,
Til sche cam ther the Launde was,   1290
Thurgh which ther ran a gret rivere.
It thoghte hir fair, and seide, 'Here
I wole abide under the schawe':
And bad hire wommen to withdrawe,
And ther sche stod al one stille,
To thenke what was in hir wille.
Sche sih the swote floures springe,
Sche herde glade foules singe,
Sche sih the bestes in her kinde,
The buck, the do, the hert, the hinde,   1300
The madle go with the femele;
And so began ther a querele
Betwen love and hir oghne herte,
Fro which sche couthe noght asterte.
And as sche caste hire yhe aboute,
Sche syh clad in o suite a route
Of ladis, wher thei comen ryde
Along under the wodes syde:
On faire amblende hors thei sete,
That were al whyte, fatte and grete,   1310
And everichon thei ride on side.
The Sadles were of such a Pride,
With Perle and gold so wel begon,
So riche syh sche nevere non;
In kertles and in Copes riche   **P. ii. 46**
Thei weren clothed, alle liche,
Departed evene of whyt and blew;
With alle lustes that sche knew
Thei were enbrouded overal.
Here bodies weren long and smal,   1320

1310 faire GEC, BΛ, H₃

The beaute faye upon her face
Non erthly thing it may desface;
Corones on here hed thei beere,
As ech of hem a qweene weere,
That al the gold of Cresus halle
The leste coronal of alle
Ne mihte have boght after the worth:
Thus come thei ridende forth.

[TALE OF ROSIPHE-
LEE.]

  The kinges dowhter, which this syh,
For pure abaissht drowh hire adryh   1330
And hield hire clos under the bowh,
And let hem passen stille ynowh;
For as hire thoghte in hire avis,
To hem that were of such a pris
Sche was noght worthi axen there,
Fro when they come or what thei were:
Bot levere than this worldes good
Sche wolde have wist hou that it stod,
And putte hire hed alitel oute;
And as sche lokede hire aboute,   1340
Sche syh comende under the linde
A womman up an hors behinde.
The hors on which sche rod was blak,
Al lene and galled on the back,
And haltede, as he were encluyed,   **P. ii. 47**
Wherof the womman was annuied;
Thus was the hors in sori plit,
Bot for al that a sterre whit
Amiddes in the front he hadde.
Hir Sadel ek was wonder badde,   1350
In which the wofull womman sat,

1321 f. *Text thus in third recension (but* faire WKH₃Magd *for* faye F
and hir H₃   the W *for* her): faye—desface *in ras.* F
     A *has*   The beaute of hire face schon
                    Wel bryhtere þan þe Cristall ston
so the others of first recension, but most have here (her) *for* hire *and
many (as* H₁GRCLB₂) *read* faces
     S *has*   The beaute of here faye face
                    Ther mai non erþly þing deface
so AdBTΔΛ *with* faire (fair) *for* faye *and some* (AdT) hir *for* here
   1341 a lynde L, BΛ   1342 vpon hors XC, BΛ   vpon an (a)
hors H₁GLB₂, AdTΔ, W, H₃   on an h. M   1348 And B
**   Z

And natheles ther was with that
A riche bridel for the nones
Of gold and preciouse Stones.
Hire cote was somdiel totore ;
Aboute hir middel twenty score
Of horse haltres and wel mo
Ther hyngen ate time tho.

　　Thus whan sche cam the ladi nyh,
Than tok sche betre hiede and syh　　　1360
This womman fair was of visage,
Freyssh, lusti, yong and of tendre age ;
And so this ladi, ther sche stod,
Bethoghte hire wel and understod
That this, which com ridende tho,
Tidinges couthe telle of tho,
Which as sche sih tofore ryde,
And putte hir forth and preide abide,
And seide, ' Ha, Suster, let me hiere,
What ben thei, that now riden hiere,　　　1370
And ben so richeliche arraied ? '

　　This womman, which com so esmaied,
Ansuerde with ful softe speche,
And seith, ' Ma Dame, I schal you teche.
These ar of tho that whilom were　　　**P. ii. 48**
Servantz to love, and trowthe beere,
Ther as thei hadde here herte set.
Fare wel, for I mai noght be let :
Ma Dame, I go to mi servise,
So moste I haste in alle wise ;　　　1380
Forthi, ma Dame, yif me leve,
I mai noght longe with you leve.'

　　' Ha, goode Soster, yit I preie,
Tell me whi ye ben so beseie
And with these haltres thus begon.'

　　' Ma Dame, whilom I was on

1361 f. *Thus in third recension* (and *om.* W)　F *has the lines written
over erasure, except* womman
　　A *has*　　The wom*m*an was riht fair of face
　　　　　　　Al þogh hire lackede oþer grace
so S *and the other copies of first and second recensions*
1367 Which J, S, F　Whiche A, B

That to mi fader hadde a king ;
Bot I was slow, and for no thing
Me liste noght to love obeie,
And that I now ful sore abeie.   1390
For I whilom no love hadde,
Min hors is now so fieble and badde,
And al totore is myn arai,
And every yeer this freisshe Maii
These lusti ladis ryde aboute,
And I mot nedes suie here route
In this manere as ye now se,
And trusse here haltres forth with me,
And am bot as here horse knave.
Non other office I ne have,   1400
Hem thenkth I am worthi nomore,
For I was slow in loves lore,
Whan I was able forto lere,
And wolde noght the tales hiere
Of hem that couthen love teche.'   **P. ii. 49**
   ' Now tell me thanne, I you beseche,
Wherof that riche bridel serveth.'
   With that hire chere awei sche swerveth,
And gan to wepe, and thus sche tolde :
' This bridel, which ye nou beholde   1410
So riche upon myn horse hed,—
Ma Dame, afore, er I was ded,
Whan I was in mi lusti lif,
Ther fel into myn herte a strif
Of love, which me overcom,
So that therafter hiede I nom
And thoghte I wolde love a kniht :
That laste wel a fourtenyht,
For it no lengere mihte laste,
So nyh my lif was ate laste.   1420
Bot now, allas, to late war
That I ne hadde him loved ar :
For deth cam so in haste bime,
Er I therto hadde eny time,

1393 And *om.* AM   1397 now] mow (mowe) J, AdB, W
1419 non AJ

[TALE OF ROSIPHE-
LEE.]

That it ne mihte ben achieved.
Bot for al that I am relieved,
Of that mi will was good therto,
That love soffreth it be so
That I schal swiche a bridel were.
Now have ye herd al myn ansuere :   1430
To godd, ma Dame, I you betake,
And warneth alle for mi sake,
Of love that thei ben noght ydel,
And bidd hem thenke upon mi brydel.'
And with that word al sodeinly   **P. ii.,50**
Sche passeth, as it were a Sky,
Al clene out of this ladi sihte :
And tho for fere hire herte afflihte,
And seide to hirself, 'Helas !
I am riht in the same cas.   1440
Bot if I live after this day,
I schal amende it, if I may.'
And thus homward this lady wente,
And changede al hire ferste entente,
Withinne hire herte and gan to swere
That sche none haltres wolde bere.

Confessor.

    Lo, Sone, hier miht thou taken hiede,
How ydelnesse is forto drede,
Namliche of love, as I have write.
For thou miht understonde and wite,   1450
Among the gentil nacion
Love is an occupacion,
Which forto kepe hise lustes save

Non quia sic se
habet veritas, set
opinio Amantum.

Scholde every gentil herte have :
For as the ladi was chastised,
Riht so the knyht mai ben avised,
Which ydel is and wol noght serve
To love, he mai per cas deserve
A grettere peine than sche hadde,
Whan sche aboute with hire ladde   1460
The horse haltres ; and forthi
Good is to be wel war therbi.
Bot forto loke aboven alle,

1454 f. *margin* Non quia—Amantum *om.* G, BΔ

These Maidens, hou so that it falle,
Thei scholden take ensample of this   P. ii. 51
Which I have told, for soth it is.
    Mi ladi Venus, whom I serve,
What womman wole hire thonk deserve,
Sche mai noght thilke love eschuie
Of paramours, bot sche mot suie   1470
Cupides lawe ; and natheles
Men sen such love sielde in pes,
That it nys evere upon aspie
Of janglinge and of fals Envie,
Fulofte medlid with disese :
Bot thilke love is wel at ese,
Which set is upon mariage ;
For that dar schewen the visage
In alle places openly.
A gret mervaile it is forthi,   1480
How that a Maiden wolde lette,
That sche hir time ne besette
To haste unto that ilke feste,
Wherof the love is al honeste.
Men mai recovere lost of good,
Bot so wys man yit nevere stod,
Which mai recovere time lore :
So mai a Maiden wel therfore
Ensample take, of that sche strangeth
Hir love, and longe er that sche changeth 1490
Hir herte upon hir lustes greene
To mariage, as it is seene.
For thus a yer or tuo or thre
Sche lest, er that sche wedded be,
Whyl sche the charge myhte bere   P. ii. 52
Of children, whiche the world forbere
Ne mai, bot if it scholde faile.
Bot what Maiden hire esposaile
Wol tarie, whan sche take mai,
Sche schal per chance an other dai   1500
Be let, whan that hire lievest were.
Wherof a tale unto hire Ere,

1501 that hire] þat sche H₁ ... B₂   hir ΔΛ   it M

Which is coupable upon this dede,
I thenke telle of that I rede.

[TALE OF JEPHTHAH'S
DAUGHTER.]

Hic ponit exem-
plum super eodem :
Et narrat de filia Iepte,
que cum ex sui patris
voto in holocaustum
deo occidi et offerri
deberet, ipsa pro eo
quod virgo fuit et pro-
lem ad augmentacio-
nem populi dei non-
dum genuisset, xl.
dierum spacium vt
cum suis sodalibus
virginibus suam de-
fleret virginitatem,
priusquam moreretur,
in exemplum aliarum
a patre postulauit.

Among the Jewes, as men tolde,
Ther was whilom be daies olde
A noble Duck, which Jepte hihte.
And fell, he scholde go to fyhte
Ayein Amon the cruel king :
And forto speke upon this thing,   1510
Withinne his herte he made avou
To god and seide, 'Ha lord, if thou
Wolt grante unto thi man victoire,
I schal in tokne of thi memoire
The ferste lif that I mai se,
Of man or womman wher it be,
Anon as I come hom ayein,
To thee, which art god sovereign,
Slen in thi name and sacrifie.'
And thus with his chivalerie   1520
He goth him forth, wher that he scholde,
And wan al that he winne wolde
And overcam his fomen alle.
    Mai noman lette that schal falle.
This Duc a lusti dowhter hadde,   P. ii. 53
And fame, which the wordes spradde,
Hath broght unto this ladi Ere
How that hire fader hath do there.
Sche waiteth upon his cominge
With dansinge and with carolinge,   1530
As sche that wolde be tofore
Al othre, and so sche was therfore
In Masphat at hir fader gate
The ferste ; and whan he com therate,
And sih his douhter, he tobreide
Hise clothes and wepende he seide :
    'O mihti god among ous hiere,
Nou wot I that in no manere

1507 duck A, F   duk J, SB   1511 auou (auov, avow) AJC,
B, F   a vou (a vowe) MH₁, S   1519 *margin* aliorum A . . . B₂, S
. . . ΔΛ, H₃   1521 wher that] so as B   1525 Duc F   duck A
duk J, SB   1532 Al AJ, S, F   Alle C, BT

This worldes joie mai be plein.

I hadde al that I coude sein   1540
Ayein mi fomen be thi grace,
So whan I cam toward this place
Ther was non gladdere man than I :
But now, mi lord, al sodeinli
Mi joie is torned into sorwe,
For I mi dowhter schal tomorwe
Tohewe and brenne in thi servise
To loenge of thi sacrifise
Thurgh min avou, so as it is.'
   The Maiden, whan sche wiste of this,   1550
And sih the sorwe hir fader made,
So as sche mai with wordes glade
Conforteth him, and bad him holde
The covenant which he is holde
Towardes god, as he behihte.   **P. ii. 54**
Bot natheles hire herte aflihte
Of that sche sih hire deth comende ;
And thanne unto the ground knelende
Tofore hir fader sche is falle,
And seith, so as it is befalle   1560
Upon this point that sche schal deie,
Of o thing ferst sche wolde him preie,
That fourty daies of respit
He wolde hir grante upon this plit,
That sche the whyle mai bewepe
Hir maidenhod, which sche to kepe
So longe hath had and noght beset ;
Wherof her lusti youthe is let,
That sche no children hath forthdrawe
In Mariage after the lawe,   1570
So that the poeple is noght encressed.
Bot that it mihte be relessed,
That sche hir time hath lore so,
Sche wolde be his leve go
With othre Maidens to compleigne,
And afterward unto the peine

[TALE OF JEPHTHAH'S DAUGHTER.]

Of deth sche wolde come ayein.
   The fader herde his douhter sein,
And therupon of on assent
The Maidens were anon asent,   1580
That scholden with this Maiden wende.
So forto speke unto this ende,
Thei gon the dounes and the dales
With wepinge and with wofull tales,
And every wyht hire maidenhiede   **P. ii. 55**
Compleigneth upon thilke nede,
That sche no children hadde bore,
Wherof sche hath hir youthe lore,
Which nevere sche recovere mai :
For so fell that hir laste dai   1590
Was come, in which sche scholde take
Hir deth, which sche may noght forsake.
Lo, thus sche deiede a wofull Maide
For thilke cause which I saide,
As thou hast understonde above.

Amans.

   Mi fader, as toward the Love
Of Maidens forto telle trowthe,
Ye have thilke vice of Slowthe,
Me thenkth, riht wonder wel declared,
That ye the wommen have noght spared   1600
Of hem that tarien so behinde.
Bot yit it falleth in my minde,
Toward the men hou that ye spieke
Of hem that wole no travail sieke
In cause of love upon decerte :
To speke in wordes so coverte,
I not what travaill that ye mente.

Confessor.

   Mi Sone, and after min entente
I woll thee telle what I thoghte,
Hou whilom men here loves boghte   1610
Thurgh gret travaill in strange londes,
Wher that thei wroghten with here hondes
Of armes many a worthi dede,
In sondri place as men mai rede.

vi. *Quem probat armorum probitas Venus approbat, et quem* **P. ii. 56**
   Torpor habet reprobum reprobat illa virum.
Vecors segnicies insignia nescit amoris,
   Nam piger ad brauium tardius ipse venit.

That every love of pure kinde
Is ferst forthdrawe, wel I finde :
Bot natheles yit overthis
Decerte doth so that it is
The rather had in mani place.
Forthi who secheth loves grace,   1620
Wher that these worthi wommen are,
He mai noght thanne himselve spare
Upon his travail forto serve,
Wherof that he mai thonk deserve,
There as these men of Armes be,
Somtime over the grete Se :
So that be londe and ek be Schipe
He mot travaile for worschipe
And make manye hastyf rodes,
Somtime in Prus, somtime in Rodes,   1630
And somtime into Tartarie ;
So that these heraldz on him crie,
'Vailant, vailant, lo, wher he goth !'
And thanne he yifth hem gold and cloth,
So that his fame mihte springe,
And to his ladi Ere bringe
Som tidinge of his worthinesse ;
So that sche mihte of his prouesce
Of that sche herde men recorde,
The betre unto his love acorde   1640
And danger pute out of hire mod,
Whanne alle men recorden good,
And that sche wot wel, for hir sake   **P. ii. 57**
That he no travail wol forsake.

Mi Sone, of this travail I meene :
Nou schrif thee, for it schal be sene
If thou art ydel in this cas.
My fader ye, and evere was :

Hic loquitur quod in amoris causa mi-licie probitas ad ar-morum laboris ex-cercicium nullatenus torpescat.

Confessor.

Confessio Amantis.

[ARGUMENTS TO THE CONTRARY.]

For as me thenketh trewely
That every man doth mor than I   1650
As of this point, and if so is
That I have oght so don er this,
It is so litel of acompte,
As who seith, it mai noght amonte
To winne of love his lusti yifte.
For this I telle you in schrifte,
That me were levere hir love winne
Than Kaire and al that is ther inne :
And forto slen the hethen alle,
I not what good ther mihte falle,   1660
So mochel blod thogh ther be schad.
This finde I writen, hou Crist bad
That noman other scholde sle.
What scholde I winne over the Se,
If I mi ladi loste at hom ?
Bot passe thei the salte fom,
To whom Crist bad thei scholden preche
To al the world and his feith teche :
Bot now thei rucken in here nest
And resten as hem liketh best   1670
In all the swetnesse of delices.
Thus thei defenden ous the vices,
And sitte hemselven al amidde ;   **P. ii. 58**
To slen and feihten thei ous bidde
Hem whom thei scholde, as the bok seith,
Converten unto Cristes feith.
Bot hierof have I gret mervaile,
Hou thei wol bidde me travaile :
A Sarazin if I sle schal,
I sle the Soule forth withal,   1680
And that was nevere Cristes lore.
Bot nou ho ther, I seie nomore.

　　Bot I wol speke upon mi schrifte ;
And to Cupide I make a yifte,
That who as evere pris deserve
Of armes, I wol love serve ;
And thogh I scholde hem bothe kepe,

1670 hem liken H₁XRCLB₂, W　hym likeþ M

Als wel yit wolde I take kepe
Whan it were time to abide,
As forto travaile and to ryde :
For how as evere a man laboure,
Cupide appointed hath his houre.
   For I have herd it telle also,
Achilles lefte hise armes so
Bothe of himself and of his men
At Troie for Polixenen,
Upon hire love whanne he fell,
That for no chance that befell
Among the Grecs or up or doun,
He wolde noght ayein the toun
Ben armed, for the love of hire.
And so me thenketh, lieve Sire,
A man of armes mai him reste
Somtime in hope for the beste,
If he mai finde a weie nerr.
What scholde I thanne go so ferr
In strange londes many a mile
To ryde, and lese at hom therwhile
Mi love ? It were a schort beyete
To winne chaf and lese whete.
Bot if mi ladi bidde wolde,
That I for hire love scholde
Travaile, me thenkth trewely
I mihte fle thurghout the Sky,
And go thurghout the depe Se,
For al ne sette I at a stre
What thonk that I mihte elles gete.
What helpeth it a man have mete,
Wher drinke lacketh on the bord?
What helpeth eny mannes word
To seie hou I travaile faste,
Wher as me faileth ate laste
That thing which I travaile fore ?

[ARGUMENTS TO THE CONTRARY.]

1690

Hic allegat Amans
in sui excusacionem,
qualiter Achilles apud
Troiam propter amo-
rem Polixenen arma
sua per aliquod tem-
pus dimisit.

1700

P. ii. 59

1710

1720

1690 As] And B   for to (forto) ride H₁ . . . B₂   1693 herd
it] it herd A, Δ   herd M   1701 the *om.* AM   1705 weie]
werre B   1706 go þan (þen) AM go þanne W   1708 þe while
H₁XE . . . B₂, W my while G þat while M, Δ

[ARGUMENTS TO THE
CONTRARY.]

O in good time were he bore,
That mihte atteigne such a mede.
Bot certes if I mihte spede
With eny maner besinesse
Of worldes travail, thanne I gesse,
Ther scholde me non ydelschipe
Departen fro hir ladischipe.   1730
Bot this I se, on daies nou
The blinde god, I wot noght hou,
Cupido, which of love is lord,   **P. ii. 60**
He set the thinges in discord,
That thei that lest to love entende
Fulofte he wole hem yive and sende
Most of his grace; and thus I finde
That he that scholde go behinde,
Goth many a time ferr tofore:
So wot I noght riht wel therfore,   1740
On whether bord that I schal seile.
Thus can I noght miself conseile,
Bot al I sette on aventure,
And am, as who seith, out of cure
For ought that I can seie or do:
For everemore I finde it so,
The more besinesse I leie,
The more that I knele and preie
With goode wordes and with softe,
The more I am refused ofte,   1750
With besinesse and mai noght winne.
And in good feith that is gret Sinne;
For I mai seie, of dede and thoght
That ydel man have I be noght;
For hou as evere I be deslaied,
Yit evermore I have assaied.
Bot thogh my besinesse laste,
Al is bot ydel ate laste,
For whan theffect is ydelnesse,
I not what thing is besinesse.   1760
Sei, what availeth al the dede,

1738 that] which AJH₁ . . . B₂   1740 So þat I not H₁ . . . B₂
1752 that] it B

Which nothing helpeth ate nede?
For the fortune of every fame   **P. ii. 61**
Schal of his ende bere a name.
And thus for oght is yit befalle,
An ydel man I wol me calle
As after myn entendement:
Bot upon youre amendement,
Min holi fader, as you semeth,   [THE CONFESSOR RE-
Mi reson and my cause demeth.   1770   PLIES.]
                                                   Confessor.
　Mi Sone, I have herd thi matiere,
Of that thou hast thee schriven hiere:
And forto speke of ydel fare,
Me semeth that thou tharst noght care,
Bot only that thou miht noght spede.
And therof, Sone, I wol thee rede,
Abyd, and haste noght to faste;
Thi dees ben every dai to caste,
Thou nost what chance schal betyde.
Betre is to wayte upon the tyde   1780
Than rowe ayein the stremes stronge:
For thogh so be thee thenketh longe,
Per cas the revolucion
Of hevene and thi condicion
Ne be noght yit of on acord.
Bot I dar make this record
To Venus, whos Prest that I am,
That sithen that I hidir cam
To hiere, as sche me bad, thi lif,
Wherof thou elles be gultif,   1790
Thou miht hierof thi conscience
Excuse, and of gret diligence,
Which thou to love hast so despended,   **P. ii. 62**
Thou oghtest wel to be comended.
Bot if so be that ther oght faile,
Of that thou slowthest to travaile
In armes forto ben absent,
And for thou makst an argument
Of that thou seidest hiere above,
Hou Achilles thurgh strengthe of love   1800

1769 you] ȝe A . . . B₂ (*except* G)   1780 Bet B

[THE CONFESSOR RE-
PLIES.]

Hise armes lefte for a throwe,
Thou schalt an other tale knowe,
Which is contraire, as thou schalt wite.
For this a man mai finde write,
Whan that knyhthode schal be werred,
Lust mai noght thanne be preferred ;
The bedd mot thanne be forsake
And Schield and spere on honde take,
Which thing schal make hem after glaae,
Whan thei ben worthi knihtes made.   1810
Wherof, so as it comth to honde,
A tale thou schalt understonde,
Hou that a kniht schal armes suie,
And for the while his ese eschuie.

[TALE OF NAUPLUS
AND ULYSSES.]

Hic dicit quod amo-
ris delectamento post-
posito miles arma sua
preferre debet : Et
ponit exemplum de
Vlixe, cum ipse a
bello Troiano propter
amorem   Penolope
remanere domi volu-
isset, Nauplus pater
Palamades eum tantis
sermonibus allocutus
est, quod Vlixes thoro
sue coniugis relicto
labores armorum vna
cum aiiis Troie mag-
nanimus subiba

Upon knyhthode I rede thus,
How whilom whan the king Nauplus,
The fader of Palamades,
Cam forto preien Ulixes
With othre Gregois ek also,
That he with hem to Troie go,   1820
Wher that the Siege scholde be,
Anon upon Penolope
His wif, whom that he loveth hote,   **P. ii. 63**
Thenkende, wolde hem noght behote.
Bot he schop thanne a wonder wyle,
How that he scholde hem best beguile,
So that he mihte duelle stille
At home and welde his love at wille :
Wherof erli the morwe day
Out of his bedd, wher that he lay,   1830
Whan he was uppe, he gan to fare
Into the field and loke and stare,
As he which feigneth to be wod :
He tok a plowh, wher that it stod,
Wherinne anon in stede of Oxes
He let do yoken grete foxes,
And with gret salt the lond he siew.
But Nauplus, which the cause kniew,

1805 knythode F   1816 Namplus T (*and so afterwards*)   1833
which] þat M . . . B₂   feigned B₂, B   1838 Namplus J, BT

Ayein the sleihte which he feigneth
An other sleihte anon ordeigneth.   1840
And fell that time Ulixes hadde
A chyld to Sone, and Nauplus radde
How men that Sone taken scholde,
And setten him upon the Molde,
Wher that his fader hield the plowh,
In thilke furgh which he tho drowh.
For in such wise he thoghte assaie,
Hou it Ulixes scholde paie,
If that he were wod or non.

The knihtes for this child forthgon;   1850
Thelamacus anon was fett,
Tofore the plowh and evene sett,
Wher that his fader scholde dryve.   **P. ii. 64**
Bot whan he sih his child, als blyve
He drof the plowh out of the weie,
And Nauplus tho began to seie,
And hath half in a jape cryd:
' O Ulixes, thou art aspyd:
What is al this thou woldest meene?
For openliche it is now seene   1860
That thou hast feigned al this thing,
Which is gret schame to a king,
Whan that for lust of eny slowthe
Thou wolt in a querele of trowthe
Of armes thilke honour forsake,
And duelle at hom for loves sake:
For betre it were honour to winne
Than love, which likinge is inne.
Forthi tak worschipe upon honde,
And elles thou schalt understonde   1870
These othre worthi kinges alle
Of Grece, which unto thee calle,
Towardes thee wol be riht wrothe,
And grieve thee per chance bothe:
Which schal be tothe double schame

1850 The] This AJH₁ . . . B₂   These M   forþgon A, F   forþ
gon JC, SB   1872 which J, B, F   whiche AC, S   1875 toþe A, F
to þe JC, B &c.

[TALE OF NAUPLUS AND ULYSSES.]

Most for the hindrynge of thi name,
That thou for Slouthe of eny love
Schalt so thi lustes sette above
And leve of armes the knyhthode,
Which is the pris of thi manhode   1880
And oghte ferst to be desired.'
Bot he, which hadde his herte fyred
Upon his wif, whan he this herde,   P. ii. 65
Noght o word therayein ansuerde,
Bot torneth hom halvinge aschamed,
And hath withinne himself so tamed
His herte, that al the sotie
Of love for chivalerie
He lefte, and be him lief or loth,
To Troie forth with hem he goth,   1890
That he him mihte noght excuse.
Thus stant it, if a knyht refuse
The lust of armes to travaile,
Ther mai no worldes ese availe,
Bot if worschipe be with al.
And that hath schewed overal ;
For it sit wel in alle wise
A kniht to ben of hih emprise
And puten alle drede aweie ;
For in this wise, I have herd seie,   1900
    The worthi king Protheselai

[EXAMPLES OF PROW-
ESS. PROTESILAUS.]

Hic narrat super
eodem qualiter Lao-
domia Regis Prothe-
selai vxor, volens
ipsum a bello Troiano
secum retinere, fata-
tam sibi mortem in
portu Troie prenun-
ciauit : set ipse mili-
ciam pocius quam
ocia affectans, Troiam
adiit, vbi sue mortis
precio perpetue laudis
Cronicam ademit.

On his passage wher he lai
Towardes Troie thilke Siege,
Sche which was al his oghne liege,
Laodomie his lusti wif,
Which for his love was pensif,
As he which al hire herte hadde,
Upon a thing wherof sche dradde
A lettre, forto make him duelle
Fro Troie, sende him, thus to telle,   1910
Hou sche hath axed of the wyse
Touchende of him in such a wise,
That thei have don hire understonde,   P. ii. 66

1892 king C, B   1893 lust AJ, SB   luste F   1901 Prothefelay
H₁G ... B₂, B

Towardes othre hou so it stonde,

[EXAMPLES OF PROW-
ESS. PROTESILAUS.]

The destine it hath so schape
That he schal noght the deth ascape
In cas that he arryve at Troie.
Forthi as to hir worldes joie
With al hire herte sche him preide,
And many an other cause alleide,   1920
That he with hire at home abide.
Bot he hath cast hir lettre aside,
As he which tho no maner hiede
Tok of hire wommannysshe drede ;
And forth he goth, as noght ne were,
To Troie, and was the ferste there
Which londeth, and tok arryvaile :
For him was levere in the bataille,
He seith, to deien as a knyht,
Than forto lyve in al his myht   1930
And be reproeved of his name.
Lo, thus upon the worldes fame
Knyhthode hath evere yit be set,
Which with no couardie is let.

Of king Saül also I finde,

[SAUL.]

Whan Samuel out of his kinde,
Thurgh that the Phitonesse hath lered,
In Samarie was arered
Long time after that he was ded,
The king Saül him axeth red,   1940
If that he schal go fyhte or non.
And Samuel him seide anon,
'The ferste day of the bataille   **P. ii. 67**
Thou schalt be slain withoute faile
And Jonathas thi Sone also.'
Bot hou as evere it felle so,
This worthi kniht of his corage
Hath undertake the viage,
And wol noght his knyhthode lette
For no peril he couthe sette ;   1950

Adhuc super eo-
dem, qualiter Rex
Saul, non obstante
quod per Samuelem a
Phitonissa suscitatum
et coniuratum respon-
sum, quod ipse in bello
moreretur, accepisset,
hostes tamen suos
aggrediens milicie
famam cunctis huius
vite blandimentis pre-
posuit

1916 the deth] þe day X ... B₂   1922 hir] his H₁ ... CB₂
this L   1928 the *om.* H₁XGE, B   1940 axeþ him H₁ ... B₂, W
1944 beslain F

Wherof that bothe his Sone and he
Upon the Montz of Gelboë
Assemblen with here enemys:
For thei knyhthode of such a pris
Be olde daies thanne hielden,
That thei non other thing behielden.
And thus the fader for worschipe
Forth with his Sone of felaschipe
Thurgh lust of armes weren dede,
As men mai in the bible rede;   1960
The whos knyhthode is yit in mende,
And schal be to the worldes ende.

[EDUCATION OF
ACHILLES.]

Hic loquitur quod
miles in suis pr̄mor-
diis ad audaciam pro-
uocari debet. Et nar-
rat qualiter Chiro
Centaurus Achillem,
quem secum ab in-
fancia in monte Pileon
educauit, vt audax
efficeretur, primitus
edocuit, quod cum ipse
venacionibus ibidem
insisteret, leones et
tigrides huiusmodike
animalia sibi resisten-
cia et nulla alia fugitiua
agitaret. Et sic A-
chilles in iuuentute
animatus famosissime
milicie   probitatem
postmodum adoptauit.

   And forto loken overmore,
It hath and schal ben evermore
That of knihthode the prouesse
Is grounded upon hardinesse
Of him that dar wel undertake.
And who that wolde ensample take
Upon the forme of knyhtes lawe,
How that Achilles was forthdrawe   1970
With Chiro, which Centaurus hihte,
Of many a wondre hiere he mihte.
For it stod thilke time thus,   **P. ii. 68**
That this Chiro, this Centaurus,
Withinne a large wildernesse,
Wher was Leon and Leonesse,
The Lepard and the Tigre also,
With Hert and Hynde, and buck and doo,
Hadde his duellinge, as tho befell,
Of Pileon upon the hel,   1980
Wherof was thanne mochel speche.
Ther hath Chiro this Chyld to teche,
What time he was of tuelve yer age;
Wher forto maken his corage
The more hardi be other weie,
In the forest to hunte and pleie
Whan that Achilles walke wolde,

1966 hardiesse AH₁XGECB₂   hardiest L   1975 *margin*
exagitaret SBΔΛ (*Latin om.* AdT)   1978 and *om.* MXGL, B, W
margin optauit A

Centaurus bad that he ne scholde
Which wolde flen out of his place,   1990
As buck and doo and hert and hynde,
With whiche he mai no werre finde ;
Bot tho that wolden him withstonde,
Ther scholde he with his Dart on honde
Upon the Tigre and the Leon
Pourchace and take his veneison,
As to a kniht is acordant.
And therupon a covenant
This Chiro with Achilles sette,
That every day withoute lette   2000
He scholde such a cruel beste
Or slen or wounden ate leste,
So that he mihte a tokne bringe   **P. ii. 69**
Of blod upon his hom cominge.
And thus of that Chiro him tawhte
Achilles such an herte cawhte,
That he nomore a Leon dradde,
Whan he his Dart on honde hadde,
Thanne if a Leon were an asse :
And that hath mad him forto passe   2010
Alle othre knihtes of his dede,
Whan it cam to the grete nede,
As it was afterward wel knowe.
    Lo, thus, my Sone, thou miht knowe   Confessor.
That the corage of hardiesce
Is of knyhthode the prouesce,
Which is to love sufficant
Aboven al the remenant
That unto loves court poursuie.
Bot who that wol no Slowthe eschuie,   2020
Upon knihthode and noght travaile,
I not what love him scholde availe ;
Bot every labour axeth why
Of som reward, wherof that I

1996 make BTA   2008 in honde MX ... B₂, W   2010 mad
(maad) AJC, T   made B, F   2012 to *om.* B   2015 hardiesce AC, F   hardinesse J, SB   2020 Bot] That H₁ ... B₂
                            A a 2

[PROWESS.]

Ensamples couthe telle ynowe
Of hem that toward love drowe
Be olde daies, as thei scholde.

Amans.

Mi fader, therof hiere I wolde.

Confessor.

Mi Sone, it is wel resonable,
In place which is honorable   2030
If that a man his herte sette,
That thanne he for no Slowthe lette
To do what longeth to manhede.   **P. ii. 70**
For if thou wolt the bokes rede
Of Lancelot and othre mo,
Ther miht thou sen hou it was tho
Of armes, for thei wolde atteigne
To love, which withoute peine
Mai noght be gete of ydelnesse.
And that I take to witnesse   2040
An old Cronique in special,
The which into memorial
Is write, for his loves sake
Hou that a kniht schal undertake.

[TALE OF HERCULES
AND ACHELONS.]

Hic dicit, quod Miles
priusquam amoris am-
plexu dignus efficia-
tur, euentus bellicos
victoriosus amplect-
ere debet. Et narrat
qualiter Hercules et
Achelons propter Dei-
aniram Calidonie Reg-
is filiam singulare du-
ellum adinuicem ini-
erunt, cuius victor
Hercules existens ar-
morum meritis amo-
rem virginis laudabi-
liter conquestauit.

Ther was a king, which Oënes
Was hote, and he under his pes
Hield Calidoyne in his Empire,
And hadde a dowhter Deianire.
Men wiste in thilke time non
So fair a wiht as sche was on;   2050
And as sche was a lusti wiht,
Riht so was thanne a noble kniht,
To whom Mercurie fader was.
This kniht the tuo pilers of bras,
The whiche yit a man mai finde,
Sette up in the desert of Ynde;
That was the worthi Hercules,
Whos name schal ben endeles
For the merveilles whiche he wroghte.
This Hercules the love soghte   2060

2034 the] þy (thi) H₁, BTΛ   *om.* Ad   2039 begete FH₃
2045 Cenes L, BΛ   seues M   2052 propter *om.* H₁ ... B₂
2055 *margin* armorum] amorum RCLB₂

Of Deianire, and of this thing
Unto hir fader, which was king,
He spak touchende of Mariage.   P. ii. 71
The king knowende his hih lignage,
And dradde also hise mihtes sterne,
To him ne dorste his dowhter werne;
And natheles this he him seide,
How Achelons er he ferst preide
To wedden hire, and in accord
Thei stode, as it was of record: 2070
Bot for al that this he him granteth,
That which of hem that other daunteth
In armes, him sche scholde take,
And that the king hath undertake.
This Achelons was a Geant,
A soubtil man, a deceivant,
Which thurgh magique and sorcerie
Couthe al the world of tricherie:
And whan that he this tale herde,
Hou upon that the king ansuerde   2080
With Hercules he moste feighte,
He tristeth noght upon his sleighte
Al only, whan it comth to nede,
Bot that which voydeth alle drede
And every noble herte stereth,
The love, that no lif forbereth,
For his ladi, whom he desireth,
With hardiesse his herte fyreth,
And sende him word withoute faile
That he wol take the bataille.   2090
Thei setten day, thei chosen field,
The knihtes coevered under Schield
Togedre come at time set,   P. ii. 72
And echon is with other met.
It fell thei foghten bothe afote,
Ther was no ston, ther was no rote,
Which mihte letten hem the weie,
But al was voide and take aweie.

2072 da�ū̃teþ F   daunteþ C, B   danteþ AJ, S   2088 hardiesse
A, F   hardinesse J, SB

Thei smyten strokes bot a fewe,
For Hercules, which wolde schewe   2100
His grete strengthe as for the nones,
He sterte upon him al at ones
And cawhte him in hise armes stronge.
This Geant wot he mai noght longe
Endure under so harde bondes,
And thoghte he wolde out of hise hondes
Be sleyhte in som manere ascape.
And as he couthe himself forschape,
In liknesse of an Eddre he slipte
Out of his hond, and forth he skipte;   2110
And efte, as he that feighte wole,
He torneth him into a Bole,
And gan to belwe of such a soun,
As thogh the world scholde al go doun :
The ground he sporneth and he tranceth,
Hise large hornes he avanceth
And caste hem here and there aboute.
Bot he, which stant of him no doute,
Awaiteth wel whan that he cam,
And him be bothe hornes nam   2120
And al at ones he him caste
Unto the ground, and hield him faste,
That he ne mihte with no sleighte   **P. ii. 73**
Out of his hond gete upon heighte,
Til he was overcome and yolde,
And Hercules hath what he wolde.
The king him granteth to fulfille
His axinge at his oghne wille,
And sche for whom he hadde served,
Hire thoghte he hath hire wel deserved.   2130
And thus with gret decerte of Armes
He wan him forto ligge in armes,
As he which hath it dere aboght,
For otherwise scholde he noght.

And overthis if thou wolt hiere
Upon knihthode of this matiere,

2118 hem SBT   2135 ouerþis A, F   ouer þis J, SB   2136 of]
in A . . . B₂

Hou love and armes ben aqueinted,
A man mai se bothe write and peinted
So ferforth that Pantasilee,
Which was the queene of Feminee,
The love of Hector forto sieke
And for thonour of armes eke,
To Troie cam with Spere and Schield,
And rod hirself into the field
With Maidens armed al a route
In rescouss of the toun aboute,
Which with the Gregois was belein.
Fro Pafagoine and as men sein,
Which stant upon the worldes ende,
That time it likede ek to wende
To Philemenis, which was king,
To Troie, and come upon this thing
In helpe of thilke noble toun ;
And al was that for the renoun
Of worschipe and of worldes fame,
Of which he wolde bere a name :
And so he dede, and forth withal
He wan of love in special
A fair tribut for everemo.
For it fell thilke time so ;
Pirrus the Sone of Achilles
This worthi queene among the press
With dedli swerd soghte out and fond,
And slowh hire with his oghne hond ;
Wherof this king of Pafagoine
Pantasilee of Amazoine,
Wher sche was queene, with him ladde,
With suche Maidens as sche hadde
Of hem that were left alyve,
Forth in his Schip, til thei aryve ;
Wher that the body was begrave
With worschipe, and the wommen save.
And for the goodschipe of this dede
Thei granten him a lusti mede,

[PENTHESILEA.]
Amazonie Regina, que
Hectoris amore colli-
gata contra Pirrum
2140 Achillis filium apud
Troiam arma ferre
eciam personaliter
non recusauit.

[PHILEMENIS.]
Nota qualiter Phi-
lemenis propter mi-
2150 licie famam a finibus
terre in defensionem
Troie veniens tres
puellas a Regno Am-
P. ii. 74 azonie quolibet anno
percipiendas sibi et
heredibus suis imper-
tuum ea de causa
habere promeruit.

2160

2170

2153 margin Amozonie H₁ . . . B₂ (except G), B   2165 þe king
H₁ . . . B₂   2166 of Amozoine H₁ . . . RLB₂ and Amozoine C

[PHILEMENIS.]

That every yeer as for truage
To him and to his heritage
Of Maidens faire he schal have thre.
And in this wise spedde he,
Which the fortune of armes soghte,
With his travail his ese he boghte;　　2180
For otherwise he scholde have failed,
If that he hadde noght travailed.

[ENEAS.]

Nota pro eo quod
Eneas Regem Turnum
in bello deuicit, non
solum amorem La-
vine, set et regnum
Ytalie sibi subiugatum
obtinuit.

　　Eneas ek withinne Ytaile,　　**P. ii. 75**
Ne hadde he wonne the bataille
And don his miht so besily
Ayein king Turne his enemy,
He hadde noght Lavine wonne;
Bot for he hath him overronne
And gete his pris, he gat hire love.

　　Be these ensamples here above,　　2190
Lo, now, mi Sone, as I have told,
Thou miht wel se, who that is bold
And dar travaile and undertake
The cause of love, he schal be take
The rathere unto loves grace;
For comunliche in worthi place
The wommen loven worthinesse
Of manhode and of gentilesse,
For the gentils ben most desired.

[GENTILESSE.]

Hic dicit, quod ge-
nerosi in amoris causa
sepius preferuntur.
Super quo querit
Amans, Quid sit gene-
rositas : cuius verita-
tem questionis Con-
fessor per singula
dissoluit.

　　Mi fader, bot I were enspired　　2200
Thurgh lore of you, I wot no weie
What gentilesce is forto seie,
Wherof to telle I you beseche.

　　The ground, Mi Sone, forto seche
Upon this diffinicion,
The worldes constitucion
Hath set the name of gentilesse
Upon the fortune of richesse
Which of long time is falle in age.
Thanne is a man of hih lignage　　2210
After the forme, as thou miht hiere,

2175 as for] for his BT　　2186 *margin* Lavine] set vine A　se
uine M　　2189 And gete] He gette (gete, get) X ... B₂　He gate
H₁　And gat M, W　　2199 ff. *margin* Hic dicit—dissoluit *om.* B

Bot nothing after the matiere.   [Gentilesse.]
For who that resoun understonde,   P. ii. 76
Upon richesse it mai noght stonde,
For that is thing which faileth ofte :
For he that stant to day alofte
And al the world hath in hise wones,
Tomorwe he falleth al at ones
Out of richesse into poverte,
So that therof is no decerte,   2220
Which gentilesce makth abide.
And forto loke on other side
Hou that a gentil man is bore,
Adam, which alle was tofore
With Eve his wif, as of hem tuo,
Al was aliche gentil tho ;
So that of generacion
To make declaracion,
Ther mai no gentilesce be.
For to the reson if we se,   2230
Of mannes berthe the mesure,
It is so comun to nature,
That it yifth every man aliche,
Als wel to povere as to the riche ;
For naked thei ben bore bothe,
The lord nomore hath forto clothe
As of himself that ilke throwe,
Than hath the povereste of the rowe.
And whan thei schulle bothe passe,
I not of hem which hath the lasse   2240
Of worldes good, bot as of charge
The lord is more forto charge,
Whan god schal his accompte hiere,   P. ii. 77
For he hath had hise lustes hiere.
Bot of the bodi, which schal deie,   Omnes quidem ad
Althogh ther be diverse weie   vnum finem tendimus,
To deth, yit is ther bot on ende,   set diuerso tramite.

2218 faileþ H₁GRCLB₂, Δ   2224 þe which al was X . . . B₂
the wiche was alle H₁   2227 gouernacioun AM   2234 the
om. H₁XECLB₂, Ad, WH₃   (to *om.* R)   2241 as of] ȝit of H₁ . . .
B₂   of W

To which that every man schal wende,
Als wel the beggere as the lord,
Of o nature, of on acord :   2250
Sche which oure Eldemoder is,
The Erthe, bothe that and this
Receiveth and alich devoureth,
That sche to nouther part favoureth.
So wot I nothing after kinde
Where I mai gentilesse finde.

For lacke of vertu lacketh grace,
Wherof richesse in many place,
Whan men best wene forto stonde,
Al sodeinly goth out of honde :   2260
Bot vertu set in the corage,
Ther mai no world be so salvage,
Which mihte it take and don aweie,
Til whanne that the bodi deie ;
And thanne he schal be riched so,
That it mai faile neveremo ;
So mai that wel be gentilesse,
Which yifth so gret a sikernesse.
For after the condicion
Of resonable entencion,   2270
The which out of the Soule groweth
And the vertu fro vice knoweth,
Wherof a man the vice eschuieth,   **P. ii. 78**
Withoute Slowthe and vertu suieth,
That is a verrai gentil man,
And nothing elles which he can,
Ne which he hath, ne which he mai.
Bot for al that yit nou aday,
In loves court to taken hiede,
The povere vertu schal noght spiede,   2280
Wher that the riche vice woweth ;
For sielde it is that love alloweth
The gentil man withoute good,

2251 Eldemoder (elde moder) AJH₁ &c., SAd, FH₃   eldirmodir
(eldermoder) L, Δ   oldmoder M   olde moder BT   alder moder W
2254 he B   2259 wene best to H₁ ... B₂, W   wene best for to M
2278 aday J, F   a day (a dai) AC, SB

Thogh his condicion be good.   [GENTILESSE.]
Bot if a man of bothe tuo
Be riche and vertuous also,
Thanne is he wel the more worth :
Bot yit to putte himselve forth
He moste don his besinesse,
For nowther good ne gentilesse   2290
Mai helpen hem whiche ydel be.
   Bot who that wole in his degre   [EFFECTS OF LOVE.]
Travaile so as it belongeth,
It happeth ofte that he fongeth
Worschipe and ese bothe tuo.
For evere yit it hath be so,
That love honeste in sondri weie
Profiteth, for it doth aweie
The vice, and as the bokes sein,
It makth curteis of the vilein,   2300
And to the couard hardiesce
It yifth, so that verrai prouesse
Is caused upon loves reule   **P. ii. 79**
To him that can manhode reule ;
And ek toward the wommanhiede,
Who that therof wol taken hiede,
For thei the betre affaited be
In every thing, as men may se.
For love hath evere hise lustes grene
In gentil folk, as it is sene,   2310
Which thing ther mai no kinde areste :
I trowe that ther is no beste,
If he with love scholde aqueinte,
That he ne wolde make it queinte
As for the while that it laste.
And thus I conclude ate laste,
That thei ben ydel, as me semeth,
Whiche unto thing that love demeth
Forslowthen that thei scholden do.
   And overthis, mi Sone, also   2320
After the vertu moral eke   Nota de amore cari-

2295 ese] eek (ek) XG, BTΛ   2300 the *om.* H₁E, BTΛ   2307
thei] þough BT   2311 areste] haue reste AM

tatis, vbi dicit, Qui non diligit, manet in morte.

To speke of love if I schal seke,
Among the holi bokes wise
I finde write in such a wise,
'Who loveth noght is hier as ded';
For love above alle othre is hed,
Which hath the vertus forto lede,
Of al that unto mannes dede
Belongeth : for of ydelschipe

[LOVE CONTRARY TO SLOTH.]

He hateth all the felaschipe.   2330
For Slowthe is evere to despise,
Which in desdeign hath al apprise,
And that acordeth noght to man :   P. ii. 80
For he that wit and reson kan,
It sit him wel that he travaile
Upon som thing which mihte availe,
For ydelschipe is noght comended,
Bot every lawe it hath defended.
And in ensample therupon
    The noble wise Salomon,   2340
Which hadde of every thing insihte,
Seith, 'As the briddes to the flihte
Ben made, so the man is bore
To labour,' which is noght forbore
To hem that thenken forto thryve.
For we, whiche are now alyve,
Of hem that besi whylom were,

Apostolus. Que-cumque scripta sunt, ad nostram doctrinam scripta sunt.

Als wel in Scole as elleswhere,
Mowe every day ensample take,
That if it were now to make   2350
Thing which that thei ferst founden oute,
It scholde noght be broght aboute.
Here lyves thanne were longe,
Here wittes grete, here mihtes stronge,
Here hertes ful of besinesse,
Wherof the worldes redinesse
In bodi bothe and in corage
Stant evere upon his avantage.

2324 awise F   2325 as hier is ded BT   2330 all the] alle
(al) A . . . CB₂   2348 ff. *margin* Apostolus—scripta sunt *om.* S . . . Δ
2351 S *has lost a leaf* (ll. 2351–2530)

And forto drawe into memoire
Here names bothe and here histoire,   2360
Upon the vertu of her dede
In sondri bokes thou miht rede.

vii. *Expedit in manibus labor, vt de cotidianis*   **P. ii. 81** [Uses of Labour.]
Actibus ac vita viuere possit homo.
Set qui doctrine causa fert mente labores,
Preualet et merita perpetuata parat.

Of every wisdom the parfit
The hyhe god of his spirit
Yaf to the men in Erthe hiere   Hic loquitur contra
Upon the forme and the matiere   ociosos quoscumque,
Of that he wolde make hem wise: et maxime contra is-
                                             tos, qui excellentis
And thus cam in the ferste apprise   prudencie   ingenium
Of bokes and of alle goode   habentes absque fruc-
Thurgh hem that whilom understode   2370 tu operum torpescunt.
                                             Et ponit exemplum de
The lore which to hem was yive,   diligencia predeces-
Wherof these othre, that now live,   sorum, qui ad tocius
Ben every day to lerne newe.   humani generis doc-
                                             trinam et auxilium suis
Bot er the time that men siewe,   continuis laboribus et
And that the labour forth it broghte,   studiis, gracia medi-
Ther was no corn, thogh men it soghte,   ante diuina, artes et
In non of al the fieldes oute ;   sciencias primitus in-
And er the wisdom cam aboute   uenerunt.
Of hem that ferst the bokes write,
This mai wel every wys man wite,   2380
Ther was gret labour ek also.
Thus was non ydel of the tuo,
That on the plogh hath undertake
With labour which the hond hath take,
That other tok to studie and muse,
As he which wolde noght refuse
The labour of hise wittes alle.
And in this wise it is befalle,
Of labour which that thei begunne
We be now tawht of that we kunne :   2390
Here besinesse is yit so seene,   **P. ii. 82**

Latin Verses vii. 1 in] de B
2373 *margin* et laboribus AM   2377 al F   att J   alle A, B   2391
so] to BTΔ

[DISCOVERERS AND INVENTORS.]

That it stant evere alyche greene;
Al be it so the bodi deie,
The name of hem schal nevere aweie.
In the Croniqes as I finde,
    Cham, whos labour is yit in minde,
Was he which ferst the lettres fond
And wrot in Hebreu with his hond:
Of naturel Philosophie
He fond ferst also the clergie.   2400
    Cadmus the lettres of Gregois
Ferst made upon his oghne chois.
    Theges of thing which schal befalle,
He was the ferste Augurre of alle:
    And Philemon be the visage
Fond to descrive the corage.
    Cladyns, Esdras and Sulpices,
Termegis, Pandulf, Frigidilles,
Menander, Ephiloquorus,
Solins, Pandas and Josephus   2410
The ferste were of Enditours,
Of old Cronique and ek auctours:
    And Heredot in his science
Of metre, of rime and of cadence
The ferste was of which men note.
    And of Musique also the note
In mannes vois or softe or scharpe,
That fond Jubal; and of the harpe
The merie soun, which is to like,
That fond Poulins forth with phisique.   2420
    Zenzis fond ferst the pourtreture,   **P. ii. 83**
And Promotheüs the Sculpture;
After what forme that hem thoghte,
The resemblance anon thei wroghte.
    Tubal in Iren and in Stel
Fond ferst the forge and wroghte it wel:
    And Jadahel, as seith the bok,
Ferst made Net and fisshes tok:
Of huntynge ek he fond the chace,

Which now is knowe in many place :
He sette up ferst and dede it make.
   Verconius of cokerie
Ferst made the delicacie.
   The craft Minerve of wolle fond
And made cloth hire oghne hond ;
   And Delbora made it of lyn :
Tho wommen were of great engyn.
   Bot thing which yifth ous mete and drinke
And doth the labourer to swinke   2440
To tile lond and sette vines,
Wherof the cornes and the wynes
Ben sustenance to mankinde,
In olde bokes as I finde,
Saturnus of his oghne wit
Hath founde ferst, and more yit
Of Chapmanhode he fond the weie,
And ek to coigne the moneie
Of sondri metall, as it is,
He was the ferste man of this.   2450
   Bot hou that metall cam a place   **P. ii. 84**
Thurgh mannes wit and goddes grace
The route of Philosophres wise
Controeveden be sondri wise,
Ferst forto gete it out of Myne,
And after forto trie and fyne.
   And also with gret diligence   [ALCHEMY.]
Thei founden thilke experience,   Nota de Alconomia.
Which cleped is Alconomie,
Wherof the Selver multeplie   2460
Thei made and ek the gold also.
And forto telle hou it is so,
Of bodies sevene in special
With foure spiritz joynt withal
Stant the substance of this matiere.
The bodies whiche I speke of hiere
Of the Planetes ben begonne :
The gold is titled to the Sonne,

2433 Herconius H₁XGECLB₂, BA   Hercenius R   Berconius T, H₃

The mone of Selver hath his part,
And Iren that stant upon Mart,   2470
The Led after Satorne groweth,
And Jupiter the Bras bestoweth,
The Coper set is to Venus,
And to his part Mercurius
Hath the quikselver, as it falleth,
The which, after the bok it calleth,
Is ferst of thilke fowre named
Of Spiritz, whiche ben proclamed;
And the spirit which is secounde
In Sal Armoniak is founde: 2480
The thridde spirit Sulphur is;   **P. ii. 85**
The ferthe suiende after this
Arcennicum be name is hote.
With blowinge and with fyres hote
In these thinges, whiche I seie,
Thei worchen be diverse weie.
For as the philosophre tolde
Of gold and selver, thei ben holde
Tuo principal extremites,
To whiche alle othre be degres   2490
Of the metalls ben acordant,
And so thurgh kinde resemblant,
That what man couthe aweie take
The rust, of which thei waxen blake,
And the savour and the hardnesse,
Thei scholden take the liknesse
Of gold or Selver parfitly.
 Bot forto worche it sikirly,
Betwen the corps and the spirit,
Er that the metall be parfit,   2500
In sevene formes it is set;
Of alle and if that on be let,
The remenant mai noght availe,
Bot otherwise it mai noght faile.
For thei be whom this art was founde
To every point a certain bounde
Ordeignen, that a man mai finde

2477 Is] The B   2501 as it is set H₁. . . B₂

This craft is wroght be weie of kinde,   [Alchemy.]
So that ther is no fallas inne.
Bot what man that this werk beginne,   2510
He mot awaite at every tyde,   **P. ii. 86**
So that nothing be left aside,
Ferst of the distillacion,
Forth with the congelacion,
Solucion, descencion,
And kepe in his entencion
The point of sublimacion,
And forth with calcinacion
Of veray approbacion
Do that ther be fixacion   2520
With tempred hetes of the fyr,
Til he the parfit Elixir
Of thilke philosophres Ston
Mai gete, of which that many on
Of Philosophres whilom write.
And if thou wolt the names wite
Of thilke Ston with othre tuo,
Whiche as the clerkes maden tho,
So as the bokes it recorden,
The kinde of hem I schal recorden.   2530

These olde Philosophres wyse   [The Three Stones
Be weie of kinde in sondri wise   of the Philoso-
Thre Stones maden thurgh clergie.   phers.]
The ferste, if I schal specefie,
                                           Nota de tribus lapi-
Was *lapis vegetabilis*,   dibus, quos philosophi
Of which the propre vertu is   composuerunt, quo-
                                           rum primus dicitur
To mannes hele forto serve,   lapis vegetabilis, qui
As forto kepe and to preserve   sanitatem conseruat,
The bodi fro siknesses alle,   secundus dicitur lapis
                                           animalis, qui membra
Til deth of kinde upon him falle.   et virtutes sencibiles
    The Ston seconde I thee behote   2540 fortificat, tercius dici-
                                      P. ii. 87 tur lapis mineralis, qui
Is *lapis animalis* hote,   omnia metalla purificat
The whos vertu is propre and cowth   et in suum perfectum
                                           naturali potencia de-
                                           ducit.

2512 lefte F   2524 many on F   2531 S *resumes*   The BT
2534 ferste S   ferst AJ, F   2535 *lapis*] cleped BT   2538 As] And
H₁ . . . B₂, Λ   2539 *margin* qui membra] que membra F
sencibiles] sanabiles H₁ . . . B₂, Λ
  **   B b

For Ere and yhe and nase and mouth,
Wherof a man mai hiere and se
And smelle and taste in his degre,
And forto fiele and forto go
It helpeth man of bothe tuo :
The wittes fyve he underfongeth
To kepe, as it to him belongeth.   2550
   The thridde Ston in special
Be name is cleped Minerall,
Which the metalls of every Mine
Attempreth, til that thei ben fyne,
And pureth hem be such a weie,
That al the vice goth aweie
Of rust, of stink and of hardnesse :
And whan thei ben of such clennesse,
This Mineral, so as I finde,
Transformeth al the ferste kynde   2560
And makth hem able to conceive
Thurgh his vertu, and to receive
Bothe in substance and in figure
Of gold and selver the nature.
For thei tuo ben thextremetes,
To whiche after the propretes
Hath every metal his desir,
With help and confort of the fyr
Forth with this Ston, as it is seid,
Which to the Sonne and Mone is leid ;   2570
For to the rede and to the whyte   **P. ii. 88**
This Ston hath pouer to profite.
It makth multiplicacioun
Of gold, and the fixacioun
It causeth, and of his habit
He doth the werk to be parfit
Of thilke Elixer which men calle
Alconomie, as is befalle
To hem that whilom weren wise.

2555 aweie F   2556 vice goth] filþe be H₁ . . . B₂, Λ (*line
om.* W)   2562 to *om.* BT   2565 thextremetes] extremites
X . . . B₂, B   2569 ffor AM   þe ston H₁ . . . B₂   2576 He]
It S . . . Δ   2578 as] which A . . . B₂

Bot now it stant al otherwise; 2580 [THE THREE STONES
Thei speken faste of thilke Ston, OF THE PHILOSO-
Bot hou to make it, nou wot non PHERS.]
After the sothe experience.
And natheles gret diligence
Thei setten upon thilke dede,
And spille more than thei spede;
For allewey thei finde a lette,
Which bringeth in poverte and dette
To hem that riche were afore:
The lost is had, the lucre is lore, 2590
To gete a pound thei spenden fyve;
I not hou such a craft schal thryve
In the manere as it is used:
It were betre be refused
Than forto worchen upon weene
In thing which stant noght as thei weene.
Bot noght forthi, who that it knewe,
The science of himself is trewe
Upon the forme as it was founded,
Wherof the names yit ben grounded 2600
Of hem that ferste it founden oute; **P. ii. 89**
And thus the fame goth aboute
To suche as soghten besinesse
Of vertu and of worthinesse.
Of whom if I the names calle,
  Hermes was on the ferste of alle, [THE FIRST AL-
To whom this art is most applied; CHEMISTS.]
Geber therof was magnefied,
And Ortolan and Morien,
Among the whiche is Avicen, 2610
Which fond and wrot a gret partie
The practique of Alconomie;
Whos bokes, pleinli as thei stonde
Upon this craft, fewe understonde;
Bot yit to put hem in assai
Ther ben full manye now aday,
That knowen litel what thei meene.

2587 all weies (alweies) XGRCLB₂   2609 Orcalan H₁ ... B₂
2615 put'AJ, S, F   putte C, B
B b 2

[THE FIRST AL-
CHEMISTS.] .

It is noght on to wite and weene ;
In forme of wordes thei it trete,
Bot yit they failen of beyete,   2620
For of tomoche or of tolyte
Ther is algate founde a wyte,
So that thei folwe noght the lyne
Of the parfite medicine,
Which grounded is upon nature.
Bot thei that writen the scripture
Of Grek, Arabe and of Caldee,
Thei were of such Auctorite
That thei ferst founden out the weie
Of al that thou hast herd me seie ;   2630
Wherof the Cronique of her lore   **P. ii. 90**
Schal stonde in pris for everemore.

[LETTERS AND
LANGUAGE.]

Bot toward oure Marches hiere,
Of the Latins if thou wolt hiere,
Of hem that whilom vertuous
Were and therto laborious,
Carmente made of hire engin
The ferste lettres of Latin,
Of which the tunge Romein cam,
Wherof that Aristarchus nam   2640
Forth with Donat and Dindimus
The ferste reule of Scole, as thus,
How that Latin schal be componed
And in what wise it schal be soned,
That every word in his degre
Schal stonde upon congruite.
And thilke time at Rome also
Was Tullius with Cithero,
That writen upon Rethorike,
Hou that men schal the wordes pike   2650
After the forme of eloquence,
Which is, men sein, a gret prudence :

2620 faile of þe beȝete H₁ . . . B₂ fallen of b. T   but þei faile ȝit
of b. Δ   2627 of *om.* M, BT, H₃   2629 out] out of AMH₁
2641 ffor B   2642 as SBTΔ   is Ad   and A . . . B₂, Λ, FWH₃
2650 schal the wordes] schal þe worde S   shal wordes W   scholde
þe wordes Ad   scholde her wordes B

And after that out of Hebreu
Jerom, which the langage kneu,
The Bible, in which the lawe is closed,
Into Latin he hath transposed;
And many an other writere ek
Out of Caldee, Arabe and Grek
With gret labour the bokes wise
Translateden. And otherwise   2660
The Latins of hemself also   **P. ii. 91**
Here studie at thilke time so
With gret travaile of Scole toke
In sondri forme forto boke,
That we mai take here evidences
Upon the lore of the Sciences,
Of craftes bothe and of clergie;
Among the whiche in Poesie
To the lovers Ovide wrot
And tawhte, if love be to hot,   2670
In what manere it scholde akiele.

   Forthi, mi Sone, if that thou fiele   Confessor
That love wringe thee to sore,
Behold Ovide and take his lore.

   My fader, if thei mihte spede   Amans.
Mi love, I wolde his bokes rede;
And if thei techen to restreigne
Mi love, it were an ydel peine
To lerne a thing which mai noght be.
For lich unto the greene tree,   2680
If that men toke his rote aweie,
Riht so myn herte scholde deie,
If that mi love be withdrawe.
Wherof touchende unto this sawe
There is bot only to poursuie
Mi love, and ydelschipe eschuie.

   Mi goode Sone, soth to seie,   Confessor.
If ther be siker eny weie
To love, thou hast seid the beste:

2662 and þilke time so H₁ . . . RLB₂   and þilke time also C   at
thilke t. also W at þilke tyme þo M   2674 take AJ, S, F tak C, BT
2676 hise A   2681 take B

For who that wolde have al his reste   2690
And do no travail at the nede,   **P. ii. 92**
It is no resoun that he spede
In loves cause forto winne;
For he which dar nothing beginne,
I not what thing he scholde achieve.
Bot overthis thou schalt believe,
So as it sit thee wel to knowe,
That ther ben othre vices slowe,
Whiche unto love don gret lette,
If thou thin herte upon hem sette.   2700

[vi. Somnolence.]   viii. *Perdit homo causam linquens sua iura sopori,*
Et quasi dimidium pars sua mortis habet.
Est in amore vigil Venus, et quod habet vigilanti
Obsequium thalamis fert vigilata suis.

Hic loquitur de
Sompnolencia, que
Accidie Cameraria
dicta est, cuius na-
tura semimortua ali-
cuius negocii vigilias
obseruare soporifero
torpore recusat: vnde
quatenus amorem
concernit Confessor
Amanti diligencius op-
ponit.

Toward the Slowe progenie
Ther is yit on of compaignie,
And he is cleped Sompnolence,
Which doth to Slouthe his reverence,
As he which is his Chamberlein,
That many an hundrid time hath lein
To slepe, whan he scholde wake.
He hath with love trewes take,
That wake who so wake wile,
If he mai couche a doun his bile,   2710
He hath al wowed what him list;
That ofte he goth to bedde unkist,
And seith that for no Druerie
He wol noght leve his sluggardie.
For thogh noman it wole allowe,
To slepe levere than to wowe
Is his manere, and thus on nyhtes,   **P. ii. 93**
Whan that he seth the lusti knyhtes
Revelen, wher these wommen are,
Awey he skulketh as an hare,   2720
And goth to bedde and leith him softe,

2704 *margin* Accidia H₁E . . . B₂, W   2707 *margin* sopori fero
MH₁ERL, Λ, WH₃   sopori sero XGCB₂, B   2710 a doun C, B, F
adoun AJ, S   2711 S *has lost two leaves* (ll. 2711–3078)

And of his Slouthe he dremeth ofte   [SOMNOLENCE.]
Hou that he stiketh in the Myr,
And hou he sitteth be the fyr
And claweth on his bare schanckes,
And hou he clymbeth up the banckes
And falleth into Slades depe.
Bot thanne who so toke kepe,
Whanne he is falle in such a drem,
Riht as a Schip ayein the Strem,   2730
He routeth with a slepi noise,
And brustleth as a monkes froise,
Whanne it is throwe into the Panne.
And otherwhile sielde whanne
That he mai dreme a lusti swevene,
Him thenkth as thogh he were in hevene
And as the world were holi his :
And thanne he spekth of that and this,
And makth his exposicion
After the disposicion   2740
Of that he wolde, and in such wise
He doth to love all his service ;
I not what thonk he schal deserve.
Bot, Sone, if thou wolt love serve,
I rede that thou do noght so.
    Ha, goode fader, certes no.   Confessio Amantis.
I hadde levere be mi trowthe,   **P. ii. 94**
Er I were set on such a slouthe
And beere such a slepi snoute,
Bothe yhen of myn hed were oute.   2750
For me were betre fulli die,
Thanne· I of such a slugardie
Hadde eny name, god me schilde ;
For whan mi moder was with childe,
And I lay in hire wombe clos,
I wolde rathere Atropos,
Which is goddesse of alle deth,
Anon as I hadde eny breth,
Me hadde fro mi Moder cast.
Bot now I am nothing agast,   2760

2743 shal F   2744 wolde A   2760 I am now H₁ ... B₂, A

[THE LOVER'S WAKE-
FULNESS.]

I thonke godd ; for Lachesis,
Ne Cloto, which hire felawe is,
Me schopen no such destine,
Whan thei at mi nativite
My weerdes setten as thei wolde ;
Bot thei me schopen that I scholde
Eschuie of slep the truandise,
So that I hope in such a wise
To love forto ben excused,
That I no Sompnolence have used.   2770
For certes, fader Genius,
Yit into nou it hath be thus,
At alle time if it befelle
So that I mihte come and duelle
In place ther my ladi were,
I was noght slow ne slepi there :
For thanne I dar wel undertake,   **P. ii. 95**
That whanne hir list on nyhtes wake
In chambre as to carole and daunce,
Me thenkth I mai me more avaunce,   2780
If I mai gon upon hir hond,
Thanne if I wonne a kinges lond.
For whanne I mai hire hand beclippe,
With such gladnesse I daunce and skippe,
Me thenkth I touche noght the flor ;
The Ro, which renneth on the Mor,
Is thanne noght so lyht as I :
So mow ye witen wel forthi,
That for the time slep I hate.
And whanne it falleth othergate,   2790
So that hire like noght to daunce,
Bot on the Dees to caste chaunce
Or axe of love som demande,
Or elles that hir list comaunde
To rede and here of Troilus,
Riht as sche wole or so or thus,
I am al redi to consente.
And if so is that I mai hente

2773 times BT   2788 mow F   mowe AJ, B   2792 a chaunce
H₁ . . . RLB₂, BT   his chaunce C   2796 wole or so] wolde so BT

Somtime among a good leisir,
So as I dar of mi desir 2800
I telle a part; bot whanne I preie,
Anon sche bidt me go mi weie
And seith it is ferr in the nyht;
And I swere it is even liht.
Bot as it falleth ate laste,
Ther mai no worldes joie laste,
So mot I nedes fro hire wende   **P. ii. 96**
And of my wachche make an ende:
And if sche thanne hiede toke,
Hou pitousliche on hire I loke, 2810
Whan that I schal my leve take,
Hire oghte of mercy forto slake
Hire daunger, which seith evere nay.
  Bot he seith often, 'Have good day,'
That loth is forto take his leve:
Therfore, while I mai beleve,
I tarie forth the nyht along,
For it is noght on me along
To slep that I so sone go,
Til that I mot algate so; 2820
And thanne I bidde godd hire se,
And so doun knelende on mi kne
I take leve, and if I schal,
I kisse hire, and go forth withal.
And otherwhile, if that I dore,
Er I come fulli to the Dore,
I torne ayein and feigne a thing,
As thogh I hadde lost a Ring
Or somwhat elles, for I wolde
Kisse hire eftsones, if I scholde, 2830
Bot selden is that I so spede.
And whanne I se that I mot nede
Departen, I departe, and thanne
With al myn herte I curse and banne
That evere slep was mad for yhe;
For, as me thenkth, I mihte dryhe

2802 bidt A, F bit J bid C, B   2822 doun *om.* AM   2826
to the] atte M, B   2833 Departen] Depart(e) and H₁ . . . B₂, BΛ

Withoute slep to waken evere,   P. ii. 97
So that I scholde noght dissevere
Fro hire, in whom is al my liht :
And thanne I curse also the nyht   2840
With al the will of mi corage,
And seie, 'Awey, thou blake ymage,
Which of thi derke cloudy face
Makst al the worldes lyht deface,
And causest unto slep a weie,
Be which I mot nou gon aweie
Out of mi ladi compaignie.
O slepi nyht, I thee defie,
And wolde that thou leye in presse
With Proserpine the goddesse   2850
And with Pluto the helle king :
For til I se the daies spring,
I sette slep noght at a risshe.'
And with that word I sike and wisshe,
And seie, ' Ha, whi ne were it day?
For yit mi ladi thanne I may
Beholde, thogh I do nomore.'
And efte I thenke forthermore,
To som man hou the niht doth ese,
Whan he hath thing that mai him plese   2860
The longe nyhtes be his side,
Where as I faile and go beside.
Bot slep, I not wherof it serveth,
Of which noman his thonk deserveth
To gete him love in eny place,
Bot is an hindrere of his grace
And makth him ded as for a throwe,   P. ii. 98
Riht as a Stok were overthrowe.
And so, mi fader, in this wise
The slepi nyhtes I despise,   2870
And evere amiddes of mi tale
I thenke upon the nyhtingale,
Which slepeth noght be weie of kinde
For love, in bokes as I finde.

2846 go now (gon now) M . . . B₂   2860 mai] might (miȝte)
H₁ . . . B₂ doth W   2867 him A . . . B₂ hem AdBTΔ, FWH₃

Thus ate laste I go to bedde, [THE LOVER'S WAKE-
FULNESS.]
And yit min herte lith to wedde
With hire, wher as I cam fro;
Thogh I departe, he wol noght so,
Ther is no lock mai schette him oute,
Him nedeth noght to gon aboute, 2880
That perce mai the harde wall;
Thus is he with hire overall,
That be hire lief, or be hire loth,
Into hire bedd myn herte goth,
And softly takth hire in his arm
And fieleth hou that sche is warm,
And wissheth that his body were
To fiele that he fieleth there.
And thus miselven I tormente,
Til that the dede slep me hente: 2890
Bot thanne be a thousand score [DREAMS.]
Welmore than I was tofore
I am tormented in mi slep,
Bot that I dreme is noght of schep;
For I ne thenke noght on wulle,
Bot I am drecched to the fulle
Of love, that I have to kepe, **P. ii. 99**
That nou I lawhe and nou I wepe,
And nou I lese and nou I winne,
And nou I ende and nou beginne. 2900
And otherwhile I dreme and mete
That I al one with hire mete
And that Danger is left behinde;
And thanne in slep such joie I finde,
That I ne bede nevere awake.
Bot after, whanne I hiede take,
And schal arise upon the morwe,
Thanne is al torned into sorwe,
Noght for the cause I schal arise,
Bot for I mette in such a wise, 2910
And ate laste I am bethoght
That al is vein and helpeth noght:
Bot yit me thenketh be my wille
I wolde have leie and slepe stille,

[DREAMS.]

Confessor.

To meten evere of such a swevene,
For thanne I hadde a slepi hevene.
  Mi Sone, and for thou tellest so,
A man mai finde of time ago
That many a swevene hath be certein,
Al be it so, that som men sein   2920
That swevenes ben of no credence.
Bot forto schewe in evidence
That thei fulofte sothe thinges
Betokne, I thenke in my wrytinges
To telle a tale therupon,
Which fell be olde daies gon.

[TALE OF CEIX AND
  ALCEONE.]

Hic ponit exemplum,
qualiter Sompnia pre-
nostice veritatis quan-
doque certitudinem
figurant. Et narrat
quod, cum Ceix Rex
Trocinie pro refor-
macione fratris sui
Dedalionis in Ancipi-
trem transmutati per-
egre proficiscens in
mari longius a patria
dimersus fuerat, Iuno
mittens Yridem nun-
ciam suam in partes
Chymerie ad domum
Sompni, iussit quod
ipse Alceone dicti Re-
gis uxori huius rei e-
uentum per Sompnia
certificaret. Quo facto
Alceona rem perscru-
tans corpus mariti sui,
vbi super fluctus mor-
tuus iactabatur, inue-
nit; que pre dolore
angustiata   cupiens
corpus amplectere, in
altum mare super ip-
sum prosiliit. Vnde dii
miserti amborum cor-
pora in aues, que ad-
huc Alceones dicte

  This finde I write in Poesie: **P. ii. 100**
Ceïx the king of Trocinie
Hadde Alceone to his wif,
Which as hire oghne hertes lif   2930
Him loveth; and he hadde also
A brother, which was cleped tho
Dedalion, and he per cas
Fro kinde of man forschape was
Into a Goshauk of liknesse;
Wherof the king gret hevynesse
Hath take, and thoghte in his corage
To gon upon a pelrinage
Into a strange regioun,
Wher he hath his devocioun   2940
To don his sacrifice and preie,
If that he mihte in eny weie
Toward the goddes finde grace
His brother hele to pourchace,
So that he mihte be reformed
Of that he hadde be transformed.
To this pourpos and to this ende
This king is redy forto wende,
As he which wolde go be Schipe;
And forto don him felaschipe   2950
His wif unto the See him broghte,

2937 *margin* demersus AM   2942 *margin* Quo facto *om.* A ... B2
2945 *margin* mortuus *om.* A ... B2

With al hire herte and him besoghte,
That he the time hire wolde sein,
Whan that he thoghte come ayein :
'Withinne,' he seith, 'tuo Monthe day.'
And thus in al the haste he may
He tok his leve, and forth he seileth   **P. ii. 101**
Wepende, and sche hirself beweileth,
And torneth hom, ther sche cam fro.
Bot whan the Monthes were ago,   2960
The whiche he sette of his comynge,
And that sche herde no tydinge,
Ther was no care forto seche :
Wherof the goddes to beseche
Tho sche began in many wise,
And to Juno hire sacrifise
Above alle othre most sche dede,
And for hir lord sche hath so bede
To wite and knowe hou that he ferde,
That Juno the goddesse hire herde,   2970
Anon and upon this matiere
Sche bad Yris hir Messagere
To Slepes hous that sche schal wende,
And bidde him that he make an ende
Be swevene and schewen al the cas
Unto this ladi, hou it was.
    This Yris, fro the hihe stage
Which undertake hath the Message,
Hire reyny Cope dede upon,
The which was wonderli begon   2980
With colours of diverse hewe,
An hundred mo than men it knewe ;
The hevene lich unto a bowe
Sche bende, and so she cam doun lowe,
The god of Slep wher that sche fond.
And that was in a strange lond,
Which marcheth upon Chymerie :   **P. ii. 102**
For ther, as seith the Poesie,

[TALE OF CEIX AND
ALCEONE.]
sunt, subito conuer-
terunt.

2954 thoghte] wolde H₁...B₂   wol L   thought to W   2955
monþes H₁ ... B₂, H₃   2973 she Λ, Magd   he Λ ... B₂, AdBTΔ,
FWKH₃   2984 so *m.* AM

The god of Slep hath mad his hous,
Which of entaille is merveilous.   2990
Under an hell ther is a Cave,
Which of the Sonne mai noght have,
So that noman mai knowe ariht
The point betwen the dai and nyht:
Ther is no fyr, ther is no sparke,
Ther is no dore, which mai charke,
Wherof an yhe scholde unschette,
So that inward ther is no lette.
And forto speke of that withoute,
Ther stant no gret Tree nyh aboute   3000
Wher on ther myhte crowe or pie
Alihte, forto clepe or crie:
Ther is no cok to crowe day,
Ne beste non which noise may
The hell, bot al aboute round
Ther is growende upon the ground
Popi, which berth the sed of slep,
With othre herbes suche an hep.
A stille water for the nones
Rennende upon the smale stones,   3010
Which hihte of Lethes the rivere,
Under that hell in such manere
Ther is, which yifth gret appetit
To slepe. And thus full of delit
Slep hath his hous; and of his couche
Withinne his chambre if I schal touche,
Of hebenus that slepi Tree   **P. ii. 103**
The bordes al aboute be,
And for he scholde slepe softe,
Upon a fethrebed alofte   3020
He lith with many a pilwe of doun:
The chambre is strowed up and doun
With swevenes many thousendfold.
Thus cam Yris into this hold,
And to the bedd, which is al blak,

2992 the *om.* AM   2994 betwen the] betwene A . . . B₂, T
(bitwen)   betwen bothe H₃   2997 Wherfor(e) AJMG . . . B₂
3023 many a XGL, AdBTΔ, WH₃

[TALE OF CEIX AND
ALCEONE.]

Sche goth, and ther with Slep sche spak,
And in the wise as sche was bede
The Message of Juno sche dede.
Fulofte hir wordes sche reherceth,
Er sche his slepi Eres perceth;   3030
With mochel wo bot ate laste
His slombrende yhen he upcaste
And seide hir that it schal be do.
Wherof among a thousend tho,
Withinne his hous that slepi were,
In special he ches out there
Thre, whiche scholden do this dede:
The ferste of hem, so as I rede,
Was Morpheüs, the whos nature
Is forto take the figure   3040
Of what persone that him liketh,
Wherof that he fulofte entriketh
The lif which slepe schal be nyhte:
And Ithecus that other hihte,
Which hath the vois of every soun,
The chiere and the condicioun
Of every lif, what so it is: P. ii. 104
The thridde suiende after this
Is Panthasas, which may transforme
Of every thing the rihte forme,   3050
And change it in an other kinde.
Upon hem thre, so as I finde,
Of swevenes stant al thapparence,
Which otherwhile is evidence
And otherwhile bot a jape.
Bot natheles it is so schape,
That Morpheüs be nyht al one
Appiereth until Alceone
In liknesse of hir housebonde
Al naked ded upon the stronde,   3060
And hou he dreynte in special
These othre tuo it schewen al.
The tempeste of the blake cloude,

3027 þe wise þat M ... CB₂   þis wise as BT, H₃   3033 schulde
BT, W   3056 was AdBTΔ   3058 vnto JH₁ ... B₂, Δ, WH₃

[TALE OF CEIX AND ALCEONE.]

The wode See, the wyndes loude,
Al this sche mette, and sih him dyen;
Wherof that sche began to crien,
Slepende abedde ther sche lay,
And with that noise of hire affray
Hir wommen sterten up aboute,
Whiche of here ladi were in doute,   3070
And axen hire hou that sche ferde ;
And sche, riht as sche syh and herde,
Hir swevene hath told hem everydel.
And thei it halsen alle wel
And sein it is a tokne of goode ;
Bot til sche wiste hou that it stode,
Sche hath no confort in hire herte,   **P. ii. 105**
Upon the morwe and up sche sterte,
And to the See, wher that sche mette
The bodi lay, withoute lette   3080
Sche drowh, and whan that sche cam nyh,
Stark ded, hise armes sprad, sche syh
Hire lord flietende upon the wawe.
Wherof hire wittes ben withdrawe,
And sche, which tok of deth no kepe,
Anon forth lepte into the depe
And wolde have cawht him in hire arm.
  This infortune of double harm
The goddes fro the hevene above
Behielde, and for the trowthe of love,   3090
Which in this worthi ladi stod,
Thei have upon the salte flod
Hire dreinte lord and hire also
Fro deth to lyve torned so,
That thei ben schapen into briddes
Swimmende upon the wawe amiddes.
And whan sche sih hire lord livende
In liknesse of a bridd swimmende,
And sche was of the same sort,
So as sche mihte do desport,   3100
Upon the joie which sche hadde

3074 falsen AM   3079 S *resumes*   3082 hir BT   3086 forth
lepte] lepte forþ AM   lepte L

Hire wynges bothe abrod sche spradde,
And him, so as sche mai suffise,
Beclipte and keste in such a wise,
As sche was whilom wont to do:
Hire wynges for hire armes tuo
Sche tok, and for hire lippes softe **P. ii. 106**
Hire harde bile, and so fulofte
Sche fondeth in hire briddes forme,
If that sche mihte hirself conforme 3110
To do the plesance of a wif,
As sche dede in that other lif:
For thogh sche hadde hir pouer lore,
Hir will stod as it was tofore,
And serveth him so as sche mai.
Wherof into this ilke day
Togedre upon the See thei wone,
Wher many a dowhter and a Sone
Thei bringen forth of briddes kinde;
And for men scholden take in mynde 3120
This Alceoun the trewe queene,
Hire briddes yit, as it is seene,
Of Alceoun the name bere.

 Lo thus, mi Sone, it mai thee stere *Confessor.*
Of swevenes forto take kepe,
For ofte time a man aslepe
Mai se what after schal betide.
Forthi it helpeth at som tyde
A man to slepe, as it belongeth,
Bot slowthe no lif underfongeth 3130
Which is to love appourtenant.

 Mi fader, upon covenant *Confessio Amantis.*
I dar wel make this avou,
Of all mi lif that into nou,
Als fer as I can understonde,
Yit tok I nevere Slep on honde,
Whan it was time forto wake; **P. ii. 107**
For thogh myn yhe it wolde take,
Min herte is evere therayein.

3129 Aman F 3132 þe couenant BTΛ 3138 For]
And BTΛ

**   C C

Bot natheles to speke it plein,   3140
Al this that I have seid you hiere
Of my wakinge, as ye mai hiere,
It toucheth to mi lady swete;
For otherwise, I you behiete,
In strange place whanne I go,
Me list nothing to wake so.
For whan the wommen listen pleie,
And I hir se noght in the weie,
Of whom I scholde merthe take,
Me list noght longe forto wake,   3150
Bot if it be for pure schame,
Of that I wolde eschuie a name,
That thei ne scholde have cause non
To seie, 'Ha, lo, wher goth such on,
That hath forlore his contenaunce!'
And thus among I singe and daunce,
And feigne lust ther as non is.
For ofte sithe I fiele this;
Of thoght, which in mi herte falleth
Whanne it is nyht, myn hed appalleth,   3160
And that is for I se hire noght,
Which is the wakere of mi thoght:
And thus as tymliche as I may,
Fulofte whanne it is brod day,
I take of all these othre leve
And go my weie, and thei beleve,
That sen per cas here loves there;   P. ii. 108
And I go forth as noght ne were
Unto mi bedd, so that al one
I mai ther ligge and sighe and grone   ⁰3170
And wisshen al the longe nyht,
Til that I se the daies lyht.
I not if that be Sompnolence,
Bot upon youre conscience,
Min holi fader, demeth ye.

Confessor.   My Sone, I am wel paid with thee,

3140 it] in H₁ ... B₂   3141 that *om.* AM   3142 walkyng
H₁RCB₂ *line om.* T   3153 ne *om.* H₁ ... B₂   3154 Ha *om.*
A ... B₂   3159 mi F   myn AJ, B   3165 all S, F   alle AJ, B

Of Slep that thou the Sluggardie
Be nyhte in loves compaignie
Eschuied hast, and do thi peine
So that thi love thar noght pleine :   3180
For love upon his lust wakende
Is evere, and wolde that non ende
Were of the longe nyhtes set.
Wherof that thou be war the bet,
To telle a tale I am bethoght,
Hou love and Slep acorden noght.

For love who that list to wake
Be nyhte, he mai ensample take
Of Cephalus, whan that he lay
With Aurora that swete may   3190
In armes all the longe nyht.
Bot whanne it drogh toward the liht,
That he withinne his herte sih
The dai which was amorwe nyh,
Anon unto the Sonne he preide
For lust of love, and thus he seide :
  'O Phebus, which the daies liht   **P. ii. 109**
Governest, til that it be nyht,
And gladest every creature
After the lawe of thi nature,—   3200
Bot natheles ther is a thing,
Which onli to the knouleching
Belongeth as in privete
To love and to his duete,
Which asketh noght to ben apert,
Bot in cilence and in covert
Desireth forto be beschaded :
And thus whan that thi liht is faded
And Vesper scheweth him alofte,
And that the nyht is long and softe,   3210
Under the cloudes derke and stille
Thanne hath this thing most of his wille.
Forthi unto thi myhtes hyhe,

[SLEEPING AND
WAKING.]

[THE PRAYER OF
CEPHALUS.]

Hic dicit quod vigilia in Amantibus et non Sompnolencia laudanda est. Et ponit exemplum de Cephalo filio Phebi, qui nocturno cilencio Auroram amicam suam diligencius amplectens, Solem et lunam interpellabat, videlicet quod Sol in circulo ab oriente distanciori currum cum luce sua retardaret, et quod luna spera sua longissima orbem circuiens noctem continuaret ; ita vt ipsum Cephalum amplexibus Aurore volutum, priusquam dies illa illucesceret, suis deliciis adquiescere diucius permittere dignarentur.

3190 þe AM   3199 *margin* sua *om.* BT   3202 *margin* ita
quod AM   3204 *margin* illa *om.* SBTΔ (*Latin om.* Ad)
3206 cilence S, F   silence AJ, B   *margin* dignaretur A . . . B₂, Λ

C C 2

As thou which art the daies yhe,
Of love and myht no conseil hyde,
Upon this derke nyhtes tyde
With al myn herte I thee beseche
That I plesance myhte seche
With hire which lith in min armes.
Withdrawgh the Banere of thin Armes,   3220
And let thi lyhtes ben unborn,
And in the Signe of Capricorn,
The hous appropred to Satorne,
I preie that thou wolt sojorne,
Wher ben the nihtes derke and longe :
For I mi love have underfonge,
Which lith hier be mi syde naked,   **P. ii. 110**
As sche which wolde ben awaked,
And me lest nothing forto slepe.
So were it good to take kepe   3230
Nou at this nede of mi preiere,
And that the like forto stiere
Thi fyri Carte, and so ordeigne,
That thou thi swifte hors restreigne
Lowe under Erthe in Occident,
That thei towardes Orient
Be Cercle go the longe weie.
   And ek to thee, Diane, I preie,
Which cleped art of thi noblesse
The nyhtes Mone and the goddesse,   3240
That thou to me be gracious :
And in Cancro thin oghne hous
Ayein Phebus in opposit
Stond al this time, and of delit
Behold Venus with a glad yhe.
For thanne upon Astronomie
Of due constellacion
Thou makst prolificacion,
And dost that children ben begete :
Which grace if that I mihte gete,   3250

3221 ben unborn] be vp (vppe) AM   3233 Thi (Thy) A . . . B₂,
S . . . Δ   This FWKH₃   3244 all] at S . . . Δ   3250 if that I]
if I H₁ . . . B₂

With al myn herte I wolde serve
Be nyhte, and thi vigile observe.'
  Lo, thus this lusti Cephalus   Confessor.
Preide unto Phebe and to Phebus
The nyht in lengthe forto drawe,
So that he mihte do the lawe
In thilke point of loves heste,   P. ii. III
Which cleped is the nyhtes feste,
Withoute Slep of sluggardie;
Which Venus out of compaignie   3260
Hath put awey, as thilke same,
Which lustles ferr from alle game
In chambre doth fulofte wo
Abedde, whanne it falleth so
That love scholde ben awaited.
But Slowthe, which is evele affaited,
With Slep hath mad his retenue,
That what thing is to love due,
Of all his dette he paieth non :
He wot noght how the nyht is gon   3270
Ne hou the day is come aboute,
Bot onli forto slepe and route
Til hyh midday, that he arise.
Bot Cephalus dede otherwise,
As thou, my Sone, hast herd above.
  Mi fader, who that hath his love   Amans.
Abedde naked be his syde,
And wolde thanne hise yhen hyde
With Slep, I not what man is he :
Bot certes as touchende of me,   3280
That fell me nevere yit er this.
Bot otherwhile, whan so is
That I mai cacche Slep on honde
Liggende al one, thanne I fonde
To dreme a merie swevene er day;
And if so falle that I may
Mi thought with such a swevene plese, P. ii. 112

3252 vigilie B   3255 nyht (night) AC, B nyhte (nihte) J, S, F
3259 of] or X . . . B₂, W   3263 S *has lost a leaf* (ll. 3263–
3442)

[THE PRAYER OF
CEPHALUS.]

Me thenkth I am somdiel in ese,
For I non other confort have.
So nedeth noght that I schal crave   3290
The Sonnes Carte forto tarie,
Ne yit the Mone, that sche carie
Hire cours along upon the hevene,
For I am noght the more in evene
Towardes love in no degree :
Bot in mi slep yit thanne I se
Somwhat in swevene of that me liketh,
Which afterward min herte entriketh,
Whan that I finde it otherwise.
So wot I noght of what servise   3300
That Slep to mannes ese doth.

Confessor.

    Mi Sone, certes thou seist soth,
Bot only that it helpeth kinde
Somtyme, in Phisique as I finde,
Whan it is take be mesure :
Bot he which can no Slep mesure
Upon the reule as it belongeth,
Fulofte of sodein chance he fongeth
Such infortune that him grieveth.
Bot who these olde bokes lieveth,   3310
Of Sompnolence hou it is write,
Ther may a man the sothe wite,
If that he wolde ensample take,
That otherwhile is good to wake :
Wherof a tale in Poesie
I thenke forto specefie.

[ARGUS AND MER-
CURY.]

Hic loquitur in amo-
ris causa contra istos
qui Sompnolencie de-
diti ea que seruare
tenentur amittunt. Et
narrat quod, cum Yo
puella pulcherima a
Iunone in vaccam
transformata et in

    Ovide telleth in his sawes,   **P. ii. 113**
How Jupiter be olde dawes
Lay be a Mayde, which Yo
Was cleped, wherof that Juno   3320
His wif was wroth, and the goddesse
Of Yo torneth the liknesse
Into a cow, to gon theroute
The large fieldes al aboute

And gete hire mete upon the griene.
And therupon this hyhe queene
Betok hire Argus forto kepe,
For he was selden wont to slepe,
And yit he hadde an hundred yhen,
And alle alyche wel thei syhen.
Now herkne hou that he was beguiled.
Mercurie, which was al affiled
This Cow to stele, he cam desguised,
And hadde a Pipe wel devised
Upon the notes of Musiqe,
Wherof he mihte hise Eres like.
And over that he hadde affaited
Hise lusti tales, and awaited
His time ; and thus into the field
He cam, where Argus he behield
With Yo, which beside him wente.
With that his Pype on honde he hente,
And gan to pipe in his manere
Thing which was slepi forto hiere ;
And in his pipinge evere among
He tolde him such a lusti song,
That he the fol hath broght aslepe.
Ther was non yhe mihte kepe
His hed, the which Mercurie of smot,
And forth withal anon fot hot
He stal the Cow which Argus kepte,
And al this fell for that he slepte.
Ensample it was to manye mo,
That mochel Slep doth ofte wo,
Whan it is time forto wake :
For if a man this vice take,
In Sompnolence and him delite,
Men scholde upon his Dore wryte
His epitaphe, as on his grave ;
For he to spille and noght to save
Is schape, as thogh he were ded.

[ARGUS AND MER-
CURY.]

Argi custodiam sic
deposita fuisset, su-
perueniens Mercurius
Argum dormientem
occidit, et ipsam vac-
3330 cam a pastura rapiens,
quo voluit secum
perduxit.

3340

P. ii. 114

3350

3360

3337 haþ AdBTΔ   3341 Wiþ þo which(e) E . . . B₂, AdT
Wiþ þo þe whiche B   3349 the *om.* H₁ . . . B₂, AdTΔ, WH₃   3355
Whan] ffor whan H₁E . . . B₂   3361 as] and BT   he] it AM

Confessor.

Forthi, mi Sone, hold up thin hed,
And let no Slep thin yhe englue,
Bot whanne it is to resoun due.

Amans.

Mi fader, as touchende of this,
Riht so as I you tolde it is,
That ofte abedde, whanne I scholde,
I mai noght slepe, thogh I wolde;
‹For love is evere faste byme,
Which takth no hiede of due time.   3370
For whanne I schal myn yhen close,
Anon min herte he wole oppose
And holde his Scole in such a wise,
Til it be day that I arise,
That selde it is whan that I slepe.
And thus fro Sompnolence I kepe
Min yhe: and forthi if ther be   P. ii. 115
Oght elles more in this degre,
Now axeth forth.

Confessor.

           Mi Sone, yis:
For Slowthe, which as Moder is   3380
The forthdrawere and the Norrice
To man of many a dredful vice,
Hath yit an other laste of alle,
Which many a man hath mad to falle,
Wher that he mihte nevere arise;
Wherof for thou thee schalt avise,
Er thou so with thiself misfare,
What vice it is I wol declare.

[vii. TRISTESSE OR
DESPONDENCY.]

ix. *Nil fortuna iuuat, vbi desperacio ledit;*
    Quo desiccat humor, non viridescit humus.
Magnanimus set amor spem ponit et inde salutem
    Consequitur, quod ei prospera fata fauent.

Hic loquitur super
vltima specie Acci-
die, que Tristicia siue
Desperacio dicitur,

Whan Slowthe hath don al that he may
To dryve forth the longe day,   3390
Til it be come to the nede,
Thanne ate laste upon the dede
He loketh hou his time is lore,

3366 telle H₁... B₂, W   3370 no M, F *the rest* non (none)
Latin Verses ix. 1 Nil fortuna valet (*rest of line blank*) AM

And is so wo begon therfore,
That he withinne his thoght conceiveth
Tristesce, and so himself deceiveth,
That he wanhope bringeth inne,
Wher is no confort to beginne,
Bot every joie him is deslaied :
So that withinne his herte affraied   3400
A thousend time with o breth
Wepende he wissheth after deth,
Whan he fortune fint adverse.   P. ii. 116
For thanne he wole his hap reherce,
As thogh his world were al forlore,
And seith, 'Helas, that I was bore !
Hou schal I live? hou schal I do?
For nou fortune is thus mi fo,
I wot wel god me wol noght helpe.
What scholde I thanne of joies yelpe,   3410
Whan ther no bote is of mi care?
So overcast is my welfare,
That I am schapen al to strif.
Helas, that I nere of this lif,
Er I be fulliche overtake !'
And thus he wol his sorwe make,
As god him mihte noght availe :
Bot yit ne wol he noght travaile
To helpe himself at such a nede,
Bot slowtheth under such a drede,   3420
Which is affermed in his herte,
Riht as he mihte noght asterte
The worldes wo which he is inne.
   Also whan he is falle in Sinne,
Him thenkth he is so ferr coupable,
That god wol noght be merciable
So gret a Sinne to foryive ;
And thus he leeveth to be schrive.
And if a man in thilke throwe
Wolde him consaile, he wol noght knowe   3430
The sothe, thogh a man it finde :

[TRISTESSE OR DE-
SPONDENCY.]
cuius obstinata con-
dicio tocius consola-
cionis spem deponens,
alicuius remedii, quo
liberari poterit, for-
tunam sibi euenire
impossibile credit.

3397 *margin* poterit *om.* BT   3401 tymes E, BT   3427 gret
JC, B   grete A, F

[Tristesse or De-
spondency.]

Obstinacio est con-
tradiccio veritatis ag-
nite.

For Tristesce is of such a kinde,
That forto meintiene his folie,   P. ii. 117
He hath with him Obstinacie,
Which is withinne of such a Slouthe,
That he forsaketh alle trouthe,
And wole unto no reson bowe;
And yit ne can he noght avowe
His oghne skile bot of hed:
Thus dwyneth he, til he be ded,   3440
In hindringe of his oghne astat.
For where a man is obstinat,
Wanhope folweth ate laste,
Which mai noght after longe laste,
Till Slouthe make of him an ende.
Bot god wot whider he schal wende.

Confessor.

Mi Sone, and riht in such manere
Ther be lovers of hevy chiere,
That sorwen mor than it is ned,
Whan thei be taried of here sped   3450
And conne noght hemselven rede,
Bot lesen hope forto spede
And stinten love to poursewe;
And thus thei faden hyde and hewe,
And lustles in here hertes waxe.
Hierof it is that I wolde axe,
If thou, mi Sone, art on of tho.

Confessio Amantis.

Ha, goode fader, it is so,
Outake a point, I am beknowe;
For elles I am overthrowe   3460
In al that evere ye have seid.
Mi sorwe is everemore unteid,
And secheth overal my veines;   P. ii. 118
Bot forto conseile of mi peines,
I can no bote do therto;
And thus withouten hope I go,
So that mi wittes ben empeired,
And I, as who seith, am despeired

3437 no *om.* AM   3443 S *resumes*   folweth] falleþ SAdBΔ
faileth TΛ   3449 more þan is B, H₃ more þan hit L   3459 o
point BT, W

To winne love of thilke swete,
Withoute whom, I you behiete,   3470
Min herte, that is so bestad,
Riht inly nevere mai be glad.
For be my trouthe I schal noght lie,
Of pure sorwe, which I drye
For that sche seith sche wol me noght,
With drecchinge of myn oghne thoght
In such a wanhope I am falle,
That I ne can unethes calle,
As forto speke of eny grace,
Mi ladi merci to pourchace.   3480
Bot yit I seie noght for this
That al in mi defalte it is ;
For I cam nevere yit in stede,
Whan time was, that I my bede
Ne seide, and as I dorste tolde :
Bot nevere fond I that sche wolde,
For oght sche knew of min entente,
To speke a goodly word assente.
And natheles this dar I seie,
That if a sinful wolde preie   3490
To god of his foryivenesse
With half so gret a besinesse
As I have do to my ladi,   **P. ii. 119**
In lacke of askinge of merci
He scholde nevere come in Helle.
And thus I mai you sothli telle,
Save only that I crie and bidde,
I am in Tristesce al amidde
And fulfild of Desesperance :
And therof yif me mi penance,   3500
Min holi fader, as you liketh.

   Mi Sone, of that thin herte siketh   Confessor.
With sorwe, miht thou noght amende,
Til love his grace wol thee sende,
For thou thin oghne cause empeirest
What time as thou thiself despeirest.

3479 eny] my AM   3484 my] me H₁RCLB₂, W (me bidde)
3489 I dar AM   3502 if þat H₁ . . . B₂, W

I not what other thing availeth,
Of hope whan the herte faileth,
For such a Sor is incurable,
And ek the goddes ben vengable :   3510
And that a man mai riht wel frede,
These olde bokes who so rede,
Of thing which hath befalle er this :
Now hier of what ensample it is.

[TALE OF IPHIS
AND ARAXARATHEN.]

Hic narrat qualiter
Iphis, Regis Theucri
filius, ob amorem cui-
usdam puelle nomine
Araxarathen, quam
neque donis aut pre-
cibus vincere potuit,
desperans ante patris
ipsius puelle ianuas
noctanter se suspen-
dit. Vnde dii com-
moti dictam puellam
in lapidem durissi-
mum transmutarunt,
quam Rex Theucer
vna cum filio suo
apud Ciuitatem Sala-
mynam in templo
Veneris pro perpetua
memoria sepeliri et
locari fecit.

Whilom be olde daies fer
Of Mese was the king Theucer,
Which hadde a kniht to Sone, Iphis :
Of love and he so maistred is,
That he hath set al his corage,
As to reguard of his lignage,   3520
Upon a Maide of lou astat.
Bot thogh he were a potestat
Of worldes good, he was soubgit   **P. ii. 120**
To love, and put in such a plit,
That he excedeth the mesure
Of reson, that himself assure
He can noght; for the more he preide,
The lasse love on him sche leide.
He was with love unwys constreigned,
And sche with resoun was restreigned :   3530
The lustes of his herte he suieth,
And sche for drede schame eschuieth,
And as sche scholde, tok good hiede
To save and kepe hir wommanhiede.
And thus the thing stod in debat
Betwen his lust and hire astat :
He yaf, he sende, he spak be mouthe,
Bot yit for oght that evere he couthe
Unto his sped he fond no weie,
So that he caste his hope aweie,   3540
Withinne his herte and gan despeire
Fro dai to dai, and so empeire,
That he hath lost al his delit

3529 *margin* Ciuitatem *om.* BT   3531 hert sche BΛ   sche
(*om.* herte) T   3535 king (kyng) JL, BT

Of lust, of Slep, of Appetit,
That he thurgh strengthe of love lasseth
His wit, and resoun overpasseth.
As he which of his lif ne rowhte,
His deth upon himself he sowhte,
So that be nyhte his weie he nam,
Ther wiste non wher he becam;   3550
The nyht was derk, ther schon no Mone,
Tofore the gates he cam sone,
Wher that this yonge Maiden was,   **P. ii. 121**
And with this wofull word, ' Helas !'
Hise dedli pleintes he began
So stille that ther was noman
It herde, and thanne he seide thus :
'O thou Cupide, o thou Venus,
Fortuned be whos ordinaunce
Of love is every mannes chaunce,   3560
Ye knowen al min hole herte,
That I ne mai your hond asterte ;
On you is evere that I crie,
And yit you deigneth noght to plie,
Ne toward me youre Ere encline.
Thus for I se no medicine
To make an ende of mi querele,
My deth schal be in stede of hele.
    Ha, thou mi wofull ladi diere,
Which duellest with thi fader hiere   3570
And slepest in thi bedd at ese,
Thou wost nothing of my desese,
Hou thou and I be now unmete.
Ha lord, what swevene schalt thou mete,
What dremes hast thou nou on honde?
Thou slepest there, and I hier stonde.
Thogh I no deth to the deserve,
Hier schal I for thi love sterve,
Hier schal a kinges Sone dye
For love and for no felonie ;   3580
Wher thou therof have joie or sorwe,
Hier schalt thou se me ded tomorwe.

3560 manes F   3576 sleplest F

O herte hard aboven alle,   P. ii. 122
This deth, which schal to me befalle
For that thou wolt noght do me grace,
Yit schal be told in many a place,
Hou I am ded for love and trouthe
In thi defalte and in thi slouthe:
Thi Daunger schal to manye mo
Ensample be for everemo,   3590
Whan thei my wofull deth recorde.'
And with that word he tok a Corde,
With which upon the gate tre
He hyng himself, that was pite.
   The morwe cam, the nyht is gon,
Men comen out and syhe anon
Wher that this yonge lord was ded:
Ther was an hous withoute red,
For noman knew the cause why;
Ther was wepinge and ther was cry.   3600
This Maiden, whan that sche it herde,
And sih this thing hou it misferde,
Anon sche wiste what it mente,
And al the cause hou it wente
To al the world sche tolde it oute,
And preith to hem that were aboute
To take of hire the vengance,
For sche was cause of thilke chaunce,
Why that this kinges Sone is spilt.
Sche takth upon hirself the gilt,   3610
And is al redi to the peine
Which eny man hir wole ordeigne:
And bot if eny other wolde,   P. ii. 123
Sche seith that sche hirselve scholde
Do wreche with hire oghne hond,
Thurghout the world in every lond
That every lif therof schal speke,

3586 ȝit schal...many a place J, S, FH₃ ȝit schalt...many a place
AM   ȝit schal...many place Ad, W   ȝit schal it...mani place TΔ
It (Hit) schal...many a place H₁XGRCLB₂   It schal...many
place E, B   3587 and] of H₁...B₂, B   3596 syhe (sihe)
AJ, SB   syh F   3612 wold(e) BT, W

Hou sche hirself it scholde wreke.
Sche wepth, sche crith, sche swouneth ofte,
Sche caste hire yhen up alofte   3620
And seide among ful pitously :
'A godd, thou wost wel it am I,
For whom Iphis is thus besein :
Ordeine so, that men mai sein
A thousend wynter after this,
Hou such a Maiden dede amis,
And as I dede, do to me :
For I ne dede no pite
To him, which for mi love is lore,
Do no pite to me therfore.'   3630
And with this word sche fell to grounde
Aswoune, and ther sche lay a stounde.
The goddes, whiche hir pleigntes herde
And syhe hou wofully sche ferde,
Hire lif thei toke awey anon,
And schopen hire into a Ston
After the forme of hire ymage
Of bodi bothe and of visage.
And for the merveile of this thing
Unto the place cam the king   3640
And ek the queene and manye mo ;
And whan thei wisten it was so,
As I have told it hier above,   **P. ii. 124**
Hou that Iphis was ded for love,
Of that he hadde be refused,
Thei hielden alle men excused
And wondren upon the vengance.
And forto kepe in remembrance,
This faire ymage mayden liche
With compaignie noble and riche   3650
With torche and gret sollempnite
To Salamyne the Cite
Thei lede, and carie forth withal
The dede corps, and sein it schal

3622 O god þou wost þat it B   O god þou wost it TΛ (wotest)
3627 S *has lost two leaves* (ll. 3627—v. 274)   3632 astounde
AMR, T, W   3638 and of] and eke of AM

Beside thilke ymage have
His sepulture and be begrave :
This corps and this ymage thus
Into the Cite to Venus,
Wher that goddesse hire temple hadde,
Togedre bothe tuo thei ladde.   3660
This ilke ymage as for miracle
Was set upon an hyh pinacle,
That alle men it mihte knowe,
And under that thei maden lowe
A tumbe riche for the nones
Of marbre and ek of jaspre stones,
Wherin this Iphis was beloken,
That evermor it schal be spoken.
And for men schal the sothe wite,
Thei have here epitaphe write,   3670
As thing which scholde abide stable :
The lettres graven in a table
Of marbre were and seiden this :   P. ii. 125
'Hier lith, which slowh himself, Iphis,
For love of Araxarathen :
And in ensample of tho wommen,
That soffren men to deie so,
Hire forme a man mai sen also,
Hou it is torned fleissh and bon
Into the figure of a Ston :   3680
He was to neysshe and sche to hard.
Be war forthi hierafterward ;
Ye men and wommen bothe tuo,
Ensampleth you of that was tho.'

Confessor.

Lo thus, mi Sone, as I thee seie,
It grieveth be diverse weie
In desespeir a man to falle,
Which is the laste branche of alle
Of Slouthe, as thou hast herd devise.
Wherof that thou thiself avise   3690

3656 Hir B   be begrave] begraue A, Δ   be graue MH₁ERLB₂, W
3666 ek om. C, BTΔ   3667 this] þat AdBTΔ   3676 tho] þe
JH₁ ... B₂, BΔ, W   3678 aman F   3687 despeir JMH₁XRLB₂,
AdBTΔ, W   vespeir H₃

Good is, er that thou be deceived,
Wher that the grace of hope is weyved.

Mi fader, hou so that it stonde, Amans.
Now have I pleinly understonde
Of Slouthes court the proprete,
Wherof touchende in my degre
For evere I thenke to be war.
Bot overthis, so as I dar,
With al min herte I you beseche,
That ye me wolde enforme and teche   3700
What ther is more of youre aprise
In love als wel as otherwise,
So that I mai me clene schryve.   **P. ii. 126**

Mi Sone, whyl thou art alyve Confessor.
And hast also thi fulle mynde,
Among the vices whiche I finde
Ther is yit on such of the sevene,
Which al this world hath set unevene
And causeth manye thinges wronge,
Where he the cause hath underfonge: 3710
Wherof hierafter thou schalt hiere
The forme bothe and the matiere.

Explicit Liber Quartus.

Incipit Liber Quintus.

[AVARICE.]

i. *Obstat auaricia nature legibus, et que*   **P. ii.** 127
   Largus amor poscit, striccius illa vetat.
Omne quod est nimium viciosum dicitur aurum,
   Vellera sicut oues, seruat auarus opes.
Non decet vt soli seruabitur es, set amori
   Debet homo solam solus habere suam.

FERST whan the hyhe god began
This world, and that the kinde of man
Was falle into no gret encress,
For worldes good tho was no press,
Bot al was set to the comune.
Thei spieken thanne of no fortune
Or forto lese or forto winne,

Hic in quinto libro intendit Confessor tractare de Auaricia, que omnium malorum radix dicitur, necnon et de eiusdem vicii speciebus: set primo ipsius Auaricie naturam describens Amanti quatenus amorem concernit super hoc specialius opponit.

Til Avarice broghte it inne;
And that was whan the world was woxe
Of man, of hors, of Schep, of Oxe,   10
And that men knewen the moneie.
Tho wente pes out of the weie
And werre cam on every side,
Which alle love leide aside
And of comun his propre made,   **P. ii.** 128
So that in stede of schovele and spade
The scharpe swerd was take on honde;
And in this wise it cam to londe,
Wherof men maden dyches depe
And hyhe walles forto kepe   20
The gold which Avarice encloseth.
Bot al to lytel him supposeth,
Thogh he mihte al the world pourchace;

Latin Verses i. 5 dicet AM ... B₂
4 þer was G, AdB

For what thing that he may embrace
Of gold, of catel or of lond,
He let it nevere out of his hond,
Bot get him more and halt it faste,
As thogh the world scholde evere laste.
So is he lych unto the helle;
For as these olde bokes telle,   30
What comth therinne, lasse or more,
It schal departe neveremore:
Thus whanne he hath his cofre loken,
It schal noght after ben unstoken,
Bot whanne him list to have a syhte
Of gold, hou that it schyneth brihte,
That he ther on mai loke and muse;
For otherwise he dar noght use
To take his part, or lasse or more.
So is he povere, and everemore   40
Him lacketh that he hath ynowh:
An Oxe draweth in the plowh,
Of that himself hath no profit;
A Schep riht in the same plit   **P. ii. 129**
His wolle berth, bot on a day
An other takth the flees away:
Thus hath he, that he noght ne hath,
For he therof his part ne tath.
To seie hou such a man hath good,
Who so that reson understod,   50
It is impropreliche seid,
For good hath him and halt him teid,
That he ne gladeth noght withal,
Bot is unto his good a thral,
And as soubgit thus serveth he,
Wher that he scholde maister be:
Such is the kinde of thaverous.
   Mi Sone, as thou art amerous,   Confessor.

30 Wher in it moste nedes dwelle H₁ ... B₂   35 asyhte F
40 ouermore B   47 that he] þat . þat A
47 f.   ffor he þer of his part ne taþ
          Bot kepeþ to anoþer þat he haþ
So H₁ ... B₂ *with some variations* (þat *for* Bot C   it hath *for* he haþ H₁)

Tell if thou farst of love so.

   Mi fader, as it semeth, no;   60
That averous yit nevere I was,
So as ye setten me the cas :
For as ye tolden here above,
In full possession of love
Yit was I nevere hier tofore,
So that me thenketh wel therfore,
I mai excuse wel my dede.
Bot of mi will withoute drede,
If I that tresor mihte gete,
It scholde nevere be foryete,   70
That I ne wolde it faste holde,
Til god of love himselve wolde
That deth ous scholde parte atuo.
For lieveth wel, I love hire so,
That evene with min oghne lif,   P. ii. 130
If I that swete lusti wif
Mihte ones welden at my wille,
For evere I wolde hire holde stille :
And in this wise, taketh kepe,
If I hire hadde, I wolde hire kepe,   80
And yit no friday wolde I faste,
Thogh I hire kepte and hielde faste.
Fy on the bagges in the kiste!
I hadde ynogh, if I hire kiste.
For certes, if sche were myn,
I hadde hir levere than a Myn
Of Gold; for al this worldesriche
Ne mihte make me so riche
As sche, that is so inly good.
I sette noght of other good;   90
For mihte I gete such a thing,
I hadde a tresor for a king;
And thogh I wolde it faste holde,
I were thanne wel beholde.
Bot I mot pipe nou with lasse,

59 farst F   fare A . . . B₂, Ad . . . Δ   73 departe AMH₁
om. Ad   82 To holde hir whil my lif may laste H₁ . . . B₂
line om. T

And suffre that it overpasse,   [AVARICE.]
Noght with mi will, for thus I wolde
Ben averous, if that I scholde.
Bot, fader, I you herde seie
Hou thaverous hath yit som weie,   100
Wherof he mai be glad; for he
Mai whanne him list his tresor se,
And grope and fiele it al aboute,
Bot I fulofte am schet theroute,
Ther as my worthi tresor is.   P. ii. 131
So is mi lif lich unto this,
That ye me tolden hier tofore,
Hou that an Oxe his yock hath bore
For thing that scholde him noght availe:
And in this wise I me travaile;   110
For who that evere hath the welfare,
I wot wel that I have the care,
For I am hadd and noght ne have,
And am, as who seith, loves knave.
Nou demeth in youre oghne thoght,
If this be Avarice or noght.
    Mi Sone, I have of thee no wonder,   Confessor.
Thogh thou to serve be put under
With love, which to kinde acordeth:
Bot, so as every bok recordeth,   120
It is to kinde no plesance
That man above his sustienance
Unto the gold schal serve and bowe,
For that mai no reson avowe.
Bot Avarice natheles,
If he mai geten his encress
Of gold, that wole he serve and kepe,
For he takth of noght elles kepe,
Bot forto fille hise bagges large;
And al is to him bot a charge,   130
For he ne parteth noght withal,
Bot kepth it, as a servant schal:

103 fiele] seche A . . . B₂   104 fulofte I A . . . B₂   ofte I H₁
110 wise] þing A . . . B₂   120 acordeþ XE . . . B₂   129
fulle AM

And thus, thogh that he multeplie
His gold, withoute tresorie
He is, for man is noght amended   **P. ii. 132**
With gold, bot if it be despended
To mannes us ; wherof I rede
A tale, and tak therof good hiede,
Of that befell be olde tyde,
As telleth ous the clerk Ovide.   140

[TALE OF MIDAS.]

Hic loquitur contra istos Auaros. Et narrat qualiter Mida Rex Frigie Cillenum Bachi sacerdotem, quem rustici vinculis ferreis alligarunt, dissoluit, et in hospicium suum benignissime recollegit ; pro quo Bachus quodcunque munus Rex exigere vellet donari concessit. Vnde Rex Auaricia ductus, ut quicquid tangeret in aurum conuerteretur, indiscrete peciit. Quo facto postea contigit quod cibos cum ipse sumere vellet, in aurum conuersos manducare non potuit. Et sic percipiens aurum pro tunc non posse sibi valere, illud auferri, et tunc ea que victui sufficerent necessaria iteratis precibus a deo mitissime postulauit.

Bachus, which is the god of wyn,
Acordant unto his divin
A Prest, the which Cillenus hihte,
He hadde, and fell so that be nyhte
This Prest was drunke and goth astraied,
Wherof the men were evele apaied
In Frigelond, where as he wente.
Bot ate laste a cherl him hente
With strengthe of other felaschipe,
So that upon his drunkeschipe   150
Thei bounden him with chenes faste,
And forth thei ladde him als so faste
Unto the king, which hihte Myde.
Bot he, that wolde his vice hyde,
This courteis king, tok of him hiede,
And bad that men him scholde lede
Into a chambre forto kepe,
Til he of leisir hadde slepe.
And tho this Prest was sone unbounde,
And up a couche fro the grounde   160
To slepe he was leid softe ynowh ;
And whanne he wok, the king him drowh
To his presence and dede him chiere,
So that this Prest in such manere,
Whil that him liketh, there he duelleth : **P. ii. 133**
And al this he to Bachus telleth,
Whan that he cam to him ayein.
And whan that Bachus herde sein

133 that he] he to H₁ . . . B₂   135 He is] He as H₁ . . . B₂
141 the om. AMB₂, T   142 his] þis A . . . B₂   143 the] is AM
146 payed CB₂, AdB   159 tho] þus BT   160 margin tunc]
tantum BT   om. G, Δ   168 that om. B

How Mide hath don his courtesie,
Him thenkth it were a vilenie,   170
Bot he rewarde him for his dede,
So as he mihte of his godhiede.
Unto this king this god appiereth
And clepeth, and that other hiereth :
This god to Mide thonketh faire
Of that he was so debonaire
Toward his Prest, and bad him seie :
What thing it were he wolde preie,
He scholde it have, of worldes good.
This king was glad, and stille stod,   180
And was of his axinge in doute,
And al the world he caste aboute,
What thing was best for his astat,
And with himself stod in debat
Upon thre pointz, the whiche I finde
Ben lievest unto mannes kinde.
The ferste of hem it is delit,
The tuo ben worschipe and profit.
And thanne he thoghte, 'If that I crave
Delit, thogh I delit mai have,   190
Delit schal passen in myn age :
That is no siker avantage,
For every joie bodily
Schal ende in wo : delit forthi
Wol I noght chese. And if worschipe   **P. ii. 134**
I axe and of the world lordschipe,
That is an occupacion
Of proud ymaginacion,
Which makth an herte vein withinne ;
Ther is no certein forto winne,   200
For lord and knave al is o weie,
Whan thei be bore and whan thei deie.
And if I profit axe wolde,
I not in what manere I scholde
Of worldes good have sikernesse ;

---

173 þe king A . . . B₂   185 þe poyntes whiche H₁, BT, W
188 Tho XGERCB₂, B   They H₁   196 the world] worldes
A . . . B₂, Λ   201 is al AM

For every thief upon richesse
Awaiteth forto robbe and stele :
Such good is cause of harmes fele.
And also, thogh a man at ones
Of al the world withinne his wones   210
The tresor myhte have everydel,
Yit hadde he bot o mannes del
Toward himself, so as I thinke,
Of clothinge and of mete and drinke,
For more, outake vanite,
Ther hath no lord in his degre.'
And thus upon the pointz diverse
Diverseliche he gan reherce
What point him thoghte for the beste ;
Bot pleinly forto gete him reste   220
He can no siker weie caste.
And natheles yit ate laste
He fell upon the coveitise
Of gold ; and thanne in sondri wise
He thoghte, as I have seid tofore,   **P. ii. 135**
Hou tresor mai be sone lore,
And hadde an inly gret desir
Touchende of such recoverir,
Hou that he mihte his cause availe
To gete him gold withoute faile.   230
Withinne his herte and thus he preiseth
The gold, and seith hou that it peiseth
Above al other metall most :
'The gold,' he seith, 'may lede an host
To make werre ayein a King ;
The gold put under alle thing,
And set it whan him list above ;
The gold can make of hate love
And werre of pes and ryht of wrong,
And long to schort and schort to long ;   240
Withoute gold mai be no feste,
Gold is the lord of man and beste,

Salomon. Pecunie
obediunt omnia.

210 þis world H₁... B₂   211 myhte *om.* H₁... B₂   (hadde
for have H₁)   212 a mannes H₁ ... B₂, Ad, W   217 the] þo GEC
þese (þeis) AdBTΔ   235 þe king BT   242 the *om.* AMH₁XRLB₂

And mai hem bothe beie and selle ;
So that a man mai sothly telle
That al the world to gold obeieth.'
Forthi this king to Bachus preieth
To grante him gold, bot he excedeth
Mesure more than him nedeth.
Men tellen that the maladie
Which cleped is ydropesie   250
Resembled is unto this vice
Be weie of kinde of Avarice :
The more ydropesie drinketh,
The more him thursteth, for him thinketh
That he mai nevere drinke his fille ;   **P. ii.** 136
So that ther mai nothing fulfille
The lustes of his appetit :
And riht in such a maner plit
Stant Avarice and evere stod ;
The more he hath of worldes good,   260
The more he wolde it kepe streyte,
And evere mor and mor coveite.
And riht in such condicioun
Withoute good discrecioun
This king with avarice is smite,
That al the world it myhte wite :
For he to Bachus thanne preide,
That wherupon his hond he leide,
It scholde thurgh his touche anon
Become gold, and therupon   270
This god him granteth as he bad.
Tho was this king of Frige glad,
And forto put it in assai
With al the haste that he mai,
He toucheth that, he toucheth this,
And in his hond al gold it is,
The Ston, the Tree, the Lef, the gras,
The flour, the fruit, al gold it was.

249 telleþ AM   253 dropesie (dropseie) AM   268 þer vpon B
273 put AJ, F   putte C, BT   274 He touched (toucheþ) al þat
by him lay H₁ . . . B₂, Λ   (toucheþ H₁GC   touchit B₂   touche X)
278 al] as AM

Thus toucheth he, whil he mai laste
To go, bot hunger ate laste   280
Him tok, so that he moste nede
Be weie of kinde his hunger fede.
The cloth was leid, the bord was set,
And al was forth tofore him fet,
His disch, his coppe, his drinke, his mete; **P. ii. 137**
Bot whanne he wolde or drinke or ete,
Anon as it his mouth cam nyh,
It was al gold, and thanne he syh
Of Avarice the folie.
And he with that began to crie,   290
And preide Bachus to foryive
His gilt, and soffre him forto live
And be such as he was tofore,
So that he were noght forlore.
This god, which herde of his grevance,
Tok rowthe upon his repentance,
And bad him go forth redily
Unto a flod was faste by,
Which Paceole thanne hyhte,
In which as clene as evere he myhte   300
He scholde him waisshen overal,
And seide him thanne that he schal
Recovere his ferste astat ayein.
This king, riht as he herde sein,
Into the flod goth fro the lond,
And wissh him bothe fot and hond,
And so forth al the remenant,
As him was set in covenant:
And thanne he syh merveilles strange,
The flod his colour gan to change,   310
The gravel with the smale Stones
To gold thei torne bothe at ones,
And he was quit of that he hadde,
And thus fortune his chance ladde.
And whan he sih his touche aweie,   **P. ii. 138**

281 him most(e) AJMG . . . B₂   288 al] as AMXERLB₂
295 þis SBT   301 waisshen F   waisschen B   wasshen (waschen)
AJ, S   306 wyssh (wissh) SB   wisshe AJ, F   314 change AM

He goth him hom the rihte weie
And liveth forth as he dede er,
And putte al Avarice afer,
And the richesse of gold despiseth,
And seith that mete and cloth sufficeth.   320
Thus hath this king experience
Hou foles don the reverence
To gold, which of his oghne kinde
Is lasse worth than is the rinde
To sustienance of mannes fode ;
And thanne he made lawes goode
And al his thing sette upon skile :
He bad his poeple forto tile
Here lond, and live under the lawe,
And that thei scholde also forthdrawe   330
Bestaile, and seche non encress
Of gold, which is the breche of pes.
For this a man mai finde write,
Tofor the time, er gold was smite
In Coign, that men the florin knewe,
Ther was welnyh noman untrewe ;
Tho was ther nouther schield ne spere
Ne dedly wepne forto bere ;
Tho was the toun withoute wal,
Which nou is closed overal ;   340
Tho was ther no brocage in londe,
Which nou takth every cause on honde :
So mai men knowe, hou the florin
Was moder ferst of malengin
And bringere inne of alle werre,   **P. ii. 139**
Wherof this world stant out of herre
Thurgh the conseil of Avarice,
Which of his oghne propre vice
Is as the helle wonderfull ;
For it mai neveremor be full,   350
That what as evere comth therinne,
Awey ne may it nevere winne.
Bot Sone myn, do thou noght so,

Let al such Avarice go,
And tak thi part of that thou hast :
I bidde noght that thou do wast,
Bot hold largesce in his mesure ;
And if thou se a creature,
Which thurgh poverte is falle in nede,
Yif him som good, for this I rede   360
To him that wol noght yiven here,
What peine he schal have elleswhere.

[The Punishment of
Tantalus.]

Nota de pena Tan-
tali, cuius amara sitis
dampnatos   torquet
auaros.

Ther is a peine amonges alle
Benethe in helle, which men calle
The wofull peine of Tantaly,
Of which I schal thee redely
Devise hou men therinne stonde.
In helle, thou schalt understonde,
Ther is a flod of thilke office,
Which serveth al for Avarice :   370
What man that stonde schal therinne,
He stant up evene unto the chinne ;
Above his hed also ther hongeth
A fruyt, which to that peine longeth,
And that fruit toucheth evere in on   **P. ii. 140**
His overlippe : and therupon
Swich thurst and hunger him assaileth,
That nevere his appetit ne faileth.
Bot whanne he wolde his hunger fede,
The fruit withdrawth him ate nede,   380
And thogh he heve his hed on hyh,
The fruit is evere aliche nyh,
So is the hunger wel the more :
And also, thogh him thurste sore
And to the water bowe a doun,
The flod in such condicioun
Avaleth, that his drinke areche
He mai noght. Lo nou, which a wreche,
That mete and drinke is him so couth,

364 Benethe] Grieueþ C &c.   368 And for no drede now wol
I wonde H₁ . . . B₂, Λ   371 ffor what man stonde B   ffor what
man þat stonde T   372 unto] to H₁ . . . B₂, BTΔ, W   vp to Λ
385 a doun J, F   adoun A, B

And yit ther comth non in his mouth !   390
Lich to the peines of this flod
Stant Avarice in worldes good :
He hath ynowh and yit him nedeth,
For his skarsnesse it him forbiedeth,
And evere his hunger after more
Travaileth him aliche sore,
So is he peined overal.
Forthi thi goodes forth withal,
Mi Sone, loke thou despende,   [AVARICE.]
Wherof thou myht thiself amende   400
Bothe hier and ek in other place.
And also if thou wolt pourchace
To be beloved, thou most use
Largesce, for if thou refuse
To yive for thi loves sake,   P. ii. 141
It is no reson that thou take
Of love that thou woldest crave.
Forthi, if thou wolt grace have,
Be gracious and do largesse,
Of Avarice and the seknesse   410
Eschuie above alle other thing,
And tak ensample of Mide king
And of the flod of helle also,
Where is ynowh of alle wo.
And thogh ther were no matiere
Bot only that we finden hiere,
Men oghten Avarice eschuie ;
For what man thilke vice suie,
He get himself bot litel reste.
For hou so that the body reste,   420
The herte upon the gold travaileth,
Whom many a nyhtes drede assaileth ;
For thogh he ligge abedde naked,
His herte is everemore awaked,
And dremeth, as he lith to slepe,
How besi that he is to kepe

---

394 forbiedeþ J, S, F   forbedeþ A, B   The more he haþ þe
more he greedeþ H₁ . . . B₂, Λ (dredeþ *for* greedeþ R)   412 tak
SB   take AJ, F   424 everemore] ouercome AM . . . B₂, Λ

His tresor, that no thief it stele.
Thus hath he bot a woful wele.

And riht so in the same wise,
If thou thiself wolt wel avise,   430
Ther be lovers of suche ynowe,
That wole unto no reson bowe.
If so be that thei come above,
Whan thei ben maistres of here love,
And that thei scholden be most glad, **P. ii. 142**
With love thei ben most bestad,
So fain thei wolde it holden al.
Here herte, here yhe is overal,
And wenen every man be thief,
To stele awey that hem is lief;   440
Thus thurgh here oghne fantasie
Thei fallen into Jelousie.
Thanne hath the Schip tobroke his cable,
With every wynd and is muable.

Amans.

Mi fader, for that ye nou telle,
I have herd ofte time telle
Of Jelousie, bot what it is
Yit understod I nevere er this :
Wherfore I wolde you beseche,
That ye me wolde enforme and teche   450
What maner thing it mihte be.

Confessor.

Mi Sone, that is hard to me :
Bot natheles, as I have herd,
Now herkne and thou schalt ben ansuerd.

Among the men lacke of manhode
In Mariage upon wifhode
Makth that a man himself deceiveth,
Wherof it is that he conceiveth
That ilke unsely maladie,
The which is cleped Jelousie :   460
Of which if I the proprete
Schal telle after the nycete,

448 vnderstod (vnderstood) AJ, B   vnderstode S, F   er this]
]is AM . . . L   I wis B₂   454 Now om. A . . . B₂   458 margin.
de om. AMXRCLB₂, Λ   459 ilke] þilke AM

So as it worcheth on a man,
A Fievere it is cotidian,
Which every day wol come aboute,   P. ii. 143
Wher so a man be inne or oute.
At hom if that a man wol wone,
This Fievere is thanne of comun wone
Most grevous in a mannes yhe :
For thanne he makth him tote and pryhe,   470
Wher so as evere his love go ;
Sche schal noght with hir litel too
Misteppe, bot he se it al.
His yhe is walkende overal ;
Wher that sche singe or that sche dance,
He seth the leste contienance,
If sche loke on a man aside
Or with him roune at eny tyde,
Or that sche lawghe, or that sche loure,
His yhe is ther at every houre.   480
And whanne it draweth to the nyht,
If sche thanne is withoute lyht,
Anon is al the game schent ;
For thanne he set his parlement
To speke it whan he comth to bedde,
And seith, ' If I were now to wedde,
I wolde neveremore have wif.'
And so he torneth into strif
The lust of loves duete,
And al upon diversete.   490
If sche be freissh and wel araied,
He seith hir baner is displaied
To clepe in gestes fro the weie :
And if sche be noght wel beseie,
And that hir list noght to be gladd,   P. ii. 144
He berth an hond that sche is madd
And loveth noght hire housebonde ;
He seith he mai wel understonde,
That if sche wolde his compaignie,

463 on] in H₁ . . . B₂   471 as *om.* H₁ . . . B₂, Δ   486 I] it AM
487 neveremore] neuer B   neue*r*more more T   493 fro] by (be)
H₁ . . . B₂, B

Sche scholde thanne afore his ÿe 500
Schewe al the plesir that sche mihte.
So that be daie ne be nyhte
Sche not what thing is for the beste,
Bot liveth out of alle reste ;
For what as evere him liste sein,
Sche dar noght speke a word ayein,
Bot wepth and holt hire lippes clos.
Sche mai wel wryte, ' Sanz repos,'
The wif which is to such on maried.

Of alle wommen be he waried, 510
For with this Fievere of Jalousie
His echedaies fantasie
Of sorghe is evere aliche grene,
So that ther is no love sene,
Whil that him list at hom abyde.
And whan so is he wol out ryde,
Thanne hath he redi his aspie
Abidinge in hir compaignie,
A janglere, an evel mouthed oon,
That sche ne mai nowhider gon, 520
Ne speke a word, ne ones loke,
That he ne wol it wende and croke
And torne after his oghne entente,
Thogh sche nothing bot honour mente.
Whan that the lord comth hom ayein, **P. ii.** 145
The janglere moste somwhat sein ;
So what withoute and what withinne,
This Fievere is evere to beginne,
For where he comth he can noght ende,
Til deth of him have mad an ende. 530
For thogh so be that he ne hiere
Ne se ne wite in no manere
Bot al honour and wommanhiede,
Therof the Jelous takth non hiede,
Bot as a man to love unkinde,
He cast his staf, as doth the blinde,
And fint defaulte where is non ;

As who so dremeth on a Ston   [JEALOUSY OF
                                                   LOVERS.]
Hou he is leid, and groneth ofte,
Whan he lith on his pilwes softe.   540
So is ther noght bot strif and cheste ;
Whan love scholde make his feste,
It is gret thing if he hir kisse :
Thus hath sche lost the nyhtes blisse,
For at such time he gruccheth evere
And berth on hond ther is a levere,
And that sche wolde an other were
In stede of him abedde there ;
And with tho wordes and with mo
Of Jelousie, he torneth fro   550
And lith upon his other side,
And sche with that drawth hire aside,
And ther sche wepeth al the nyht.
Ha, to what peine sche is dyht,
That in hire youthe hath so beset   **P. ii. 146**
The bond which mai noght ben unknet !
I wot the time is ofte cursed,
That evere was the gold unpursed,
The which was leid upon the bok,
Whan that alle othre sche forsok   560
For love of him ; bot al to late
Sche pleigneth, for as thanne algate
Sche mot forbere and to him bowe,
Thogh he ne wole it noght allowe.
For man is lord of thilke feire,
So mai the womman bot empeire,
If sche speke oght ayein his wille ;
And thus sche berth hir peine stille.

   Bot if this Fievere a womman take,
Sche schal be wel mor harde schake ;   570
For thogh sche bothe se and hiere,
And finde that ther is matiere,
Sche dar bot to hirselve pleine,
And thus sche suffreth double peine.

   Lo thus, mi Sone, as I have write,   Confessor.
Thou miht of Jelousie wite

        545 at *om.* AM   551 his] þat B
**   E e

His fievere and his condicion,
Which is full of suspecion.
Bot wherof that this fievere groweth,
Who so these olde bokes troweth,   580
Ther mai he finden hou it is :
For thei ous teche and telle this,
Hou that this fievere of Jelousie
Somdel it groweth of sotie
Of love, and somdiel of untrust.   **P. ii.** 147
For as a sek man lest his lust,
And whan he may no savour gete,
He hateth thanne his oughne mete,
Riht so this fieverous maladie,
Which caused is of fantasie,   590
Makth the Jelous in fieble plit
To lese of love his appetit
Thurgh feigned enformacion
Of his ymaginacion.
  Bot finali to taken hiede,
Men mai wel make a liklihiede
Betwen him which is averous
Of gold and him that is jelous
Of love, for in on degre
Thei stonde bothe, as semeth me.   600
That oon wolde have his bagges stille,
And noght departen with his wille,
And dar noght for the thieves slepe,
So fain he wolde his tresor kepe ;
That other mai noght wel be glad,
For he is evere more adrad
Of these lovers that gon aboute,
In aunter if thei putte him oute.
So have thei bothe litel joye
As wel of love as of monoie.   610
  Now hast thou, Sone, at my techinge
Of Jelousie a knowlechinge,
That thou myht understonde this,
Fro whenne he comth and what he is,

601 bagge BT   606 euere more AJ, F   eueremore SB
611 at] of B

And ek to whom that he is lik.   [JEALOUSY OF
Be war forthi thou be noght sik   LOVERS.]
Of thilke fievere as I have spoke,
For it wol in himself be wroke.
For love hateth nothing more,
As men mai finde be the lore   620
Of hem that whilom were wise,
Hou that thei spieke in many wise.
Mi fader, soth is that ye sein.   Amans.
Bot forto loke therayein,
Befor this time hou it is falle,
Wherof ther mihte ensample falle
To suche men as be jelous
In what manere it is grevous,
Riht fain I wolde ensample hiere.
My goode Sone, at thi preiere   630   Confessor.
Of suche ensamples as I finde,
So as thei comen nou to mynde
Upon this point, of time gon
I thenke forto tellen on.

Ovide wrot of manye thinges,   [TALE OF VULCAN
Among the whiche in his wrytinges   AND VENUS.]
He tolde a tale in Poesie,
Which toucheth unto Jelousie,
Upon a certein cas of love.
Among the goddes alle above   640   Hic ponit exem-
It fell at thilke time thus :   plum contra istos mar-
The god of fyr, which Vulcanus   itos quos Ialousia mac-
Is hote, and hath a craft forthwith   ulauit. Et narrat qua-
Assigned, forto be the Smith   liter Vulcanus, cuius
Of Jupiter, and his figure   vxor Venus extitit,
                                    suspicionem inter ip-
Bothe of visage and of stature   sam et Martem con-
                                    cipiens, eorum gestus
Is lothly and malgracious,   diligencius explor-
Bot yit he hath withinne his hous   abat : vnde contigit
As for the likynge of his lif   quod ipse quadam
The faire Venus to his wif.   vice ambos inter se
                                    pariteramplexantes in
Bot Mars, which of batailles is   lecto nudos inuenit,
The god, an yhe hadde unto this :   650 et exclamans omnem
                                    cetum deorum et dea-
                                    rum ad tantum spec-
                                    taculum conuocauit :

[TALE OF VULCAN
AND VENUS.]

super quo tamen de-
risum pocius quam
remedium a tota co-
horte consecutus est.

As he which was chivalerous,
It fell him to ben amerous,
And thoghte it was a gret pite
To se so lusti on as sche
Be coupled with so lourde a wiht :
So that his peine day and nyht
He dede, if he hire winne myhte ;
And sche, which hadde a good insihte　　　660
Toward so noble a knyhtli lord,
In love fell of his acord.
Ther lacketh noght bot time and place,
That he nys siker of hire grace :
Bot whan tuo hertes falle in on,
So wys await was nevere non,
That at som time thei ne mete ;
And thus this faire lusti swete
With Mars hath ofte compaignie.
Bot thilke unkynde Jelousie,　　　　　670
Which everemor the herte opposeth,
Makth Vulcanus that he supposeth
That it is noght wel overal,
And to himself he seide, he schal
Aspie betre, if that he may ;　　　　P. ii. 150
And so it fell upon a day,
That he this thing so slyhli ledde,
He fond hem bothe tuo abedde
Al warm, echon with other naked.
And he with craft al redy maked　　　680
Of stronge chenes hath hem bounde,
As he togedre hem hadde founde,
And lefte hem bothe ligge so,
And gan to clepe and crie tho
Unto the goddes al aboute ;
And thei assembled in a route
Come alle at ones forto se.
Bot none amendes hadde he,
Bot was rebuked hiere and there

654 auerous BTΛ　　　659 And sche þan þoughte how sche
mighte B　Grete it was *and* sore he sight Λ　*line om.* T　　660 As
sche BTΛ　　　671 apposeþ AM, W　　　681 him AMECLB₂

Of hem that loves frendes were;   690   [TALE OF VULCAN
And seiden that he was to blame,   AND VENUS.]
For if ther fell him eny schame,
It was thurgh his misgovernance:
And thus he loste contienance,
This god, and let his cause falle;
And thei to skorne him lowhen· alle,
And losen Mars out of hise bondes.
Wherof these erthli housebondes
For evere myhte ensample take,
If such a chaunce hem overtake: 700
For Vulcanus his wif bewreide,
The blame upon himself he leide,
Wherof his schame was the more;
Which oghte forto ben a lore
For every man that liveth hiere,   **P. ii. 151**
To reulen him in this matiere.
Thogh such an happ of love asterte,
Yit scholde he noght apointe his herte
With Jelousie of that is wroght,
Bot feigne, as thogh he wiste it noght: 710
For if he lete it overpasse,
The sclaundre schal be wel the lasse,
And he the more in ese stonde.
For this thou myht wel understonde,
That where a man schal nedes lese,
The leste harm is forto chese.
Bot Jelousie of his untrist
Makth that full many an harm arist,
Which elles scholde noght arise;
And if a man him wolde avise   720
Of that befell to Vulcanus,
Him oghte of reson thenke thus,
That sithe a god therof was schamed,
Wel scholde an erthli man be blamed
To take upon him such a vice.
   Forthi, my Sone, in thin office   Confessor.
Be war that thou be noght jelous,

691 that] how þat H₁XRCLB₂ how GE   698 ʝe BT
702 he leide] is leid(e) H₁ . . . B₂ was leyed W

[TALE OF VULCAN
AND VENUS.]

Amans.

Which ofte time hath schent the hous.
Mi fader, this ensample is hard,
Hou such thing to the heveneward   730
Among the goddes myhte falle :
For ther is bot o god of alle,
Which is the lord of hevene and helle.
Bot if it like you to telle
Hou suche goddes come aplace,   P. ii. 152
Ye mihten mochel thonk pourchace,
For I schal be wel tawht withal.

Confessor.

Mi Sone, it is thus overal
With hem that stonden misbelieved,
That suche goddes ben believed :   740
In sondri place sondri wise
Amonges hem whiche are unwise
Ther is betaken of credence ;
Wherof that I the difference
In the manere as it is write
Schal do the pleinly forto wite.

[THE GODS OF THE
NATIONS.]

ii. *Gentibus illusis signantur templa deorum,*
    Vnde deos cecos nacio ceca colit.
  Nulla creatori racio facit esse creatum
    Equiperans, quod adhuc iura pagana fouent.

[i. BELIEF OF THE
CHALDEANS.]

Quia   secundum
Poetarum fabulas in
huius libelli locis
quampluribus nomi-
na et gestus deorum
falsorum intitulantur,
quorum infidelitas vt
Cristianis clarius in-
notescat, intendit de
ipsorum origine se-
cundum varias Paga-
norum Sectas scribere
consequenter.
  Et primo de Secta
Chaldeorum tractare
proponit.

Er Crist was bore among ous hiere,
Of the believes that tho were
In foure formes thus it was.
Thei of Caldee as in this cas   750
Hadde a believe be hemselve,
Which stod upon the signes tuelve,
Forth ek with the Planetes sevene,
Whiche as thei sihe upon the hevene.
Of sondri constellacion
In here ymaginacion
With sondri kerf and pourtreture
Thei made of goddes the figure.
  In thelementz and ek also
Thei hadden a believe tho ;   760

Latin Verses ii. 1 Mentibus H1 . . . B2, BTΛ, W   4 Equiperans
A Equipans J, B, F

And al was that unresonable :   **P. ii. 153**
For thelementz ben servicable
To man, and ofte of Accidence,
As men mai se thexperience,
Thei ben corrupt be sondri weie ;
So mai no mannes reson seie
That thei ben god in eny wise.
And ek, if men hem wel avise,
The Sonne and Mone eclipse bothe,
That be hem lieve or be hem lothe,   770
Thei soffre ; and what thing is passible
To ben a god is impossible.
These elementz ben creatures,   *Et nota quod Nem-*
So ben these hevenly figures,   *broth quartus a Noe*
Wherof mai wel be justefied   *ignem tanquam deum*
That thei mai noght be deified :   *in Chaldea primus*
And who that takth awey thonour *adorari decreuit.*
Which due is to the creatour,
And yifth it to the creature,
He doth to gret a forsfaiture.   780
Bot of Caldee natheles
Upon this feith, thogh it be les,
Thei holde affermed the creance ;
So that of helle the penance,
As folk which stant out of believe,
They schull receive, as we believe.   *De Secta Egipcio-*
    Of the Caldeus lo in this wise   *rum.*
Stant the believe out of assisse :
Bot in Egipte worst of alle
The feith is fals, hou so it falle ;   790
For thei diverse bestes there   **P. ii. 154**
Honoure, as thogh thei goddes were :
And natheles yit forth withal
Thre goddes most in special
Thei have, forth with a goddesse,

---

764 experience H₁ ... B₂, Δ   773 ff. *margin* Et nota—decreuit
om. BT   781 of] as E ... B₂   os X   786 And wol (woln) non
oþer maner leue H₁ ... B₂ (whi *for* wol R)   787 lo] so B *om.* ME
margin De Secta Egipciorum *om.* B   792 thogh *om.* AMH₁B₂, Δ
795 forth] feiþ L   seþ C   seintis B₂

In whom is al here sikernesse.
Tho goddes be yit cleped thus,
Orus, Typhon and Isirus :
Thei were brethren alle thre,
And the goddesse in hir degre   800
Here Soster was and Ysis hyhte,
Whom Isirus forlai be nyhte
And hield hire after as his wif.
So it befell that upon strif
Typhon hath Isre his brother slain,
Which hadde a child to Sone Orayn,
And he his fader deth to herte
So tok, that it mai noght asterte
That he Typhon after ne slowh,
Whan he was ripe of age ynowh.   810
Bot yit thegipcienes trowe
For al this errour, which thei knowe,
That these brethren ben of myht
To sette and kepe Egipte upriht,
And overthrowe, if that hem like.
Bot Ysis, as seith the Cronique,
Fro Grece into Egipte cam,
And sche thanne upon honde nam
To teche hem forto sowe and eere,
Which noman knew tofore there.   820
And whan thegipcienes syhe   **P. ii. 155**
The fieldes fulle afore here yhe,
And that the lond began to greine,
Which whilom hadde be bareigne,—
For therthe bar after the kinde
His due charge,—this I finde,
That sche of berthe the goddesse
Is cleped, so that in destresse
The wommen there upon childinge
To hire clepe, and here offringe   830
Thei beren, whan that thei ben lyhte.
Lo, hou Egipte al out of syhte

811 þegipcienes (þe Egipcienes) YGEC, BΔ   þe Egipcianis X
thegipciens (þe Egipciens) AJMH₁RB₂, SAdT, FWH₃ . egipcens L.
821 *as in* 811 *but* Egipcienes Y   þegipciens L

Fro resoun stant in misbelieve
For lacke of lore, as I believe.

[iii. BELIEF OF THE
GREEKS.]

   Among the Greks, out of the weie
As thei that reson putte aweie,
Ther was, as the Cronique seith,
Of misbelieve an other feith,
That thei here goddes and goddesses,
As who seith, token al to gesses   840
Of suche as weren full of vice,
To whom thei made here sacrifice.
The hihe god, so as thei seide,
To whom thei most worschipe leide,
Saturnus hihte, and king of Crete
He hadde be ; bot of his sete
He was put doun, as he which stod
In frenesie, and was so wod,
That fro his wif, which Rea hihte,
Hise oghne children he to plihte,   850
And eet hem of his comun wone.   **P. ii. 156**
Bot Jupiter, which was his Sone
And of full age, his fader bond
And kutte of with his oghne hond
Hise genitals, whiche als so faste
Into the depe See he caste ;
Wherof the Greks afferme and seie,
Thus whan thei were caste aweie,
Cam Venus forth be weie of kinde.
And of Saturne also I finde   860
How afterward into an yle
This Jupiter him dede exile,
Wher that he stod in gret meschief.
Lo, which a god thei maden chief!
And sithen that such on was he,
Which stod most hihe in his degre
Among the goddes, thou miht knowe,

De Secta Grecorum.

Nota qualiter Sa-
turnus deorum sum-
mus appellatur.

833 Fro] Of A . . . B₂   835 *margin* De Secta Grecorum] De
secta egipciorum B   *om*. E   836 that *om*. XRCLB₂   850 he to
plihte (toplighte &c.) J, SAdBTΔ, FWH₃   al to plyhte (alto plight
&c.) AM . . . B₂   ˅   862 dede him H₁ . . . B₂, Δ, W   866 hihe
A, S, F   hih BT

[BELIEF OF THE
    GREEKS.]

Iupiter deus deli-
ciarum.

These othre, that ben more lowe,
Ben litel worth, as it is founde.
For Jupiter was the secounde,   870
Which Juno hadde unto his wif;
And yit a lechour al his lif
He was, and in avouterie
He wroghte many a tricherie;
And for he was so full of vices,
Thei cleped him god of delices :
Of whom, if thou wolt more wite,
Ovide the Poete hath write.
Bot yit here Sterres bothe tuo,
Saturne and Jupiter also,   880
Thei have, althogh thei be to blame, **P. ii. 157**
Attitled to here oghne name.

Mars deus belli.

Mars was an other in that lawe,
The which in Dace was forthdrawe,
Of whom the clerk Vegecius
Wrot in his bok, and tolde thus,
Hou he into Ytaile cam,
And such fortune ther he nam,
That he a Maiden hath oppressed,
Which in hire ordre was professed,   890
As sche which was the Prioresse
In Vestes temple the goddesse,
So was sche wel the mor to blame.
Dame Ylia this ladi name
Men clepe, and ek sche was also
The kinges dowhter that was tho,
Which Mynitor be name hihte.
So that ayein the lawes ryhte
Mars thilke time upon hire that
Remus and Romulus begat,   900
Whiche after, whan thei come in Age,
Of knihthode and of vassellage
Ytaile al hol thei overcome
And foundeden the grete Rome;
In Armes and of such emprise
Thei weren, that in thilke wise

893 he BT   901 Whiche A, S   Which J, B, F

Here fader Mars for the mervaile
The god was cleped of bataille.
Thei were his children bothe tuo,
Thurgh hem he tok his name so,   910
Ther was non other cause why :   **P. ii. 158**
And yit a Sterre upon the Sky
He hath unto his name applied,
In which that he is signified.
   An other god thei hadden eke,
To whom for conseil thei beseke,
The which was brother to Venus,
Appollo men him clepe thus.
He was an Hunte upon the helles,
Ther was with him no vertu elles,   920
Wherof that enye bokes karpe,
Bot only that he couthe harpe ;
Which whanne he walked over londe,
Fulofte time he tok on honde,
To gete him with his sustienance,
For lacke of other pourveance.
And otherwhile of his falshede
He feignede him to conne arede
Of thing which after scholde falle ;
Wherof among hise sleyhtes alle   930
He hath the lewed folk deceived,
So that the betre he was received.
Lo now, thurgh what creacion
He hath deificacion,
And cleped is the god of wit
To suche as be the foles yit.
   An other god, to whom thei soghte,
Mercurie hihte, and him ne roghte
What thing he stal, ne whom he slowh.
Of Sorcerie he couthe ynowh,   940
That whanne he wolde himself transforme, **P. ii. 159**

Margin notes:

[Belief of the Greeks.]

Appollo deus Sapiencie.

Mercurius deus Mercatorum et furtorum.

915 *margin* Sciencie A   923 whane F   928 feigneþ B
936 be the] beþ þe AMXE . . . B₂   ther beth H₁   ben (*om.* the) J,
Δ, W   937 f. *margin* Mercurius—furtorum *om.* X . . . CB₂, H₃
Mercurius deus latronum L   Mercurie deus H₁   939 stal] dide
(dede) H₁ . . . B₂

[BELIEF OF THE
GREEKS.]

Fulofte time he tok the forme
Of womman and his oghne lefte;
So dede he wel the more thefte.
A gret spekere in alle thinges
He was also, and of lesinges
An Auctour, that men wiste non
An other such as he was on.
And yit thei maden of this thief
A god, which was unto hem lief,   950
And clepede him in tho believes
The god of Marchantz and of thieves.
Bot yit a sterre upon the hevene
He hath of the planetes sevene.

Vulcanus deus Ignis.

But Vulcanus, of whom I spak,
He hadde a courbe upon the bak,
And therto he was hepehalt:
Of whom thou understonde schalt,
He was a schrewe in al his youthe,
And he non other vertu couthe   960
Of craft to helpe himselve with,
Bot only that he was a Smith
With Jupiter, which in his forge
Diverse thinges made him forge;
So wot I noght for what desir
Thei clepen him the god of fyr.

Eolus deus vento-
rum.

King of Cizile Ypolitus
A Sone hadde, and Eolus
He hihte, and of his fader grant
He hield be weie of covenant   970
The governance of every yle   **P. ii. 160**
Which was longende unto Cizile,
Of hem that fro the lond forein
Leie open to the wynd al plein.
And fro thilke iles to the londe
Fulofte cam the wynd to honde:
After the name of him forthi
The wyndes cleped Eoli
Tho were, and he the god of wynd.

948 ðn F   951 tho] þe X . . . B₂, Ad   967 *margin* Eolus
deus ventorum *om.* B   979 Tho] They (þai &c.) H₁ . . . B₂, B

Lo nou, hou this believe is blynd!   980   [BELIEF OF THE
   The king of Crete Jupiter,   GREEKS.]
The same which I spak of er,   Neptunus   deus
Unto his brother, which Neptune   maris.
Was hote, it list him to comune
Part of his good, so that be Schipe
He mad him strong of the lordschipe
Of al the See in tho parties ;
Wher that he wroghte his tyrannyes,
And the strange yles al aboute
He wan, that every man hath doute   990
Upon his marche forto saile ;
For he anon hem wolde assaile
And robbe what thing that thei ladden,
His sauf conduit bot if thei hadden.
Wherof the comun vois aros
In every lond, that such a los
He cawhte, al nere it worth a stre,
That he was cleped of the See
The god be name, and yit he is
With hem that so believe amis.   1000
This Neptune ek was thilke also,   P. ii 61
Which was the ferste foundour tho
Of noble Troie, and he forthi
Was wel the more lete by.
   The loresman of the Schepherdes,   Pan deus nature.
And ek of hem that ben netherdes,
Was of Archade and hihte Pan :
Of whom hath spoke many a man ;
For in the wode of Nonarcigne,
Enclosed with the tres of Pigne,   1010
And on the Mont of Parasie
He hadde of bestes the baillie,
And ek benethe in the valleie,

981 *margin* Neptunus deus maris *om.* X . . . B₂   Iubiter deus
deliciarum H₁   986 mad J, S, F   made AC, B   987 tho] þe
H₁ . . . B₂   989 al *om.* BT   992 wold(e) hem H₁ . . . B₂, Δ
he wolde hem M   1006 ben *om.* AM   1009 Nonarigne (Noua-
rigne, Nonareigne &c.) H₁ . . . B₂, B   Nonartigne (Nonartyne) M,
WH₃   1013 benethe in] beneþe (by neþe, benethen &c.)
H₁ . . . B₂, BT   beneþin A

[BELIEF OF THE
GREEKS.]

Wher thilke rivere, as men seie,
Which Lȧdon hihte, made his cours,
He was the chief of governours
Of hem that kepten tame bestes,
Wherof thei maken yit the festes
In the Cite Stinfalides.
And forth withal yit natheles   1020
He tawhte men the forthdrawinge
Of bestaile, and ek the makinge
Of Oxen, and of hors the same,
Hou men hem scholde ryde and tame :
Of foules ek, so as we finde,
Ful many a soubtiel craft of kinde
He fond, which noman knew tofore.
Men dede him worschipe ek therfore,
That he the ferste in thilke lond
Was which the melodie fond   1030
Of Riedes, whan thei weren ripe,   **P. ii. 162**
With double pipes forto pipe ;
Therof he yaf the ferste lore,
Til afterward men couthe more.
To every craft for mannes helpe
He hadde a redi wit to helpe
Thurgh naturel experience :
And thus the nyce reverence
Of foles, whan that he was ded,
The fot hath torned to the hed,   1040
And clepen him god of nature,
For so thei maden his figure.

Bachus deus vini.   An other god, so as thei fiele,
Which Jupiter upon Samele
Begat in his avouterie,
Whom, forto hide his lecherie,
That non therof schal take kepe,
In a Montaigne forto kepe,
Which Dyon hihte and was in Ynde,
He sende, in bokes as I finde :   1050
And he be name Bachus hihte,
Which afterward, whan that he mihte,

1050 sende] sayde B *line om.* T

A wastour was, and al his rente
In wyn and bordel he despente.
Bot yit, al were he wonder badde,
Among the Greks a name he hadde ;
Thei cleped him the god of wyn,
And thus a glotoun was dyvyn.
Ther was yit Esculapius
A godd in thilke time as thus.   1060
His craft stod upon Surgerie,   **P. ii. 163**
Bot for the lust of lecherie,
That he to Daires dowhter drowh,
It fell that Jupiter him slowh :
And yit thei made him noght forthi
A god, and was no cause why.
In Rome he was long time also
A god among the Romeins tho ;
For, as he seide, of his presence
Ther was destruid a pestilence,   1070
Whan thei to thyle of Delphos wente,
And that Appollo with hem sente
This Esculapius his Sone,
Among the Romeins forto wone.
And there he duelte for a while,
Til afterward into that yle,
Fro whenne he cam, ayein he torneth,
Where al his lyf that he sojorneth
Among the Greks, til that he deide.
And thei upon him thanne leide   1080
His name, and god of medicine
He hatte after that ilke line.
An other god of Hercules
Thei made, which was natheles
A man, bot that he was so strong,
In al this world that brod and long
So myhti was noman as he.
Merveiles tuelve in his degre,
As it was couth in sondri londes,

Esculapius   deus
medicine.

Hercules deus for-
titudinis.

1058 a glotoun] þe glotoun B   1059 *margin* Esculapius deus
medicine *om.* B   1065 thei *om.* AMXRCLB₂   1072 him
AM . . . CB₂, BT, WH₃   1083 *margin* Hercules &c. *om.* B.

[Belief of the
Greeks.]

He dede with hise oghne hondes   1090
Ayein geantz and Monstres bothe,   **P. ii. 164**
The whiche horrible were and lothe,
Bot he with strengthe hem overcam :
Wherof so gret a pris he nam,
That thei him clepe amonges alle
The god of strengthe, and to him calle.
And yit ther is no reson inne,
For he a man was full of sinne,
Which proved was upon his ende,
For in a rage himself he brende ;   1100
And such a cruel mannes dede
Acordeth nothing with godhede.

Pluto deus Inferni.

Thei hadde of goddes yit an other,
Which Pluto hihte, and was the brother
Of Jupiter, and he fro youthe
With every word which cam to mouthe,
Of eny thing whan he was wroth,
He wolde swere his commun oth,
Be Lethen and be Flegeton,
Be Cochitum and Acheron,   1110
The whiche, after the bokes telle,
Ben the chief flodes of the helle :
Be Segne and Stige he swor also,
That ben the depe Pettes tuo
Of helle the most principal.
Pluto these othes overal
Swor of his commun custummance,
Til it befell upon a chance,
That he for Jupiteres sake
Unto the goddes let do make   1120
A sacrifice, and for that dede   **P. ii. 165**
On of the pettes for his mede
In helle, of which I spak of er,
Was granted him ; and thus he ther

1103 *margin* Pluto &c. *om.* AH₁XE . . . B₂ (*ins. later* M), B
1105 fro] for H₁, BT   of W   1107 euery H₁ . . . B₂   1109
fflagetoun AMH₁, W   fflogetoun GECLB₂, B   1112 of the helle]
of helle AM . . . B₂, AdBΔΛ, W   1119 Iupiteres (Iubiteres &c.)
MYXGERC, SB   Iupiters (Iubiters) AJLB₂, FH₃ Iupiter (Iubiter)
H₁, AdTΔ, W

Upon the fortune of this thing
The name tok of helle king.
  Lo, these goddes and wel mo
Among the Greks thei hadden tho,
And of goddesses manyon,
Whos names thou schalt hiere anon,   1130
And in what wise thei deceiven
The foles whiche here feith receiven.

So as Saturne is soverein
Of false goddes, as thei sein,
So is Sibeles of goddesses
The Moder, whom withoute gesses
The folk Payene honoure and serve,
As thei the whiche hire lawe observe.
Bot forto knowen upon this
Fro when sche cam and what sche is,   1140
Bethincia the contre hihte,
Wher sche cam ferst to mannes sihte ;
And after was Saturnes wif,
Be whom thre children in hire lif
Sche bar, and thei were cleped tho
Juno, Neptunus and Pluto,
The whiche of nyce fantasie
The poeple wolde deifie.
And for hire children were so,
Sibeles thanne was also   1150
Mad a goddesse, and thei hire calle   **P. ii. 166**
The moder of the goddes alle.
So was that name bore forth,
And yit the cause is litel worth.
  A vois unto Saturne tolde
Hou that his oghne Sone him scholde
Out of his regne putte aweie ;
And he be cause of thilke weie,
That him was schape such a fate,
Sibele his wif began to hate   1160

[BELIEF OF THE GREEKS.]

Nota, qualiter Si-
beles Dearum Mater
et origo nuncupatur.

Iuno Dea Regno-
rum et diuiciarum.

1134 *margin* dearum JY, S . . . Δ, FH₃   deorum AM . . . B₂, W
1138 the *om.* H₁ . . . B₂, Δ, W   lawes H₁ . . . B₂   1149 here (her)
B, W   his C   1155 f. *margin* Iuno &c. *om.* AM . . . B₂   et
diuiciarum *om.* BT   1156 him *om.* B
  **   F f

And ek hire progenie bothe.
And thus, whil that thei were wrothe,
Be Philerem upon a dai
In his avouterie he lai,
On whom he Jupiter begat ;
And thilke child was after that
Which wroghte al that was prophecied,
As it tofore is specefied :
So that whan Jupiter of Crete
Was king, a wif unto him mete　　　　1170
The Dowhter of Sibele he tok,
And that was Juno, seith the bok.
Of his deificacion
After the false oppinion,
That have I told, so as thei meene ;
And for this Juno was the queene
Of Jupiter and Soster eke,
The foles unto hire sieke,
And sein that sche is the goddesse
Of Regnes bothe and of richesse :　　　　1180
And ek sche, as thei understonde,　　**P. ii. 167**
The water Nimphes hath in honde
To leden at hire oghne heste ;
And whan hir list the Sky tempeste,
The reinbowe is hir Messager.
Lo, which a misbelieve is hier !
That sche goddesse is of the Sky
I wot non other cause why.

Minerua Dea sapi-
enciarum.

　　An other goddesse is Minerve,
To whom the Greks obeie and serve :　　　　1190
And sche was nyh the grete lay
Of Triton founde, wher sche lay
A child forcast, bot what sche was
Ther knew noman the sothe cas.
Bot in Aufrique sche was leid
In the manere as I have seid,
And caried fro that ilke place
Into an Yle fer in Trace,

1165 Iupiter he SAdΔ　　1172 was *om.* H₁ ... B₂　as seiþ H₁ ... B₂
1176 And *om.* BT

The which Palene thanne hihte,
Wher a Norrice hir kepte and dihte. 1200
And after, for sche was so wys
That sche fond ferst in hire avis
The cloth makinge of wolle and lyn,
Men seiden that sche was divin,
And the goddesse of Sapience
Thei clepen hire in that credence.
　Of the goddesse which Pallas
Is cleped sondri speche was.
On seith hire fader was Pallant,
Which in his time was geant, 1210
A cruel man, a bataillous :
An other seith hou in his hous
Sche was the cause why he deide.
And of this Pallas some ek seide
That sche was Martes wif; and so
Among the men that weren tho
Of misbelieve in the riote
The goddesse of batailles hote
She was, and yit sche berth the name.
Now loke, hou they be forto blame. 1220
　Saturnus after his exil
Fro Crete cam in gret peril
Into the londes of Ytaile,
And ther he dede gret mervaile,
Wherof his name duelleth yit.
For he fond of his oghne wit
The ferste craft of plowh tilinge,
Of Eringe and of corn sowinge,
And how men scholden sette vines
And of the grapes make wynes ; 1230
Al this he tawhte, and it fell so,
His wif, the which cam with him tho,
Was cleped Cereres be name,
And for sche tawhte also the same,

[BELIEF OF THE GREEKS.]

Pallas Dea bello-
rum.

1210

P. ii. 168

Ceres dea frugum.

1199 Palon(e) H₁ . . . B₂　　1201 after þat for sche was w. AM . . . B₂
1203 The] To H₁E . . . B₂　　1207 *margin* Pallas &c. *om.* C, BT
1221 *margin* Ceres dea frugum *om.* JH₁ . . . B₂　Saturnus dea
frugum B　　1230 grape AM . . . B₂, Δ　　1232 the *om.* AM, W

[BELIEF OF THE
GREEKS.]

And was his wif that ilke throwe,
As it was to the poeple knowe,
Thei made of Ceres a goddesse,
In whom here tilthe yit thei blesse,
And sein that Tricolonius
Hire Sone goth amonges ous   1240
And makth the corn good chep or dere, **P. ii. 169**
Riht as hire list fro yer to yeere;
So that this wif be cause of this
Goddesse of Cornes cleped is.

Diana Dea Moncium
et Siluarum.

King Jupiter, which his likinge
Whilom fulfelde in alle thinge,
So priveliche aboute he ladde
His lust, that he his wille hadde
Of Latona, and on hire that
Diane his dowhter he begat   1250
Unknowen of his wif Juno.
And afterward sche knew it so,
That Latona for drede fledde
Into an Ile, wher sche hedde
Hire wombe, which of childe aros.
Thilke yle cleped was Delos;
In which Diana was forthbroght,
And kept so that hire lacketh noght.
And after, whan sche was of Age,
Sche tok non hiede of mariage,   1260
Bot out of mannes compaignie
Sche tok hire al to venerie
In forest and in wildernesse
For ther was al hire besinesse
Be daie and ek be nyhtes tyde
With arwes brode under the side
And bowe in honde, of which sche slowh
And tok al that hir liste ynowh
Of bestes whiche ben chacable:
Wherof the Cronique of this fable   1270
Seith that the gentils most of alle   **P. ii. 170**

1238 her tilþes B   1245 *margin* et Siluarum *om.* AM   1252 And]
Bot (But) SAdBTΔΛ   1253 ledde BT   1256 was cleped BTΛ
1262 al to] vnto B

Worschipen hire and to hire calle,
And the goddesse of hihe helles,
Of grene trees, of freisshe welles,
They clepen hire in that believe,
Which that no reson mai achieve.

Proserpina, which dowhter was   Proserpina Dea In-
Of Cereres, befell this cas :   fernorum.
Whil sche was duellinge in Cizile,
Hire moder in that ilke while   1280
Upon hire blessinge and hire heste
Bad that sche scholde ben honeste,
And lerne forto weve and spinne,
And duelle at hom and kepe hire inne.
Bot sche caste al that lore aweie,
And as sche wente hir out to pleie,
To gadre floures in a pleine,
And that was under the monteine
Of Ethna, fell the same tyde
That Pluto cam that weie ryde,   1290
And sodeinly, er sche was war,
He tok hire up into his char.
And as thei riden in the field,
Hire grete beaute he behield,
Which was so plesant in his ÿe,
That forto holde in compainie
He weddeth hire and hield hire so
To ben his wif for everemo.
And as thou hast tofore herd telle
Hou he was cleped god of helle,   1300
So is sche cleped the goddesse   **P. ii. 171**
Be causè of him, ne mor ne lesse.

Lo, thus, mi Sone, as I thee tolde,   Confessor.
The Greks whilom be daies olde
Here goddes hadde in sondri wise,
And thurgh the lore of here aprise
The Romeins hielden ek the same.

1279 Whil sche was] Which was H₁ . . . B₂   1286 hir
om. H₁ . . . B₂   1287 To gedre ARCLB₂   To gedres M
1290 Than BTΛ   þe weie H₁E . . . B₂   1297 hield] tok(e)
H₁ . . . B₂

[BELIEF OF THE
GREEKS.]

And in the worschipe of here name
To every godd in special
Thei made a temple forth withal,   1310
And ech of hem his yeeres dai
Attitled hadde ; and of arai
The temples weren thanne ordeigned,
And ek the poeple was constreigned
To come and don here sacrifice ;
The Prestes ek in here office
Solempne maden thilke festes.
And thus the Greks lich to the bestes
The men in stede of god honoure,
Whiche mihten noght hemself socoure,   1320
Whil that thei were alyve hiere.
And over this, as thou schalt hiere,

Nota, quod dii Mon-
tium Satiri vocantur.

The Greks fulfild of fantasie
Sein ek that of the helles hihe
The goddes ben in special,
Bot of here name in general
Thei hoten alle Satiri.

Oreades   Nimphe
Montium.

Ther ben of Nimphes proprely
In the believe of hem also :
Oreades thei seiden tho   1330
Attitled ben to the monteines ;   **P. ii. 172**

Driades Siluarum.

And for the wodes in demeynes
To kepe, tho ben Driades ;

Naiades fontium.

Of freisshe welles Naiades ;
And of the Nimphes of the See

Nereides Marium.

I finde a tale in proprete,
Hou Dorus whilom king of Grece,
Which hadde of infortune a piece,—
His wif forth with hire dowhtres alle,
So as the happes scholden falle,   1340
With many a gentil womman there
Dreint in the salte See thei were :
Wherof the Greks that time seiden,
And such a name upon hem leiden,

1308 in *om.* AM   for H₁ ... B₂   1318 to bestes ER, BTΔ, W
1331 Attitred AMXRB₂   1333 tho] þer H₁ ... B₂   1336 *margin*
Nereides Marium *om.* B   1339 forth *om.* AM ... B₂

Nereïdes that thei ben hote,
The Nimphes whiche that thei note
To regne upon the stremes salte.
Lo now, if this believe halte!
Bot of the Nimphes as thei telle,
In every place wher thei duelle   1350
Thei ben al redi obeissant
As damoiselles entendant
To the goddesses, whos servise
Thei mote obeie in alle wise;
Wherof the Greks to hem beseke
With tho that ben goddesses eke,
And have in hem a gret credence.
  And yit withoute experience   Manes dii mortuo-
Salve only of illusion,   rum.
Which was to hem dampnacion,   1360
For men also that were dede   **P. ii. 173**
Thei hadden goddes, as I rede,
And tho be name Manes hihten,
To whom ful gret honour thei dihten,
So as the Grekes lawe seith,
Which was ayein the rihte feith.
  Thus have I told a gret partie;
Bot al the hole progenie
Of goddes in that ilke time
To long it were forto rime.   1370
Bot yit of that which thou hast herd,
Of misbelieve hou it hath ferd,
Ther is a gret diversite.
  Mi fader, riht so thenketh me.   Amans.
Bot yit o thing I you beseche,
Which stant in alle mennes speche,
The godd and the goddesse of love,
Of whom ye nothing hier above
Have told, ne spoken of her fare,
That ye me wolden now declare   1380
Hou thei ferst comen to that name.

1349 the *om.* AM . . . B₂   1353 goddes BΛ, W   goddesse
AM . . . B₃   1358 *margin* Manes &c. *om.* B   1381 comen
ferst AM   came first W

[BELIEF OF THE
    GREEKS.]
Qualiter Cupido et
Venus deus et dea
amoris nuncupantur.

Mi Sone, I have it left for schame,
Be cause I am here oghne Prest ;
Bot for thei stonden nyh thi brest
Upon the schrifte of thi matiere,
Thou schalt of hem the sothe hiere :
And understond nou wel the cas.
Venus Saturnes dowhter was,
Which alle danger putte aweie
Of love, and fond to lust a weie ;   1390
So that of hire in sondri place   P. ii. 174
Diverse men felle into grace,
And such a lusti lif sche ladde,
That sche diverse children hadde,
Nou on be this, nou on be that.
Of hire it was that Mars beyat
A child, which cleped was Armene ;
Of hire also cam Andragene,
To whom Mercurie fader was :
Anchises begat Eneas   1400
Of hire also, and Ericon
Biten begat, and therupon,
Whan that sche sih ther was non other,
Be Jupiter hire oghne brother
Sche lay, and he begat Cupide.
And thilke Sone upon a tyde,
Whan he was come unto his Age,
He hadde a wonder fair visage,
And fond his Moder amourous,
And he was also lecherous :   1410
So whan thei weren bothe al one,
As he which yhen hadde none
To se reson, his Moder kiste ;
And sche also, that nothing wiste
Bot that which unto lust belongeth,
To ben hire love him underfongeth.
Thus was he blind, and sche unwys :
Bot natheles this cause it is,

1383 ff. *margin* Qualiter &c. *om.* H₁ ... B₂   1383 here] hire (hir)
JL, Ad, W   ȝour(e) X ... CB₂   1384 þe brest A ... B₂, Ad,
H₃   1405 lay] haþ AM

Why Cupide is the god of love,
For he his moder dorste love.   1420
And sche, which thoghte hire lustes fonde, **P. ii. 175**
Diverse loves tok in honde,
Wel mo thanne I the tolde hiere:
And for sche wolde hirselve skiere,
Sche made comun that desport,
And sette a lawe of such a port,
That every womman mihte take
What man hire liste, and noght forsake
To ben als comun as sche wolde.
Sche was the ferste also which tolde   1430
That wommen scholde here bodi selle;
Semiramis, so as men telle,
Of Venus kepte thilke aprise,
And so dede in the same wise
Of Rome faire Neabole,
Which liste hire bodi to rigole;
Sche was to every man felawe,
And hild the lust of thilke lawe,
Which Venus of hirself began;
Wherof that sche the name wan,   1440
Why men hire clepen the goddesse
Of love and ek of gentilesse,
Of worldes lust and of plesance.
  Se nou the foule mescreance
Of Greks in thilke time tho,
Whan Venus tok hire name so.
Ther was no cause under the Mone
Of which thei hadden tho to done,
Of wel or wo wher so it was,
That thei ne token in that cas   1450
A god to helpe or a goddesse.   **P. ii. 176**
Wherof, to take mi witnesse,
  The king of Bragmans Dindimus
Wrot unto Alisandre thus:
In blaminge of the Grekes feith

1423 telle X, B, W   1429 a comun AM   all comyn X
1438 hild J, F hield SB huld A   1447 no] þe AM . . . B₂
1453 Bragmas AM . . . B₂, H₃

[BELIEF OF THE
GREEKS.]
cit quod Greci tunc
ad corporis conserua-
cionem pro singulis
membris singulos de-
os specialiter appro-
priari credunt.

And of the misbelieve, he seith
How thei for every membre hadden
A sondri god, to whom thei spradden
Here armes, and of help besoghten.
Minerve for the hed thei soghten,　　1460
For sche was wys, and of a man
The wit and reson which he can
Is in the celles of the brayn,
Wherof thei made hire soverain.

Mercurie, which was in his dawes
A gret spekere of false lawes,
On him the kepinge of the tunge
Thei leide, whan thei spieke or sunge.

For Bachus was a glotoun eke,
Him for the throte thei beseke,　　1470
That he it wolde waisshen ofte
With swote drinkes and with softe.

The god of schuldres and of armes
Was Hercules; for he in armes
The myhtieste was to fihte,
To him tho Limes they behihte.

The god whom that thei clepen Mart
The brest to kepe hath for his part,
Forth with the herte, in his ymage
That he adresce the corage.　　1480
And of the galle the goddesse,　　**P. ii. 177**
For sche was full of hastifesse
Of wraththe and liht to grieve also,
Thei made and seide it was Juno.

Cupide, which the brond afyre
Bar in his hond, he was the Sire
Of the Stomak, which builleth evere,
Wherof the lustes ben the levere.

To the goddesse Cereres,
Which of the corn yaf hire encress　　1490
Upon the feith that tho was take,

1476 tho] þe H₁XGCLB₂, AdB, W　　1477 whom that] þe whom B
whom H₁B₂, TΔ, W　　1482 hastifesse J, S, F　hastifnesse A
hastiuesse B　　1485 of fire H₁E . . . B₂, Δ, WH₃　　1486 Bar]
Bereþ (Berþ) XG　But AME . . . B₂　　1489 To] Lo AMH₁XG

The wombes cure was betake;
And Venus thurgh the Lecherie,
For which that thei hire deifie,
Sche kept al doun the remenant
To thilke office appourtenant.
Thus was dispers in sondri wise
The misbelieve, as I devise,
With many an ymage of entaile,
Of suche as myhte hem noght availe;
For thei withoute lyves chiere
Unmyhti ben to se or hiere
Or speke or do or elles fiele;
And yit the foles to hem knele,
Which is here oghne handes werk.
Ha lord, hou this believe is derk,
And fer fro resonable wit!
And natheles thei don it yit:
That was to day a ragged tre,
To morwe upon his majeste
Stant in the temple wel besein.
How myhte a mannes resoun sein
That such a Stock mai helpe or grieve?
Bot thei that ben of such believe
And unto suche goddes calle,
It schal to hem riht so befalle,
And failen ate moste nede.
Bot if thee list to taken hiede
And of the ferste ymage wite,
Petornius therof hath write
And ek Nigargorus also;
And thei afferme and write so,
That Promotheüs was tofore
And fond the ferste craft therfore,
And Cirophanes, as thei telle,
Thurgh conseil which was take in helle,
In remembrance of his lignage
Let setten up the ferste ymage.

[Origin of Idol-
worship.]

Nota de prima ydol-
orum cultura, que ex
1500 tribus precipue Sta-
tuis exorta est; qua-
rum prima fuit illa,
quam in filii sui me-
moriam quidam prin-
ceps nomine Ciropha-
nes a sculptore Pro-
motheo fabricari con-
stituit.

1510

P. ii. 178

1520

1495 kept J, B, F kepte A   1517 ate] at here (atte her) AM . . . B₂
at hor W   1520 Petornius A, S, F Petronius J, B   1526 which om.
E . . . B₂ þat W to helle E . . . B₂   1527 hir(e) E . . . B₂ (her R)

Of Cirophanes seith the bok,
That he for sorwe, which he tok　　　1530
Of that he sih his Sone ded,
Of confort knew non other red,
Bot let do make in remembrance
A faire ymage of his semblance
And sette it in the market place,
Which openly tofore his face
Stod every dai to don him ese.
And thei that thanne wolden plese
The fader, scholden it obeie,
Whan that they comen thilke weie.　　　1540

Secunda Statua fuit
illa, quam ad sui patris
Beli culturam Rex
Ninus fieri et adorari
decreuit.　Et sic de
nomine Beli postea
Bel et Belzebub ydo-
lum accreuit.

And of Ninus king of Assire　　P. ii. 179
I rede hou that in his empire
He was next after the secounde
Of hem that ferst ymages founde.
For he riht in semblable cas
Of Belus, which his fader was
Fro Nembroth in the rihte line,
Let make of gold and Stones fine
A precious ymage riche
After his fader evene liche;　　　1550
And therupon a lawe he sette,
That every man of pure dette
With sacrifice and with truage
Honoure scholde thilke ymage:
So that withinne time it fell,
Of Belus cam the name of Bel,
Of Bel cam Belzebub, and so
The misbelieve wente tho.

Tercia Statua fuit
illa, que ad honorem
Apis Regis Grecorum
sculpta fuit, cui postea
nomen Serapis impo-
nentes, ipsum quasi
deum Pagani colue-
runt.

The thridde ymage next to this
Was, whan the king of Grece Apis　　　1560
Was ded, thei maden a figure
In resemblance of his stature.
Of this king Apis seith the bok
That Serapis his name tok,
In whom thurgh long continuance
Of misbelieve a gret creance
Thei hadden, and the reverence

1535 sette SB　set AJ, F

Of Sacrifice and of encence
To him thei made: and as thei telle,
Among the wondres that befelle,   1570
Whan Alisandre fro Candace   **P. ii. 180**
Cam ridende, in a wilde place
Undur an hull a Cave he fond ;
And Candalus, which in that lond
Was bore, and was Candaces Sone,
Him tolde hou that of commun wone
The goddes were in thilke cave.
And he, that wolde assaie and have
A knowlechinge if it be soth,
Liht of his hors and in he goth,   1580
And fond therinne that he soghte :
For thurgh the fendes sleihte him thoghte,
Amonges othre goddes mo
That Serapis spak to him tho,
Whom he sih there in gret arrai.
And thus the fend fro dai to dai
The worschipe of ydolatrie
Drowh forth upon the fantasie
Of hem that weren thanne blinde
And couthen noght the trouthe finde.   1590
   Thus hast thou herd in what degre
Of Grece, Egipte and of Caldee
The misbelieves whilom stode ;
And hou so that thei be noght goode
Ne trewe, yit thei sprungen oute,
Wherof the wyde world aboute
His part of misbelieve tok.
Til so befell, as seith the bok,
That god a poeple for himselve
Hath chose of the lignages tuelve,   1600
Wherof the sothe redely,   **P. ii. 181**
As it is write in Genesi,
I thenke telle in such a wise
That it schal be to thin apprise.

1573 Vndur A, F   Vnder J, S, B   1578 And he] He AM ... B₂
1593 mysbelieue H₁E ... B₂

[iv. Belief of the Jews.]

De Hebreorum seu Iudeorum Secta, quorum Sinagoga, ecclesia Cristi superueniente, defecit.

After the flod, fro which Noë
Was sauf, the world in his degre
Was mad, as who seith, newe ayein,
Of flour, of fruit, of gras, of grein,
Of beste, of bridd and of mankinde,
Which evere hath be to god unkinde : 1610
For noght withstondende al the fare,
Of that this world was mad so bare
And afterward it was restored,
Among the men was nothing mored
Towardes god of good lyvynge,
Bot al was torned to likinge
After the fleissh, so that foryete
Was he which yaf hem lif and mete,
Of hevene and Erthe creatour.
And thus cam forth the grete errour, 1620
That thei the hihe god ne knewe,
Bot maden othre goddes newe,
As thou hast herd me seid tofore :
Ther was noman that time bore,
That he ne hadde after his chois
A god, to whom he yaf his vois.
Wherof the misbelieve cam
Into the time of Habraham :
Bot he fond out the rihte weie,
Hou only that men scholde obeie 1630
The hihe god, which weldeth al, **P. ii. 182**
And evere hath don and evere schal,
In hevene, in Erthe and ek in helle ;
Ther is no tunge his miht mai telle.
This Patriarch to his lignage
Forbad, that thei to non ymage
Encline scholde in none wise,
Bot here offrende and sacrifise
With al the hole hertes love
Unto the mihti god above 1640
Thei scholden yive and to no mo :
And thus in thilke time tho

1624 bore] bifore BT   1628 habraham F   *rest* Abraham
(J *defective here*) *so also l.* 1650   1633 and erþe E . . . B₂, Ad

Began the Secte upon this Erthe,
Of rihtwisnesse it was conceived,
So moste it nedes be received
Of him that alle riht is inne,
The hihe god, which wolde winne
A poeple unto his oghne feith.
On Habraham the ground he leith,   1650
And made him forto multeplie
Into so gret a progenie,
That thei Egipte al overspradde.
Bot Pharao with wrong hem ladde
In servitute ayein the pes,
Til god let sende Moïses
To make the deliverance ;
And for his poeple gret vengance
He tok, which is to hiere a wonder.
The king was slain, the lond put under,   1660
God bad the rede See divide,   **P. ii. 183**
Which stod upriht on either side
And yaf unto his poeple a weie,
That thei on fote it passe dreie
And gon so forth into desert :
Wher forto kepe hem in covert,
The daies, whan the Sonne brente,
A large cloude hem overwente,
And forto wissen hem be nyhte,
A firy Piler hem alyhte.   1670
And whan that thei for hunger pleigne,
The myhti god began to reyne
Manna fro hevene doun to grounde,
Wherof that ech of hem hath founde
His fode, such riht as him liste ;
And for thei scholde upon him triste,
Riht as who sette a tonne abroche,

1643 the Secte] þat secte S . . . Δ   this secte W   to sette AMH₁X
this] þe AM . . . B₂   1646 And alle mysbelieue weyued E . . . B₂,
Λ (misbelieues RLB₂)   1647 is] was E . . . B₂   1653 al *om.*
XE . . . B₂   1662 on] in BT   1664 on fote (foote) passen
ECLB₂, B   on fete p. R   on fote myght p. W   in fote it p. X
1667 The daies] Be (By) daies S . . . Δ   A dayes W

He percede the harde roche,
And sprong out water al at wille,
That man and beste hath drunke his fille: 1680
And afterward he yaf the lawe
To Moïses, that hem withdrawe
Thei scholden noght fro that he bad.
And in this wise thei be lad,
Til thei toke in possession
The londes of promission,
Wher that Caleph and Josuë
The Marches upon such degre
Departen, after the lignage
That ech of hem as Heritage   1690
His porpartie hath underfonge.   **P. ii. 184**
And thus stod this believe longe,
Which of prophetes was governed;
And thei hadde ek the poeple lerned
Of gret honour that scholde hem falle;
Bot ate moste nede of alle
Thei faileden, whan Crist was bore.
Bot hou that thei here feith have bore,
It nedeth noght to tellen al,
The matiere is so general: 1700
Whan Lucifer was best in hevene
And oghte moste have stonde in evene,
Towardes god he tok debat;
And for that he was obstinat,
And wolde noght to trouthe encline,
He fell for evere into ruine:
And Adam ek in Paradis,
Whan he stod most in al his pris
After thastat of Innocence,
Ayein the god brak his defence   1710
And fell out of his place aweie:
And riht be such a maner weie
The Jwes in here beste plit,
Whan that thei scholden most parfit

1678 perced(e) þo þe RCLB₂, Λ, W   1685 toke (tooke) C, SB
tok (took) A, F   1698 lore MH₁XGLB₂, AdBT, W   (hath lore
H₁L, W)   1713 Iwes F   Iewes A, SB

Have stonde upon the prophecie,
Tho fellen thei to most folie,
And him which was fro hevene come,
And of a Maide his fleissh hath nome,
And was among hem bore and fedd,
As men that wolden noght be spedd   1720
Of goddes Sone, with o vois   **P. ii. 185**
Thei hinge and slowhe upon the crois.
Wherof the parfit of here lawe
Fro thanne forth hem was withdrawe,
So that thei stonde of no merit,
Bot in truage as folk soubgit
Withoute proprete of place
Thei liven out of goddes grace,
Dispers in alle londes oute.
And thus the feith is come aboute,   1730
That whilom in the Jewes stod,
Which is noght parfihtliche good.
To speke as it is nou befalle,
Ther is a feith aboven alle,
In which the trouthe is comprehended,
Wherof that we ben alle amended.

[Belief of the Jews.]

The hihe almyhti majeste,
Of rihtwisnesse and of pite,
The Sinne which that Adam wroghte,
Whan he sih time, ayein he boghte,   1740
And sende his Sone fro the hevene
To sette mannes Soule in evene,
Which thanne was so sore falle
Upon the point which was befalle,
That he ne mihte himself arise.
Gregoire seith in his aprise,

[The Christian Faith.]

De fide Cristiana, in qua perfecte legis complementum, summi misterii sacramentum, nostreque saluacionis fundamentum infallibiliter consistere credimus.

1715 stonde AC, B stond F   1742 Which mannes soule
haþ set in euene S . . . Δ
   1743   And haþ his grace reconciled
                ffro which þe man was ferst exiled
                And in himself so sore falle
So S . . . Δ (inserting a couplet between 1742 and 1743)   1743 margin
ineffabiliter . . . creditur B   1745 auise E . . . B₂   1746 margin
Gregorius.   Nichil nobis nasci profuit, nisi redimi profuisset SBΔ
(proficit for profuit B)
**   G g

It helpeth noght a man be bore,
If goddes Sone were unbore;
For thanne thurgh the ferste Sinne,
Which Adam whilom broghte ous inne,   1750
Ther scholden alle men be lost;   **P. ii. 186**
Bot Crist restoreth thilke lost,
And boghte it with his fleissh and blod.
And if we thenken hou it stod
Of thilke rancoun which he payde,

Gregorius. O ne-
cessarium Ade pecca-
tum! O felix culpa,
que talem ac tantum
meruit habere re-
demptorem!

As seint Gregoire it wrot and sayde,
Al was behovely to the man:
For that wherof his wo began
Was after cause of al his welthe,
Whan he which is the welle of helthe,   1760
The hihe creatour of lif,
Upon the nede of such a strif
So wolde for his creature
Take on himself the forsfaiture
And soffre for the mannes sake.
Thus mai no reson wel forsake
That thilke Senne original
Ne was the cause in special
Of mannes worschipe ate laste,
Which schal withouten ende laste.   1770
For be that cause the godhede
Assembled was to the manhede
In the virgine, where he nom
Oure fleissh and verai man becom
Of bodely fraternite;
Wherof the man in his degre
Stant more worth, as I have told,
Than he stod erst be manyfold,
Thurgh baptesme of the newe lawe,
Of which Crist lord is and felawe.   1780
     And thus the hihe goddes myht,   **P. ii. 187**
Which was in the virgine alyht,

1756 ff. *margin* O certe necessarium Ade peccatum etc*etera* B   O
felix—redemptorem *om.* SBΔ(AdT) *The note stands at l.* 1746 *in* H₃
1763 wolde he AdB   1772 to] wiþ BT
     1781-1793   Thurgh vertu of his hihe myht
                         Which in Marie was alyht

The mannes Soule hath reconsiled,
Which hadde longe ben exiled.
So stant the feith upon believe,
Withoute which mai non achieve
To gete him Paradis ayein :
Bot this believe is so certein,
So full of grace and of vertu,
That what man clepeth to Jhesu   1790
In clene lif forthwith good dede,
He mai noght faile of hevene mede,
Which taken hath the rihte feith ;
For elles, as the gospel seith,
Salvacion ther mai be non.
And forto preche therupon
Crist bad to hise Apostles alle,
The whos pouer as nou is falle
On ous that ben of holi cherche,
If we the goode dedes werche ;   1800
For feith only sufficeth noght,
Bot if good dede also be wroght.
  Now were it good that thou forthi,
Which thurgh baptesme proprely
Art unto Cristes feith professed,
Be war that thou be noght oppressed
With Anticristes lollardie.
For as the Jwes prophecie

[THE CHRISTIAN FAITH.]

1790

1800   Iacobus. Fides sine operibus mortua est.

Confessor.

Nota hic contra istos qui iam lollardi dicuntur.

> To begge mannes soule aȝein
> And þis belieue is so certein
> So full of grace and of vertu
> That what man clepeþ to Jhesu
> In clene lif forþwiþ good dede
> He mai noght faile of heuene mede   1790*
> So þat it stant vpon belieue
> That euery man mai wel achieue
> Which taken haþ &c. SAdBTΔ

1791 forþwiþ F   forþ wiþ AJ, B   1800 þe goode dede J E . . . B₂
(þo C)   the goodenesse (þe goodnesse) H₁X   goode dedes G
1800 f. *margin* Iacobus &c. *om.* S . . . Δ
   1801 f.   ffor feiþ . bot if þer be good dede
                  Thapostel seiþ is worþ no mede SAdBTΔ
1807 f. *margin* Nota hic—dicuntur *om.* BΔ(AdT), W   Nota contra
istos qui lollardi dicuntur S   Nota contra lollardos C   1808 Iwes F
Iewes AJ, SB

[The Christian
Faith.]

Was set of god for avantage,
Riht so this newe tapinage   1810
Of lollardie goth aboute   **P. ii. 188**
To sette Cristes feith in doute.
The seintz that weren ous tofore,
Be whom the feith was ferst upbore,
Ťhat holi cherche stod relieved,
Thei oghten betre be believed
Than these, whiche that men knowe
Noght holy, thogh thei feigne and blowe
Here lollardie in mennes Ere.
Bot if thou wolt live out of fere,   1820
Such newe lore, I rede, eschuie,
And hold forth riht the weie and suie,
As thine Ancestres dede er this :
So schalt thou noght believe amis.

*Incepit Jhesus fa-
cere et docere.*

   Crist wroghte ferst and after tawhte,
So that the dede his word arawhte ;
He yaf ensample in his persone,
And we the wordes have al one,
Lich to the Tree with leves grene,
Upon the which no fruit is sene.   1830
   The Priest Thoas, which of Minerve

*Nota quod, cum
Anthenor Palladium
Troie a templo Mi-
nerue abstulit, Thoas
ibidem summus sacer-
dos auro corruptus
oculos auertit, et sic
malum quasi non vi-
dens scienter fieri
permisit.*

The temple hadde forto serve,
And the Palladion of Troie
Kepte under keie, for monoie,
Of Anthenor which he hath nome,
Hath soffred Anthenor to come
And the Palladion to stele,
Wherof the worschipe and the wele
Of the Troiens was overthrowe.
Bot Thoas at the same throwe,   1840
Whan Anthenor this Juel tok,   **P. ii. 189**
Wynkende caste awei his lok
For a deceipte and for a wyle :
As he that scholde himself beguile,
He hidde his yhen fro the sihte,
And wende wel that he so mihte

1826 his dede þe BT   his dede his Λ, W   1835 Anthenor
AJ, SB   Antenor F

Excuse his false conscience.
I wot noght if thilke evidence
Nou at this time in here estatz
Excuse mihte the Prelatz,   1850
Knowende hou that the feith discresceth
And alle moral vertu cesseth,
Wherof that thei the keies bere,
Bot yit hem liketh noght to stere
Here gostliche yhe forto se
The world in his adversite;
Thei wol no labour undertake
To kepe that hem is betake.
Crist deide himselve for the feith,
Bot nou our feerfull prelat seith,   1860
'The lif is suete,' and that he kepeth,
So that the feith unholpe slepeth,
And thei unto here ese entenden
And in here lust her lif despenden,
And every man do what him list.
Thus stant this world fulfild of Mist,
That noman seth the rihte weie :
The wardes of the cherche keie
Thurgh mishandlinge ben myswreynt,
The worldes wawe hath welnyh dreynt   1870
The Schip which Peter hath to stiere,   P. ii. 190
The forme is kept, bot the matiere
Transformed is in other wise.
Bot if thei weren gostli wise,
And that the Prelatz weren goode,
As thei be olde daies stode,
It were thanne litel nede
Among the men to taken hiede
Of that thei hieren Pseudo telle,
Which nou is come forto duelle,   1880
To sowe cokkel with the corn,
So that the tilthe is nyh forlorn,
Which Crist sew ferst his oghne hond.

1849 estatz F   estates J   astatz (astates) A, SB   1855 goodly
goodlich) BT   1879 Pseudo telle] Pheudo telle E   Pfeudo t. C
hem telle A   om. T   1883 sew A, S, F   siew B

[The Christian
Faith.]

Nou stant the cockel in the lond,
Wher stod whilom the goode grein,
For the Prelatz nou, as men sein,
Forslowthen that thei scholden tile.
And that I trowe be the skile,
Whan ther is lacke in hem above,
The poeple is stranged to the love   1890
Of trouthe, in cause of ignorance ;
For wher ther is no pourveance
Of liht, men erren in the derke.
Bot if the Prelatz wolden werke
Upon the feith which thei ous teche,
Men scholden noght here weie seche
Withoute liht, as now is used :
Men se the charge aldai refused,
Which holi cherche hath undertake.

Gregorius. Quan-
do Petrus cum Judea,
Andreas cum Achaia,
Thomas cum Yndea,
et Paulus cum gente
venient, quid dicemus
nos moderni, quorum
fossum talentum pro
nichilo computabitur ?

Bot who that wolde ensample take,   1900
Gregoire upon his Omelie   **P. ii. 191**
Ayein the Slouthe of Prelacie
Compleigneth him, and thus he seith :
' Whan Peter, fader of the feith,
At domesdai schal with him bringe
Judeam, which thurgh his prechinge
He wan, and Andrew with Achaie
Schal come his dette forto paie,
And Thomas ek with his beyete
Of Ynde, and Poul the routes grete   1910
Of sondri londes schal presente,
And we fulfild of lond and rente,
Which of this world we holden hiere,
With voide handes schul appiere,
Touchende oure cure spirital,
Which is our charge in special,
I not what thing it mai amonte
Upon thilke ende of oure accompte,
Wher Crist himself is Auditour,

1893 erren] crepen E . . . B2, Λ
1906 f.   Which haþ conuert wiþ his prechinge
                 And whan þat Andrew E . . . B2, Λ
(conuerted . . . teching L   conuer E)   1911 schal] to B

Which takth non hiede of vein honour.' 1920
Thoffice of the Chancellerie
Or of the kinges Tresorie
Ne for the writ ne for the taille
To warant mai noght thanne availe;
The world, which nou so wel we trowe,
Schal make ous thanne bot a mowe:
So passe we withoute mede,
That we non otherwise spede,
Bot as we rede that he spedde,
The which his lordes besant hedde 1930
And therupon gat non encress. **P. ii. 192**
Bot at this time natheles,
What other man his thonk deserve,
The world so lusti is to serve,
That we with him ben all acorded,
And that is wist and wel recorded
Thurghout this Erthe in alle londes
Let knyhtes winne with here hondes,
For oure tunge schal be stille
And stonde upon the fleisshes wille. 1940
It were a travail forto preche
The feith of Crist, as forto teche
The folk Paiene, it wol noght be;
Bot every Prelat holde his See
With al such ese as he mai gete
Of lusti drinke and lusti mete,
Wherof the bodi fat and full
Is unto gostli labour dull
And slowh to handle thilke plowh.
Bot elles we ben swifte ynowh 1950
Toward the worldes Avarice;
And that is as a sacrifice,
Which, after that thapostel seith,
Is openly ayein the feith
Unto thidoles yove and granted:

1923 no writ . . . þe taile A no writ . . . no t. YE . . . B2 to write
. . . to taile B   1925 which now we see and trowe E . . . B2, A
1946 and] of YEC, BT   1952 as a sacrifice] a good s. E . . . B3
1953 þat after E . . . B3

Bot natheles it is nou haunted,
And vertu changed into vice,
So that largesce is Avarice,
In whos chapitre now we trete.

Amans.

Mi fader, this matiere is bete   1960
So fer, that evere whil I live   P. ii. 193
I schal the betre hede yive
Unto miself be many weie :
Bot over this nou wolde I preie
To wite what the branches are
Of Avarice, and hou thei fare
Als wel in love as otherwise.

Confessor.

Mi Sone, and I thee schal devise
In such a manere as thei stonde,
So that thou schalt hem understonde.   1970

1965 the] þo E . . . L   1969 a *om.* BT, W   1970 hem *om.* BT
wel Ad

(Libri Quinti §§ iii–xiii *in sequenti volumine continentur*)

NOTES

PROLOGUS

Latin Verses. i. 1 f. The author acknowledges his incapacity for higher themes, as at the beginning of the first book. The subject of the present work is a less exalted one than that of those which preceded it.

3 f. *Qua tamen* &c. The couplet may be translated, 'Yet in that tongue of Hengist in which the island of Brut sings, I will utter English measures by the aid of Carmentis.'

5 f. *Ossibus ergo carens* &c. That is, ' Let the evil tongue be far away.' The reference is to Prov. xxv. 15, 'A soft tongue breaketh the bone,' taken here in a bad sense : cp. iii. 463 ff.

---

7. 'Moved by the example of these wise men of old.' For this use of 'ensampled' cp. *Traitié*, xv. l. 4,

'Pour essampler les autres du present.'

13. *Who that al* &c. ' If one writes of wisdom only ' : a common form of expression in Gower's French and English both ; see note on *Mirour*, 1244. In English we have ' who that,' ' who so (that) ' or ' what man (that),' sometimes with indic. and sometimes with subjunctive: cp. Prol. 460, 550, i. 383, 481, ii. 88, iii. 971, 2508, &c. See also note on l. 460.

writ, present tense, syncopated form.

16. *if that ye rede*, ' if ye so counsel me,' i. e. if you approve, equivalent to the ' si bon vous sembleroit ' of the *Mirour*, l. 33.

24. The marginal note is wanting in F and S, and may perhaps have been added after the year 1397, when Henry became Duke of Hereford, cp. ' tunc Derbie comiti,' or even later, for in the *Cron. Tripertita* Gower calls him Earl of Derby at the time of his exile, using the same expression as here, 'tunc Derbie comiti.' Caxton, followed by

---

24*—92*. For this variation see the Introduction. The text of B, which is here followed, is as good as any other, but none of the copies which give the passage are thoroughly good in spelling, and the text has in this respect been slightly normalized. A and E are here defective,

Berthelet, gives the following: 'Hic in primis declarat Ioannes Gower quam ob causam presentem libellum composuit et finaliter compleuit, An. regni regis Ric. secundi 16.'

31. That is, compared with what it was in former time: cp. l. 133.

41. *write . . . stode* : subjunctive. For the subjunctive in indirect question cp. ii. 1243, 1943, iii. 708, 771, &c.

43. *as who seith,* i.e. ' as one may say,' a qualification of what follows, a gret partie': the phrase is a common one, e.g. i. 1381, 'as who seith, everemo,' 2794, ii. 696, 'as who seith, ded for feere,' &c.

46. *schewen,* used absolutely, ' set forth their histories.'

52. *a burel clerk,* 'a man of simple learning,' esp. 'a layman'; cp. Chaucer, *Cant. Tales,* B 3145, D 1872: 'burel' was a coarse cloth.

54. *tok,* 'took place,' 'existed': cp. Chaucer, *Troilus,* iv. 1562,

> ' And if so be that pees herafter take.'

So 'prendre' in French, e.g. *Mir.* 831,

> 'Le mariage devoit prendre.'

---

and J, which is the best available MS., has eccentricities of spelling ('Richardus,' 'wyche,' 'hyt,' 'hys,' 'aftur,' 'resonabul,' 'ȝef,' 'be heste,' 'be ginne,' &c.), which make it rather unsuitable as a basis for the text. It will be found however that J and B mutually correct each other to a great extent, and we have also MGRCL as additional witnesses of a respectable character. Thus in regard to some of the variations in spelling from B we have as follows :—

24* bok J   25 belongeþ MC   27* euere JML   31* Preiende G Preiend MCL   36* betyde (betide) GCL   40* be JML   43* f. nyh : syh (sih) JL   47* f. seid : leyd J   49* besinesse J   51* boke JM   52* myhte loke J   53* f. wrytinge : comandinge J   55* herte JMGCL   59* wiþoute GC   62* non JGC   65* handleþ JMGL   66* preye (preie) JMGCL   heuene JMG   69* befalle J   75* bit JMCL   80 longe JML   82* bok J   87* begynneþ (beginneþ) ML   89* f. bok : tok J   92* begynne MCL.

34* ff. A very loosely constructed sentence. It means apparently, 'I consider how it befell, as a thing destined then to come to pass, namely that as on Thames I came rowing by boat &c., I chanced to meet my liege lord.' The disorder in which the clauses are thrown together is a feature which we shall notice elsewhere in our author's style. 'The toun of newe Troye' is of course London, supposed to have been founded by Brut of Troy, whence was derived 'Britain,' the 'insula Bruti' of the opening lines.

52*. *loke,* 'examine': cp. ii. 733, vi. 1959.

65*. There is here a corruption which affects all the existing copies. The various readings are given in the critical notes, and evidently 'outkrong' is that which has most support. I conjecture that the author wrote 'onwrong,' i.e. 'awrong,' which being an unusual word suffered corruption at the hand of the first transcriber, the 'w' being

72. *the god,* so 198, ii. 594 ; cp. 'the vertu,' 116, 'the manhode,' 260, 'the man,' 546, 582, 'The charite,' 319, &c.

74. *ended,* 'continued to the end.'

77 ff. Apparently a reference to the treatise on the duties of a ruler contained in the seventh book : 'I shall make a discourse also with regard to those who are in power, marking the distinction between the virtues and the vices which belong to their office.'

81 ff. 'But as my wit is too small to correct the faults of every one, I send this book unto my own lord Henry of Lancaster ... to be amended at his command.' For 'upon amendement to stonde' cp. ii. 583. The suggestion of amendment at the hands of the author's patron is of course a mere compliment, like that paid by Chaucer to Gower at the conclusion of *Troilus,* but it gives a modest appearance to the general censure.

It is not likely that the expression 'upon amendement' refers to the change made in this part of the text, to which the author would hardly have called attention thus. Also, unless we explain as above, the meaning would seem to be 'as my wit is too small to admonish every one, I send my work as now revised to my own lord Henry of Lancaster,' a much too pointed application of the coming admonitions.

It is hardly needful to add that 'to tellen every man his tale' is not a reference to the *Canterbury Tales,* as some have supposed.

Latin Verses. ii. 2. *vertit in orbe,* 'turns round,' as upon her wheel.

4. Cp. 111 f.

11. 'And thus those regions which were once the strongest fall into

---

mistaken, as it easily might be, for 'tk': cp. Chaucer, *H. of Fame,* ii. 403, where 'tokne' is apparently a corruption of 'towne.'

66*. *the hevene king,* 'the king of hevene.' Gower regularly writes the final 'e' in 'hevene,' 'evene,' 'evere,' 'nevere,' &c. The preceding syllable is of course syncopated in pronunciation.

69*. *what befalle,* 'whatsoever may befall': cp. iii. 325, 'what it were.'

75*. *bit,* i. e. 'biddeth.'

85*. The true reading is probably 'listen pleie,' which is preferable both as regards form and construction: cp. iv. 3147, 'whan the wommen listen pleie.' The readings are as follows: 'listen pleye' J, 'lusten pleie' M, 'luste pley' B₂; the rest mostly 'lust to pleye.' The verb seems usually to be followed by a preposition when used impersonally, as i. 147, 1403, and otherwise more generally not, as i. 2741, iv. 3147, but there are exceptions both ways, e. g. iv. 907 and iii. 111, iv. 3187.

90*. Cp. 54 ff.

92*. *for to newe.* This is the reading of the better MSS., and 'schewe' is probably the correction of a copyist who did not understand it. The word 'newe' means here 'produce,' but in l. 59 'neweth' is intransitive and means 'comes into being.'

decay throughout the world, and have no centre of rest there.' (The first 'que' is the relative, for 'quae.') It is possible however that 'per orbem' may refer again to Fortune's wheel, cp. 138 ff., where the sense of this couplet seems to be expressed, and in that case the meaning is, 'fall into decay as they turn upon the wheel.'

116. *the vertu* : for this French use of the article, which is often found in Gower, see note on l. 72.

122 ff. 'And in witness of that I take the common voice of every land, which may not lie.' This appeal to the common voice, the 'commune dictum,' is characteristic of our author, who repeats the proverb 'Vox populi vox dei' several times in various forms, e. g. *Mirour*, 12725. For the use of 'that' in such expressions cp. l. 907, and iv. 2040.

133. *to loke* &c., 'when we look on all sides': cp. 31, i. 1060, 2278, &c.

139. *blinde fortune*. 'Fortune' must here be taken as a proper name, and hence the definite form of adjective : cp. i. 3396, 'wyse Peronelle,' ii. 588, 2721, 'of grete Rome,' ii. 2304, 'false Nessus,' iii. 2100, 'false Egiste,' &c.

143. *upon a weer*, i. e. in doubt or distress : cp. iii. 1148, and Chaucer, *House of Fame*, 979,

'Tho gan I wexen in a wer.'

144 ff. 'And especially if the power of the rulers of the world be not kept upright by good counsel in such wise that' &c.

152. *heved*, always a monosyllable in the metre : the word also appears as 'hefd' i. 199, and frequently as 'hed.'

154. *her trowthe allowe*, 'approve of their loyalty,' i.e. accept it.

155. 'And welcome them with all his heart.' For the position of the conjunction cp. 521, 756, 759, 1014, i. 854, 863, &c., and note on *Mirour*, 415. Mr. Liddell points out to me that the same usage occurs frequently in the ME. Palladius.

156 (margin). The quotation is from Ecclus. xxxii. 24, 'Fili, sine consilio nihil facias.' This book is often cited as Solomon in the *Mirour*.

162. A truce with both France and Scotland was made for three years in 1389, but peace was not finally concluded till 1396.

166 f. Cp. *Praise of Peace*, 190.

172. *at alle assaies*, 'in every way': cp. ii. 2447.

Latin Verses. iii. 1. *Iohannes*: St. John the Evangelist, who is mentioned either as the teacher of brotherly love or because his Gospel contains the exhortations to St. Peter, 'Feed my sheep,' 'Feed my lambs.'

2. *ista*, 'this.'

3. *bina virtute*, perhaps charity and chastity, cp. 464 ff.

4. *inculta*, nominative in spite of metre, so *auaricia* in l. 8.

8. *tepente*, 'being lukewarm,' that is, held in a lukewarm manner.

196 (margin). *Roberti Gibbonensis*, Robert of Geneva, elected pope in opposition to Urban VI, under the title of Clement VII.

198. *the god*, see note on l. 72.

204. *Simon*, i. e. Simon Magus, whence simony has its name : cp.
442 ff., *Mirour*, 18451 ff., and *Vox Clamantis*, iii. 249, 1217, &c.

207 ff. The reference is to Lombard bankers employed as inter-
mediaries in obtaining Church preferment. The 'letter' referred to is
the papal provision, or perhaps the letter of request addressed to the
pope in favour of a particular person : cp. *Vox Clam.* iii. 1375 f.,

> ' Littera dum Regis papales supplicat aures,
> Simon et est medius, vngat vt ipse manus.'

210. *provende*, equivalent to prebend, and in fact 'prebende' is
a var. reading here. Littré quotes from Wace,

> ' Cil me dona et Diez li rende
> À Baiex une provende,'

and from Rutebeuf,

> ' Qui argent porte a Rome, assés tot provende a.'

212. ' The authority of the Church' (symbolized by the key) ' did not
then lie at the mercy of armed bands or depend upon the issue of
battle.' For 'brigantaille,' meaning bands of irregular troops, cp.
Mir. 18675.

218. *defence*, ' prohibition': cp. iv. 1026, v. 1710, and Chaucer, *Troil.*
iii. 138, 'if that I breke your defence.'

220. ' was then no charge of theirs,' i. e. did not come under their
authority: 'baillie' means the charge or government of a thing, as
Trait. xi. 19, ' Le duc q'ot lors Ravenne en sa baillie,' hence a thing
placed in a person's charge.

221. *The vein honour*: the definite form is rather less regularly
used by Gower in adjectives taken from French than in others, e. g. iii.
889, ' For with here fals compassement'; but on the other hand,
i. 864, ' the pleine cas,' ii. 412, ' And thurgh his false tunge endited,' and
824, ' This false knyht upon delay.'

246. *is went*: cp. iii. 878 and Chaucer, *Cant. Tales*, E 1013, F 567.

247. *here lawe positif*: the 'lex positiva' is that which is not
morally binding in itself, but only so because imposed by (eccle-
siastical) authority: cp. *Vox Clam.* iii. 227 ff. This is naturally the
sphere within which Church dispensations of all kinds take effect.

248. *Hath set*. Apparently 'set' is intransitive, ' Since their positive
law hath set itself to make,' &c. There is no good authority for reading ' hire.'

252. There is hardly another instance of 'but' for 'bot' in F, and the
form 'right' for 'riht' in the preceding line is very unusual.

260. *the manhode*, i.e. human nature: see note on l. 72. For 'thenkth'
see note on 461.

263. *withholde*, 'retained as her servant.'

268. *in the point* &c., i. e. so soon as it is collected. The allusion is
to the circumstances of the campaign of the Bishop of Norwich in

1385 ; cp. *Vox Clam.* iii. 373 (margin), and see Froissart (ed. Letten-hove), vol. x. p. 207.

278. *That scholde be* &c., i. e. the papacy, which by reason of the schism has become a cause of war and strife.

289. *Gregoire.* The reference is to such passages as *Regula Pastoralis,* i. cap. 8, 9. The quotation in the margin at l. 298 is loosely taken from the Homilies on the Gospel (Migne, *Patrol.* vol. 76. p. 1128), 'Mercenarius quippe est qui locum quidem pastoris tenet, sed lucra animarum non quaerit : terrenis commodis inhiat, honore praelationis gaudet, temporalibus lucris pascitur, impensa sibi ab hominibus reverentia laetatur.' The idea expressed by 'non vt prosint sed vt presint' often occurs in Gregory's writings, e.g. *Reg. Past.* ii. cap. 6, 'nec praeesse se hominibus gaudent sed prodesse.'

299. *manie* : the final 'e' counts as a syllable and the preceding vowel is absorbed ; see note on 323 : but 'many' is also used as the plural.

305. Cp. *Vox Clam.* iii. 1271, 'In cathedram Moysi nunc ascendunt Pharisei,' and see *Rom. de la Rose,* 11809 ff. (ed. Méon), English version, 6889 ff.

311. *is noght foryete,* an impersonal use, 'there is no forgetting' : cp. 338.

323. Here 'studie' is reduced by elision to the value of a monosyllable: see note on *Mirour,* 296. The rule applies to substantives like 'accidie,' 'Mercurie,' 'chirie,' adjectives like 'manie' (l. 299), and verbs like 'studie,' 'carie,' 'tarie.'

329. *If Ethna brenne* &c. What is meant is the fire of Envy, which is often compared to that of Etna, ii. 20, 2337, &c.

338 f. The verb is used impersonally, 'there is cause for us all to be sorry.'

348. 'it causeth this new sect to be brought in.' The subject must be supplied from the previous clause.

366 f. That is, the various claimants to the papacy are supported in various lands by national partiality or interest.

380 f. 'They use no other reasoning than this as to the peril of religion.'

383. *his world,* i. e. his fortune, cp. 1081, i. 178, &c.

388 f. That is, the right cause has no defence but in the rule of personal inclination and interest, the principle expressed by 'Where I love, there I hold.'

407 ff. This is a charge against those who hold office in the Church of deliberately throwing temptation in the way of their people, in order to profit by the fines which may be imposed for breaches of morality and discipline. The meaning is fully illustrated by parallel passages in the *Mirour de l'omme,* 20161 ff., and the *Vox Clamantis,* iii. 195 ; cp. Chaucer, *Pers. Tale,* 721. The sentence here is a little disorderly and therefore obscure : 'Men say that they drive forth their flock from the smooth meadow into the briars, because they wish to seize and by such

ill-treatment take away the wool which shall remain upon the thorns, torn out by the briars,' &c. The archdeacon's court is chiefly referred to.

416. *chalk for chese,* cp. ii. 2346: it is a proverbial expression still current.

430. 'We see the lot drawn amiss': for 'merel' cp. *Mir.* 23496.

434. Hebr. v. 4.

452. *in audience,* 'in public assembly' : cp. ii. 2556.

454. *a chirie feire,* taken as an emblem of delights which are transitory: cp. vi. 890 f.,

> 'And that endureth bot a throwe,
> Riht as it were a cherie feste.'

460. *understode,* past subj. with indefinite sense: cp. i. 383, ii. 88, iii. 971, iv. 2597, 2728, vi. 1474. 'Whoso understood their words, to him it seems likely,' &c., instead of 'to him it would seem likely'; cp. l. 520.

461. The distinction between 'thinke' and 'thenke' is completely lost in Gower's usage: 'thenke' is the regular form for both, but 'thinke' is admitted equally for both in rhyme, as v. 213, 254.

480. 'For fear that (On the chance that) I may say wrong.' The subject is a delicate one and the author shows similar caution when dealing with it in the *Mirour.*

492. *as of,* 'as regards' : cp. i. 557, iii. 1479, &c.

Latin Verses. iv. 4. *velle,* used as a noun, 'will' : so 'de puro velle' in the lines at the beginning of the second book.

509 f. 'Which with great difficulty man shall restrain, if he shall restrain it ever.'

521. For the position of 'and' see note on 155.

525. *stonde upon* : cp. 214.

529. *som men* : 'som' is uninflected in this expression: on the other hand we have 'somme clerkes,' l. 355.

546. *the man,* so 582 : see note on 72.

550 f. 'If any one thinks otherwise, look at the people of Israel' : 'Behold' is 2nd sing. imperative. The unusual form 'Irael' is given by the best MSS. here and elsewhere, and we must suppose that it proceeds from the author.

558. *stonde full* : perhaps a reference to 503 ff., or a metaphor from the tides.

567 (margin). The quotation is from *Cons. Phil.* ii. Pr. 4 : 'Quam multis amaritudinibus humanae felicitatis dulcedo respersa est.' The constant references to Fortune and her wheel may probably be suggested by Boethius, e. g. ii. Pr. 1.

578. i. e. till the end of all things.

585 ff. This vision of Nebuchadnezzar, which our author takes as his guide to universal history, is made the subject of illustration in those MSS. which have miniatures at or near the beginning of the *Confessio Amantis.*

618. *Fel doun*: cp. iii. 2492, 'That have I herd the gospell seith.'

668. *hol*: see note on 683.

676. 'And he kept himself in this condition undisturbed,' the subject being supplied from l. 671, 'Was in that kinges time tho.' For omission of pronoun cp. Prol. 348, i. 1895, 2083, 2462, &c. However, the fall of the Empire took place not in the reign of Nebuchadnezzar but of Belshazzar (see l. 685).

683. Here and in 693 the best MSS. have 'put' for 'putte,' and this entire suppression of the inflexional syllable in cases where it is lost to the metre by elision is sufficiently well-attested to justify us in accepting it as an occasional practice of the author, both in the case of verbs and adjectives ; cp. 668, 739, &c. It is especially common with this particular verb, e.g. i. 1578, 1807, 3213, ii. 93, 1021, &c., where 'put' is used for infinitive as well as for the preterite. Much more rarely in cases where there is no elision, as i. 732. On the other hand, we have 'putte' pret. before an elision, l. 1069, i. 2797, 'pute' inf. i. 462, iv. 1641.

702. In the marginal summary here F gives 'Imparatoris,' and sometimes in other places where the word is fully written, as i. 1417, ii. 593, 2506, 3201. However, 'Imperator' is also found in various places of the same MS., as vii. 2416, and the contracted form 'Impator' has in this edition been written out so.

725. *Of that honour which tok*, i. e. 'of such honour that he took.'

738. *so vileins*: a clear case of French plural of the adjective, used here for the sake of the rhyme.

739. *fals*: see notes on 221, 683.

745 ff. It is hardly necessary to point out that our author's history is here incorrect. Charlemagne was not called in against the Emperor Leo, who died in the year before he was born, but against the Lombards by Adrian I, and then against the rebellious citizens of Rome by Leo III, on which latter occasion he received the imperial crown.

756. *Of Rome and*: cp. ll. 759, 766, and note on 155.

761. *doth restore*, i. e. 'causeth to be restored.'

772 ff. Here again the story is historically inaccurate, but it is not worth while to set it straight.

786 ff. The meaning seems to be, 'But this after all is what we might expect, for prosperity (they say) seldom endures.'

795. *hath no felawe*, 'hath no supporter or champion': cp. *Praise of Peace*, 266, 'And in this wise hath charite no brother.'

809. The punctuation follows F.

823. *expondeth*. This form occurs also in ll. 663, 873, as a reading of F. The French terminations '-on,' '-oun,' had the same sound and rhymed together, and the same is true of '-ance,' '-aunce.' Probably on the same principle therefore 'expondeth' may stand for 'expoundeth,' and rhyme with 'foundeth': cp. viii. 235 f. On the other hand, in i. 2867 we have expo*u*nde, founde. It may be noted that 'exponde' is the form used in the French works, e. g. *Mir.* 22192, *Trait.* xi. 20, where it rhymes with *Rosemonde, responde, immonde.* As a rule in the *Mirour* this class of words is given without 'u,' but in one stanza we have 'responde,' 'monde,' 'blo*u*nde' in rhyme together, 8681 ff.

836. *Cit*: this is the true reading; the word occurs also *Mir.* 7197.

843. *now with that beforn*, 'the present with the past,' 'now' being used as a substantive.

850. *the sothe seie*: this is the reading of the third recension; the others have 'the soth schal seie.' Either text is admissible, for 'soth' is used as a substantive, but 'the sothe' is usually preferred, as in l. 834, and i. 981, iii. 765.

858. Cp. ii. 3490.

881. *writ*: syncopated present, 'writeth.' The reference is to 1 Cor. x. 11.

891. *Statue*: a dissyllable in Gower and Chaucer (equivalent to 'statwe'), and here reduced to one syllable by elision : cp. *Cant. Tales,* A. 975. The longer form 'stature' occurs vi. 1524.

900. *these clerkes* : demonstrative for definite article, as in French ; cp. i. 608, and see note on *Mir.* 301.

905. See l. 965. Perhaps here 'cause of' means 'because of,' as 'whos cause' for 'because of which' 1040 ; but I suspect rather an inversion of order, for 'Man is cause of al this wo.'

907. *that in tokne*, cp. 122.

910 ff. This matter of the corruption of all creation through man's fall is discussed at length both in the *Mirour*, 26605 ff., and in the *Vox Clamantis*, vii. 509 ff.

945 ff. This is one of Gower's favourite citations : it occurs also *Mir.* 26869, *Vox Clam.* vii. 639. It is quoted here from *Moralia*, vi. 16 (Migne, *Patr.* vol. 75, p. 740) : 'Homo itaque, quia habet commune esse cum lapidibus, vivere cum arboribus, sentire cum animalibus, discernere cum angelis, recte nomine universitatis exprimitur.' In the *Mirour* it is given as from the Homilies ; see *Hom. in Ev.* xxix. 2. The passage is also quoted in the *Roman de la Rose*, 19246 ff. (ed. Méon),

> 'Il a son estre avec les pierres,
> Et vit avec les herbes drues,
> Et sent avec les bestes mues,' &c.

947. *the lasse world*, i.e. a microcosm : cp. *Vox Clam.* vii. 645,

> 'Sic minor est mundus homo, qui fert singula solus.'

The saying is attributed to Aristotle in *Mirour*, 26929.

953. That is, the stones have existence and so hath he, this being the only point in common.

955. *as telleth the clergie*, 'as learning informs us.'

975. *The which*, resumed by 'He' in 978 : *for*, i.e. 'since.'

979. That is, the·opposite elements in his constitution ('complexioun') are so much at variance with one another.

985. 'Without separation of parts.'

**   H h

995. *also*, a repetition of 'yit over this,' 991.

1013. *sende*, pret., cp. i. 851, 992, 1452, &c. (but 'sente' in rhyme i. 3095, ii. 613, v. 1072), so 'bende' ii. 2235.

1047. That is, there can be no conciliation of the discord.

1055 ff. Cp. Ovid, *Fasti*, ii. 83 ff.

1066. *commun*: this form, as well as 'commune,' occurs in the *Mirour*.

1085. *The horse side*: cp. i. 1536, 2301, &c.

After 1088 the Sidney Coll. MS. (Δ) has the following lines,

> 'So were it gode at þis tide
> þat eueri man vpon his side
> besowt and preied for þe pes
> wiche is þe cause of al encres
> of worschep and of werldis welþe
> of hertis rest of soule helþe
> withouten pes stant no þing gode
> forthi to crist wiche sched his blode
> for pes beseketh alle men
> Amen amen amen amen.'

These were printed by Caxton, and after him by Berthelet, with some slight variations of spelling, and the reading 'and soules helthe' for 'of soule helþe.' No other MS. contains them, so far as I know, except Hatton 51, which is copied from Caxton's edition. If we read 'So were it good as at þis tide,' and correct the spelling throughout, the lines will be such as Gower might have written, and I rather suspect that they may have been contained in the Stafford MS. (S), to which Δ is nearly allied. S has lost a leaf here, on which ample room for them could have been found, the number of lines missing being only 156, while the number for a full leaf is 184. The authority of S would be conclusive in their favour.

LIB. I.

After setting forth in the Prologue the evils of the existing state of society and tracing them for the most part to lack of love and concord between man and man, the author now deliberately renounces the task of setting right the balance of the world, an undertaking which he has not shrunk from in former years, but recognizes now as too great for his strength. He proposes to change the style of his writings and to deal with something which all may understand, with that emotion of love which Nature has implanted both in man and beast, which no one is able to keep within rule or measure, and which seems to be under the dominion of blind chance, like the gifts of fortune.

Latin Verses. i. 7 f. Cp. the lines 'Est amor in glosa pax bellica, lis pietosa,' &c., which follow the *Traitié*.

10. *of thing is*, i.e. 'of thing which is': cp. ii. 1393, 'Withinne a Schip was stiereles,' so iii. 219, v. 298 &c., and *Mirour*, 16956.

21. *natheles*: as in Prol. 36, this seems to mean here 'moreover,' or perhaps 'in truth,' rather than 'nevertheless.'

37. That is, 'Wheresoever it pleases him to set himself,' 'him' serving a double function.

50. *went* : present tense, 'goes.'

62. *I am miselven* &c. Note, however, that the author guards himself in the margin with 'quasi in persona aliorum, quos amor alligat, fingens se auctor esse Amantem.'

88. *jolif wo*, cp. 'le jolif mal sanz cure,' *Bal.* xiii. 24.

98 ff. The construction is broken off, and then resumed in a new form : cp. i. 2948, iii. 1595, 2610, iv. 3201, v. 1043, 1339, &c.

116. *other* : this must be regarded as a legitimate plural form beside 'othre': cp. iv. 1183, and see Morsbach, *Schriftsprache*, p. 23. On the other hand, 'othre' is sometimes used as singular, e.g. l. 481, ii. 283.

178. *Mi world*, i.e. ' my fortune': cp. Prol. 383.

196. The idea of 'Genius' is taken from the *Roman de la Rose*, where Genius is the priest of Nature, ' Qui célébroit en sa chapelle,' and she confesses to him, 16487 ff. (ed. Méon).

205. *Benedicite*: the regular beginning of a confessor's address to his penitent.

213. Cp. *Rom. de la Rose*, 16927 f. (of Nature confessing to Genius),

'Qui dit par grant dévocion
En plorant sa confession.'

225. *my schrifte oppose*, 'question me as to my confession,' cp. the use of ' opponere ' in the margin here and 299, 708, &c.

232. *tome*. This is Gower's usual form of combination where the accent is to be thrown on the preposition. We have also ' byme,' ii. 2016, &c., tome, l. 294, ii. 3160, &c., ' untome,' iii. 99, ' tothe,' iv. 1875. In such cases, as is seen below, l. 294, the final syllable becomes weak and subject to elision.

279. *remene*, ' bring back,' from Fr. ' remener': cp. ' demenen.'

299 ff. See note on *Mir*. 16597.

320. The punctuation is here determined by that of F, which has a stop after ' love.' Otherwise the meaning might be, ' And doth great mischief to love,' the conjunction being transposed, as often.

333 ff. The story is from Ovid, *Metam.* iii. 138 ff.

350. *cam ride*. For this use of the infin. see *New Engl. Dict.*, ' come,' B. i. 3. f. : so ' thei comen ryde,' iv. 1307.

367. For the use of 'hire' as a dissyllable in the verse, cp. 872, 1667 : on the other hand, 884, 887, 939, 1673, &c.

383. That is, if a man gave heed to the matter, he would see that it was, &c. : cp. Prol. 460.

389. Ovid, *Metam.* iv. 772 ff. This, however, is not Gower's only authority, for he mentions details, as for example the names of Medusa's

sisters, which are not given by Ovid. The confusion which we find here between the Graeae and the Gorgons appears in Boccaccio, *De Gen. Deorum*, x. 10, which possibly our author may have seen ; but I suspect he had some other authority. The names which Gower gives as Stellibon and Suriale are properly Stheno (Stennio in Boccaccio) and Euryale.

422. *Mercurie* : see note on Prol. 323. Mercury's sword is not mentioned either by Ovid or Boccaccio.

431. *gan enbrace*, 'placed on his arm ' ; see the quotations in *New Engl. Dict.* under 'embrace *v.* 1,' e.g. *K. Alis.* 6651, ' His scheld enbraceth Antiocus.'

452. *To tarie with*, 'with which to vex ' : cp. i. 2172, ii. 283, 1081, v. 925, &c., and *Cant. Tales*, F 471, 'To hele with youre hurtes hastily.'

463 ff. Cp. *Mirour*, 15253. The legend is founded upon Psalm lviii. 4 f. (*Vulg.* lvii. 5 f.), ' Furor illis secundum similitudinem serpentis ; sicut aspidis surdae et obturantis aures suas, quae non exaudiet vocem incantantium,' &c. (Hence the genitive form ' Aspidis ' in our author.) The moral application is connected with the Gospel precept, ' Be ye wise as serpents,' to which reference is made in the *Mirour*. The serpent's method of stopping his ears was perhaps first suggested by Augustine, *In Ps.* lvii, who is followed by Isid. *Etym.* xii. 4, but there is nothing in these authorities about the carbuncle.

481. *an othre thing* : for 'othre' cp. i. 1496, ii. 511.

who that recordeth, ' if a man calls it to mind ' : see note on Prol. 13.

483. *tale of Troie*, i. e. Guido di Colonna, *Hist. Troiana*, lib. 32 (02, ed. Argent. 1494), which is here followed. Benoît mentions the Sirens, but does not describe their form nor state that Ulysses stopped his men's ears.

492 ff. This manner of piling up consecutive clauses is observable in the author's French style, and the use of relatives like ' wherof,' 'which' (l. 771) to introduce them is parallel to that of 'Dont,' ' Par quoy,' &c. in the French : e.g. *Mir.* 219 ff.,

> ' Et tant luy fist plesant desport,
> Dont il fuist tant enamouré,
> Que sur sa fille,' &c.

Cp. *Mir.* 681.

527. ' plus quam mille ex eis interfecimus,' Guido, *Hist. Troi.*, lib. 32.

532. *hiere*, subjunctive : cp. ii. 252, iii. 665, &c.

574. *othre thing* : plural no doubt, but we have also ' othre (other) thinges,' i. 2464, iv. 1183.

Latin Verses. v. i. *que Leone*. This position of 'que' is quite common in our author's Latin writings : see the lines after the *Praise of Peace*, ll. 10, 49, 50, &c.

8. *sub latitante*, 'lurking underneath,' ' sub ' being an adverb. The best copies have the words separate.

577. *applied*, ' assigned ' ; cp. iv. 2607, v. 913, vii. 1100.

585. *seid*, 'named.'

595. *feigneth conscience*, that is, makes pretence as to his feeling, or state of mind, ('As thogh it were al innocence '): cp. iii. 1504, 'Mi conscience I woll noght hyde.' The explanation suggested in the *New Engl. Dict.* that ' conscience' stands for ' conscientiousness ' or ' rightful dealing,' will hardly do, and the word does not seem to be used early in this sense.

599. *the vein astat*: see note on Prol. 221.

608. *these ordres*, i. e. ' the orders ' (of religion) : so ' these clerkes,' Prol. 900.

where he duelleth, that is, the hypocrite, standing for Hypocrisy in general.

623. *religioun*, the members of the religious orders, as distinguished from the rest of the clergy.

626. *It scheweth*, ' it appears ' : cp. Prol. 834.

636. *devolte apparantie* : the words are pure French, and the French feminine form is as naturally used for the adjective, as in the ' seinte apparantie ' of *Mir.* 1124. We cannot apply the English rule of the definite adjective to such combinations as this : cp. note on Prol. 221. However, ' devoute ' in l. 669 seems to be the plural form.

637. *set*, present tense : so ll. 650, 707, &c.

648. *these othre seculers*, 'the men of the world also.'

650. ' He makes no reckoning in his account.'

695. *As he which* &c.; that is simply, 'feigning to be sick,' so iv. 1833, 'As he who feigneth to be wod ' ; cp. vii. 3955. The expression ' as he which,' ' as sche which,' is very commonly used by Gower in this sense ; cp. i. 925, 1640, &c., and *Mir.* 27942, ' Comme cil q'est tout puissant,' ' being all-powerful.'

698. Cp. iv. 1180, 'And thus mi contienance I pike.' It means ' he makes many a pretence.'

709. *Entamed*, 'wounded': used in a similar moral sense in *Mir.* 25161, ' Car Covoitise les entame.'

713. *As forto feigne*, i. e. ' as regards feigning': so l. 723, ' as to my ladi diere.'

718 ff. For the form of sentence, which is a favourite one with our author in all his three languages, but especially perhaps in Latin, cp. *Mirour*, 18589 ff.,

> ' Unques le corps du sainte Heleine
> Serchant la croix tant ne se peine,
> Qe nous ovesque nostre Court,
> Assetz n'y mettons plus du peine,' &c.

Vox Clam. i. 263 ff.,

> ' In Colchos tauri, quos vicit dextra Iasonis,
> Non ita sulphureis ignibus ora fremunt,
> Quin magis igne boues isti,' &c.

So also *Bal.* vii. 23, xviii. 8, xxx. 10 ; *Vox Clam.* i. 355, 449, 499, &c.; *Conf. Am.* i. 1259, 1319, &c.

733. 'For I shall not declare this in my defence, that' &c.; a somewhat different use of the word from that which we find in the quotations given by the *New Engl. Dict.*, 'Excuse *v.*' i. 1. d.

761 ff. The story of Mundus and Paulina is historical, related by Josephus, *Ant.* xviii. 66 ff., and after him by Hegesippus, ii. 4, from whom it was taken by Vincent of Beauvais, *Spec. Hist.* vii. 4, and also doubtless, directly or indirectly, by Gower. It is told in verse by Godfrey of Viterbo, *Pantheon*, xv, but it is certain that this was not Gower's source.

771. *Which*: for this use of the relative in a consecutive clause, which is very common in our author's style, see note on 492, and cp. 801.

773. *thilke bore frele kinde.* Human nature is described as frail from birth, and by its weakness causing blindness of the heart.

776 f. 'And such were the fortunes of this tale of which I would speak,' i. e. this was the passion which determined its course.

816. *his thonk pourchace*, 'win their gratitude towards himself.'

833. 'In which a false heart was concealed,' an instance of inverted order, for which cp. ii. 565,

> 'Whiche as he wot is puyson inne.'

872. *hire*, cp. 367.

894. *which stod thanne upon believe*, 'which then was thought to be possible.'

938. *homward*, i. e. 'goes towards home'; cp. iii. 1021, 2451.

940 ff. In Hegesippus the address is as follows : ' Beata Paulina concubitu dei. Magnus deus Anubis cuius tu accepisti mysteria. Sed disce te sicut diis ita et hominibus non negare, quibus dii tribuant quod tu negaveras : quia nec formas suas dare nobis nec nomina dedignantur. Ecce ad sacra sua deus Anubis vocavit et Mundum, ut tibi iungeret. Quid tibi profuit duritia tua, nisi ut te xx milium quae obtuleram defraudaret compendio? Imitare deos indulgentiores, qui nobis sine pretio tribuunt quod abs te magno pretio impetrari nequitum est. Quod si te humana offendunt vocabula, Anubem me vocari placuit, et nominis huius gratia effectum iuvit.' It must be allowed that our author has improved upon this offensive prolixity.

987. *sche may ther noght*, 'she hath no power in the matter': cp. 725, 'there I lye noght.'

1006. *Citezeine.* Gower uses several of these feminine forms of substantives. Besides ' citezeine' we have cousine, ii. 1201, capiteine, v. 1972, enemie, v. 6753, anemie, viii. 1355 (all of which also occur in the *Mirour*), and occasionally adjectives, as 'veine' (gloire), i. 2677 ff., (vertu) ' sovereine,' ii. 3507, 'seinte' (charite), iv. 964, 'soleine,' v. 1971, and probably 'divine,' ii. 3243, 'gentile,' viii. 2294.

1013 ff. 'questioni subicit, confessos necat.' Our author here expands his original.

1040. *Whos cause*, 'for the sake of which.'

1051. *put*, pres. tense, 'putteth.'

1067. *menable*, 'fit to guide,' the ship; cp. ii. 1123, 'A wynd menable fro the londe.' The word occurs several times in our author's French, as *Mirour*, 3676, 11882, 17392. The meaning in English is not always the same, the word being, like others of this form, sometimes active and sometimes passive : cp. 'deceivable' (ii. 1698, 2202). Here and in the passage quoted the meaning is 'leading,' 'fit to guide': elsewhere it stands for 'easily led,' 'apt to be guided,' as in iii. 390 and the French examples.

1068. 'tobreken' is the reading of JH₁XGL, SBΔ, W, and is evidently required by the sense.

1077 ff. Here Gower mainly follows Benoît de Sainte-More (*Roman de Troie*, 25620 ff.), but he was of course acquainted also with Guido (*Historia Troiana*, lib. 27: in 5, ed. Argent. 1494). The name Epius is from Benoît, for Guido has 'Apius': on the other hand, Guido and not Benoît describes the horse as made of brass. In speaking of the discussion about pulling down a portion of the walls, and of the walls themselves as built by Neptune, 1146, 1152 ff., our author is certainly drawing from Benoît. Some points of the story and many details are original.

Of hem that &c., 'As regards those who have such deceit in their hearts,' i. e. hypocrites : cp. 956, 'O derke ypocrisie.'

1102. The MS. can hardly be right in punctuating after 'Togedre.'

1129 f. So Lydgate, perhaps with this passage in his mind,

'Makynge a colour of devocion
    Through holynesse under ypocrisie.'
                    Tale of Troye, bk. iv.

1133. *trapped.* 'In quo construentur quedam clausure sic artificiose composite, quod' &c. *Hist. Troiana*, m 4 v⁰. Gower does not say that men were contained within, though this is stated by his authorities, of whom Benoît places Sinon inside the horse, while Guido finds room there for a thousand armed men. The 'twelve' wheels seem to be due to Gower, as also the picturesque touch, 'And goth glistrende ayein the Sunne.'

1146 ff. Cp. *Roman de Troie*, 25814 ff. (ed. Joly),

'Et quant ço virent Troien,
    Conseil pristrent que des terralz
    Abatroient les granz muralz,
    Les biax, les granz, que Neptunus
    Ot fet, M. anz aveit et plus,
    Et qu' Apollo ot dedié.'

1165. *crossen seil*, 'set their sails across (the mast).'

1172. *Synon*. The reading of F may be right, for 'Simon' is the form of the name given in many copies of Guido. Here however the whole of the second recension and the better copies of the first give 'Synon,' and a copyist's alteration would be towards the more familiar name.

1225. *lok*. In l. 1703 we have 'loke' for the imperative, which must be regarded as more strictly correct.

Latin Verses. vi. 1 f. *olle Fictilis ad cacabum*, a proverb derived from Ecclus. xiii. 3, 'Quid communicabit cacabus ad ollam? quando enim se colliserint confringetur.'
6. The elephant was supposed to have no joints.

1262 f. *That I . . . ne bowe more*. For the form of expression see note on 718. Pauli makes the text here quite unintelligible by reproducing an error of Berthelet's edition and adding to it another of his own.
1293. A proverbial expression like that in vi. 447, 'For selden get a domb man lond.'
1328. *retenue*, 'engagement of service': cp. *Bal*. viii. 17, .

'Q'a vous servir j'ai fait ma retenue.'

1354. *the decerte Of buxomnesse*, i. e. 'the service of obedience.' For both the spelling and meaning of 'decerte' cp. *Mir*. 10194,

'Qe ja ne quiert ou gaign ou perte
Du siecle avoir pour sa decerte.'

1407 ff. The 'Tale of Florent' is essentially the same as Chaucer's 'Wife of Bath's Tale,' but the details are in many ways different. According to Chaucer the hero of the adventure is a knight of Arthur's court and the occasion of his trouble a much less creditable one than in the case of Florent. In Chaucer's tale the knight sees a fairy dance of ladies in the forest before he meets his repulsive deliverer, and she gets from him a promise that he will grant her next request if it lies in his power, the demand of marriage being put off until after the question has been successfully solved by her assistance. The rather unseasonable lectures on gentilesse, poverty, and old age are not introduced by Gower. On the other hand, Chaucer's alternative, 'Will you have me old and ugly but a faithful wife, or young and fair with the attendant risks?' is more pointed and satisfactory than the corresponding feature in Gower's tale. Finally, Chaucer has nothing about the enchantment by which the lady had been transformed.

It is tolerably certain that neither borrowed the story from the other, though there are a few touches of minute resemblance which may suggest that one was acquainted with the other's rendering of it: see ll. 1587, 1727.

We cannot point to the precise original of either; but a very similar story is found in *The Weddynge of Sir Gawene and Dame Ragnell*, published in the collection of poems relating to Gawain edited by Sir F. Madden (Bannatyne Club, 1839) and contained in MS. Rawlinson C. 86. In this ballad Arthur's life is spared by a strange knight who meets him unarmed in the forest, on condition of answering his question, 'What do women love best,' at the end of twelve months. He is assisted by Dame Ragnell, who demands in return to be married to

Sir Gawain. Sir Gawain accepts the proposal from loyalty to his lord, and the rest is much as in Gower's version. It should be noted that the alternative of day or night appears in the ballad and was a feature of the original story, which Chaucer altered.

The Percy fragment of *The Marriage of Sir Gawain*, also printed in Sir F. Madden's volume, is the same story as we have in the other ballad. The name Florent and that of the Emperor Claudius are probably due to Gower, who is apt to attach to his stories names of his own choosing: cp. Lucius and Dionys (*Conf. Am.* v. 7124*, *Mir.* 7101).

Shakespeare refers to Gower's story in the line,

> ' Be she as foul as was Florentius' love.'
> *Tam. of the Shr.* i. 2. 69.

1427. *his oghne hondes*: cp. iii. 2011, 2142 ; v. 1884, 5455 ('seide his oghne mouth ').

1509. *schape unto the lere*, 'prepared for the loss' (OE. lyre).

1521. *par aventure*, or ' per aventure ' as given by J. The former of the two words is as usual contracted in F.

1536. *his horse heved*, 'his horse's head ' : cp. Prol. 1085, iv. 1357, &c. The word 'heved,' also written 'hefd,' 'hed,' is a monosyllable as regards the metre.

1541. *Florent be thi name* : cp. Chaucer, *Cant. Tales*, B 3982, 'dan Piers be youre name.'

1556. ' I ask for nothing better (to be imposed) as a task.'

1587. *Have hier myn hond*: so in Chaucer, ' Have heer my trouthe,' D 1013.

1662. This is one of the closest parallels with the ballad,

> ' And she that told the nowe, sir Arthoure,
> I pray to god I maye se her bren on a fyre.'
> *Weddynge of Syr Gawene*, 475.

1676. *what* : cp. the use of ' quoy ' in French, e.g. *Mir.* 1781.

1677. *caste on his yhe*, ' cast his eye upon.'

1714. ' He must, whom fate compels.' The words 'schal,' 'scholde' are regularly used by Gower to express the idea of destiny, e.g. iii. 1348, iv. 92, 377.

1722. ' Placing her as he best could.'

1727. *Bot as an oule* &c. So in Chaucer,

> ' And al day after hidde him as an owle,
> So wo was hym, his wyf looked so foule.'
> D 1081 f.

1767. *tok thanne chiere on honde*, ' began to be merry.'

1771. *And profreth him ... to kisse*, i.e. offers to kiss him: cp. v. 6923, ' Anon he profreth him to love.'

1886. *til it overthrowe*, i.e. till it fall into calamity, ' overthrowe ' being intransitive, as 1962.

1888. *Hadde I wist*: cp. ii. 473, iv. 305.

1895. *And is*, i.e. 'And he is,' the pronoun being frequently omitted : cp. Prol. 348, 676, i. 2083, 2462, ii. 258, 624, 2071, 2985, iii. 1063, &c.

1917 f. A proverbial expression : cp. Lydgate, *Secrees of the Philosophres*, 459, 'Yit wer me loth ovir myn hed to hewe.'

1934. *ne schal me noght asterte*, 'shall not escape me,' in the sense of letting a fault be committed by negligence in repressing it : cp. i. 722.

1967. *unbende*, 1st sing. pret., 'I unbent (my bow).' For the form cp. 'sende,' Prol. 1013.

1980 ff. The example of Capaneus is probably from Statius. The medieval romances (e.g. the French *Roman de Thèbes*) do not represent Capaneus as slain by a lightning stroke. The impious speech alluded to here, 'Primus in orbe deos fecit timor!' is Statius, *Theb.* iii. 661, and the death of Capaneus, *Theb.* x. 827 ff.

2007. *it proeveth*, i.e. 'it appears': cp. Prol. 926.

2021 ff. This story was probably taken by Gower from the *Vita Barlaam et Josaphat*, cap. vi (Migne, *Patrol.* vol. 74. p. 462 f.). The incidents are the same, but amplified with details by Gower, who has also invented the title of the king. In the original he is only 'magnus quidam et illustris rex.' The story is found in several collections, as *Gesta Romanorum*, 143, Holkot, 70, see *Gesta Romanorum*, ed. Oesterley.

2030. *ride amaied*: cp. Chaucer, *Cant. Tales*, C 406, and Skeat's note.

2049. *par charite*. Rather perhaps 'per charite,' following J. F and A both have the contracted form. So also 'per chance,' 'per chaunce,' in ll. 2225, 2290, 3203, and 'per aventure,' l. 2350.

2073. *was the same . . . which*, cp. viii. 3062 *.

2078. This line, which would more naturally follow the next, seems to be thrown in parenthetically here.

2106. So also ii. 895, 2670.

2172. *to tendre with*, 'whereby to soften': cp. i. 452, 'To tarie with a mannes thoght,' and ii. 283.

2176. *sihe*: the mixture of past with present tenses is common in Gower.

2214 ff. 'O stulte ac demens, si fratris tui, cum quo idem tibi genus et par honos est, in quem nullius omnino sceleris tibi conscius es, praeconem ita extimuisti, quonam modo mihi reprehensionis notam idcirco inussisti, quod Dei mei praecones, qui mortem, ac Domini, in quem me multa et gravia scelera perpetrasse scio, pertimescendum adventum mihi quavis tuba vocalius altiusque denuntiant, humiliter ac demisse salutarim?' *Barl. et Jos.* cap. vi.

2225. See note on 2049.

2236. *obeie*, 'do obeisance to': cp. v. 1539.

2275 ff. The tale of Narcissus is no doubt from Ovid, *Met.* iii. 402 ff., but the account of his death is different from that which we find there. Ovid relates that he pined away gradually, and that his body was not found, but in place of it a flower.

2290. *par chance*: see note on 2049.

2316 f. Cp. Bocc. *Gen. Deorum*, vii. 59, 'existimans fontis Nympham.' By the margin we find that the nymph here meant is Echo, who is represented by Ovid as having wasted away for love of Narcissus and as giving an answer now to his cries.

2317. *as tho was faie*, 'as then was endued with (magic) power,' 'faie' being an adjective, as in ii. 1019, v. 3769.

2320. *of his sotie*, to be taken with what follows.

2340 ff. I know of no authority for this manner of his death.

2343-2358. This pretty passage is a late addition, appearing only in the third recension MSS. and one other copy, so far as I know. According to Ovid, the nymphs of the fountains and of the woods mourned for Narcissus,

'Planxere sorores
Naides, et sectos fratri posuere capillos;
Planxerunt Dryades, plangentibus assonat Echo,'

but when they desired to celebrate his obsequies, they found nothing there but a flower.

2350. *par aventure* : see note on 2049.

2355 ff. This application of the story, founded on the fact that the narcissus blooms in early spring, seems to be due to our author : cp. ii. 196, iii. 1717.

2377. *a place*, equivalent to 'aplace,' which we find in l. 1888, i.e. 'on place,' 'into place.' We might read 'aplace' here also, for though the words were at first written separately in F, there seems to have been an intention of joining them afterwards. However, such separations are often found elsewhere, as 'a doun,' iv. 2710, v. 385; 'a ferr,' i. 2335; 'a game,' viii. 2319; and most MSS. have 'a place' here.

2398. The reading of F, 'Which elles scholde haue his wille,' is a possible one, but the preservation of final 'e' before 'have' used unemphatically, as here, would be rather unusual. Instances such as l. 2465, 'a werre hadde,' are not to the point, and in l. 2542, where there is a better example, 'Of such werk as it scholde have,' the word 'have' is made more emphatic by standing in rhyme.

Latin Verses. ix. 2. *cilens*. Such forms of spelling are not uncommon in Gower's Latin : cp. 'cenatore,' v. 4944 (margin).

2410. *wynd*. The curious corruption 'hunt,' which appears in one form or another in all the copies of the unrevised first recension, must have been one of the mistakes of the original copyist. The critical note here should be, 'hunt(e) H₁YX ... C hante L haunt B₂,' and the actual reading in L is, ' Haþ þilke errour hante in his office,' which seems due to a marginal note having been incorporated in the text.

2411. *Which,* for 'that' in consecutive sense, answering to 'thilke,' see note on l. 492. In this case it does not even stand as the subject of the verb, for we have ' he overthroweth.'

2421. *tok.* This is second person singular, and we might rather expect ' toke,' which in fact is the reading of some good copies: cp. ii. 234, iii. 2629, viii. 2076.

2443. *daunger.* See note on *Balades,* xii. 8. The name represents the influences which are unfavourable to the lover's suit, and chiefly the feelings in the lady's own mind which tend towards prudence or prompt her to disdain. The personification in the *Roman de la Rose* is well known. There Danger is the chief guardian of the rose-bush, and has for his helpers Malebouche, who spreads unfavourable reports of the lover, with Honte and Paour, who represent the feelings in the lady's mind which lead her to resist his advances : see *Roman de la Rose,* 2837 ff., Chaucer, *Leg. of G. Women,* B 160, *Troilus,* ii. 1376. Danger, however, also stands without personification for scornfulness or reluctance in love, and so the adjective 'dangereus' *Rom. de la Rose,* 479 (Eng. 'dangerous,' *Cant. Tales,* D 1090, 'Is every knight of his so dangerous ? ').

In the *Confessio Amantis* the principal passages relating to Danger as a person are iii. 1537 ff. and v. 6613 ff. Such expressions also frequently occur as ' hire daunger,' iv. 2813 ; 'thi Daunger,' iv. 3589; 'make daunger,' ii. 1110 ; 'withoute danger,' iv. 1149 : cp. Chaucer, *Troilus,* ii. 384.

For the references to Danger in Lydgate see Dr. Schick's note on *Temple of Glas,* 156 (E. E. T. S.).

2459 ff. The story of Alboin and Rosemund is related by Paulus Diaconus, *Gest. Langob.* ii. 28, and after him by many others. This historian declares that he has himself seen the cup made of a skull from which the queen was invited to drink. According to him, Helmichis, the king's foster-brother and shield-bearer, plotted with Rosemunda against the king and induced her to gain the support of one Peredeus by the device of substituting herself for her waiting-maid. In some versions of the story this Peredeus was omitted. For example, in the *Pantheon* of Godfrey of Viterbo (xvii), where the story is related first in prose and then in verse, he is only slightly mentioned in the prose account and not at all in the verse, Helmegis being substituted for him in both as the object of the queen's artifice. It seems probable that Gower followed this author, with whose book we know he was acquainted (viii. 271). The name of the waiting-maid, Glodeside, seems to have been supplied by our author, who took it no doubt from ' Glodosinda,' the name of Alboin's former wife. Helmege the king's ' boteler ' is the ' Helmegis pincerna regis' of the *Pantheon,* and some expressions correspond closely, as 2474 (margin), ' ciphum ex ea gemmis et auro circumligatum ... fabricari constituit,' with the line ' Arte scyphum fieri statuens auroque ligari.'

The tale is well told by Gower, but he alters the final catastrophe, so as not to lengthen the story unnecessarily and divert attention from his principal object, which has to do with Alboin's punishment for boasting and not with the fate of the adulterous pair. He is responsible for most of the details: in the *Pantheon* the story occupies only sixty lines of Latin verse and is rather meagre in style. Compare, for example, the following with the account given by Gower of the holding of the banquet, the cruel boast of Alboin, and the feelings of the queen (2495-2569),

> 'Ipse caput soceri, quem fecerat ense necari,
> Arte scyphum fieri statuens auroque ligari,
>   Vina suae sponsae praecipit inde dari.
> Femina nescisset quod testa paterna fuisset,
> Vina nec hausisset, nisi diceret impius ipse,
>   "Testa tui patris est, cum patre, nata, bibe."
> Dum bibit immunda data vina gemens Rosimunda,
> Pectora pessumdat, lacrymae vehementer inundant,
>   Occisique patris res fit amara satis.'

2485 (margin). *Bibe cum patre tuo* : these are the exact words of the prose account in the *Pantheon*.

2504. There is a stop after 'ordeine' in F, therefore 'sende' should be taken as a past tense rather than as infinitive dependent on 'let.'

2533. 'And took a pride within his heart.'

2548. The punctuation is that of the MSS.

2569. *had mad.* The use of 'had' for 'hadde' in a position like this, where it is followed by a consonant (or of 'hadde' with the value of a monosyllable in such a position), is most unusual in Gower's verse. If there were a little more authority for it, we might read 'hath,' as given by J: cp. iv. 170, where many of the best copies read 'Had mad' for 'Hath mad.' It is possible that the author meant here 'hath had mad' ('had' being past participle), but I cannot quote any clear example of this form of speech at so early a date.

2642 ff. Here Gower departs from the authorities and winds up the story abruptly. According to the original story, Longinus the prefect of Ravenna conspired with Rosemunda to poison Helmichis; and he, having received drink from her hand and feeling himself poisoned, compelled her to drink also of the same cup.

2677. *veine gloire.* The adjective here adopts the French feminine from, as we have it in this very combination in the *Mirour*, e. g. l. 1219. On the other hand, where the words are separated, as l. 2720, the uninflected form is used. See note on l. 1006.

Latin Verses. x. 5. *strigilare fauellum*, 'to curry favel.'

2684. 'Heaven seems no gain to him.' The forms 'þinken' and 'þenken' are identified by Gower under 'þenken'; but 'þinke' is sometimes used in rhyme, and indifferently for either, e.g. v. 213, 254.

2701. *unavised*, adv., 'in a foolish fashion.'

2703 ff. Cp. *Mir.* 27337 ff., where the author pleads guilty to these crimes, as the lover also does below.

2705 (margin). Ecclus. xix. 27, 'Amictus corporis et risus dentium et ingressus hominis enunciant de illo.'

2706 f. *the newe guise of lusti folk,* i.e. the latest fashion for men of pleasure.

2713 f. This is one of the cases in which the third recension reading has been introduced over erasure into the text of F : cp. Prol. 336, iv. 1321, 1361, vii. *Lat. Verses* after ll. 1640 and 1984.
The original lines are given in the foot-note in accordance with S. They were altered perhaps to avoid repetition of 2681 f.

2745. *songe,* so here in F and A, elsewhere 'song.'

2746. *Wherof*: cp. l. 498.

2764. *hire good astat.* For the loss of inflexion cp. ii. 2341, 'his slyh compas.'

2769. *whiche*: often treated as a monosyllable in the verse, as ii. 604, iv. 1498, &c., but cp. l. 2825.

2787. Prol. 585 ff.

2795. *bere*: pret., as shown both by sense and rhyme.

2801. *good.* The original reading was 'godd,' which perhaps may be thought better, but the alteration may have been made by the author to avoid a repetition of the same word that he had used in l. 2796. The meaning is, 'he did not remember that there was anything else of worth except himself.'

2830. *And fedden hem,* i.e. 'And that they fed themselves,' &c. ; cp. 2833, 'and seide.'

2883. *sein*: so ii. 170, iii. 757, in rhyme always.

2890. Written in F 'vnder the þe kinges,' as if to make a distinction, but 'þee' in the next line.

2939. The punctuation after 'godd' is on the authority of F : otherwise it would be better to take 'with godd and stonde in good acord' together.

2951. *He let it passe* &c. The preceding sentence is broken off, and a new one begins which takes no account of the negative : see note on i. 98. This seems better than to make 'it' refer to his pride, for 'mynde' can hardly mean anything here but memory.

3032. 'He found the same gentlenes in his God.'

3050. *can no love assise,* 'can adapt no love to his liking.'

3067 ff. The tale of the Three Questions is one of which I cannot trace the origin, notwithstanding the details of name and place which are given at the end, viz. that the king was of Spain and was called Alphonso, that the knight's name was Pedro and his daughter's Petronilla. A reference to the second and third questions occurs in the *Mirour de l'omme,* 12601 ff.

3153. *herd you seid*: so v. 1623, 7609, 'herd me told.' This form of expression, for 'herd you seie,' 'herd me telle,' may have sprung from such a use of the participle as we have in v. 3376, 'Sche hadde herd spoke of his name ': cp. the use of participle for infinitive with 'do' in ii. 1799 and Chaucer, *Cant. Tales*, A 1913, 'Hath Theseüs doon wroght,' E 1098, 'Hath doon yow kept.'

3203. *par chaunce*: see note on 2049.

3246. *ansuerde*. This seems to be a plural form of the participle, used here for the rhyme: so iv. 1810, v. 6789.

3296. *leste*: elsewhere 'lest'; cp. 3106, 3313. Here we have 'leste' A, F, 'lest' JC, B. The form 'moste' is undoubtedly used for 'most' (adv.) i. 307.

3308. *reprise*, 'trouble,' as we have 'paine et reprise' in *Mirour*, 3968.

3365 f. *lete That I ne scholde be*: cp. iv. 454. In both cases 'lete' is the past participle of 'leten' (lǽtan), and not from 'letten,' meaning 'hinder.' In these expressions 'lete' means 'left' in the sense of 'omitted' (like 'lete Of wrong to don,' vii. 2726), and in this usage is naturally followed by a negative: cp. v. 4465, 'I wol noght lete, What so befalle of mi beyete, That I ne schal hire yive and lene.' The same phrase occurs with the past participle 'let' (meaning 'hindered') in ii. 128, and the sense is nearly the same.

3369 ff. Several corrections have been made by the author in this passage, either to make the verse run more smoothly, as 3369 'it mot ben holde' for 'mot nede be holde,' 3374 'mad a Pier' for 'an Erl hier,' 3412 'vice be received' for 'vice schal be received,' or to improve the sense and expression, as 3381 'maide' for 'place,' 3396 'wyse Peronelle' for 'name Peronelle,' 3414 'worth, and no reprise' for 'worthy, and no prise,' 3416 'If eny thing stond in contraire' for 'And it is alway debonaire,' an awkward parenthesis. It should be noted that Λ (the Wollaton copy of the second recension) here goes with the unrevised first recension, whereas B agrees with the revised form, except in ll. 3369, 3381.

3381. *the maide asterte*, 'escape the influence of the maiden.'

3442 f. The hellish nature of Envy consists in the fact that it wrongs both itself and others without cause, that is without having any further object to gain. It rejoices in evil for the sake of the evil itself and not for any advantage to be won from it. Cp. ii. 3132 ff.

LIB. II.

11. *if it be so*, equivalent to 'is it so,' from the form 'I ask if it be so.'

20. *Ethna*: cp. *Mirour*, 3805 ff.,

> Ly mons Ethna, quele art toutdiz,
> Nulle autre chose du paiis
> Forsque soy mesmes poet ardoir;
> Ensi q' Envie tient ou pis
> En sentira deinz soy le pis.'

The idea is that Envy, like Mount Etna, burns within itself continually, but is never consumed: cp. Ovid, *Met*. xiii. 867 (in the tale which follows below of Acis and Galatea),

> 'Uror enim, laesusque exaestuat acrius ignis,
> Cumque suis videor translatam viribus Aetnam
> Pectore ferre meo.'

83. *Write in Civile*. 'Civile' is certainly the Civil Law, for so we find it in *Mirour*, 15217, 16092, &c., and also personified in *Piers Plowman*. The reference here has puzzled me rather, but the following, I believe, is the explanation of it, strange as it may seem at first sight.

In the Institutions of Justinian, i. 7, 'De lege Furia Caninia sublata,' we read that this law, which restricted the power of owners of slaves to manumit them by will, was repealed 'quasi libertatibus impedientem et quodammodo invidam.' It seems that medieval commentators upon this, reading 'canina' for Caninia in the title of the law, explained the supposed epithet by reference to the adjective 'invidam' used in the description of it, and conceived the law to have been called 'canina' because it compelled men to imitate the dog in the manger by withholding liberty from those for whom they no longer had any use as slaves. In Bromyard's *Summa Predicantium* we find the following under the head of 'Invidia': 'Omnes isti sunt de professione legis Fusie canine. Ille enim Fusius inventor fuit legis cuius exemplum seu casus est iste. Quidam habet fontem quo non potest proprium ortum irrigare ... posset tamen alteri valere sine illius nocumento ; ipse tamen impedit ne alteri prosit quod sibi prodesse non potest, ad modum canis, sicut predictum est : a cuius condicione lex canina vocata est inter leges duodecim tabularum, que quia iniqua fuit, in aliis legibus correcta est, sicut patet Institut. lib. i. de lege Fusia canina tollenda.' It seems likely then that Gower took the fable from some comment on this passage of the Institutions.

88. *who that understode*, 'if a man understood,' subjunctive: see notes on Prol. 13, 460.

104 ff. From Ovid, *Met*. xiii. 750 ff., where it is told at greater length. The circumstance, however, of Polyphemus running round Etna and roaring with rage and jealousy before he killed Acis, is added by Gower, possibly from a misunderstanding of l. 872. It is certainly an improvement.

128. *it myhte noght be let* &c. See note on i. 3365.

196. *as he whilom* &c. This suggestion is due to our author : cp. i. 2355 ff.

252. *who overthrowe, Ne who that stonde*. The verbs are probably singular and subjunctive: cp. iii. 665.

258. *And am* : cp. note on i. 1895.

261. Cp. Chaucer, *Cant. Tales*, G 746 ff., where the Ellesmere MS. has in the margin 'Solacium miseriorum' &c. The quotation does not seem to be really from Boethius.

265 f. 'When I see another man labour where I cannot achieve success.' For this use of 'to' cp. Prol. 133, &c.

283. *to hindre with,* 'whereby to hinder': cp. i. 452, 2172.

291 ff. This story, as Prof. Morley points out, is to be found among the fables of Avian, which were widely known. Gower has amplified it considerably. The fable is as follows:

xxii. 'Iuppiter, ambiguas hominum praediscere mentes,
    Ad terram Phoebum misit ab arce poli.
Tunc duo diversis poscebant numina votis,
    Namque alter cupidus, invidus alter erat ;
His sese medium Titan scrutatus utrumque
    Obtulit et, "Precibus Iuppiter aecus," ait,
"Praestandi facilis ; nam quae speraverit unus,
    Protinus haec alter congeminata feret."
Sed cui longa iecur nequiit satiare cupido,
    Distulit admotas in sua dona preces,   10
Spem sibi confidens alieno crescere voto,
    Seque ratus solum munera ferre duo.
Ille ubi captantem socium sua praemia vidit,
    Supplicium proprii corporis optat ovans ;
Nam petit extincto iam lumine degat ut uno,
    Alter ut hoc duplicans vivat utroque carens.
Tum sortem sapiens humanam risit Apollo,
    Invidiaeque malum rettulit ipse Iovi,
Quae dum proventis aliorum gaudet iniquis,
    Laetior infelix et sua damna cupit.'   20

l. 6. Iuppiter aecus *Lachmann* vt peteretur *codd.*

309. *Now lowde wordes* &c., i.e. Now with loud words, &c.; cp. vii. 170.

317. *That on,* 'The one.'

323 (margin). *maculauit.* Du Cange has, '*Maculare,* Vulnerare, vel vulnerando deformare.'

389. *Malebouche,* cp. *Roman de la Rose,* 2847 ff., *Mirour de l'omme,* 2677 ff.

390. *pyl ne crouche,* 'pile nor cross,' cross and pile being the too sides of a coin, head and tail.

399 f. The meaning of 'heraldie' is rather uncertain here. Probably it stands for 'office of herald,' and the passage means, 'Holding the place of herald in the court of liars'; but the *New Engl. Dict.* apparently takes it in the sense of 'livery,' comparing the French 'heraudie,' a cassock, and an eighteenth-century example in English. In this case we must understand the lines to mean 'wearing the livery of those who lie,' that is, being in their service.

401 ff. Cp. *Mirour,* 3721 ff.

404. *fals,* see note on Prol. 221. Just below (l. 412) we have 'his false tunge.'

**   I i

413 ff. Cp. *Mirour*, 2893 ff.,

> 'La hupe toutdis fait son ny,
> Et l'escarbud converse auci,
> Entour l'ordure et la merdaille;
> Mais de ces champs qui sont flori
> N'ont garde: et par semblance ensi
> Malvoise langue d'enviaille,' &c.

447. 'That many envious tale is stered,' 'many' being a monosyllable for the metre before the vowel, as frequently in the expression 'many a,' and 'envious' accented on the penultimate syllable. For the use of 'many' by itself in the singular cp. ii. 89, iv. 1619, &c.

473. That is, she is on her guard against doing that of which she might afterwards repent. For 'hadde I wist' cp. i. 1888.

510 f. *I myhte noght To soffre* &c. A very unusual construction.

547 ff. 'I cannot find that I have spoken anything amiss by reason of envy,' &c.

565. 'In which he knows that there is poison': for the arrangement of words cp. i. 833.

583. 'To be amended': cp. Prol. 83.

587 ff. The tale of Constance is Chaucer's *Man of Law's Tale*, and the story was derived by the two authors from the same source, Nicholas Trivet's Anglo-Norman chronicle. The story as told by him has been printed for the Chaucer Society from MS. Arundel 56, with collation of a Stockholm copy (*Originals and Analogues*, 1872). The quotations in these Notes, however, are from the Bodleian MS., Rawlinson B. 178.

Gower has followed the original more closely than Chaucer, but he diverges from it in a good many points, as will be seen from the following enumeration:

(1) Gower says nothing of the proficiency of Constance in sciences and languages, on which Trivet lays much stress. (2) He abridges the negotiations for marriage with the Souldan (620 ff.). (3) He does not mention the seven hundred Saracens with whom the Souldan's mother conspired. (4) He brings Constance to land in Northumberland in the summer instead of on Christmas day (732). (5) He omits the talk between Constance and Hermyngeld which leads to the conversion of the latter (cp. 752 ff.). (6) According to Trivet the blind man who received his sight was one of the British Christians who had remained after the Saxon conquest, and he went to Wales to bring the bishop Lucius. (7) The knight who solicited Constance had been left, according to Trivet, in charge during Elda's absence, and planned his accusation against her for fear she should report his behaviour to Elda on his return (cp. 792 ff.). (8) The words spoken when the felon knight was smitten are not the same. Gower moreover makes him confess his crime and then die, whereas in the French book he is put to death by the king (cp. 879 ff.). (9) The reasons for Domilde's

hatred of Constance are omitted by Gower. (10) Trivet says that Domilde gave the messenger a drugged potion on each occasion (cp. 952 ff., 1008 ff.). (11) The communication to Constance of the supposed letter from the king, and her acceptance of her fate, are omitted by Gower. (12) The prayers of Constance for herself and her child upon the sea and her nursing of the child are additions made by Gower (1055–1083). (13) According to Trivet, Constance landed at the heathen admiral's castle and was entertained there, going back to her ship for the night. Then in the night Thelous came to her, and professing to repent of having denied his faith, prayed that he might go with her and return to a Christian country. So they put out at sea, and he, moved by the devil, tempted her to sin. She persuaded him to look out for land, with a promise of yielding to his desires on reaching the shore, and while he is intent on this occupation, she pushes him overboard (cp. 1084–1125). (14) The vengeance of king Alle on his mother is related by Trivet immediately after this, by Gower later. According to Trivet he hewed her to pieces (cp. 1226–1301). In the ballad of *Emaré* the mother is condemned to be burnt, but her sentence is changed to exile. (15) Gower omits the entry of king Alle into Rome and the incident of his being seen by Constance as he passed through the streets. (16) Trivet says that when Morice took the message to the Emperor, the latter was struck by his resemblance to his lost daughter. (17) Gower adds the incident of Constance riding forward to meet her father (1500 ff.). (18) According to Trivet, Constance returned to Rome because of the illness of her father (cp. 1580 ff.).

These differences, besides others of detail, show that Gower treated the story with some degree of freedom.

Before Trivet was known as the common source for Chaucer and Gower, Tyrrwhitt suggested that Chaucer's tale was taken from Gower. Chaucer in fact criticizes and rejects one feature of the tale which occurs in Gower's version of it, namely the sending of ' the child Maurice' to invite the Emperor. This incident however comes from Trivet, and it is probably to him that Chaucer refers.

It has been argued however in recent times from certain minute resemblances in detail and forms of expression between Chaucer's tale and Gower's, that Chaucer was acquainted with Gower's rendering of the story as well as with Trivet's (E. Lücke in *Anglia*, vol. xiv); and the same line of reasoning has been employed by others, e.g. Dr. Skeat in his edition of Chaucer, to prove that Gower borrowed to some extent from Chaucer. It seems probable that Chaucer's tale of Constance was written earlier than Gower's, and it is likely enough that Gower was acquainted with his friend's work and may have conveyed some expressions from it into his own. Lücke adduces twenty-seven instances, more than half of them trivial or unconvincing, but amounting on the whole to a tolerably strong proof that one of the two poets was acquainted with the other's story. The most convincing of the parallels are the following: Gower, 'Let take anon this Constantine' 706, Chaucer, 'And Custance have they take anon' *Cant. Tales*, B 438; Gower, 'lich hir oghne lif Constance loveth' 750, Chaucer, 'loved hire right as hir lif' B 535; Gower, 'yif me my sihte' 765, Chaucer, 'yif me my sighte again' B 560, Trivet, 'qe tu me facetz le signe de la croiz sur mes eux enveugles' f. 34; Gower, 'The king with many another mo Hath christned' 907, Chaucer, 'The kyng and many another in that place converted was' B 685; Gower, 'to kepe his wif' 925, Chaucer, 'his wyf to kepe' B 717; Gower, 'goth to seke Ayein the Scottes for to fonde The werre' 928 ff.; Chaucer, 'whan he is gon To Scotlondward, his fomen for to seke' B 717 f.; Gower, 'The time set of kinde is come, This lady hath hir chambre nome' 931 f. Chaucer, 'She halt hire chambre abiding Cristes wille. The tyme is come' B 721 f. These resemblances of phrase are such as we might expect to find if Gower had read Chaucer's story before writing his own. In all essentials he is independent, and it is surely not necessary to suppose, as Dr. Skeat does, that a quarrel between them was caused by such a matter as this.

590. Tiberius Constantinus was Emperor (at Constantinople) for four years only, 578–582; his wife's name was Anastasia. He selected Maurice of Cappadocia to succeed him, and gave him his daughter in marriage. The romance related by Trivet seems to have no historical foundation, but it was during the reign of Maurice that the mission went from Rome for the conversion of the English, and this may have had something to do with the story that Maurice himself was partly of English origin. Trivet himself mentions the historical form of the story, but pretends that he finds a different account in the old Saxon chronicles, 'les aunciens croniques des Sessouns,' or 'l'estoire de Sessons.'

594. *the god*: cp. Prol. 72. We find both 'god' and 'godd' as forms of spelling, so 'rod' and 'rodd,' 'bed' and 'bedd.' Here 'godd' has been altered in F by erasure.

613. Both Chaucer and Gower make the Souldan send for the merchants, whereas in Trivet they are brought before him on accusation: but in fact here Gower agrees in essentials with Trivet, while Chaucer invents a quite different occasion for the interview.

653. *Betwen hem two*, 'by themselves together': cp. 752, 3517, iii. 1466.

684. *Hire clos Envie*: see note on Prol. 221. The metaphor here may be from spreading a net, or perhaps it means simply she displayed her secret envy.

693 f. Compare Chaucer's development of the idea with examples, *Cant. Tales*, B 470 ff.

709. *withoute stiere*: Chaucer says 'a ship al steereles' where Trivet has 'sanz sigle et sanz naviroun,' or 'sanz viron' (MS. Rawl.): but either 'viron' or 'naviron' might stand for the oar with which the ship was steered.

709 ff. Note the free transposition of clauses for the sake of the
rhymes. The logical order would be 709, 711, 710, 713, 712.

711. *for yeres fyve.* Trivet says 'pur treis aunz,' but he keeps her
at sea nevertheless for nearly five.

736. *gon,* plural, 'he and his wife go': cp. 1152.

749 ff. In the MSS. the paragraph begins at 'Constance loveth,'
l. 751.

752. 'They speaking every day together alone,' an absolute use:
cp. 1723. For 'betwen hem two' cp. 653.

762. Punctuated after 'hire' in F.

771. *Thou bysne man.* The word 'bysne' is taken from the original
story. Trivet says she spoke in the Saxon language and said, 'Bisne
man, en Ihesu name in rode yslawe haue þi siht' (MS. Rawl. f. 34).

785. *As he that.* The reference is to the king, so that we should
rather expect 'As him that,' but the phrase is a stereotyped one and
does not always vary in accordance with grammatical construction:
cp. 1623. We find however also 'As him which,' iii. 1276.

791. 'The time being appointed moreover': an absolute use of the
participle.

831. 'trencha la gowle Hermigild': therefore the fact that Gower
and Chaucer agree in saying that he cut her throat has no special
significance.

833. The reading 'that dier,' or 'that diere,' was apparently a mistake of the original copyist. It appears in all the unrevised copies of
the first recension and also in B. Λ however has the corrected reading.

857. *After,* 'In accordance with.'

880 ff. Here Chaucer follows the original more closely than Gower,
as also just above, 'him smoot upon the nekke boon.' The words of
the miraculous voice are given in Latin by Trivet, 'Aduersus filiam
matris ecclesie ponebas scandalum: hoc fecisti et tacui' ('et non tacui'
Rawl. Stockh.). Chaucer has (B 674 ff.),

'And seyde, "Thou hast desclaundred gilteles
The doughter of holy chirche in heigh presence:
Thus hastou doon and yet holde I my pees."'

895. This line occurs several times, e.g. i. 2106, ii. 2670.

905. *Lucie,* apparently to be pronounced 'Lucíe.' Such names
usually appear either in the Latin forms 'Lucius,' 'Tiberius,' 'Claudius,' 'Virginius,' or with accent on the antepenultimate syllable
'Tibérie,' 'Mercúrie,' the 'i' not being counted as a syllable.

947. What the right name really is we can hardly say for certain.
The printed text of the French gives 'Domulde' or 'Domilde,' the
Rawlinson MS. has 'Downilde,' and Chaucer makes it 'Donegild.'

964. *which is of faierie.* In the French book the letter states
that the queen has been transformed since the king's departure
into the likeness of another creature and is an evil spirit in woman's
form.

994 f. 'comaunda qe sanz nul countredit feissent sa femme sauvement garder' f. 34 v⁰.

1001. I punctuate after 'Knaresburgh' on the authority of F.

1010. The manuscript has a stop after 'drunke' and this seems best.

1020. Here we have apparently one of the original corruptions of the author's text.

1046 ff. The original has only 'grant duel et grant dolour demeneient.'

1081. *To rocke with*: cp. i. 452.

1110. *if sche him daunger make*, 'if she resist his desire': see note on i. 2443.

1123. *menable*: see note on i. 1067.

1132. *er it be falle And hath* &c.; that is, 'until it be so come that it hath,' &c.

1152. *scholden*: note the plural verb after 'I forth with my litel Sone': cp. 736.

1163. Trivet adds 'qar issit l'apelerent les Sessoneis' f. 35 v⁰.

1164. *for noght he preide* &c., 'for none of his prayers to be told,' &c.

1173. The stop after 'Romeward' is on the authority of F, with which A agrees. We can say either, 'He was coming from Barbarie towards Rome, and was going home,' or 'He was coming from Barbarie, and was going home towards Rome'; but the latter perhaps is the more natural.

1191. *made sche no chiere.* This must mean here, 'she gave no outward sign of her thought.' Usually 'to make cheer' means to be cheerful.

1243. *what child that were*, subjunctive in indirect question: cp. 1943, iii. 708, 771, &c. See note on Prol. 41.

1259. *alle wel*: 'wel' seems to be a substantive.

1275. *as seith the bok.* The 'book' only says 'ia tut enflammé de ire.'

1285. *I schal be venged*: cp. v. 6766. The first and second recensions have 'It schal.'

1300. *was after sunge.* The French book does not say this. It seems probable that Gower was acquainted with ballads on the subject, such as that of *Emaré*, printed in Ritson's *Metrical Romances*, ii. 204 ff. It is to be noted that *Emaré* is taken from a Breton lay:

> 'Thys ys of Brytayne layes,
> That was used by olde dayes
> Men callys playn the garye.'

1317. According to Trivet he came especially to get absolution for having killed his mother, and Chaucer follows him here.

1329. *In help to ben his herbergour.* This seems to mean that the question was asked with a view to helping to provide a lodging for the king. The expression is rather obscure however.

1351. *seknesse of the See.* This is absurd here, but not so in the original story. Constance attributes her weakness to the effects produced by her long wanderings at sea, 'se acundut par feblesce de sa cervele que lui avint en la mere' f. 36.

1369. *sihe*, subjunctive, 'so that the king might see him.'

1381 f. Cp. viii. 1702 ff.

1393. 'a ship which was,' cp. i. 10.

1405 f. See note on 1163. Trivet speaks here only of the name of Moris.

1423 f. Gower's more usual form would be, 'Desireth not the heaven so much, that he ne longeth more,' as i. 718, &c.

1464 ff. The connexion of this remark is clearer in the original story, which says that Constance told her husband, if the Emperor should refuse his prayer, to ask 'pur l'amur q'il avoit al alme sa fille Constaunce'; because she knew that he denied no one who prayed in this form.

1586 ff. *after that*, 'according as': cp. Prol. 544, iii. 1074. The book says in fact with much apparent accuracy that Alla died nine months after his return, that Constance returned to Rome half a year after, 'pur la novele qe ele oit de la maladie son pere,' that on the thirteenth day after her arrival the Emperor died in the arms of his daughter, and she followed him in a year, the date being St. Clement's day of the year 585. It is further stated that Elda, who had accompanied Constance to Rome, died at Tours on his way back to England.

1599. *the wel meninge of love.* In spite of the variations there can hardly be a doubt about the true reading here. The word is clearly 'meninge' both in F and S, and the change to 'whel' was suggested no doubt by the misreading 'meuinge.' For the expression cp. iii. 599, 'To love and to his welwillinge.'

1613 ff. Gower apparently pieced together this story of Demetrius and Perseus from several sources, for it does not seem to occur in any single authority precisely as he gives it. The first part, which has to do with the false accusation brought against Demetrius and its consequences, agrees with the account given in Justin, *Epitome*, lib. xxxii. The story of the daughter of Paulus Emilius and her little dog is told by Valerius Maximus, *Mem.* i. 5. 3. Finally, the details of the defeat of Perseus seem to be taken from the account of a catastrophe which about the same time befell the Basternae, a Thracian tribe allied with Perseus, who according to Orosius (iv. 20), when crossing the Danube in winter with large numbers of men and horses, were almost annihilated by the breaking of the ice. The same author mentions that after the defeat and capture of Perseus his son exercised the craft of a brass-worker at Rome.

It is possible of course that Gower had before him some single account in which these elements were already combined. In Vincent of Beauvais, *Speculum Hist.* v. 65 f., we find first the catastrophe of the Basternae, taken from Orosius, then the Macedonian war from Justin and Orosius, with the incident of the dog inserted from Valerius.

1631 (margin). *testibus que iudicibus*, 'witnesses and judges,' a common use of the conjunction in Gower's Latin : cp. 'Celsior est Aquila que Leone ferocior,' *Latin Verses after* i. 574.

1633. *dorst*, so here in the best MSS. for 'dorste.'

1711. *apparant*, for 'heir apparant,' which was the original reading of the first recension : cp. *Mirour*, 5580,

'Car d'autre bien n'est apparant.'

1723. *livende his father* : for this absolute use cp. 752.

1757. *upon depos*, that is, having his power given to him as a temporary charge. See the examples in the *New Engl. Dict.*

1778. *And he.* 'As he' is an error which crept into the third recension. The interchange of 'As' with 'And' in Gower MSS. is very common.

1793 f. 'For such an omen of an hound was most like to him,' the words being transposed for the sake of the metre.

1799. *do slain.* This is apparently past participle by attraction for infinitive : cp. i. 3153, iv. 249, 816.

1817 ff. This incident is not related of the army of Perseus in any history, so far as I know : see note on 1613.

Latin Verses. iv. 7 f. As punctuated in F the couplet runs,

'Quod patet esse fides in eo, fraus est que politi
Principium pacti, finis habere negat.'

This does not seem to give any sense. The text may be translated thus : 'What appears to be faith in him is in fact fraud, and the end of the smooth covenant disowns the beginning' (*lit.* 'denies that it has the beginning').

1921. *it scheweth*, 'there appeareth' : cp. iii. 809.

1943. *how it were* : subjunctive of indirect question ; cp. 1243.

1950. *of love, and.* The punctuation is that of F.

2016. *byme* : see note on i. 232.

2018. *For this I weene*, 'the other cause is because I ween,' &c.

2025. *Forwhy and*, 'provided that' : the same line occurs again in v. 2563. Compare the use of 'for why that' in *Le Morte Arth.* 389 (Roxb.), 'Thou shalt haue yiftis good, For why þat thou wilte dwelle wyth me,' quoted in the *New Engl. Dict.*

2066. *of his oghne hed.* It may be questioned whether 'hed' is not here from an O.E. '*hǽd,' a collateral form of 'hád,' like the termination '-hed' for '-hod.' See *New Engl. Dict.*, 'hede.' In that case, 'of his oghne hed' would mean 'about his own condition.' The rhyme with 'red' is no guide to us.

2071. *Bot hield*, i. e. 'But I held'; see note on i. 1895.

2098 ff. With this attack on the Lombards compare *Mirour de l'omme*, 25429 ff. It is the usual popular jealousy of foreign rivals in trade.

2122. *Fa crere*, 'make-believe,' the art by which they acquired credit in business. The form 'crere' is used in Gower's French, e. g. *Mirour*, 4474.

2124. *hem stant no doute*, 'they have no fear,' 'they are sure': cp. iii. 1524, v. 7244. In v. 2118, 'which stant of him no doute,' we have a somewhat different form of the expression: cp. iii. 2536.

2157 ff. The story is mainly taken from Ovid, *Metam*. ix. 101 ff., but probably Gower was acquainted also with the epistle *Deianira Herculi*, and he has (naturally enough) supposed that what is there said of Hercules and Omphale, the exchange of clothes &c., referred to the relations of Hercules and Iole: see 2268 ff. 'The kinges dowhter of Eurice' is no doubt derived from the expression 'Eurytidosque Ioles': cp. *Traitié*, vii. 2. Ovid's account of the death of Hercules is very much shortened by our author, and not without good reason.

2160. That is, 'it befell him to desire,' &c.

2297. Ovid, *Met*. ix. 229 ff.

2299. *al of*: so the first and second recension copies generally, and also W. The sense seems to require it, rather than 'of al,' given by FH₃.

2341. *his slyh compas*: a clear case of the loss of inflexion in the adjective, notwithstanding that it is a native English stem. The same word occurs in the definite form in l. 2374 'with his slyhe cast.'

2346. *chalk for chese*: cp. Prol. 416.

2366. *axeth no felawe*, 'requires none to share it.'

2392. The metre requires the form 'bote,' which is etymologically correct, and is given in the best MSS.

2403. *Me roghte noght*: pret. subjunctive, 'I should not care.'

2423. *I wolde*: cp. iii. 78. We should expect the negative 'I nolde,' as in i. 2750 f.,

> 'I wol noght say
> That I nam glad on other side.'

The conditional clause thrown in has broken the thread of the sentence.

2430. *tant ne quant*: so *Mirour de l'omme*, 3654, 23358.

2437. *A man to ben*, cp. vi. 57.

2447. *in a wayt*: so given by the best copies, cp. 2999, but 'upon await' iii. 955, 1016.

2451 ff. In the MSS. the paragraph is marked as beginning with the next line, 'At Troie how that,' the line before being insignificant. As to the first story referred to in the text, Gower may have known it from Hyginus (*Fab*. cvi), or from Ovid, *Her. Ep*. iii. The example of Diomede and Troilus had been popularized by Chaucer, who had the name 'Criseide' 'from Boccaccio's 'Griseida.' In Benoît and Guido the name is 'Briseida,' but Boccaccio was aware that Briseis was a different person (*Gen. Deorum*, xii. 52).

2459 ff. I am unable to say where Gower found this version of the story. The name Geta is quite unknown in the classical form of it. It may be suspected that our author himself modified the story in order to make it more suitable for his purpose by substituting a mortal

friend for Jupiter. We may note that he has also reversed the part
played by Amphitryon.

2501 ff. I cannot indicate the source of this tale.

2537. *As thei.* The sense seems to require this reading, which is
found however in only two MSS., so far as I know, and those not the
best. It appears as a correction in Berthelet's second edition.

2550. *which that him beclipte.* Either this means 'who was encom-
passing him,' that is pressing upon his borders, referring to the Caliph
of Egypt, or 'which encircled his territory,' referring to what follows,
'in a Marche costeiant.' In the latter case we should have a very bold
inversion of clauses for the sake of rhyme, but hardly more so than in
709 ff.

2558. *unto Kaire.* It is evident that the author conceives this as
the capital not of Egypt but of Persia : cp. 2648.

2578. *hair.* The form of the word is accommodated to the rhyme :
so iv. 1252.

2642. *Upon hire oth* &c., inverted order, 'how it was a token that
she should be his wife upon her oath,' i. e. in accordance with her oath.

2670. The same line occurs also i. 2106, ii. 895.

2680. *tome,* i. e. 'leisure,' 'opportunity,' from the adjective 'tom,'
empty. The reading 'come' is due probably to the misunderstanding
of a rather unusual word, but the rhyme 'Rome : come' (past
partic.) is not an admissible one (cp. K. Fahrenburg in *Archiv für
neuere Sprachen,* vol. 89, p. 406, who of course is not aware of the
corruption).

2803. The account of Boniface VIII which was most current in
England is that which we find given in Rishanger's Chronicle and repeated by Higden and Walsingham. It is as follows, under the year
1294 :—

Papa cedit.

'Coelestinus Papa se minus sufficientem ad regendam Ecclesiam
sentiens, de consilio Benedicti Gaietani cessit Papatui, edita prius
constitutione super cessione Pontificum Romanorum.

Supplantatio Papae.

'In vigilia Natalis Domini apud Neapolim in Papam eligitur Bene-
dictus Gaietanus. . . . De quo praedecessor eius Coelestinus, vir vitae
anachoriticae, eo quod eum ad cedendum Papatui subdole induxisset,
prophetavit in hunc modum, prout fertur : "Ascendisti ut vulpes,
regnabis ut leo, morieris ut canis." Et ita sane contigit ; nam ipsum
Papam ut Papatui cederet et ut Papa quilibet cedere posset, constitu-
tionem edere fecit ; quam quidem postmodum ipsemet Papa effectus
revocavit. Deinde rigide regens generosos quosdam de Columpna
Cardinales deposuit ; Regi Francorum in multis non solum obstitit,
sed eum totis viribus deponere insudavit. Igitur Senescallus Franciae,
Willelmus de Longareto, vir quidem in agibilibus admodum circum-
spectus, et fratres de Columpna praedicti, foederatis viribus Bonifa-

cium Papam comprehenderunt et in equum effrenem, versa facie ad
caudam, sine freno posuerunt ; quem sic discurrere ad novissimum
halitum coegerunt, ac tandem fame necaverunt.'

It remains to be asked where Gower found the story of the speaking-
trumpet by means of which Celestin was moved to his abdication, why
he supposed that the capture of Boniface took place near Avignon, and
whence came such additional details as we have in l. 3028.

As to the first, it was certainly a current story, because we find it
repeated by later writers, as Paulus Langius, *Chron. Citiz.*, ann. 1294,
' Per fistulam etiam frequentius noctu in cubili per parietem missam,
velut coelica vox esset, loquebatur ei : " Celestine, Celestine, renuncia
papatui, quia aliter saluari non poteris, nam vires tuas excedit." '

As to the death of Boniface, it was commonly reported that he had
been starved in prison, the fact being that after the episode of his
captivity he refused to take food, and the biting of his hands was
observed as a symptom of extreme vexation, ' saepe caput muro
concussit et digitos momordit,' ' per plures dies ira feruidus manus sibi
arrodere videbatur,' &c.   Ciacon. *Vita Pont.* p. 655.

2837 f. cp. Prol. 329.

2875. *of such prolacioun,* ' with so prolonged a note.'

2889. *hedde* : cp. v. 1254.

2966. *Lowyz.* This of course is a mistake historically.

2985. *And seiden.* For omission of pronoun cp. i. 1895.

2995. *de Langharet.* We find this form of the name, or something
equivalent, in the English Chronicles quoted, and also in Villani. The
true name was apparently ' de Nogaret.'

3001. *at Avinoun.* This is quite unhistorical, and the precise
mention of ' Pontsorge ' (or as our author first wrote it, ' Poursorge ')
seems to point to the use of some particular form of the story, which
cannot at present be indicated.

3033 ff. This saying is sometimes given in the form of a prophecy,
and attributed to the predecessor of Boniface, whose resignation he
was said to have procured : see the passage quoted on l. 2803.

3037. *to the houndes like,* ' after the likeness of the hound ': cp. i.
2791, ' to his liche.' The form ' like ' would hardly be admissible here
as an adjective for ' lik.'

3056. This prophecy no doubt was current among the many attributed to the Abbot Joachim, but I do not find it exactly in the form
here given. The quotation of it in the margin of F is in a different
hand from that of the text and of the heading ' Nota de prophecia ' &c.
The omission of the Latin altogether in some manuscripts, as AdT, W,
has no special significance for this passage.

3081 f. ' He shall not be able to abstain from hindering him.'

3095. This saying, which is here attributed to Seneca, and which
appears also in the *Mirour de l'omme* in a slightly different form,
3831 ff., may be based really upon the well-known passage of Dante,
Inf. xiii. 64.

Latin Verses. vi. 4. *Dumque,* for 'Dum,' as sometimes in the *Vox Clamantis.*

ethnica flamma : see note on l. 20.

3122 ff. Cp. *Mirour,* 3819 ff.

3160. See note on i. 232.

3187. The Latin books referred to are the current lives of Saint Silvester, the substance of which is reproduced in the *Legenda Aurea.* Gower tells the story in considerably better style than we have it there, with amplifications of his own, especially as regards the reflections of Constantine, 3243 ff., and the preaching of Silvester to the Emperor, 3383 ff. There are some variations in detail from the current account which may or may not point to a special source. For example, in the Life of Silvester we are told that the Emperor met the lamenting mothers as he was riding up to the Capitol to take his bath of blood, and in all forms of the legend that I have seen the mountain where Silvester lay in hiding was Soracte (or Saraptis) and not Celion. The name may however have been altered by Gower for metrical reasons, as was sometimes his habit; see note on i. 1407 (end).

3210. *of Accidence.* 'Accidentia' in its medical sense is explained as 'affectus praeter naturam': cp. v. 763.

3243 ff. These reflections, continued to l. 3300, are an expanded and improved form of the rather tasteless string of maxims given in the legend, the most pointed of which is that with which our author concludes, 'Omnium se esse dominum comprobat, qui servum se monstraverit pietatis.'

3260. *his oghne wone.* This appears to mean 'according to his own habits,' like 'his oghne hondes' (i. 1427), 'his oghne mouth' (v. 5455), for 'with his own hands,' &c.

3507. *vertu sovereine*: a clear case of the French feminine inflexion, which must have been a very natural variation in such expressions as this ; cp. i. 2677. In French as in English our author would feel at liberty to adapt the form to the rhyme or metre : so we have 'sa joye soverein' *Mir.* 4810, but 'ma sovereine joie' *Bal.* ix. 7.

3517. *betwen ous tweie,* i. e. 'together'; cp. l. 653.

LIB. III.

4. *ther nis on.* Note the repetition of the negative from the clause above.

71. *the leng the ferre,* i. e. 'the lengere the ferre.'

78. *mihte I,* for 'ne mihte I': cp. ii. 2423.

83. *redy to wraththe*: cp. ii. 3444, 'redi to the feith.'

143 ff. The story is from Ovid, *Her. Ep.* xi. It is that which is referred to by Chaucer, *Cant. Tales,* B 77,

> 'But certeinly no word ne writeth he
> Of thilke wikke ensample of Canacee,
> That loved hir owene brother synfully.'

(Note that the name 'Canace' is used by Gower so as to rhyme with 'place.')

In spite of the character of the subject, it must be allowed that Gower tells the story in a very touching manner, and he shows good taste in omitting some of Ovid's details, as for example those in *Ep.* 39–44. The appeal of Canace to her father as given by Gower is original, and so for the most part is the letter to her brother and the picturesque and pathetic scene of her death. On the whole this must be regarded as a case in which our author has greatly improved upon his authority. Lydgate obviously has Gower's story before him when he introduces the tale (quite needlessly) into his *Fall of Princes.* It may be noted that in Ovid also the catastrophe is given as a consequence of ungoverned anger :

> 'Imperat, heu! ventis, tumidae non imperat irae.'

172. *lawe positif*: see note on Prol. 247. Gower's view is that there is nothing naturally immoral about an incestuous marriage, but that it is made wrong by the 'lex positiva' of the Church. This position he makes clear at the beginning of the eighth book, by showing that in the first ages of the world such marriages must have been sanctioned by divine authority, and that the idea of kinship as a bar to marriage had grown up gradually, cousins being allowed to marry among the Jews, though brother and sister might not, and that finally the Church had ordered,

> 'That non schal wedden of his ken
> Ne the seconde ne the thridde.'   viii. 147 f.

If attacked by Chaucer with regard to the subject of this story, he would no doubt defend himself by arguing that the vice with which it dealt was not against nature, and that the erring brother and sister were in truth far more deserving of sympathy than the father who took such cruel vengeance. Notwithstanding his general strictness in matters of morality, Gower was something of a fatalist, cp. the recurring phrases of 1222, 1348, 1677, iv. 1524, &c., and he repeatedly emphasizes the irresistible character of the impulses of nature in love ; cp. i. 17 ff., 1051 ff., 2621, vi. 1261 ff., and here l. 161 (margin), 'intollerabilem iuuentutis concupiscenciam.'

219. 'the child which was,' cp. i. 10.

253 f. Ovid, *Her. Ep.* xi. 96,

> 'Et iubet ex merito scire quid iste velit.'

279 ff. This letter is for the most part original. That which we have in Ovid is mainly narrative.

292. *If that* &c. The point of this as it occurs in Ovid depends upon the fact that her child has already been exposed and, as she conceives, torn by wild beasts, and she entreats her brother if possible to collect his remains and lay them by her,—a very natural and pathetic request. Gower has chosen for the sake of picturesque effect in this

scene to make the exposure of the child come after the death of the mother, and he should therefore perhaps have omitted the reference to the child's burial.

300 f. Ovid, *Her. Ep.* xi. 3, 4,

> 'Dextra tenet calamum, strictum tenet altera ferrum,
> Et iacet in gremio charta soluta meo.'

315. The word 'baskleth' is perhaps a genuine alternative reading.

331. 'Of such a thing done as that was.' We must not be tempted by the correction 'tho' for 'that.'

352. A fatalistic maxim which is often repeated, e. g. i. 1714, 'nede he mot that nede schal.'

355. The revision of this line for the third recension may indicate a preference for throwing back the accent of 'nature' in the English fashion : so ii. 1376, but 'natúre' ll. 175, 350.

361 ff. This is from Ovid, *Met.* iii. 324 ff. Gower has chosen to omit the sequel of the story, which was that after seven years Tiresias saw the same snakes again, and by striking them a second time recovered his former sex. This being so, he is obliged to make a separate story (736 ff.) of the dispute between Jupiter and Juno, which gave Ovid occasion for mentioning the incident of the snakes.

382. *Wherof,* ' In regard to which.'

390. *menable,* 'apt to be led'; see note on i. 1067. For the variations of reading cp. ii. 1599, and below, 519.

417. 'Cheste' is that form of contention which expresses itself in angry words. Gower seems to have taken it to be connected with the verb 'chide,' see 443, 492, 534, 552 ff.

431. Cp. *Mirour,* 4146 ff.,

> 'ly sage auci
> Ce dist, que deinz le cuer de luy
> Folie buylle tresparmy,
> Comme du fontaine la liquour.'

The reference is to Proverbs xv. 2, ' os fatuorum ebullit stultitiam.'

436. *oppose,* 'inquire.'

463 ff. See note on the Latin verses at the beginning of the Prologue, 5 f.

479. That is, rather than sing such a creed, I would choose to be unlearned and know no creed at all.

487. *Upon hirself,* i. e. upon her authority.

515. *balketh.* A 'balk' is a ridge left unploughed, and 'to balk' in ploughing is to leave a ridge either between two furrows or in the furrow itself, the plough being permitted to pass over a piece of ground without breaking it. Here it is referred to as an accident arising either from not ploughing straight or not keeping the ploughshare regularly at the proper depth. From this idea of leaving out something come most of the other meanings of the verb : see *New Engl. Dict.*

544. *Hire oghte noght be.* For this impersonal use with the simple infinitive cp. 704.

545. *For I,* i. e. 'For that I': cp. 820, &c.

585. This expression, which Pauli for some reason calls an 'obscene proverb,' seems to be nearly equivalent to the saying about the bird that fouls his own nest (cp. *Mirour,* 23413), and refers apparently to recriminations between the owl and the stock upon which he sits, on the matter of cleanliness. The application is to the case of the man who quarrels with his own performances, and naturally has the worst of it himself.

626. 'World' seems to be the true reading here, though 'word' stood in the earlier form of text. The meaning is 'that state of things shall never be permitted by me.' The use of 'world' is like that which we have in i. 178, where 'mi world' means 'my condition': cp. Prol. 383, 1081. The verb 'asterte' is used in the sense of escaping notice and so being allowed to pass or to happen: cp. i. 1934,

> 'Bot that ne schal me noght asterte,
> To wene forto be worthi,' &c.

Cp. i. 722.

The expression 'that word schal me nevere asterte' is a more ordinary one (and therefore more likely to have been introduced by a copyist), but it gives no satisfactory sense here.

641 ff. The story was a hackneyed one, and occurs in many places. It is shortly told by Jerome, *Adv. Jovin.* i. 48.

665. *what labour that sche toke.* The verb is subjunctive, either because the form of speech is indirect, cp. 708, or because the expression is indefinite.

699. Cp. *Mirour,* 4185 ff., where after telling the same story the author roundly declares that he shall not follow the example.

704. *Him oghte . . . . bere:* cp. 544, 1666.

708. *how that it stode:* subjunctive of indirect speech, under rhyme influence: cp. ii. 1243 and l. 771 below, and see note on Prol. 41.

736. *Met.* iii. 316 ff. We have here the rest of the story which was referred to above, 361 ff. The point of the incident as told by Ovid is (perhaps purposely) missed by Gower, who does not mention the reason why Tiresias was selected as judge.

737. That is, according to the religious belief which then prevailed.

762. 'And yet the other state would have pleased him better, to have had' &c.

771. *what he mene:* for the subjunctive cp. 708.

782. *of olde ensample:* for 'olde' in this expression cp. 1683; but 'of old time,' i. 1072, 'an old ensample,' iv. 75.

783. This is from Ovid, *Met.* ii. 542 ff. The Cornide of Gower's story is Coronis. The story is told at greater length by Chaucer as the *Manciple's Tale.*

818 ff. From Ovid, *Fasti,* ii. 585 ff.

889. *fals*: see note on Prol. 221.

918. F alone gives 'overmor,' but it is probably what the author intended, though his first editions had the common variation 'evermor.' S is here defective.

957. *sleth*, 'strikes.'

971. *who so rede*: subjunctive because indefinite; cp. 2508 and note on Prol. 460.

973 ff. This story may be found in Benoît's *Roman de Troie*, 27551 ff. and in Guido, lib. 32 (n 3 v°, ed. Argent.). We must note however that for the classical Nauplius we find in Gower 'Namplus,' whereas in Benoît and Guido both it is 'Naulus' : therefore it would seem that our author had before him also some other form of the story, where he found the name 'Nauplius' or 'Nauplus,' which he read 'Nanplus' or 'Namplus.' Perhaps this may have been Hyginus, *Fab.* cxvi. Elsewhere Gower usually follows Benoît rather than Guido, but here several expressions occur which seem to be suggested by Guido's form of the story: see notes on 1030 and 1063. Also Gower says nothing of the incident of rocks being hurled down on the Greeks (*Rom. de Troie*, 27795 ff.), which is also omitted by Guido.

1002. The name which appears here and in the Latin margin as 'Namplus,' with no important variation of reading, is quite clearly 'Nauplus' in iv. 1816 ff.

1021. *Homward*, i.e. going towards home: cp. 2451.

1030 f. *Hist. Troiana*, n 4, 'qui necesse habebant per confinia regni sui transire.'

1036. *it sihe*, 'might see it.'

1049. *ten or twelve*. Guido says two hundred. Benoît does not specify the number of ships, but says that ten thousand men were lost. Gower has judiciously reduced the number.

1063. Cp. *Hist. Troiana*, n 4 v°, 'fugiunt et se immittunt in pelagus spaciosum.'

1065. 'what' for 'war,' which appears in the unrevised form of the first recension, must be an error of the original scribe : on the other hand, 'tyme' for 'dai' proceeded no doubt originally from the author and was altered in order to make the verse run more smoothly.

Latin Verses. iv. 1. *et sit spiritus eius Naribus*: a reference to Isaiah ii. 22, 'Quiescite ergo ab homine, cuius spiritus in naribus eius est.' The same passage is quoted in *Mirour*, 4754, and it is evident there that the 'breath in the nostrils' was understood by our author to stand for fury of anger.

1113. *war hem wel*, 'let them beware.'

1158. The contest in the heart between Wit and Reason on the one hand and Will and Hope on the other is quite in the style of the *Roman de la Rose*, where Reason and the Lover have an endless controversy (2983 ff.). Though the agencies are clearly personified here, the author has not assigned capital letters to their names.

1166. *out of retenue,* ' out of my service.'

1173. *jeupartie,* ' discord,' one side being matched against the other. The first reading was ' champartie,' which may have proceeded from the author. It is clear that this word was used by Lydgate in the sense of ' rivalry' or ' contest ' in the phrase ' holde champartie,' and this may either have come from the idea of partnership, implying division of power and so rivalry, as in Chaucer, *Cant. Tales,* A 1949, or from the legal sense, with which Gower and Lydgate would doubtless be acquainted, meaning partnership for a contentious purpose. There seems no sufficient reason for supposing (with the *New Engl. Dict.*) that Lydgate's use was founded on a misunderstanding of Chaucer.

1183. *and til.* Caxton and Berthelet both have ' tyl that ' for ' and til,' and one is tempted to suggest that ' and til ' was meant to stand for ' until.'

1201 ff. The story of the visit of Alexander to Diogenes was a common one enough, and it is hardly worth while to investigate its source for Gower. He probably here combined various materials into one narrative, for the usual form of the story as given by Vincent of Beauvais, *Spec. Hist.* iii. 68 f., and in the *Gesta Romanorum,* does not include the conversation about the Reason and the Will. This may have been derived from Walter Burley, *De Vita Philosophorum,* cap. l., ' Dum Alexander rex coram Diogene transiret, Diogenes tanquam illum spernens non respexit ; cui dixit Alexander, " Quid est Diogenes quod me non respicis, quasi mei non indigeas ? " Cui ille, " Ad quid necesse habeo servi servorum meorum ? " Et Alexander, " Numquid servorum tuorum servus sum ? " Ait, " Ego prevaleo cupiditatibus meis refrenans illas et subiciens mihi illas ut serviant : tibi autem cupiditates prevalent, et servus earum efficeris, earum obtemperans iussioni : servus igitur es servorum meorum." ' Burley gives the other part of the conversation separately.

The incident of the messenger sent to inquire and of the answer which he brought back is no doubt due to Gower, as also the idea of the 'tun' being set on an axle and adapted for astronomical observations.

1212. The ' dolium ' was of course popularly regarded as a wooden cask.

1222. 'As fate would have it' : see note on 172 (end), and cp. 1442.

1224. *the Sonne ariste,* i. e. the rising of the sun : so iv. 1285, 'and that was er the Sonne Ariste.'

1310. *to schifte,* ' to dispose of.' In Burley, ' rogo ne auferas quod dare non potes.'

1331 ff. The tale of Pyramus and Thisbe is from Ovid, *Met.* iv. 55–166. Chaucer has taken it from the same source in the *Legend of Good Women.* When we compare the results. we find that in this instance it is Chaucer who has followed his authority closely, while Gower gives a paraphrase in his own language and with several variations of detail. He says, for example, that the lovers themselves made the hole in the wall through which they conversed ; he omits Ninus'

**   K k

tomb; he speaks of a lion, not a lioness; he says that Thisbe hid herself in a bush (not a cave), and that then the lion slew and devoured a beast before drinking at the spring; he cuts short the speech of Pyramus before killing himself; he represents that Pyramus was slain at once instead of living until Thisbe came; he invents an entirely new speech for Thisbe; and he judiciously omits, as Chaucer does also, the mention of the mulberry-tree and its transformation.

In short, Gower writes apparently from a general recollection of the story, while Chaucer evidently has his Ovid before him and endeavours to translate almost every phrase, showing thereby his good taste, for Ovid tells the story well.

The following points in Ovid (among others) are reproduced by Chaucer and not by Gower : l. 56, 'quas Oriens habuit'; 58, 'Coctilibus muris'; 59, 'Notitiam primosque gradus vicinia fecit' (which Chaucer misunderstands, however); 62, 'Ex aequo captis' &c.; 64, 'Quoque magis tegitur, tectus magis aestuat ignis'; 65, 'Fissus erat tenui rima,' &c.; 68, 'Quid non sentit amor?'; 73-77, the speeches of the lovers to the wall; 81 f., 'Postera nocturnos aurora' &c.; 85, 'Fallere custodes'; 87, 'Neve sit errandum' &c.; 94, 'adopertaque vultum'; 97, 'leaena'; 99, 'ad lunae radios'; 100, 'in antrum'; 105, 'vestigia vidit in alto Pulvere' &c.; 108, 'Una duos nox, inquit, perdet amantes,' and the rest of this speech; 117 f., 'Utque dedit notae lacrimas,' &c.; 122, 'Non aliter quam cum vitiato fistula plumbo Scinditur'; 130, 'Quantaque vitarit narrare pericula gestit'; 133, 'tremebunda videt pulsare cruentum Membra solum'; 134 f., 'oraque buxo' &c.; 140, 'Vulnera supplevit' &c.; 145, 'oculos iam morte gravatos'; 148 ff., the speech of Thisbe, except the reference to the mulberry-tree.

Gower's rendering of the story is inferior to that of Chaucer, as might be expected, but nevertheless it is simple and pathetic. It has even some points of superiority, as 1386 f., the passage of Thisbe through the town at night; 1400, 'with his blodi snoute'; 1411, the terror of Thisbe when concealed in the bush; and finally 1486 ff., where instead of deliberately resolving on death and inflicting it with calm resolution, she is more naturally represented as overcome by a sudden impulse in the midst of her mourning and killing herself almost without consciousness of what she did.

1348. *as it scholde be*: cp. 1222, 'As thing which scholde so betyde.'

1356. All the best copies have 'miht' or 'might' here: cp. 1440. The distinction, however, between 'miht' (=mayest) and 'mihte' is usually well preserved by our author.

1394. *In haste and*: so ll. 1396, 1415. On the other hand, in 1430 we have a stop after 'folhaste' (in F), while 1447 remains doubtful.

1442. *as it schal betide*, cp. 1222.

1448. *For sche*, a reference to the 'folhaste' of the previous line. It was his haste that destroyed him, for if he had waited but a little he would have seen her come.

1466 f. 'If it be only by this mishap which has befallen my love and me together.' For the use of 'betwen' see note on ii. 653. The position of ' Only ' is affected by metrical requirements : see note on ii. 709.

1473. *oure herte bothe*, 'the hearts of us both.' The singular 'herte' is given by the best copies of each recension.

1496. *Bewar* : thus written several times in F, e. g. 1738. Here A also has ' Bewar.'

1524. *him stant of me no fere* : cp. ii. 2124.

1537. *Daunger* : see note on i. 2443.

1593 ff. The construction of the sentence is interrupted, but the sense is clear : ' For if I, who have given all my will and wit to her service, should in reward thereof be suffered to die, it would be pity.' For this kind of irregularity cp. i. 98, 2948, &c.

1605. The reading 'in such,' though given by both S and F, must be wrong.

1630. *overthrewe*. The verb no doubt is intransitive, as often, e. g. i. 1886, 1962, and below, l. 1638.

1666. *him oghte have be* : cp. 704.

1685 ff. Ovid, *Met.* i. 453–567. Gower cuts the story short.

1701. Ovid, *Met.* i. 470,

' Quod facit auratum est et cuspide fulget acuta.'

(Merkel alters ' auratum' to ' hamatum,' but this is certainly wrong.)

1704. Note that the final syllable of ' Daphne' is subject to elision here and in 1716: so ' Progne' v. 5574, &c.

1718 ff. The suggestion is Gower's own, as in other similar cases, e. g. i. 2355.

1743. 'And it is to be desired that a man,' &c.

1757 ff. This story is chiefly from Benoît, *Roman de Troie*, 28025 ff. Guido omits many details which are given by Gower. Note that in l. 28025, where Joly's edition has ' Samas,' Guido and Gower both have ' Athemas.' Our author has treated his materials freely and tells the story at greater length. The speech which he assigns to Nestor is for the most part original.

1885 ff. The tale of Orestes is from Benoît de Sainte-More, *Rom. de Troie*, 27925–27990, 28155–28283, and 28339–28402. Guido omits the visit of Orestes to Athens to obtain help for his expedition, the portion of the oracle which bad him tear away his mother's breasts, and the name of Menetius (or Menesteus), who defended Orestes, and Gower's details are in general more in accordance with those of Benoît. A few exceptions may be found, however. For example, Gower says that Agamemnon was murdered as he lay in bed (1915), Guido, ' dum suo soporatus dormiret in lecto,' but Benoît only, ' L'ont la première nuit ocis.' Again, Guido calls Idomeneus ' consanguineum eius,' and Gower says, ' So as he was of his lignage,' of which Benoît says nothing. No doubt Gower was acquainted with both, and preferred the French because he perceived it to be better.

1911. ' To set her love in place where it cannot be secure.'

2022 f. *Cropheon . . . Phoieus.* The names are given as 'Trofion' and 'Florentes' by Benoît (Joly's text), 'Troiesem' ('Croeze' MS.) and 'Forensis' by Guido. They are originally derived from a misunderstanding of a passage in Dictys, *Bell. Troi.* vi. 3, 'armatus cum praedicta manu ad Strophium venit : is namque Phocensis, cuius filia,' &c.

2055 ff. This speech is introduced by Gower.

2112 f.
> 'Li un dient qu'il a fet dreit,
> Et li autre que non aveit.'
>
> *Rom. de Troie,* 28275.

2145. *Menesteüs.* This is a more correct form of the name than the 'Menetius,' which we have in Joly's text of Benoît.

2148. *of the goddes bede.* Here we perhaps have Guido rather than Benoît.

2173. *Egiona.* The name is properly Erigona, and so it is given by Benoît. The moralization on her fate, 2183 ff., is due to our author, and it is rather out of place, considering the circumstances of the story.

2346. *the trew man.* In F we have 'trew,' altered apparently from 'trewe,' which is the usual and the more correct form : 'the trew man to the plowh' means the labourer who truly serves the plough.

2358. This is simply a repetition of 2355, 'thei stonde of on acord.' 'As of corage' means as regards their feeling or inclination : for this use of 'as' cp. Prol. 492, i. 557, &c.

2363 ff. A very common story, found shortly in Augustine, *Civ. Dei,* iv. 4, and repeated in the *Gesta Romanorum* and many other books. Gower has expanded it after his own fashion.

2424 f. 'that men set their hearts to make gain by such wrong doing.'

2451. *homward,* i. e. 'going homeward.' The word included something of a verbal sense, as we see in i. 938, iii. 1021 : so also 'toward' in l. 2643.

2458. *the world mistimed.* The verb 'mistime' means properly 'to happen amiss,' with the suggestion that it is by the fault of the person concerned. Gower uses it here transitively for 'to manage amiss,' while in vi. 4 'was mystymed' means 'came unhappily about.'

2508. *what man . . . . rede* : for the subjunctive see note on Prol. 460.

2536. 'Hardly have any fear' : see note on ii. 2124.

2555. Acastus was king of Iolcos. He purified Peleus, as some say of the murder of Eurytion, but according to others of that of Phocus : cp. Bocc. *Gen. Deorum,* xii. 50, 'ad Magnetas abiit, ubi ab Achasto fraterna caede purgatus est.'

2563 f. Alcmaeon, son of Amphiaraus, was purified by Achelous, whom our author here takes for a priest.

2599 ff. This anecdote is told also in the *Miiour,* 5029-5040, and there also it is ascribed to Solinus. I do not find it, however, in his book.

2608 ff. For the irregularity of this sentence cp. 1593 ff.

2639 ff. The story is taken from Benoît (*Rom. de Troie,* 6497-6590), as we may see at once from the name 'Theucer,' which Guido gives rather more correctly as 'Theutran.' Also ll. 2674-2680, *Roman de Troie*, 6545-6553, have nothing corresponding to them in Guido. Guido here certainly referred to a copy of the so-called Dares, where the name occurs in its classical form 'Teuthras.' He is particularly interested in the story on local grounds, being concerned to show that the 'Messe' which he found in Benoît might be connected with the name of his place of residence, Messina, and that the events related occurred actually in Sicily. Accordingly he speaks of certain columns popularly called 'columns of Hercules,' which existed in his own time in Sicily, 'ex parte Barbarorum,' i.e. on the south coast, and takes them as evidence of the connexion of Hercules with the island, and hence of the probability that this story (which in the original has to do with Hercules, though Gower has excluded him from it) had its scene in Sicily. Dares, he admits, says nothing of this, and his reference to Dares is here in more precise form than usual, 'in suo codice' according to the Bodleian MS., though the printed editions give 'in suo opere' (MS. Add. A. 365, f. 50 v).

He says of the place where these columns are, 'qui locus dicitur adhuc columpnarum,' and adds that the emperor Frederic II has established a town there, and that the place is now called 'terra nova.' This is obviously identical with the modern Terranova, founded by Frederic II near the site of the ancient Gela. It seems probable that Guido may have been himself a native of this place or of its immediate neighbourhood, and that he chose to call himself after its former designation, 'Columpna ' or 'Columpnae,' instead of by the new name which had come into use during his own lifetime[1].

2643. *His Sone.* This is a mistake on the part of Gower. Both Benoît and Guido state quite clearly that Telephus was the son of Hercules, and that it was to Hercules that the obligation was due which is referred to in 2690 ff. Perhaps the copy of the *Roman de Troie* which Gower used had 'Thelefus fu filz Achilles ' for 'Thelefus fu filz Hercules,' in l. 6506.

2756. We should rather have expected 'That I fro you wol nothing hele.'

LIB. IV.

9. Cp. *Mirour*, 5606,

'Lachesce dist, Demein, Demein.'

38. *Thou schalt mowe*: cp. ii. 1670, where we have 'mow' for 'mowe.'

60. *a fin.* This is a French expression, which appears repeatedly in the *Mirour* as ' au fin.'

77 ff. The only definite indication of sources here is the reference (such as it is) to Ovid, *Her. Ep.* vii., contained in ll. 104-115.

92. *as it be scholde*, cp. iii. 1348.

[1] On inquiry in the locality I find that Terranova, which has always had a column for its emblem, claims Guido as a native : see *Memorie Gelesi* by Sign. S. D. Navarra, Terranova 1896, pp. 72 f.

104 ff. This picture seems to be constructed partly from a misreading or misunderstanding of Ovid, *Her. Ep.* vii. 1 f.,

> 'Sic ubi fata vocant, udis abiectus in herbis
> Ad vada Maeandri concinit albus olor.'

It is difficult to see how our author translated these lines, but the result, which must have been chiefly due to his imagination, is rather creditable to him. Chaucer gives the true sense in the *Legend of Good Women*, 1355 ff.,

> 'Ryght so,' quod she, 'as that the white swan
> Ayenst his deth begynneth for to synge.
> Ryght so to yow I make my compleynynge.'

128. *such a lak of Slowthe*, ' such a fault of Sloth.'

137. That is, to put all the slothful in mind (of their duty).

147 ff. The general idea of this is taken from the letter of Penelope to Ulysses, Ovid, *Her. Ep.* i, but this is not closely followed in details, and it will be noticed that Gower represents the letter as sent while the siege of Troy still continued, and apparently he knows nothing of the great length of the wandering afterwards : cp. 226 ff.

170. The reading ' Had' for 'Hath' is given by many MSS., including F. We find 'Hath' in the following, H₁C, SAdTΔ, W, and it must certainly be the true reading.

196 ff. Ovid, *Her. Ep.* i. 2, ' Nil mihi rescribas, attamen ipse veni.'

234. Robert Grosteste's reputation for learning in the sciences earned for him, as for his contemporary Roger Bacon, the character of a student of magic. In the metrical life of Grosteste by Robert of Bardney (Wharton, *Anglia Sacra*, i. 333) one chapter is ' De aeneo capite quod Oxoniae fecit Grosthede ad dubia quaeque determinanda.' This author says only that by some accident the head fell and was broken, and that its inventor thereupon abandoned the study of forbidden sciences.

Naudé in his *Apologie pour les grands hommes soupçonnez de Magie* classes ' Robert de Lincolne' and Albertus Magnus together as supposed makers of speaking images, but the former only on the authority of Gower, with whom he had been made acquainted by Selden.

242 f. That is, he lost all that he had done from the time when he first began to work ; an inversion of clauses for the sake of the rhyme : cp. ii. 709 ff.

249. *kept* : more properly 'kepe,' but the infinitive is attracted into the form of the participle ' wold,' much as the participle of the mood auxiliary in modern German takes the form of the infinitive : see note on ii. 1799.

305. *hadde I wist*, cp. i. 1888, ii. 473. It is the exclamation of those who fall into evil by neglect of proper precaution. The same sentiment is expressed more fully in l. 899,

> ' Ha, wolde god I hadde knowe ! '

345. *dar*. This form stands as plural here and l. 350.

371 ff. The story of Pygmalion is from Ovid, *Metam*. x. 243–297.

377. 'Being destined to the labours of love': cp. note on iii. 143 (end).

415. *how it were*, i. e. 'how so ever it were': cp. l. 1848.

448. *a solein tale*, 'a strange tale.' This word 'solein' (or 'soulein'), which English etymologists in search for the origin of 'sullen' report as hardly to be found in French, occurs repeatedly in the *Mirour de l'omme* in the sense of 'alone,' 'lonely.' For the meaning here assigned to it we may compare the modern use of the word 'singular,' which in Gower's French meant 'lonely.' There is no authority for Pauli's reading 'solempne,' and it gives neither sense nor metre.

451 ff. The tale of Iphis is from Ovid, *Metam*. ix. 666–797, abbreviated and altered with advantage.

453 ff. The authority of the MSS. is strongly in favour of 'grete : lete' in these lines, and this reading is certainly right. We must take 'lete' as the past participle of the strong verb 'leten' (from 'lǣtan'), meaning 'leave,' 'omit,' and 'grete' as accommodated to the rhyme. The negative construction following rather suggests 'let,' meaning 'hindered.' as ii. 128 ff., but the rhyme 'let : gret' would be an impossible one. See note on i. 3365 and cp. l. 1153.

585. *And stonde*, i. e. 'And I stonde': cp. i. 1895, &c., and below, l. 697.

624. *on miself along*, so below l. 952, 'It is noght on mi will along,' and Chaucer, *Troilus*, ii. 1001,

'On me is nought along thyn yvel fare.'

The use of 'on' for 'of' in this phrase is still known in some dialects.

647 ff. For the Ring of Forgetfulness here spoken of see Petrus Comestor, *Exodus* vi., where it is related that Moses in command of the Egyptians captured the chief city of the Ethiopians by the help of Tarbis, daughter of their king, and married her in recompense of her services. Then, wishing to return to Egypt and being detained by his wife, 'tanquam vir peritus astrorum duas imagines sculpsit in gemmis huius efficaciae, ut altera memoriam, altera oblivionem conferret. Cumque paribus anulis eas inseruisset, alterum, scilicet oblivionis anulum, uxori praebuit, alterum ipse tulit; ut sic pari amore sic paribus anulis insignirentur. Coepit ergo mulier amoris viri oblivisci, et tandem libere in Aegyptum regressus est' (Migne, *Patrol.* vol. 198, p. 1144). Cp. Godfr. Viterb., *Pantheon*, v. (p. 115).

731 ff. Partly from Ovid, *Her. Ep*. ii. and *Rem. Am*. 591–604 ; but there was probably some other source, for our author would not find anything in Ovid about the transformation into a tree. Many of the details seem to be of his own invention, and he is probably responsible for the variation which makes the visit of Demophon to Thrace take place on the way to Troy instead of on the return. Chaucer's form of the story in the *Legend of Good Women* is quite different.

733. F is here followed in punctuation.

776. *a Monthe day*: Ovid, *Her. Ep.* ii. 3 f.,

> 'Cornua cum lunae pleno semel orbe coissent,
> Litoribus nostris ancora pacta tua est.'

782. Cp. Ovid, *Ars Am.* ii. 354,

> 'Exarsit velis acrius illa datis.'

787 ff. Except the idea of a letter being sent, Gower takes little here from Ovid.

816 ff. This passage seems mostly of Gower's invention, partly perhaps on the suggestion of the story of Hero and Leander in Ovid, *Her. Ep.* xix. 33 ff. See Bech in *Anglia*, v. 347.

do set up. Apparently 'set' is the participle, cp. ii. 1799.

833. *al hire one.* This idea is emphasized by Ovid, *Rem. Am.* 591 f.

869. This piece of etymology is perhaps due to our author, who usually adds something of his own to the stories of transformation which he relates; see note on i. 2355. Lydgate says that Phyllis hanged herself upon a filbert-tree, but he perhaps took the notion from Gower:

> 'Upon the walles depeint men myght se
> Hou she was honged upon a filbert tre.'
> *Temple of Glas*, 88.

See the note in Dr. Schick's edition, E. E. T. S. 1891.

893. Cp. *Mirour*, 5436,

> 'Lors est il sage apres la mein,'

of which this line is an exact reproduction.

904. *pleith an aftercast.* This looks like a metaphor from casting dice, but it is difficult to see the exact application. It means of course here that he is always too late in what he says and does.

914. *come at thin above*, i.e. attain to success : cp. *Mirour*, 25350,

> 'Car lors est Triche a son dessus.'

964. See note on i. 2677.

979 ff. The story may probably enough be taken from Ovid, *Metam.* ii. 1-324, but if so it is much abbreviated.

which is the Sonne hote, 'which is called the Sun'; cp. ii. 131 f. Possibly, however, 'hote' may be the adjective, with definite termination for the sake of the rhyme. There would be no objection to rhyming with it the adverb of the same form.

1030 ff. The moral drawn by Gower from the story of Phaeton is against going too low, that is abandoning the higher concerns of love owing to slothful negligence. The next story is against aiming too high and neglecting the due claims of service.

1035 ff. Ovid, *Metam.* viii. 183–235.

1090 f. Cp. *Mirour*, 5389 ff.

1096. *who as evere take*: so 'what man' is very commonly used with subjunctive, iii. 2508 &c., but the uncertainty of the construction is shown by 'And thinkth' in the next line. See notes on Prol. 13, 460.

1108 ff. Cp. *Mirour*, 5395 ff.

1131. A superfluous syllable, such as we have at the pause in this line, is very unusual in Gower's verse ; but cp. v. 447.

1153. *lete I ne mai*, 'I may not neglect': see note on i. 3365.

1180. Cp. i. 698, 'And many a contenance he piketh.' It means here perhaps 'thus I keep up a pretence (for staying).'

1245 ff. A somewhat similar story to this is to be found in Andreas Capellanus, *De Amore*, to which my attention was first called by Mr. Archer. This book (written about 1220) gives imaginary colloquies between different kinds of persons, to illustrate the ways of courtship, 'Plebeius loquitur plebeiae,' 'Plebeius nobili,' 'Nobilis plebeiae,' 'Nobilis nobili.' In this last occurs the story of a squire who saw the god of love leading a great company of ladies in three bands, the first well mounted and well attended, the second well mounted but attended by so many that it was a hindrance rather than a help, and the third in wretched array with lame horses and no attendance. The meaning of the sight is explained to the squire by one of these last, and he is taken to see the appropriate rewards and punishments of each band. He relates what he has seen to his mistress in order to make her more ready to accept his suit (pp. 91–108, ed. Trojel, 1892).

There are some expressions which resemble those which Gower uses, as 'quarum quaelibet in equo *pinguissimo* et formoso et *suavissime ambulante* sedebat' (p. 92), cp. 1309 f.,

> 'On faire amblende hors thei sete
> That were al whyte, fatte and grete.'

And again, 'domina quaedam . . . habens equum macerrimum et turpem et tribus pedibus claudicantem,' cp. 1343 ff. The story, however, is different in many ways from that of Gower. For other similar stories see the article in *Romania* for January 1900 on the 'Purgatory of Cruel Beauties' by W. A. Neilson.

The tale of Rosiphelee is well told by Gower, and in more than one passage it bears marks of having been carefully revised by the author. The alteration of 1321 f. is peculiarly happy, and gives us one of the best couplets in the *Confessio Amantis*.

1285. *the Sonne Ariste*: cp. iii. 1224. The capital letter was perhaps intended to mark 'Ariste' as a substantive.

1307. *comen ryde*: cp. i. 350.

1309. 'hors' is evidently plural here : so i. 2036 and often.

1320. *long and smal*, i.e. tall and slender. Adjectives used predicatively with a plural subject take the plural inflection or not according to convenience. Thus in Prol. 81 we have 'Bot for my wittes ben to smale' in rhyme with 'tale.'

1323. *beere*. This is pret. plur., as 1376: the same form for pret. subj. 2749.

1330. *For pure abaissht*: cp. Chaucer, *Troilus*, ii. 656, 'And with that thought for pure ashamed she Gan in hir hed to pulle.' The parallel, to which my attention was called by Prof. McCormick, suggests the idea that 'abaissht' is a participle rather than a noun, and the use of the past participle with 'for' in this manner occurs several times in Lydgate, e. g. 'for unknowe,' 'meaning from ignorance,' *Temple of Glas*, 632, 'for astonied,' 934, 1366, and so with an adjective, 'for pure wood' in the English *Rom. of the Rose*, 276. See Dr. Schick's note on Lydgate, *Temple of Glas*, 632.

1422. *That I ne hadde*, 'I would that I had': cp. v. 3747,

'Ha lord, that he ne were alonde!'

'to late war' is in a kind of loose apposition to the subject.

1429. *swiche*. Rather perhaps 'swich,' as ii. 566 f., v. 377. Most MSS. have 'such.'

1432 ff. *warneth ... bidd*. The singular of the imperative seems to be freely interchanged with the plural in this form of address.

1454 (margin). The author dissociates himself personally from the extreme doctrines enunciated in the text, as at first he took care to remind his readers that the character of a lover was for him only an assumed one (i. 63 ff. margin).

1490. *and longe er that sche changeth* &c. This is a puzzling sentence, and we are not helped by the punctuation of the MSS., which for the most part have a stop after 'herte.' I can only suppose that it means 'and is long before she changes her heart in her youth to marriage.' We can hardly make 'longe' a verb, 'and may be eager until she changes,' because of the lines which follow.

1505 ff. Judges xi. Our author has expanded the story so far as regards the mourning for the virginity of Jephthah's daughter, that being the point with which he was particularly concerned here.

1516. 'Whether it be of man or woman.'

1537 ff. In the original this is different, 'Heu me, filia mea, decepisti me et ipsa decepta es : aperui enim os meum ad Dominum, et aliud facere non potero.' Gower deals freely here as elsewhere with the narrative, especially in the matter of speeches.

1563. *fourty daies*: in the original 'duobus mensibus.'

1632 ff. Cp. *Mirour*, 11694.

1649. *as me thenketh ... That*, equivalent to 'me thinketh ... That,' either 'as' or 'That' being redundant.

1659. The best MSS. give 'heþen' here, not 'heþene.'

1693 ff. *Roman de Troie*, 18385 ff. In the medieval Tale of Troy it is the love of Polyxena which serves as motive for the withdrawal of Achilles from the war.

1723. *which I travaile fore*. We have here rather a remarkable instance of emphasis thrown on the preposition, with a modification of form for the sake of the rhyme: cp. ii. 565.

1741. *On whether bord*, i. e. on which tack : technical terms of the sea occur several times in the *Confessio Amantis*, e.g. v. 3119, 7048, viii. 1983.

1810. *made*: cp. Prol. 300.

1815 ff. Gower seems to have dealt rather freely with this story. The usual form of it gives Palamedes, not Nauplius, as the person who came to fetch Ulysses, and makes Ulysses yoke a horse and an ox together in a plough as a sign of madness : see Hyginus, *Fab.* xcv. As to the name of Nauplus, see notes on iii. 973, 1002.

1833. That is, 'feigning to be mad,' not 'like one who feigns to be mad' : see note on i. 695.

1847 ff. 'He thought to try if he were mad or no, however it might please Ulysses,' that is, whether it pleased him or not. 'Hou' seems to be for 'How so evere' : cp. l. 415.

1875. *tothe*, written so when the emphasis falls on the preposition, see note on i. 232.

1901 ff. Ovid, *Her. Ep.* xiii.

1927. F has a stop after 'londeth,' thus throwing the clause, 'and was the ferste there Which londeth,' into a parenthesis.

1935 ff. 1 Sam. xxviii., where the witch is called 'mulier pythonem habens.'

1968 ff. The story of the education of Achilles by Chiron, as we have it here, is apparently taken, directly or indirectly, from Statius, *Achill.* ii. 121 (407) ff.,

> 'Nunquam ille imbelles Ossaea per avia damas
> Sectari, aut timidas passus me cuspide lyncas
> Sternere, sed tristes turbare cubilibus ursos
> Fulmineosque sues, et sicubi maxima tigris
> Aut seducta iugis fetae spelunca leaenae.
> Ipse sedens vasto facta exspectabat in antro,
> Si sparsus magno remearem sanguine ; nec me
> Ante nisi inspectis admisit ad oscula telis.'

2014 ff. The argument is to the effect that Prowess, which is acknowledged to be the virtue opposed to Sloth, see *Mirour*, 10136 &c., must show itself partly in the spirit of warlike boldness, 'the corage of hardiesce,' leading to such undertakings as those of which the Lover had disputed the necessity.

2040. *And that*, i. e. 'And as to that' : cp. Prol. 122.

2045 ff. The fight between Hercules and Achelous is related in detail by Ovid, *Metam.* ix. 31-88. Some parts of this seem to be reproduced by Gower, but the details are not very exactly copied. For the story generally he had some other authority, whence he got for example the names 'Oënes' and 'Calidoyne.'

It is to be noted that Gower gives 'Achelons' instead of Achelous, as he does also in the *Traitié*, vii. 5, where the story is shortly told in the same way as here, and there we find 'Achelontis' in the margin as the genitive case. He ought to have been preserved from the mistake by the occurrence of the name in Ovid's verse.

2054. For these two pillars cp. Chaucer, *Cant. Tales*, B 3307 f., but Gower supposes them to have been both set up in the 'desert of India,'

'El grant desert d'Ynde superiour' as he has it in *Traitié*, vii. 1, whereas according to Chaucer one was set up in the East and the other in the West, to mark the extreme bounds of the world.

2123 f. Such forms of spelling as 'sleighte,' 'heighte' are unusual with our author, but cp. vii. 1121, 1227 f.

2135. For the stories of 'Pantasilee' and Philemenis we may refer to the *Roman de Troie*, 23283 ff. and 25663–25704.

2200 ff. From this question arises the inevitable discussion of the nature of 'gentilesse' and how far it depends upon birth, riches or personal merit. Gower accepts only the last qualification, and argues for it after the fashion of John Ball, though he was neither a Lollard nor a social revolutionist : cp. *Mirour*, 23389 ff. For the general subject cp. Dante, *Convito*, iv. 10, *Roman de la Rose*, 18807 ff. (ed. Méon), Chaucer, *Cant. Tales*, D 1109 ff.

To Gower we must grant the merit of clearness and conciseness in handling the well-worn theme.

2208 f. Cp. Dante, *Convito*, iv. 3.

2305 ff. 'And love is of profit also as regards women, so that they may be the better "affaited." '

2314. *make it queinte*, 'behave gently': cp. 'make it tough,' Chaucer, *Troilus*, v. 101. For the meaning of 'queinte' see the quotations in Godefroy's Dictionary under 'cointe.'

2325. 1 John iii. 14.

2342. This is from Job v. 7.

2396 ff. Many of these names are unknown to me, and Warton's conjectures on the subject are very wild, but some points may be illustrated from Godfrey of Viterbo. For example, as regards the first we find,

'Septem quas legimus Cham primus scripserat artes.'

Pantheon, iii. (p. 88).

2401. Godf. Vit., *Pantheon*, vi. (p. 133), 'Tunc Cadmus Graecas literas sedecim fecit.'

2410. *Termegis*. The word is a dissyllable for the metre. Probably this name stands for Termegistus (i. e. Trismegistus), and in that case we must throw the accent upon the final syllable and pass lightly over the preceding one.

2418 ff. I suspect that 'Poulins' means Apollo or Apollinis : cp. *Pantheon*, vi. (p. 133), 'Apollo etiam citharam condidit et artem medicinalem invenit.'

2421. *Zenzis*, i. e. Zeuxis, who is referred to in the *Rom. de la Rose* (for example) as the chief of painters, 16387 ff. (ed. Méon).

2422. Cp. Godf. Vit., *Panth.* v. (p. 121),

'Tunc et Prometheus, qui filius est Atlantis
Dat statuas hominis humano more meantes.'

2427. 'Jadahel' is the Jabal (or Jebal) of the Bible (Gen. iv. 20). Godfrey of Viterbo calls him by the same name and makes the same statement about his hunting and fishing :

> ' In mundo Iadahel posuit tentoria primus,
> Venator prior ipse fuit feritate ferinus,
> Primus et invalidis retia mersit aquis.'
>
> *Panth.* ii. (p. 77).

2439 ff. Godf. Vit., *Panth.* iv. (p. 98),

> ' Saturnus statuit super aequora vela moueri,
> Denarios posuit commercia rite mereri.
>
> . . . .
>
> Aedificans Sutrium dum vivit ibi dominatur,
> Triticeum semen primus in urbe serens.'

2462 ff. For the seven bodies and four spirits of Alchemy cp. Chaucer, *Cant. Tales*, G 818 ff. Mercury, it will be noticed, is reckoned both as a body and as a spirit, but some authorities called this a spirit only and reckoned six metallic bodies.

2476. *after the bok it calleth*, ' according as the book calls it.'

2488 ff. Cp. 2565 ff.

2501. The seven forms are those enumerated in 2513 ff., viz. distillation, congelation, solution, descension, sublimation, calcination, fixation.

2522. Cp. Chaucer, *Cant. Tales*, G 862 f.

2533. *Thre Stones.* According to some authors, as Hortulanus (MS. Ashmole 1478, iv.), there was but one stone, the Elixir, which had vegetable, animal and mineral qualities or functions; but in Lydgate, *Secrees of the Philosophres*, l. 530 (E.E.T.S.), we have,

> ' And of stones, specially of three,
> Oon mineral, another vegetatyff,' &c. ;

and the editor quotes from *Rosarium Philosophorum*, ' Tres sunt lapides et tres sales sunt, ex quibus totum magisterium consistit, scilicet mineralis, plantalis et animalis.' In the *Secreta Secretorum*, however, the stone seems to be one only, see the chapter ' De lapide animali vegetabili.'

2597. *who that it knewe* : cp. ii. 88, and see note on Prol. 460.

2606. *Hermes*, i. e. Hermes Trismegistus, to whom the invention of the science was attributed.

on the ferste, ' the very first ', cp. vi. 1481. It may be questioned, however, whether the theory put forward by C. Stoffel in *Englische Studien*, xxvii. 253 ff., is the correct explanation of this expression, which survived to Elizabethan times (Shaksp., *Cymb.* i. 6. 165, ' he is one the truest mannered '). He takes ' on ' in the sense of the Latin ' unus ' in ' iustissimus unus,' to mean ' alone,' ' above all.' It is perhaps more likely that the usual explanation, which regards it as an elliptical expression for ' one who was the first,' is correct, especially in view of such expressions as ' two the first,' ' three the noblest,' &c., which also occur in the fourteenth century. The use of ' on ' (' oon ') for ' a person' is common enough, as in the expressions ' so good on,'

'so worthi on,' ii. 1217, 1240, and 'Oon Theloüs,' ii. 1092. We find
a similar expression in Gower's French, e. g. *Mirour*, 2462.

2608. A work by Geber, 'Super Artem Alkemie,' in six books, translated from Arabic into Latin, may be found in MS. Ashmole 1384.
It seems to treat in a practical and systematic manner of the method
of transmutation of metals into gold.

2609. 'Ortolan' is the Englishman John Garland, called Hortulanus,
for which name see the note in MS. Ashmole 1471 iv. prefixed to an
English translation of his 'Commentary on the Smaragdine Table of
Hermes.'

Morien is said to have been a hermit in the mountains near
Jerusalem. The two 'books of Morien' in the form of dialogues
between him and Kalid the son of Gesid may be read in Latin
(translated from Arabic) in MS. Digby 162.

2610. A short treatise of Avicen on Alchemy may be found in MS.
Ashm. 1420.

2624. *the parfite medicine*. The inflexion is perhaps in imitation of
the definite form of the English adjective, as in vii. 2168, 4994, while
in l. 2522, where the accent is thrown back, we have 'the parfit Elixir.'
It is possible, however, that this is a case of the French feminine
form such as we have in i. 2677, ii. 3507, iv. 964, cp. i. 636. So
perhaps ii. 3243, 'O thou divine pourveance,' and viii. 23, 'O thou
gentile Venus.'

2637. *Carmente*: cp. Godf. Vit., *Panth.* vi. (p. 135).

2641. Dindymus here means the grammarian Didymus, a follower
of the school of Aristarchus and a very voluminous writer on Greek
language and literature. Our author here classes Aristarchus and
Didymus with Donatus, and supposes them all to be concerned with
the Latin tongue.

2648. *Tullius with Cithero*. It is apparent from this passage,
which has been differently given without any authority in the printed
editions, that Gower supposed Tullius and Cicero to be two different
persons. There would have been reason to suspect this from the passage in the seventh book where he refers to the debate on the death
sentence of the Catiline conspirators, speaking of Tullius as his
authority for the rules of rhetoric there illustrated, and 'Cithero' as
the consul, without any hint that they are the same person (vii. 1588 ff.).
In Gower's French works Tullius (Tulles) is the only name used. The
form Cithero (or Scithero) is used also by Chaucer, *Cant. Tales*, F 722.

2738 ff. Cp. *Mirour*, 5185 ff.

2749. *beere*, past tense subjunctive, cp. 1323.

2756 ff. Gower seems to be exceptionally well informed on the subject of the Fates and their separate functions.

2792. This casting with the dice would not be for ordinary gambling,
but for divining characters and telling fortunes in matters of love.
Each combination produced by the three dice thrown would have
a certain meaning determined beforehand, as we see by the piece

called *The Chaunces of the Dyse* in the Bodleian MSS. Fairfax 16 and Bodl. 638. For example, the throw of six, four and ace is there explained by the following stanza :

> ' O mekenesse of vertu principal,
> That may be founde in eny creature !
> In this persone of kunnynge ordinal
> Is ful assembled, I yow dar assure,
> The lorde of vertu and al vices cure,
> Perfit beaute grounded without envye,
> Assured trust withoute gelousye.'

And similarly there is a stanza, complimentary or otherwise, for each possible throw.

2813. *Hire daunger* : see note on i. 2443.

2855. *whi ne were it*, ' would it were ' : cp. the expression ' that he ne were,' vii. 3747, &c.

2895 f. Apparently he means that his dreams were of no such harmless things as sheep and their wool, or perhaps not of business matters, alluding to wool as the staple of English commerce.

2901 ff. Cp. *Roman de la Rose*, 2449-2479.

2905. *I ne bede nevere awake* : cp. *Romaunt of the Rose*, 791, ' Ne bode I never thennes go.' It means apparently ' I should desire never to awake ' (' I should not pray ever to awake ').

2924. *in my wrytinges.* The author forgets here that he is speaking in the person of the Confessor.

2927 ff. This is from Ovid, *Metam.* xi. 266-748, where the story is told at great length. Gower follows some parts of it, as the description of the House of Sleep and its surroundings, very closely.

Chaucer tells the story in the *Book of the Duchess*, but he has not been so successful in reproducing it as Gower. It is here introduced only as an illustration of the truth of dreams, but with its description of the House of Sleep it is very appropriate also in other respects to the subject of Somnolence, which is under discussion.

2928. *Trocinie*, from the adjective ' Trachinia,' in such expressions as ' Trachinia tellus,' *Metam.* xi. 269.

2973. The reading of all the best MSS. in this line is ' he ' : (S however is defective). We cannot doubt that the author meant to write ' sche,' for in what follows he regularly refers to Iris as female ; but the mistake apparently escaped his notice, and we must regard the reading ' she ' in the two copies in which I have found it as an unauthorized correction. Chaucer makes the messenger male, but does not name him.

2977-3055. This passage very happily follows Ovid, *Met.* xi. 589-645. Our author gives all the essential features, but rearranges them freely and adds details of his own.

2996. *Metam.* xi. 608,

> ' Ianua, ne verso stridores cardine reddat,
> Nulla domo tota.'

3009 ff. *Metam.* xi. 602 ff.,

> 'saxo tamen exit ab imo
> Rivus aquae Lethes, per quem cum murmure labens
> Invitat somnos crepitantibus unda lapillis.'

3015 ff. *Metam.* xi. 610 ff.,

> 'At medio torus est ebeno sublimis in antro,
> Plumeus, unicolor, pullo velamine tectus,
> Quo cubat ipse deus membris languore solutis.
> Hunc circa passim varias imitantia formas
> Somnia vana iacent,' &c.

3044. 'Ithecus' is a misreading of 'Icelos,' as 'Panthasas' in l. 3049 of 'Phantasos.'

3061 ff. Here Gower has made a real improvement in the story by employing the two other ministers of Sleep, whose functions have been described, to represent the scene of the tempest and the wreck, while Morpheus plays the part of Ceyx in the same scene. Ovid introduces the characters of Icelos and Phantasos, but makes no use of them, sending Morpheus alone to relate what has taken place, instead of representing it in action, as it would more naturally appear in a dream.

3159. *mi herte*: more usually 'min herte' as 3139, and so generally before 'h,' whether aspirated or not, e. g. 3561; but 'for mi housebondes were,' vii. 4813, (with 'myn housebonde' below, 4829).

3187 ff. This seems to be for the most part original. A hint may have been given by the lines of Ovid in which it is suggested that Aurora might have used a somewhat similar prayer :

> 'At si quem manibus Cephalum complexa teneres,
> Clamares, Lente currite, noctis equi.'
>
> *Amor.* i. 13, 39.

3222. The sun enters Capricorn on Dec. 21.

3273. *that he arise* : so 3374, 'Til it be dai that I arise,' and v. 3422, 'Til dai cam that sche moste arise.'

The verb seems here to be attracted into the subjunctive by the indefinite meaning of 'Til.' In the other passages the mood is uncertain.

3317 ff. Ovid, *Metam.* i. 588–723, much abbreviated. It was, however, Jupiter who turned Io into a cow.

3386. *for thou thee schalt avise,* 'in order that thou mayest consider.'

3414. *that I nere of this lif,* 'would that I were out of this life.' For 'that I nere' cp. note on 1422. For 'of this lif' cp. vii. 2883, 'whan he were of dawe.'

3438 f. 'And yet he (Obstinacy) cannot support his own cause by any argument but by headstrong wilfulness.'

For the expression 'of hed' we may compare the Latin expression quoted by Du Cange 'de testa esse,' explained 'esse obstinatum' (Ital. 'essere di testa'), and the French adjective 'testu,'

> 'Car fol estoient et testu,' &c.

Froissart says of Pope Urban VI that after his election 'il s'en outrecuida et enorguilli, et volt user de poissance et de teste,' which is translated by Berners, 'he waxed proude and worked all on heed.' We find also the Latin adjective 'capitosus' used by Gower in the margin at the beginning of the *Cronica Tripertita,* and the adverb 'capitose,' meaning 'in a headstrong manner,' in Walsingham, *Hist. Anglica,* e.g. 'Regem contra regni consuetudinem Cancellarium deposuisse capitose,' vol. ii. p. 70 (Rolls Series).

The usual way of reading the sentence has been to punctuate after 'skile' and to take 'bot of hed' with the next line, 'but he wastes away in his condition' ('hed' from a supposed 'hǽd' akin to the suffix '-hed' or '-hede'). This word perhaps occurs *Conf. Am.* ii. 2066, but it would give no very good sense here, and it is doubtful whether it would be rhymed with 'ded.' The suffix '-hed' '-hede' apparently has 'e' in Gower's rhymes. Again, if so marked a break in the middle of the line were intended, the Fairfax MS. would almost certainly have had a stop to indicate it, as in 3423, 3431, 3458, 3459, 3484, 3485, to quote instances only from the same page of the MS.

For the use of 'avowe' in this sense, cp. v. 124.

3515 ff. The story is based upon Ovid, *Metam.* xiv. 698–761. Our author, however, has reversed the position of the lover and his mistress. In Ovid Anaxarete is a high-born maid of the race of Teucer, while Iphis is 'humili de stirpe creatus.' Moreover, the story is considerably developed by Gower, to whom belong the speech of Iphis, the whole account of the grief and self-condemnation of Araxarathen, the details of the funeral and the tomb, and finally the very successful epitaph. Ovid says that she saw from a window the body of Iphis being carried by for burial, and was forthwith turned into stone, and that as witness of the truth of his tale a statue may still be seen at Salamis. There is nothing said about remorse on her part, rather the opposite is implied.

3516. Our author supposes this to be the same as the person mentioned in iii. 2645 ff. (who is really Teuthras king of Mysia). This is Teucer son of Telamon, founder of Salamis in Cyprus.

3520 f. These lines are transposed for the sake of the rhyme. It means 'on a maid of low estate compared with his': cp. ii. 709, and below, l. 3616.

3542. Punctuated in accordance with F.

3589. *Thi Daunger,* 'thy unwillingness to love': see note on i. 2443.

3658 f. Naturally the expression of Ovid,

> 'Veneris quoque nomine templum
> Prospicientis habet,'

was not understood.

**   L l

LIB. V.

18. *it cam to londe, wherof,* 'the occasion arose, whence,' &c.

22. *him supposeth*: the verb is used impersonally, like 'him thenketh.' Probably the confusion between 'thinke' and 'thenke' gave rise to this expression.

29 ff. So below, 348 ff.: cp. *Mirour*, 7585 ff.

47 f. This seems, as it stands at present, to be an application of the instances to the case of the avaricious man, 'Thus he so possesses his wealth that he in truth possesses nothing,' ('that' for 'so that'). The original couplet however, as read by all the unrevised class of manuscripts, applies to the case of the sheep, and we may take it so also in its revised form ('Thus' being answered by 'that').

49 ff. Cp. *Mirour*, 7645 ff.,

> 'L'en dist, mais c'est inproprement,
> Qe l'averous ad grant argent;
> Mais voir est que l'argent luy a:
> En servitude ensi le prent,' &c.

65. *nevere hier.* Note that there is no elision before 'hier.'

81 f. 'And yet, though I held her fast (as a miser his hoard), my life would be a perpetual feast, even on Fridays.' If he possessed the treasure, his avarice would not allow him to let it go, and yet he would not keep it unused, as a miser does his gold. So later, 93, 'Though I should hold it fast, I should so be doing that which I were bound to do.'

95. *pipe,* 'be content': perhaps from the idea of a bird-catcher piping or whistling for birds, but failing to snare them.

127-136. Note the repetition of the word 'gold' in an emphatic position.

141 ff. Ovid, *Metam.* xi. 85-147, freely treated as usual. The debate of Midas as to which of three things he should prefer (ll. 180-245) is all due to our author. In Ovid he chooses without hesitation.

143. *Cillenus,* i.e. Silenus.

154 f. Gower attributes the action of the king to pure courtesy, Ovid to the fact that Midas recognized in Silenus a fellow-mystic.

249 ff. Cp. *Mirour*, 7603 ff.

272 ff. Ovid, *Metam.* xi. 106,

> 'Laetus abit gaudetque malo Berecyntius heros:
> Pollicitique fidem tangendo singula temptat.
> Ilice detraxit virgam, virga aurea facta est:
> Tollit humo saxum, saxum quoque palluit auro': &c.

298. See note on i. 10.

315-332. This is an expansion of *Metam.* xi. 146 f.,

> 'Ille perosus opes silvas et rura colebat,
> Panaque montanis habitantem semper in antris.'

363 ff. The punishment referred to is certainly more appropriate for

avarice than for the offence committed by Tantalus : cp. Hor. *Sat.* i. 1.
68. The story of Tantalus is alluded to several times in Ovid, as *Metam.*
iv. 458, and told by Hyginus, *Fab.* lxxxii. Perhaps our author rather
followed Fulgentius, *Mythol.* ii. 18, who quotes from Petronius,

> 'Divitis haec magni facies erit, omnia late
> Qui tenet, et sicco concoquit ore famem.'

Cp. *Mirour*, 7621 ff.,

> 'Dame Avarice est dite auci
> Semblable au paine Tantali,' &c.

370. This seems to mean that it serves for the punishment of the
avaricious ; but from what follows in 391 ff. we gather that the pains of
avarice in this life also are to be compared with this particular pain
of hell, and so the application is made in the *Mirour*, 7621–7632.

388. *which a wreche*, 'what a punishment.'

418. *suie* : cp. Prol. 460.

447. For the superfluous syllable at the pause in the middle of this
line cp. iv. 1131.

496. *berth an hond* : equivalent to 'berth on hond,' l. 546.

519. Count 'evel' as a monosyllable for the verse ; so regularly, e. g.
iii. 1272, vii. 2773.

526. *janglere*. The final '-e' is not pronounced here.

558 f. *the gold ... The which was leid upon the bok*. The gold
in question is that which is laid upon the service-book in payment of
the marriage fees : 'and the Man shall give unto the Woman a Ring,
laying the same upon the book with the accustomed duty to the Priest
and Clerk.' *Marriage Service.*

564. 'though he will not praise it,' i. e. he gives her no credit for
it : cp. Prol. 154.

635 ff. Ovid, *Ars Am.* ii. 561–592, but the original is not very closely
followed.

665. Cp. iii. 1362 ff.

729 ff. From this arises the very ill-advised digression of ll. 747–1970
about the various forms of Religion. There is no more reason why
this should come in here than anywhere else, indeed if the question of
false gods was to be raised at all, it ought to have come in as an
explanation of the appearance of Venus and Cupid in the first book.
Many stories have been told, for example those of Acteon, of the
Gorgons, of Tiresias, of Phoebus and Daphne, of Phaeton, of Ceix, of
Argus, and of Midas, which required the explanation quite as much as
this one, and the awkwardness of putting it all into the mouth of the
priest of Venus is inexcusable.

The main authority followed in this account of the religions of
Chaldea, Egypt, and Greece is the *Vita Barlaam et Josaphat*, cap. xxvii.
(Migne, *Patrol.* vol. 73, p. 548 ff.), but Gower adds much to it, especially
as regards the gods and goddesses of Greece.

763. *of Accidence* : cp. ii. 3210.

774. *hevenly*: so Prol. 918, but 'hevenely' i. 834, 3136, the second syllable in that case being syncopated, as regularly in 'hevene.' So also in the case of 'evermore' and 'everemore' as compared with 'evere.'

782. *les*, that is, 'falsehood.'

798. *Isirus*, i. e. Osiris.

811. *thegipcienes*. This must be the true reading for the sake of the metre, both here and in l. 821, though the best copies fail to give it. A similar case occurs in l. 1119, but there the authority for 'Jupiteres' is made much stronger by the accession of S.

897. *Mynitor*, i. e. Numitor.

899 f. *that Remus and Romulus*. For the position of 'that' cp. 1166, 1249.

925. *To gete him with*: cp. i. 452.

1004. *wel the more lete by*, 'much the more esteemed': cp. *Piers Plowman*, A vi. 105, 'to lete wel by thyselve,' and xi. 29: also with 'of,' v. 5840; cp. *Piers Plowm*. iv. 160, 'Love let of hire lighte and lewte yit lasse,' *Orm*. 7523, 'uss birrth. . . lætenn wel off othre menn.'

1009. *Nonarcigne*. The name is taken no doubt from the adjective 'Nonacrinus' (from Nonacris), used as in Ovid, *Met*. i. 690, where it occurs in the story of Pan and Syrinx, told by Mercury to lull Argus to sleep: cp. *Conf. Am*. iv. 3345 ff.

1040. Cp. Prol. 118.

1043 ff. The sentence is interrupted and then begun again at l. 1051: see note on i. 98.

1063. *That he*, i. e. 'In that he.' Gower has here mistaken his authority, which says 'post autem eum propter Tyndarei Lacedaemonii filium a Jove fulmine percussum interiisse narrant.' *Vita Barl. et Jos*. xxvii.

1071. Delphi and Delos are very naturally confused in the medieval Tale of Troy and elsewhere; but Delos is mentioned correctly enough below, 1256.

1097. *no reason inne*: cp. i. 3209.

1163. *Philerem*, presumably Philyra, but there is no authority for making her the mother of Jupiter.

1249. *that*: cp. 899. Apparently it means, 'that Diane of whom I am to speak.' The necessities of rhyme are responsible for these forms of speech.

1276. 'Which may not attain to reason.'

1323. The paragraph is made to begin here in the MSS. with what is, strictly speaking, its second line, because it is marked by a proper name which indicates its subject, the first line being a mere formal introduction. So also below, 1453: cp. ii. 2451.

1337. The name 'Dorus' seems to have been suggested by that of Doris, mother of the Nereids.

1389. *alle danger*, that is, all reluctance or coyness.

1397. *Armene*, i. e. Harmonia.

1398. *Andragene* Androgynus or Hermaphroditus.

1428. *noght forsake To ben*, i. e. ' not refuse to be.'

1449. ' whether it was of weal or wo' : ' wher' for ' whether.'

1453. See note on 1323.

As for the letters said to have been exchanged between Alexander and the king of the Bragmans (or Brahmins), we find them at length in the *Historia Alexandri Magni de Preliis*, which was the source of most of the current stories about Alexander. The passage referred to is as follows: ' Tot deos colis quot in tuo corpore membra portas. Nam hominem dicis paruum mundum, et sicut corpus hominis habet multa membra, ita et in celo dicis multos deos existere. Iunonem credis esse deum cordis, eo quod iracundia nimia mouebatur. Martem vero deum pectoris esse dicis, eo quod princeps extitit preliorum. Mercurium deum lingue vocas, ex eo quod plurimum loquebatur. Herculem deum credis brachiorum, eo quod duodecim virtutes exercuit preliando. Bachum deum gutturis esse putas, eo quod ebrietatem primus inuenit. Cupidinem esse deam dicis, eo quod fornicatrix extitit ; tenere dicis facem ardentem, cum qua libidinem excitat et accendit, et ipsam deam iecoris etiam existimas. Cererem deam ventris esse dicis, et Venerem, eo quod fuit mater luxurie, deam genitalium membrorum esse profers' (e 2, ed. Argent. 1489).

Cp. the English alliterative *Wars of Alexander*, E. E. T. S., 1886, ll. 4494 ff. There is no mention of Minerva in either of these.

1520 ff. The usual account is to the effect that Ninus set up the first idol: see below, **1541.** What we have here seems to be taken from Fulgentius, *Mythol.* ii. 9, where the authorities here cited, Nicagoras and Petronius, are quoted. The passage is apparently corrupt, and our author obviously did not quite understand it: ' Et quamvis Nicagoras in Disthemithea libro quem scripsit, primum illum formasse idolum referat, et quod vulturi iecur praebeat livoris quasi pingat imaginem : unde et Petronius Arbiter ait,

    " Qui vultur iecor intimum pererrat " ' &c.

From the same author, *Mythol.* i. 1, he got the story about Syrophanes, who set up an image of his dead son, to which offerings were made by those who wished to gain his favour.

1541. Cp. Godfr. Vit., *Panth.* iv. (p. 102), whose account agrees very nearly with what we have here, though he represents this image as the first example of an idol, under the heading, ' Quare primum idolum in mundo et quo tempore fuit.' Cp. Guido, *Hist. Troiana*, lib. x (e 5, ed. Argent. 1494).

1559. Godf. Vit., *Panth.* iv. (p. 112) : ' His temporibus apud Egyptios constructum est idolum magnum in honorem Apis, Regis Argivorum ; quidam tamen dicunt in honorem Ioseph, qui liberavit eos a fame ; quod idolum Serapis vocabatur, quasi idolum Apis.'

1571 ff. *Hist. Alexandri*, f 1v°, ed. Argent. 1489 : ' Exiens inde Alexander cum Candeolo profecti sunt iter diei vnius, et venerunt ad quandam speluncam magnam et hospitati sunt ibi. Dixitque Candeolus,

" Omnes dii concilium in ista spelunca concelebrant." Cum hoc audisset
Alexander, statim fecit victimas diis suis, et ingressus in speluncam
solus vidit ibi caligines maximasque nubes stellasque lucentes, et inter
ipsas stellas quendam deum maximum,' &c.

Cp. the English alliterative *Wars of Alexander*, ll. 5387 ff.

1624. *herd me seid*: see note on i. 3153.

1636. There is a stop after 'Forbad' in F. The meaning is that
he gave a prohibition commanding them not to bow to an image.

1677. *Riht as who sette*: the verb apparently is subjunctive.

1746 ff. What purports to be the original passage is quoted in the
margin of the second recension.

1747. For the form of expression cp. vi. 56 f.,

> 'O which a sorwe
> It is a man be drinkeles!'

1756 ff. The substance of this is to be found in Gregory, *In* i. *Reg.*
viii. 7 f. (Migne, *Patrol.* vol. 79. p. 222): 'Et quidem, nisi Adam peccaret,
Redemptorem nostrum carnem suscipere nostram non oporteret.... Si
ergo pro peccatoribus venit, si peccata deessent, eum venire non oporteret . . . Magna quippe sunt mala quae per primae culpae meritum
patimur, sed quis electus nollet peiora perpeti, quam tantum Redemptorem non habere ?'

1781 ff. Note that here twelve lines are replaced in the second
recension by ten, one of the couplets (or the substance of it) having
been inserted earlier, after l. 1742.

1826. 'So that his word explained his deed': 'arawhte' from
'arechen' (āreccan).

1831 ff. *Roman de Troie*, 25504-25559.

1848-1959. With this compare Prol. 193-498.

1865. 'And they do every man what he pleases,' the verb being plural.

1879. *Pseudo*: cp. *Mirour*, 21625 ff.,

> 'Il estoit dit grant temps y a
> Q'un fals prophete a nous vendra,
> Q'ad noun Pseudo le decevant;
> Sicomme aignel se vestira,
> Et cuer du loup il portera.
> O comme les freres maintenant
> A Pseudo sont bien resemblant!'

So also *Vox Clam.* iv. 787 f.,

> 'Nomine sunt plures, pauci tamen ordine fratres;
> Vt dicunt aliqui, Pseudo prophetat ibi.'

It seems that the word 'pseudopropheta,' used Rev. xix. 20 and
elsewhere, was read 'Pseudo propheta,' and 'Pseudo' was taken as a
proper name. This was combined with the idea of the wolf in sheep's
clothing suggested by Matt. vii. 15, 'Attendite a falsis prophetis,' &c.,
and the application was made especially to the friars.

1888. 'And this I am brought to believe by the argument that where those above neglect their duty, the people are ignorant of the truth, (as they now are).'

1900 ff. Cp. *Mirour*, 20065 ff., and *Vox Clamantis*, iii. 903. The reference is to Gregory, *Hom. in Evang.* xvii. (Migne, *Patrol.* vol. 76, p. 1148): 'Ibi Petrus cum Iudaea conversa, quam post se traxit, apparebit: ibi Paulus conversum, ut ita dixerim, mundum ducens. Ibi Andreas post se Achaiam, ibi Iohannes Asiam, Thomas Indiam in conspectu sui regis conversam ducet . . . . Cum igitur tot pastores cum gregibus suis ante aeterni pastoris oculos venerint, nos miseri · quid dicturi sumus, qui ad Dominum nostrum post negotium vacui redimus?'

1919. Cp. *Mirour*, 16662, 'U q'il ert mesmes auditour.' The metaphor from rendering accounts in the Exchequer is especially appropriate here for the prelates.

1930. *his lordes besant hedde* : Matt. xxv. 18.

1944. *every Prelat holde*, 'let every Prelate hold.'

1952 ff. Coloss. iii. 5, 'avaritiam, quae est simulacrorum servitus.'